UNDERSTANDING SERVICES MANAGEMENT

UNDERSTANDING SERVICES MANAGEMENT

Integrating Marketing, Organisational Behaviour, Operations and Human Resource Management

Edited by
William J. Glynn,
University College Dublin
and
James G. Barnes,
Memorial University of Newfoundland

WILEY

JOHN WILEY & SONS

Chichester • New York • Brisbane • Toronto • Singapore

Published by   John Wiley & Sons Ltd
Baffins Lane, Chichester
West Sussex PO19 1UD, England

National   Chichester 01243 779777
International   (+44) 1243 779777

Published in the Republic of Ireland and Northern Ireland
by Oak Tree Press

The University College Dublin Centre for Quality & Services
Management gratefully acknowledges the generous support and
encouragement provided by its founding sponsor, Telecom Ireland.

Other Wiley Editorial Offices

John Wiley & Sons, Inc., 605 Third Avenue
New York, NY 10158-0012, USA

Jacaranda Wiley Ltd, 33 Park Road, Milton,
Queensland 4064, Australia

John Wiley & Sons (Canada) Ltd, 22 Worcester Road
Rexdale, Ontario M9W 1L1, Canada

John Wiley & Sons (SEA) Pte Ltd, 37 Jalan Pemimpin #05-04
Block B, Union Industrial Building, Singapore 2057

ISBN 0-471-96066-7
Printed in the Republic of Ireland

CONTENTS

ABOUT THE CONTRIBUTORS

THE EDITORS

WILLIAM J. GLYNN is a lecturer in services marketing at the University College Dublin Graduate School of Business. He was appointed as Director of the B.Comm. (International) Degree in 1992 and as the first Director of the University College Dublin Centre for Quality & Services Management in 1994. His previous employments include: Dublin City University, Groupe ESSEC (France), Swedish Match and Abbott Laboratories. He has published services marketing articles in France (Institut d'Administration des Entreprises, Université Aix-Marseille), Ireland (European Marketing Academy Conference), United Kingdom (Marketing Educators Group and *Journal of Marketing Management*) and most recently with the First Interstate Center for Services Marketing at Arizona State University in the United States.

JAMES G. BARNES is Professor of Marketing and former Dean of the Faculty of Business Administration, Memorial University of Newfoundland, Canada. He is also co-founder and Chairman of Omnifacts Research Limited, a full-service marketing research company with offices in eastern Canada and specialising in service quality research. Dr Barnes holds undergraduate degrees in Commerce and Economics from Memorial University, an MBA from the Harvard Business School, and a PhD from the University of Toronto. He is a widely-published author of textbooks and articles in Marketing and related fields. He serves as a consultant in marketing research and service quality to a large number of national and international companies.

THE CHAPTER AUTHORS

MARY JO BITNER is Associate Professor at Arizona State University (ASU), Program Co-Director of the Services Marketing Institute, and a member of the Board of Directors of the International Service Quality Association. Dr Bitner was Chair of the American Marketing Association (AMA) Faculty Consortium on Services Marketing, which was held at ASU in 1993, and she served as co-chair of the 1988 AMA

Services Conference. She is a frequent presenter on services marketing topics at conferences and executive education programs. Dr Bitner pioneered the development of new courses in Services Marketing for both MBA and undergraduate students and was the recipient of the 1992–93 ASU College of Business Graduate Teaching Excellence Award. She has consulted with numerous service businesses, primarily in the travel and tourism industries. Her current research is concerned with how customers evaluate service encounters, and the role of physical environments and contact employee behaviours in determining customer satisfaction with services. She has published articles relevant to service industry management in the *Journal of Marketing, Journal of Business Research, Journal of Retailing, Journal of Travel Research,* and the *Cornell Hotel and Restaurant Administration Quarterly*. She has her PhD in Marketing from the University of Washington, Seattle.

DAVID E. BOWEN is Associate Professor of Management, Business Programs at Arizona State University West. Previously, he was with the School of Business Administration at the University of Southern California. He received his PhD from Michigan State University. His research, consulting, and executive education interests include: (1) Managing organisation culture and human resource issues in services, with a special emphasis on employee empowerment; (2) Managing customer involvement in co-producing services and, (3) Creating customer-focused corporate staffs. His articles have appeared in *Academy of Management Review, Journal of Applied Psychology, Sloan Management Review, Human Resource Management, and Organizational Dynamics*. He has co-authored two books, *Service Management Effectiveness* (Jossey-Bass, 1990) and *Advances in Services Marketing & Management* (JAI Press 1992), and is currently writing a book with Benjamin Schneider, on managing the culture of service organisations. He serves on the editorial review boards of the *Academy of Management Review* and *Human Resource Management*.

DR FRANK BRADLEY is R & A Bailey Professor of International Marketing, Head of the Department of Marketing, and Director of the Centre of International Marketing Studies at University College Dublin where he teaches Marketing and International Marketing on undergraduate and postgraduate programmes in the Faculty of Commerce. Professor Bradley has lectured at the European Institute for Advanced Studies in Management (EIASM), Brussels, the University of California at Berkeley, the National Management Training Centre, Beijing, PRC, the University of Gothenburg, Sweden, at the École Supérieure de

Commerce de Paris and at IAE-Aix-en-Provence. He has also lectured on international management development programmes in Barbados, Belgium, Chile, China (PRC), Costa Rica, Egypt, France, India, Italy, Jamaica, Peru, Philippines, Spain, Sweden, Switzerland, Trinidad and Tobago, and the US. His research interests lie in the area of marketing strategy for firms expanding into international markets. The second edition of his textbook, *International Marketing Strategy,* was published by Prentice Hall in Spring 1995. His research has also been published widely in management journals such as: *Irish Marketing Review, Journal of Irish Business and Administrative Research (IBAR), Management Decision (UK), Industrial Marketing Management (US), Research in Marketing (US), and Journal of Business Research* (US) and as chapters in numerous books. He has edited works on international marketing including a recently published *Symposium on International Marketing.* He also serves on the editorial board of the *Journal of International Marketing* and the *Journal of Business Research.* His new textbook, *Marketing Management: Providing, Communicating & Delivering Value,* was published by Prentice Hall in Spring 1995.

STEPHEN W. BROWN is Professor of Marketing and Director of the First Interstate Center for Services Marketing at Arizona State University in Tempe. The FICSM is North America's first university-based centre for research and education on the topics of services marketing and management. Twenty-five leading firms, including IBM, AT&T, Xerox, Marriott and First Interstate Bank provide support to the centre in their role as charter members. Dr Brown's recent work focuses on service quality and the unique marketing situations confronting service organisations. His call for attention to services marketing research and education has been featured in major speeches at international conferences, in various articles he has written and in the business press, including *Wall Street Journal, Business Week* and *Fortune.* Dr Brown is a past president of the 50,000-member American Marketing Association, and he was instrumental in the establishment of the AMA's services marketing division and Academy for Health Services Marketing. His capabilities have been recognised with various prestigious honours, including ASU's Faculty Achievement Award. He is co-author of over 100 articles and 12 books, including *Marketing Strategies for Physicians*, and *Patient Satisfaction Pays* — health-care industry best sellers. Dr Brown is also a co-editor of the new books, *Service Quality* and *Advances in Services Marketing and Management.* He serves on the editorial boards of the *Journal of Marketing, Journal of the Academy of Marketing Science* and four other professional journals. He is also an advisor, researcher and board member for various respected firms and professions.

JANE KINGMAN-BRUNDAGE is a pioneer and master practitioner of the service mapping technique. Service mapping is used by such diverse clients as AT&T, the Xerox Corporation, Merill Lynch and the Swedish Railroad in the design and implementation of new services. Jane has also applied service mapping across a wide spectrum of industry segments, including The Cooperators (Canadian insurance company) and Pemex Gas & Basic Petrochemicals (Mexico) in support of their continuous improvement activities. Her work enjoys international recognition, and she has introduced service mapping to quality professionals at the International Service Quality Association (Sweden) and the International Service & Quality Forum (France). Co-author of *The Fundamentals of Trade Finance* (John Wiley & Sons, 1985), she holds Master of Arts degrees from Columbia University (Personnel Psychology) and The New School for Social Research (Sociology).

SEÁN DE BURCA worked on a number of engineering projects in Ireland, the UK and Australia, following his engineering studies. He returned to University College Dublin to complete a Bachelor of Commerce Degree and Master of Business Studies Degree in Marketing. He joined FÁS (Training & Development Authority) and held responsibility for the management design and development of Business Development programmes and gained extensive management development experience assisting a wide variety of industrial, commercial and government clients. He currently lectures in International Marketing and Business-to-Business Marketing in the Department of Marketing, University College Dublin. He has lectured on a number of MBA programmes in France, Hungary and Romania. His main research interest and consultancy work have focused on how firms internationalise from a network perspective.

DAVID CARSON is Professor of Marketing at the University of Ulster, Northern Ireland. His teaching and research interests are in small-to-medium-sized enterprise (SME) marketing and services marketing. He is primarily concerned with adapting existing marketing frameworks and exploring new approaches to marketing for use in the context of SMEs and services. He has published widely in these areas. He has been editor of the *European Journal of Marketing* for the past seven years and is a review board member of several international academic journals in marketing. He is also the lead author of a forthcoming text on marketing and entrepreneurship, to be published by Prentice Hall. David has been an active entrepreneur involved with several enterprises over the past 20 years. Currently, he is a partner in an import/export trading company, based in Ireland and operating throughout Europe. He is an active consultant engaged in long-term relationships with Eurodisney and Stena Sea Ferries in the area of marketing strategies. Coming from Ireland, with its economic reliance on SMEs and international trading, David Carson is widely experienced in international marketing and strategic alliances.

MOIRA CLARK. Prior to joining Cranfield as a Teaching Fellow in Services Marketing, Moira was an international marketing consultant based in Munich, where she was involved with a wide range of industries including construction and related fields, engineering, local radio, consumer and industrial goods manufacturers and services industries. She has also held marketing positions with the toiletries subsidiary of Dunhill and an international health-food manufacturer. She is a graduate in Business Studies and Marketing and has an Executive MBA from Cranfield Institute of Technology. She has held lecturing posts at the University of Maryland and Leicester Business School. Her work covers a range of business areas including strategic marketing planning, international marketing and relationship marketing. Her special area of interest is internal marketing and the linkages between employee satisfaction and customer retention.

JUDITH A. CUMBY is Assistant Professor of Accounting at the Faculty of Business Administration, Memorial University of Newfoundland, Canada. She holds an undergraduate degree in Business Administration from St Francis Xavier University and an MBA from Memorial University of Newfoundland. She is also a Chartered Accountant, who was in public practice in Newfoundland for several years before returning to academia. She continues to provide accounting-related services for selected business and individual clients in Newfoundland. Her present research interests span accounting and marketing, and include cost of service quality, accounting for brand names, and environmental accounting.

SEAN ENNIS graduated from Dublin University and the College of Marketing and Design in 1979 with a Bachelor of Science — Management Degree and from University College Dublin with a Master of Business Studies Degree in 1980. Having worked for the *Irish Press* newspaper and as a marketing consultant to a number of Irish and international companies, he joined the College of Marketing and Design as a lecturer in Marketing in 1984. He served as Vice-Chairman (Education) for the Marketing Institute of Ireland in 1986 and 1987, participating actively in the redesign of their education programmes. He is currently completing his PhD which examines the planning practices of the indigenous Irish firms in the electronics sector. His teaching interests are in the areas of small-business marketing, retailing and supply-chain management. He is currently employed as a lecturer in marketing at the University of Strathclyde in Glasgow, Scotland. In addition to his research and teaching, he is engaged in consultancy projects with a number of Scottish companies.

DR RAYMOND P. FISK is Associate Professor of the Department of Marketing, at the University of Central Florida. He earned his BS, MBA, and PhD from Arizona State University. Previously, he served as Interim Head and Associate Professor of the Department of Marketing, Oklahoma State University. Dr Fisk served as a Fulbright Scholar to Klagenfurt University of Education Sciences, Austria. He has also taught at Arizona State University and the American Graduate School of International Management (Thunderbird). Dr Fisk's research has focused on services marketing and marketing theory. He has published in the *Journal of Marketing, Journal of Retailing, Journal of the Academy of Marketing Science, Journal of Health Care Marketing, Journal of Professional Services Marketing, Marketing Education Review,* and numerous national and regional marketing conferences. Dr Fisk has published three books: *Marketing Theory: Distinguished Contributions, AIRWAYS: A Marketing Simulation,* and *Services Marketing: An Annotated Bibliography.* He served for many years on the editorial review board of the *Journal of Health Care Marketing* and was the editor of the *AMA Services Marketing Newsletter.* Dr Fisk created *SERVMARK: The Electronic Bibliography of Services Marketing Literature.*

BRIAN FYNES lectures in the Department of Business Administration at University College Dublin, where he specialises in Manufacturing and Operations Management. Previously he held positions in the Dublin Institute of Technology and at the Centre for Transport Studies in University College Dublin. He has carried out assignments on behalf of the European Commission, the International Labour Organisation, the OECD, and has lectured extensively in Eastern Europe. His research interests include leadership roles in total quality management, manufacturing strategy and the future of advanced telecommunications systems in supply-chain relationships. In addition, he is co-author of a forthcoming book on the future of work sharing and temporal flexibility in the workplace. The European Commission has recently awarded him a Research Fellowship in Total Quality Management at London Business School.

AUDREY GILMORE is a lecturer in marketing at the University of Ulster, Northern Ireland. Her teaching and research interests are in Quality in Marketing and Marketing in Service Industries, particularly in travel and tourism. She is interested in developing an holistic approach to quality in services marketing within specific contexts. Audrey has published widely in the area of quality in services marketing and management. The main focus of her current research is on improving quality in marketing within a travel service company. Prior to her academic career, she had considerable experience in a variety of managerial roles in the service and retail sectors.

EVERT GUMMESSON graduated from the Stockholm School of Economics and received his Doctorate in Business Administration at Stockholm University, Sweden, where he is Professor of Service Management and Marketing. He has been professor and scientific leader at the Service Research Centre, the first research centre in the world to focus on research in service management, and is one of the founders of QUIS, the Quality in Services international research conferences. His original interest is marketing and his marketing textbook has been reprinted and revised continuously in Sweden since 1976. His most recent book is on relationship marketing. He is also active as a management consultant and a frequent speaker at conferences, companies and universities throughout the world.

JAMES L. HESKETT is UPS Foundation Professor of Business Logistics at the Graduate School of Business Administration, Harvard University. He holds a PhD from Stanford University, and has been a member of the faculty of the Ohio State University. He is a member of the Board of Directors of Cardinal Health, Inc.; the Equitable of Iowa Companies; Anchor Glass Container Corporation; First Security Services Corporation; Boston Police Foundation; the Advisory Board of IPADE (a Mexican business school); the Advisory Board of INCAE (a Central American business school) and has served as a consultant to companies in North America, Latin America and Europe. He is a member of the editorial boards of the *Journal of Business Logistics* and the *International Journal of Service Industry Management*. In 1974 he received the John Drury Sheahan Award of the Council of Logistics Management and the 1992 Marketing Educator of the Year Award of Sales and Marketing Executives International. Among his publications are books, including co-authorship of *Corporate Culture and Performance* (The Free Press, 1992); co-authorship of *Services Breakthroughs: Changing the Rules of the Game* (The Free Press, 1990); co-authorship of *The Service Management Course* (The Free Press, 1991); *Managing in the Service Economy* (Harvard Business School Press, 1986); co-authorship of *Logistics Strategy: Cases and Concepts* (MN: West Publishing Co., 1985); *Marketing* (Macmillan Publishing Co., 1976); co-authorship of *Business Logistics*, Revised Edition (The Ronald Press Company, 1974); and numerous articles in such publications as the *Harvard Business Review, Journal of Marketing, Sloan Management Review, California Management Review*, and others. A member of the faculty of the Harvard Business School since 1965, he has taught courses in marketing, business logistics, the management of service operations, and business policy, and is currently teaching service management.

EDWARD E. LAWLER III is a Professor of Management and Organisation at the University of Southern California. In 1979, he founded, and became director of, the university's Center for Effective Organizations. He has consulted with more than 200 organisations and four national governments on such issues as employee involvement, organisational change, and compensation. As an author of more than 200 articles and 20 books, he is widely recognised as a contributor to the fields of organisational development and organisational behaviour. His most recent books include *High Involvement Management, Strategic Pay* (Jossey-Bass 1990), *Employee Involvement & Total Quality Management* (Jossey-Bass 1992) and *The Ultimate Advantage* (Jossey-Bass 1992).

UOLEVI LEHTINEN is a Professor of Marketing at the University of Tampere, Finland. His fields of expertise are services marketing, international marketing and marketing decision-making. He has published over 100 scientific publications, more than one third of which are referred to in international journals or proceedings. He has been a visiting professor or scholar at the University of California, Los Angeles; Keio University, Tokyo; State University of Moscow and University of Delhi, New Delhi. He has also lectured in 20 other countries, and has worked as an entrepreneur and a consultant.

BARBARA R. LEWIS is Senior Lecturer in the Manchester School of Management. Her teaching and research interests are concerned with marketing in service-sector industries. Current research activities are focused on Service Quality and Customer Service and projects include: customer care in financial services; patient satisfaction with health-care services; service quality in tourism; internal marketing in financial services; service recovery; and buyer behaviour in the service sector. Founder editor of the *International Journal of Bank Marketing*, she is also special issue editor and an editorial review board member for several marketing journals, co-editor of a forthcoming encyclopaedia of Marketing, and organiser of the annual UK Services Marketing Conference. Dr Lewis is a member of the Executive Committee of the British Academy of Management.

CHRISTOPHER LOVELOCK is an internationally-recognised world authority on marketing and managing services. A teacher and consultant, he is also a prolific author with 12 titles to his credit. Business-school students around the world use his textbooks, including *Service Marketing* and *Managing Services: Marketing, Operations and Human Resources*. For more than 20 years, Lovelock's work in teaching and consulting to senior executives has focused on developing service strategies that will create value for customers and the firm. He holds an MBA from Harvard University and a PhD from Stanford University.

LIONELLO NEGRI is the scientific co-ordinator of a research team on "Geoeconomy of Services for Innovation and Quality Improvement of Enterprises" within the activities of the CNR Strategic Project, "Technological Change and Industrial Development". Negri's major research interests deal with innovation management; policies and strategies to implement *Company-Wide Quality Control*; methodologies and tools for quality improvement in commodities and services production and strategies to rationalise the modal split and to optimise the service level in transportation systems. He is currently responsible for the "Innovation Valorisation and Management" division of the Office for Innovation Transfer, Patents, Technical Standards and Regulations of the Italian Research Council, and is a widely-published editor of *S&R — Studio e Ricerca*. He received his undergraduate degree in mechanical engineering and holds a Master of Industrial Management Degree.

A. "PARSU" PARASURAMAN is a Professor and holder of the James W. McLamore Chair in Marketing at the University of Miami. He obtained his Bachelor of Technology degree in 1970 and Masters of

Business Administration degree in 1972 from leading universities in India. His Doctor of Business Administration degree, which he obtained in 1975, is from Indiana University, Bloomington, Indiana. Parsu teaches courses in the areas of services marketing, marketing research, and research methodology. His research interests focus on service-quality measurement and improvement, and on services marketing strategy. He is a recipient of several teaching and research awards. In 1988, Parsu was selected as one of the "Ten Most Influential Figures in Quality" by the editorial board of *The Quality Review,* co-published by the American Quality Foundation and the American Society for Quality Control. He has written numerous articles in journals such as the *Journal of Marketing, Journal of Marketing Research, Journal of Services Marketing, and Business Horizons.* He is the author of *Marketing Research*, a college textbook, and co-author of *Delivering Quality Service: Balancing Customer Perceptions and Expectations.* His newest book, *Marketing Services: Competing Through Quality*, was published by the Free Press in August, 1991. Parsu is an active consultant to a number of major corporations.

ADRIAN PAYNE is Professor of Services Marketing and Director of the Centre for Services Management at the Cranfield School of Management, Cranfield University. He has wide experience as an educator and has lectured and run courses at many institutions including Oxford University, Cambridge University, INSEAD, IMD, EAP — European Management Centre, Manchester Business School, Copenhagen Business School, University of Bangkok and University of Melbourne. His current research interests are in strategic marketing and management in service industries, customer service, corporate acquisitions, global competition and developing marketing-oriented organisations. He has published three books and many papers in the areas of strategy, marketing and financial markets.

LAUREN K. WRIGHT is an Associate Professor of Marketing at California State University, Chico, where she teaches services marketing courses that emphasise student interaction, team-work and active application of service-marketing concepts. She won an undergraduate teaching award in 1983. Dr Wright has been involved in the area of services marketing since 1987, when she received the Marketing Science Institute Doctoral Dissertation Award for her thesis proposal on the factors affecting the success of new business services. She received her PhD in Marketing from Penn State University in 1990. Dr Wright's research interests include service quality, issues related to new service success and effective practices for teaching services marketing. She has published in these areas and has presented her work at numerous national and international conferences. She is on the editorial board of the *Journal of Marketing Education.* Dr Wright is currently the research director of the International Service Quality Association and is a member of the Leadership Council of the American Marketing Association's Special Interest Group for Services Marketing. She is an internal consultant for California State University, Chico, on how to implement innovative teaching techniques into university classrooms. Dr Wright is also a co-director of the Centre for Information Systems Research on the California State University campus.

PRÉCIS AUTHORS

Michael J. Bannon, University College Dublin, Ireland.

Robert H. Collins, University of Nevada — Las Vegas, USA.

Anthony C. Cunninghan, University College Dublin, Ireland.

Andrew J. Deegan, University College Dublin, Ireland.

Andy Lowe, University of Strathclyde, Scotland.

Aidan O'Driscoll, Dublin Institute of Technology, Ireland.

Eleanor O'Higgins, University College Dublin, Ireland.

Paul O'Sullivan, Dublin Institute of Technology, Ireland.

George G. Panigyrakis, Athens University of Economics and Business, Greece.

Hervé Mathe, ESSEC, France.

William K. Roche, University College Dublin, Ireland.

Kate Stewart, University of Ulster — Magee College, Northern Ireland.

Christodoulos Stylianides, Cyprus International Institute of Management, Cyprus.

Eamonn Walsh, University of Limerick, Ireland.

James J. Ward, University College Galway, Ireland.

Helen Woodruffe, University of Salford, England.

DEDICATION

*This book is dedicated to
the most important people in our lives:
Muriel, Françoise, Diane, Jennifer, Stephanie and Karen.*

PREFACE

The growth and growth of services as the engine of modern-day economic prosperity has resulted in a veritable explosion of academic literature dealing with the diverse territory of services management. Contributors to this literature have drawn their expertise from the areas of Marketing, Organisational Behaviour, Operations and Human Resource Management. The reasons for this mix of disciplinary approaches are the characteristics of services and the key role of "people, people and people" in the service exchange process. In recent years, a growing number of researchers have begun to pool their knowledge across disciplines in order to extend the frontiers of services management thought into the twenty-first century. A small number of interdisciplinary conferences, journal articles and collections of readings and books have emerged as evidence of this movement. *Understanding Services Management* is the culmination of much of the pioneering work. The writings of many of the world's most prolific services management authors are included together in this book which has been prepared to reflect the essential interdisciplinary approach to the study of services management.

Today, no undergraduate or postgraduate business programme is complete without a services course. Our experience as teachers of services marketing and management courses has led us to collect a diverse range of materials from marketing, organisational behaviour, operations and human resource management. In developing the author guidelines for this book, we set out to integrate materials dealing with the broad range of issues which challenge services managers. The book provides final-year undergraduate business students, postgraduate business students, and services managers with an integrated view of these inter-related services management issues. Service industry examples from around the world are used to illustrate the concepts and principles of services marketing and management and to aid in the learning process. Many of the authors also indicate future research directions which are intended to inspire others to join in the new interdisciplinary approach to the study of services.

The preparation of this book involved extensive co-ordination among authors in order to integrate their work into a single publication. Many personal contacts, meetings, reviews and redrafts employing audio, video and other electronic communications enabled this book to emerge. Each chapter is designed to direct readers to other related chapters and thereby take them on a guided tour of the entire range of the latest services management thought.

As part of the review process, a number of chapter discussants agreed to read, present and chair discussions among all of the authors. Their contribution is also reflected in a précis at the beginning of each chapter.

Stephen Brown, Raymond Fisk and Mary Jo Bitner, open the book with the definitive history of services marketing thought. They present their personal interpretations as participant-observers of the evolution of the services marketing literature. Bibliographic analysis of more than 1,000 English-language, general services marketing publications spanning four decades provides an additional resource for the chapter. They use an evolutionary metaphor as a framework to trace the literature in services marketing through three stages: Crawling Out (1953–79); Scurrying About (1980–85); and Walking Erect (1986–present). The discussion of the three stages shows how the literature has evolved from the early services-marketing-is-different debate to the maturation of specific topics (e.g., service quality, service encounters) and the legitimisation of the services marketing literature by major marketing journals. A classification and summary of publications and authors is also presented.

Lauren Wright continues with a similar theme and considers services marketing, using the three-stage Brown, Fisk and Bitner services evolutionary metaphor, in the wider context of the marketing paradigm. The maturity of the services marketing subdiscipline is positively assessed in terms of its contribution to general marketing literature. The author then presents several contingency factors that may allow services marketers to determine more precisely the types of marketing strategies that will be most effective in creating and sustaining a distinctive competitive advantage.

Barbara Lewis concentrates on the themes of customer care, including customer satisfaction: putting the customer first, anticipating needs and problems, tailoring products and services to meet needs, and establishing customer relationships. Interdisciplinary issues emphasised include: the need to focus on products/services, delivery systems and environment, and the management of employees so as to provide an efficient and caring service, getting things right the first time and maintaining standards. The background to the present emphasis on customer care and service is presented, followed by a discussion of the external customer. The dimensions of customer care and service and their measurement are also discussed. Attention is then turned to the internal customer's role in customer care, and the need for internal marketing and enlightened personnel policies. The final section deals, briefly, with service delivery, in particular service recovery strategies.

William Glynn and Uolevi Lehtinen explore the concept of exchange in services marketing and interpret traditional, interactive, internal and relationship marketing in the context of a more complex three-way interactive relationship involving the external customer, the internal customer and the service organisation. This chapter proposes a model of service exchange depicting this relationship. A number of services marketing inferences are drawn from the model. Illustrative case materials are also used to represent this material.

The issue of designing service systems to meet customer needs is discussed by Jane Kingman-Brundage. Her ground-breaking service mapping technique is explained and illustrated as a management tool for service system design. The service mapping methodology sees service systems as arrangements of people and technique. A service template, derived from key findings in services research, is introduced. Investigation of customer, technical and employee logics uncovers the fundamental principles that govern service system operation. Control over service system design and management increases when these principles are explicitly understood.

Service quality is a topic of increasing interest both to academics and to practitioners. A. Parasuraman begins his chapter by reviewing the literature on the conceptualisation and assessment of service quality. He then traces the development and refinement of SERVQUAL, a multiple-item instrument for measuring service quality. A number of studies involving the application of SERVQUAL — in both "academic" and "practical" settings — are presented, and relevant results from those studies are discussed. The most recent enhancements to SERVQUAL are described, and questions that have been raised about SERVQUAL's soundness are addressed, based on results from a major study that tested the enhanced versions of the instrument.

Impetus for escalation in the level of service provided to customers has come from the desire by firms to increase profitability levels in a marketplace where consumers are demanding more in the way of true value, and where gaining a competitive advantage through product and price is less feasible and less desirable. These demanding consumers are willing to switch their loyalties to firms that can meet their demands for exceptional service. The result has been a proliferation of quality initiatives and programmes, to the point where the word "quality" may no longer be synonymous with something over and above the norm. Such quality initiatives have resulted in considerable investment of time and money in the development of service quality initiatives, and in many cases no assessment has been made of when, or even if, such expenditures will return benefits to the firm. James Barnes and Judith Cumby contend that, as with any other disbursement, expenditures on service quality should be evaluated to determine if they are justified in terms of their future benefit to the firm. Judicious management of service quality must be supported by improved cost information and a shift towards evaluating the total benefits and costs associated with serving a customer, not just the immediate financial returns.

Christopher Lovelock examines Human Resource Management issues that are particularly relevant for managing service employees whose jobs entail extensive contact with customers. Not all services are the same, of course, since the nature of the service affects both the extent of customer–employee contact and the proportion of all employees who regularly encounter customers. Useful insights can be obtained from a theatrical analogy in which service is delivered "on stage" by employees playing defined roles as actors in a service drama before an often participatory audience of customers. The analogy of casting actors for roles leads into a review of key issues in job design and recruitment, followed by a discussion of the distinction between hiring people for their innate personal characteristics as opposed to teaching technical skills through training. Particular attention is given to issues relating to job design, hiring, and training in today's new technology-driven service environments. The notion of service jobs as relationships — with the firm and with individual customers — is also examined. Unwillingness to invest up-front in selective recruitment, training, and higher wages can result in either a "cycle of failure", leading to rapid turnover of both staff and customers, or in the "cycle of mediocrity", encountered when unmotivated staff trapped in secure but boring jobs provide unresponsive service to unhappy customers who lack a choice of alternatives. Breaking out of these vicious cycles requires not just new practices, but a reworking of the sociology of the workplace to empower employees and increase their levels of involvement and discretion. The chapter concludes with the challenges involved in managing human re-sources in a multicultural environment.

In Chapter 9, Evert Gummesson contributes a theoretical discourse on relationship marketing. He discusses relationship marketing's role as contributor to the success of the contemporary service society, approaching relationship marketing from four directions: marketing, organisation, management, and economics. He establishes that relationship marketing's emphasis on collaboration through relationships, networks and interaction is a significant contribution to marketing and to the functioning of a service-oriented market economy. He sees relationship marketing as a paradigmatic shift away from a manipulative seller perspective toward a win-win reciprocal relationship.

In the field of organisational behaviour, David Bowen and Edward Lawler III take up the recent debate in management practice and research about which of two alternative models of organisation is most effective. One is the control model, which relies heavily on hierarchy, procedures, and work standardisation. The other is the involvement model, which is grounded more in participation and self-management. This general debate is offered as the background for addressing the specific question: should the production-line approach to service be replaced by an empowerment approach? In recent years, there has been a rush to adopt an empowerment approach, in which employees face the customer "free of rulebooks", encouraged to do whatever is necessary to satisfy the customer. The production-line approach is a very different management style. Employees face the customer via standardised, procedurally-driven operations. The authors offer a detailed examination of the empowerment approach by considering: what empowerment really means; why to empower — there are benefits and costs; how to empower — a range of management practices are possible; and when to empower. Some important contingencies are considered and it is argued that in some situations, the production-line approach may be the best.

Audrey Gilmore and David Carson consider the internal marketing approach as a means of finding and retaining customer-conscious employees. Internal marketing is also identified as a means of developing and maintaining a "service ethos" which has often been used as a competitive advantage for organisations when they can get it to work! The scope and parameters of internal marketing are discussed in this chapter, together with some of the shortfalls of well-tried attempts to implement internal marketing. Finally, an alternative approach to managing internal customers, based on contemporary marketing management thought, is discussed.

In the next chapter, Adrian Payne and Moira Clark focus on marketing services to external markets. The chapter begins with a recognition that there are a number of external markets, as well as internal markets within the organisation, to which marketing frameworks and principles can be applied. The importance of creating focus through integrating business definition, segmentation and positioning is then discussed — a critical set of activities in achieving direction with intangible services. The key elements of a marketing mix for services are then presented. It is argued that, although imperfect, an augmented marketing mix consisting of seven key elements, is a useful approach to managing services marketing. However, this marketing mix approach will be suboptimal if these elements are not focused on relationship building, are confined to the marketing function rather than being cross-functional in orientation, and are not integrated and used to best advantage.

Brian Fynes, Sean Ennis and Lionello Negri continue the interdisciplinary focus by addressing the theme of quality in the context of the manufacturing/operations management school and the services and marketing school. The interface between both schools of thought is addressed and the traditional perception of the existence of an adversarial relationship between manufacturing and marketing is challenged. This chapter focuses on the issue of quality in both a manufacturing and a logistics context, the latter labelled by Drucker as "management's last frontier". A case study of the journey to lean production at Microsoft Ireland's manufacturing plant and the implications of such changes for the sales and service subsidiaries in Europe is included. Changes in channel structure and relationships, the management of logistics from a peripheral location, and trust, are key elements of the case.

Traditional approaches to the management of services have been criticised for failing to absorb new developments and for being incomplete and manipulative, especially in the services and business-to-business marketing area. The relationship marketing concept has a number of progenitors. In his chapter, Seán de Burca concentrates on one such source: the network perspective. The network perspective has provided fresh insights into how business is co-ordinated, and specifically, is credited with the provision of a rich source of ideas which has given rise to developments in the traditional services marketing literature. The purpose of this chapter is to analyse the contribution and conflicts that the network perspective holds for relationship marketing. The first section presents the theoretical foundations, the assumptions and characteristics of the network perspective. The basic model of industrial networks is presented to illuminate the perspective. The second section concentrates on the current debate within the services marketing literature which deals with how traditional marketing thinking, developed in a consumer goods context, has damaged marketing, in failing to capture the dynamics of services management. Instead, the new marketing concept of "relationship marketing", taking its provenance from the network perspective, is presented. The final section of this chapter analyses the contribution and conflicts that the network perspective holds for the relationship marketing concept.

In recent years, there has been a very considerable growth in the international marketing of services. Much of the motivation for international product marketing can be found in services marketing. Most of the growth which has occurred in international services has been concentrated in a few key sectors such as advertising accounting and financial services. Other services — health services, for example — are becoming important. Developing countries are taking an interest in the international marketing of services because of low-cost factors and the ability to compete in nearby developing country markets. In his chapter, Frank Bradley maintains that the unique status of the international marketing of services offers rich potential for creative new approaches and analysis. Interest in service marketing has reached a considerable height in recent years and this book focuses on services as an important area of academic research. The need for the management of trade-offs in international marketing of services to be addressed by marketing scholars is highlighted. Unless service marketing is perceived by managers to be at least as important as product marketing, now that its importance is recognised, opportunities in the international marketplace will continue to be lost.

In the final chapter, James Heskett takes a strategic view of services management and recognises the influence of many of the interdisciplinary authors in this book on thinking about management in general. This interdisciplinary research movement reflects trends already taking place in practice. Phenomena ranging from the service encounter to other initiatives with stronger prescriptive components, such as research associated with service quality, are also discussed. The application of the concepts of manufacturing management to the service sector and ways in which service management concepts can be used to advantage in manufacturing firms are considered to be significant. The emergence of the holistic view of businesses as a composite of both services and manufacturing, with an increasing emphasis on information as an important element of the business mix and a source of profit, is charted. This chapter reviews a portion of the significant contributions to strategic management thinking resulting from this work while raising questions about future directions of the research itself. This is done in the context of three integrative frameworks: the strategic service vision; the cycle of failure; and the service profit chain.

William J. Glynn
James G. Barnes
Dublin, May 1995

ACKNOWLEDGEMENTS

In preparing this book we called upon the co-operation of over forty authors from a dozen countries. Their extraordinary dedication to the difficult and challenging tasks presented by this multidisciplinary project is evidenced in the excellence of their contributions and the cohesion across the sixteen chapters of this book.

The University College Dublin Centre for Quality & Services Management is indebted to the inspired financial support provided by Telecom Ireland both for this book and all the activities of the Centre in the pursuit of excellence in quality and services management.

We also thank our other corporate supporters: R & A Bailey, Bank of Ireland, Ballygowan, Campbell-Bewley Group, Cantrell & Cochrane, Fred Hanna, Lir Chocolates, The Marketing Institute of Ireland, and Irish Distillers.

We thank our colleagues in University College Dublin and Memorial University of Newfoundland for their support and advice in the preparation of this book.

The continued personal support and intellectual stimulation provided by Alan Corbett, Michael G. Ryan and Andrew Conlan is much appreciated.

We also offer our special thanks to:

Angela O'Farrell, Breda Bradley and Maeve Cunningham, Marie Byrne, Maureen Clinton, Elena Day, Amanda Horan, Barbara Hurley, Carol Kellegher, Fionnuala McCarthy, Dean McGuinness, Deirdre Linehan-O'Brien, Mary Rose O'Shea, Jean Reddan and Anne Woods.

1

SERVICES MANAGEMENT LITERATURE OVERVIEW:

A Rationale for Interdisciplinary Study[*]

Raymond P. Fisk
University of Central Florida, USA

Stephen W. Brown
Arizona State University, USA

Mary Jo Bitner
Arizona State University, USA

PRÉCIS

This participant-observer study is presented from the unique perspective of its authors who have had the opportunity of being actual participants in the development of the services marketing literature. They eloquently describe and report on this process using a three-stage evolutionary metaphor: Crawling Out (1953–79), Scurrying About (1980–85) and Walking Erect (1986–present). Their discussion details how the services marketing literature has evolved over four decades; from an early defensive posture of "services are different," to its current position as a more established discipline within marketing, containing numerous important sub-specialities. In keeping with the marketing concept, customer focus is a central part of the evolution of this body of literature.

The authors trace the evolution of the key ideas within the relevant

---

[*] This chapter is adapted from a prior publication. An extended version appears as follows: Fisk, R.P., Brown, S.W. and Bitner, M.J. "Tracking the Evolution of the Services Marketing Literature," *Journal of Retailing*, Vol. 69, No. 1, 1993, pp. 61–103.

The support of the First Interstate Center for Services Marketing, Arizona State University is also acknowledged.

literature, documenting the prolific authors who contributed to this stream of research. They chronicle the significant events which helped to move the field forward, such as the holding of special interest conferences, the establishment of research institutes, the introduction of new journals, and the provision of industry and financial support for research programmes. All of these various events served to trigger the explosive growth in services marketing research, which has been especially apparent since the mid-1980s.

The authors describe the distinctive nature of the literature in services marketing; with its focus on the "3 I's": Interaction between academics and service practitioners; Interdisciplinary orientation, especially between operations management and human resources; and an International or global focus from the beginning. The chapter closes with speculation on the future direction of the literature. This particular piece of work is valuable not only for its contribution to an understanding of the evolution of the services marketing literature, but also for its bibliography. For this set of references is a single source of the important works in services marketing knowledge, as we know it today.

Robert H. Collins
University of Nevada — Las Vegas, USA

1. INTRODUCTION

The services literature is driven by a rapidly growing population of services scholars and publication outlets. The scholars and the publications have been influenced by economic changes and the changing needs of management, especially during the last 10–15 years. Not since the strong emergence of consumer behaviour in the 1960s has a field developed within the marketing discipline with the passion and determination of services marketing.

Academe is conservative and hidebound by nature. New ideas and concepts gain acceptance slowly. In this context, early services marketing scholars were true risk-takers. They found relatively few publication outlets enthusiastic about their work, and they confronted a discipline debating whether services marketing was different. Today services marketing scholars work in a far more receptive environment. Between 1990 and 1992, for example, 20 books and more than 150 scholarly papers and journal articles were published on the general topic of services marketing — several in the top marketing journals.[1] And now numerous conferences are held annually in Europe and the US, allowing services researchers to present their work.

In addition to the exuberance and the risk-taking that have characterised the discipline's development, three other factors influenced the evolution of the literature. First, considerable interaction has occurred between academics and practitioners. This has resulted in a lively literature anchored in managerial issues and sometimes authored or co-authored by practitioners. Second, the literature has a strong inter-disciplinary orientation especially involving operations and human resource management. Numerous academics from the management field have regularly attended services marketing conferences. Their work has significantly influenced the thinking and writing of services marketing scholars.[2] Third, the services literature has been international from the beginning, with academics in France, Scandinavia, the UK, and the US intensely involved. These factors are essential cross-fertilising ingredients in the evolution of the services marketing literature.

This chapter traces the rapid progress of the general services marketing literature, as opposed to literature on specific services industries; further, the literature examined concentrates on English-language publications.[3] The history of the literature in an academic field can focus on key ideas, authors, or events. This history focuses primarily on the key ideas in the services literature, but prolific authors and significant events are also chronicled.

We have been fortunate to participate in the period described in this chapter. While a personal perspective cannot be completely unbiased, we think that the reader will benefit from our eyewitness accounts of the ideas, authors, and events that created the services marketing literature.

The evolution and legitimisation of services marketing as reflected in the literature can be described in three stages: Crawling Out (Pre-1980), Scurrying About (1980–85), and Walking Erect (1986–Present). A summary tally of the services marketing literature across the three evolutionary stages is presented in Table 1.1. In the Crawling Out stage, 120

---

[1] This tally does not include the myriad publications in every sub-field of services marketing (such as health care, financial, professional, non-profit, education, hospitality, government).

[2] Both the management and marketing fields have found considerable common ground in the pursuit of services knowledge.

[3] The authors acknowledge that there are many services publications in languages other than English, especially in Danish, Dutch, Finnish, French, German, Italian, Norwegian, and Swedish-language publications.

publications were found. During the Scurrying About stage, the literature grew rapidly to 287 publications. Growth accelerated in the Walking Erect stage to 720 publications. A combined total of 1,127 publications have been identified across the history of the services marketing field. Details on the bibliographic data used here are in the Appendix at the end of this chapter.

TABLE 1.1: GENERAL SERVICES MARKETING LITERATURE
(as of November 1992)

	Journals/ Articles	Books	Proceedings Papers and Book Chapters	Dissertations	Total
Crawling Out (pre-1980)[*]	59	10	32	19	120
Scurrying About (1980–85)	104	26	141	16	287
Walking Erect (1986–Present)	361	50	272	37	720
Total	524	86	445	72	1,127

* The first services publication included in the data base is dated 1953. Thus, the Crawling Out stage represents a 27-year time period.

Scholars in the services marketing field first asserted the discipline's right to exist — the Crawling Out stage. This stage began with the first services marketing scholars struggling to publish their work and culminated with a fierce debate over whether "services marketing is different." The debate questioned the very legitimacy of services marketing as a field within the discipline; its outcome could have been the early demise of the field had the debate been lost. In the Scurrying About stage, a thriving colony of nimble scholars created a rapidly growing literature. This was a bustling period when enthusiastic scholars contributed to the rapid development of multiple topics. In the Walking Erect stage, scholars achieved a respected stance as services marketing became an established field within the marketing discipline. Publications on many of the primary topics matured considerably.

To trace this evolution through the literature, major contributions to the general services marketing literature across all three periods are discussed. The final section offers speculations about the future of services literature.

2. CRAWLING OUT: PRE-1980

The Crawling Out stage was a time of discovery and risk-taking. The period captures the embryonic beginnings of the services marketing literature in 1953 and continues through the goods marketing v. services marketing debate that marks the end of this stage. The entire output of the 27 years spanned by this stage is 120 publications, most of which were published in the 1970s (see Table 1.1). Many of the prominent services marketing authors today (including John Bateson, Leonard Berry, Stephen Brown, John Czepiel, Pierre Eiglier, William George, Christian Grönroos, Evert Gummesson, Eugene Johnson, Eric Langeard, Christopher Lovelock and Lynn Shostack) began writing and publishing during this stage.

2.1. General Observations

The early history of the marketing discipline (Bartels, 1988) focused on selling agricultural products. Subsequently, the discipline's scope expanded to marketing physical goods. Services were given little attention in this early literature.[4] In textbooks and other publications, the accepted wisdom that marketing meant goods marketing was rarely challenged.

As the industrialised nations began the transition to service economies, the development received little notice in academe. Although some of these nations' economies were dominated by services as early as the mid-1940s, some time elapsed before scholars began to discuss and study service economies and the marketing that occurred within these settings.

As noted, many of the early scholars took significant risks by writing about the new topic of services marketing. Many began their services research as doctoral students or as untenured professors. Yet one of the traditions of academe is the building of new knowledge "on the shoulders of giants." When the early services scholars chose to pioneer their area, however, they put themselves in the difficult position of developing new knowledge with virtually no research model. They found themselves "seeking to be giants". The personal challenges these early scholars faced are documented by Berry and Parasuraman (1993).

Most of the literature in the Crawling Out stage is conceptual. Assertions defining the nature of services and their marketing were often

---

[4] This is illustrated in the following quote: "Still the main function of 'business' is to market goods. Accounting, banking, insurance, and transportation are only aids, very important aids it is true, to the production and marketing of goods." (Converse, 1921, p. vi).

key parts of these papers. Few publications included empirical investigations. Further, the newness of the services marketing field meant that publishing outlets for the early literature were somewhat limited.

2.2. Early Publications

Most of the scholars studying services marketing in the 1950s did so through their dissertation research (McDowell, 1953; Parker, 1958). These academics began a pattern of innovation that was continued by 17 other budding scholars completing services marketing dissertations during the Crawling Out stage. Several of these scholars went on to significant prominence in the services marketing field. Johnson's dissertation (1969) was the first to ask the question, "Are goods and services different?" and launched the goods v. services debate. At least a dozen dissertations were completed on services marketing topics during the 1970s; 10 were written during the late 1970s. George studied the marketing of service industries, and his dissertation (1972) led to an early publication in the *Journal of Marketing* (George and Barksdale, 1974). George (1977) also wrote the first article in the *Journal of Retailing* on retailing services. Weinberger's dissertation (1976) tested information on services v. goods in a laboratory setting. This became the basis for the first services marketing article in the *Journal of the Academy of Marketing Science* (Weinberger and Brown, 1977). Grönroos' dissertation (1979) focused on the marketing function of service firms, and he continues that emphasis in his recent work (Grönroos, 1990).

Regan (1963) wrote the first of three services marketing articles to appear in the *Journal of Marketing* during the 1960s. He described the US as well advanced into a "service revolution" that would significantly change consumer behaviour. Judd (1964) proposed redefining services and created a services typology. Rathmell (1966) argued that marketing people should devote more attention to the service sector and offered a definition of services still used by scholars today.

Blois (1974) wrote the first services marketing article to appear in the *European Journal of Marketing*. He noted the importance of the service economy in the UK and emphasised the scarcity of services literature sources. Another noteworthy article from the 1970s was Donnelly's (1976) examination of distribution channels for services. He demonstrated that marketing channels for services are significantly different from those for physical goods.

The first book on services marketing was actually a research monograph by Johnson (1964). Based on personal interviews, case studies, trade association contacts and literature review, he sought to show marketing managers how to address the intangibility issues associated with services. The first full-length book was authored by Rathmell (1974). He sought to introduce the service sector to marketing and marketing to the service sector.

Johnson's research monograph on the service economy (1968) was the first of many monographs published by the Marketing Science Institute (MSI). Eiglier et al. (1977) produced the first output of MSI's new consumer services marketing research programme. This collection of five lengthy papers served as a valuable resource to many early researchers. The MSI followed this monograph with *Testing a Conceptual Framework for Consumer Service Marketing* (Bateson et al. 1978).

Perhaps the major outcome of the Crawling Out stage is the literature's delineation of services characteristics. These features — intangibility, inseparability, heterogeneity, and perishability — provided the underpinnings for the case that services marketing is a field distinct from goods marketing. The advocacy for this new field, however, was met with some challenge.

2.3. Goods *v.* Services Marketing Debate

As the literature grew, a fundamental questioning of the legitimacy of services marketing emerged and became most intense during the latter years of the Crawling Out stage. The goods marketing *v.* services marketing debate represented a fundamental challenge to the right of the services marketing field to exist. If the marketing discipline concluded that services marketing was different, the field might gain sufficient acceptance to grow and thrive. However, if the discipline concluded that services marketing was simply a modest extension of goods marketing, the field would be deemed illogical and would die. Today, outside observers looking back at the literature might assume that the debate was primarily one-sided. This is because virtually all services marketing authors during the 1970s felt compelled to argue — at least in the introductions to their articles and papers — that services marketing was different. Few of the critics, however, felt compelled to publish their arguments. Indeed, most advocates were reacting to criticism by reviewers and conference participants. Within academic departments, this questioning continued as informal discussion and among dissertation committee members. Virtually all early services scholars recognised these informal comments as questioning the legitimacy of their research and writing. Such challenges were career threatening, especially because many of the pioneers were young and untenured. In this context, the vigour of the response to these criticisms is not surprising. One of the few early published criticisms of services marketing appeared in the *European Journal of Marketing* by Wyckham, Fitzroy and Mandry (1975). They concluded that a taxonomy of goods *v.* services is dysfunctional.

In the late 1970s, a landmark article altered the evolution of the services marketing field. Lynn Shostack, then a vice president at Citibank, published "Breaking Free From Product Marketing" in the *Journal of Marketing* (1977). Philip Kotler (in Grönroos, 1990, p. xii) has commented, "This article was to alter the course of our thinking about services marketing, if not general marketing itself." In her article, Shostack made the following provocative assertions (p. 73):

> Could marketing itself be 'myopic' in having failed to create relevant paradigms for the service sector?
>
> … service industries have been slow to integrate marketing into the mainstream of decision making and control because marketing offers no guidance, terminology, or practical rules that are clearly relevant to services.

Shostack's criticisms stung all the more because they came from someone outside the academic community. Her article became a rallying cry that inspired numerous services marketing scholars.

Thomas (1978), in an influential *Harvard Business Review* article, also argued that strategy differs for services businesses. More specifically, he stated that traditional strategies developed for physical goods are inappropriate for services and that services managers need to take advantage of the unique strategies available to them.

At an American Marketing Association (AMA) conference on marketing theory, Bateson (1979) and Lovelock (1979) strongly argued that marketing concepts needed to be broadened to encompass services marketing. Berry (1980) wrote one of the definitive assertions (titled "Services Marketing is Different") near the end of the goods marketing *v.* services marketing era.

3. SCURRYING ABOUT (1980–85)

The Scurrying About period represents a time of high interest and enthusiasm in services marketing. For the first time in North America, conferences on the topic brought together established and novice contributors. The first half of the 1980s also represents a bridging period for the literature. The services *v.* goods debate began to wane, and the foundation was laid for the flourishing "Walking Erect" stage (1986–present). During the Scurrying About period, the literature increased significantly, including four pieces in a premier journal, the *Journal of Marketing*.

3.1. General Observations

Two major developments during 1980–85 helped to trigger an exponential growth in the literature that continues to this day. These were the deregulation of service industries and the interaction among participants at a series of AMA conferences.

Deregulation was ushered in at the beginning of the decade, especially in North America. Firms in air transportation, financial services, health care, and telecommunications woke up to an environment of new rivals, intensified price competition, and rising consumer expectations. The role of marketing within these firms was transformed from being modestly important to being a core function vital to the survival of the organisation. With most of these firms recognising the greater significance of the discipline, they were hungry to acquire and understand marketing knowledge.

For some academics, the first exposure to services marketing occurred almost before they fully realised what was happening. Through writing, executive education programmes, and consulting, many scholars attempted to respond to the needs of specific services industries. These educators quickly realised that services marketing differs from goods marketing. Many also recognised the need for research that transcends specific company and industry boundaries.

At the same time, a series of services marketing conferences were sponsored by the AMA. Selected AMA leaders (such as past presidents Leonard Berry and Stephen Brown) convinced the AMA to make a special commitment to the rising interest in services. The Services Marketing Conferences of 1981–3 and 1985 stimulated excitement and productive interchanges between academics and business people in Europe and the US. In 1985, the first AMA Services Marketing Faculty Consortium was held at Texas A&M University, and in 1985 the Marketing Science Institute and New York University also sponsored a special conference on service encounters. Much of the literature of the 1980s and 1990s emerged from discussions at these events. A result has been an on-going sensitivity to both European and North American contributions and to managerial implications.

During the Scurrying About stage, two new journals were created: the *Services Industries Journal (SIJ)* in 1980 and the *Journal of Professional Services Marketing (JPSM)* in 1985. The First Interstate Center for Services Marketing (FICSM) at Arizona State University was established in 1985. The centre further legitimised the field by encouraging scholarly research and establishing ties with the business community. Collectively, deregulation, the practitioner–academic dialogue, and the European–North American connection had a pronounced impact on the literature of the time and on subsequently published work.

3.2. Contributions

During the 1980–85 period, the quantity of literature increased as illustrated in Table 1.1. Although the goods *v.* services debate was dying out in the mid-1980s, the proceedings of the AMA services conferences suggest a lingering dispute. More and more scholars, however, began to investigate substantive issues unique to the field, such as service quality and service encounters.

The appearance in the *Journal of Marketing* of four services articles within three years (1983–85) encouraged many services scholars and further legitimated the field. Christopher Lovelock's "Classifying Services to Gain Strategic Marketing Insights" (1983) proposed five classification schemes for services that transcend industry boundaries. The article received the journal's prestigious Alpha Kappa Psi Award and strengthened the case for the uniqueness of services marketing.

Two significant *Journal of Marketing* articles by A. Parasuraman, Valarie Zeithaml and Leonard Berry were published in 1985. In the first article, the authors presented a conceptual framework summarising the unique characteristics of services. They reported findings from a survey of service managers, concerning the strategies used to respond to marketing problems (Zeithaml, Parasuraman and Berry, 1985). The authors compared the problems and strategies cited in the literature with those reported by the managers and offered suggestions for reflection. Two issues later, the same author team published their "Conceptual Model of Service Quality" (1985). This piece launched a highly successful research programme supported by the MSI. This landmark article and subsequent studies by Parasuraman et al. stimulated others to contribute to the area (for example, Brown and Swartz, 1989; Cronin and Taylor, 1992). It led to service quality becoming a core topic for services marketing. A third services marketing article by Solomon, Surprenant, Czepiel and Gutman (1985) in the *Journal of Marketing* established "service encounters" as a research topic.

Although the preceding works are among the most notable articles of the Scurrying About stage, other important contributions were made during this period. Papers from the AMA services conferences proceedings are some of the most widely cited literature (e.g., Donnelly and George,

1981; Berry, Shostack and Upah, 1983; Bloch, Upah and Zeithaml, 1985). Papers having a profound impact, among others, include Berry (1983) on relationship marketing, Booms and Bitner's (1981) expanded marketing mix for services, Grönroos (1981) on internal marketing, and Zeithaml (1981) on consumer evaluation processes for services.

In addition to the *Journal of Marketing,* the *Harvard Business Review (HBR)* has long been an outlet for literature on services. During this period, the *HBR* published articles by Levitt (1981) on marketing intangibles, Takeuchi and Quelch (1983) on service quality, Canton (1984) on the service economy, and Shostack (1984) on service design. Levitt's widely cited piece, in particular, offered significant services marketing insights, to both business and academic audiences. The *Journal of Retailing* also furthered the development of the field, publishing contributions by Berry (1980) on the time-buying consumer, by Kelly and George (1982) on strategic issues for retailing of services, and by Bateson (1985) on the self-service consumer. The work of management and psychology academics, such as Richard Chase, Peter Mills and Benjamin Schneider, also had a significant impact. Their work began to enlighten marketing scholars on the human resource and operations management issues associated with services. Further, the contributions of Europeans John Bateson, K.J. Blois, Christian Grönroos, Evert Gummesson, Richard Normann and others significantly influenced the services literature.

A number of noteworthy books appeared in the early to mid-1980s, each having a different orientation but pronounced influence. Lovelock (1984) published the first services marketing textbook. By bringing together cases, articles, and text material in a single text, his book provided a major resource to faculty teaching of the emerging courses in the discipline. The holistic work of the "Nordic School" became particularly influential during this period as illustrated in Normann's (1984) *Service Management* and Grönroos' and Gummesson's (1985) *Services Marketing — Nordic School Perspectives.* In 1985, *The Marketing of Services* by British academic Donald W. Cowell was also published. Fisk and Tansuhaj (1985) edited the first bibliography of services marketing literature. Some of the articles, papers, and books published during the Scurrying About period continued to defend services as fundamentally different from goods. Others, however, targeted new areas of inquiry, such as service design and mapping and service encounters; they laid the groundwork for the Walking Erect period.

4. WALKING ERECT: 1986–PRESENT

This stage in the services marketing literature can be characterised as a period of explosive growth in numbers of publications and increasing empirical and theoretical rigor in their content. The literature has focused on specific marketing problems of service businesses. These topics include managing quality given the heterogeneity of the service experience, designing and controlling intangible processes, managing supply and demand in capacity-constrained services, and organisational issues resulting from the overlap in marketing and operations functions. This problem focus has resulted in the field becoming increasingly cross-functional because many of the research issues have multiple roots that span traditional functional boundaries.

4.1. General Observations

The Walking Erect period has produced an increasing number of marketing academics conducting research in services marketing. From the handful of marketing academics who provided enthusiastic moral support to each other at the first AMA Services Conference in 1981, the numbers of services researchers mushroomed during the late 1980s and continues to the present. Researchers in other areas (Claes Fornell, Richard Oliver, Linda Price, Roland Rust, Steven Shugan, for example) began developing their research to address marketing issues in services, while every year more doctoral students have pursued dissertations in services marketing. In addition, virtually all of those who met at the early AMA conferences (e.g., John Bateson, Leonard Berry, Mary Jo Bitner, Bernard Booms, Stephen Brown, James Donnelly, Raymond Fisk, William George, Christian Grönroos, Evert Gummesson, Eric Langeard, Christopher Lovelock, Carol Surprenant and Valarie Zeithaml) continue to contribute to the development of the field. The boom in research was encouraged by the AMA Services Conferences that continued through 1991.

Research was also encouraged by the first Quality in Service (QUIS 1) meeting in Karlstad, Sweden, in 1988, which was jointly sponsored by the Service Research Center at the University of Karlstad and the FICSM at Arizona State University. This meeting brought academics and business practitioners together from 10 different countries. It was pivotal in moving services research ahead. QUIS 2, held in 1990 in Norwalk, Connecticut, and QUIS 3, held again in Karlstad in 1992 with 15 countries represented, encouraged the enthusiastic continuation of research in the field. The international and cross-functional dimensions of the field also are evident in the services management and marketing research seminars sponsored since 1988 by the Université d'Aix-Marseille III in France and hosted by two of the field's early and still active academics, Eric Langeard and Pierre Eiglier.

The establishment of the Center for Services Marketing at Vanderbilt University and its sponsorship of four conferences on services marketing between 1990 and 1993 provided impetus as well. The FICSM at Arizona State University also flourished during this period. The centre's working paper series resulted in publications in the *Journal of Marketing, Journal of Retailing, Journal of Marketing Research* and others. In 1992, the FICSM also produced the first volume of an annual series (*Advances in Services Marketing*, edited by Teresa Swartz, David Bowen, and Stephen Brown 1992a). In June, 1993, the AMA Faculty Consortium was held on services marketing at Arizona State University. This was the second Services Marketing Faculty Consortium and it provided another forum for leading services marketing scholars. These meetings and seminars, as well as the establishment of university-based centres, suggest that the research momentum generated in this period will continue.

4.2. Explosive Growth

The explosion in the number of books, journal publications, conference proceedings, and dissertations dealing with services marketing during the Walking Erect stage is documented in Table 1.1. Growing numbers of general services marketing publications in the top academic marketing journals characterise this period. The *Journal of Marketing* has been the primary outlet for academic services marketing research among the field's top journals. The *Journal of Marketing* published 13 services marketing papers since 1987 (compared to a total of four between 1980 and 1985). The *Journal of Consumer Research* published three services articles. The *Journal of Marketing Research* published two services papers. while the *Journal of Retailing* published 11 general services marketing pieces. In addition, two journals dealing specifically with services marketing and management were started: the *Journal of Services Marketing* in 1987, and the *International Journal of Service Industry Management* in 1990.

Along with the rapid growth in journal publications, the number of dissertations in services marketing doubled in the Walking Erect stage when compared to the preceding period. Because a number of years often elapse from the time a dissertation is completed until a journal article is published, the rising number of dissertations is an early indicator of journal articles to come.

A number of significant books have been written in the field of services (Heskett, 1986; Johnson, Scheuing and Gaida, 1986; Lovelock, 1988; 1991; 1992; Bateson, 1989; 1992; Grönroos, 1990; Heskett, Sasser and Hart, 1990; Bowen, Chase and Cummings, 1990; Zeithaml, Parasuraman and Berry, 1990; Brown, Gummesson, Edvardsson, and Gustavsson, 1991; Berry and Parasuraman, 1991; Sasser, Hart and Heskett, 1991; Swartz, Bowen and Brown, 1992). A new services marketing textbook by John Bateson was added in 1989, with a second edition in 1992. Also, Christopher Lovelock published a second edition of his Services Marketing text in 1991. In addition, numerous books on topics closely related to services marketing, such as customer service, relationship management, and service quality, have been published.

4.3. Focus

The cross-disciplinary and international nature of the field is becoming increasingly evident in the literature. In reviewing the citations of any major journal article on services, the cross-functional and international sources that support nearly all research in this area are immediately apparent. For example, a recent *Journal of Marketing* article on service environments (Bitner, 1992) cites research from management, human resources, operations, and social psychology journals as well as from marketing. Similarly, a journal article on managing service organisations in the prestigious *Academy of Management Review* (Larsson and Bowen, 1989) includes 20 marketing citations. Clearly, while the research has become more focused and rigorous, services researchers have drawn from related fields to solve problems and build theories for services marketing. The international focus is expanding similarly. This is apparent in article citations as well as in the addition of the *International Journal of Service Industry Management* published in the United Kingdom, the QUIS meetings, and the biannual research seminars in France.

Journal publications in services marketing have become more empirically based and theory driven, as opposed to presenting conceptual discussions or debates. Differences between goods and services appear to be assumed, and researchers have begun to focus on substantive business issues and problems stemming from the implications of these basic service differences. Topics that gained substantial attention are rooted in relatively isolated pieces of research published during the preceding periods. However, not until the Walking Erect period could a cohesive core of research be identified under these topics.

4.4. Specific Topics

Service Quality. The single most researched area in services marketing, to date, is service quality. The interest in service quality parallels the focus on quality, total quality management, and customer satisfaction in business during the last decade. The roots of the service quality research reside in early conceptual work from Europe (Grönroos, 1983; Lehtinen and Lehtinen, 1982, for example), and customer satisfaction theory (Oliver, 1980, for example). Most of the recent work on service quality in marketing can be credited to the pioneering contributions of A. Parasuraman, Leonard Berry and Valarie Zeithaml. Their ongoing research, has produced a well-received conceptual framework (the Gaps Model) and a measurement instrument, SERVQUAL, for assessing service quality. While there is healthy—and for the most part productive—debate regarding the dimensional nature of SERVQUAL across industries, and the precise wording of the SERVQUAL items, researchers generally agree that the scale items are good predictors of overall service quality (Babakus and Boller, 1992; Bolton and Drew, 1991a, b; Brown and Swartz, 1989; Carman, 1990; Cronin and Taylor, 1992; and Parasuraman, Berry and Zeithaml, 1991). The debate underscores the importance of the topic and the significance of the contributions to date. Such interchange helps refine the meaning of service quality.

Researchers have contributed empirical studies on service satisfaction, a closely related topic that is sometimes difficult to distinguish from service quality (Bitner, 1990; Bitner, Booms and Tetreault, 1990; Crosby, Evans and Cowles, 1990; Oliva, Oliver and MacMillan, 1992). Researchers do not share common definitions of the terms, nor is there clear understanding of how the two relate. Discussion of these issues will certainly continue in the near future (see Rust and Oliver, 1993).

Service Encounters/Experiences. Another prominent stream of research relates to service encounters/experiences or "moments of truth" (Carlzon, 1987). The underlying assumption is that customer perceptions of service encounters are important elements of customer satisfaction, perceptions of quality, and long-term loyalty. Research published recently can be traced to the book entitled *The Service Encounter* (Czepiel, Solomon and Surprenant, 1985), the first *Journal of Marketing* article on service encounters (Solomon, Surprenant, Czepiel and Gutman, 1985), and numerous conference proceedings papers from the early 1980s.

Currently the research on service encounters can be divided into three primary types. First, considerable attention is being paid to the *management* of customer and employee interactions in service encounters and to understanding how customers evaluate individual service encounters (for example, Bitner, 1990; Bitner, Booms and Tetreault, 1990; Czepiel, 1990; Lewis and Entwistle, 1990; Mills, 1990;

Surprenant and Solomon, 1987). A second research focus is on customer involvement in service encounters and the customer's role in service production and delivery (for example, Goodwin, 1990; Kelley, Donnelly, and Skinner, 1990; Larsson and Bowen, 1989). The roots of this research are in Bateson's early work on self-service customers (Bateson, 1983). The third research focus on service encounters examines the role of tangibles and physical environment in the customer's evaluation of encounters (Berry and Parasuraman, 1991; Bitner, 1992; Hui and Bateson, 1991, for example).

Service Design. Because services are processes, the actual steps involved in delivering and receiving the service (traditionally called the service "operation"), assume tremendous marketing importance. The growth of Total Quality Management (TQM) has provided another catalyst for research on service processes because TQM is process-oriented. Unlike manufacturing, however, service industries typically do not apply rigorous process design standards prior to introducing new services, and service processes are typically less controllable because of the human element. Although this topic is likely to receive greater attention in the near future, most contributions to date have been in service blueprinting and service mapping, an area pioneered by Lynn Shostack (1984; 1987; 1992) and Jane Kingman-Brundage (1989; 1991). A primary difference between service blueprinting and typical operations flowcharts is that a blueprint incorporates the customer and the customer's actions on the same flow diagram.

Others have contributed to an increased understanding of the marketing impact and role of service operations and process design (Baum, 1990; George and Gibson, 1991; Scheuing and Johnson, 1989, for example). The role of technology in service process design and its impact on service quality are topics that have received attention outside marketing; they are sure to influence services design research (Quinn and Paquette, 1990; Quinn, Doorley and Paquette, 1990, for example).

Customer Retention and Relationship Marketing. Services researchers since the early 1980s have drawn attention to the need to retain, as well as attract, customers (Berry, 1983). Relationship marketing recognises the value of current customers and the need to continue providing services to existing customers so that they will remain loyal. For marketers, this is a definite shift away from more traditional marketing approaches.

The research on relationship marketing and customer retention has taken various forms. For example, some research focuses on constructs, such as trust and relationship commitment and how these constructs relate to customer satisfaction and loyalty (for example, Crosby and

Stephens, 1987; Crosby, Evans and Cowles, 1990). Other researchers have focused on specific breakthrough strategies for retaining customers, such as building an effective recovery strategy for service failure situations (for example, Berry and Parasuraman, 1991; Hart, Heskett and Sasser, 1990) or offering service guarantees to reduce risk and build loyalty (Hart, 1988, for example). Understanding and calculating both the long-term value of a customer and the lost revenue-profits for defecting customers (Reichheld and Sasser, 1990, for example) are two other research topics that fall within the relationship marketing focus. These latter topics (recovery, guarantees, and the cost of defecting customers) have been embraced quickly by business practitioners.

Internal Marketing. Two basic ideas underlie the concept of internal marketing. First, "everyone in the organisation has a customer" (Grönroos, 1981). It is not just contact personnel who need to be concerned with satisfying their customers. Everyone in the organisation has someone whom they must serve. The second basic idea is that internal customers must be sold on the service and happy in their jobs before they can effectively serve the final customer. This idea suggests that marketing tools and concepts (such as segmentation and marketing research) can be used internally with employees (Berry, 1981).

The basic premise of internal marketing is that satisfied employees (or well-served internal customers) will lead to satisfied customers (or well-served external customers). George (1990) provides an excellent review of internal marketing, a concept that has quickly pervaded the business community. A number of recent contributions on internal marketing have appeared in both the marketing and management literature (Berry and Parasuraman, 1991; Grönroos, 1990; Gummesson, 1987; Schlesinger and Heskett, 1991a, b; Tansuhaj, Randall and McCullough, 1988). Empowerment is highly relevant to internal marketing, and this topic has received solid and thought-provoking coverage in a recent services management publication by Bowen and Lawler (1992).

5. PUBLICATION ANALYSIS ACROSS THE THREE EVOLUTIONARY STAGES

The preceding sections examined the three stages of evolution of the services marketing literature by discussing the themes, ideas and key contributions to the literature during each separate period. Before concluding and offering speculations for the future, we want to quantify and summarise the literature as it has evolved *across* all three periods according to type of publication, where publications have appeared and who the most prolific contributors are.

TABLE 1.2: THE 56 MOST PROLIFIC GENERAL SERVICES
MARKETING AUTHORS[1] (as of November 1992)

Author	Frequency[2]	Author	Frequency
Berry, Leonard	35	Upah, Gregory	8
Grönroos, Christian	31	Blois, K.J.	7
Lovelock, Christopher	27	Congram, Carole	7
Parasuraman, A.	24	Edvinsson, Leif	7
Gummesson, Evert	22	Guseman, Dennis	7
Zeithaml, Valarie	22	Quinn, James Brian	7
Bateson, John	21	Stern, Barbara	7
Fisk, Raymond	20	Swartz, Teresa	7
Bitner, Mary Jo	19	Collier, David	6
Bowen, David	19	Drew, James	6
George, William	19	Evans, Kenneth	6
Schneider, Benjamin	19	Orsini, Joseph	6
Chase, Richard	17	Shaw, John	6
Brown, Stephen	14	Babakus, Emin	5
Langeard, Eric	14	Bowers, Michael	5
Shostack, G. Lynn	14	Cowell, Donald	5
Mills, Peter	11	Cravens, David	5
Crosby, Lawrence	10	Davis, Duane	5
Czepiel, John	10	Edvardsson, Bo	5
Heskett, James	10	Hart, Christopher	5
Johnson, Eugene	10	Hoffman, K. Douglas	5
Scheuing, Eberhard	10	Hui, Michael	5
Booms, Bernard	9	Kelly, J. Patrick	5
Eiglier, Pierre	9	Lamb, Charles	5
Goodwin, Cathy	8	Schlesinger, Leonard	5
Grove, Stephen	8	Tansuhaj, Patriya	5
Sasser, W. Earl	8	Zinkhan, George	5
Solomon, Michael	8	**Total**	**613**
Surprenant, Carol	8		

1. A number of these authors consider their primary discipline to be an area
   other than marketing.
2. Frequencies reflect each time an author's name appears, regardless of
   whether the publication has single or multiple authors.

The literature is categorised into four types in Table 1.1 (p. 4): Journal articles (524); books (86); proceedings papers and book chapters (445); and dissertations (72). The five journals publishing the most services marketing articles as of November 1992 are the *Journal of Services Marketing* (84), *International Journal of Service Industry Management* (41), *Harvard Business Review* (34), *Services Industries Journal* (30) and *Journal of Marketing* (25). The most frequent authors of books are Christian Grönroos (3), Eugene Johnson (3) and Christopher Lovelock (three, not counting two second editions).

Fifty-six services marketing authors are listed in Table 1.2 (p. 18) according to how many general services marketing publications they have contributed to the literature. A cut-off of five citations was imposed on the listing. Numerous other scholars have published two, three, and four contributions. The numbers in the table are frequencies and therefore do not necessarily translate directly into relative contribution or impact on the discipline. The reader is cautioned that this list of authors is based solely on publications in English. Several authors have published numerous works in other languages (Christian Grönroos, Evert Gummesson, Eric Langeard, for example). This list does not include the industry-specific publications that most of these authors have published.

Together, the 56 authors named in Table 1.2 have published 613 general services marketing pieces. These works, however, are not separate publications. Significant co-authorship is represented. Several authors are from a discipline other than marketing (Bernard Booms, David Bowen, Richard Chase, and Benjamin Schneider). Finally, the list includes two noteworthy executives, Lynn Shostack and Gregory Upah, and at least four former academics whose current careers focus on business (John Bateson, Lawrence Crosby, Christopher Lovelock and Valarie Zeithaml). Several of these services authors have maintained a steady publication flow from the Crawling Out stage through the Walking Erect stage.

6. CONTINUING EVOLUTION: ENVISIONING THE FUTURE LITERATURE

This chapter has documented the founding, emergence, and legitimation of a whole new literature. The explosion of articles, papers, books, and dissertations has been remarkable, leading us naturally to ask: What will the literature of the future be like? What will the next stage of the evolution generate? Based on documentation of the past and our positions as active researchers and participants in the field, we will attempt to look ahead. Recognising that the past often predicts the future, we are fairly comfortable in projecting from the present trends. However, we also take this opportunity to speculate, dream, and envision the next era. We will not attempt to name the next stage or to predict a precise time frame. We leave that task to future authors.

Based on the previous 40 years, but particularly the last 15, we expect a continued broadening, deepening, and sharpening of the research. By increasing breadth, we mean a continuation of the trend to incorporate theories and ideas from disciplines outside marketing, particularly management, operations, and human resources. This trend is consistent with the desire of businesses to break down functional barriers in their organisations to improve effectiveness, which is often particularly essential for service businesses. By increasing depth, we mean extended development and deeper thinking on current research topics such as service quality, service satisfaction, service encounters and service design. We also expect that the literature will continue to sharpen in theoretical and methodological rigour, making ever greater contributions in all these areas.

With the recent entry into the field of researchers whose expertise is in measurement, statistics and decision support modelling, we would also expect more quantitative contributions. The practical focus and managerial relevance of services research is likely to develop even further as a result of the continuing involvement of practitioners in helping to formulate research issues and supporting the research efforts of scholars. The involvement of a global community of scholars will continue as well. We envision even closer working relationships and co-authoring among scholars from different countries, as opportunities to interact become more frequent, and service business problems become increasingly global.

We also expect the interest in services marketing to continue to grow among academic researchers. Given the dramatic increase in services dissertations, we expect journal contributions from new scholars. In addition, we note a rising number of established, well-respected academics turning their research interests at least partially to services issues. The field is attractive both to new and to established academics because the research issues are practical and plentiful, the community of researchers and practitioners is receptive and open, and a growing number of outlets for services publications exists. Further, there are more opportunities for these researchers to interact through various events, both in Europe and in North America.

We will also speculate about topics that will continue to draw research interest, as well as new areas for contributions. We recognise that we cannot predict the future with certainty, so our ideas are based in part on our understanding of the current trends and on our knowledge from brainstorming sessions at recent symposia gatherings (see also Swartz, Bowen and Brown, 1992b).

6.1. Service Design and Delivery

Service blueprinting and mapping have received some attention in the literature, but compared to the engineering and production emphasis associated with the development and manufacturing of goods, research on the parallel activities for services is meagre. We believe that service engineering, design, and execution will be key areas for scholarly and managerial inquiry. Services marketing scholars have special opportunities to incorporate the customer's needs into design and delivery of services.

6.2. Service Encounters and Service Experiences

As noted earlier, literature on contact personnel and customer relationships emerged recently. As customer expectations increase, we anticipate front-line service employees assuming the role of consultant and salesperson more frequently. In other words, organisations will rely on these representatives not only to provide the service but also to solve customers' problems, gather information on customer needs and preferences, and cross-sell additional services. We foresee research on long-term service experiences beyond once-off, brief transactions. We also expect greater focus on the relationships among service encounter issues and other organisational concerns such as quality and profitability.

6.3. Service Quality and Customer Satisfaction

Certainly the dominant theme in recent services research has been quality. We foresee this interest continuing and assuming broader, deeper dimensions. We expect more research on internal and external quality and the interrelationships between the two areas. The dynamics of quality are also likely to be investigated by researchers through studies of multiple exchanges over time and through a hierarchy of quality measurements ranging from individual service encounters to overall firm or even industry assessments. Finally, we see a coming together (if not a merging) of the heretofore independent research streams of customer satisfaction and service quality. How to establish clear links between customer satisfaction and quality on the one hand and internal measures of efficiency and employee compensation on the other are important future directions for research.

6.4. Other Future Topics

Although the observations on the preceding three areas are reasonable predictions given the past, we also envisage a future that could — and undoubtedly should — include research on some of the following topics:

- *Service Recovery.* Despite TQM's call for "zero defects" and "doing it right the first time," service providers typically cannot meet these high expectations. Unlike tangible goods, 100 per cent quality cannot be engineered into a service, especially when even the definition of the service is in the eyes of the beholder. This recognition indicates opportunities for research on topics such as consumer complaining behaviour, managerial responses to these behaviours, and employee–customer complaint interactions and resolution.

- *Reverse Marketing.* This topic focuses on the service provider improving relationships with suppliers and vendors to provide the final customer with higher service quality. Some organisations, for example, are asking their suppliers to meet or exceed the same customer satisfaction standards that they set for themselves. To date, services researchers have virtually ignored the value-added chain and instead have chosen to focus on the final consumer. We see a need to broaden the scope of services research to embrace topics like reverse marketing and other forms of organisational alliances.

- *Internal Marketing and Support Services.* The view of employees as customers has been discussed in the literature but not subjected to extensive research. Further, the considerations associated with providing a service internally or outsourcing to the external market is an additional area of needed research. For example, can we transfer our understanding of external service encounters and customer satisfaction to the provision of *internal* services? Also, can internal service guarantees work and what should be guaranteed?

- *Modelling and Measurement.* The existing literature is replete with unsubstantiated principles about service excellence, service quality and related topics. Yet too little evidence exists to substantiate whether these principles result in outcomes such as long-term customer satisfaction and profitability. Understanding the links between customer satisfaction and employee satisfaction also demands further research. Furthermore, alternative measures and methods for understanding these principles and related factors still need to be developed and refined. For example, while SERVQUAL is a popular measure for service quality, refinements and alternative approaches are needed in measuring this important construct.

- *Technology Infusion.* The current services literature is implicitly mired in the paradigm of "low tech and high touch". The typical need for high levels of human interaction has led some writers to downplay the potential contributions of technology to services marketing. In the work place, however, new technology is empowering service employees by quickly giving them more information for use in deciding how best to serve customers. Technology can also help organisations to design and engineer services processes. Researchers have opportunities to break out of the prevailing low-tech paradigm and study customers' relative preferences for high-tech service in and of itself and in conjunction with high-touch experiences. The impact of technology on the entire service industry and organisational structures and business methods demands further research too (see Quinn, 1992).

This discussion of future research needs is far from exhaustive. Topics such as customer retention and customer value, managing supply and demand for a perishable inventory or capacity, and service quality and productivity in the public sector could easily be added to this list. In pursuing future services research, scholars should recognise and incorporate relevant contributions made outside their geographical sphere and the marketing discipline. Contributions by colleagues in operations management, human resources management and psychology are highly relevant as well.

7. CONCLUSION

The evolution of the services literature can be tracked across three metaphorical evolutionary stages from its early beginnings in the Crawling Out stage to the most recent publications in the Walking Erect stage. As with human evolution, the outcomes at each of the three stages would have been difficult to predict precisely at an earlier stage. Thus, while we have speculated on future literature, we cannot give a precise label or time frame for the next phase of the evolution. The face of the literature at each stage, the ideas that emerged, and even the contributors who chose to write in the field truly evolved and were shaped by a variety of forces (documented in Berry and Parasuraman, 1993).

Clearly the risk-taking of services marketing researchers (particularly in the Crawling Out phase) was a key element shaping the literature. However, as the debate over whether services marketing is distinct died out, it became less risky for academics to enter the field. During the second (Scurrying About) phase, specific problems faced by business practitioners in service industries influenced the large numbers of topics that were researched. The problems first identified in this phase were carried forward in the Walking Erect stage and, in fact, the roots of all the major topic areas (such as service quality, service encounters, internal marketing) can be tracked to the Scurrying About phase. This problem-centred research focus later branched into the issues faced by manufacturing companies that were beginning (during the Walking Erect stage) to view service as a competitive advantage, if not a competitive necessity. As the term *Walking Erect* implies, the literature published during this evolutionary phase stands on its own and is a solid contribution to management practice and academic theories of marketing in a variety of topic areas.

As with human evolution, evidence of past stages is always apparent in later evolutionary stages. The entrepreneurial spirit of the early services marketing researchers in the Crawling Out stage is still evident in the topics selected for research and in the excitement and enthusiasm with which they are pursued. The business problem-centred nature of the research in the Scurrying About phase has also been carried forward. We expect that the strong international nature of the research in the Walking Erect phase will continue and will rapidly expand as scholars all over the world emerge to pursue new research agendas. We also expect that the strong interdisciplinary nature of the research in the Walking Erect phase will continue and expand. Further, we expect that the interest in service issues from manufacturing businesses will also carry forward into the next stage of evolution. All of these influences promise that the cross-fertilisation of ideas that has been a hallmark of services research will continue.

We are certain of one thing: the community of scholars, the wealth of issues, and methods for understanding them will continue to grow. The future for scholarship and for scholars in services marketing has never been brighter. We foresee the services literature of the future burgeoning in quantity, but more importantly, in quality. This growth will raise new unanswered questions in need of research that will represent future opportunities. The literature documented here, and future contributions, will shape the next evolutionary stage, enriching not only the services marketing literature but also the marketing discipline.

APPENDIX

The bibliographic data used in this chapter are derived and expanded from prior bibliographic work by Fisk and Tansuhaj (1985) and from an electronic data base known as SERVMARK developed by Fisk,

Tansuhaj and Crosby (1988). These bibliographies contain both general services marketing literature and industry-specific services marketing literature. This chapter, however, focuses exclusively on the general services marketing literature containing 1,127 sources as of November 1992.

Four major kinds of general services marketing literature are included in the bibliography: journal articles, books, conference proceedings papers, and dissertations. These represent the principal outlets for disseminating marketing knowledge. In addition, the bibliography includes original book chapters and a few early monographs from the Marketing Science Institute. Books from the popular press are included. Services marketing articles from thousands of newspapers and magazines are not included. Nor are cases and working papers a part of this review. The services marketing literature discussed in this chapter is primarily North American, although many worldwide English-language publications are listed.

Scholarly services marketing literature is primarily discussed in this chapter — that is, publications written primarily by academics for an academic audience. As noted earlier, the boundaries between the fields of services marketing and services management are somewhat fluid. Several services marketing topics, in other words, are not the exclusive domain of marketers. Thus, numerous publications listed were judged to be of significant interest and value to services marketing scholars, even though they were written by management professors and published in management journals.

REFERENCES

Babakus, E. and Boller, G.W., "An Empirical Assessment of the SERVQUAL Scale", *Journal of Business Research*, 24 May, 1992, pp. 253–68.

Bartels, R., *The History of Marketing Thought*, Third Edition, Publishing Horizons, Inc., Columbus, OH, 1988.

Bateson, J.E.G., "Why We Need Service Marketing", in O.C. Ferrell, S.W. Brown, and C.W. Lamb (Eds.), *Conceptual and Theoretical Developments in Marketing*, American Marketing Association, Chicago, IL, 1979, pp. 131–46.

Bateson, J.E.G., "The Self-Service Customer — Empirical Findings", in L.L. Berry, L.G. Shostack, and G.D. Upah (Eds.), *Emerging Perspectives on Services Marketing,* American Marketing Association, Chicago, IL, 1983, pp. 50–3.

Bateson, J.E.G., "Self-Service Consumer: An Exploratory Study", *Journal of Retailing,* Vol. 61, Fall, 1985, pp. 49–76.

Bateson, J.E.G., *Managing Services Marketing: Text and Readings,* Dryden Press, Hinsdale, IL, 1989.

Bateson, J.E.G., *Managing Services Marketing: Text and Readings,* Second Edition, Dryden Press, Orlando, FL, 1992.

Bateson, J.E.G., P. Eiglier, E. Langeard, and C.H. Lovelock, *Testing a Conceptual Framework for Consumer Service Marketing*, Marketing Science Institute, Cambridge, MA, 1978.

Baum, S.H., "Making Your Service Blueprint Pay Off", *Journal of Services Marketing,* Vol. 4, Summer, 1990, pp. 45–52.

Berry, L.L. (a), "Services Marketing is Different", *Business*, Vol. 30, May/June, 1980, pp. 24–29.

Berry, L.L. (b), "The Time Buying Consumer", *Journal of Retailing,* Vol. 56, Winter, 1980, pp. 58–69.

Berry, L.L., "Perspectives on the Retailing of Services", in R.W. Stampfl, and E.C. Hirschman (Eds.), *Theory in Retailing: Traditional and Non-traditional Sources,* American Marketing Association, Chicago, IL, 1981, pp. 9–20.

Berry, L.L., "Relationship Marketing", in L. Berry, L.G. Shostack, and G.D. Upah (Eds.), *Emerging Perspectives on Services Marketing,* American Marketing Association, Chicago, IL, 1983, pp. 25–28.

Berry, L.L. and A. Parasuraman., *Marketing Services: Competing Through Quality,* The Free Press, New York, 1991.

Berry, L.L. and A. Parasuraman, "Building a New Academic Field — The Case of Services Marketing", *Journal of Retailing,* Vol. 69, Spring, 1993.

Berry, L.L., A. Parasuraman, and V.A. Zeithaml, "The Service Quality Puzzle", *Business Horizons*, Vol. 31, September/October, 1988, pp. 35–43.

Berry, L.L., G.L. Shostack, and G.D. Upah (Eds.), *Emerging Perspectives on Services Marketing*, American Marketing Association, Chicago, IL, 1983.

Berry, L.L., V.A. Zeithaml, and A. Parasuraman, "Five Imperatives for Improving Service Quality", *Sloan Management Review*, Vol. 31, Summer, 1990, pp. 29–38.

Bitner, M.J., "Evaluating Service Encounters: The Effects of Physical Surroundings and Employee Responses", *Journal of Marketing*, Vol. 54, April, 1990, pp. 69–82.

Bitner, M.J., "Servicescapes: The Impact of Physical Surroundings on Customers and Employees" *Journal of Marketing,* Vol. 56, April, 1992, pp. 57–71.

Bitner, M.J., B.H. Booms, and M.S. Tetreault, "The Service Encounter: Diagnosing Favorable and Unfavorable Incidents", *Journal of Marketing,* Vol. 54, January, 1990, pp. 71–84.

Bloch, T.M., G.D. Upah, and V.A. Zeithaml, (Eds.), *Services Marketing in a Changing Environment*, American Marketing Association, Chicago, IL, 1985.

Blois, K.J., "The Marketing of Services: An Approach", *European Journal of Marketing,* Vol. 8, Summer, 1974, pp. 137–145.

Bolton, R.N. and J.H. Drew (a), "A Longitudinal Analysis of the Impact of

Service Changes on Consumer Attitudes", *Journal of Marketing*, Vol. 55, January, 1991, pp. 1–9.

Bolton, R.N. and J.H. Drew (b), "A Multistage Model of Customers' Assessments of Service Quality and Value", *Journal of Consumer Research*, Vol. 17 No. 4, 1991, pp. 375–84.

Booms, B.H. and M.J. Bitner, "Marketing Strategies and Organizational Structures for Service Firms", in J.H. Donnelly and W.R. George (Eds.), *Marketing of Services,* American Marketing Association, Chicago, IL, 1981, pp. 47–51.

Bowen, D.E. and E.E. Lawler, "The Empowerment of Service Workers: What, Why, How, and When", *Sloan Management Review,* Vol. 33, Spring, 1992, pp. 31–9.

Bowen, D.E., R.B. Chase, and T.G. Cummings (Eds.), *Service Management Effectiveness: Balancing Strategy, Organization and Human Resources, Operations and Marketing,* Jossey-Bass Inc., San Francisco, CA, 1990.

Brown, S.W. and T.A. Swartz, "A Gap Analysis of Professional Service Quality", *Journal of Marketing*, Vol. 53, April, 1989, pp. 92–98.

Brown, S.W., E. Gummesson, B. Edvardsson and B. Gustavsson (Eds.), *Service Quality: Multidisciplinary and Multinational Perspectives*, Lexington Books, Lexington, MA, 1991.

Canton, I.D., "Learning to Love the Service Economy", *Harvard Business Review*, May/June, 1984, pp. 89–97.

Carlzon, J., *Moments of Truth,* Harper & Row Publishers, New York,1987.

Carman, J.M., "Consumer Perceptions of Service Quality: An Assessment of the SERVQUAL Dimensions", *Journal of Retailing,* Vol. 66, Spring, 1990, pp. 33–55.

Converse, P.D., *Marketing: Methods and Policies,* Prentice-Hall, Inc., New York, 1921

Cowell, D.W., *The Marketing of Services,* W. Heinemann Ltd., London, 1985.

Cronin Jr., J.J. and S.A. Taylor, "Measuring Service Quality: A Reexamination and Extension" *Journal of Marketing*, Vol. 56, July, 1992, pp. 55–68.

Crosby, L.A. and D. Cowles, "A Role Consensus Model of Satisfaction with Service Interaction Experiences", in M. Venkatesan, D.H. Schmalensee and C.E. Marshall (Eds.), *Creativity in Services Marketing: What's New, What Works, What's Developing*, American Marketing Association, Chicago, IL, 1986, pp. 40–3.

Crosby, L.A. and N. Stephens, "Effects of Relationship Marketing on Satisfaction, Retention, and Prices in the Life Insurance Industry", *Journal of Marketing Research*, Vol. 24, November, 1987, pp. 404–11.

Crosby, L.A., K.R. Evans, and D. Cowles, "Relationship Quality in Services Selling: An Interpersonal Influence Perspective", *Journal of Marketing,* Vol. 54, July, 1990, pp. 68–81.

Czepiel, J.A., "Service Encounters and Service Relationships: Implications for Research", *Journal of Business Research*, Vol. 20, January, 1990, pp. 13–21.

Czepiel, J.A., M.R. Solomon, and C.F. Surprenant (Eds.), *The Service*

Encounter: Managing Employee/Customer Interaction in Service Businesses, Lexington Books, Lexington, MA, 1985.

Donnelly, J.H., Jr., "Marketing Intermediaries in Channels of Distribution for Services", *Journal of Marketing,* Vol. 40, January, 1976, pp. 55–7.

Donnelly, J.H., Jr. and W.R. George (Eds.), *Marketing of Services.* American Marketing Association, Chicago, IL, 1981.

Eiglier, P., E. Langeard, C.H. Lovelock, J.E.G. Bateson and R.F. Young (Eds.), *Marketing Consumer Services: New Insights,* Marketing Science Institute, Cambridge, MA, 1977.

Fisk, R.P. and P.S. Tansuhaj, *Services Marketing: An Annotated Bibliography,* American Marketing Association, Chicago, IL, 1985.

Fisk, R.P., P.S. Tansuhaj, and L.A. Crosby, *SERVMARK: The Electronic Bibliography of Services Marketing Literature,* The First Interstate Center for Services Marketing, Arizona State University, Tempe, AZ, 1988.

George, W.R., "Marketing in the Service Industries", Ph.D. dissertation, University of Georgia, 1972.

George, W.R., "The Retailing of Services — A Challenging Future", *Journal of Retailing,* Vol. 53, Fall, 1977, pp. 85–98.

George, W.R., "Internal Marketing and Organizational Behavior: A Partnership in Developing Customer-Conscious Employees at Every Level", *Journal of Business Research,* Vol. 20, January, 1990, pp. 63–70.

George, W.R. and B.E. Gibson, "Blueprinting: A Tool for Managing Quality in Service", in S.W. Brown, E. Gummesson, B. Edvardsson and B. Gustavsson (Eds.), *Service Quality: Multidisciplinary and Multinational Perspectives,* Lexington Books, Lexington, MA, 1991, pp. 73–91.

Goodwin, C.F., "I Can Do it Myself: Training the Service Consumer to Contribute to Service Productivity", *Journal of Services Marketing,* Vol. 2, Fall, 1990, pp. 71–8.

Grönroos, C., "Marketing of Services: A Study of the Marketing Function of Service Firms", ECON.D. dissertation, Swedish School of Economics, Helsinki, Finland, 1979.

Grönroos, C., "Internal Marketing — An Integral Part of Marketing Theory", in J.H. Donnelly and W.R George (Eds.), *Marketing of Services,* American Marketing Association, Chicago, IL, 1981, pp. 236–8.

Grönroos, C., *Strategic Management and Marketing in the Service Sector,* Marketing Science Institute, Cambridge, MA, 1983. (Also published by Swedish School of Economics and Business Administration, 1982).

Grönroos, C. (a), "Relationship Approach to Marketing in Service Contexts: The Marketing and Organizational Behavior Interface", *Journal of Business Research,* Vol. 20, January, 1990, pp. 3–11.

Grönroos, C. (b), *Service Management and Marketing: Managing the Moments of Truth in Service Competition,* Lexington Books, Lexington, MA, 1990.

Grönroos, C. and E. Gummesson (Eds.), *Service Marketing — Nordic School Perspectives,* Swedish School of Economics, Stockholm, Sweden, 1985.

Gummesson, E., "Using Internal Marketing to Develop a New Culture — The

Case of Ericsson Quality", *Journal of Business and Industrial Marketing*, Vol. 2, Summer, 1987, pp. 23–8.

Hart, C.W.L., "The Power of Unconditional Service Guarantees", *Harvard Business Review,* July/August, 1988, pp. 54–62.

Hart, C.W.L., J.L. Heskett and W.E. Sasser, Jr., "The Profitable Art of Service Recovery", *Harvard Business Review*, July/August, 1990, pp. 148–56.

Heskett, J.L., *Managing in the Service Economy,* Harvard Business School Press, Boston, MA, 1986.

Heskett, J.L., W.E. Sasser, Jr., and C.W.L. Hart, *Service Breakthroughs: Changing The Rules of the Game,* The Free Press, New York,1990.

Hui, M.K. and J.E.G. Bateson, "Perceived Control and the Effects of Music on High- and Low-Involvement Consumers' Processing of Ads", *Journal of Consumer Research,* Vol. 18, September, 1991, pp. 174–84.

Johnson, E.M., *An Introduction to Service Marketing Management,* University of Delaware, Newark, NJ, 1964.

Johnson, E.M., *Our Service Economy: Trends and Implications*, Marketing Science Institute, Philadelphia, PA, 1968.

Johnson, E.M., "Are Goods and Services Different? An Exercise in Marketing Theory", Ph.D. dissertation, Washington University, 1969.

Johnson, E.M., E.E. Scheuing, and K.A. Gaida, *Profitable Services Marketing,* Dow Jones-Irwin, Inc., Homewood, IL, 1986.

Judd, R.C., "The Case for Redefining Services", *Journal of Marketing,* Vol. 28 January, 1964, pp. 58–9.

Kelley, S.W., J.H. Donnelly, Jr., and S.J. Skinner, "Customer Participation in Service Production and Delivery", *Journal of Retailing,* Vol. 66, Fall, 1990, pp. 315–35.

Kelly, J.P. and W.R. George, "Strategic Management Issues for the Retailing of Services", *Journal of Retailing* Vol. 58, Summer, 1982, pp. 26–43.

Kingman-Brundage, J., "The ABC's of Service System Blueprinting", in M.J. Bitner and L.A. Crosby (Eds.), *Designing a Winning Service Strategy: 7th Annual Services Marketing Conference Proceedings,* American Marketing Association, Chicago, IL, 1989, pp. 30–3.

Kingman-Brundage, J., "Technology, Design and Service Quality", *International Journal of Service Industry Management*, Vol. 2, No. 3, 1991, pp. 47–59.

Larsson, R. and D.E. Bowen, "Organization and Customer: Managing Design and Coordination of Services", *Academy of Management Review*, Vol. 14, April, 1989, pp. 213–33.

Lehtinen, J.R. and U. Lehtinen, "Service Quality: A Study of Quality Dimensions", Unpublished Working Paper, Service Management Institute, Helsinki, Finland, 1982.

Levitt, T., "Marketing Intangible Products and Product Intangibles", *Harvard Business Review*, May/June, 1981, pp. 94–102.

Lewis, B.R. and Entwhistle, T.W., "Managing the Service Encounter: A Focus on the Employee", *International Journal of Service Industry Management,* Vol. 1, No. 3, 1990, pp. 41–52.

Lovelock, C.H., "Theoretical Contributions from Services and Nonbusiness Marketing", in O.C. Ferrell, S.W. Brown, and C.W. Lamb, Jr. (Eds.), *Conceptual and Theoretical Developments in Marketing,* American Marketing Association, Chicago, IL, 1979, pp. 147–65.

Lovelock, C.H., "Classifying Services to Gain Strategic Marketing Insights", *Journal of Marketing,* Vol. 47, Summer, 1983, pp. 9–20.

Lovelock, C.H., *Services Marketing: Text, Cases, and Readings,* Prentice-Hall, Inc., Englewood Cliffs, NJ, 1984.

Lovelock, C.H., *Managing Services: Marketing, Operations, Human Resources,* Prentice-Hall, Inc., Englewood Cliffs, NJ, 1988.

Lovelock, C.H., *Services Marketing,* Second Edition, Prentice-Hall, Inc., Englewood Cliffs, NJ, 1991.

Lovelock, C.H., *Managing Services: Marketing, Operations, Human Resources,* Second Edition, Prentice-Hall, Inc., Englewood Cliffs, NJ, 1992.

McDowell, W.J., "The Marketing of Consumer Services", Ph.D. dissertation, University of Iowa, Iowa City, 1953.

Mills, P.K., "On the Quality of Services in Encounters: An Agency Perspective", *Journal of Business Research,* Vol. 20, January, 1990, pp. 31–41.

Normann, R., *Service Management: Strategy and Leadership in Service Businesses,* John Wiley, Chichester, England, 1984.

Oliva, T.A., R.L. Oliver, and I.C. MacMillan, "A Catastrophe Model for Developing Service Satisfaction Strategies" *Journal of Marketing,* Vol. 56, July, 1992, pp. 83–95.

Oliver, R.L., "A Cognitive Model of the Antecedents and Consequences of Satisfaction Decisions", *Journal of Marketing Research,* Vol. 17, November, 1980, pp. 460–9.

Parasuraman, A., L.L. Berry and V.A. Zeithaml (a), "Refinement and Reassessment of the SERVQUAL Scale", *Journal of Retailing,* Vol. 67, Winter, 1991, pp. 420–50.

Parasuraman, A., L.L. Berry, and V.A. Zeithaml (b), "Understanding, Measuring, and Improving Service Quality: Findings from a Multiphase Research Program", in S.W. Brown, E. Gummesson, B. Edvardsson and B. Gustavsson (Eds.), *Service Quality: Multidisciplinary and Multinational Perspectives,* Lexington Books, Lexington, MA, 1991, pp. 253–68.

Parasuraman, A., V.A. Zeithaml and L.L. Berry, "A Conceptual Model of Service Quality and its Implications for Future Research", *Journal of Marketing,* Vol. 49, Fall, 1985, pp. 41–50.

Parasuraman, A., V.A. Zeithaml and L.L. Berry, "SERVQUAL: A Multiple-item Scale for Measuring Consumer Perceptions of Service Quality", *Journal of Retailing,* Vol. 64, Spring, 1988, pp. 12–37.

Parker, D.D., "The Marketing of Consumer Services", D.B.A. dissertation, University of Washington, Seattle, 1958.

Quinn, J.B., *Intelligent Enterprise,* The Free Press, New York, 1992.

Quinn, J.B. and P.C. Paquette, "Technology in Services: Creating Organizational Revolutions", *Sloan Management Review,* Winter, 1990, pp. 67–78.

Quinn, J.B., T.L. Doorley and P.C. Paquette "Beyond Products: Services-Based Strategy", *Harvard Business Review,* March/April, 1990, pp. 58–68.

Rathmell, J.M., "What is Meant by Services?", *Journal of Marketing,* Vol. 30 October, 1966, pp. 32–6.

Rathmell, J.M., *Marketing in the Service Sector,* Cambridge, Winthrop Publishers, Inc., MA, 1974.

Regan, W.J., "The Service Revolution", *Journal of Marketing,* Vol. 27, July, 1963, pp. 57–62.

Reichheld, F.F., and W.E. Sasser, Jr., "Zero Defections: Quality Comes to Services", *Harvard Business Review,* September/October, 1990, pp. 105–11.

Rust, R.T. and R.L. Oliver, "Frontiers in Service Quality" in Rust, R.T. and R.L. Oliver (Eds.), *Frontiers in Service Quality,* Sage Publications, Beverly Hills, CA, 1993.

Sasser, W.E., Jr., W.L. Christopher and J.L. Heskett, *The Service Management Course,* The Free Press, New York,1991.

Scheuing, E.E. and E.M. Johnson, "A Proposed Model for New Service Development", *Journal of Services Marketing,* Vol. 3, Spring, 1989, pp. 25–34.

Schlesinger, L.A. and (a), "Breaking the Cycle of Failure in Services", *Sloan Management Review,* Vol. 32, Spring, 1991, pp. 17–28.

Schlesinger, L.A. and J.L. Heskett (b), "Enfranchisement of Service Workers", *California Management Review,* Summer, 1991, pp. 83–100.

Shostack, G.L., "Breaking Free from Product Marketing", *Journal of Marketing,* Vol. 41, April, 1977, pp. 73–80.

Shostack, G.L., "Designing Services that Deliver", *Harvard Business Review,* January/February, 1984, pp. 133–9.

Shostack, G.L., "Service Positioning through Structural Change", *Journal of Marketing,* Vol. 51, January, 1987, pp. 34–43.

Shostack, G.L., "Understanding Services through Blueprinting" in T.A. Swartz, D.E. Bowen and S.W. Brown (Eds.), *Advances in Services Marketing, and Management: Research and Practice,* Vol., 1, JAI Press Inc., Greenwich, CT, 1992, pp. 75–90.

Solomon, M.R., C. Surprenant, J.A. Czepiel and E.G. Gutman, "A Role Theory Perspective on Dyadic Interactions: The Service Encounter", *Journal of Marketing,* Vol. 49, Winter, 1985, pp. 99–111.

Surprenant, C.F. and M.R. Solomon, "Predictability and Personalization in the Service Encounter", *Journal of Marketing,* Vol. 51, April, 1987, pp. 86–96.

Swartz, T.A., D.E. Bowen and S.W. Brown (Eds.) (a), *Advances in Services Marketing and Management,* Vol., 1, JAI Press, Greenwich, CT, 1992.

Swartz, T.A., D.E. Bowen, and S.W. Brown (b), "Fifteen Years After Breaking Free: Services Then, Now and Beyond", in T.A. Swartz, D.E. Bowen, and S.W. Brown (Eds.), *Advances in Services Marketing and Management,* Vol. 1, JAI Press Inc., Greenwich, CT, 1992, pp. 1–21.

Takeuchi, H. and J.A. Quelch, "Quality is More than Making a Good Product", *Harvard Business Review,* July/August, 1983, pp. 139–45.

Tansuhaj, P., D. Randall and J. McCullough, "A Services Marketing

Management Model: Integrating Internal and External Marketing Functions", *Journal of Services Marketing*, Vol. 2, Winter, 1988, pp. 31–8.

Thomas, D.R.E., "Strategy is Different in Service Businesses", *Harvard Business Review*, July/August, 1978, pp. 158–65.

Weinberger, M.G., "Services and Goods: A Laboratory Study of Informational Influences", PhD dissertation, Arizona State University, Tempe, AZ, 1976.

Weinberger, M.G. and S.W. Brown, "A Difference in Informational Influences: Services vs. Goods", *Journal of the Academy of Marketing Science,* Vol. 5, Winter, 1977, pp. 389–407.

Wyckham, R.G., P.T. Fitzroy and G.D. Mandry, "Marketing of Services — An Evaluation of the Theory", *European Journal of Marketing*, Vol. 9, Spring, 1975, pp. 59–67.

Zeithaml, V.A., "How Consumer Evaluation Processes Differ Between Goods and Services", in J.H. Donnelly, and W.R. George (Eds.), *Marketing of Services*, American Marketing Association, Chicago, IL, 1981, pp. 186–190.

Zeithaml, V.A., L.L. Berry, and A. Parasuraman, "Communication and Control Processes in the Delivery of Service Quality", *Journal of Marketing,* Vol. 52, April, 1988, pp. 35–48.

Zeithaml, V.A., A. Parasuraman and L.L. Berry, "Problems and Strategies in Services Marketing", *Journal of Marketing,* Vol. 49, Spring, 1985, pp. 33–46.

Zeithaml, V.A., A. Parasuraman and L.L. Berry, *Delivering Quality Service: Balancing Customer Perceptions and Expectations,* Free Press, New York, 1990.

2

AVOIDING SERVICES MARKETING MYOPIA

Lauren K. Wright
California State University, Chico, USA

PRÉCIS

Now that services marketing has truly established its domain in the marketing firmament, there is an apprehension that a certain intro-spection or myopia may occur. In the rush to establish the legitimate differences between services marketing and other areas of marketing activity, there is a danger that differences within and similarity without may be underestimated. A greater consideration of some key contin-gency variables is proffered as a way of minimising any such myopia.

The three phrases in marketing services evolution are described in the context of Kuhn's view about the nature of paradigm shift. This growing corpus of knowledge is seen to have made a substantive contri-bution not only to the services marketing subdiscipline itself, but also to the general marketing field. This is to be observed, for example, in the broadened comprehension of product to include people, a deepened understanding about distribution and pricing and an appreciation that product benefits rather than just attributes are key. But what are the implications of this hard-won maturity now that the services marketing subdiscipline is "walking erect"? Kuhn argues that "the full acceptance of a paradigm is unavoidably accompanied by drastically reduced vision". There is danger of myopia on a number of fronts: ignoring the variation within the service sector; ignoring the similarity between goods and services; further, the ability to develop comprehensive prod-uct marketing strategies may be inhibited. There are, in effect, limita-tions to the services marketing paradigm. Examples of growing variance within the services sector on the four key service dimensions are set forth. For instance, on the inseparability dimension we are witnessing a greater separation of consumption and production, e.g., ATMs. Equally, there is evidence that the goods/services and consumer/industrial dichotomy is being exaggerated. It is suggested that scholarly thinking in the area might benefit from attempting to find similarities between services and other marketing activities, in an integrated rather than a dual path of theory development. Indeed companies in both the manufacturing and service sectors are starting to look beyond their own traditional paradigms for more effective ways of meeting customers' needs. The "service factory" concept is an example. By studying such common dimensions, such contingency factors, more informative explanations of successful marketing theory and practice may emerge. The development of such a contingency approach could be nurtured by analysing at least three important contingency variables: tangibility, the nature of production requirements, and stages in the life cycle.

To conclude, the traditional division between goods and services is outdated and may well lead to myopic behaviour in both manufacturing and service sectors. Contingency models may help overcome this myopia by addressing the variance within each of the sectors as well as the similarities across the two groups, thus enabling a more tailored response to customers' needs.

Aidan O'Driscoll
Dublin Institute of Technology
Ireland

1. INTRODUCTION

Like all sciences, the marketing discipline is in a constant state of change. It has evolved over time as a result of efforts systematically to explain and predict phenomena that affect both businesses and consumers. The discipline traces its roots to the early twentieth century, when the major emphasis was on selling agricultural products (Bartels, 1988). As the industrial revolution progressed, the scope expanded to include the marketing of physical goods. This led to an emphasis on distribution issues and how to move these physical goods (especially commodities) most effectively from producers to consumers (Lovelock, 1979). Services were viewed as merely aiding the production and marketing of goods. This focus on physical goods remained intact for over 75 years, even though the United States began its transition to a service economy as early as the mid-1940s. The goods-centred paradigm was so deeply rooted in the marketing discipline that almost another 30 years passed before scholars began to discuss the marketing implications of a service economy (Fisk, Brown and Bitner, 1993; Chapter 1). The emergence of services marketing in the early 1970s signalled a paradigm shift from the marketing discipline's traditional focus on marketing physical goods. Early services researchers faced constant challenges from established marketing scholars as they struggled to establish services marketing as a valid subdiscipline.

There is little doubt that services marketing has proved its legitimacy (see Berry and Parasuraman, 1993). However, the determination of services marketing pioneers to demonstrate that services are significantly different from goods may have led researchers deliberately to ignore both variance *within* the service sector (Swartz, Bowen and Brown, 1992) and similarities *across* the goods and services sectors. According to Swartz et al., the principles of services marketing that have emerged from the literature to date may not be equally valid across all service industries. They suggest that there is a need to develop contingency theories that identify which marketing practices are appropriate for different types of services under various conditions.

This chapter has two related goals. The first is to provide a brief history of the evolution of services marketing and to describe some of its contributions and limitations. The second objective is to present several contingency factors that may allow services marketers to determine more precisely the types of marketing strategies that will be most effective in creating and sustaining a distinctive competitive advantage.

2. EMERGENCE AND EVOLUTION OF SERVICES MARKETING

While the evolution of services marketing has been well documented in the literature (Berry and Parasuraman, 1993; Fisk, Brown and Bitner, 1993; Chapter 1), it is useful to review it from the perspective of Kuhn's (1970) discussion of the nature of scientific revolutions. Fisk, Brown and Bitner categorise the evolution of services marketing in three different stages: Crawling Out (pre-1980); Scurrying About (1980–1985); and Walking Erect (1986–present). These stages run closely parallel to the events described by Kuhn (1970) as necessary for a paradigm shift to occur. Closer examination of these three stages should provide insights into both the contributions made by the services marketing literature and the ways in which the services marketing paradigm may now be preventing a richer understanding of marketing phenomena.

According to Kuhn, a paradigm is "an entire constellation of beliefs, values and techniques shared by the members of a given community" (p. 175). Paradigms are theories, perspectives or frames of reference that determine how people perceive, interpret and understand the world. Kuhn argues that well-established paradigms do not encourage explorations into anomalies or alternative points of view, but that the discovery of new and unexplained phenomena is inevitable as research in a discipline continues. A few scholars become increasingly aware that these phenomena somehow violate the rules of the game that govern the existing paradigm. They continue to investigate the anomalies until one of two things happens:

1. The anomalies are assimilated into the current paradigm; or

2. A new paradigm begins to emerge that offers a better explanation of the phenomena under investigation.

Early in the Crawling Out stage, services marketing researchers began to build a case for the second alternative by maintaining that services and goods were fundamentally different in nature. They argued that the unique characteristics of services made traditional marketing theories and practices inapplicable to the service sector.

When services marketers in the Crawling Out stage first asserted the subdiscipline's right to exist, they encountered fierce opposition. They were challenging the existing marketing paradigm whose very roots were tied to the production and distribution of physical goods. These early services researchers found it difficult to publish their work since established marketing scholars insisted that services were just a modest extension of goods marketing and thus did not merit special attention (Fisk, Brown and Bitner, 1993; Chapter 1). This sparked a fierce debate on "whether services are different" that lasted throughout the entire Crawling Out period. The debate represented a fundamental challenge to the legitimacy of services marketing as a subdiscipline, and the outcome would determine the fate of the entire services marketing paradigm. Services marketers understood the seriousness of this challenge: in virtually all of their papers and articles written during this period, they argued that services marketing was different. The heated "goods *v.* services" controversy led to the identification of four unique services characteristics — intangibility, inseparability, heterogeneity and perishability — which provided the foundation for the services marketing subdiscipline.

Toward the end of the Crawling Out period, an event occurred that altered the course of services marketing. In 1977, the *Journal of Marketing* published Shostack's article "Breaking Free of Product Marketing", in which she accused the marketing discipline of failing to offer relevant theories or practical rules that were relevant for the service sector. This article, which asserted that the marketing field had not provided relevant paradigms for services, helped to crystallise support for the fledgling services marketing subdiscipline as other influential scholars argued that services marketing required new concepts (Bateson, 1979; Lovelock, 1979; Berry, 1980). All of these activities helped to push services marketing towards the next evolutionary stage.

According to Kuhn (1970), if a new paradigm is destined to win the fight for survival, the strength of the persuasive arguments in its favour will increase. More researchers will be converted as they are convinced of the logic of the approach, and the number of articles and books based on the paradigm will increase. This is exactly what occurred in the Scurrying About stage described by Fisk, Brown and Bitner (1993; Chapter 1). An unexpected environmental event also accelerated interest in the emerging services marketing discipline. In the early 1980s, many American industries were deregulated, including air transportation, telecommunications, health care and financial services (Fisk, Brown and Bitner, 1993; Chapter 1). Firms in these industries needed marketing skills to cope with the increasingly competitive environment and rising consumer expectations. They turned to academics for advice, but these scholars quickly realised that traditional marketing concepts did not fully address issues that arose in the service sector. This external validation helped to establish the services marketing paradigm even more, since it was more effective than traditional goods-focused marketing at explaining services-related phenomena.

Interest in services marketing continued to increase dramatically. For the first time, special services marketing conferences were held under the auspices of the American Marketing Association. These conferences were attended both by academics and by practitioners who had discovered that traditional marketing approaches were not adequate for their businesses. The First Interstate Center for Services Marketing was established in 1985. This further legitimised the subdiscipline by supporting scholarly research and strengthening ties with service businesses. Four services marketing articles were published in the *Journal of Marketing* (a top North American marketing journal) during this period. Two new journals, the *Services Industries Journal* and the *Journal of Professional Services Marketing*, were introduced as an outlet for services marketing research.

While some of the articles and books published during the Scurrying About stage still explicitly defended services as fundamentally different from goods, many researchers began to explore the implications of the unique service characteristics (such as service design issues or the nature of the service encounter.) This signalled the acceptance of services marketing as a legitimate paradigm. According to Kuhn (1970), a paradigm can be taken for granted when its researchers no longer need to build a case for the field in every article by starting from basic principles (for example, services *are* fundamentally different) and justifying each new concept introduced after that. Scholars can then concentrate on more subtle and esoteric aspects of the discipline. More rigorous theoretical and empirical work is done to articulate the paradigm's premises. Thus, the implicit acceptance of the services marketing paradigm and the appearance of more rigorous research indicated that the services marketing subdiscipline had started to mature.

With its entrance into the Walking Erect stage, the services marketing subdiscipline has continued to show signs of this maturity. Journal publications in services marketing have become more empirically based and theory-driven as opposed to presenting conceptual discussions, and they have been published in many of the top marketing journals. There has been almost no discussion of the services versus goods debate in the marketing literature since 1985 (although the issue is still being argued in other disciplines, including economics and operations management). In marketing, these differences appear to be generally accepted. Services researchers are now focusing on business issues and problems related to the established set of unique service characteristics. A cohesive core of literature exists for several different topics, including: service quality; service encounters; service design; customer retention and relationship marketing; and internal marketing. The areas that are attracting substantial attention in the field today stem from relatively isolated pieces of research published during the Crawling Out stage (Fisk, Brown and Bitner, 1993; Chapter 1). They are evidence that the field is now engaging in the increasingly rigorous research that Kuhn describes.

There are other signs that services marketing has become an accepted discipline within the broader marketing field. Kuhn (1970) states that "the formation of specialized journals, specialist associations and institutes, and the claim for a special place in the academic curriculum are usually associated with the acceptance of a paradigm" (p. 19). This has certainly occurred in services marketing. Along with the two specialised journals that emerged during the previous stage, other publications have been added that focus specifically on services marketing issues (the *Journal of Services Marketing* and *Advances in Services Marketing and Management*, for example). New institutes (most notably the Center for Services Marketing at Vanderbilt University) have joined the First Interstate Center for Services Marketing in supporting scholarly activity in the field. Professional associations like the International Service Quality Association sponsor both conferences and research, and the American

Marketing Association has established a Services Marketing Division and a Special Interest Group for Services Marketing. Finally, services marketing has claimed its place in the academic curriculum. There are currently several services marketing texts (Bateson, 1992; Lovelock, 1991), and most traditional introductory marketing texts have added a chapter on the special issues faced by services marketers. Many business schools now offer a course that is entirely dedicated to services marketing.

What are the implications of this hard-won maturity now that the services marketing subdiscipline is "walking erect?" According to Kuhn (1970), the acceptance of a paradigm is unavoidably accompanied by drastically reduced vision as disciples of the new approach seek more precise and robust solutions to the issues that the paradigm has identified as important. In the services marketing field, this has created a tendency to emphasise similarities between different types of services while explicitly ignoring the variation within the service sector. A few scholars have recently noted these discrepancies (see Bharadwaj, Varadarajan and Fahy, 1993; Dobholkar, 1994; Swartz, Bowen and Brown, 1993; Wright, 1993). But the literature to date has focused primarily on identifying and resolving marketing issues that relate primarily to what might be termed "classic services" — those market offerings that have most or all of the characteristics that the discipline has established as unique (that is, intangibility, inseparability, heterogeneity and perishability).

This restricted focus has served a useful purpose in the evolution of the services marketing discipline. The reduced parameters developed as a result of confidence in the services marketing paradigm (which is based on the argument that services are fundamentally different from goods). These assumptions have been essential to the development of the services marketing discipline by focusing attention on "classic" services — those referred to by Fisk, Brown and Bitner (1993) as "low tech and high touch". The paradigm has encouraged researchers to investigate in greater detail and depth than would otherwise be possible the implications of those market offerings farthest from the domain of the traditional goods-centred paradigm. In exploring these issues, scholars have contributed substantially to both the services marketing subdiscipline and to the general marketing field. Some of these contributions are discussed below.

3. SERVICES MARKETING CONTRIBUTIONS

The proliferation of articles on services marketing has led to some significant contributions over the past 20 years. Our definition of product has expanded as a result of the extensive research directed at delineating services from goods. This research has ultimately re-emphasised the concept that all products are a mixture of tangible and intangible elements bundled by marketers to satisfy consumers' needs. The broadening of the product scope to include people and operations (often within the context of the service encounter) has also facilitated a greater understanding of the nature of both goods and services. Finally, research on determining and implementing service quality has extended our understanding of the various components of product quality in general (McIntyre and Brown, 1988).

Services marketing has also added to our knowledge of distribution in several ways. Channels concepts have been extended to include the distribution of intangible products. Our understanding of franchising as a means of distribution has also grown dramatically with the expansion of the service sector. Franchising offers answers to some of the most challenging distribution problems facing services marketers, including intangibility (which can be offset by the brand name of service franchises like Kinko's Copies or Mrs Fields' Cookies) and quality control (which McDonald's has handled by standardising its entire delivery process).

An additional contribution of services marketing research to the element of pricing is a greater appreciation of the expanded role that price may play in defining a product. Price may be used as a convenient surrogate for quality in appraising relatively intangible offerings (Rushton and Carson, 1985). Customers may also use price as a "social cue" to help assess the suitability of specific service establishments. For example, casually dressed tourists may use the menu prices posted outside a restaurant in San Francisco to determine whether they will be appropriately attired — so that their dining experience will be a pleasant one for them as well as for other restaurant patrons. This assessment may not be based on affordability; rather it is used as an indicator of the social atmosphere of the restaurant.

The services marketing literature has focused attention on the need to promote product benefits rather than attributes. It has also highlighted the need for marketers to communicate intangible benefits for tangible products and tangible benefits for intangible products. McIntyre and Brown (1988) provide a good illustration of these concepts by describing a promotional campaign for Singapore Airlines that was initially reported in *Asian Business* (Astbury, 1986). When Singapore Airlines planned its initial promotional strategy in 1972, it was tempted to advertise its new Boeing 747 aircraft as a way of achieving competitive advantage. But the company realised that this strategy might not provide a sustainable advantage, since other Asian airlines could purchase the same aircraft. Singapore Airlines decided instead to position itself as a world leader in quality inflight service. This presented a challenge, since inflight service quality was a highly intangible attribute. The firm's solution was to build an advertising campaign around the concept of a "Singapore Girl". Actual flight attendants were used in the campaign to make service quality attributes more tangible; the "Singapore Girl" symbolised warmth, friendliness, efficiency and professionalism.

While it is obvious from the preceding discussion that the services marketing literature has contributed substantially to the marketing discipline, its historic focus on separating services from goods may now be limiting our ability to develop comprehensive *product* marketing strategies. To determine whether the services marketing paradigm is robust across the entire services domain, the basic assumptions that have been used to distinguish services from goods must be re-examined.

4. LIMITATIONS OF THE SERVICES MARKETING PARADIGM

The services marketing paradigm is based on the belief that there are fundamental differences between goods and services. Researchers have vigorously and successfully defended this claim in their arguments for a separate services marketing subdiscipline. However, the emphasis on the goods/services dichotomy has led to an oversimplified assumption that services are relatively homogeneous and that the same marketing factors are important for most service offerings. Within the broad group of market offerings categorised as services, a great deal of heterogeneity exists in terms of such characteristics as level of intangibility, extent of direct contact with the customer and amount of technology or equipment used to produce the service. There is also increasing homogeneity between the goods and services sectors. Many companies that sell manufactured goods include services as an intrinsic part of their products (Enis and Roering, 1981; Swartz, Bowen and Brown, 1992), while many service firms rely on equipment and technology to meet the needs of their customers effectively (Dabholkar, 1994).

Because the services marketing discipline has been so intent on defending its legitimacy, differences among services have been minimised or overlooked. Aside from a few dissenters (see Brown and Fern, 1981; Enis and Roering, 1981; Ghingold and Maier, 1987), the services marketing literature has been based on the assumption that services possess four unique characteristics — intangibility, inseparability, heterogeneity and perishability — that distinguish them from tangible goods (Zeithaml, Parasuraman and Berry, 1985). These characteristics are at the foundation of the existing services marketing paradigm, and they have guided most of the research that has been conducted in the field to date. Ironically, it is the mature, well-articulated status of the paradigm itself that has caused some researchers to insist recently that the basic tenets of services marketing may not be valid across the entire service sector (Bharadwaj, Varadarajan and Fahy, 1993; Dabholkar, 1994; McIntyre and Brown, 1988; Swartz, Bowen and Brown, 1992; Wright, 1993). As the implications of each of the four service characteristics have been more thoroughly explored, anomalies have begun to emerge that call into question the feasibility of developing global strategies that apply across the entire service sector. Examples of the variance *across* services on the four key service dimensions help illustrate this issue.

4.1. Intangibility

Intangibility is at the heart of the initial debate about whether services and goods are fundamentally different. Early arguments about the goods/ services "dichotomy" gave way to the concept of a "continuum" of products based on levels of tangible versus intangible attributes. "Goods" (that is, products that possess mainly tangible attributes and a tangible core) are at one extreme of the continuum, while services (that is, products consisting of primarily intangible attributes and an intangible core) are at the other extreme. The products that fall between the two extremes are composed of varying combinations of tangible and intangible attributes (Shostack, 1977). Services marketing theories work well for the products toward the far end of the intangibility scale, while traditional marketing practices apply to highly tangible offerings. The problem lies with the products in the middle, since they contain a mixture of intangible and tangible elements. Classifying these products as *either* goods *or* services may be misleading unless the classification is accompanied by a clear understanding on the part of the marketer about which attributes are determinant from the customer's perspective.

Several researchers have argued that the goods/services distinction is dysfunctional from the standpoint of developing effective marketing strategies because it focuses attention on the product rather than on the customer. Two decades ago, Wyckham, Fitzroy and Mandry (1975) maintained that marketers should be concerned not with distinguishing between goods and services, but with creating sets of needs satisfiers or utilities for particular market segments. They argued that clusters of similar offerings should share common marketing strategies regardless of whether the core was tangible or intangible. Brown and Fern (1981) suggested that marketers should emphasise the *total* market offering (that is, the aggregate of all benefits the customer receives as a result of the core offering plus all other supplemental tangible and intangible benefits), because customers consider total market offerings when they evaluate product alternatives.

Buyers are seeking certain utilities from products, and they may not necessarily care whether the core offering is tangible or intangible (Enis and Roering, 1981; Gummesson, 1987; 1994). Customers can sometimes choose between a good or a service to meet the same need. For example, customers' needs to record phone messages can be satisfied in several ways. They can purchase an answering machine (tangible core) and accept the responsibility for retrieving messages and maintaining the equipment themselves. Or they might choose to subscribe to an answering service (intangible core) where an employee answers calls, provides some limited information to callers and records messages. Technology has recently made a third option available. Customers can now subscribe to voice or electronic mail services that use electronic technology (either via personal computer or the telephone) to relay and record messages. They will choose one of these three product options based on which offers the best bundle of benefits to meet their specific needs. Although two of the alternatives are services, these services are produced in very different ways. The differences might be masked if marketers focus only on the fact that both offerings have intangible cores.

In fact, the demarcation between goods and services is becoming increasingly blurred. Companies in the manufacturing sector are redefining their missions to emphasise customer service rather than the goods they produce (for example, Xerox, IBM and Hewlett-Packard all define themselves as providers of "solutions" rather than hardware, and Ford attempts to make their cars more attractive by advertising a customer contact person who is responsible for guiding a car and its customer safely through dealer-provided maintenance and repair). In the service sector, businesses are relying more and more on technology and tangible equipment to meet the needs of their customers.

4.2. Inseparability

Inseparability implies that services are first sold, then produced and consumed simultaneously through interaction between customers and service producers. On the other hand, goods are assumed to be produced, then sold and consumed. While some services are simultaneously produced and consumed, many are not. Riddle (1986) identifies three basic types of service production: co-production; isolated production; and self-service. In co-production, the service provider and the customer work together to produce the service (students and faculty interacting in a traditional classroom setting, for example). Co-production corresponds to what Chase (1981) calls "pure services". In self-service production, customers use equipment and services provided and maintained by the seller to produce the service (for example, service stations where pumping petrol and paying for purchases are fully automated.) Isolated production relates closely to Chase's concept of "quasi-manufacturing", where part (or in some cases, nearly all) of the service is performed outside the customer's presence. For example, the entertainment industry relies on isolated production when films are produced and taped for later distribution to cinemas, video stores and television stations.

In an effort to improve efficiency, many service producers are actively searching for ways to separate customer involvement from production activities. This corresponds to observations by Chase (1981) and Levitt (1972) that production efficiency is directly related to the extent of time customers are directly involved with the service facility and employees. As service businesses face increasingly competitive environments, they are finding more ways to separate production and consumption activities. An example of this is the banking industry's use of automatic teller machines (ATMs) to reduce customer/personnel contact while expanding business hours for basic services from eight to twenty-four! In the food service industry, fast-food restaurants often separate production and consumption by keeping prepared food on hand (this improves efficiency and allows faster customer services).

4.3. Heterogeneity

Heterogeneity refers to the potential for variance in service production. Inconsistencies can occur because:

- Different service-providers perform a given service on different occasions

- The service performed by an individual provider may differ over time

- Interactions between customers and providers may vary by customer (Zeithaml, Parasuraman and Berry, 1985).

Since it is difficult to predict the nature and extent of variations, especially when there is direct interaction between service providers and customers, consumers may feel that there is greater risk attached to purchasing services rather than goods. Services marketers have historically claimed that standardisation and quality control are difficult for service businesses because of inherent heterogeneity (Berry, 1980;

Booms and Bitner, 1981; Langeard et al., 1981; Levitt, 1972; 1976).

The concern with service quality has triggered an ongoing dialogue in the services marketing literature. According to Fisk, Brown and Bitner (1993; Chapter 1), service quality is the single most researched area in the services marketing literature to date. Many quality-related issues have been explored in the literature, including the impact of both delivery method and technology in reducing heterogeneity. Thomas (1978) distinguished between equipment-based and people-based services. Lovelock (1983) expanded this concept by proposing that firms could choose to emphasise either people-intensive or equipment-intensive production factors, or they could use some combination of both delivery types. Firms that are high in equipment-based or technology-based attributes and low in people-based attributes tend to be the least heterogeneous services. Examples of these services include automatic car washes, ATM machines at banks, video rental outlets and residential telephone services. The greatest variations in quality occur in people-based services, especially those where the customer goes to the service facility and other customers are present during service consumption. In this case, variance can occur as a result of interactions between the service provider and a particular customer, the service provider and other customers or among customers themselves. Legal services, education, restaurant dining and hairdressing are illustrations of these types of services. Equipment-based services lend themselves more readily to standardisation through the use of technology and traditional operations management techniques. However, even people-based services can utilise technology and equipment-based operations whenever possible to reduce the heterogeneity that often occurs from interactions between customers and providers. McDonald's provides a classic example of "a production-line approach to services". The restaurant's employees have claimed that every aspect of the operations is standardised down to the width of the smile that each customer should be greeted with!

4.4. Perishability

Services marketing researchers have maintained that services are more perishable than goods — in other words, that they can not be easily saved, stored or inventoried. This assumption is intimately tied to the other basic service assumptions. Services scholars have made the case that because of the intangibility and simultaneity characteristics, services are not easy to standardise or inventory (Berry, 1980; Sasser, 1976). If services can't be stored, transported or saved, these researchers reason, then distribution channels can't exist for services (or if they do, they must be very short). However, Evans and Brown (1983) point out that many services use intermediaries in their distribution systems (for example, the entertainment industry uses cinemas and video rental stores as intermediaries to distribute its products). Services that are high in technology or equipment-based attributes can more easily be standardised, and in many cases they can be inventoried as well. In the entertainment example mentioned above, film producers like Paramount and Universal Pictures store their films on tapes to be distributed to cinemas and video outlets. They employ strict quality control procedures during production, and the films can be stored and distributed by channel intermediaries for long periods of time.

5. A COMPREHENSIVE APPROACH TO CLASSIFYING MARKETING PHENOMENA

It is obvious from the discussion above that there can be significant variance between different services and homogeneity among services and goods in certain cases. These observations are very similar to those made by Fern and Brown (1984) in their article questioning the validity of the industrial/consumer dichotomy. Fern and Brown maintain that while the organisation of phenomena into related groups is often a prerequisite to the development of marketing theory and practice, classification schemes must meet certain criteria to be considered truly robust. Advocates of the industrial marketing paradigm have argued that industrial and consumer marketing are fundamentally different, based on such factors as: the type of goods being purchased (Corey, 1976); the buyer's decision-making process (Sheth, 1979); characteristics of the product market (Corey, 1976); and the nature of the selling firm's marketing activities (Sheth, 1979). But according to Fern and Brown (1984), the industrial/consumer dichotomy does not stand up to Hunt's (1976) criteria for evaluating classification schemata.

Hunt (1976) suggests several criteria for determining the strength of a particular classification approach, including: adequacy of the characteristics used in classification; mutual exclusiveness of categories; and collective exhaustiveness of categories. Fern and Brown (1984) maintain that the industrial/consumer dichotomy is a relatively weak classification scheme based on these criteria. For example, the characteristics of the products being purchased do not always differ substantially between consumer and industrial markets. Thus, there are not mutually exclusive sets of consumer versus industrial products. It is relatively easy to think of products that do not fit neatly into one category or the other, though industrial marketers have tended to focus on extreme examples to accentuate the differences and have played down the large numbers of products common in both types of markets. The industrial/consumer dichotomy also does not provide mutually exclusive categories for the other marketing mix variables (Fern and Brown, 1984). In addition, this classification scheme fails to provide categories that are mutually exhaustive. Fern and Brown (1984) identify several other specialised areas of marketing knowledge, including non-profit marketing, international marketing and services marketing. They suggest that a more useful way of classifying marketing phenomena might be built around some dimensions that are common across all of these categories.

Fern and Brown (1984) present a final argument against the consumer/industrial dichotomy. According to the industrial marketing advocates, variations *between* the consumer and industrial groups should be greater than the variance *within* each of the two categories. However, there is evidence (Fern and Brown, 1984) that the differences *within* the industrial marketing and consumer marketing groups are actually more substantial than those separating the two areas. Thus, it should be possible (and desirable) to formulate marketing strategies that explicitly account for the within-group variance and are generalisable across both categories. Ironically, this is similar to the argument Brown and Fern made against the goods/services dichotomy when they maintained that:

> Rather than looking for differences between goods and services core offerings, marketing scholars might better serve the discipline and marketing practitioners by examining their commonalities. These are best seen when the total market offering is examined.... Researchers should further explore the underlying characteristics of total market offerings. If marketing scholars can uncover a more exhaustive list and if they can relate these characteristics to marketing strategy, they will have progressed that much closer to the elusive general theory of marketing. Marketing managers should carefully assess their total marketing offerings to identify the underlying characteristics. These characteristics can then be used to develop proper marketing strategies for the total market offering (Brown and Fern, 1981, pp. 206–7).

These authors' argument against both the consumer/industrial and goods/services classification schemes is that they require the development of marketing theory along two similar but separate paths. If these dichotomies are removed and marketing phenomena are examined for similarities, common dimensions may be identified that provide the opportunity for developing a richer, more comprehensive theory of marketing (Fern and Brown, 1984).

There is evidence that this synergistic approach may prove very useful. For example, companies in both the manufacturing and service sectors are starting to look beyond their own traditional paradigms for more effective ways of meeting customer needs. Service companies (particularly those that rely heavily on equipment or technology for production) have begun to incorporate manufacturing-based techniques in their efforts to improve product quality, while goods-producing firms are focusing on service attributes as sources of added value and competitive advantage. Bowen, Siehl and Schneider (1989; 1990) suggest that to be truly service-oriented, manufacturers must adopt the strategies, practices and organisational arrangements that characterise the prototypical service organisation. They must value customer contact, treat customers as co-producers/producers, integrate production and marketing and learn to compete on intangibles as well as tangibles. In their article on the "service factory", Chase and Garvin (1989) describe how manufacturers can involve customers before, during and after the production process. Heskett (Chapter 16) describes how a clothing manufacturer such as Benetton characterises itself as a "service system" that is dedicated to meeting the fashion needs of its youthful market.

General Motors' approach to marketing its Saturn line provides an excellent example of a goods-manufacturing company that has tried to create the "service factory" described by Chase and Garvin (1989). GM has worked hard to create a competitive advantage by incorporating services marketing concepts into both the production and sales of its cars. Saturns are designed and manufactured by cross-functional teams. After the sale, the company maintains a relationship with its customers by contacting them frequently for feedback, inviting them to barbecues with other Saturn customers, and providing each customer with their own Saturn representative to contact if the car should need to be serviced or repaired. Ford Motor Company has recently followed suit with its "service advisers", who form the liaison between the dealer's service shop and the customer whose car is being serviced.

The car manufacturers described above have integrated marketing knowledge and tools from both the goods and services sectors to create the most effective marketing strategy for each market offering. This approach could be systematically built into the marketing discipline by developing contingency models for marketing theories and practices. Contingency approaches may provide an effective way of "handling the same bundle of data as before, but placing them in a new system of relations with one another by giving them a different framework" (Kuhn, 1970).

Contingent relationships and contingency modelling have been explored in several disciplines (see, for example, Hayes, 1977; Hofer,

1975; Lawrence and Lorsch, 1967; Lilien and Weinstein, 1984; Reukert, Walker and Roering, 1985; Tellis and Fornell, 1988). Hofer argues that universal models of complex outcomes are inadequate for explaining variability in outcomes. Lee (1989) suggests that any theory of business strategy must be a contingency theory, since no universal set of strategies is optimal for all businesses. Steiner (1979) maintains that:

> [T]he contingency approach is richer than the universal principles approach to theory building. Inherent in it is more rigor, a deeper appreciation of interrelationships in situations, and an effort to identify causal relationships.

By considering contingency factors — the "common dimensions" referred to by Fern and Brown (1984) — more informative models of business strategy have emerged (see, for example, Anderson and Zeithaml, 1984; Bowen and Lawler, Chapter 10; Hambrick and Lei, 1985; Thietart and Vivas, 1984). Many different contingencies have been explored in the literature (for example, type of relationship with customers, level of technology, nature of production requirements, and life cycle stage); the goods/services and consumer/industrial dichotomies could also be characterised as contingency factors. Several of these contingency variables are described in more detail below.

5.1. Tangibility

The boundary separating goods and services can be extremely fluid (Bharadwaj, Varadarajan and Fahy, 1993; Quinn and Paquette, 1990; Swartz, Bowen and Brown, 1992). The augmented product that is marketed to consumers consists of varying levels of tangible and intangible attributes (Shostack, 1977). Customers purchase bundles of benefits to satisfy current or anticipated needs with little explicit thought about whether the product core is tangible or intangible. The task of the marketer is to determine the combination of features and attributes that will best meet the needs of a specific market. If the resulting market offering is composed primarily of intangible attributes, then it may be classified as high in "serviceness" dimensions, and strategies from the services marketing literature may be most applicable. If tangible attributes are dominant, the traditional goods-centred marketing concepts may be most appropriate. However, there are many products that fall between the extremes on the tangibility continuum. A combination of goods and services marketing strategies will probably work best for these offerings.

5.2. Nature of Production Requirements

While the traditional focus in the manufacturing sector has been on equipment and/or technology-based production of tangible goods, the belief in the service sector has been that "services are invariably and undeviatingly personal ... something performed by individuals for individuals" (Levitt, 1972). This is certainly true for some services — especially the ones Fisk, Brown and Bitner (1993) refer to as "low-tech and high touch", such as barber shops or beauty salons. However, other businesses (like basic cable or telephone service) rely very heavily on equipment for service delivery. The strategic requirements for equipment-based services may differ substantially from those in which people perform services directly for others (Chase, 1978; Lovelock, 1983; Schmenner, 1986).

Thomas (1978) proposed dividing services into two broad categories — people-intensive and capital-intensive — to understand better the marketing challenges and opportunities for each type of service. Lovelock (1983) argued that this broad distinction between people-based and capital-based services was too general to provide useful information about how customers actually perceive and evaluate services. He developed a matrix with three levels of equipment and people intensity. Lovelock's classification scheme was intended to help managers to determine appropriate marketing strategy for their services by referring to other (sometimes seemingly unrelated) businesses with similar levels of people- or equipment-intensity.

Other researchers have used related classification schemes to explain differences in customer behaviour and marketing strategies (Bowen, Siehl and Schneider, 1989; Dudek, 1988; Guiltinan, 1987; Kotler, 1988; Levitt, 1981; Solomon et al., 1985; Surprenant and Solomon, 1987; Zeithaml, 1981). Their work suggests that the level of people- versus equipment-intensity may have strategic implications for the factors that ultimately lead to successful product performance. Wright (1993) has demonstrated empirically that the factors related to new service success varied depending on whether people- or equipment-based attributes were dominant.

5.3. Life Cycle Stage

Of the contingency variables explored to date, stage in the life cycle has received the most attention. Hofer (1979) proposes that life cycle stage is the "most fundamental variable in determining an appropriate business strategy" (p. 798). The basic premise of the life cycle concept is that different variables become critical as products evolve through the life cycle stages. Research in marketing as well as strategic management indicates that the product life cycle does have a significant impact on product strategy. A number of researchers have conceptually related different business strategies with successful product performance for each stage of the product life cycle (Day, 1981; Kotler, 1988; Levitt, 1965; Porter, 1981; Rink and Swan, 1979). Other researchers have demonstrated empirically that key determinants of business performance vary across life cycle stage (Anderson and Zeithaml, 1984; Thietart and Vivias, 1984; Thorelli and Burnett, 1981; Wright and Toy, 1989). The life cycle concept has proven to be a versatile framework for organising contingent hypotheses about critical strategic factors for business success. It also directs management attention toward potential consequences of the underlying environmental dynamics in a given market (Day, 1981; Polli and Cook, 1969).

The contingencies described above represent only a few of the variables for classifying similarities across different marketing offerings. Other interesting possibilities exist, including type of relationship with customers (which has received increased attention with the recent interest in relationship marketing: de Burca, Chapter 14; Gummesson, Chapter 9, for example) and level of technology (for example, Dabholkar, 1994). These individual contingencies offer interesting insights into underlying product characteristics. However, it is likely that a market offering is affected by several contingencies simultaneously (Dabholkar, 1994; McIntyre and Brown, 1988; Wright, 1990). For example, technology and life cycle stage can interact in several ways. Technological innovations can move existing products through the life cycle stages more quickly. And as a product moves through the life cycle, technology may play a greater part as consumers become more educated and companies experience increasing pressure to become efficient and cost-effective. A multidimensional contingency framework may ultimately be necessary to depict accurately the effects of these types of interactions.

6. CONCLUSION

As we enter the "information and technology" age, managers are under increasing pressure to make strategic decisions quickly and effectively. They will need more flexible models that allow them to identify and access the marketing theories and practices that are most appropriate for their market offerings. As Gummesson (1987) suggests, "the theories and models that constitute the present marketing concept are too limited in scope, exaggerate some aspects of marketing and suppress others. The old marketing concept needs to be replaced". The traditional division between goods and services is outdated and may lead to myopic behaviour in both the manufacturing and service sectors. Contingency models can help overcome this myopia by addressing the variance within each of the sectors, as well as similarities across the two groups. This type of approach should help companies to tailor their marketing efforts to meet customers' needs more effectively.

REFERENCES

Anderson, Carl R. and Valarie A. Zeithaml, "Stage of the Product Life Cycle", *Academy of Management Journal*, Vol. 27, 1984, pp. 5–24.

Astbury, Sid, "Singapore Girl — A Great Way to Sell", *Asian Business*, April, 1986, p. 26.

Ayal, Igal, "Effects of Success Measure Choice and Sample Selection on Recommended Development Strategies", in Lilien, Gary and Jacques Laban (Eds.) *Industrial and New Technologies Marketing*, Institut d'administration des entreprises, IRET La Londe les Maures, France, 1989.

Bartels, Robert, *The History of Marketing Thought*, Third Edition, Publishing Horizons, Inc., Columbus, OH, 1988.

Bateson, John E.G., "Why We Need Services Marketing", in O.C. Ferrell, S.W. Brown and C.W. Lamb Jr. (Eds.), *Conceptual and Theoretical Developments in Marketing*, American Marketing Association, Chicago, IL, 1979, pp. 131–146.

Berry, Leonard L., "Services Marketing is Different", *Business*, Vol. 30, May/June, 1980, pp. 24–9.

Berry, Leonard L. and A. Parasuraman, "Building a New Academic Field — The Case of Services Marketing", *Journal of Retailing*, Vol. 69, Spring, 1993, pp. 13–60.

Bharadwaj, Sundar G., P. Rajan Varadarajan and John Fahy, "Sustainable Competitive Advantage in Service Industries", *Journal of Marketing*, Vol. 57, October, 1993, pp. 83–99.

Booms, Bernard H. and Mary Jo Bitner, "Marketing Strategies and Organization Structures for Service Firms", in James H. Donnelly, and William R. George (Eds.), *Marketing of Services*, American Marketing Association, Chicago, IL, 1981, pp. 47–51.

Bowen, D.E., C. Siehl and B. Schneider, "A Framework for Analyzing Customer Service Orientations in Manufacturing", *Academy of Management Review*, Vol. 14, No. 1, 1989, pp. 75–95.

Brown, James R. and Edward F. Fern, "Goods vs. Services Marketing: A

Divergent Perspective", in James H. Donnelly and William R. George (Eds.), *Marketing of Services*, American Marketing Association, Chicago, IL, 1981, pp. 205–7.

Chase, Richard B., "Where Does the Customer Fit in a Service Organization?" *Harvard Business Review*, November/December, 1978, pp. 137–42.

Chase, Richard B., "Customer Contact Approach to Services: Theoretical Approaches and Practical Extensions", *Operations Research*, Vol. 29, 1981, pp. 698–706.

Chase, Richard B. and D. Garvin, "The Service Factory", *Harvard Business Review*, July/August, 1989, pp. 61–76.

Collier, David A., *Service Management: The Automation of Services*, Reston Publishing Company, Inc., Reston, VA, 1985.

Corey, E. Raymond, *Industrial Marketing*, Prentice-Hall, Englewood Cliffs, NJ, 1976.

Dabholkar, Prathiba A., "Technology-Based Service Delivery: A Classification Scheme for Developing Marketing Strategies", in Teresa A. Swartz, David E. Bowen and Stephen W. Brown (Eds.), *Advances in Services Marketing and Management: Research and Practice,* Vol. 3, JAI Press Inc., Greenwich, CT, 1994.

Day, George, "The Product Life Cycle: Analysis and Application Issues", *Journal of Marketing*, Vol. 45, Fall, 1981, pp. 60–7.

Drucker, Peter, *Management: Tasks, Responsibilities, Practices*, Harper and Row, New York,1974.

Dudek, Evan, "Profiting from the Turmoil in Service Industries", *The Journal of Business Strategy*, September/October, 1988, pp. 32–6.

Enis, Ben M. and Kenneth J. Roering, "Services Marketing: Different Products, Similar Strategy", in James H. Donnelly and William R. George (Eds.), *Marketing of Services*, American Marketing Association, Chicago, IL, 1981, pp. 1–4.

Evans, Kenneth R. and Stephen W. Brown, "Services Marketing: The Misconstrued Distribution Variable", in Irene Lange and Bruce Walker (Eds.), *Striking a Balance in Marketing Education*, Western Marketing Educators' Association, San Francisco, CA, 1983.

Fern, Edward F. and James R. Brown, "The Industrial/Consumer Marketing Dichotomy: A Case of Insufficient Justification", *Journal of Marketing*, Vol. 48, Spring, 1984, pp. 68–77.

Fisk, Raymond P., Stephen W. Brown and Mary Jo Bitner, "Tracking the Evolution of the Services Marketing Literature", *Journal of Retailing*, Vol. 69, Spring, 1993, pp. 61–103.

Ghingold, Morry and Kurt C. Maier, "Questioning the Unquestioned Importance of Personal Service in Services Marketing: Discussion and Implications", in J.A. Czepiel, C.A. Congram, and J. Shanahan (Eds.), *The Service Challenge: Integrating for Competitive Advantage*, Proceedings Series, American Marketing Association, Chicago, IL, 1987.

Guiltinan, Joseph P., "The Price Bundling of Services: A Normative

Framework", *Journal of Marketing*, Vol. 51, April, 1987, pp. 74–85.

Gummesson, Evert, "The New Marketing: Developing Long-Term Interactive Relationships", *Long Range Planning*, Vol. 20, No. 4, 1987, pp. 10–20.

Gummesson, Evert, "Service Management: An Evaluation and the Future", *The International Journal of Service Industry Management*, Vol. 5, No. 1, 1994, pp. 77–96.

Hambrick, Donald C. and David Lei, "Toward an Empirical Prioritization of Contingency Variables for Business Strategy", *Academy of Management Journal*, Vol. 28, 1985, pp. 763–788.

Hayes, David C., "The Contingency Theory of Management Accounting", *The Accounting Review*, Vol. 2, January, 1977, pp. 22–39.

Hiam, Alexander and Charles D. Schewe, *The Portable MBA in Marketing*, John Wiley and Sons, Inc., New York, 1992.

Hofer, Charles W., "Toward a Contingency Theory of Business Strategy", *Academy of Management Journal*, Vol. 18, December, 1975, pp. 784–810.

Hunt, Shelby D., *Marketing Theory*, Grid Publications, Columbus, Ohio, OH, 1976.

Kotler, Philip, *Marketing Management: Analysis, Planning, Implementation and Control*, 6th Edition, Prentice-Hall, Englewood Cliffs, NJ, 1988.

Kuhn, Thomas S., *The Structure of Scientific Revolutions*, The University of Chicago Press, Chicago, IL, 1970.

Langeard, Eric, John E.G. Bateson, Christopher H. Lovelock and Pierre Eiglier, *Service Marketing: New Insights from Consumers and Managers*, Marketing Science Institute, Cambridge, MA, August 1981, Report Number 81–104.

Lawrence, P. and J. Lorsch, "Differentiation and Integration in Complex Organizations", *Administrative Science Quarterly*, Vol. 12, 1967, pp. 1–47.

Lee, Moonkyu, "Contingency Approach to Strategies for Service Firms", *Journal of Business Research*, Vol. 19, 1989, pp. 293–301.

Levitt, Theodore, "Production-Line Approach to Services", *Harvard Business Review*, September/October, 1972, pp. 42–52.

Levitt, Theodore, "Exploit the Product Life Cycle", *Harvard Business Review*, November/December, 1965, pp. 81–94.

Levitt, Theodore, "The Industrialization of Service", *Harvard Business Review*, September/October, 1976, pp. 63–74.

Levitt, Theodore, "Marketing Intangible Products and Product Intangibles", *Harvard Business Review*, May/June, 1981, pp. 94–102.

Lilien, Gary and David Weinstein, "An International Comparison of the Determinants of Industrial Marketing Expenditures", *Journal of Marketing*, Vol. 48, Winter, 1984, pp. 46–53.

Lovelock, Christopher H., "Theoretical Contributions from Services and Nonbusiness Marketing", in O.C. Ferrell, S.W. Brown and C.W. Lamb, Jr. (Eds.), *Conceptual and Theoretical Developments in Marketing*, American Marketing Association, Chicago, IL, 1979, pp. 147–165.

Lovelock, Christopher H., "Classifying Services to Gain Strategic Marketing Insights", *Journal of Marketing*, Vol. 47, Summer, 1983, pp. 9–20.

McIntyre, Roger P. and Stephen W. Brown, "Is Marketing Really Services Marketing?" unpublished manuscript written at Arizona State University, Tempe, AZ, 1988.

Polli, Rolando and Victor Cook, "Validity of the Product Life Cycle", *Journal of Business,* Vol. 42, October, 1969, pp. 385–401.

Porter, Michael E., *Competitive Advantage: Techniques for Analyzing Industries and Competitors,* The Free Press, New York,1981.

Quinn, J. and P. Paquette, "Strategic Implications of Service Technologies", in D.E. Bowen, R.B. Chase and T. Cummings (Eds.), *Service Management Effectiveness,* Jossey-Bass, Inc., San Francisco, CA, 1990, pp. 97–125.

Riddle, Dorothy I., *Service-Led Growth: The Role of the Service Sector in World Development,* Praeger Publishers, New York,1986.

Rink, David R. and John E. Swan, "Product Life Cycle Research: A Literature Review", *Journal of Business Research,* Vol. 7, 1985, pp. 219–42.

Ruekert, Robert W., Orville C. Walker, Jr. and Kenneth J. Roering, "The Organization of Marketing Activities: A Contingency Theory of Structure and Performance", *Journal of Marketing,* Vol. 49, Winter, 1985, pp. 13–25.

Rushton, Angela M. and David J. Carson, "The Marketing of Services: Managing the Intangibles", *European Journal of Marketing,* Vol. 19, 1985, pp. 19–40.

Sasser, W. Earl, Jr., "Match Supply and Demand in Service Industries", *Harvard Business Review,* November/December, 1976, pp. 133–40.

Schmenner, Roger W., "How Can Service Businesses Survive and Prosper?" *Sloan Management Review,* Vol. 27, 1986, pp. 21–32.

Sheth, Jagdish N., "The Specificity of Industrial Marketing", *P. U. Management Review,* Vol. 2, December/January, 1979, pp. 53–6.

Shostack., G. Lynn, "Breaking Free of Product Marketing", *Journal of Marketing,* Vol. 41, April, 1977, pp. 73–80.

Solomon, Michael R., Carol Surprenant, John A. Czepiel and Evelyn G. Gutman, "A Role Theory Perspective on Dyadic Interactions: The Service Encounter", *Journal of Marketing,* Vol. 49, Winter, 1985, pp. 99–111.

Surprenant, Carol and Michael R. Solomon, "Predictability and Personalization in the Service Encounter", *Journal of Marketing,* Vol. 51, April, 1987, pp. 86–96.

Steiner, George A., "Contingency Theories of Strategy and Strategic Management", in Dan E. Schendel and Charles W. Hofer (Eds.), *Strategic Management,* Little, Brown & Company, Boston, MA, 1979, pp. 405–16.

Swartz, Teresa A., David E. Bowen and Stephen W. Brown, "Fifteen Years After Breaking Free: Services Then, Now and Beyond", in Teresa A. Swartz, David E. Bowen and Stephen W. Brown (Eds.), *Advances in Services Marketing and Management: Research and Practice,* Vol. 1, JAI Press Inc., Greenwich, CT, 1992, pp. 1–21.

Tellis, Gerald J. and Claes Fornell, "The Relationship Between Advertising and Product Quality Over the Product Life Cycle", *Journal of Marketing Research,* 25 February, 1988, pp. 64–71.

Thietart, R.A. and R. Vivas, "An Empirical Investigation of Success Strategies for Businesses Along the Product Life Cycle", *Management Science*, Vol. 30, December, 1984, pp. 1405–23.

Thomas, Dan R.E., "Strategy is Different in Service Business", *Harvard Business Review*, July/August, 1978, pp. 158–65.

Thorelli, Hans B. and Stephen C. Burnett, "The Nature of Product Life Cycles for Industrial Goods Businesses", *Journal of Marketing*, Vol. 45, Fall, 1981, pp. 97–108.

Wright, Lauren K. and Daniel R. Toy, "Service Success Over Stages of the Life Cycle: A Contingent Approach", in Gary Lilien and Jacques Laban (Eds.), *Industrial and New Technologies Marketing*, Institut d'administration des entreprises, IRET La Londe les Maures, France, 1989.

Wright, Lauren K., *Characterizing Successful New Business Services*, The Pennsylvania State University, University Park, PA, 1990.

Wright, Lauren K., "The Effects of Service Type on New Service Success", in Teresa A. Swartz, David E. Bowen and Stephen W. Brown (Eds.), *Advances in Services Marketing and Management: Research and Practice*, Vol. 2, JAI Press Inc., Greenwich, CT, 1993.

Wyckham, Robert G., Peter T. Fitzroy and G.D. Mandry, "Marketing of Services: An Evaluation of Theory", *European Journal of Marketing*, Vol. 9, No. 1, 1975, pp. 59–67.

Zeithaml, Valarie A., "How Consumer Evaluation Processes Differ Between Goods and Services", in J.H. Donnelly and William R. George (Eds.), *Marketing of Services*, American Marketing Association, Chicago, IL, 1981.

Zeithaml, Valarie A., A. Parasuraman and Leonard L. Berry, "Problems and Strategies in Services Marketing", *Journal of Marketing*, Vol. 49, Spring, 1985, pp. 33–46.

3

CUSTOMER CARE IN SERVICES

Barbara R. Lewis
Manchester School of Management — UMIST
England

PRÉCIS

In this comprehensive chapter by Barbara Lewis, she points out that customer care is concerned with customer satisfaction; that is, putting the customer first, anticipating needs and problems, tailoring products and services to meet needs, and establishing customer relationships. In other words, she is describing what I was taught as a description for marketing some 30 years ago! She does, however, go on to describe with a great deal of insight and understanding, the achievement of this desired state, incorporating into the process such relatively new concepts as "internal marketing" and "service recovery strategies".

The background to the current emphasis on customer care is well presented, showing how organisations need to focus on service delivery systems, the environment, and especially the need to manage their employees so as to provide an efficient and caring service — getting things right the first time and maintaining standards. She demonstrates how to measure the dimensions of customer care and service through some European case examples and then turns her attention to the internal customers' role in external customer care, emphasising the need for a full understanding of internal marketing and enlightened personnel policies. The final section deals briefly with service delivery and, in particular, service recovery strategies, including the role of service guarantees. In concluding her chapter, Barbara very usefully highlights avenues for continuing and future research, including a plea for the consideration of all aspects of this research on customer care and service from a cross-cultural perspective — a potentially fruitful field indeed!

Anthony C. Cunningham
University College Dublin, Ireland

1. INTRODUCTION

In the service sector, the provision and delivery of service involves a variety of interactions between an organisation and its customers. In particular, personnel are instrumental in the creation and provision of service quality and, in so doing, they need to "care" for the customer. The concept of "customer care" is, however, wider and includes service to the customer (providing what is required and being "nice" to the customer), delivery/operations, employee relationships with customers and internal relationships between employees and management.

In developing customer care strategies and programmes, organisations are managing products and services, systems, environment and people, which, inevitably, brings together marketing, operations management and human resource management. Further, customer care/service quality programmes may be integral to TQM initiatives within organisations. Therefore, in this chapter no apology is made for the wide-ranging nature of material, some of which is discussed in detail in other chapters. All is required to understand the necessity for well-managed customer care activities.

In the first section of the chapter, the reasons for developing customer care initiatives are outlined, together with a brief overview of steps in a customer care programme and the ensuing benefits.

Attention is then focused on the external customer. The elements of customer care are presented, followed by a review of conceptualisations of dimensions of customer care/service quality. It is also appropriate here to consider the measurement of care/service and associated problems. This section continues with a summary of several European research projects which investigated external customers in financial services, tourism, health care, retailing and manufacturing.

The third section involves consideration of the internal customer to include the development of internal marketing and personnel policies (the province of human resource management) to embrace recruitment, selection, training and rewards and recognition.

The final section, on service delivery, highlights some of the current issues pertaining to "managing promises" to customers, namely service guarantees and service recovery procedures to handle customer problems and complaints. In the conclusion, a number of continuing and developing research initiatives are commented on.

2. THE DEVELOPMENT OF CUSTOMER CARE

2.1. The Need For Customer Care

The need for customer care is driven by customers, employees and a changing business environment.

Customers, be they individuals, households or organisations, are increasingly aware of alternatives on offer, in relation to services and provider organisations, and also of rising standards of service. Consequently, expectations rise and consumers become more critical of the quality of service received, and so companies can never be complacent. In addition, knowledge of the costs and benefits of keeping customers relative to attracting new ones, draws companies' attention to looking after present customers, responding to their needs and problems, and developing long-term relationships. Companies realise that looking after customers does not conflict with profitability.

Looking after *employees* is also an opportunity for an organisation. As companies become large, they may also become anonymous and bureaucratic. Communications may deteriorate and relationships (between customers and customer contact personnel, between customer contact staff and back-room staff, and between staff and management) may suffer. Further, in a recession climate, cost-cutting exercises and reorganisations can impact on staff morale, motivation and performance. However, companies are realising that commitment to employees brings rewards.

The *business environment* is characterised by economic, legal and technological changes. For example, in financial services, the law resulting in deregulation has increased competition between financial service providers and brought retailers into the industry, thus providing more choice for the consumer. In air travel, deregulation has brought not only competition but also problems of survival. In a competitive environment companies can react by emphasising operations and financial efficiency and/or more focused product and market strategies. Additionally, they can focus on customer care (service and quality) in their corporate and marketing strategies. Superior customer care may be seen as a mechanism to achieve differentiation and a competitive advantage, and so become integral to the overall direction and strategy of an organisation.

2.2. Customer Care Programmes

Customer care programmes involve a number of stages, typically:

- Identifying the dimensions of customer care/service from internal and external customer research — their needs and expectations from a company
- Measuring the importance of these dimensions

- Translating customer needs into appropriate service specifications

- Setting measurable standards and systems for service delivery

- Managing employees, to include recruitment, selection, training, rewards and recognition

- Managing the delivery process, to include complaint handling and service recovery

- Monitoring the customer care programme, e.g. developing systems to research and evaluate customer satisfactions and dissatisfactions, and employee performance

- Reviewing organisation structures and customer care objectives.

2.3. Benefits of Customer Care

With a focus on customer care/service quality an organisation can expect a number of benefits:

Customer loyalty through satisfaction. Looking after present customers can generate repeat and increased business and may lead to attraction of new customers from positive word-of-mouth communication. Customer retention is more cost-effective than trying to attract new customers. Cost savings also accrue from "getting things right the first time".

Increased opportunities for cross-selling. Comprehensive and up-to-date product knowledge and sales techniques among employees, combined with developing relationships and rapport with customers, enables staff to identify customer needs and suggest relevant products/services.

Employee benefits which may be seen in terms of increased job satisfaction and morale and commitment to the company, successful employer-employee relationships and increased staff loyalty, which contribute to reducing the rate of staff turnover and the associated costs of recruitment, selection and training activities. Committed and competent employees will also make fewer mistakes (and in turn lead to fewer customer complaints), and so contribute to further cost savings.

In addition, good customer care/service enhances corporate image and may provide insulation from price competition; some customers may pay a premium for reliable service. Overall, successful service leads to reduced costs (of mistakes, operating, advertising and promotion), and increased productivity and sales, market shares, profitability and business performance.

3. THE EXTERNAL CUSTOMER

3.1. The Elements of Customer Care

Customer care for the external customer requires an organisation to pay attention to its products/services, delivery systems, delivery environment, technology and employees — which are highly interdependent.

Product/Service Range. This will include both basic products: namely, what the customers will receive, to include a core service with facilitating and supporting services; and the augmented service offering, to include the service process and the interaction between customer and organisation (Grönroos, 1987).

Delivery Systems and procedures need to operate efficiently and effectively; they should be responsive and reliable. Silvestro et al. (1992) refer to three types of service process/delivery. Professional services are characterised by few transactions, highly customised services, a process orientation, relatively long contact time, with most value added in the front office. Mass services (McDonald's or a bank, for example) are typified by many customer interactions, limited contact time and customisation, a product orientation, and with value being added in the back office. Service shops would come between the other two types. The extent of direct interaction between service providers and customers in the delivery process has been referred to as Service Encounters or Moments of Truth (see Albrecht and Zemke, 1985; and Czepiel, et al., 1985 for examples*)*. Service encounters have impact both on customers in their impression and evaluation of the service experienced, and also on employees with respect to their motivation, performance, job satisfaction and rewards. Recent perspectives and research activities relating to service encounters are reported by Bitner (1990), Bitner et al. (1990) and Larsson (1990).

The *Delivery Environment* includes both physical design and access aspects, and also emotional or atmospheric impact; and is experienced by both customers and employees. Physical design includes layout, signposting, furnishings, noise and music, space, colour, lighting, temperature and comfort. Access includes hours, availability, convenience of location and privacy. Tangible clues are integral in design of a service environment and may be essential/facilitating (e.g. wrapping of dry cleaning, aircraft, rental cars) or peripheral and/or of no independent value (e.g. toiletries in a hotel room, clothes of a hairdresser, waiting room décor, report folders). Significant research relating to the physical environment has been carried out by Bitner (1990 and 1992). She introduces the concept of "servicescapes" which may involve customers only (e.g. in self-service), employees only (e.g. remote services), or customer–employee interactions — in most service delivery. She indicates that the physical environment needs to be conducive both to customer satisfaction and employees' ability to work, and that perceptions of the environment lead to emotions, attitudes and subsequent behaviours. So, pleasurable environments lead to positive customer evaluations of service and a desire to spend more time and money there, whereas unpleasant servicescapes lead to avoidance.

Technology may be integral to a service product, its environment and delivery, and advances have made major contributions to facilitating customer–company exchanges and to increasing levels of service. For example, mechanisation and computerisation can increase speed, efficiency and accuracy of service (e.g. in stocktaking, ordering and distribution, operations, reservations systems, management and marketing information systems, and security systems), but can also depersonalise service. Depersonalised service can free staff for other activities which may detract from customer contact and lead to less customer loyalty; or to concentrate on developing interactions and relationships to maintain customer loyalty. Ultimately, technology will not replace people in the provision of service, and "high tech" and "high touch" go hand-in-hand — better personal service with enhanced technological efficiency.

Employees. The role of employees in customer care cannot be overstated and includes their personal qualities, ability to understand and satisfy customer needs, and their skills and knowledge — including flexibility. In the following sections frameworks for identifying the dimensions of service are summarised, all of which include employee characteristics, which are again brought to light in the various empirical research examples. Employees then become the focus of the section on the internal customer.

3.2. Dimensions of Customer Care

As the understanding of customer care and service quality has emerged, researchers have developed conceptualisations of the dimensions of care/service. Lehtinen and Lehtinen (1982) refer to process quality, as judged by consumers during a service, and output quality judged after a service is performed. They also make a distinction between physical quality (products or support), interactive quality (where the dimensions of quality originate in the interaction between the customer and the service organisation), and corporate quality (Lehtinen and Lehtinen, 1991).

Grönroos (1984) discusses the technical (outcome) quality of service encounters — i.e., what is received by the customer — and the functional quality of the process — i.e., the way in which the service is delivered, to include the attitudes and behaviour, appearance and personality, service-mindedness, accessibility and approachability of customer contact personnel — together with the corporate image dimension of quality. Gummesson and Grönroos (1987) synthesised the Grönroos model with one from manufacturing and incorporate design, production, delivery and relational dimensions of quality. Edvardsson et al. (1989) present four aspects of quality: technical, integrative, functional and outcome. And LeBlanc and Nguyen (1988) suggest that corporate image, internal organisation, physical support of the service producing system, staff–customer interaction and degree of customer satisfaction all contribute to service quality.

Parasuraman et al. (1985 and 1988) offer the most widely reported set of service quality dimensions: tangibles, reliability, responsiveness, communication, credibility, security, competence, courtesy, understanding/knowing the customer, and access. Subsequent factor analysis and testing by Parasuraman et al. (1988) condensed these into five categories (tangibles, reliability, responsiveness, assurance and empathy) to which Grönroos (1988) added a sixth dimension — recovery.

Service researchers and providers might also consider the contribution of Johnston et al. (1990) and Silvestro and Johnston (1990), investigating service quality in UK organisations, who identified 15 dimensions of service quality which they categorised as: *hygiene* factors — expected by the customer and where failure to deliver will cause dissatisfaction; *enhancing* factors — which lead to customer satisfaction but where failure to deliver will not necessarily cause dissatisfaction; and *dual threshold* factors — where failure to deliver will cause dissatisfaction and delivery above a certain level will enhance customers' perceptions of service and lead to satisfaction.

3.3. Measurement of Customer Care/Service

Success with respect to customer care/service has traditionally been assessed by measurement of consumer satisfaction. However, as the literature has evolved, customer service/quality has come to be defined in terms of the difference between consumer expectations and perceptions. Expectations are desires or wants, what people feel a service provider *should* offer, and are formed on the basis of previous experience of a company and all the elements of its marketing mix (to include process, people and physical evidence (Booms and Bitner, 1981), competition and word-of-mouth communication. Perceptions are consumer judgments about actual service performance/delivery by a company and so, if there is a shortfall in the comparison between predicted and perceived service, then a service quality "gap" exists which providers would wish to close. Definitions of service (quality) are offered by Grönroos (1982 and 1984), Berry et al. (1985 and 1988) and Parasuraman et al. (1985 and 1988). The consumer service quality gap is influenced by four other gaps or shortfalls which were identified from the extensive research of Berry and his colleagues (Parasuraman et al., 1985; and Zeithaml et al., 1988). These gaps relate to management assessment of customer needs, development of service systems, employees' involvement in service delivery, and external communications about service delivery; and become relevant in subsequent sections of this chapter.

Researchers have developed increasingly sophisticated mechanisms to assess levels of consumers' expectations and perceptions of actual service delivered. Many use rating scales and are similar to, or are adapted from, the SERVQUAL instrument developed by Parasuraman, Zeithaml and Berry (1988). SERVQUAL has 22 pairs of Likert-type scales. The first 22 items are designed to measure customer expectations of service for a particular industry and the second 22 to measure the perceived level of service provided by a particular organisation. It provides an indication of the relative importance of Parasuraman et al's five dimensions which influence customers' service perceptions, but is limited to current and past customers, as respondents need knowledge and experience of the company being assessed. Parasuraman discusses the assessment of service quality in more detail later in this book (Parasuraman, Chapter 6).

Such scales allow researchers and organisations not only to measure performance against customers' expectations, but also to track service quality trends over time; compare branches/outlets of an organisation; measure performance against competition (competitor mapping); measure the relative importance of service quality dimensions; compare service performance with customer service priorities; and categorise customers (see Parasuraman et al., 1990 and Berry et al., 1990). The relative importance of key customer care/service components may also be established from rankings, point allocations, and by trade-off analysis (Christopher and Yallop, 1990). Christopher and Yallop also provide examples of competitor mapping.

3.3.1 *Measurement Problems*
Measurement of service dimensions is, however, fraught with methodological problems relating to the dimensions themselves, variations in customer expectations, and the nature of the measurement tools.

Dimensions. Companies need to be aware that some elements of service are easier to evaluate than others (Parasuraman et al., 1985 and 1988). For example, tangibles and credibility are known in advance, but most elements are *experience* criteria and can only be evaluated during or after consumption. Some, such as competence and security, may be difficult or impossible to evaluate, even after purchase and consumption. In general, consumers rely on experience properties when evaluating services.

Customer expectations are usually reasonable but vary depending on circumstances and experience, and experience with one service provider may influence expectations of others. In addition, consumers have what Parasuraman et al. (1991a) refer to as Zones of Tolerance, the difference between *desired* and *adequate* expectations. The desired level of service expectation is what they hope to receive, a blend of what "can" and "should" be, which is a function of past experience. The adequate level is what is acceptable, based on an assessment of what the service "will be" — the "predicted" service — and depends on the alternatives which are available. Tolerance zones vary between individuals and companies, service aspects, and with experience. In addition, if options are limited, tolerance zones/levels may be higher than if many alternatives are available and it is easy to switch service providers.

Further, it is necessary to realise that as customers are increasingly aware of the alternatives on offer and rising standards of service, expectations may change over time. Higher levels of performance lead to higher expectations. Also, over time, the dimensions of care/service may change and also the relative importance of such factors. In addition, research and measurement usually focus on routine service situations. Organisations also need to consider non-routine service encounters, which may have a major impact on consumer (and employee) evaluations and satisfactions. An example would be service recovery situations — what happens when something goes wrong.

Measurement Tools. Problems with SERVQUAL are highlighted by the authors themselves (Parasuraman et al., 1991b) and in other research studies (Babakus and Boller, 1992; Carmen, 1990; Lewis and Mitchell, 1990; Smith, 1992; Lewis, 1993; and Lewis, Orledge and Mitchell, 1994). They relate to respondent difficulties with negatively worded statements; using two lists of statements for the same items; the number of dimensions of service being assessed; ease of consumer assessment; and timing of measurement — before, during or after a service encounter. Parasuraman et al. (1991b and 1993) have addressed some of these issues and made amendments to SERVQUAL. Again, for further detail, see Parasuraman's work in this book (Parasuraman, Chapter 6).

Rating scales in general raise questions with respect to verbal labels and the use of extremes; interpretation of the mid-point of unlabelled scales; the propensity to indicate only positive or desirable answers; the number of scale points; and the measurement of desired as against adequate levels of care/service. Researchers also need to be aware of cultural differences in attitudes and behaviour, and the cultural context of a rating scale assessment and consumer willingness to respond and if necessary to criticise companies and service, both of which affect responses.

3.4. Customers: European Research Examples

A number of consumer-based research projects uncover the dimensions of care and service, relating to products/services, systems and technology, environment and employees. Several will be cited from financial services, tourism and health care, retailing and manufacturing in Europe.

3.4.1 Financial Services

Buswell (1983) identified five key service elements for a major British clearing bank: knowledge of staff, communications, expertise of staff, willingness to lend and branch design. Consumer attitudes towards these dimensions enabled the bank to develop benchmarks and a system which could reveal changes in service at a branch over time and distinguish between branches.

Subsequent research has been carried out in the Financial Services Research Centre at the Manchester School of Management. Lewis and Smith (1989) investigated the expectations and perceptions of bank and building society retail customers with regard to 39 elements of service, grouped into four dimensions: physical features and facilities, reliability, characteristics of staff with whom customers come into contact, and responsiveness to customer needs. Half the respondents had come to expect a better service in recent years, many believed that service had improved, and there was a great deal of satisfaction with the overall quality of service received. In particular, the organisations were successful with respect to elements of reliability (e.g. accuracy of transactions, ability to do things right, ability to keep promises, and competence of back-room staff). Nevertheless, a number of service quality gaps came to light, such as problems in relation to staff not knowing personal needs, insufficient individualised attention, lack of information about new services, and perceptions of not enough staff available.

The responses from these retail bank customers were compared with a sample from the US using a slightly modified questionnaire (Lewis, 1991). The international comparison provided evidence of cultural differences in attitudes and behaviour which impact on expectations and perceptions. For example, the US customers appeared to be less satisfied than their UK counterparts with the overall quality of service they received.

In addition, Smith (1989, 1990a and 1990b) investigated relationships between banks and their small business customers. She found, from in-depth interviews, that the key elements of service related to bank personnel, organisation and structure of banks, pricing policies and product offerings. Fifty-five elements of service were then incorporated into structured rating questions for respondents to indicate expectations and perceptions-satisfactions. The most important elements were accuracy or competence aspects; confidentiality and trustworthiness of the bank manager; promises being kept; reliability in the branch and at head office; and speed with regard to decision-making, transactions and dealing with customers. In relation to perceptions of service, a number of problem areas emerged, — for example, queueing with personal customers, charges, lack of explanations and collateral requirements.

A further study (Orledge, 1991; and Lewis, Mitchell and Orledge, 1994) took account of some of the problems associated with SERVQUAL and scaling techniques, and used a graphic positioning scale to assess the opinions of university students with respect to their banks' and building societies' provision of service in general, and loan and overdraft facilities and arrangements in particular. A typical question was:

> Indicate how well you feel banks and building societies in general should perform by marking an 'E' on the scale. On the same scale, please indicate with a 'P' how well your bank or building society performs.

> Smart and tidy appearance .........E.........P........ Untidy appearance
> of employees   of employees

> Up-to-date equipment ...........E.........P.......... Outdated equipment

Measuring expectations and perceptions at the same time enabled the students to visualise the distance between their bank and banks in general. Further, the gap scores were weighted by the expectation scores to reflect the importance of the factors and the magnitude of the gaps. Findings indicated that, overall, the banks and building societies were performing well in relation to their employees' personal characteristics, but could improve with respect to knowledge aspects, speed and efficiency, queuing and convenience. In relation to loan and overdraft facilities, a number of service shortfalls were identified, mainly in relation to explanations of charges and conditions, approachability of managers, and privacy.

3.4.2 Tourism

Examples from the tourism industry concern package holidays and transportation. Lewis and Owtram (1986) researched package holidays with respect to expectations and anticipated benefits prior to travel; and satisfactions and dissatisfactions and future purchase intentions, after the holidays. The most desirable features of a forthcoming holiday, which included a number of elements of service and care, were: good weather, clean hotel, good food, on-time flights, friendly hotel staff, efficient service in the hotel, and plenty to do in the resort. When asked how certain they were that these would be met, respondents were fairly confident about some (weather, cleanliness, things to do) but not about others (e.g. efficiency, friendliness and on-time flights). On their return almost all felt that their expectations had been met, even though this might have been below their "desired" levels. A further, important finding was that expectations were, in part, related to the price being paid. This was also evidenced in respondents' attitudes towards tour operators with regard to reliability, value for money and standards of service.

In the transport sector, British Rail (see Gilbin, 1986) research customers with respect to important aspects of service. Continuing consumer concerns are: customer information — the need to be reassured about times, platforms and delays; time keeping; train service quality; and conduct of staff. British Airways (Hamill and Davies, 1986) are aware of four important dimensions of service: care and concern on the part of customer–contact staff; problem-solving capability; spontaneity — customers want front-line staff to have the authority and discretion to deal with problems that do not fit the procedure book; and service recovery — in the event of something going wrong, customers want someone to make a special effort to put it right and apologise.

Lewis and Sinhapalin (1991) focused on assessment of elements of service by both executives and passengers of an international airline. Senior managers considered 37 aspects of airline service (general, in-flight and ground service), and indicated how important they felt these aspects were in the provision of customer service and how good they perceived the airline's performance to be for each aspect. They believed they were doing well, especially with regard to employees' responsiveness and performing the service right the first time; but could improve with regard to schedules, technology and on-time departures. Passengers' expectations and perceptions were measured for the same 37 elements, and gaps were evident with respect to: security; on-time departure; and information and care during delays. Further, it appeared that the managers were more concerned than passengers with employee appearance, and were not fully aware of passengers' concerns and needs for information and care when their flights were delayed.

3.4.3 Health Care

Concern for service levels and customer care in the public sector is evidenced, for example, in the UK by initiatives and programmes within the National Health Service, prompted by various government white papers and reports, and consequent changes in the organisation and management of the national health-care delivery system — for example, self-governing hospital trusts with an increasing focus on markets and marketing.

At community level, the Griffiths Report (1983) on the National Health Service stated that management should "ascertain how well the service is being delivered at local level by obtaining the experience and perceptions of patients and the community" and a white paper, *Promoting Better Health* (Secretaries of State for Social Services, 1987) called for greater account to be taken of consumer opinion of the primary health care services. The government stated its intent to take steps to ensure that the public's comments are sought on the services provided. Patient research has been developed by the Institute for Social Studies in Medical Care and by the Centre for Health Economics at York University, but increasingly area health authorities and Family Health Service Authorities are initiating their own projects.

A recent project (White et al., 1993) investigated the quality of general practitioner services with data collected from GPs and other practice personnel, which focused on the services they provide, and their perceptions of patient needs. This was undertaken together with a large survey of patients ($N = 6728$), to measure their views of service (quality) with respect to discrete aspects of GP services, and to determine the relative importance of dimensions of service influencing their overall quality perceptions. Areas of service covered:

- Structure: for example, choice of GP; accessibility of care in the practice, at home and out-of-hours; facilities; and information

- Process: the nature of the care to include consultations, procedures and prescribing, range of services; and doctor–patient interaction

- Outcome: satisfactions.

A major part of the patient questionnaire was an adaptation of

SERVQUAL covering 55 elements of service. Patients were asked about the service features doctors should provide, how important they believed these features were in their overall satisfaction with the service provided, and their perceptions about the service that their doctor does provide. The patients perceived assurance to be the most important dimension of service quality, followed by reliability and responsiveness. Typically, reliability has been given most priority, but the relationship between patient and GP requires a greater degree of trust than that between the producer and consumer of other services, which would seem to explain why assurance is the more important dimension. The difficulties that the patient has in evaluating the performance of the GP mean that the patient must have a degree of faith in their doctor.

Hospital in-patients were the focus of pioneering research by Thompson (1983 and 1986), who developed a substantive questionnaire to measure expectations and perceptions. Patients were presented with hundreds of attitude statements for elements of service, ranging from physical aspects, medical and nursing care, to interpersonal relationships and communications in the hospital. For example, a question relating to confidence in medical staff offered a choice between:

> "I had absolute confidence in everything the doctors did for me."
>
> "Overall, my confidence in the doctors was quite high."
>
> "My confidence in the doctors was not as high as I felt it should have been."
>
> "I had no confidence in the doctors who treated me."

In some questions, respondents were asked to compare their expectations and perceptions: for example, "ward conditions were:

> "considerably better than I expected"
>
> "better than I expected"
>
> "just as I expected"
>
> "not as good as I expected"
>
> "much worse than I expected."

From factor analysis, Thompson identified dimensions of service and patient satisfaction: medical care and information; food and physical facilities; ward atmosphere; nursing care; and visiting arrangements. The best aspects of health care were found to be people- and relationship-based, and the worst aspects were mainly concerned with tangibles and the environment. Thompson concluded that expectations were an important element in reported levels of satisfaction and he developed indices of patient satisfaction and dissatisfaction, as well as identifying dimensions in need of improvement.

A third empirical example is focused on consumers' evaluation of family planning services (Smith, 1993). Her research objectives were to compare the requirements (expectations) that women have of a family planning service with their perceptions of the performance of their general practitioner and a particular specialist family planning clinic, thus achieving a measure of the quality of service offered by the two providers. Respondents were initially asked about their satisfaction with 29 aspects of the service offered by the clinic and its staff, and by their general practice and its personnel. Expectations of an excellent family planning service were then assessed for the same 29 features, together with perceptions of the family planning clinic and the general practice. Smith found that "consumers" felt the most important features to be people-related qualities, such as staff expertise, knowledge and manner/understanding. In addition, the family planning clinic was perceived to perform exceptionally well, compared to the general practices, with respect to specific family planning services; to the extent that, on the whole, expectations were met.

3.4.4 Retailing

Retailers have, for many years, been concerned with customer service and have researched the critical elements in store environment and delivery systems, including the role of employees. For example, Jaeger, a vertically integrated retailer with a corporate commitment to service excellence, have established the importance of:

- Friendly and approachable staff
- Honest opinions of staff when trying on clothes
- Consistent service on every visit
- You can reserve garments
- Staff are not waiting to pounce on you
- Window displays enticing
- Staff can quickly locate any stock
- Merchandise in window clearly priced
- Branch looks well stocked
- Fitting rooms of a high standard

3.4.5 Manufacturing

Although this chapter is focused on the service sector, a final research example deals with service in the manufacturing sector, which is no less relevant than in the service sector as a part of corporate and marketing strategy. Early research in industrial buyer behaviour identified buyers' concerns with respect to customer service, which were developed more fully by the International Marketing and Purchasing Group in their Inter-action Model of Buyer–Seller Relationships (see Ford, 1990, and de Burca, Chapter 14). Craven (1991) took account of this work, and recent developments in measuring service, in an investigation of the relationships between a major supplier of industrial gases and its business (manufacturing) customers. He identified dimensions of service quality relating to: *products*, e.g. quality of products, record of tech-nological innovation, range of products, technical specifications, product availability; *the organisation* and its personnel, e.g. reputation, previous experience, helpful personnel, technical support, after sales service, location of supplier, communication/response time; and *operations/ systems*, e.g. delivery reliability and speed, ease of contact, adminis-trative efficiency, electronic aspects of ordering. Craven was able to identify three dimensions of service:

- Reliability services, which reduce the uncertainty of buyers' purchase decisions

- Convenience services, which add value to the product offering by adapting it to individual customer needs and by simplifying the work of the industrial buyer

- Interaction services, which enhance buyer–seller relationships by reducing friction at the customer interface and by encouraging the exchange of information.

4. THE INTERNAL CUSTOMER

The role of an organisation's employees in customer care has come increasingly to the forefront, and investment in people becomes integral to the service-profit chain as offered by Schlesinger and Heskett (1991b) and Heskett (Chapter 16):

Internal service quality→Employee satisfaction→Employee retention→ External service quality→Customer satisfaction→Customer retention→ → Profit

Much of the attention given to employees relates to the concept of internal marketing.

4.1. Internal Marketing

Internal marketing views employees as internal customers and jobs as internal products (Berry, 1980), and a company needs to sell the jobs to employees before selling its service to external customers (Sasser and Arbeit, 1976). In other words, satisfying the needs of internal customers upgrades the capability to satisfy the needs of external customers. Grönroos (1981 and 1985) referred to three objectives of internal marketing:

- Overall: to achieve motivated, customer-conscious and care-oriented personnel

- Strategic: to create an internal environment which supports customer-consciousness and sales-mindedness among personnel

- Tactical: to sell service campaigns and marketing efforts to employees — the first marketplace of the company — via staff training programmes and seminars.

Internal marketing is primarily the province of human resource management within a company, who have responsibilities for developing enlightened personnel policies to include recruitment, selection and training, and also appraisal, rewards and recognition. A number of these topics are well covered later in this book (Gilmore and Carson, Chapter 11; Lovelock, Chapter 8).

4.1.1 Recruitment, Selection and Training

Successful personnel policies include recruitment and selection of the "right" people. Key characteristics for employees to perform effectively may relate to: process and technical skills, interpersonal and communication skills, teamwork skills, flexibility and adaptability, and empathy with the external customer. In general, employees must be able and willing to deliver desired levels of service, and so avoid Gap 3 (Zeithaml et al., 1988). Employees' contributions in meeting customer needs cannot be overemphasised.

4.1.2 Training

Schlesinger and Heskett (1991a) stress that companies should realise that, regardless of education levels, people need training. Training needs will, however, vary as a function of the amount of contact (visible and non-visible) with customers, the skills and equipment/technology required, and the extent of relationships with customers and with other employees (Grönroos, 1990). Such needs, of both new and present employees, may be identified by a training audit, and translated into training activities.

Training programmes cover a variety of dimensions including: product, company and systems knowledge; awareness of employees' role in assessing and meeting customer needs; and the economic impact of everyone working together to support company goals. Critical to this is a focus on service encounters or relationships within organisations, at *all* levels and *between levels* (Lewis and Entwistle, 1990), which contribute to the service delivered to external customers. This includes relationships between customer contact and back-room staff, between operations and non-operations staff, and between staff and management at all levels and locations.

In addition to product/technical knowledge and relationship management, personal skills and interpersonal communication skill development is vital. This allows organisations to *empower* employees to respond to customer needs and problems (see Schlesinger and Heskett, 1991a; and Bowen and Lawler, Chapter 10). Empowerment should lead to better job performance and improved morale. It is a form of job enrichment, evidenced by increased commitment to jobs and reflected in attitudes towards customers. Knowing that management has confidence in employees helps create positive attitudes in the work place and good relationships between employees, and between employees and customers.

Zeithaml et al. (1988) indicated that successful training programmes will lead to:

- Teamwork: evidenced by a caring management and involved and committed employees

- Employee-job fit: the ability of employees to perform a job

- Technology-job fit: are the "tools" appropriate for the employee and the job?

- Perceived control: e.g. do employees have flexibility in dealing with customers? If not, stress levels may rise and performance decrease

- Supervisory control systems: based on behaviours rather than output quality

- Avoidance of role conflict: for employees in satisfying employees' expectations of the company and expectations of customers

- Avoidance of role ambiguity: employees should know what is expected of them and how performance will be evaluated.

4.1.3 Rewards

Employee rewards, typically motivating factors, were considered some years ago by Berry (1981) who discussed the associated possibilities for market research and segmentation. He suggested that organisations should carry out research among employees to identify their needs, wants and attitudes with respect to working conditions, benefits and company policies. Further, he indicated that people are as different as employees as they are as consumers, and might be segmented in a number of ways, — for example, with respect to flexible working hours which lead to increased job satisfaction, increased productivity and decreased absenteeism. In addition, "cafeteria benefits" could be appropriate with respect to health insurance, pensions and holidays — the notion being that employees use "credits" (a function of salary, service, age, etc.) to choose their benefits. Berry was indicating a need for staff fringe benefits to embrace the heterogeneity of the labour force. Present-day staff benefits and facilities include restaurants, sports facilities, and crèches and nurseries. Koula (1992) also refers to pensions, mortgages, loans and insurance at reduced rates for financial services employees, and share options and profit-sharing schemes. Recent attention of service companies is focused on issues of supervision, appraisal and performance evaluation together with performance-related pay, recognition and reward schemes for excellent employees. Customer service awards may be financial or not, and may involve career development.

Research in the UK. A number of the first major organisations in the UK to invest significant amounts of money in customer care training programmes were researched by Smith and Lewis (1988, 1989) at an early stage of their development. Expenditure was viewed as long-term investment, and the programmes were designed to move a company to a service-oriented culture by breaking down barriers and improving internal communications, which necessitated changes in employee and management attitudes. Objectives with respect to management training were:

- To gain their commitment

- To change their attitudes and behaviour: to focus on internal and external customers, devolve responsibility and authority, lead by example, and communicate

- To change the organisational culture and improve relationships between management and staff.

Objectives with regard to staff activities were:

- To increase staff commitment to the organisation and the programme
- To develop attitudes and behaviour to create an environment where all work together towards shared values and goals
- To improve staff–management relationships
- To improve relationships with colleagues
- To improve relationships with external customers.

Overall, the organisations wanted to: emphasise the need for high levels of service and the importance of the customer; train staff to deal effectively with customers; motivate staff through encouragement and rewards; and develop new styles of leadership and management. Consequently, they developed an array of management and staff training activities with variable success at that time. However, most, it not all, are now significantly further down the road in understanding the customer care concept and the principles that guide success.

Successful Personnel Policies do require human resource managers to develop relationships not only with employees but also with marketing managers and operations management. Collins and Payne (1991) highlight some of the challenges and opportunities confronting inter-departmental organisational relationships. Success should also lead to an appropriate service culture to support relationships with external markets.

4.2. European Research Examples

Several European research examples are now referred to, which focus on the internal customer; three are based in financial services, one is from a survey among a large sample of organisations, and the final one is focused on the need for a multidisciplinary approach to internal marketing.

Lewis (1989) reported findings from (previously referred to) leading UK banks and building societies, which had recently embarked on extensive and expensive customer care training programmes. A total of 1,419 employees provided opinions with respect to: internal service encounters and relationships, perceptions of customer service in their organisations, training for customer service, and areas for service

improvement. At this time, there was evidence of a number of deficiencies with regard to personnel initiatives and customer care training
activities, resulting in: problems in meeting customer expectations and
providing good service (including insufficient product knowledge) to all
customers, all of the time; and criticisms of internal interpersonal
relationships, at all levels.

More recently, Koula (1992) looked at Parasuraman's Gap 3 in a
major Cyprus bank, with surveys among senior managers and other
personnel. Comparisons were made in a number of areas to include: customer and service orientation; the role of personnel in service delivery;
corporate objectives with regard to personnel; internal communications;
recruitment and training procedures; interpersonal attitudes and behaviour (e.g. relationships, teamwork and co-operation); employee
commitment; and appraisal, rewards and benefits.

Koula's findings showed that the senior managers realised the importance of a motivated workforce and of its personnel in the delivery of
service, and the personnel appeared to have both the requisite capabilities and the confidence in themselves to perform well. There was also
evidence of a good teamwork spirit and good interpersonal relationships
and communications between customer contact and non-contact employees. Nevertheless, a number of shortfalls were evident between
management and personnel perspectives, which affected morale and
motivation, quality of work and subsequently, the quality of service provided to the external customer. There was evidence of: role ambiguity —
some staff being uncertain about what was expected of them; policies
and procedures that limited the freedom of some employees to act in the
delivery of service to external customers; role conflict — although they
were confident in their ability to satisfy customers, some employees felt
overworked; and differences of opinion with respect to the objectives of
the control and reward systems — which again affect morale and
performance.

The third research activity focused on banks in Norway (Gabrielsen,
1993) where recent severe economic pressures have led to government
intervention and control, and significant rationalisation and restructuring
(including layoffs) among the major banks. Even so, service quality
initiatives and customer care training are a strategic priority. Gabrielsen
interviewed senior managers and then developed a structured survey
questionnaire completed by more than 300 employees. He developed 82
attitude statements covering a number of key dimensions of organisation, staffing and training:

• Culture and environment: to include communication, focus on service quality, role of managers, working environment, focus on customers

- Individual attitudes: to selves, service, customers, selling, the company and the job

- Attitudes towards management: competence, communications, emphasis on service and on the customer and employees, their visibility and interest in employees

- Role perception and training: extent and value of training

- Organisational structure: role of technology, centralisation, authority, communications and targets

- Evaluation and rewards: role of feedback

- Service recovery: routine, compensation, responsibility, authority, training

- Improvements which could be made with regard to: service, internal working environment, customer orientation, personal competence, relationships and communications, training, evaluations and rewards, service recovery systems.

The findings, to be reported in a forthcoming paper, again point to the successes and potential failure points of internal marketing.

Further, an empirical piece of work by Piercy and Morgan (1991) provided evidence from 200 UK companies of their knowledge and practice of internal marketing. They highlighted a number of communication problems between top management and others in the organisations, and problems with respect to recruitment and training — not geared to support marketing strategies and plans. They referred to an "Internal Marketing Gap" and the need for "Internal Marketing Strategies".

These issues are central to present research in the Sheffield Hallam Business School in which the role of internal marketing in corporate strategy is being investigated, in particular the increasing logical and practical concerns between marketing and human resource management as a way of changing the nature of the work climate and employee involvement in organisation management. The research aims to build a theory of internal marketing based on observed evolution in the process of achieving customer orientation in service organisations.

5. SERVICE DELIVERY

When an organisation has assessed key variables of customer care/

service, translated them into service standards and systems, and recruited and trained employees, it then has to "manage its promises" so as to avoid Gap 4 (Parasuraman et al., 1985; Zeithaml et al., 1988). What is said about the service in external communications should match the service that is delivered. Advertising and promotion can influence consumers' expectations and perceptions and, therefore, it is important not to promise more than can be delivered or fail to present relevant information. Realistic communications are needed so as not to increase expectations unnecessarily and decrease perceptions and satisfaction.

As consumer expectations and company standards rise, service providers become competitive in the promises they make to consumers, and there is now increasing evidence of "service guarantees" in both the public and private sectors. Examples of unconditional service guarantees include Marriott hotels, which offer cash compensation if difficulties are not resolved in 30 minutes; a Pizza delivery which becomes free after a certain time delay; British Telecom promises with regard to waiting periods for telephone installations and repair of faults; the Royal Mail's compensation for late/lost delivery and damaged items; and Government Charters for health care and other public services.

5.1. Service Guarantees

Hart (1988) summarises key considerations relating to service guarantees. Some aspects of service and customer satisfaction cannot be guaranteed — e.g. unconditional on-time arrival of planes — and so guarantees must be realistic. A good service guarantee should be unconditional, easy to understand and communicate, easy to invoke and easy to collect on. It should also be meaningful, in particular with respect to payout which should be a function of the cost of the service, seriousness of failure and perception of what is fair, e.g. 15-minute lunch service in a restaurant or a free meal.

Ideally, a service guarantee should get everyone in a company to focus on good service, and to examine service delivery systems for possible failure points. However, inevitably, failures may occur and some customers will become dissatisfied, of whom (only) a small proportion will complain. The reasons why dissatisfied people keep quiet are discussed by Goodman et al. (1986) and Horovitz (1990) and include:

- Fear of hassle or too much trouble to complain

- No one is available to complain to or there is no easy channel by which to communicate disquiet

- No one cares and it won't do any good
- Do not know where to complain to
- Customers attributing themselves as a source of service problems by their failure to perform in the creation of a service.

Hart et al. (1990) discuss the additional costs of replacing customers over those of trying to retain customers who may be dissatisfied. They also refer to evidence of customers who complain and who then receive a satisfactory response subsequently being more loyal to an organisation, more likely to buy other services/products, and more likely to engage in positive word-of-mouth communication. Reichheld and Sasser (1990) also refer to financial benefits of retaining customers and the need, if possible, to monitor defecting customers and their reasons for leaving a company.

Consequently, organisations are encouraging dissatisfied customers to complain, in order to discourage negative word-of-mouth communication and to retain rather than replace customers. In so doing, they are managing Service Recovery.

5.2. Service Recovery

The service recovery process is presented by Hart et al. (1990) and Mason (1993). Service organisations, typically, strive for zero defects in their service delivery, i.e. 100 per cent customer satisfaction, to get things right the first time. So they develop their systems and personnel policies accordingly. But problems do occur (bad weather may delay a plane, for example, or employees may be sick and absent), and mistakes will happen (e.g. a hotel room not ready on time, a lost chequebook or suitcase). The challenge for service providers is to recover the problem or mistake and get it very right the second time — to turn frustrated customers into loyal ones.

Service recovery has been defined as "a planned process/strategy of returning an aggrieved/dissatisfied customer to a state of satisfaction with a company/service", making a special effort to put things right when something is wrong. This includes focus on critical service encounters and anticipating and preventing possible failure points. It also includes: identifying service problems; making it easy to complain (toll-free telephone numbers, for example); conducting research (phoning customers to check on services delivered, for example); tracking and analysing failures; offering rewards for improvement suggestions; and measuring performance against standards (pizza delivery, for example).

When problems do occur, companies have to expedite service recovery to meet customers' recovery expectations — which may now be even higher than initial expectations. It is increasingly accepted that companies should first believe the customer, acknowledge the problem, take responsibility and avoid defensiveness. They should also apologise, and then fix the problem and recompense explicit and hidden costs if appropriate. Service recovery is "emotional and physical repair". Organisations need to deal with the customer first and then with the problem (Hart et al., 1990).

Service recovery strategies should be flexible, and integral to this is the role of front-line employees and the extent to which they have been *empowered* to respond to the customer. Do they have the authority, responsibility and incentives/rewards to identify, care about and solve customer problems and complaints? Are they allowed to use their judgment and creative and communication skills to develop solutions to satisfy customers?

Successful service recovery has economic benefits in terms of customer retention and loyalty. It is also a means to identify organisational problems with respect to all the dimensions of customer care, and to improve overall customer awareness and care.

One major company, known for its high levels of customer care is the retailer, Marks and Spencer. Even so, many thousands of complaints are handled at head office. To do this they have a highly professional customer service department, which aims to: re-establish customer goodwill; supply buying groups with information; and provide store personnel with feedback and training. Critical to success is their use, in this department, of established personnel, recruited internally, appropriately trained, with annual appraisal and performance-related pay.

A research project underway in the Manchester School of Management is investigating complaints and service recovery to include determinants of dissatisfaction and complaining "styles": directly to a company — via voice, letter or in person; to third parties, such as consumer protection bodies or the media; via negative word-of-mouth communication; and exit from the company. Research objectives include comparisons between industries, and the influence of consumer demographics, together with company response styles with regard to complaints.

6. CONCLUSIONS

Customer care programmes are currently high priorities in many organisations, with expenditure viewed as long-term investment for future growth and profitability. Successful customer care strategies, of necessity, require substantial investments of time, money and the need to:

1. Research and understand customer needs and expectations at all service encounters, i.e. at all stages in the service delivery process. To identify the key components of customer care/service quality.

2. Develop enlightened personnel policies. Research and understand employee needs and expectations. Structure training programmes to: meet these needs; motivate employees towards commitment to the organisation and its objectives; understand customer needs and the needs/wants of other employees; and provide product/service knowledge, personal and communication skills. Reward appropriately.

3. Develop: products/services to meet customer needs; systems and procedures that are customer- and employee-focused, responsive, flexible and reliable; and a suitable delivery environment — including retail design.

4. Make best use of technology in products/services, systems and environment — to ensure speed, accuracy and efficiency.

5. Pay attention to potential failure points and service recovery procedures, which become integral to employee training — in other words, empowering employees to exercise responsibility, judgment and creativity in responding to customers' problems.

6. Management commitment to customer care and the creation of an appropriate culture. The organisational culture may require change, towards employee orientation to the company, and everyone's orientation to the external customer. This change starts at the top; the customer care process must begin with senior management commitment to employees and customers, ideally with strong and visible leaders.

6.1. Continuing Research

Throughout this chapter reference has been made to a variety of research focused on both conceptualisations and empirical investigations. Research continues apace, in several directions.

A number of researchers have investigated the gap between customers' expectations and perceptions of services and their delivery, using SERVQUAL and associated measurement tools. There is continuing work to refine measurement tools including scaling techniques (e.g. Parasuraman et al., 1991b and 1993; Brown et al., 1993).

There is also a focus on other aspects of customer care pertaining to services, employees and delivery; that is, consideration of all the service quality gaps. Managing these gaps involves an integrated effort from marketing, human resource and operations management.

Further attention is being addressed to the service process, for example, by Grönroos (1992) who talks about the need for a dynamic model of service quality and by Boulding et al. (1993). A current project (based in Napier University and the Manchester School of Management) is looking at the process of service delivery, to include the extent to which the attributes of customer care, and their importance, vary during the process, and the impact that the timing of measurement activities has on the findings.

Consumer behaviour researchers are also addressing service quality issues, for example, the role of risk perception in consumer expectations. And, as customer loyalty and retention is increasingly linked with profitability and success, research needs to incorporate the relationships between customer satisfaction and customer loyalty/retention. This is a major focus for research at Cranfield Management School (see, for example, Payne and Rickard, 1993; and Clark, 1993).

Projects to date have paid limited attention to relationships between price, and customer expectations and perceptions, that is, the concept of value for money. For example, the "cost" of service quality to customers is not only the "price" that is paid; one also has to consider their time and effort required in the service delivery process. Exceptions include projects by Lewis and Owtram (1986), Smith (1989 and 1990b) and Zeithaml (1988), so there is certainly scope for development in this area. Further, the costs of quality to all organisations are the focus of continuing research by Barnes and Cumby (Chapter 7).

In relation to employee impact on customer care, research agendas typically evolve with human resource management. With respect to service delivery, current interest includes a focus on complaint management which may be considered from the perspectives of customers, employees and management. In particular, most reported complaints are written, but in reality, complaints are typically voiced as they arise during service encounters/delivery: this leads into research focused on service recovery.

In addition, one can point towards developments in the manufacturing sector, where relationships and customer care have traditionally been well established, but where a focus on customer care/service is increasingly at the forefront.

Finally, all aspects of research might be considered from a cross-cultural perspective, among both internal and external customers/ markets — that is, the extent to which cultural differences in attitudes and behaviour impact on product and service needs, delivery requirements, and the role of service organisations' personnel and intra-organisational personnel issues: that is, on customer care and service.

REFERENCES

Albrecht, K. and R. Zemke, *Service America: Doing Business in the New Economy*, Dow Jones-Irwin, Homewood, IL, 1985.

Babakus, E. and G. W. Boller, "An Empirical Assessment of the SERVQUAL Scale", *Journal of Business Research*, Vol. 24, 1991, pp. 253–68.

Berry, L.L., "Services Marketing is Different", *Business*, Vol. 30 No. 3, May/June, 1980, pp. 24–9.

Berry, L.L., "The Employee as Customer", *Journal of Retail Banking*, Vol. 3, No. 1, 1981, pp. 33–40.

Berry, L.L., V.A. Zeithaml, and A. Parasuraman, "Quality Counts in Services Too", *Business Horizons*, Vol. 28, No. 3, 1985, pp. 44–52.

Berry, L.L., A. Parasuraman, and V.A Zeithaml, "The Service-Quality Puzzle", *Business Horizons*, July/August, 1988, pp. 35–43.

Berry, L.L., V.A. Zeithaml, and A. Parasuraman, "Five Imperatives for Improving Service Quality", *Sloan Management Review*, Vol. 31, No. 4, Summer, 1990, pp. 29–38.

Bitner, M.J., "Evaluating Service Encounters: The Effects of Physical Surroundings and Employee Responses", *Journal of Marketing*, Vol. 54, No. 2, April, 1990, pp. 69–82.

Bitner, M.J., "Servicescapes: The Impact of Physical Surroundings on Customers and Employees", *Journal of Marketing*, Vol. 56, April, 1992, pp. 57–71.

Bitner, M.J., B.M. Booms, and M.S. Tetreault, "The Service Encounter: Diagnosing Favourable and Unfavourable Incidents", *Journal of Marketing*, Vol. 54, No. 1, 1990, pp. 71–84.

Booms, B.H. and M.J. Bitner, "Marketing Strategies and Organisation Structures for Service Firms", in Donnelly, J.H. and W.R. George (Eds.), *Marketing of Services*, American Marketing Association, Chicago, IL, 1981, pp. 47–51.

Boulding, W., A. Katra, R. Staelin and V.A. Zeithaml, "A Dynamic Process Model of Service Quality: from Expectations to Behavioural Intentions", *Journal of Marketing Research*, Vol. 30, 1993, pp. 7–27.

Brown, T.J., G.A. Churchill, and J.P. Peter, "Improving the Measurement of Service Quality", *Journal of Retailing*, Vol. 69, No. 1, Spring, 1993, pp. 127–39.

Buswell, D., "Measuring the Quality of In-Branch Customer Service", *International Journal of Bank Marketing*, Vol. 1, No. 1, 1983, pp. 26–41.

Carmen, J.M., "Consumer Perceptions of Service Quality: An Assessment of the SERVQUAL Dimensions", *Journal of Retailing*, Vol. 66, No. 1, 1990, pp. 33–56.

Christopher, M. and R. Yallop, "Audit Your Customer Service Quality", *Physical Distribution and Logistics Management*, Vol. 9, No. 5, 1990, pp. 4–9.

Clark, M., "Factors Affecting Customer Retention: A Conceptual Model", *British Academy of Management Annual Conference*, Milton Keynes, UK, 1993.

Collins, B. and A. Payne, "Internal Marketing: A New Perspective for HRM", *European Management Journal*, Vol. 9, No. 3, 1991, pp. 261–70.

Craven, P., *Sustaining Competitive Advantage: The Importance of Customer*

Service in Industrial Markets, unpublished M.Sc. Dissertation, Manchester School of Management, UK, 1991.

Czepiel, J.A., M.R. Solomon and C.F. Surprenant (Eds.), *The Service Encounter: Managing Employee/Customer Interaction in Service Businesses*, Lexington Books, Lexington, MA, 1985.

Edvardsson, B., B.O. Gustavsson and D.I. Riddle, *An Expanded Model of the Service Encounter with Emphasis on Cultural Context*, Research Report 89:4, CTF Services Research Centre, University of Karlstad, Sweden, 1989.

Ford, D. (Ed.), *Understanding Business Markets: Interaction, Relationships, Networks*, Academic Press, London, 1990.

Gabrielsen, G.O.S., *An Intra-Organisational Approach Towards the Implementation of Service Quality Management in Norwegian Banking*, unpublished M.Sc. Thesis, Manchester School of Management, UK, 1993.

Gilbin, D., "Customer Care in British Rail", in Moores, B., (Ed.), *Are They Being Served?*, Philip Allan Publishing Limited, Oxford, UK, 1986, pp. 57–66.

Goodman, J.A., T. Marra and L. Brigham, "Customer Service: Costly Nuisance or Low Cost Profit Strategy?", *Journal of Retail Banking*, Vol. 8, No. 3, 1986, pp. 7–16.

Griffiths, R., *National Health Service Inquiry Report*, DHSS, London, UK, 1983.

Grönroos, C., "Internal Marketing — an Integral Part of Marketing Theory", in Donnelly, J.H. and W.R. George (Eds.), *Marketing of Services*, American Marketing Association, Chicago, IL, 1981, pp. 236–38.

Grönroos, C., *Strategic Management and Marketing in the Service Sector*, Vol. 2, Swedish School of Economics, Helsinki, Finland, 1982.

Grönroos, C., *Strategic Management and Marketing in the Service Sector*, Studentlitteratur/Chartwell-Bratt, Lund, Sweden/Bromley, UK, 1984.

Grönroos, C., "Internal Marketing: Theory and Practice", in Bloch, T.M., G.D. Upah, and V.A. Zeithaml (Eds.), *Services Marketing in A Changing Environment*, American Marketing Association, Chicago, IL, 1985, pp. 41–7.

Grönroos, C., *Developing the Service Offering — A Source of Competitive Advantage*, September, Swedish School of Economics and Business Administration, Helsinki, Finland, 1987.

Grönroos, C., "Service Quality; the Six Criteria of Good Perceived Service Quality", *Review of Business*, Vol. 9, No. 3, Winter, 1988, pp. 10–13.

Grönroos, C., "A Relationship Approach to Marketing in Service Contexts: the Marketing and Organisational Behaviour Interface", *Journal of Business Research*, (USA), Vol. 20, No. 1, January, 1990, pp. 3–11.

Grönroos, C., "Towards a Third Phase in Service Quality Research: Challenges and Future Directions", in *Frontiers in Services*, American Marketing Association Conference, Nashville, TN, September, 1992.

Gummesson, E. and C. Grönroos, *Quality of Products and Services: A Tentative Synthesis between Two Models*, Research Report 87:3, Services Research Centre, University of Karlstad, Sweden, 1987.

Hamill, B. and R. Davies, "Quality in British Airways", in Moores, B. (Ed.), *Are They Being Served?*, Philip Allan Publishers Limited, Oxford, UK, 1986, pp. 77–87.

Hart, C.W.L., "The Power of Unconditional Service Guarantees", *Harvard Business Review*, July/August, 1988, pp 54–62.

Hart, C.W.L., J.L. Heskett and W.E. Sasser, Jr., "The Profitable Art of Service Recovery", *Harvard Business Review*, July/August, 1990, pp. 148–56.

Horovitz, J., *Winning Ways: Achieving Zero Defect Service*, Productivity Press, Cambridge, MA, 1990.

Johnston, R., R. Silvestro, L. Fitzgerald and C. Voss, "Developing the Determinants of Service Quality", in Langeard, E. and P. Eiglier (Eds.), *Marketing, Operations and Human Resources Insights into Services*, First International Research Seminar on Services Management, IAE, Aix-en-Provence, France, 1990, pp. 373–400.

Koula, S., *Service Quality and Internal Marketing in the Hellenic Bank in Cyprus*, unpublished M.Sc. Dissertation, Manchester School of Management, UK, 1992.

Larsson, L., "Service Encounter Evaluation: Different Perspectives", in Langeard, E. and P. Eiglier (Eds.), *Marketing, Operations and Human Resources Insights Into Services*, First International Research Seminar in Service Management, IAE, Aix-en-Provence, France, 1990, pp. 426–49.

LeBlanc, G. and N. Nguyen, "Customers' Perceptions of Service Quality in Financial Institutions", *International Journal of Bank Marketing*, Vol. 6, No. 4, 1988, pp. 7–18.

Lehtinen, U. and J.R. Lehtinen, *Service Quality: A Study of Quality Dimensions*, Working Paper, Service Management Institute, Helsinki, Finland, 1982.

Lehtinen, U. and J.R. Lehtinen, "Two Approaches to Service Quality Dimensions", *The Service Industries Journal*, Vol. 11, No. 3, 1991, pp. 287–303.

Lewis, B.R., *Customer Care in the Service Sector: The Employees' Perspective*, Financial Services Research Centre, Manchester School of Management, UK, 1989.

Lewis, B.R., "Service Quality: an International Comparison of Bank Customers' Expectations and Perceptions", *Journal of Marketing Management*, Vol. 7, No. 1, 1991, pp. 47–62.

Lewis, B.R., "Service Quality Measurement", *Marketing Intelligence and Planning*, Vol. 11, No. 4, 1993, pp. 4–12.

Lewis, B.R. and M.T. Owtram, "The Growth of International Tourism and Package Holidays", in Moores, B. (Ed.), *Are They Being Served?*, Philip Allan Publishers Limited, Oxford, UK, 1986, pp. 201–13.

Lewis, B.R. and A.M. Smith, *Customer Care in the Service Sector: The Customers' Perspective*, Financial Services Research Centre, Manchester School of Management, UK, 1989.

Lewis, B.R. and T.W. Entwistle, "Managing the Service Encounter: a Focus on the Employee", *International Journal of Service Industry Management*, Vol. 1, No. 3, 1990, pp. 41–52.

Lewis, B.R. and V.W. Mitchell, "Defining and Measuring the Quality of Customer Service", *Marketing Intelligence and Planning*, Vol. 8, No. 6, 1990, pp. 11–7.

Lewis, B.R. and D. Sinhapalin, "Service Quality: An Empirical Study of Thai Airways", in *Quality Management in Services*, EIASM, Brussels, Belgium, 16–17 May 1991.

Lewis, B.R., J. Orledge and V. Mitchell, "Service Quality: Students' Assessments of Banks and Building Societies", *International Journal of Bank Marketing*, forthcoming.

Mason, J.B., "The Art of Service Recovery", *Arthur Andersen Retailing Issues Letter*, Texas A and M University, College Station, TX, Vol. 5, No. 1, January, 1993.

Orledge, J., *Service Quality: An Empirical Investigation of Two Measurement Techniques*, unpublished M.Sc. Dissertation, Manchester School of Management, UK, 1991.

Parasuraman, A., V.A. Zeithaml and L.L. Berry, "A Conceptual Model of Service Quality and its Implications for Future Research", *Journal of Marketing*, Vol. 49, Fall, 1985, pp. 41–50.

Parasuraman, A., V.A. Zeithaml and L.L. Berry, "SERVQUAL: a Multiple Item Scale for Measuring Consumer Perceptions of Service Quality", *Journal of Retailing*, Vol. 64, No. 1, Spring, 1988, pp. 14–40.

Parasuraman, A., L.L. Berry and V.A. Zeithaml, "Guidelines for Conducting Service Quality Research", *Marketing Research*, December 1990, pp. 34–44.

Parasuraman, A., L.L. Berry and V.A. Zeithaml, (a), "Understanding Customer Expectations of Service", *Sloan Management Review*, Vol. 32, No. 3, 1991, pp. 39–48.

Parasuraman, A., L.L. Berry and V.A. Zeithaml, (b), "Refinement and Reassessment of the SERVQUAL Scale", *Journal of Retailing*, Vol. 67, No. 4, Winter, 1991, pp. 420–450.

Parasuraman, A., V.A. Zeithaml and L.L. Berry, "More on Improving Service Quality", *Journal of Retailing*, Vol. 69, No. 1, 1993, pp. 140–147.

Payne, A. and J. Rickard, "Relationship Marketing: Customer Retention, and Service Firms Profitability", *British Academy of Management Annual Conference*, Milton Keynes, UK, 1993.

Piercy, N. and N. Morgan, "Internal Marketing: the Missing Half of the Marketing Programme", *Long Range Planning*, Vol. 24, No. 2, 1991, pp. 82–93.

Reichheld, F.F. and W.E. Sasser Jr., "Zero Defections: Quality Comes to Services", *Harvard Business Review*, September/October, 1990, pp. 105–11.

Sasser, W.E. Jr. and S.P. Arbeit, "Selling Jobs in the Service Sector", *Business Horizons*, Vol. 19, 1976, pp. 61–5.

Schlesinger, L.A. and J.L. Heskett, (a), "The Service-Driven Company", *Harvard Business Review*, September/October, 1991, pp. 71–81.

Schlesinger, L.A. and J.L. Heskett, (b), "Breaking the Cycle of Failures in Services", *Sloan Management Review*, Vol. 32, No. 3, Spring, 1991, pp. 17–28.

Secretaries of State for Social Services, *Promoting Better Health*, HMSO, London, UK, 1987.

Silvestro, R. and R. Johnston, *The Determinants of Service Quality — Hygiene and Enhancing Factors*, Warwick Business School, Warwick, UK, 1990.

Silvestro, R., L. Fitzgerald, R. Johnston and C. Voss, "Towards a Classification of Service Processes", *International Journal of Service Industry Management*, Vol. 3, No. 3, 1992, pp. 62–75.

Smith, A.M., "Service Quality: Relationships between Banks and Their Small Business Clients", *International Journal of Bank Marketing*, Vol. 7, No. 5, 1989, pp. 28–35.

Smith, A.M. (a), "Quality Aspects of Services Marketing", *Marketing Intelligence and Planning*, Vol. 8, No. 6, 1990, pp. 25–32.

Smith, A.M. (b), *Quality Service and The Small Business-Bank Relationship*, unpublished M.Sc. Thesis, Manchester School of Management, UK, 1990.

Smith, A.M., "The Consumers' Evaluation of Service Quality: Some Methodological Issues", in Whitelock, J. (Ed.), *Marketing in the New Europe and Beyond*, MEG, proceedings of the 1992 Annual Conference, University of Salford, UK, 1992, pp. 633–48.

Smith, A., *The Consumers' Evaluation of the Quality of Family Planning Services*, September, Manchester School of Management, UK, 1993.

Smith, A.M. and B.R. Lewis, *Customer Care in the Service Sector: The Suppliers' Perspective*, Financial Services Research Centre, Manchester School of Management, UK, 1988.

Smith, A.M. and B.R. Lewis, "Customer Care in Financial Service Organisations", *International Journal of Bank Marketing*, Vol. 7, No. 5, 1989, pp. 13–22.

Thompson, A.G.H., *The Measurement of Patients' Perceptions of the Quality of Hospital Care*, unpublished Ph.D. Thesis, Manchester School of Management, UK, 1983.

Thompson, A.G.H., "What the Patient Thinks", in Moores, B. (Ed.) *Are They Being Served?*, Philip Allan Publishers Limited, Oxford, UK, 1986, pp. 91–103.

White, B., I. Robertson and B. Lewis, *A Survey of Patient Satisfaction with General Practitioner Services*, Manchester School of Management, UK, 1993.

Zeithaml, V.A., "Consumer Perceptions of Price, Quality and Value: A Means-End Model and Synthesis of Evidence", *Journal of Marketing*, Vol. 52, July, 1988, pp. 2–22.

Zeithaml, V.A., L.L. Berry and A. Parasuraman, "Communication and Control Processes in the Delivery of Service Quality", *Journal of Marketing*, Vol. 52, April, 1988, pp. 35–48.

4

THE CONCEPT OF EXCHANGE:
Interactive Approaches in Services Marketing

William J. Glynn
University College Dublin, Ireland

Uolevi Lehtinen
University of Tampere, Finland

PRÉCIS

Essentially this chapter falls into two main parts. In the first part, the authors argue that the marketing concept has been revised or re-interpreted to accommodate a core made up of relationships and an emphasis on activities which maintain relationships. This view supplants the original view of exchanges as the core and the marketing mix as the key marketing activities. Landmarks along the road of the development of relationship marketing are pointed out: the increased emphasis on the service component of goods; the rise of customer retention and the concentration on service quality issues. Long-term relationships are seen to make sense in terms of being more economically efficient than the acquisition of new customers, providing cross-selling opportunities, a source of new product ideas, and goodwill assets. Long-term relationships are also seen as having different demands from one-off transactions, these being interactive marketing, service quality management and internal marketing. In particular, the authors emphasise interactive marketing. Drawing on the work of the IMP group and the Nordic School of Services, they suggest that interaction bridges production and consumption. Contact personnel have an enhanced role and perform a bridging function between internal and external customers. Glynn and Lehtinen see the exchange process as characterised by complexity, interaction and interdependence. Exchange is not confined to a restricted interpretation of "customer" and "business". Exchanges take place between the organisation and the external customer; between the organisation and the internal customer/service provider; and between the internal customer/service provider and the external customer. Each party brings to the exchange process their objectives, expectations and perceptions. These extensions, revisions and developments of marketing are structured in a model of the exchange process. This is a useful device, which reduces some very complex and far-reaching issues and offers some structure for scholars.

The second part of the paper presents findings from case study research exploring the intensity of relationship/interactive marketing in five Finnish companies from service and manufacturing sectors. The intensity of relationship marketing is measured using dimensions gathered from marketing theory. These dimensions are evaluated along a continuum representing transaction marketing at one end and relationship marketing at the other. The main groups of dimensions are those concerning organisation, interactive marketing and internal marketing. Although service companies are often thought to be closest to the relationship paradigm, this research suggests that the type of company which could be positioned closest is the business-to-business case company. All the case companies considered the fulfilment of promises and trust as critical marketing practice.

Kate Stewart
University of Ulster — Magee College
Northern Ireland

1. INTRODUCTION: EXTENDING THE MARKETING CONCEPT

Reinterpreting and extending the traditional marketing concept to cater more adequately for the services marketing challenge has proven to be a fruitful exercise. The marketing concept, which views marketing as a philosophy and extols the virtues of finding and filling customer wants, fits just as well in the services context as it does in its physical product-oriented birthplace. Descriptions of the marketing concept centre on the fulfilment of needs and wants of target market segments, and adaptation of organisations to deliver desired satisfactions more efficiently and effectively than competitors (McKitterick, 1957; Borch, 1957).

The prevailing marketing philosophy revolving around the concept of exchange on the one hand, and the application of the marketing mix paradigm on the other, are frequently cited as playing prime roles in the definition of marketing (Culliton, 1948; McCarthy, 1960; Borden, 1965; Levy and Zaltman, 1975; Bagozzi, 1975 and 1979; Hunt, 1976). This definition has been updated by the American Marketing Association in 1985 to encompass services as well as goods (American Marketing Association, 1985):

> Marketing is the process of planning and executing the conception, pricing, promotion and distribution of ideas, goods and services to create exchange and satisfy individual and organisational objectives.

Several authors have expressed their dissatisfaction with the limitations of the American-based marketing concept in the context of both services and industrial marketing (de Ferrer, 1986; Gummesson, 1987). The established exchange and marketing mix view of marketing is considered still to be overly production-oriented, in that it originates with the supplier and not with the customer (Grönroos, 1990a). Limiting study to single isolated exchanges fails to recognise the need to build long-term relationships with customers (Houston and Gassheimer, 1987). The marketing mix paradigm alone does not account for the many marketing-like activities, interactions and resources that go towards maintaining the customer relationship over time (Grönroos and Gummesson, 1986; Grönroos, 1990b). The relationship paradigm adds to the marketing mix paradigm in that it recognises the value of related exchanges and the need to maintain customer relationships over time. The relationship paradigm is best represented in the services literature under the heading of relationship marketing.

2. RELATIONSHIP VIEW OF MARKETING

During the 1980s, increasing competition and deregulation in many industries had, and still has, a number of far-reaching effects on the competitive environment. Firstly, the ability to replicate physical products at lower and lower costs facilitated price undercutting by domestic and international competitors. This encouraged many manufacturers to augment their physical products with services in order to compete and even to survive. Many large firms have been transformed from predominantly manufacturing organisations into predominantly service organisations by bundling services with products (Peters, 1988; Chase and Garvin, 1989). Secondly, the need to keep existing customers became a priority in the face of intense competition and the higher comparative marketing costs of acquiring new customers (Reichheld and Sasser, 1990). Thirdly, increased competition and deregulation in many service-dominated industries resulted in a concentration on service quality as a means of achieving a competitive advantage (Grönroos, 1987; Barnes, 1994; Fisk, Brown and Bitner, Chapter 1).

The term "relationship marketing" was first coined in the early 1980s in the services literature (Berry, 1983). Prior to that time several authors had discussed the need to concentrate on customer retention, customer loyalty and reselling efforts (George, 1977; Schneider, 1980; Grönroos, 1981). The Conference Board, as early as 1970, proposed that selling to the prospective customer was only half the battle and that winning repeat sales was the other half (Hopkins and Bailey, 1970). The need to develop and maintain profitable long-term relationships with customers has received particular attention both in the industrial network inter-action theory and in the services marketing theory (Håkansson, 1982; Rosenberg and Czepiel, 1984; Jackson, 1985; McKenna, 1985 and 1991; Gummesson, 1987). The long-term holistic approach of relationship marketing can be contrasted with the short-term focus of transaction marketing and the predetermined structure of decision-making variables presented by the reductionist marketing mix approach (Jackson, 1985; Grönroos, 1991b). Relationship and transaction marketing have been opposed on a marketing strategy continuum and equated with the marketing of services and consumer packaged goods respectively (Grönroos, 1990c and 1991). This approach is illustrated and examined in the case study material included in this chapter.

Keeping and improving customer relationships is important for a number of reasons:

1. There are higher marketing costs associated with generating interest in new customers as opposed to already informed existing customers.

   > The marketing costs involved in the creation of interest in an un-informed new customer far outweigh those involved in maintaining the relationship necessary to continue exchanges between buyer and seller (Barnes and Glynn, 1992).

   > It has been estimated that the cost of attracting new customers can be as high as six times that of retaining existing customers (Desatnick, 1987; Sellers, 1989; Congram, 1991).

2. Close and long-term relationships with customers imply continuing exchange opportunities with existing customers at a lower marketing cost per customer (Grönroos, 1990b). Reichheld and Sasser observe:

   > Across a wide range of businesses, the pattern is the same: the longer a company keeps a customer, the more money it tends to make (Reichheld and Sasser 1990).

3. Viewing customer exchanges as a revenue stream, as opposed to a compendium of isolated transactions, enables cross-selling of related services over time and premium pricing for the customer's confidence in the business (Reichheld and Sasser, 1990; Congram, 1991).

4. Strong customer relationships with a high degree of familiarity and communications on both sides can generate more practical new product ideas from customers and contact personnel (Kiess-Moser and Barnes, 1992).

5. Good relationships with customers can result in good word-of-mouth from successful exchanges and minimal bad word-of-mouth in the event of unsuccessful exchanges. Service quality cracks can often be papered over where good relationships have existed previously.

The relationship paradigm views marketing as revolving around relationships between the parties to the exchange. Exchanges take place in order to establish and develop these relationships. The relationship marketing approach also recognises the importance of fulfilment of promises in the maintenance of long-term relationships with customers (Calonius, 1986 and 1988; Grönroos, 1990c and 1991). The establishment, maintenance and development of relationships by sellers involves giving and fulfilling promises concerning goods, services, systems, finances, information, materials, social contacts and future commitments (Grönroos, 1990b). Reciprocal promises concerning customer commitment to the relationship makes for continuity over the long term. Customer and business relationships have been described as significant intangible marketing assets of the firm which need to be cultivated and sustained (Carson and Gilmore, 1989; Normann, 1991; Forsgren and Johanson, 1992).

The relationship paradigm also applies to other relationships with and among partners/stakeholders which are more or less peripheral to the central direct customer–seller exchange process. Relationships with and among customers, technology and people — employees, peers, union officials and suppliers — are often critical and interrelated success factors in the competitive environment (Blount, 1988).

Grönroos's relationship definition of marketing endeavours to capture many of the concepts discussed above:

> Marketing is to establish, maintain, and enhance [usually but not necessarily always long-term] relationships with customers and other partners, at a profit, so that the objectives of the parties involved are met. This is achieved by a mutual exchange and fulfilment of promises (Grönroos 1990c at p. 138).

This definition is valuable in so far as it extends the list of resources and activities necessary in the application of the marketing concept. These activities include interactive marketing, service quality management and internal marketing. While emphasising the lack of empirical testing, Grönroos is eager to point out that the importance of the elements of the marketing mix are not diminished by the above definition (Grönroos, 1990c). On a similar note, Lehtinen forecast that the importance of the marketing mix will not be diminished but rather will be completed and improved through the interactive approach (Lehtinen, 1983). However, the absence of reference to any element of the marketing mix in the definition would seem to imply the contrary. The definition of marketing outlined below has been developed as a working definition and research guide for the purposes of this chapter:

Marketing is the establishment, maintenance and enhancement of mainly long-term profitable relationships with customers and other stake-holders. This is achieved by an on-going mutually beneficial exchange process, including the fulfilment of promises, and is facilitated by the application of the marketing mix.

The relationship paradigm places the exchange activities of interactive marketing, between service provider and service consumer, at the heart of the services marketing function. In relationships, the core interaction consists of an exchange of values and supporting joint activities (Gummesson, Chapter 9). Organising for the diverse interactive marketing roles played within and without the boundaries of the service organisation presents the organisation with a complex management task. This task will be explored in the remainder of this chapter.

3. INTERACTIVE MARKETING AND TRADITIONAL MARKETING

The forging of exchange relationships necessarily involves buyers and sellers in interactive relationships. The literature dealing with the concepts of interactive relationships and interactive marketing/relationship marketing emanates from two sources: industrial marketing and services marketing. In the industrial context, empirical research has been carried out by the Industrial Marketing and Purchasing (IMP) Group at the University of Uppsala and the Stockholm School of Economics, Sweden, in the development of network interaction theory (Håkansson, 1982 and 1987; Turnbull and Valla, 1986; Johansson and Mattsson, 1987; Lindquist, 1987). The IMP Group views the development of relationships over time, through an interactive network, as a core concept of industrial marketing — that is, bilateral and multilateral supplier–customer activities to produce and deliver goods and services mainly through interpersonal communication. Bradley describes four underlying constructs of an interactive paradigm: organisations and individuals involved in interactions, the interaction/exchange process, the environment in which interactions take place and the atmosphere of the interaction (Bradley, 1991).

In the service context, the Nordic School of Services, with researchers based in Sweden and Finland, have emphasised the importance of interactions and interactive marketing (Grönroos and Gummesson, 1985). The predominance of the characteristics of intangibility, inseparability and heterogeneity in service exchanges bring buyers and sellers into intimate and multiple contacts (Wright, Chapter 2). These exchange occasions are often related either directly or indirectly over time, transaction and situation. Consequently they effect long-term relationships. The nature of the exchanges can also vary by taking the form of information, goods, service and social exchanges (Grönroos, 1990a).

Service customer–provider contact points and exchange occasions have been popularly referred to as "Moments of Truth or Opportunity", (Normann, 1984; Carlzon, 1987; Gummesson, 1987; Blount, 1988; Beatty and Gup, 1989; Albrecht and Zemke, 1990; George, 1990; Grönroos, 1988 and 1990b; Mayo, 1990). All preparations, support, expectations and perceptions on both sides are confronted in individual moments of interpersonal contact. During these interactions the customer has the opportunity to form an impression of the service supplier. These interactions have both short-term effects and longer-term cumulative effects on the all important customer relationship. Ensuring the successful outcome of every moment of truth through good interactive marketing is the primary objective of the services marketing strategy.

A number of interactive relationships have been identified (Lehtinen, 1985; Gummesson, 1987 and 1991; Martin and Pranter, 1989):

- Internal interactions within a marketing organisation

- Internal interactions within a customer organisation

- Interaction between the customer and the service provider's contact person (front-line employees)

- Interaction between the buyer and the seller's systems, machinery and routines

- Interaction between the customer and service provider's physical environment and/or tangible products

- Interaction among customers who produce the service amongst themselves

- Interaction between the organisation, facilitating agencies and customer's customers

- Interaction between the organisation and its competitors.

Buyer–seller interactions utilise three main resources (Eiglier and Langeard, 1977):

- The employees who come into contact with the customers (contact personnel)

- Resources present in the physical environment where the service is produced and consumed (physical/technical resources)

- The consumers.

Grönroos sees the management of interactions between these resources as a task of marketing which he calls interactive marketing (Grönroos, 1981). The total marketing function in services is composed of traditional marketing and interactive marketing (Grönroos, 1972). The interactive marketing tasks of handling the moments of truth differ significantly from those tasks involved in traditional marketing activities such as advertising and pricing (Grönroos, 1981). Traditional marketing activities can be managed separately from other functions in the company. These activities are normally planned and implemented by sales and marketing specialists.

Grönroos has described the interactive marketing function as the marketing activities outside the marketing mix (Grönroos, 1991b). The traditional marketing efforts are seen as occasional supports to the interactive marketing activities performed during the moments of truth (Grönroos, 1990c). While this description attempts to differentiate the interactive marketing function from the traditional marketing mix, it fails to capture the marketing mix implementation role played by every employee in every customer interaction or moment of truth, or indeed marketing's interest in influencing that role. Lehtinen describes the nature of service interaction as necessarily linking marketing with production and consumption on several levels (Lehtinen, 1985). Figure 4.1 illustrates the link between production, consumption, traditional marketing and interactive marketing in the context of services.

FIGURE 4.1: THE TRADITIONAL/INTERACTIVE MARKETING LINK IN SERVICES

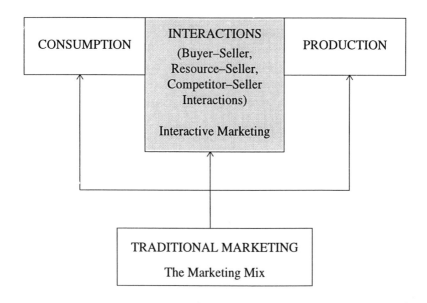

With the exception of the sales function, interactive marketing is carried out for the main part by contact personnel outside the marketing department — for example, production, technical services, claims handling, accounts and deliveries. These non-marketing personnel have been referred to as "Part-Time Marketers". (George and Compton, 1985; Gummesson, 1987 and Chapter 9; George, 1990; Grönroos, 1990b). The part-time marketer concept places all non-marketing employees in the role of service marketers. The part-time marketer tends to be a non-marketing specialist who predominates in the vast majority of interactive marketing tasks. Part-time marketers have been classified into internal and external groupings (Gummesson, 1990 and 1991). Internal part-time marketers comprise top management, support personnel and front-line contact personnel other than the full-time marketers of the marketing department. External part-time marketers comprise marketing facilitation agencies, suppliers, investors, trade unions, environmentalists, the media and other stakeholders including customers. Services customers can also be classed as external part-time marketers in so far as they are often involved in the production, delivery and consumption of the service. The marketing department can influence the interactive marketing function by directing marketing interventions internally at part-time marketers. Figure 4.2 interprets the marketing function in the context of traditional and interactive marketing and the relationship between internal and external part-time marketers and the marketing department.

FIGURE 4.2: THE SERVICES MARKETING FUNCTION

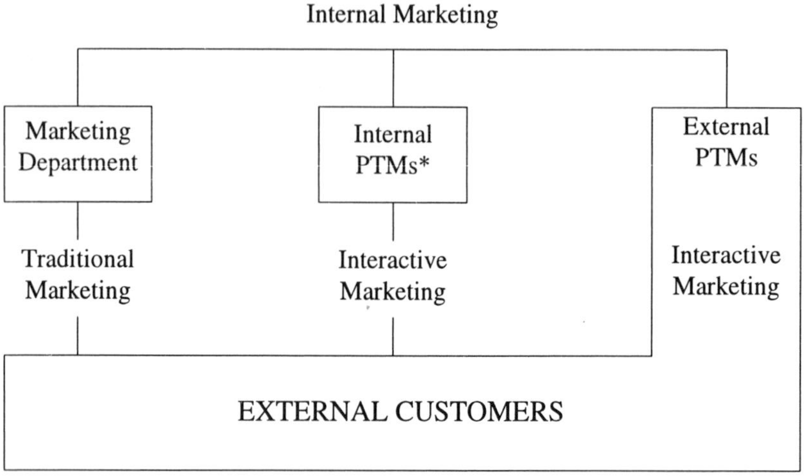

Internal Marketing

Marketing Department	Internal PTMs*	External PTMs
Traditional Marketing	Interactive Marketing	Interactive Marketing

EXTERNAL CUSTOMERS

* PTMs = Part-time Marketers.

4. AN EXCHANGE MODEL APPLIED TO SERVICES

The fundamental keystone of marketing theory has been identified as the broad exchange relationships including the theory of market transactions and the exchange of values between parties (Kotler and Levy, 1969; Kotler, 1972; Hunt, 1976). In proposing a formal theory of marketing exchanges, Bagozzi considers the basic subject matter of marketing science to be the explanation and prediction of marketing exchanges (Bagozzi, 1974). Hunt's fundamental explanation of marketing science attempts to describe four interrelated elements of exchange relationships, namely, the behaviours of buyers, the behaviours of sellers, the facilitating institutional framework and the consequences on society (Hunt, 1983). This macro-perspective focuses on the organisation as synonymous with the seller and the institutions facilitating exchange as outside the organisation. In the context of the highly interactive people-oriented area of service exchange, the macro-level of abstraction is beyond the scope of the model proposed in this chapter. However, mega exchange relationships and mega marketing points the way for future research in this area. (Gummesson, Chapter 9).

The model of exchange proposed here can best be understood by considering the organisation as an involved exchange facilitator with service provider and service consumer interactions. The elements of the exchange process illustrated in the model are marketing-oriented in nature and form part of the overall exchange process which also includes other exchanges such as costs incurred and potential benefits to be gained by the various parties to the exchange. This model concentrates on the consideration of three of the four fundamental explanations (Hunt, 1983).

There remains considerable scope for theory development regarding the consequences on society of the interactive and interdependent behaviours of service customers, service providers and service facilitators. Viewed from the three-way perspective of service organisation, internal customer and external customer, the overall service exchange process can be characterised by complexity, interaction and interdependence. All three exchanging parties are involved in a three-way exchange and it is not possible to isolate any party from the overall exchange process. Figure 4.3 offers a model to integrate the service exchange process.

FIGURE 4.3: THE EXCHANGE PROCESS APPLIED TO SERVICES

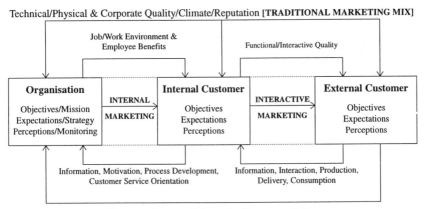

At the broadest level, the organisation is exchanging technical/physical quality, a physical and corporate climate of interaction and a level-of-service reputation in return for patronage, payment, information and recommendation. At this level, exchange is mainly facilitated by the traditional marketing mix. Each exchanging party brings objectives, expectations and perceptions to the exchange process. In the case of the organisation, these objectives, expectations and perceptions are formalised in terms of a mission, strategies and monitoring/evaluations of exchange performance. The operation of this exchange process, over time and in context, enables organisational learning and cultural development.

At another level, the service provider or internal customer exchanges a functional/interactive service quality for varying amounts of external customer interaction in the production, delivery and consumption of the service. This is a complex exchange process with unclear boundaries between service provider and service customer. In addition, the external customer provides information as to the nature of the service required, the delivery and production process and the nature of the developing relationship. This information is part of the exchange process itself. Traditional market information is also gathered by the service provider during the exchange process. At this level of exchange, the service provider plays the role of part-time marketer in the interactive marketing mode. The relationship marketing paradigm is expressed through the application of traditional and interactive marketing activities over time. Again, the individual service provider brings objectives, expectations and perceptions to the external customer exchange process.

Additional objectives, expectations and perceptions are brought to the internal exchange process between the service organisation and the internal customer. These objectives, expectations and perceptions are reflected in the nature of the internal exchange process between the internal customer and the service organisation and between internal customers and internal suppliers. In the service organisation/internal customer exchange case, the organisation is exchanging a job and work environment for a customer service quality orientation, a holistically-based motivation, an informed input to service process development and external market information. At this level, the marketing process is mainly internal in nature with some related cross-market impact of external traditional marketing activities aimed at both external and internal customers.

From this model it can be seen that the traditional dividing lines between organisation, internal customer and external customer are to a large extent blurred. The service organisation itself is composed of its own internal customers, the external customers occupy boundary-spanning roles as part-time employees, and the internal customer occupies a part-time marketing role both in internal and external exchange relationships.

In order to manage the service exchange process successfully, the service organisation needs to develop market intelligence, which not only endeavours to understand the needs of the external customer, but also examines the needs of the internal customer in themselves, and their relationship to the needs of the external customer. The process of understanding needs, wants and demands is basic to marketing (Kotler, 1980). What is emphasised in relation to services marketing is the inter-relationship between internal and external customers.

Examination of the process of exchange in the context of services marketing, requires consideration of the notions of boundary spanning, employees as partial customers, customers as partial employees, and exchanges between external customers, the service organisation and the individual service provider(s) (Parkington and Schneider, 1979; Mills and Moberg, 1982; Mills, Chase and Margulies, 1983; Bowen and Schneider, 1985; George and Compton, 1985; Bowen, 1986; Mills, 1986; Gummesson, 1987; Bowen and Schneider, 1988; George, 1990; Grönroos, 1990b).

Services marketing exchanges are complex in nature and occur at a number of levels: between the organisation and the external customer; between the service provider and the external customer; and between the organisation and the service provider or internal customer. Almost all services are provided, to some extent or other, by people. The following discussion examines the service exchange from the *people* perspective.

At the most basic level the external customer exchanges custom/patronage for technical service quality; the physical service encounter climate; and the organisation's service quality reputation. This exchange occurs against a background of the organisation's mission/objectives, strategy/expectations and evaluations/perceptions; and the customer's objectives, expectations and perceptions of the service exchange. At this service exchange level, traditional marketing is largely used to facilitate the exchange process.

However, the customer wants more from the exchange than mere technical service quality. In order for the service exchange to take place, a functional service quality must be provided and a personal interaction process must occur. This direct level of exchange occurs between the service provider, namely the front-line employee, and the external customer. Each exchanging party brings their own objectives, perceptions and expectations to the service exchange encounter. The exchange flows consist of functional quality, as delivered to the external customer, and varying levels of external customer inputs including production, delivery, consumption and information exchange. The variation is a function of the nature and dramaturgy of the service exchange (Grove and Fisk, 1983). This level of exchange is of vital importance to the retention of external customers through good interactive marketing by the service provider or part-time marketer (Grönroos, 1981 and 1991b). Interactive marketing can be likened to the building blocks upon which the external customer relationship house is constructed over time. The service organisation needs to ensure that the individual builders — service providers — have adequate tools and instruction to enable them to build a customer relationship house that will last a lifetime.

5. INTERNAL MARKETING AND SERVICE EXCHANGE

Attention has been drawn to the need for the service organisation to achieve a level of control over the personal and dynamic exchange interaction between service provider/internal customer and external customer (Bowen and Schneider, 1988; Bowen, 1990). Acceptance of this principle draws attention to a third interrelated exchange between the service organisation and the internal customer, — in other words, between the front-line, support and management employees in the organisation. Again, each party brings their own objectives, expectations and perceptions to the internal exchange relationship. In this case, the exchange flow comprises a job and work environment in exchange for a desired level of customer service quality orientation, motivation, process development input and external customer market intelligence feedback. The role of internal marketing to internal customers is thus one of facilitating internal exchange within the context of the overall exchange process. Internal marketing consists of the organisation informing internal customers of target external customer service levels — the *"What service?"* question; providing the means of service delivery, that is, selection, training, internal communications and support — the *"How to serve?"* question; and developing and communicating the exchange offer and external marketing plan to internal customers — the *"Why serve?"* question (Berry, Bennett and Brown, 1989). The "Why serve?" offer includes the external marketing plan, the job description itself, monetary reward, bonuses, non-monetary benefits-in-kind, promotion opportunities, new skills, prestige, status, recognition, power, authority, responsibility and job security, to name but a few. Figure 4.4 illustrates the "what?", "how?", and "why serve?" internal marketing function.

Once recognised and appreciated, the interactive and interdependent nature of the complex service exchange process can be facilitated, through a dedicated relationship marketing approach, combining interactive, internal and traditional marketing, aimed at building long-term relationships with customers. The case materials summarised in the remainder of this chapter provide evidence of the success of this approach. A transaction marketing–relationship marketing continuum is employed to present the empirical results.

FIGURE 4.4: THE INTERNAL MARKETING FUNCTION IN
SERVICE EXCHANGE

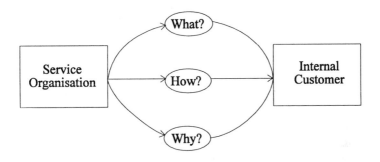

5.1. A Case Study of Relationship/Interactive Marketing Intensity

The nature and methodological difficulties of empirical research in services have to a great extent given services marketing concepts a "life of their own" in the literature. The research presented here attempts to redress this imbalance by testing the model of service exchange and its associated concepts in a number of diverse environments. The following case material is based on data collected in Finland in 1993. Five companies from different lines of business were selected for empirical study of the intensity of relationship/interactive marketing within the overall context of the model (Lehtinen, Hankimaa and Mittila, 1994). Two of the companies were service firms (hotels) and the others were manufacturers (consumer durables, consumer non-durables and industrial goods). The inclusion of manufacturing organisations in the research study allowed the authors scope to make additional comparisons and to test the generalised use of the model.

In each company, a person responsible for marketing strategy formulation and decision making was interviewed in detail. Interviews were structured, semi-structured and theme-type in nature.

The study was theoretically based on the dimensional examination of the transaction (or traditional) relationship–interactive marketing continuum. Dimensions evaluated to be suitable for empirical measurement of the intensity of relationship marketing were collected from the marketing theory literature. A number of sources, including Grönroos's marketing strategy continuum, were utilised to identify dimensions (or marketing and management implications) upon which to describe the intensity of relationship marketing in the five firms (Oldano, 1987; Frazier, Spekman and O'Neal, 1988; Grönroos, 1989 and 1991; Copulsky and Wolf, 1990; Christopher, Payne and Ballantyne, 1991; Webster, 1992; Blomqvist, Dahl and Haeger, 1993).

The generation of dimensions, while essentially guided by theory, was supplemented by additional dimensions evidenced during the course of the five case study interview and analysis processes. The identified dimensions, which even theoretically are not clear continuums, are divided into three natural sections. Each section is then considered as an individual continuum on which the five companies can be placed.

In the context of this research, the data is used in the examination of the exchange model from three basic viewpoints, namely, organisation, interactive marketing and its exchange objects, and internal marketing and its exchange objects. The dimensions can then be approximately classified into the groups that belong to the different areas of examination. The following dimensions could be considered as dimensions concerning *organisation,* especially its strategic basis:

- Time perspective

- Focus of marketing

- Marketing definition

- Target of marketing activities

- Customer service emphasis

- Quality.

Marketing dimensions such as the following concern *interactive marketing*:

- Dominating marketing function

- Communication

- Advertising media

- Collecting, recording and utilising customer information.

Dimensions measuring the intensity of *internal marketing* include:

- Role of internal marketing

- Interdependency between marketing and other functions in the firm.

The main results of the case study research are summarised in Table 4.1.

TABLE 4.1: INTENSITY OF RELATIONSHIP/INTERACTIVE MARKETING EMPIRICAL RESULTS

	TRANSACTION MARKETING		RELATIONSHIP MARKETING
Time Perspective	Short-term focus C(c), D(c)	H(1), H(2)	Short-term focus I C(c), D(c)
Focus of Marketing	Product C D	Customer H(2)	Customer relationship H(1) I
Marketing Definition	Mass markets C(c)	Segments D(c) H(2) C(b) D(b)	Individual customer I H(1)
Target of Marketing Activities	Gaining new customers	D (a) H(2)	Maintaining old customers H(1) I C D(f)
Dominating Marketing Function	Marketing mix C(c) D(c)		Interactive marketing (supported by marketing mix activities) C(b) D(b) H(1) H(2) I
Price Elasticity	Customers tend to be more sensitive to price	C H(1) H(2)	Customers tend to be less sensitive to price D I
Communication	Campaigns C(c) D(c)	Ongoing	Interactive H(1), H(2) I, C(b), D(b)
Advertising Media	Mass media C(c), D (c)	Direct media H(2) H(1)	Interactive direct media C(b), D(b)
Measurement of Customer Satisfaction	Monitoring market share (indirect approach) C(c) D (c)		Managing the customer base (direct approach) H(1), H(2) C(b), D(b), I
Customer Information System	Ad hoc customer satisfaction surveys C(c), D(c)		Real-time customer feedback system H(1), H(2) I, C(b), D(b)
System of Collecting Customer Information	Marketing research C(c), D(c)		Dialogue with customers H(1), H(2) I, C(b), D(b)
Recording of Customer Data	Disintegrated system C(c), D(c) H(2)		Integrated system H(1) I, C(b), D(b)
Main Utiliser of Customer Information System	Marketing department C(c), D(c) H(2)		All customer contact persons H(1) I, C(b), D(b)
Dominating Quality Dimension	Quality of output C(b), D(c), I		Quality of interactions C(b), D(b) H(2) H(1)
Production of Quality	Primary concern of production C(c) D(c) I		The concern of all C(b), D(b) H(2) H(1)
Customer Service Emphasis	Low C(c), D(c)		High C(b), D(b) H(2) H(1), I
The Role of Internal Marketing	No or limited importance to success		Substantial strategic importance to success C D I H(2) H(1)
Interdependency between Marketing and Other Functions of the Firm	Interface of no or limited strategic importance	C	Interface of substantial strategic importance D H(2) H(1), I

Notes: I = Manufacturer of industrial goods
C = Manufacturer of non-durable consumer goods
D = Manufacturer of durable consumer goods
H(1) = Private hotel
b= business customers
a = abroad

H(2) = SBU of a chain of hotels
c = consumers
f = in Finland

It is emphasised here that in the case of manufactured durable and non-durable goods, it is possible to market directly to consumers and through intermediaries. This can, to a large extent, differentiate the nature of marketing activity. The remainder of this chapter discusses a number of the dimensions in the context of the generalised service exchange model under the headings of organisation, interactive marketing and internal marketing.

5.1.1 Organisation: Different Strategies and Marketing Approaches

The need for long-term marketing planning and strategies used to be obvious in every company, but the prevailing turbulent economic situation forced the companies towards increased flexibility and short-term decision making. The *time perspective* was clearly illustrated in this respect. In this case, marketing to consumers was represented by short-term transaction marketing activity whereas marketing to business was a long-term relationship-based marketing activity. The hotels H(1) and H(2) can be placed between the two approaches. The difficulty faced by the researchers in the hotel case was one of customer differentiation, that is, differentiating private from business customers. The business customer marketing approach in hotels can be considered more relationship-based marketing.

The dimensions labelled *focus of marketing* and *marketing definition* were more easily defined in so far as transaction marketing tends to be concentrated on products and mass markets, whereas relationship marketing — emphasising individual relationships with customers — dominated in the case of the private hotel H(1) and the manufacturer of industrial goods (I). In the case of the manufacturer of non-durable consumer goods (C) and the manufacturer of durable goods (D), the *focus of marketing* was on the product and its various characteristics including price. Customer relationships were important, but they were less emphasised than the product. For the manufacturer of industrial goods (I) the *focus of marketing* was on the customer relationship with some emphasis on the price/quality aspect of the product. Both of the hotels placed emphasis on customers, but in the private hotel H(1) customer relationships were more important than for the SBU hotel chain member H(2). The number of outlets/branches and the nature of the marketing channel were typical determinants of the nature of marketing activity along these dimensions. The dimension labelled *marketing definition,* in the firms manufacturing consumer non-durables (C) and consumer durables (D), is two-dimensional in nature in that consumers were often seen as comprising a transactional mass market, or at most, segments, while business customers were treated as individuals. The private hotel H(1) individualised its marketing approach to a greater extent than any of the other four companies.

Responses to questions regarding the *target of marketing activities* dimension reflected a strong emphasis on maintaining existing (old) customers. In this context, comments such as "this year" or "at least at the moment" reveal, however, that the objectives of marketing activities are not always planned in the long-term perspective.

The five case companies described the *customer service emphasis* dimension as being primarily concerned with the building of bonds with customers to ensure long-term mutually advantageous relationships. Service was placed in a broader context as a multidimensional issue with an impact on relationships with specific target groups across a broad range of company activities. The line between the service as a core product, or as a supplementary activity, is deliberately somewhat blurred. As one interviewee dealing with consumer goods put it: "Our whole activity is serving the customers". The manufacturer of industrial goods (I) placed the highest emphasis on the physical aspects of customer service, such as installation, repair and maintenance services, licensed services. In both hotels H(1) and H(2), a heavy emphasis was placed on customer service which was considered to be bound to their image. This is to be expected in so far as service comprises the main part of the total product offering. The private hotel H(1) maintained the strongest desire to serve customers in all possible ways and situations. This desire was expressed as a willingness to tailor all services according to customer wants and thereby maximise service to the customer.

In both the non-durable (C), durable (D) and industrial (I) manufacturing operations, the *dominating quality dimension* was described as technical (output) quality of the goods with some emphasis on the interaction between the buyer and the seller in the exchange process. The importance of interaction grew where manufacturers needed to co-operate with intermediaries on a regular basis. In the case of both hotels, H(1) and H(2), a large part of their services was produced in the interactions between employees and customers. The interactive skills of employees were emphasised here.

The *production of quality* dimension was identified as the primary concern of production in the case of the manufacturer of non-durable consumer goods (C). While the first buy of a consumer good is often influenced by the promotional elements of the marketing mix — advertising, for example — subsequent re-buys are more influenced by technical quality. In the case of the manufacturer of durable consumer goods for consumer markets D(c), the customer perceived quality was mostly influenced by the quality of the interaction. The manufacturer of industrial goods (I) maintained that the *production of quality* was the concern both of production and of all those dealing with customers. Manufacturers of non-durable goods for business customers C(b) and durable goods for business customers D(b) saw functional quality as being the concern of all internal customers in the exchange process. In the case of the private hotel H(1), the *production of quality* was considered to be the concern of all employees in their roles as quality producers and marketers. The strong employee role as producer of quality in the private hotel can be attributed to the entrepreneurial spirit exhibited by the company. This perceived production role, combined with job rotation, served to encourage a strategic vision of quality among all employees of the private hotel. In the SBU hotel H(2), not all employees were considered to be in charge of quality to the same extent as those in the private hotel. The production of quality was primarily the concern of those employees actually producing the services and interacting with external customers. This difference can be attributed to the larger size and more functional structure of this hotel.

All case companies made use to varying degrees of both traditional transaction marketing and relationship marketing. However, the emphasis varied both between and within industries. In examining company profiles across dimensions, the private hotel H(1) can be considered to practise more relationship-type marketing than the SBU hotel H(2). On the basis of these results, it could be argued that the theoretical juxtapositioning of transaction marketing against relationship marketing is unjustified. All case firms utilised the broadest level of the exchange model, that is, traditional or transaction marketing. Traditional marketing is most at home in firms manufacturing non-durable consumer goods and to a slightly lesser extent in those manufacturing durable goods. However, it is more difficult to evaluate the relative importance of traditional marketing in the case of services or industrial products. Contextual variables such as numbers of customers and various strategic issues would influence any evaluation of the importance of traditional marketing in such cases.

Another consideration is the variation in exchange objects from firm to firm. In the case of the manufacturing firms, the emphasis seemed to be more on the technical quality and image/reputation of their products and services as the primary exchange offering. The hotels, and the private hotel H(1) in particular, considered the functional quality of the service and its consequent image and reputation as being of primary importance in addition to that of the technical quality exchange offering.

In this case, the image and climate of interaction were strongly associated in the minds of respondents.

5.1.2 Interactive Marketing

Interactive marketing issues were emphasised by respondents in relation to the *dominating marketing function* dimension. Most service operations, by their nature, involve personnel and customer interaction in the simultaneous production, marketing and consumption of the service. Functional quality is a major exchange item in the service provider/ customer exchange process — in both hotels, for example. Technical service quality was also used to improve interactions between manufacturers and intermediaries — linked information technology, for example. The level of interaction between consumer goods manufacturers and retailers was evidenced by in-store promotional stands in retail outlets. A greater level of interaction and co-operation was reported between consumer goods manufacturers and wholesalers. The level of interaction between the industrial goods manufacturing company (I) and its potential customers was high due to the customised nature of the jobbing process requiring extensive sales negotiation and planning on a job-by-job basis. The time factor was a feature of this interaction — some larger projects could take 3–5 years to negotiate. The highly individualised nature of many projects often necessitated the formation of teams from both exchanging parties. Extensive and prolonged interaction and information exchange regarding production and delivery planning was the norm in industrial exchanges.

Interviewees from manufacturing firms singled out word-of-mouth as the most important way/*system of collecting business customer information*. Information was gathered from partners and co-operatives, salespeople and colleagues. However, there were big differences in all dimensions of information collection and use regarding consumers and business customers. All five case companies used some kind of real time customer feedback system. In the case of the hotels, customer information forms were placed in the guests rooms on a daily basis.

The dimensions labelled *recording of customer data* and *main utiliser of customer information system* were represented to differing degrees in the two hotels. The private hotel H(1) maintained databases on contact level, use of services and special (individual) customer requirements. In addition to the individual hotel customer database, the SBU hotel H(2) used the chain's central register of larger customers and their usage patterns, including meetings at any of the chain's hotels. It was interesting to note that the hotels also used feedback in different ways. In the private hotel H(1), the manager read each guest comment personally.

Individual thank-you notes were dispatched to each guest and their requests were facilitated immediately. The private hotel H(1) interviewee mentioned that customers were more than willing to give positive and negative feedback. The main users of customer information in this hotel were marketing and reception. Marketers in such a small hotel were also customer contact personnel. In contrast, the marketing department was more defined in the SBU hotel H(2). Customer comments were followed up by telephone or post. In this respect, customers were also treated on an individual basis via the customer feedback system. Although both hotels could be said to possess real-time customer feedback systems, they did not systematically collect this data in databases. Neither of the hotels employed market research methods in the development of customer information, preferring instead to concentrate on personal interaction with customers. This personalised market intelligence system was crucial to both hotels in the ongoing monitoring of external customer needs and wants. The same approach was used in the collection of internal customer intelligence and was used as input in the development of hotel marketing strategy. The nature, quantity and quality of external and internal customer information collection and utilisation can be a useful indicator of whether a company's marketing approach is transaction- or relationship-oriented.

In summary, the dimensions labelled *recording of customer data* and *main utiliser of customer information system* offered preliminary evidence of interactive marketing activity within the overall model of service exchange.

5.1.3 Internal Marketing

The *role of internal marketing* was clearly emphasised as a crucial success factor in all five case companies. The construction of a solid customer orientation requires the development of the new service-oriented attitude in the mind of every employee of the firm. Employees of both consumer goods manufacturers, (C) and (D), were encouraged towards a greater customer orientation by their attendance at external and internal educational courses. Further evidence of internal marketing was uncovered in the non-durable consumer goods manufacturer (C) in the form of an in-company magazine. The durable consumer goods manufacturer (D) used an internal video system to broadcast part-time marketer contacts and negotiations with customers. The private hotel H(1) maintained good internal communications and high motivation levels among employees. The high motivation levels and consequent congruence of marketing thinking were achieved through a close co-operative work environment, management by example — that is, full management participation in all customer service tasks — and a functioning job rotation scheme. The less personalised approach to internal marketing in the SBU hotel H(2) was considered to be a function of its larger size. Nevertheless, the educational course approach and interactive internal information flow were also strongly in evidence here.

Case companies were also examined for their level of *interdependency between marketing and other functions*. The marketing department of the non-durable consumer goods manufacturer (C) had firm connections with product development and some connections with the buying and production departments. In the durable consumer goods manufacturer (D), marketing and product development were also closely related. Marketing and production were particularly closely related because the firm was a producer of raw material for the dynamic clothing industry. The financial and marketing departments worked together in the creation of franchising solutions to manage the intermediate customer base better. In the case of the industrial goods manufacturer (I) interaction was evident among all functions because of the size and jobbing orientation of the company. The interdependency among functional areas was also strong in the private hotel H(1) because of the high level of commitment to job rotation. Similarly, in order to facilitate job rotation, the SBU hotel H(2) plans to increase co-operation between marketing, service production and finance. However, the size and more disintegrated organisational structure of the SBU hotel H(2), made for less interdependency than was the case in the private hotel H(1).

Although the case material presented here is limited in terms of the number of firms surveyed and the complexity of the exchange process modelled, the depth of the survey in each case offers useful illustration of the different elements of the action of the proposed model in both services and manufacturing-based organisations. For the same reason, the researchers were also afforded the possibility of drawing some additional conclusions related to the nature of the service exchange process. Firstly, the importance of the fulfilment of promises and trust was considered a key element in the marketing practice of all case companies. The importance of the fulfilment of promises is discussed by a number of authors in this book (Gummesson, Chapter 9; Heskett, Chapter 16; Lewis, Chapter 3 and Parasuraman, Chapter 6). Secondly, although services marketing is considered to be close to the relationship juxtaposition of the transaction–relationship marketing continuum (Grönroos, 1990c), this study has positioned business-to-business marketing at the same extreme and in many cases even further along the continuum than the services companies surveyed. This second point would seem to argue that the exchange model may have significant application in the business-to-business exchange process.

6. CONCLUSIONS

The interactive and interdependent nature of the process of service exchange requires the marketer to formulate interactive, internal and traditional marketing plans, which themselves are integrated from first principles. Dependence on the traditional marketing planning approach alone, or the *post hoc* addition of interactive and/or internal marketing elements, fails to cater for the complexity of the three-way exchange relationship between service organisation, internal customer and external customer. A first step in this process is the establishment of an integrated marketing information system, designed to understand and monitor internal and external customers' service demands in tandem. The proposed exchange model and associated case research presents some arguments against the juxtapositioning of transaction- and relationship-marketing in the context of service exchange.

In addition, the preliminary evidence regarding business-to-business marketing activity places it at least beside services marketing in terms of its relationship focus and points to the possible extension and/or modification of the model to include the business-to-business exchange process. The relationship and networking paradigms focus on the concept of exchange and emphasise contextuality and time (Knoke and Kuklinski, 1982; de Burca, Chapter 14). The operation of the exchange process over time and in context, provides ample space for future research in marketing. Another fruitful area for model extension is at the mega-relationship level, including mega-alliances at organisation, market and societal levels (Gummesson, Chapter 9). There remains considerable scope for theory development regarding the consequences on society of the interactive and interdependent behaviours of service customers, service providers and service facilitators. Marketing researchers have many challenging and exciting frontiers to cross in the future.

REFERENCES

Albrecht, Karl and Ron Zemke, *Service America!: Doing Business in the New Economy*, Dow Jones-Irwin, Homewood, IL, 1985.
American Marketing Association, "American Marketing Association Approves New Marketing Definition", *Marketing News*, No. 5, 1 March 1985.

Bagozzi, R.P., "Marketing as an Organised Behavioural System of Exchange", *Journal of Marketing*, Vol. 38, October 1974, pp. 77–81.

Bagozzi, R.P., "Marketing as Exchange", *Journal of Marketing*, Vol. 39, October 1975, pp. 32–9.

Bagozzi, R.P., "Towards a Formal Theory of Marketing Exchange", in O. Ferrel, S.W. Brown and C.W. Lamb Jr., (Eds.), *Conceptual and Theoretical Developments in Marketing*, American Marketing Association, Proceedings Series, Chicago, IL, 1979, pp. 431–47.

Barnes, James G., "Relationship Marketing: A Useful Concept for All Firms?" *Working Paper*, No. 94–2, Centre for Quality and Services Management, Graduate School of Business, University College Dublin, Ireland, 1994.

Barnes, James G. and William J. Glynn, "Beyond Technology: What the Consumer Wants Now is Service", 2nd International Research Seminar in Service Management, Institut d'Administration des Entreprises, Université d'Aix-marseille III, Proceedings, L'Agelonde, France, 1992, pp. 25–41.

Beatty, Sharon E. and Benton E. Gup, "A Guide to Building a Customer Service Orientation", *Journal of Retail Banking*, Vol. 11, No. 2, Summer 1989, pp. 15–22.

Berry, Leonard L., "Relationship Marketing", in Leonard L. Berry, G. Lynn Shostack and Gregory D. Upah (Eds.), *Emerging Perspectives in Services Marketing*, American Marketing Association, Proceedings Series, Chicago, IL, 1983, pp. 25–28.

Berry, Leonard L., David R. Bennett and Carter W. Brown, *Service Quality: A Profit Strategy for Financial Institutions*, Dow Jones-Irwin, Homewood, IL, 1989, p. 147.

Blomqvist, R., I. Dahl and T. Haeger, *Relationsmarknadssföring. Strategy och method för service konkurrens,* IMH-Förlag AB, Göteborg, Sweden, 1993.

Blount, W.F., "AT&T Service Quality and Renewal", *AT&T Technology*, Vol. 3, No. 1, 1988, pp. 2–7.

Borch, Fred J., "The Marketing Philosophy as a Way of Business Life", in *The Marketing Concept: Its Meaning to Management*, American Management Association, Marketing Series, No. 99, New York, 1957, pp. 3–5.

Borden, N. H., "The Concept of the Marketing Mix", in G. Schwartz (Ed.), *Science in Marketing*, John Wiley and Sons, New York, 1965.

Bowen, David E., "Managing Customers as Human Resources in Service Organisations", *Human Resource Management*, Vol. 25, 1986, pp. 371–84.

Bowen, David E., "Interdisciplinary Study of Service: Some Progress, Some Prospects", *Journal of Business Research*, Vol. 20, No. 1, January 1990, pp. 71–9.

Bowen, David E. and Benjamin Schneider, "Boundary-Spanning-Role Employees and the Services Encounter: Some Guidelines for Management and Research", in John A. Czepiel, Michael R. Solomon and Carol F. Surprenent (Eds.), *The Service Encounter: Managing Employee/Customer Interaction in Service Businesses*, D.C. Heath and Company, Lexington, MA, 1985, pp. 127–47.

Bowen, David E. and Benjamin Schneider, "Services Marketing and Management: Implications for Organisational Behavior", *Research in Organisational Behavior*", Vol. 10, 1988, pp. 43–80.

Bradley, M. Frank, *International Marketing Strategy*, Prentice-Hall International (UK) Ltd., Hertfordshire, UK, 1991.

Calonius, Henrik, "A Market Behaviour Framework", in Kristian Möller and M. Paltschik (Eds.), *Contemporary Research in Marketing*, Proceedings of the 15th European Marketing Academy Conference, Helsinki, Finland, 1986.

Calonius, Henrik, "A Buying Process Model", in Keith Blois and Stephen Parkinson, (Eds.), *Innovative Marketing: A European Perspective*, Proceedings of the 17th European Marketing Academy Conference, University of Bradford, UK, May 1988, pp. 86–103.

Carlzon, Jan, *Moments of Truth*, Ballinger, New York, 1987.

Carson, David and Audrey Gilmore, "Customer Care: The Neglected Domain", *Irish Marketing Review*, Vol. 4, No. 3, 1989/90, pp. 49–61.

Chase, Richard B. and David A. Garvin, "The Service Factory", *Harvard Business Review*, July/August, 1989, pp. 30–8.

Christopher, Martin, Adrian Payne and David Ballantyne, *Relationship Marketing: Bringing Quality, Customer Service and Marketing Together*, Butterworth-Heinemann, Oxford, UK, 1991.

Congram, Carole A., "Building Relationships that Last", in Carole A. Congram and Margaret L. Friedman (Eds.), *The AMA Handbook of Marketing for the Service Industries*, AMACOM, American Management Association, New York, 1991, pp. 263–79.

Copulsky, Jonathan R. and Michael J. Wolf, "Relationship Marketing: Positioning for the Future", *Journal of Business Strategy*, July/August, 1990, pp. 16–20.

Culliton, J.W., *The Management of Marketing Costs*, Andover Press, Andover, MA, 1948.

Desatnick, Robert L., *Managing to Keep the Customer: How to Achieve and Maintain Superior Customer Service Throughout the Organisation*, Jossey-Bass Incorporated, San Francisco, CA, 1987.

Eiglier, Pierre, Eric Langeard, Christopher H. Lovelock, John E.G. Bateson and Robert F. Young, *Marketing Consumer Services: New Insights*, Marketing Science Institute, Report 77–115, December, Cambridge, MA, 1977.

de Ferrer, Robert J., "A Case for European Management", *The Information Management Development Review*, Vol. 2, 1986, pp. 275–81.

Forsgren, Mats and Jan Johanson, "Managing Internationalisation in Business Networks", in Mats Forsgren and Jan Johanson (Eds.), *"Managing Networks in International Business"*, Gordon and Breech Science Publishing, Philadelphia, PA, 1992, Chapter 1, pp. 1–15.

Frazier, G.L., R.E. Spekman and C.R. O'Neal, "Just-in-Time Exchange Relationships in Industrial Markets", *Journal of Marketing*, Vol. 52, October 1988, pp. 52–67.

George, William R., "The Retailing of Services: A Challenging Future", *Journal of Retailing*, Vol. 53, Fall, 1977, pp. 85–98.

George, William R. and Fran Compton, "How to Initiate a Marketing Perspective in a Health Services Organisation", *Journal of Health Care Marketing*, Vol. 5, No. 1, Winter, 1985, pp. 29–37.

George, William R., "Internal Marketing and Organisational Behaviour — A Partnership in Developing Customer-Conscious Employees At Every Level", *Journal of Business Research*, Vol. 20, 1990, pp. 63–70.

Grönroos, Christian, "Internal Marketing: An Integral Part of Marketing Theory", in James H. Donnelly and William R. George (Eds.), *Marketing of Services*, Proceedings Series, American Marketing Association, 1981, pp. 236–8.

Grönroos, Christian, "An Applied Service Marketing Theory", *European Journal of Marketing*, Vol. 16, No. 7, 1982, pp. 30–41.

Grönroos, Christian and Evert Gummesson (Eds.), *Service Marketing — Nordic School Perspectives*, Research Report, No. R 1985:2, University of Stockholm, Department of Business Administration, Sweden, 1985.

Grönroos, Christian and Evert Gummesson, "Service Orientation in Industrial Marketing", in M. Venkatesan, Diane M. Schmalensee and Claudia Marshall, (Eds.), *Creativity in Services Marketing: What's New, What Works, What's Developing*, American Marketing Association, Proceedings Series, Chicago, IL, 1986, pp. 23–6.

Grönroos, Christian, "Developing the Service Offering — A Source of Competitive Advantage", *Working Paper* 161, Swedish School of Economics, Helsinki, Finland, 1987.

Grönroos, Christian, "Service Quality: The Six Criteria of Good Perceived Service Quality", *Review of Business*, Vol. 9, No. 3, Winter 1988, pp. 10–13.

Grönroos, Christian, "A Relationship Approach to Marketing: The Need for a New Paradigm", *Working Papers,* Swedish School of Economics, Helsinki, Finland, 1989.

Grönroos, Christian (a), "Marketing Redefined", *Management Decision*, Vol. 28, No. 8, 1990, pp. 5–9.

Grönroos, Christian (b), "Relationship Approach to Marketing in Service Contexts: Marketing and Organisational Behaviour Interface", *Journal of Business Research*, Vol. 20, 1990, pp. 3–11.

Grönroos, Christian (c), *Service Management and Marketing: Managing the Moments of Truth in Service Competition*, Lexington Books, Lexington, MA, 1990.

Grönroos, Christian, "The Marketing Strategy Continuum: Towards a Marketing Concept for the 1990's", *Management Decision*, Vol. 29, No. 1, 1991, pp. 7–13.

Grove, Stephen J. and Raymond P. Fisk, "The Dramaturgy of Services Exchange: An Analytical Framework for Services Marketing", in Leonard L. Berry, G. Lynn Shostack and Gregory D. Upah (Eds.), *Emerging Perspectives in Services Marketing*, American Marketing Association, Proceedings Series, Chicago, IL, 1983, pp. 45–49.

Gummesson, Evert, "The New Marketing — Developing Long-term Interactive Relationships", *Long Range Planning*, Vol. 20, No. 4, 1987, pp. 10–20.

Gummesson, Evert, "Marketing Organisation in Service Businesses: The Role of the Part-Time Marketer", in R. Teare, Luiz Moutinho and Neil Morgan (Eds.), *Managing and Marketing Services in the 1990's*, Cassell Education Limited, London, 1990, pp. 35–48.

Gummesson, Evert, "Marketing-Orientation Revisited: The Crucial Role of the Part-time Marketer", *European Journal of Marketing*, Vol. 25, No. 2, 1991, pp. 60–75.

Håkansson, Hakan (Ed.), *International Marketing and Purchasing of Industrial Goods*, John Wiley and Sons, Chichester, UK, 1982.

Håkansson, Hakan (Ed.), *Industrial Technological Development*, Croom Helm, London, 1987.

Hopkins, D.S. and E.L. Bailey, *Customer Service — A Progress Report*, The Conference Board, New York, 1970.

Houston, Franklin S. and J.B. Gassenheimer, "Marketing and Exchange", *Journal of Marketing*, Vol. 51, October 1987, pp. 3–18.

Hunt, Shelby D., "The Nature and Scope of Marketing", *Journal of Marketing*, Vol. 40, July, 1976, pp. 17–28.

Hunt, Shelby D., "General Theories and the Fundamental Explanada of Marketing", *Journal of Marketing*, 46, Fall, 1983, pp. 9–17.

Jackson, Barbara Bund, "Build Customer Relationships that Last", *Harvard Business Review*, November/December, 1985, pp. 120–28.

Johansson, Jan and Lars Gunnar Mattsson, "Interorganizational Relations in Industrial Systems: A Network Approach Compared with the Transaction-Cost Approach", *International Studies of Management and Organisation*, Vol. 17, No. 1, Spring, 1987.

Kiess-Moser, Eva, and James G. Barnes, *Emerging Trends in Marketing Research: The Link with Customer Satisfaction*, The Conference Board of Canada, Report 82–92, Ottawa, Ontario, Canada, 1992.

Knoke, D. and J. H. Kuklinski, *Network Analysis*, 1982, Sage, Beverly Hills, CA, pp 9–21.

Kotler, Philip and S. J. Levy, "Broadening the Concept of Marketing", *Journal of Marketing*, Vol. 33, January, 1969, pp. 10–15.

Kotler, Philip, "A Generic Concept of Marketing", *Journal of Marketing*, Vol. 36, April, 1972, pp. 46–54.

Kotler, Philip, *Marketing Management: Analysis, Planning and Control*, 4th Edition, Prentice Hall, Englewood Cliffs, NJ, 1980.

Lehtinen, Uolevi, "Changes in Interpreting International Marketing", *The Finnish Journal of Business Economics*, Vol. 32, No. 1, 1983, pp. 94–6.

Lehtinen, Uolevi, "Functional Interactions and International Services Marketing", *2nd Open International I.M.P. Research Seminar on International Marketing*, Uppsala, Sweden, September, 1985.

Lehtinen, Uolevi, Anna Hankimaa and Tuula Mittilä, "Measuring the Intensity of Relationship Marketing", in *Relationship Marketing: Theory, Methods and Applications*, Jagdish N. Sheth, and Atul Parvatiyar (Eds.), Proceedings, Relationship Marketing Conference, Center for Relationship Marketing, Roberto C. Goizueta Business School, Emory University, Atlanta, GA, 1994.

Levy, S. J. and Gerald Zaltman, *Marketing Society and Conflict*, Prentice Hall, Englewood Cliffs, NJ, 1975.

Lindquist, Lars J., "Quality and Service Value in the Consumption of Services", in Carole F. Surprenant, (Ed.), *Add Value to Your Service*, American Marketing Association, Chicago, IL, 1987.

Martin, Charles L, and Charles A. Pranter, "Compatibility Management: Customer-to-Customer Relations in Service Environments", *Journal of Services Marketing*, Vol. 3, No. 3, Summer, 1989, pp. 5–15.

Mayo, Michael C., "The Services Marketing Literature: A Review and Critique", *Canadian Journal of Marketing Research*, Vol. 9, 1990, pp. 33–41.

McCarthy, E. Jerome, *Basic Marketing*, Irwin, Homewood, IL, 1960.

McKenna, Regis, *The Regis Touch*, Addison-Wesley, Reading, MA, 1985.

McKenna, Regis, *Relationship Marketing: Successful Strategies for the Age of the Customer*, Addison-Wesley, Reading, MA, 1991.

McKitterick, John B., "What is the Marketing Management Concept?" in *Frontiers of Marketing Thought and Action*, American Marketing Association, Chicago, IL, 1957, pp. 71–82.

Mills, Peter K. and D.J. Moberg, "Perspectives on the Technology of Service Operations", *Academy of Management Review*, Vol. 7, No. 3, 1982, pp. 467–78.

Mills, Peter K., Richard B. Chase and Newton Marguilies, "Motivating the Client/Employee System as a Service Production Strategy", *Academy of Management Review*, Vol. 8, No. 2, 1983, pp. 301–10.

Mills, Peter K., *Managing Service Industries: Organisational Practices in a Post-Industrial Economy*, Ballinger, Cambridge, MA, 1986.

Normann, Richard, *Service Management: Strategy and Leadership*, John Wiley and Sons, Chichester, UK, 1984.

Normann, Richard, *Service Management: Strategy and Leadership in Service Businesses*, 2nd Edition, John Wiley and Sons, Chichester, UK, 1991.

Oldano, T. L., "Relationship Segmentation", in T. Surpenant (Ed.), *Add Value to Your Service*, American Marketing Association, Chicago, IL, 1987, pp. 143–6.

Parkington, J.J. and Benjamin Schneider, "Some Correlates of Experienced Job Stress: A Boundary Role Study", *Academy of Management Journal*, Vol. 22, 1979, pp. 270–81.

Peters, Tom, "New Products, New Markets, New Competition, New Thinking", *The Economist*, March, 1988, p. 20.

Reichheld, Frederick F. and W. Earl Sasser, "Zero Defections: Quality Comes to Services", *Harvard Business Review*, September/October, 1990, pp. 105–11.

Rosenberg, Larry J. and John A. Czepiel, "A Marketing Approach for Customer Retention", *Journal of Consumer Marketing*, Vol. 1, 1984, pp. 45–51.

Schneider, Benjamin, "The Service Organisation: Climate is Crucial",

Organizational Dynamics, Autumn, 1980, p. 54.

Sellers, Patricia, "Getting Customers to Love You", *Fortune,* 13 March, 1989, pp. 38–49.

Turnbull, Peter W. and Jean-Paul Valla (Eds.), *Strategies for International Industrial Marketing*, Croom Helm, London, 1986.

Webster, F.E. Jr., "The Changing Role of Marketing in the Corporation", *Journal of Marketing*, Vol. 56, October, 1992, pp. 1–17.

5

SERVICE MAPPING:
Back to Basics

Jane Kingman-Brundage
Kingman-Brundage Inc.
Connecticut, USA

PRÉCIS

This chapter deals with service mapping as a tool for service system design and management, and is divided into sections. Following the introduction, the second section comprises a brief examination of the literature to summarise the nature and characteristics of the service operation. The service encounter, or instrumental interaction between consumers and service providers, as it is termed here, is considered, and two main components of the service system — people and technique — are discussed in more detail. Section three deals with the service logic template, which is a generic model of the service operation, represented through a "universal service map". The service map models the service system in a manner which shows clearly the logic of decision-making and service activity against a background of organisation structure. An important aspect of the service map is that it assists in the identification of critical success factors, and the sub-processes and decision points most influential in effective system performance. Section four examines the use of service mapping in service system design, with an application to a car repair service system. In particular, the separate mapping of customer logic, technical logic, and employee logic, is detailed through separate service maps, facilitating analysis of how they work, possibly conflict, and in general contribute to the characteristic instrumental interaction of the system. These three service maps, representing different dimensions of the service system, are ultimately synthesised to produce a desired state map of the system. Future research directions are then suggested.

This chapter constitutes a valuable addition to the literature on the design and management of service systems. The service mapping technique outlined, builds on previous work in the applications of process mapping to service organisations. The suggested methodology for producing a desired state map involves an analytical approach that gives full weighting to customer, technical and employee perspectives, and supports a clearer evaluation of the criticality of various sub-processes and decisions. Many of the advantages claimed for graphical modelling approaches from the world of systems development are available — clarity, brevity, flexibility, standardisation, and so on — through the effective application of a methodology such as this. Points of possible difficulty with service mapping might include the application of the approach to particularly complex systems, or systems that legitimately require extensive flexibility at the operational level. The level of detail at which the service mapping approach is pitched is crucial. Another issue to consider is the automation of the technique, and its integration with other re-engineering philosophies (as mentioned by the author) that embrace multilevel process modelling, data modelling and organisation charting.

In summary, there is no doubt that the service map, properly used, constitutes an invaluable analytical and communications tool for those charged with responsibility for the quality of the service system.

Andrew J. Deegan
University College Dublin
Ireland

1. INTRODUCTION

The purpose of this chapter is to describe how service mapping can be used as a tool for service system design and management. Service mapping is a form of process mapping in the tradition of service blue-printing (Shostack, 1984), but service mapping alone uses the vertical and horizontal planes of a flat surface to depict service system structure and process. The creation of effective service systems requires "... the ability to think in terms of *wholes* and [in terms] of the *integration of structure and process*..." (Normann, 1986). The service mapping methodology is thus a valuable management tool for improving the effectiveness of service system design.

Although there is now widespread agreement that services are different from products, it is, nonetheless, difficult to operationalise the differences because many of our ideas about the nature of production are rooted in an industrial logic that has dominated much of our century. The industrial paradigm is grounded in the twin ideas of the division of labour (specialisation) and the assembly line. Unfortunately, much of our thinking about services is captive to our assumptions about the manufacture of products. Service mapping suggests that a different logic applies to services — one derived from understanding operationally the characteristics inherent in services.

This chapter is divided into three sections. First, a Service Story is constructed out of key research findings in the field of services marketing theory. Second, a Service Template is created by arranging key research findings according to the dictates of the service mapping format. And, finally, the Design Story presents a specific example — car repair — to demonstrate how service mapping works in tandem with the service story to facilitate service system design and management.

2. THE SERVICE STORY

We begin with a review of the characteristics accepted as inherent to services: namely, a high degree of intangibility, simultaneity of production and consumption, and active customer participation in service production, which is typically entrepreneurial or non-standard especially in the early stages (Zeithaml, 1981). Service delivery is effected by means of a *system*, that is, by means of a group of inter-related elements forming a collective entity that is open to the consumer. It is this characteristic openness that distinguishes the structure of service systems from the manufacturer's assembly line, which is closed to the consumer (Fitzsimmons and Sullivan, 1982).

The differences between service production and the manufacture of product can also be expressed in terms of their respective inputs. Raw materials and supplies are the natural inputs used in the manufacture of products, whereas the natural inputs of service production include task-related information delivered by consumers to service providers. (In the car repair example that follows in section 3, the consumer delivers the automobile with information about needed repairs.)

The goal-oriented human interactions that punctuate the service system, and which generally feature the exchange of task-related information, have been labelled service encounters (Czepiel, Solomon, Surprenant, and Gutman, 1985). Now, the choice of the word "encounter" to describe these interactions is unfortunate. According to the *American Heritage Dictionary,* an *encounter* is "a meeting, especially when casual and unplanned", or a "hostile confrontation; a contest".

Neither definition represents service interactions favourably. Further-more, the term "encounter" suggests an exchange between *people*, while many service situations are now automated. For these reasons, the term "encounter" is outdated and should be replaced.

We have proposed the term *instrumental interactions* (Kingman-Brundage, 1989; 1991) to describe the goal-directed exchanges by con-sumers and service providers of the task-related information and task-results required for production of specific service outcomes.

Selected services research yields insight into the nature of these instrumental interactions, which are profoundly influenced by the fact, noted above, that service production and consumption often occur simul-taneously (Glynn and Lehtinen, Chapter 4). Early researchers observed in this regard that service firms' marketing managers, unlike their counterparts in product firms, do not have the luxury of assuming responsibility for the product only as it leaves the factory gate. They have suggested that the operations, marketing and personnel functions in service firms in effect form a service trinity, and hypothesised that an action taken by any one of the three would automatically affect the other two (Langeard, Bateson, Lovelock and Eiglier, 1981).

What is the nature of the instrumental interactions that comprise the service system? These interactions vary subtly depending on the specific realities of a given industry — or even of a given firm with an industry — but generally comprise two critical elements: people and technique.

2.1. People

As consumers and as service providers, people are an integral part of the instrumental interactions that comprise a service system. Psychological factors thus constitute key elements of service success and, in fact, they have received considerable research attention. Research into consumer behaviour in service firms appears to be an extension of product-oriented consumer research. For example, it has been found that con-sumers experience a greater *sense of uncertainty or risk* when purchas-ing services than when purchasing goods (George, Weinberger and Kelly, 1985). In a service vein, the proposition has been advanced that the *psychological experience* of waiting (in queues, for example) can be managed (Maister, 1985). Moreover, the SERVQUAL research indicates that customer *expectations* — whether derived by new customers from advertising and promotion or by repeat customers from their preceding service experiences — affect customer satisfaction levels (Parasuraman, Berry and Zeithaml, 1991).

Although the universal applicability of the SERVQUAL factors has been recently challenged, they nonetheless remain a useful survey of the key elements of service quality:

- *Tangibles* — the physical facilities, equipment, and appearance of personnel

- *Reliability* — the ability to perform the desired service dependably, accurately and consistently

- *Responsiveness* — the willingness to provide prompt service and help customers

- *Assurance* — employees' knowledge, courtesy, and *ability to convey trust and confidence*

- *Empathy* — the provision of caring, individualised attention to customers (Zeithaml, Berry and Parasuraman, 1988).

In order to apply the SERVQUAL factors to a particular service system, it is necessary to operationalise them, that is, to define them in terms of the particular behaviours or activities that, for example, typify *reliability*, or *responsiveness*, or *empathy* to the customers within a specific service system. Put differently, the service mapping methodology requires the ability to perceive factors of service quality in the day-to-day activities that constitute service operations.

Research attention has also been focused on the role of employees in service interactions. Techniques have been advanced to promote control of employees who work directly with customers (Mills, 1985; Bowen and Schneider, 1988). On the other hand, the challenges and benefits associated with self-direction (empowerment) have also been explored (Bowen and Lawler, 1992). The individual behaviour of service employees has been investigated for its impact on service interactions (Tansik, 1985; Hochschild, 1983).

2.2. Technique

If the human element represents the subjective dimension of instrumental interactions, then technical issues constitute their objective dimension (Fynes, Ennis and Negri, Chapter 13). However, technical issues have up to now received less attention from services researchers — a fact unsurprising among a group whose skills tend to the social rather than engineering sciences. What is the unique role of technical issues in creating service quality?

Technique is defined as the systematic procedure by which a complex task is accomplished; it is also the degree of skill or command of fundamentals exhibited in any performance. Service technique, then, is the systematic and personal mastery of the service task — whether it is manual or automated (Kingman-Brundage, 1991).

In the past decade, many service firms have used technical means to standardise operations that had traditionally been more entrepreneurial or dependent on individual judgment and initiative. Wendy's, the US-based fast-food chain, developed an ingenious technique, based on the number of cars arriving in the parking lot, for determining how many hamburgers to put on the grill in order to assure that freshly prepared hamburgers were ready as customers reached the front of the queue!

To improve service quality, Disney installed a system of pneumatic tubes at 20-foot intervals throughout their theme parks in order to assist litterpickers to dispose of the rubbish they had "picked". The purpose was two-fold: first, to assure that litter itself became nearly invisible, but the second purpose was based on the knowledge that most guests when lost turn to litterpickers for directions. Thus management sought to liberate the litterpickers from the physical effort associated with rubbish disposal in order to assure that they would have the time and energy (i.e., motivation) to serve as informal park guides. The Disney anecdote is a particularly dramatic example of how technical — that is, "hard" — means can be used to support what appear on the surface to be "psychological" or "soft" goals (Pope, 1979).

Technical issues have played an increasingly important part in instrumental interactions over the last decade, as changes in the field of information technology are radically transforming how information is transmitted, manipulated, and accessed (Zuboff, 1988). Databases and telecommunications are altering the service landscape in ways that were unimaginable only a short time ago. At the extreme, instrumental interactions are conducted electronically with minimal interaction between persons, as exemplified in the automatic teller machine.

The service template, introduced below, dramatises the ways in which such concepts as consumer uncertainty and expectations, service quality factors, and service technique work together to form a logic that governs service systems. A clear understanding of their combined influence is essential to the design and management of effective service systems.

3. THE SERVICE LOGIC TEMPLATE

A manager once observed that improving a service system is like trying to change the wings on an airliner cruising at 40,000 feet. The fact that most service systems are already in operation constitutes a serious problem for service system design, and an unmet challenge to the field. The service template responds to this challenge by creating a pattern and guide for the identification and analysis of the complex dynamics inherent in the instrumental interactions that make up service systems.

Figure 5.1 presents a generic template constructed from research findings introduced in the previous section. Although it applies in a general sense to most service systems, it is probably insufficiently specific for any single system, and would hence require modification to reflect research findings for a specific industry and company. Thus modified, the service template could spotlight recalcitrant service problems and even the service benchmarks that characterise a specific service, company or industry.

3.1. Service Mapping Format

The service template takes the form of a service map on which organisational structure is depicted on the vertical axis and service process on the horizontal axis. Structurally, the service map reflects an inverted pyramid, with client activities at the top of the map and management activities at its base. (To use another image, the service map might be seen as a sandwich in which the customer and management are the slices of bread, and the service operations are the filling that connects management to customers.)

On the service template, four horizontal lines create the structural frontiers that help to locate the moments of instrumental interaction. The *line of interaction* is a broken line that demarcates client activities from those of front-line personnel; the *line of visibility* separates activities that are visible from those that are invisible to clients; the *line of internal interaction* delineates the activities of support teams from those of the front line; and the *line of implementation* separates management functions from the day-to-day activities of service operation. Instrumental interactions occur at the line of interaction, which represents the customer–front-line interface; and at the line of internal interaction, which marks the front-line-support team interface.

3.2. Customer Thresholds

Before proceeding to read the map, notice that the eye is drawn to the three shaded diamonds located across the top of the customer zone. These "decision diamonds" represent fundamental principles that organise the service system from the *customer's* point of view. They contain the key questions that customers asks themselves at three service thresholds:

"Shall I *respond?*" [7]

"Shall I *buy?*" [10], and

"Shall I buy *again?*" [20].

Obtaining positive answers at these service thresholds is the ultimate responsibility of marketing, sales and service operations, respectively. When these three areas are integrated, customers experience "seamless service" and reward the service firm with the repeat business that is key to long-term profitability (Buzzell and Gale, 1987).

Service maps cultivate operational understanding by articulating the sequence of activities that *precede* each service threshold. *Effective service system design assumes detailed understanding of the relationship between and among service activities in terms of one or more of the customer thresholds.* Service maps establish these critical connections by elaborating practical answers to the fundamental issue, "How do our firm's policies, practices and procedures affect the ability of our customers to *achieve their own goals?*"

3.3. Service System Walkthrough

To read the service template, begin at the management level with the three fundamental activities:

1. Management defines or refines the service concept through marketing management.

2. Management allocates resources through the budget process.

3. Management co-ordinates functions through the process of organisational design.

These three steps in the template allow assessment of current management practice, and how it affects the existing service system.

Once management has established guidelines:

4. *Marketing develops advertising and sales promotion* to introduce the service to prospective customers, and the sales force offers the service concept to prospective customers.

FIGURE 5.1: UNIVERSAL SERVICE MAP

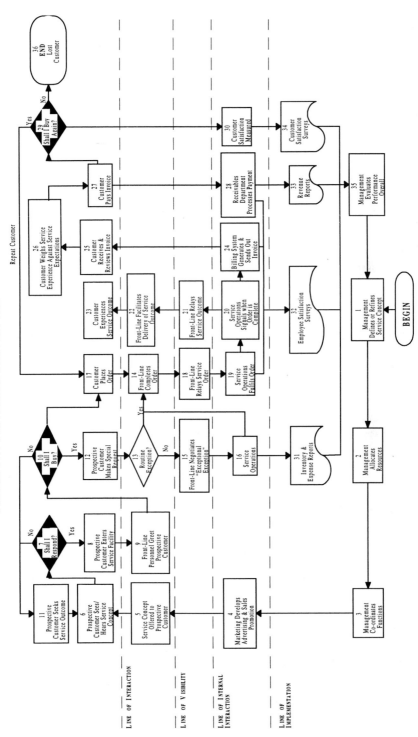

© Kingman-Brundage, Inc., October 1994
Used with permission

6. *Prospective customer sees/hears service concept.* This is the moment when the advertising and promotional campaign reaches the customer.

7. *"Shall I respond?"*, asks the customer poised at the first customer threshold. If the answer is no, the prospective customer returns to the market "pool".

8. *Prospective customer enters the service facility.* A proper assessment of this moment seeks answers to these questions: What service elements increase the customer's sense of uncertainty or even risk? How do elements of the service system serve to reduce customer uncertainty and/or mitigate risk? How does the customer apprehend the service by means of the five senses — sight, sound, touch, even taste or smell? (Bitner, 1991; Lewis, Chapter 3.)

9. *Front-line personnel greet the prospective customer.* Interpersonal factors such as the SERVQUAL factors of responsiveness ("willingness to provide prompt service") and assurance ("ability to foster confidence in the service firm") couple with technical issues ("service capability is congruent with customer needs and wants") and play a role in promoting a positive answer at the second customer threshold.

10. *"Shall I buy?"*, asks the customer while evaluating sources of uncertainty or outright risk. In this evaluation, the customer considers, "What is the likelihood that I will *pay* (in time and money) more than I receive?"

12. *Prospective customer makes special request.* The SERVQUAL factor of empathy ("provision of caring, individualised attention") is operationalised here as *service flexibility.*

Within the service operation, special requests are treated as exceptions that break down into two types: "routine exceptions" that the service provider knows in advance can be made; and "exceptional exceptions", for which the co-operation of others must be enlisted.

The distinction between these two types is an important one. Exceptional exceptions serve as an early warning system to signal the direction in which the market is evolving. Then, as exceptional exceptions are standardised, they become "routine exceptions". Over time, these routine exceptions may become accepted and even promoted as service variations.

17. *Customer places order.* The SERVQUAL factors of responsiveness

and assurance again come into play. The key issues are: What are the objective behaviours that constitute "responsiveness" at this moment of instrumental interaction? What actions must front-line personnel take in order to foster customer confidence (assurance)? How is the consumer role best structured to make it easy for the consumer to contribute essential inputs — either task-information or task-results?

19. *Service operations fulfils order.* The SERVQUAL factor of reliability ("ability to do it right the first time") dominates service process at this point. The key issues are: "How effective is the service system in allowing employees to 'get it right the first time'? Is employee performance helped or hindered by available tools, techniques and/or knowledge?"

23. *Customer experiences service outcome.* Customer, technical and employee interact intricately to create outcomes that customers value.

24. *Billing system generates and sends invoice.* The SERVQUAL factors of reliability, responsiveness and assurance all come into play in the invoicing system. Not only must the invoice be "right the first time", but it must be timely and credible. That is, the client must both understand and believe the invoice information.

26. *Customer weighs Service Experience against Service Expectations.* Clients invest time and money when they purchase services. Inevitably, they weigh actual service experiences against their service expectations by asking, "Is what I'm *getting* worth what I'm *paying*?"

29. *"Shall I buy again?"*, asks the customer at the third customer threshold. The goal of service system design is to arrange activities that increase the likelihood of obtaining a positive answer to this vital question. Repeat customers are valuable. They do not have to be "sold". Because they are knowledgeable, they do not require education in how to use the system. Last but not least, they may be responsible for extending positive word of mouth.

Management monitors the service system by means of such indicators as *customer satisfaction levels* [34] (Parasuraman, Chapter 6), *revenue levels* [33], *employee satisfaction surveys* [32] and *inventory and expense measures* [31]. Management uses these indicators to *evaluate performance overall* [35] prior to refining the service concept, which begins the cycle again (Barnes and Cumby, Chapter 7).

This in brief is the service template.

4. THE DESIGN STORY

We turn now to the task of service system design in order to plan the means by which the service concept is to be implemented. The critical success factors are those activities whose positive performance is essential for the achievement of optimal service outcomes. Hence, central to the design task is construction of the service techniques needed to assure positive performance of the critical success factors. Service system design draws its planning efficacy — and its imaginative power — from a deep understanding of the interrelationships between the instrumental interactions and the critical success factors.

Service maps are a tool for uncovering critical success factors by the deceptively simply tactic of identifying all possible processing paths. Whether volunteered spontaneously ("Well, that's how we *usually* do it" — or even, "Do you want us to tell you how we're *supposed* to do it, or how we *really* do it?"), or offered in response to a probing question ("Tell me, is that the *only* way you do it?"), operations personnel describe alternative processing paths. They are then asked, "How do you *decide* which processing path to take?" Their answer to this question typically uncovers a critical success factor, which is shown on the service map as the question within the decision diamond that points to the alternative paths.

A brief example may clarify the dynamic. Suppose, for example, that a customer service representative says, "*Sometimes* we call the customer to schedule the delivery date and time as soon as we receive the sales order." Clearly, the word "sometimes" implies that the call is not made at "other times". When asked, "How do you decide whether or not to make the call?", the representatives answered, "If we have product in stock, we make the call; if not, we wait until the product shows up on our computer screens before we make the call." Product availability is the underlying critical success factor identified by the service map: a gap in customer service occurs when product is not available for scheduling.

The practical value of the service maps is evident here: by spotlighting the *service intersections* where one or more alternative paths are possible, decision diamonds facilitate identification of the underlying, objective issues that govern and even control service system performances. Although the service intersections are familiar to the people who perform the service task every day, they are usually invisible to managers and counterparts in other departments. In sum, the service mapping methodology uncovers underlying issues by articulating the question that triggers the branching into alternative paths.

These questions are complex because they often reflect the three types of dynamics that comprise instrumental interactions: customer logic, technical logic and employee logic (Kingman-Brundage, George and Bowen, forthcoming). An understanding of these three logics, then, is crucial to accurate diagnosis of any service situation, and we define them here. *Customer logic* is the underlying rationale, based on customer needs and wants, that drives customer behaviour. *Technical logic* is the "engine" of the service system. Comprising the fundamental principles that govern objective production of service outcomes, technical logic derives from relevant technologies, from applicable law, and from corporate policy, rules and regulations. *Employee logic* is the underlying rationale, based on personal and professional needs, wants and requirements, that drives employee behaviour. It should be noted that the "people logics" (customer and employee) are subjective in nature, whereas the technical logic is characteristically objective in its content and operation.

Now, instrumental interactions occur at the interfaces between two or more of the logics. To complicate matters, all three logics are potentially at work simultaneously in any given situation! First, though, let us observe the three logics at work, as applied to a service example regarding car repair.

The purpose of this example is to show how the elements of the service mapping methodology can be used to identify and understand the components of the key instrumental interactions that make up a service system. As a base line for comparison, an Actual State Map (Figure 5.2) is introduced first. The Actual State Map represents how the service system functions *today*. The Desired State Map [Figure 5.5] depicts how the service system might function in the *future*. The example assumes that the Desired State Map is the result of the work of a cross-disciplinary service design team (Shostack and Kingman-Brundage, 1991). In order to make Figure 5.5 easier to interpret, the Desired State Map is broken down into segments: thus Customer Logic is analysed in Figure 5.3, and Technical Logic is investigated in Figure 5.4. Employee Logic is explored in connection with Figure 5.5.

4.1. Actual State Map

The traditional approach to process mapping is adapted from an example given in *Service Breakthroughs* (Heskett, Sasser and Hart, 1990). For purposes of analysis, the process steps have been put into the service mapping format. The "Points Critical to the Success of the Service", identified with a single asterisk (*), and the "Points Where Failure is Experienced", identified by a double asterisk (**) are preserved from the original example.

FIGURE 5.2: ACTUAL STATE MAP

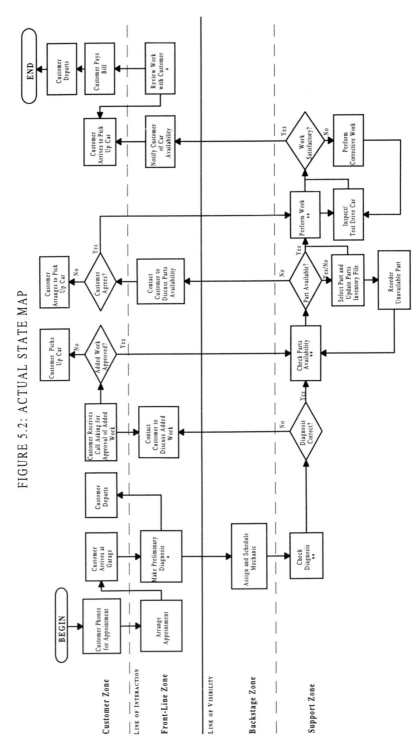

Now, to judge from the map, car repair is a straightforward service transaction. The customer calls for an appointment, communicates information about the vehicle's performance problems and delivers the car at the appointed hour. When the repair is completed, the customer picks up the car, pays and departs. An open and shut case. Or is it?

Before answering this question, let us briefly consider the Actual State Map from a service mapping perspective — specifically from the perspective of customer logic. Instantly, several questions are raised. First, the Actual State Map shows that a preliminary diagnosis is made and customer approval of a repair limit is obtained. These agreements create customer expectations, but the map neither shows customer expectations nor demonstrates how customer uncertainty is reduced and/ or sense of risk is mitigated. The consequences of this omission ripple through the interpretation of the map and undermine its value. For example, the map shows that when the diagnosis is incorrect, the customer may refuse to approve additional work; however, it neglects to show how the customer is affected when a *part is not available*. It does not chart the possibility that the customer will *not* agree to a time delay caused by parts unavailability. In short, the Actual State Map appears to reflect an operations perspective on service process and so fails to interpret the service operation consistently from the *customer's point of view*.

4.2. Customer Logic

Figure 5.3 explores the customer logic inherent in our customer repair example. In so doing, it spotlights the critical success factors from the customer's viewpoint. The decision diamonds that form the customer thresholds in the Customer Contact Zone are eye-catching — as are the blocks that show *customer adjusts expectation* when cost or delivery time are changed. In this way, the service map dramatises cost and delivery time as the customer's primary values. Moreover, the service map extends the customer logic by posing the question, *"Does the problem stay fixed?"* From a quality perspective, this question is essential with regard to the critical issue of rework. Finally, the customer logic poses the classic question, "Shall I buy *again*?"

Once the critical success factors are identified, the instrumental interactions can be analysed. Customer–front-line contacts occur across the line of interaction. Figure 5.3 suggests as the optimal contact points: call for appointment; deliver car; authorise repair limit and set pick-up time; pick up car and pay. In the event of incorrect diagnosis or an unavailable part, the customer is contacted to approve additional expense and/or late delivery. If the problem recurs, the customer will contact the garage.

FIGURE 5.3: CUSTOMER LOGIC MAP

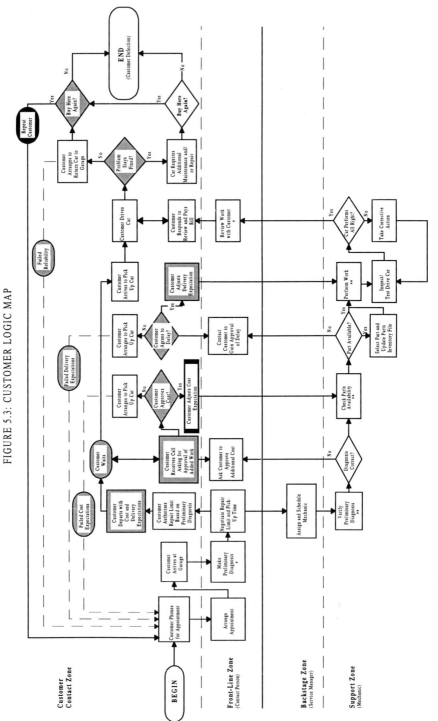

Each of these customer contact points is an instrumental interaction, governed by fundamental principles. By making explicit the logic inherent in these principles, the service map plays a critical role in developing explicit service principles, or a "service logic" (Kingman-Brundage, George, Bowen, forthcoming), that can help service personnel understand how their task fits into the service "big picture" (Payne and Clark, Chapter 12). Service failure is sometimes attributed to a lack of adequate training of personnel. "Training", however, is not a magic answer; training content does not appear full-blown from nowhere. The kind of analysis suggested by the service mapping methodology provides a solid foundation for training front-line and support personnel in the fundamental realities that govern their instrumental interactions.

4.3. Technical Logic

The objective principles of production constitute a second perspective through which to interpret the car repair service system.

The Technical Logic Map (Figure 5.4) takes the points at which failure is most often experienced, as identified on the Actual State Map ("verification of preliminary diagnosis", "parts availability" and "work performance"), and reconsiders these fail-points — no longer in isolation, but within the context of customer logic.

What the technical logic map critically contributes to our understanding of the car repair service system is a sensitivity to the ways in which technical events impact upon the customer's experience. For service personnel, who probably lack direct contact with customers, this awareness of what their actions do to customers is indispensable. For example, the technical logic map demonstrates the connections between the *preliminary diagnosis*, which is made by the contact person in the presence of the customer; *verification* of the preliminary diagnosis, which is made by the mechanic in the service area; *parts availability*, which is made by the inventory clerk in the service area; and *work performance*, which is executed by the mechanic. The connecting link is the potential impact on customer expectations. Each of these variables carries the potential to create a positive or negative response to the question, "Is what I *received* worth what I *paid*?" The ultimate question, of course, is, "Shall I buy *again*?"

In general, the service map helps the design team to look at the service system as a unified whole and mentally to test design options prior to their implementation. In order to assure reliable performance around the critical success factors, service maps encourage the team to seek potential solutions across the entire service system.

FIGURE 5.4: TECHNICAL LOGIC MAP

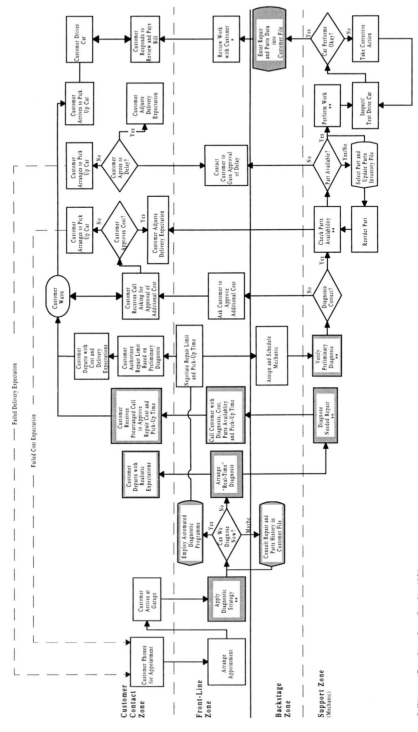

To take an example regarding technical logic, for instance, the design team might identify parts availability as a discrete issue and charge an independent design team with the task of creating a parts strategy that assures "parts are available when we need them". The shadow on the parts process symbol indicates a lower level, or more detailed map.

The practical benefits of an enhanced awareness of technical logic are substantial. A design team seeking to improve the congruence between the preliminary diagnosis and subsequent verification of that diagnosis will test various scenarios on a series of technical logic maps. It will explore ways to use information to improve the accuracy of the preliminary diagnosis. For example, a customer database supplying repair and parts data for each car might also be accessed by the service manager looking for historical data to support the preliminary diagnosis. The Technical Logic Map shows the feedback loop from the end of the repair process through the customer file into the front-end diagnostic process. An automated diagnostic programme might be installed to identify certain types of repair problems. Finally, exploration of alternative scenarios on service maps might challenge the design team to redefine the problem. The team might decide it can improve diagnostic accuracy in some instances by *delaying* the diagnosis until after the mechanic examines the car. In this scenario, the customer establishes a minimal repair limit when the car is delivered and agrees to approve a realistic repair limit by means of an additional phone call when the diagnosis is complete. Figure 5.4 shows how the design team used the decision diamond to integrate the various design options into a single, unified diagnostic strategy that is easily understood by employees and customers alike.

By connecting the mechanic's job performance ("perform work") to consequences for the customer, the Technical Logic map operationalises repair quality as the likelihood that the problem will stay fixed. This critical success factor contains elements of all three logics: employee, technical and customer. Employee components are discussed in the next section. With regard to customer logic, we are reminded that in the final analysis, it is *customers* who bear the consequences of service failures by additional expenditures of time, effort and money. For that reason, the design team may choose to develop a *recovery strategy* in response to customers who must return to gain resolution of their car troubles.

4.4. Employee Logic

As the third ingredient in the service logic, employee logic has two dimensions: personal and professional (Lovelock, Chapter 8). The personal dimensions of employee logic are concerned with the quality of the work life — physical environment, supervisory practices, compensation schemes, etc. The professional dimension of employee logic is essentially the analysis of technical and customer logic from the employee perspective. We have just looked at the ways in which technical failure affects consumers. We now train our attention on the ways in which these same technical failures affect employees. Just as all disorders in a service system eventually reflect themselves in customer dissatisfaction, so too do they travel along invisible lines to make themselves felt, unhappily, among employees.

As our first example, consider the job task, "Perform work". The mechanic's total job performance is a function of the mechanic's skill level (competence), the tools and procedures available for performing the work, and the mechanic's willingness to do the job well (motivation). Clearly, Technical Logic governs tools and procedures, and Employee Logic governs skill level and motivation — which may be viewed as the emotional and physical *energy* employees are willing to expend to produce results. Hence, within the realm of Employee Logic, compensation and benefits, supervisory practices and other cultural elements affect employee performance positively or negatively.

As a second example, let us look again at the activity "Customer phones for appointment". In the Actual State Map, this activity appears to occur in isolation from any inputs. This isolation suggests that front-line employees, in order to do their jobs well, need only be prepared to arrange the requested appointment.

But how far from the truth this is! Closer analysis of the Desired State Map (Figure 5.5) shows that when the telephone rings [3], the front-line person confronts at least four possible scenarios:

- *New customer* seeks appointment

- Existing customer seeks to pick up car because cost and/or delivery *expectations are not met*

- Recent customer seeks to drop off car for second try to *fix old problem*

- *Repeat customer* seeks appointment to repair new problem.

Until and unless employees are prepared to field any one of these types of phone calls, their performance (and morale) are likely to be less than optimal. This example illustrates how service mapping depicts the intricate links between service logic elements. As such, the methodology is explicitly valued by service design teams as a technique for arranging the microelements implied in the customer, technical and employee logics in structures that can produce outcomes of value to customers.

FIGURE 5.5: DESIRED STATE MAP

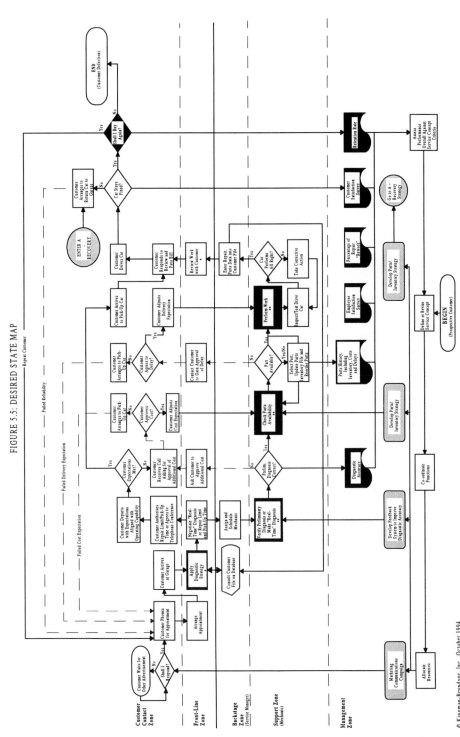

4.5. Desired State Map

Figure 5.5 shows the full Desired State Map for the car repair service. Critical success factors are shaded and shadowed, as is the service threshold question, "Shall I buy *again*?" The symbol "Apply Diagnostic Strategy" holds Technical Logic (Figure 5.4) as a lower level map. The Desired State Map suggests the underlying diagnostic strategy, but doesn't present all the details. The broken lines show where the service path goes astray by frustrating customer expectations.

The management zone is dominated by the key indicators of performance and shows the strategic initiatives intended to assure optimal performance of the critical success factors: diagnostic accuracy, parts availability, percentage of repair "rework", and retention rate. These indicators are the inputs for the core management functions: evaluation of performance overall, refinement of the service concept, allocation of resources, and co-ordination of functions.

4.6. Future Research Directions

The service mapping methodology suggests several areas for future research. The re-engineering methodology challenges organisations to rethink how they perform their core processes. A promising research opportunity might be found in constructing explicit links between the service mapping and re-engineering methodologies.

Another direction is suggested by the need to dramatise service offerings for consumer research. Simplified service maps — using attractive graphics to spotlight key elements of the service concept — might be used effectively to introduce new services in focus group and other consumer research settings.

In the future, activity-based costing is likely to have widespread application for services (Barnes and Cumby, Chapter 7). The service mapping methodology may be useful in identifying appropriate service activities and in delineating realistic boundaries for them.

Finally, it should be noted that the service maps themselves (the boxes) do not communicate the full power of the service mapping methodology. The exercise of defining "who does what, to whom, how often, and under what conditions" changes forever the way in which people in service systems view their customers, their jobs and themselves (George and Gibson, 1988). In other words, service maps uncover and operationalise the norms and values that constitute organisational culture. Research focused on interpreting service maps in terms of how they reveal cultural dimensions of the service organisation would make an important contribution to the development of service management practice.

5. CONCLUSION

The service mapping exercise reveals underlying assumptions about customers, service operation and fellow workers. It tends to explode old myths, and it makes *explicit* the taken-for-granted ways of doing things that under normal conditions remain *implicit*. As what is normally invisible is exposed to the light, the creative imagination of service managers is liberated to explore new possibilities for creating outcomes that are valued by customers. In this context, service maps are an invaluable tool for testing new ideas and assessing their impact not only on customers, but on disparate areas within the organisation as well.

REFERENCES

American Heritage Dictionary, American Heritage Publishing Company, New York, 1969.

Bitner, M., "Servicescapes: The Impact of Physical Surroundings on Customers and Employees", *Journal of Marketing*, April, 1991, pp. 57–71.

Bowen, D.E. and B. Schneider, "Services Marketing and Management: Implications for Organizational Behavior", *Research in Organizational Behavior,* Vol. 10, 1988, pp. 43–80.

Bowen, D.E. and E.E. Lawler III, "The Empowerment of Service Workers: What, Why, How, and When", *Sloan Management Review,* Vol. 33, 1992, pp. 31–9.

Buzzell, R.D. and B.T. Gale, *The PIMS Principles*, The Free Press, New York, 1987.

Czepiel, J.A., M.R. Solomon, C.F. Surprenant and E.G. Gutman, "Service Encounters: An Overview", in J.A. Czepiel, M.R., Solomon, and C. Surprenant (Eds.), *The Service Encounter*, Lexington Books, Lexington, MA, 1985.

Fitzsimmons, J.A. and R.S. Sullivan, *Service Operations Management*, McGraw-Hill, New York, 1982.

George, W.R., M.G Weinberger and J.P. Kelly, "Consumer Risk Perceptions: Managerial Tool for the Service Encounter", in J.A. Czepiel, M.R. Solomon, and C. Surprenant (Eds.), *The Service Encounter,* Lexington Books, Lexington, MA, 1985.

Heskett, J.L., W.E. Sasser Jr. and C.W.L. Hart, *Service Breakthroughs: Changing the Rules of the Game,* The Free Press, New York, 1990.

Kingman-Brundage, J., "Service Mapping: Gaining a Concrete Perspective on Service System Design", in E.E. Scheuing and W.F. Christopher, *The Service Quality Handbook,* Amacon (a division of the American Management Association), New York, 1993.

Kingman-Brundage, J., "Technology, Design and Service Quality", *International Journal of Service Industry Management*, Vol. 2, 1991, pp. 47–59.

Kingman-Brundage, J., "The ABC's of Service System Blueprinting", in M. Bitner and L. Crosby (Eds.), *Designing a Winning Service Strategy*, American Marketing Association, Chicago, IL, 1989, pp. 30–33.

Kingman-Brundage, J., W.R. George and D.E. Bowen, "'Service Logic': Achieving Service System Integration", *International Journal of Service Industry Management* (forthcoming).

Langeard, E., J. Bateson, C. Lovelock and P. Eiglier, *Marketing of Services: New Insights from Consumers and Managers,* Report No. 81–104, Marketing Science Institute, Cambridge, MA, 1981.

Maister, D.H., "The Psychology of Waiting Lines", in J.A. Czepiel, M.R. Solomon and C. Surprenant (Eds.), *The Service Encounter*, Lexington Books, Lexington, MA, 1985.

Mills, P.K., "The Control Mechanisms of Employees at the Encounter of Service Organizations", in J.A. Czepiel, M.R. Solomon and C. Surprenant (Eds.), *The Service Encounter,* Lexington Books, Lexington, MA, 1985.

Normann, R., *Service Management*, John Wiley and Sons, New York, 1986.

Parasuraman, A., L.L. Berry and V.A. Zeithaml, "Understanding Customer Expectations of Service", *Sloan Management Review*, Spring, 1991, pp. 39–48.

Pope, N.W., "Mickey Mouse Marketing", *American Banker*, 25 July; and "More Mickey Mouse Marketing", *American Banker*, 12 September, 1979.

Shostack, G.L., "Designing Services That Deliver", *Harvard Business Review*, January/February, 1984, pp. 133–9.

Shostack, G.L. and J. Kingman-Brundage, "Service Design and Development", in C.A. Congram and M.L. Friedman (Eds.), *Handbook of Services Marketing,* AMACOM (a division of the American Management Association), New York, 1990.

Tansik, D.A., "Nonverbal Communication and High-Contact Employees", in J.A. Czepiel, M.R. Solomon and C. Surprenant (Eds.), *The Service Encounter,* Lexington Books, Lexington, MA, 1985.

Zeithaml, V.A., "How Consumer Evaluation Processes Differ between Goods and Services", in J.H. Donnelly and W.R. George (Eds.), *Marketing of Services*, American Marketing Association, Chicago, IL, 1981, pp. 186–200.

Zuboff, S., *In the Age of the Smart Machine,* Basic Books, New York, 1988.

6

MEASURING AND MONITORING SERVICE QUALITY

A. Parasuraman
University of Miami, USA

PRÉCIS

In the competitive environment of the 1990s, service quality provided to customers has become the focus of many organisations. Customer satisfaction is well recognised as being of paramount importance for the existence of many organisations. For over a decade, academics and practitioners alike have been trying to conceptualise and assess service quality. Research papers have appeared in many reputable journals, both in Europe and the US, offering insights into what service quality is and how it can be measured. Parasuraman, Zeithaml and Berry (PZB) have published extensively on this subject and have defined service quality as "the degree and direction of discrepancy between customers' service perceptions and expectations". Building on this definition, Parasuraman, in the following pages, presents the development of the SERVQUAL model, a multiple-item instrument for measuring and monitoring service quality. He begins with a thorough review of the current literature on service quality and proceeds to establish, through his research, five quality dimensions: tangibles, reliability, responsiveness, assurance and empathy. These dimensions influence customer evaluation of service quality. The author describes the research methodology used by PZB to construct and refine the SERVQUAL model and demonstrates its practical application in an Australian bank and in the Ceramic Products Division of Corning, Inc., US. Both organisations reported great benefits to their service quality systems as a result of using the model.

The author also addresses the most recent questions raised in the literature regarding the soundness of the model and argues that these concerns should not be allowed to reduce the importance of the model

*or hinder its use, especially when used to track customer expectations
and perceptions over time. The model is a generic, skeletal instrument
that can be adapted for use in a variety of contexts, including industrial-
product and internal-service contexts. In the final part of this chapter,
Parasuraman presents a number of issues for further investigation.
These issues include: the dimensionality of the SERVQUAL items; the
alleged psychometric deficiencies of difference-score measures of service quality; the exploration of upwardly biased ratings produced by
direct measures of service quality; the underlying causes and managerial implications of the empirical correlations among the dimensions;
and the need to incorporate practical criteria such as diagnostic value
into the traditional scale-assessment paradigm. Investigating these
issues further will increase our knowledge about service quality
measurement and monitoring and will allow organisations to serve their
internal and external customers better.*

Christodoulos Stylianides
Cyprus International Institute of Management
Cyprus

1. INTRODUCTION

The growing recognition that superior customer service is necessary for
competitive differentiation in a wide variety of markets has spawned
considerable practitioner interest in assessing and improving service
quality. Commensurate with this practitioner interest has been academic
interest in defining and measuring the service quality construct. As of
the early 1980s, only a handful of writings, including several by European scholars, had discussed the nature of service quality (Grönroos,
1982; Lehtinen and Lehtinen, 1983; Lewis and Booms, 1983, Sasser,
Olsen, and Wyckoff, 1978). However, since the mid-1980s, service
quality and its measurement have been occupying an increasingly prominent position in the published literature. As acknowledged by Fisk,
Brown, and Bitner in Chapter 1 of this book, "service quality is the
single most researched area in services marketing to date".

The objectives of this chapter are:

1. To provide an overview of the literature on service quality measurement, including the development and applications of SERVQUAL (a
   service quality scale developed by the author along with colleagues
   Leonard Berry and Valarie Zeithaml)

2. To present and respond to concerns raised about the SERVQUAL instrument

3. To discuss refinements to the instrument

4. To provide future research directions pertaining to service quality measurement.

2. CONCEPTUALISATION OF SERVICE QUALITY

2.1. Definition of Service Quality

Early writings on the topic of service quality (Grönroos, 1982, Lehtinen and Lehtinen, 1983, Lewis and Booms, 1983, Sasser, Olsen, and Wyckoff, 1978) have suggested that service quality results from a comparison of what customers feel a service provider should offer (i.e., their expectations) with the provider's actual performance. For instance, according to Lewis and Booms (1983):

> Service quality is a measure of how well the service level delivered matches customer expectations. Delivering quality service means conforming to customer expectations on a consistent basis.

The notion that service quality is a function of the expectations-performance gap was confirmed by an extensive multi-sector study conducted by Parasuraman, Zeithaml, and Berry — hereafter referred to as PZB — (1985). This study involved twelve customer focus group interviews — three in each of four different service sectors (retail banking, credit card, stock brokerage, and appliance repair and maintenance) — to understand how customers assessed service quality. Based on common insights from the focus groups, PZB formally defined service quality, as perceived by customers, as *the degree and direction of discrepancy between customers' service perceptions and expectations.*

PZB also proposed a "continuum" of service quality:

> Perceived service quality is further posited to exist along a continuum ranging from ideal quality to totally unacceptable quality, with some point along the continuum representing satisfactory quality. The position of a consumer's perception of service quality on the continuum depends on the nature of the discrepancy between the expected service (ES) and perceived service (PS). When ES > PS, perceived quality is less than satisfactory and will tend toward totally unacceptable quality, with increased discrepancy between ES and PS; when ES = PS, perceived quality is satisfactory; when ES < PS, perceived quality is

more than satisfactory and will tend toward ideal quality, with increased discrepancy between ES and PS. (PZB, 1985, pp. 48–9)

It should be noted that the PZB (1985) study produced a comprehensive "gaps model" delineating various organisational shortfalls within a company, which contribute to the external gap between customers' expectations and perceptions. Because the focus of this chapter is on the external gap, readers interested in details about potential causes of poor service quality are encouraged to review PZB (1985) and PZB (1990).

2.2. Dimensions of Service Quality

Early conceptualisations suggested several general service attributes that customers might use to assess service quality. Sasser, Olsen, and Wyckoff (1978) proposed three different dimensions of service performance (all apparently dealing with the *process* of service delivery): *levels of material, facilities* and *personnel*. Grönroos (1982) proposed two types of service quality: *technical quality*, which involves what customers actually receive from the service provider (i.e., the *outcome* of the service) and *functional quality*, which involves the manner in which customers receive the service (i.e., the *process* of service delivery). Lehtinen and Lehtinen (1982) discussed three kinds of quality: *physical quality*, involving physical aspects associated with the service such as equipment or building; *corporate quality*, involving a service firm's image or reputation; and *interactive quality*, involving interactions between service personnel and customers, as well as among customers.

A consistent theme emerging from these dimensions is that customers might use more than just the service outcome or "core" in assessing service quality. Customer assessments may also be influenced by the service process and the "peripherals" associated with the service. The customer focus group research conducted by PZB (1985) confirmed that both outcome and process dimensions influence customers' evaluation of service quality. In addition, common patterns of responses from the focus group interviews revealed 10 key evaluative criteria that customers might use, regardless of the type of service sector. These criteria, while consistent with the service attributes mentioned earlier, are more specific and, as a group, constitute a more comprehensive set of service quality dimensions. Listed below are the 10 dimensions, their definitions, and illustrative questions pertaining to them based on responses from the focus group participants.

- Tangibles: *appearance of physical facilities, equipment, personnel, and communication personnel* — Is my credit card statement easy to read and understand? Do the tools used by the repair person look modern?

- Reliability: *ability to perform the promised service dependably and accurately* — When a loan officer in my bank promises to call me back in an hour, is that promise kept? Does my stockbroker follow my exact instructions to buy or to sell?

- Responsiveness: *willingness to help customers and provide prompt service* — Is my stockbroker willing to answer my questions? When there is a problem with my bank statement, does the bank resolve the problem quickly?

- Competence: *possession of the required skills and knowledge to perform the service* — When I call my credit card company, is the person at the other end able to answer my questions? Does the repair person appear to know how to deal with the job in hand?

- Courtesy: *politeness, respect, consideration, and friendliness of contact personnel* — Does the bank teller have a pleasant demeanour? Does my broker refrain from acting busy or being rude when I ask questions?

- Credibility: *trustworthiness, believability, and honesty* — Does my bank have a good reputation? Does the repair firm guarantee its services?

- Security: *freedom from danger, risk, or doubt* — Is it safe for me to use the bank's automatic teller machines? How confident can I be that my appliance was repaired properly?

- Access: *approachability and ease of contact* — How easy is it for me to get through to my broker over the telephone? Does the credit card company have a 24-hour, toll-free telephone number?

- Communication: *keeping customers informed in language they can understand and listening to them* — Does my broker avoid using technical jargon? Does the repair firm call when they are unable to keep a scheduled repair appointment?

- Understanding the Customer: *making the effort to know customers and their needs* — Does someone in my bank recognise me as a regular customer? Is the credit limit set by my credit card company consistent with what I can afford (i.e., neither too high nor too low)?

The definitions and illustrations of the 10 dimensions suggest that some of them may be interrelated. PZB (1985) acknowledged the possibility of overlapping dimensions, but added:

> Because the research was exploratory, measurement of possible overlap
> across the ten criteria (as well as determination of whether some can be
> combined) must await future empirical investigation (p.46).

Such empirical research, which served as the foundation for the
SERVQUAL instrument, is discussed in section 3.

3. DEVELOPMENT AND REFINEMENT OF SERVQUAL

3.1. Operationalisation of the Service Quality Gap

Consistent with the definition of service quality (that is, the discrepancy
between customers' service perceptions and expectations), PZB (1988)
operationalised the construct as the difference between two 7-point
rating scales — one to measure customers' expectations about companies in general within the service sector or category being investigated, and the other to measure customers' perceptions about a particular company whose service quality was to be assessed. Both rating scales
were anchored by "Strongly Agree" (7) at one end and "Strongly Disagree" (1) at the other. The expectations scale measured the extent to
which customers felt companies in the sector in question *should* possess
a specified service attribute. The corresponding perceptions scale
measured the extent to which customers felt a given company (say XYZ
Company) *did* posses the attribute. The attributes were cast in the form
of statements with which customers were asked to express their degree
of agreement or disagreement on the 7-point scale. The following statements illustrate:

3.1.1 Expectations Statements

- The physical facilities at banks should be visually appealing.
- The behaviour of employees of banks should instil confidence in
  customers.
- Banks should give customers individual attention.

3.1.2 Corresponding Perceptions Statements

- The physical facilities at XYZ Bank are visually appealing.
- The behaviour of employees of XYZ Bank instils confidence in
  customers.
- XYZ Bank gives customers individual attention.

3.2. Construction of SERVQUAL

PZB, drawing upon insights and examples from their extensive focus group interviews, developed a comprehensive set of statements (such as the ones listed in the preceding section) to represent various specific facets of the 10 service-quality dimensions. This process yielded 97 statements (approximately 10 per dimension). These statements formed the basis for constructing an initial two-part instrument. The first part consisted of 97 expectations statements. The corresponding set of 97 perceptions statements formed the second part. In accordance with recommended procedures for scale development (Churchill, 1979), roughly half of the expectations statements and the corresponding perceptions statements were worded negatively.

To purify the initial instrument, PZB administered it to a sample of 200 customers representing five different service categories — appliance repair and maintenance, retail banking, long-distance telephone, securities brokerage, and credit cards. Analyses of the perception-minus-expectation gap scores on the 97 items resulted in a more parsimonious, 34-item instrument whose statements seemed to group into seven rather than the original 10 dimensions. The details of these analyses — which included item-to-total correlation analysis, factor analysis, and assessment of internal consistency of the items making up each dimension (i.e., computation of coefficient alpha) — are documented in PZB (1988).

To assess the reliability, validity, and dimensionality of the 34-item instrument further, PZB used it to collect data pertaining to the service quality of four nationally-known, US-based companies (a bank, a company offering appliance repair and maintenance services, a credit-card company, and a long-distance telephone company). Four independent samples, consisting of 200 customers each from the four companies, participated in this phase of the instrument-development process. Results of analyses (similar to those mentioned above) of the perception–expectation gap scores were remarkably consistent across the four independent samples. The common pattern of findings resulted in two changes to the instrument:

1. Further elimination of items to create a 22-item instrument

2. Grouping of the 22 items into just five general dimensions.

Strong evidence supporting the reliability, validity, and dimensionality of this condensed instrument — labelled SERVQUAL — is documented in PZB (1988). A complete listing of statements in the two parts of SERVQUAL — as well as instructions for the two parts — is also provided in PZB (1988). A number of other chapters in this book make reference to the structure, dimensions, and applications of SERVQUAL, in particular the chapters by Fynes, Ennis and Negri, Chapter 13; Lewis, Chapter 3; Payne and Clark, Chapter 12; and Heskett, Chapter 16.

Three of the original 10 dimensions remained intact in the final set of five SERVQUAL dimensions. These three dimensions were tangibles (with four items), reliability (with five items), and responsiveness (with four items). The remaining seven original dimensions clustered into two broader dimensions. Based on the content of the items falling under these two dimensions, PZB labelled them *assurance* (with four items) and *empathy* (with five items). Definitions of these two new dimensions are as follows:

- Assurance: knowledge and courtesy of employees and their ability to inspire trust and confidence.

- Empathy: caring, individualised attention the firm provides its customers.

Assurance is basically a combination of the original dimensions of competence, courtesy, credibility, and security. Empathy represents the remaining dimensions of access, communication, and understanding the customer. Thus, although SERVQUAL contains only five dimensions, these dimensions represent the essence of all 10 original dimensions. However, SERVQUAL is not a "panacea" for all service-quality measurement problems, nor should it be treated by companies as the *sole* basis for assessing service quality (more on this later). As PZB (1988) have observed:

> The instrument has been designed to be applicable across a broad spectrum of services. As such, it provides a basic skeleton through its expectations/perceptions format encompassing statements for each of the five service-quality dimensions. The skeleton, when necessary, can be adapted or supplemented to fit the characteristics or specific research needs of a particular organisation. SERVQUAL is most valuable when it is used periodically to track service quality trends, *and when it is used in conjunction with other forms of service quality measurement* [emphasis added] (pp. 30–31).

3.3. Refinement of SERVQUAL

In another major multi-sector study, discussed in PBZ (1991), SERVQUAL was further refined. In this study, customer assessments of service quality were measured for three types of services: telephone repair, retail banking, and insurance. Five nationally-known companies — one telephone company, two insurance companies, and two banks — participated in the study. The refinements to SERVQUAL were suggested by results from a pre-test of the original version through a mail survey of a sample of 300 customers of the telephone company that participated in the study. The refined SERVQUAL was then further tested in the main study, wherein data were collected through mail surveys of independent samples of customers of each of the five companies (the number of completed questionnaires received ranged from 290 to 487 across the five companies, for a combined sample size of 1,936).

The refinements involved changes to the instructions and to some of the statements in the original SERVQUAL, but not to its 5-dimensional structure or to the 7-point rating scale. The refinements and brief rationale for them are outlined below (a more detailed discussion is available in PBZ, 1991).

The distribution of expectations ratings obtained in the pre-test was highly skewed toward the upper end of the 7-point scale (mean expectation score was 6.22). Suspecting that the "should" terminology in the expectations statements might be responsible for the high ratings, the statements were revised to capture what customers *will* expect from companies delivering *excellent* service. For example, the original expectations statement "Banks *should* give customers individual attention" was revised to read "*Excellent* banks *will* give customers individual attention". The instructions for the expectations section were also appropriately altered.

The negatively worded statements in the original SERVQUAL instrument were problematic for several reasons:

- They were awkward
- They might be confusing respondents (the pre-test data showed substantially higher standard deviations for the negatively worded statements than for those worded positively)
- They seemed to lower the reliabilities (coefficient alpha values) for the dimensions containing them. Therefore, all negatively worded statements were changed to a positive format.

Finally, two original items — one each under tangibles and assurance — were replaced with two new items to reduce redundancy and to capture more fully the dimensions. These changes also reflected suggestions from company managers who reviewed the pre-test questionnaire.

The psychometric properties of the refined SERVQUAL instrument were reassessed with data from the five companies. The results indicated strong reliability for the five multiple-item components of the instrument — the coefficient alpha values for all components exceeded .7, the value recommended by Nunnally (1978) as an acceptable minimum. Across the five companies, the coefficient alpha values ranged from .80 to .86 for tangibles, .88 to .92 for reliability, .88 to .93 for responsiveness, .87 to .91 for assurance, and .85 to .89 for empathy. The five components also possessed high predictive and convergent validity as indicated, for example, by their ability to explain the variance in customers' perceptions of the companies' overall service quality on a 10-point scale, anchored by "extremely poor" (1) at one end and "extremely good" (10) at the other. Regression analyses, in which overall service quality was the dependent variable and the mean perception–expectation gap scores on the five SERVQUAL dimensions were the independent variables, yielded adjusted R-squared values ranging from .57 to .71 across the five companies.

The evidence of reliability and validity reported above was stronger than the corresponding results obtained for the original SERVQUAL instrument (PZB, 1988). Thus the refinements seem to have improved the cohesiveness of the items under each dimension and the ability of the gap scores on the dimensions to predict overall service quality. However, results of factor analyses of the gap scores obtained from the refined instrument revealed somewhat greater overlap among the five dimensions — especially responsiveness and assurance — than in the case of the original SERVQUAL. Thus, some question exists about the discriminant validity or uniqueness of the five components of the refined SERVQUAL instrument. This issue is further explored in a later section.

3.4. Using SERVQUAL

The refined SERVQUAL statements (including instructions to respondents) used in the five-company study are shown in Appendix 1. In addition to the expectations and perceptions sections, this appendix contains a "point-allocation question", which was used to ascertain the relative importance of the five dimensions by asking respondents to allocate a total of 100 points among the dimensions. Results from this question were consistent across the five company samples: reliability always emerged as the most critical dimension (its average allocation was 32 points) and tangibles as the least critical dimension (its average allocation was 11 points). The average allocations for responsiveness, assurance, and empathy were 23, 19, and 17 points, respectively.

Data gathered through a questionnaire incorporating the three sections in Appendix 1 (after appropriate adaptations, if necessary) can be used for a variety of purposes as outlined below (analytical and other details concerning these potential applications are available in ZPB, 1990, pp. 175–80):

- To determine the average gap score (between customers' perceptions and expectations) for each service attribute.

- To assess a company's service quality along each of the five SERVQUAL dimensions.

- To compute a company's overall *weighted* SERVQUAL score, which takes into account not only the service quality gap on each dimension but also the relative importance of the dimension (as reflected by the number of points allocated to it).

- To track customers' expectations and perceptions (on individual service attributes and/or on the SERVQUAL dimensions) over time.

- To compare a company's SERVQUAL scores against those of competitors.

- To identify and examine customer segments that significantly differ in their assessments of a company's service performance.

- To assess internal service quality (i.e., the quality of service rendered by one department or division of a company to others within the same company).

4. APPLICATIONS OF SERVQUAL

4.1. Applications in Published Studies

The SERVQUAL instrument has generated considerable interest in service quality measurement among academic researchers. The instrument has served as the basis for measurement approaches used in published studies examining service quality in a variety of contexts — e.g., real estate brokers (Johnson, Dotson and Dunlop, 1988); physicians in private practice (Brown and Swartz, 1989); public recreation programmes (Crompton and Mackay, 1989); a dental school patient clinic, a business school placement centre, and a tyre shop (Carman, 1990); motor carrier companies (Brensinger and Lambert, 1990); an accounting firm (Bojanic, 1991); discount and department stores (Finn and Lamb, 1991; Teas, 1993); a gas and electric utility company (Babakus and

Boller, 1992); hospitals (Babakus, Mangold, 1992; Carman, 1990); banking, pest control, dry cleaning, and fast food (Cronin and Taylor, 1992); higher education (Boulding et al., 1993; Ford, Joseph and Joseph, 1993).

The SERVQUAL instrument, in addition to stimulating interest in measuring service quality in different settings, has spawned an ongoing debate in the literature about its soundness and usefulness. Some of the aforementioned studies that critically evaluated SERVQUAL and its psychometric properties have raised concerns about the instrument. These concerns are outlined and addressed in Section 5.

4.2. Practical Applications

SERVQUAL has been productively used in several countries for measuring service quality in commercial as well as public-sector orga- nisations. The nature of and findings from virtually all of these applications are unpublished and/or proprietary. However, based on the author's knowledge of some of these applications, and with appropriate disguise to protect their confidentiality, two are briefly described below to provide readers with a flavour for the use of SERVQUAL in "real life" contexts.

4.2.1 *Consumer-Service Context*

A large Australian bank recently used SERVQUAL to measure its quality of service as evaluated by several segments of individual cus- tomers. The three sections in Appendix 1 were incorporated virtually unchanged into the bank's mail-survey questionnaire. The bank analysed the data to accomplish objectives similar to the first three potential uses of SERVQUAL data listed in section 3.4 above — namely, to assess service quality deficiencies on individual attributes and on the five SERVQUAL dimensions, and to compute weighted gap scores. The bank also "benchmarked" its SERVQUAL scores against those of two similar banks in the US that had participated in studies conducted by the author and his colleagues. While there were some differences between the results for the Australian and US banks, especially on specific ser- vice attributes, there were also some striking similarities in the overall pattern of results. For instance, the relative importance of the five dimensions (as measured by the point-allocation question) were as shown in Table 6.1 below.

At the time of writing, the Australian bank was in the process of setting up a measurement system to track service quality at regular inter- vals and to assess the impact of service improvement efforts.

TABLE 6.1

	Points Allocated		
	Australian Bank	**US Bank 1**	**US Bank 2**
Tangibles	13	10	11
Reliability	28	31	32
Responsiveness	22	22	22
Assurance	19	20	19
Empathy	18	17	16

4.2.2. Industrial-Product Context

The Ceramic Products Division of Corning, Inc., a large manufacturing company in the US, developed a systematic process for monitoring and improving its service quality as perceived by customer organisations to which it supplied its manufactured products. The SERVQUAL approach was an integral component of this process. Details about the development and implementation of the process are documented in Farley, Daniels and Pearl (1990). Only an overview of the adaptation and application of SERVQUAL in the process is provided here.

Corning's Ceramic Products Division is a major, worldwide supplier of a line of ceramics that form the core of catalytic-converter sub-assemblies installed on the underside of cars. As such, its product line undergoes transformations at several levels of intermediaries — from "coaters" (which apply a precious-metal coating to the ceramic core, and which are the Division's *immediate* customers in the supply chain) to car manufacturers. The Ceramic Products Division began its service-improvement process by focusing on just the coater-level customers. Within this level, the Division first used the SERVQUAL approach to get service-quality feedback from its largest customer, a multinational coater company.

An interfunctional team from the Division reviewed the standard SERVQUAL (shown in Appendix 1) and adapted it to measure the customer company's assessment of the quality of service delivered by Corning, as well as that of Corning's major competitor. A section of the adapted instrument, focusing on reliability attributes, is shown in Appendix 2. The instrument had similar sections for the other four SERVQUAL dimensions, as well as a section containing the point-allocation question to measure the relative importance of the five dimensions.

A comparison of the reliability statements in Appendices 1 and 2 indicates that the *content* of the statements and the *number* of response choices are basically the same for the adapted instrument and the standard SERVQUAL. However, there are several significant differences. The adapted instrument:

- Does not have separate expectations and perceptions sections

- Anchors the upper end of the 7-point scale as "world class" (thereby "fixing" customers' expectations at a level of 7)

- Obtains customers' assessment of not only Corning but also its competitor relative to world class.

Thus, although the adapted instrument assumes that the expectation level is the same for all service attributes and customers (i.e., a level of 7 representing world class) — perhaps a debatable assumption — it is more parsimonious by virtue of its not repeating the battery of statements in two different sections. The interfunctional team that adapted SERVQUAL justifiably felt that the ability to measure actual expectation levels was worth giving up in return for the ability to measure parsimoniously customers' assessment of Corning's service quality relative to "world class" and to its leading competitor.

The target customer company had individuals at various functional levels — from employees at the receiving docks where Corning's products were delivered, to senior managers who negotiated purchase agreements with Corning. Thus, different segments of personnel at the customer company interacted with Corning. The interfunctional team from Corning's Ceramics Products Division held a meeting with managers representing these segments to explain the SERVQUAL approach and its purpose, and to obtain their co-operation in completing the survey. Copies of the survey instrument were delivered personally to potential respondents in the various segments. Completed questionnaires were returned directly to the interfunctional team.

The team analysed the responses to identify seven service attributes on which Corning's performance was weakest relative to world class. It further condensed this short-list of attributes to four "vital few" attributes on which Corning's performance was worse than that of its major competitor. Interestingly, all these attributes pertained to reliability, the most critical dimension (respondents in the customer company on average allocated over 40 points out of 100 to reliability). Corning's team then held a meeting with a team of managers from the customer company to share the survey findings and to brainstorm specific issues and action plans to improve Corning's quality on the "vital few" service attributes. This exchange of information augmented the spirit of partnership between the two companies to such an extent that a "corrective action team" with representatives from *both* companies was set up to oversee the implementation of the action plans.

The SERVQUAL survey was re-administered a year later to assess the impact of Corning's corrective actions. The results indicated significant improvements in most of the targeted attributes and also identified additional areas for further corrective action. The success of using SERVQUAL in this pilot application prompted Corning to make this process an ongoing activity in the Ceramics Product Division and to expand its implementation to other divisions and customer groups. In discussing the impact of this process, several members of the inter-functional team wrote:

> An enhanced atmosphere of partnership has been realised with our external customers, along with an internal focus on service quality within the Ceramics Products business. Service improvement programs are now a focal point of our business with SERVQUAL as the vehicle to obtain results. Other businesses at Corning are using SERVQUAL.... During the past 18 months over 30 different Corning units world-wide have attended SERVQUAL workshops and developed questionnaires for use with their customers. Approximately half of these units are suppliers to internal customers and half are suppliers to external customers. In all cases where the survey has been used, areas where customer expectations were not being met have been exposed and targeted for improvement (Farley, Daniels, and Pearl, 1990).

Corning's use of SERVQUAL touches on virtually all of the potential applications of the instrument listed in Section 3.4. It also illustrates the fact that SERVQUAL is a generic, skeletal instrument that can be adapted for use in a variety of contexts, including industrial-product and internal-service contexts.

5. CONCERNS RAISED ABOUT SERVQUAL

As mentioned in Section 4.1, several of the published SERVQUAL-based studies have critically examined the instrument and raised questions about its psychometric soundness and its usefulness. Specifically, these questions relate to the need for SERVQUAL's expectations component (see, for example, Babakus and Mangold, 1992; Cronin and Taylor, 1992), the interpretation and operationalisation of expectations (Teas, 1993), the reliability and validity of SERVQUAL's *difference-*

score formulation (Babakus and Boller, 1992; Brown, Churchill, and Peter, 1993, for example), and SERVQUAL's dimensionality (Carman, 1990; Finn and Lamb, 1991, for example). In response to these questions, the author and his colleagues have presented counter arguments, clarifications, and additional evidence to reaffirm the instrument's psychometric soundness and practical value (PBZ, 1991; 1993; PZB, 1994a). As details of this ongoing debate are well documented in the sources cited, they are not repeated here. However, the major unresolved questions are outlined below.

1. *Is it necessary to measure expectations?* Studies have consistently shown that scores on the perceptions-only component of SERVQUAL are able to explain significantly more variance in customers' overall evaluations of an organisation's service quality (measured on a single-item, overall-perceptions rating scale) than are the perception-expectation difference scores. Thus, from a strictly *predictive-validity* standpoint, it appears that measuring expectations is not warranted. Moreover, measuring expectations increases survey length. However, SERVQUAL's developers have argued that measuring expectations has *diagnostic value* (i.e., generates information that would pinpoint *shortfalls* in service quality) and that basing service-improvement decisions solely on perceptions data might lead to suboptimal or erroneous resource allocations (PZB, 1994a). Thus, an important unresolved issue is the trade-off between the empirical and diagnostic value of expectations in service quality measurement.

2. *How should the expectations construct be operationalised?* Although the definition of service quality as the gap between customers' expectations and perceptions is conceptually simple, the operationalisation of this definition has been controversial because of the multiple ways the term "expectation" can be and has been interpreted. While service quality researchers have generally viewed expectations as *normative* standards (customers' beliefs about what a service provider *should* offer), researchers working in the area of customer satisfaction/ dissatisfaction have typically considered expectations to be *predictive* standards (what customers feel a service provider *will* offer). However, both "should" and "will" expectations have been used in measuring service quality (Boulding et al., 1993). Furthermore, other types of expectations ("ideal", "deserved", for example) have also been proposed and defended as appropriate comparison standards (for a comprehensive review, see Woodruff et al., 1991).

   The multiplicity of comparison standards and the absence of a comprehensive theoretical framework delineating their inter-relationships are implicit in a call issued by Woodruff et al. (1991) for developing "a classification scheme ... to reduce the many possible standards to a relatively few categories" (p. 108). In an attempt to address unresolved issues in the area of customer expectations, the author and his colleagues (ZBP, 1993) developed a conceptual model of expectations by combining insights from past research with findings from a multi-sector study aimed at understanding the nature and determinants of customers' service expectations. The core of this model served as the foundation for the latest enhancements to the SERVQUAL instrument and will be discussed in Section 6.

3. *Is it appropriate to operationalise service quality as a difference score?* Operationalising any construct as a difference between two other constructs has been questioned for psychometric reasons, especially if the difference scores are to be used in multivariate analyses (for a recent review of the concerns raised, see Peter, Churchill and Brown, 1993). SERVQUAL's difference-score formulation has also been questioned for the same psychometric reasons (Babakus and Boller, 1992; Brown, Churchill and Peter, 1993). Critics of difference scores have suggested that direct (that is, non-difference score) measures of the perception-expectation gap will be psychometrically superior (see, for example, Carman, 1990; Peter, Churchill and Brown, 1993). However, the available empirical evidence comparing SERVQUAL and direct measures of service quality has not conclusively established that the alleged psychometric problems are present in SERVQUAL or that direct measures are superior (PBZ, 1993). Thus, the relative superiority of the direct *v.* difference-score operationalisation of service quality is another unresolved issue.

4. *Does SERVQUAL have five distinct dimensions that transcend different contexts?* Replication studies incorporating SERVQUAL have not been able to reproduce as "clean" a five-dimensional factor structure as was obtained in the original study that produced the instrument (PZB, 1988). For instance, in an article comparing and synthesising results from several replication studies, PBZ (1991) point out that the number of final SERVQUAL dimensions vary from two (Babakus and Boller, 1991) to five (Brensinger and Lambert, 1990) to eight (Carman, 1990). PZB (1991) also offer alternative explanations for these differences:

To some extent this variation across studies may be due to differences in [the] data collection and analysis procedures [across the various replications]. However, there is another, perhaps more plausible, explanation: Respondents may indeed consider the SERVQUAL dimensions to be conceptually distinct ... however, if their evaluations of a specific company on individual scale items are similar *across* dimensions, fewer than five dimensions will result as in the Babakus and Boller (1991) study. Alternatively, if their evaluations of a company on scale items *within* a dimension are sufficiently distinct, more than five dimensions will result as in Carman's (1990) study. In other words, differences in the number of empirically derived factors across replications may be primarily due to across-dimension similarities and/or within-dimension differences in customers' evaluations of a *specific* company involved in each setting. At a *general* level, the five-dimensional structure of SERVQUAL may still serve as a meaningful framework for summarising the criteria customers use in assessing service quality (p. 440).

Nevertheless, the dimensionality of SERVQUAL continues to be debated (see, for example, Cronin and Taylor, 1992; PZB, 1994a) and, as such, is an issue warranting further research.

The next section describes additional refinements to SERVQUAL which were made to address the concerns raised herein. It also discusses findings from a study that was conducted to evaluate the refinements. The findings are then used as the basis for proposing an agenda for future research on service quality measurement.

6. RECENT ENHANCEMENTS TO SERVQUAL

The core of the conceptual model of expectations developed by ZBP (1993), and alluded to in the preceding section, is that customers have two different service levels that serve as comparison standards in assessing service quality: *Desired Service* — the level of service representing a blend of what customers believe "can be" and "should be" provided; and *Adequate Service* — the minimum level of service customers are willing to accept. Separating these two levels is a *Zone of Tolerance* that represents the range of service performance a customer would consider satisfactory.

Because SERVQUAL's expectations component measures *normative* expectations, the construct represented by it reflects the *desired service* construct defined above. However, the current SERVQUAL's structure does not capture the *adequate service* construct. Therefore, in a recent multi-sector study conducted by the author and his colleagues (PZB, 1994b), SERVQUAL was augmented and refined to capture not only the discrepancy between perceived service and desired service — labelled as *measure of service superiority* (or MSS) — but also the discrepancy between perceived service and adequate service — labelled as *measure of service adequacy* (or MSA).

To assess the merits and demerits of a difference-score operationalisation (relative to a direct operationalisation) of the service quality gap measures (i.e., MSS and MSA), two measurement formats were tested in the study:

- *Three-Column Format* — this format involves obtaining separate ratings of desired, adequate, and perceived service with three identical, side-by-side scales. It requires computing differences between ratings to quantify MSS and MSA. Thus, its operationalisation of service quality is similar to that of SERVQUAL. However, unlike SERVQUAL, it does not repeat the battery of items.

- *Two-Column Format* — unlike SERVQUAL, this format involves obtaining *direct* ratings of MSS and MSA with two identical, side-by-side scales.

Appendix 3 illustrates the two questionnaire formats. Only one sample SERVQUAL item is shown in Appendix 3. The questionnaires used in the study contained the full battery of items in Appendix 1 (but after each item was abbreviated to a form similar to the sample item in Appendix 3). The term *minimum service* rather than *adequate service* was used in the questionnaires based on the recommendation of customers in focus groups who pre-tested earlier questionnaire drafts.

The two questionnaire formats were used in mail surveys of independent samples of customers from four large companies in the US — a computer manufacturer, a retail chain, a car insurance company and a life insurance company. Across companies, the response rates ranged from 14 per cent to 28 per cent for the two-column format, and from 17 per cent to 28 per cent for the three-column format. Initial sample sizes were the same for both formats and ranged from 800 to 1757 across companies. Relevant results from the mail surveys are discussed next, to address the four issues raised in Section 5.

6.1. Is it Necessary to Measure Expectations?

Consistent with findings from earlier studies, the perceptions-only ratings (obtained from the third column of the three-column format) had the most predictive power. Specifically, regressing customer ratings on a 9-point, overall service quality scale (with anchors 1 = "extremely poor" and 9 = "extremely good") on the perceptions scores on the five SERVQUAL dimensions yielded R-squared values ranging from .72 to .86 across the four companies. In contrast, when difference-score ratings of MSS (that is, perception-minus-desired service ratings) on the five dimensions were used as independent variables in the regression analyses, the R-squared values ranged from .51 to .60 across companies. When direct ratings of MSS (from the two-column format questionnaire) were used as independent variables, the R-squared values ranged from .45 to .74 across companies. Thus, measuring perceptions alone should suffice if the sole purpose of service quality measurement on individual attributes is to try to maximise the explained variance in overall service ratings. However, from a practitioner's standpoint, an equally important (if not *more* important) purpose is to pinpoint service quality shortfalls and take appropriate corrective action. From this *diagnostic-value* perspective, it is prudent to measure perceptions against expectations as discussed below.

The importance of assessing perceptions relative to expectations (rather than in isolation) was evident from several patterns of results for the four companies. For instance, consider the following mean ratings (on a 9-point scale) obtained for the computer company on the reliability and tangibles dimensions:

TABLE 6.2

	Desired Service	Adequate Service	Perceptions
Reliability	8.5	7.2	7.5
Tangibles	7.5	6.0	7.5

On the basis of perceptions ratings alone, the company's performance is identical on both dimensions and, as such, the company may place the same level of service-improvement emphasis on each. That such a strategy will be suboptimal becomes evident when the perceptions ratings are interpreted in conjunction with the desired- and adequate-service expectations. Performance on tangibles far exceeds the adequate service level (the MSA rating is 1.5) and actually meets the desired service level (the MSS rating is 0). In contrast, performance on reliability barely exceeds the adequate service level (the MSA rating is

.3) and is substantially short of the desired service level (the MSS rating is -1). Clearly, devoting equal attention to both dimensions would be wasteful; instead, the company should give far higher priority to improving performance on reliability.

Thus, measuring expectations is warranted from the standpoint of being able to pinpoint the most serious service shortfalls and make wise resource-allocation decisions. Before expending effort to make improvements on any service attribute, a company should ascertain, at a minimum, whether perceived performance on the attribute falls below, within, or above the customers' zone of tolerance. Such a comparative assessment is not possible if perceptions alone are measured. For instance, the retail-chain customers' mean perceptions ratings on the 9-point scale for reliability, responsiveness, assurance, empathy and tangibles were 6.6, 6.2, 6.7, 6.2 and 7.2, respectively. Although these ratings suggest room for improvement, the chain might still consider them to be "decent" ratings, especially since even the lowest rating of 6.2 is more than a full point above the scale's midpoint of 5. However, the adequate service ratings for reliability, responsiveness, assurance, empathy and tangibles were 7.1, 6.6, 6.9, 6.6 and 6.6, respectively. Thus, except on the dimension of tangibles, the retail chain's perceived performance does not even meet customers' minimum expectations. The retail chain's service quality is much worse than one might infer from the perceptions ratings alone.

The results from the study also shed light on whether increased questionnaire length — due to measuring expectations — adversely affects response rate. Both the two-column and three-column format questionnaires (illustrated in Appendix 3) are physically shorter than the current two-part SERVQUAL (shown in Appendix 1) because they do not repeat the battery of items. However, the two-column format is "shorter" than the three-column format in that the former requires one less set of ratings. Thus, if questionnaire length (reflected by the number of sets of ratings respondents are requested to provide) has a detrimental effect on response rate, one would predict a higher response rate for the two-column format than for the three-column format. The actual response rates obtained run counter to this prediction — in all four companies the response rate for the three-column format was equal to or higher than the response rate for the two-column format (the mean response rates across companies for the two-column and three-column formats were 22 per cent and 24 per cent, respectively). These results suggest that measuring expectations separately is not likely to lower response rates.

6.2. How Should the Expectations Construct be Operationalised?

Although the results of the study do not directly address this issue, they provide support for the meaningfulness of using the zone of tolerance (bounded by the desired and adequate service expectations) as a yardstick against which to compare perceived service performance. As implied by the illustrative findings discussed in the preceding section, operationalising customer expectations as a zone or range of service levels is not only feasible empirically but also valuable from a diagnostic standpoint. Using the zone of tolerance as a comparison standard in evaluating service performance can help companies in understanding how well they are at least meeting customers' minimum requirements, and how much improvement is needed before they achieve the status of service superiority.

6.3. Is it Appropriate to Operationalise Service Quality as a Difference Score?

As already discussed, while the two-column format measures the gap between perceptions and expectations *directly*, the three-column format involves operationalising the gap as a difference score. Therefore, relevant results from the comparative study can be used to assess the reliability, validity, and diagnostic value of the direct and difference-score measures.

Based on values of coefficient alpha — the conventional criterion for assessing the reliability (or internal consistency) of items making up a scale — both the direct and difference-score measures of service quality fared quite well. For instance, the range of coefficient alpha values across companies for the five SERVQUAL dimensions based on the MSS scores (representing the measure of service superiority or the gap between perceptions and desired-service expectations) were as follows:

TABLE 6.3

	Direct Measure	**Difference-Score Measure**
Reliability	.90 to .96	.87 to .95
Responsiveness	.83 to .95	.84 to .91
Assurance	.88 to .94	.81 to .90
Empathy	.91 to .97	.85 to .93
Tangibles	.88 to .97	.75 to .88

As the results in Table 6.3 indicate, although the reliability coefficients are somewhat higher for the direct measure than for the difference-score measure, all the values for the latter measure exceed the lower threshold value of .7 suggested by Nunnally (1978). However, some concern has been raised in the psychometric literature about the appropriateness of computing coefficient alphas for difference scores, and an alternative formula has been recommended specifically for assessing the reliability of a difference-score measure (Peter, Churchill and Brown, 1993). The reliability coefficients obtained through this formula for the difference-score operationalisation of MSS were somewhat lower than the co-efficient alpha values reported above, but were still quite high. In fact, the coefficient values for the SERVQUAL dimensions across all companies exceeded .8 with just two exceptions in one company (the coefficients for assurance and tangibles in the computer company were .71 and .65, respectively). Thus, the reliability of the difference-score operationalisation of service quality, although somewhat lower than that of the direct measure, seems to be quite respectable.

Both the direct and the difference-score measures of service quality have *face validity* in that both are consistent with the conceptual definition of service quality as the discrepancy between perceptions and expectations. And, as implied by the regression results reported in Section 6.1, both measures have good *predictive validity* — the R-squared values for the regressions with overall quality as the dependent variable range from .45 to .74 for the direct measure and .51 to .60 for the difference-score measure.

Because service quality is proposed in the literature, (Zeithaml, 1988, for example) to be an antecedent of *perceived value*, one can assess the *nomological validity* of the service quality measures by the degree to which they are related to perceived value. In the present study, customers rated the "overall value for the money" offered by their respective companies on a 9-point scale with anchors 1 = "poor value" and 9 = "excellent value". As in the case of the overall quality ratings, the overall value ratings for each company were regressed on the MSS scores for the five SERVQUAL dimensions. The range of R-squared values from these regression analyses was .34 to .57 for the direct measure and .31 to .58 for the difference-score measure. These results support the nomological validity of both measures. Moreover, comparing these ranges of R-squared values for the value regressions with the corresponding ranges reported above for the quality regressions reveals that the variance explained is higher for quality — the construct the direct and difference-score formats purport to measure — than for value, a different construct. This pattern of results offers some support for the *discriminant validity* of both measures as well.

The two measures did differ in terms of possible *response error*, a potential threat to their validity. Response error was assessed by examining the logical consistency of the MSA and MSS ratings from the two-column format, and of the adequate-service and desired-service ratings from the three-column format. An instance of response error occurs when the MSS rating on an item exceeds the MSA rating, or when the adequate-service rating exceeds the desired-service rating. The percentages of respondents who committed one or more such errors ranged from 8.6 per cent to 18.2 per cent for the two-column format, and from 0.6 per cent to 2.7 per cent for the three-column format. Thus, the validity threat because of possible response error is much greater for the direct measure than for the difference-score measure.

The study's results also suggested a need for caution in interpreting the direct-measure ratings because of possible upward bias in them. To illustrate, with just two exceptions, the mean values for the direct measures of service superiority (i.e., MSS) along the five SERVQUAL dimensions were *greater than* 5, the scale point at which the desired and perceived service levels are equal (the exceptions were mean ratings of 4.9 and 5.0 for the retail chain's responsiveness and empathy, respectively). This consistent pattern implied that perceived service performance was *above* the desired service level for virtually all dimensions in each company. In contrast, except for tangibles in the computer company, the difference-score values of MSS were negative, implying that perceived service performance was *below* the desired service level. Given that the desired service level represents a form of "ideal" standard, perceived performance falling below that level (on at least several dimensions) seems a more plausible and "face valid" finding than a consistent pattern of perceptions exceeding the desired service level. As such, the direct measures may be producing upwardly biased ratings that can mislead executives into believing that their companies' service performance is better than it actually is.

From a practical or diagnostic-value standpoint, the three-column format questionnaire (from which the difference-score measures are derived) has yet another advantage — by virtue of its generating separate ratings of the adequate-service, desired-service, and perception levels, this format is capable of *pinpointing* the position of the zone of tolerance and the perceived service level relative to the zone. The direct measures obtained from the two-column format questionnaire can indicate whether the perceived service level is above the tolerance zone (MSS score greater than 5), below the tolerance zone (MSA score less than 5), or within the tolerance zone (MSS score less than or equal to 5 and MSA score greater than or equal to 5). However, ratings from the two-column format cannot identify the tolerance zone's position on a continuum of expectation levels; nor can they pinpoint the perceived service level relative to the zone.

In summary, the difference-score operationalisation of service quality appears to have psychometric properties that are as sound as that of the direct-measure operationalisation. Moreover, the three-column format questionnaire yields richer, and perhaps more trustworthy, diagnostics than the two-column format questionnaire. Thus, operationalising service quality as difference scores seems appropriate.

6.4. Does SERVQUAL Have Five Distinct Dimensions that Transcend Different Contexts?

To verify the dimensionality of the direct-measure and difference-score versions of SERVQUAL, the MSA and MSS scores on the individual items were factor analysed to extract five factors. The results showed that for both questionnaire versions the reliability items formed a distinct factor. The responsiveness, assurance and empathy items primarily loaded on the same factor. The tangibles items, though distinct from the other dimensions, were split among the three remaining factors. The splitting of tangibles into several factors has occurred in past studies as well (PBZ, 1991), and might be an artefact of extracting five factors (in other words, because the items for the other four dimensions were captured by just two factors, the tangibles items may have split up to represent the remaining factors).

To evaluate further the distinctiveness of the SERVQUAL dimensions, confirmatory factor analyses were conducted using LISREL to assess the tenability of two alternative measurement models. One was a five-construct model in which the items loaded on the five SERVQUAL dimensions according to the a priori groupings of the items. The second model was a three-construct model in which the reliability and tangibles items loaded on two distinct constructs, while the remaining items loaded on the third construct (acknowledging the possible unidimensionality of responsiveness, assurance and empathy). The analyses showed both models to be tenable on the basis of the traditional criteria of GFI (Goodness-of-Fit Index), AGFI (Adjusted GFI), and RMSR (Root-Mean-Squared Residual). Additional analyses conducted to assess the *relative* fit of the two models and to explore further the distinctiveness of the five dimensions provided stronger support for the five-dimensional structure than for the three-dimensional structure (details of these analyses are available in PZB, 1994b). In summary, although the results showed evidence of discriminant validity among SERVQUAL's five dimensions, they also support the possibility of a three-dimensional structure wherein responsiveness, assurance and empathy meld into a single factor.

7. DIRECTIONS FOR FUTURE RESEARCH

The most recent refinements to SERVQUAL, and the empirical results from analyses conducted to reassess them, raise a number of issues for further investigation. First, although the three-column format is superior to the two-column format, especially in terms of diagnostic value, administering it in its entirety may pose practical difficulties, particularly in telephone surveys or when the list of generic items is supplemented with more context-specific items as suggested by PBZ (1991). Therefore, it would be useful to explore the soundness of administering logical subsections of the questionnaire (sections pertaining to the five dimensions, for example) to comparable subsamples of customers, so as to continue to achieve its full diagnostic value.

Second, research is needed to explore why the actual results from this study as well as earlier studies (cf. Brown, Churchill and Peter, 1993; PBZ, 1993) apparently do not fully support the alleged psychometric deficiencies of difference-score measures of service quality. Such research might provide a more enlightened understanding of the pros and cons of using difference scores in service-quality measurement.

Third, based on this study's findings, and consistent with recent calls issued by PZB (1994b) and Perreault (1992), there is a need explicitly to incorporate practical criteria such as diagnostic value into the traditional scale-assessment paradigm that is dominated by psychometric criteria.

Fourth, the possibility that direct measures of service quality tend to produce upwardly biased ratings warrants further exploration. Insights from research aimed at understanding the causes of this tendency and estimating the extent of upward bias it produces would be helpful in reducing the bias, or at least in correcting it in interpreting direct-measure ratings.

Finally, this study's findings call for additional research on the dimensionality of the SERVQUAL items. Although the findings showed some support for SERVQUAL's five-dimensional configuration, they also revealed considerable interdimensional overlap, especially among responsiveness, assurance, and empathy. PBZ (1991) have speculated about possible reasons for similar overlaps observed in earlier studies, and have proffered directions for future research on this issue. The present study's findings reiterate the need for such research, especially exploratory research for uncovering the underlying causes and managerial implications of the empirical correlations among the dimensions.

APPENDIX 1

REFINED SERVQUAL INSTRUMENT

Note: In what follows, telephone repair services are used as an illustrative context.

DIRECTIONS: Based on your experiences as a customer of telephone repair services, please think about the kind of telephone company that would deliver excellent quality of repair service. Think about the kind of telephone company with which you would be pleased to do business. Please show the extent to which you think such a telephone company would possess the feature described by each statement. If you feel a feature is *not at all essential* for excellent telephone companies such as the one you have in mind, circle the number "1". If you feel a feature is *absolutely essential* for excellent telephone companies, circle "7". If your feelings are less strong, circle one of the numbers in the middle. There are no right or wrong answers — all we are interested in is a number that truly reflects your feelings regarding telephone companies that would deliver excellent quality of service.

Note: Each of the statements was accompanied by a 7-point scale anchored at the ends by the labels "Strongly Disagree" (1) and "Strongly Agree" (7). Intermediate scale points were not labelled. Also, the headings (TANGIBLES, RELIABILITY, etc.), shown here to indicate which statements fall under each dimension, were not included in the actual questionnaire.

Tangibles

1. Excellent telephone companies will have modern-looking equipment.

2. The physical facilities at excellent telephone companies will be visually appealing.

3. Employees of excellent telephone companies will be neat-appearing.

4. Materials associated with the service (such as pamphlets or statements) will be visually appealing in excellent telephone companies.

Reliability

5. When excellent telephone companies promise to do something by a certain time, they will do so.

6. When customers have a problem, excellent telephone companies will show a sincere interest in solving it.

7. Excellent telephone companies will perform the service right the first time.

8. Excellent telephone companies will provide their services at the time they promise to do so.

9. Excellent telephone companies will insist on error-free records.

Responsiveness

10. Employees of excellent telephone companies will tell customers exactly when services will be performed.

11. Employees of excellent telephone companies will give prompt service to customers.

12. Employees of excellent telephone companies will always be willing to help customers.

13. Employees of excellent telephone companies will never be too busy to respond to customer requests.

Assurance

14. The behaviour of employees of excellent telephone companies will instil confidence in customers.

15. Customers of excellent telephone companies will feel safe in their transactions.

16. Employees of excellent telephone companies will be consistently courteous with customers.

17. Employees of excellent telephone companies will have the knowledge to answer customer questions.

Empathy

18. Excellent telephone companies will give customers individual attention.

19. Excellent telephone companies will have operating hours convenient to all their customers.

20. Excellent telephone companies will have employees who give customers personal attention.

21. Excellent telephone companies will have the customers' best interests at heart.

22. The employees of excellent telephone companies will understand the specific needs of their customers.

PERCEPTIONS SECTION

DIRECTIONS: The following set of statements relate to your feelings about XYZ Telephone Company's repair service. For each statement, please show the extent to which you believe XYZ has the feature described by the statement. Once again, circling a "1" means that you strongly disagree that XYZ has that feature, and circling a "7" means that you strongly agree. You may circle any of the numbers in the middle that show how strong your feelings are. There are no right or wrong answers — all that we are interested in is a number that best shows your perceptions about XYZ's repair service.

Tangibles

1. XYZ has modern-looking equipment.

2. XYZ's physical facilities are visually appealing.

3. XYZ's employees are neat-appearing.

4. Materials associated with the service (such as pamphlets or statements) are visually appealing at XYZ.

Reliability

5. When XYZ promises to do something by a certain time, it does so.

6. When you have a problem, XYZ shows a sincere interest in solving it.

7. XYZ performs the service right the first time.

8. XYZ provides its services at the time it promises to do so.

9. XYZ insists on error-free records.

Responsiveness

10. Employees of XYZ tell you exactly when services will be performed.

11. Employees of XYZ give you prompt service.

12. Employees of XYZ are always willing to help you.

13. Employees of XYZ are never too busy to respond to your requests.

Assurance

14. The behaviour of employees of XYZ instils confidence in customers.

15. You feel safe in your transactions with XYZ.

16. Employees of XYZ are consistently courteous with you.

17. Employees of XYZ have the knowledge to answer your questions.

Empathy

18. XYZ gives you individual attention.

19. XYZ has operating hours convenient to all its customers.

20. XYZ has employees who give you personal attention.

21. XYZ has your best interests at heart.

22. Employees of XYZ understand your specific needs.

POINT-ALLOCATION QUESTION

DIRECTIONS: Listed below are five features pertaining to telephone companies and the repair services they offer. We would like to know how important each of these features is to *you* when you evaluate a telephone company's quality of repair service. Please allocate a total of 100 points among the five features *according to how important each feature is to you* — the more important a feature is to you, the more points you should allocate to it. Please ensure that the points you allocate to the five features add up to 100.

1. The appearance of the telephone company's physical facilities, equipment, personnel, and communications materials	_____ points
2. The ability of the telephone company to perform the promised service dependably and accurately	_____ points
3. The willingness of the telephone company to help customers and provide prompt service	_____ points
4. The knowledge and courtesy of the telephone company's employees and their ability to convey trust and confidence	_____ points
5. The caring, individualised attention the telephone company provides its customers	_____ points
TOTAL POINTS ALLOCATED	100 points

APPENDIX 2

EXCERPT FROM ADAPTED SERVQUAL USED BY CORNING

Note: Respondents were instructed to rate Corning and a leading competitor ("alternate supplier") against "world class" on each attribute.

Reliability: Ability to perform the promised service dependably and accurately.

Scale: "7" = "World Class".

	Corning *v.* World Class	Alternate Supplier *v.* World Class
1. When _____ promises to do something by a certain time, it does so.	1 2 3 4 5 6 7	1 2 3 4 5 6 7
2. When you have a problem, _____ shows a sincere interest in solving it.	1 2 3 4 5 6 7	1 2 3 4 5 6 7
3. _____ performs the service right the first time.	1 2 3 4 5 6 7	1 2 3 4 5 6 7
4. _____ is dependable.	1 2 3 4 5 6 7	1 2 3 4 5 6 7
5. _____ insists on error-free records.	1 2 3 4 5 6 7	1 2 3 4 5 6 7

APPENDIX 3

ENHANCED VERSIONS OF SERVQUAL

Note: Both formats are for the auto insurer (one of four companies that participated in the study) and only one illustrative item is shown in each.

Three-Column Format

We would like your impressions about _____'s service performance relative to your expectations. Please think about the two different levels of expectations defined below:

MINMIMUM SERVICE LEVEL — the *minimum* level of service performance you consider adequate.

DESIRED SERVICE LEVEL — the level of service performance you desire.

For each of the following statements, please indicate: (a) your *minimum service level* by circling one of the numbers in the *first* column; (b) your *desired service level* by circling one of the numbers in the *second* column; and (c) your *perception of* _____'s service by circling one of the numbers in the *third* column.

When it comes to:	My *Minimum* Service Level is: Low　　　High	My *Desired* Service Level is: Low　　　High	My Perception of _____'s Service Performance is: Low　　　High　　No Opinion
1. Prompt service to policy-holders	1 2 3 4 5 6 7 8 9	1 2 3 4 5 6 7 8 9	1 2 3 4 5 6 7 8 9　　　N

Two-Column Format

Please think about the quality of service _____ offers compared to the two different levels of service defined below:

MINMIMUM SERVICE LEVEL — the *minimum* level of service performance you consider adequate.

DESIRED SERVICE LEVEL — the level of service performance you desire.

For each of the following statements, please indicate: (a) how _____'s performance compares with your *minimum service level* by circling one of the numbers in the *first* column; and (b) how _____'s performance compares with your *desired service level* by circling one of the numbers in the *second* column.

	Compared to My *Minimum* Service Level, _____'s Service Performance is:				Compared to My *Desired* Service Level, _____'s Service Performance is:			
When it comes to:	Lower	The Same	Higher	No Opinion	Lower	The Same	Higher	No Opinion
1. Prompt service to policy-holders	1 2 3	4 5 6	7 8 9	N	1 2 3 4	5 6	7 8 9	N

REFERENCES

Babakus, Emin and Gregory W. Boller, "An Empirical Assessment of the SERVQUAL Scale", *Journal of Business Research*, Vol. 24, 1992, pp. 253–68.

Babakus, Emin and W. Glynn Mangold, "Adapting the SERVQUAL Scale to Hospital Services: An Empirical Investigation", *Health Services Research*, Vol. 26, No. 6, 1992, pp. 767–86.

Bojanic, David C., "Quality Measurement in Professional Services Firms", *Journal of Professional Services Marketing*, Vol. 7, No. 2, 1991, pp. 27–36.

Boulding, William, Ajay Kalra, Richard Staelin, and Valarie Zeithaml, "A Dynamic Process Model of Service Quality: From Expectations to Behavioral Intentions", *Journal of Marketing Research*, Vol. 30, February, 1993, pp. 7–27.

Brensinger, Ronald P. and Douglas M. Lambert, "Can The SERVQUAL Scale be Generalized to Business-to-Business Services?", *Knowledge Development in Marketing*, 1990 AMA's Summer Educators' Conference Proceedings, 1990, p. 289.

Brown, Stephen W. and Teresa A. Swartz, "A Gap Analysis of Professional Service Quality", *Journal of Marketing*, Vol. 53, April, 1989, pp. 92–8.

Brown, Tom J., Gilbert A. Churchill Jr. and J. Paul Peter, "Improving the Measurement of Service Quality", *Journal of Retailing*, Vol. 69, No. 1, 1993, pp. 127–39.

Carman, James M., "Consumer Perceptions of Service Quality: An Assessment of the SERVQUAL Dimensions", *Journal of Retailing*, Vol. 66, No. 1, 1990, pp. 33-55.

Churchill, Gilbert A., Jr., "A Paradigm for Developing Better Measures of Marketing Constructs", *Journal of Marketing Research*, Vol. 16, February, 1979, pp. 64–73.

Crompton, John L. and Kelly J. Mackay, "Users' Perceptions of the Relative Importance of Service Quality Dimensions in Selected Public Recreation Programs", *Leisure Sciences*, Vol. 11, 1989, pp. 367–75.

Cronin, J. Joseph, Jr. and Stephen A. Taylor, "Measuring Service Quality: A Reexamination and Extension", *Journal of Marketing*, Vol. 56, July, 1992, pp. 55–68.

Farley, John M., Carson F. Daniels and Daniel H. Pearl, "Service Quality in a Multinational Environment", *Proceedings* of ASQC Quality Congress Transactions, San Francisco, CA, 1990.

Finn, David W. and Charles W. Lamb Jr., "An Evaluation of the SERVQUAL Scales in a Retail Setting", in Rebecca H. Holman and Michael R. Solomon (Eds.), *Advances in Consumer Research*, Vol. 18, Association for Consumer Research, Provo, UT, 1991.

Ford, John B., Mathew Joseph and Beatriz Joseph, "Service Quality in Higher Education: A Comparison of Universities in the United States and New Zealand Using SERVQUAL", in *Enhancing Knowledge Development in Marketing*, 1993 AMA Educators' Proceedings, 1993, pp. 75–81.

Grönroos, Christian, "Strategic Management and Marketing in the Service Sector", Swedish School of Economics and Business Administration, Helsinki, Finland, 1982.

Johnson, Linda L, Michael J. Dotson and B.J. Dunlop, "Service Quality Determinants and Effectiveness in the Real Estate Brokerage Industry", *The Journal of Real Estate Research*, Vol. 3, 1988, pp. 21–36.

Lehtinen, Uolevi and Jarmo R. Lehtinen, "Service Quality: A Study of Quality Dimensions", unpublished research report, Service Management Group OY, Finland, 1982.

Lewis, Robert C. and Bernard H. Booms, "The Marketing Aspects of Service Quality", in L Berry, G. Shostack, and G. Upah (Eds.), *Emerging Perspectives on Services Marketing*, American Marketing Association, Chicago, IL, 1983, pp. 99–107.

Nunnally, Jim C., *Psychometric Theory*, 2nd. Edition, McGraw-Hill Book Company, New York, 1978.

Parasuraman, A., Valarie A. Zeithaml and Leonard L. Berry, "A Conceptual Model of Service Quality and Its Implications for Future Research", *Journal of Marketing*, Vol. 49, Fall, 1985, pp. 41–50.

Parasuraman, A., Valarie A. Zeithaml and Leonard L. Berry, "SERVQUAL: A Multiple-Item Scale for Measuring Consumer Perceptions of Service Quality", *Journal of Retailing*, Vol. 64, No. 1, 1988, pp. 12–40.

Parasuraman, A., Leonard L. Berry and Valarie A. Zeithaml, "Refinement and Reassessment of the SERVQUAL Scale", *Journal of Retailing*, Vol. 67,

Winter, 1991, pp. 420–50.

Parasuraman, A., Leonard L. Berry and Valarie A. Zeithaml, "More on Improving Service Quality Measurement", *Journal of Retailing*, Vol. 69, Spring, 1993, pp. 40–147.

Parasuraman A., Valarie A. Zeithaml and Leonard L. Berry, (a), "Reassessment of Expectations as a Comparison Standard in Measuring Service Quality: Implications for Further Research", *Journal of Marketing*, Vol. 58, No. 1, 1994, pp. 111–24.

Parasuraman A., Valarie A. Zeithaml and Leonard L. Berry, (b), "Moving Forward in Service Quality Research: Measuring Different Levels of Customer Expectations, Comparing Alternative Scales, and Examining the Performance-Behavioral Intentions Link", Working Paper, 1994.

Perreault, William D., Jr., "The Shifting Paradigm in Marketing Research", *Journal of the Academy of Marketing Science*, Vol. 20, Fall, 1992, pp. 367–75.

Peter, J. Paul, Gilbert A. Churchill Jr. and Tom J. Brown, "Caution in the Use of Difference Scores in Consumer Research", *Journal of Consumer Research*, Vol. 19, March, 1993, pp. 655–62.

Sasser, W. Earl, Jr., Paul R. Olsen and D. Daryl Wyckoff, *Management of Service Operations: Text and Cases*, Allyn and Bacon, Boston, MA, 1978.

Teas, R. Kenneth, "Expectations, Performance Evaluation and Consumer's Perceptions of Quality", *Journal of Marketing*, Vol. 57, No. 4, 1993, pp. 18–34.

Woodruff, Robert B., D. Scott Clemons, David W. Schumann, Sarah F. Gardial and Mary Jane Burns, "The Standards Issue in CS/D Research: A Historical Perspective", *Journal of Consumer Satisfaction, Dissatisfaction and Complaining Behavior*, Vol. 4, 1991, pp. 103–9.

Zeithaml, Valarie A., "Consumer Perceptions of Price, Quality, and Value: A Conceptual Model and Synthesis of Research", *Journal of Marketing*, Vol. 52, July, 1988, pp. 2–22.

Zeithaml, Valarie A., Leonard L. Berry and A. Parasuraman, "The Nature and Determinants of Customer Expectations of Service", *Journal of the Academy of Marketing Science*, Vol. 21, No. 1, 1993, pp. 1–12.

Zeithaml, Valarie A., A. Parasuraman and Leonard L. Berry, *Delivering Quality Service*, The Free Press, New York, 1990.

7

THE COST OF SERVICE QUALITY:

Extending the Boundaries of Accounting Systems to Enhance Customer Value

James G. Barnes and Judith A. Cumby
Memorial University of Newfoundland
Canada

PRÉCIS

Consider a one-armed bandit that always pays a jackpot: everyone will be infinitely rich (other than the owner of the machine). Some advocates of service quality initiatives appear to believe that they have found such a slot machine: a dollar spent on quality always returns more than a dollar. In this chapter, Barnes and Cumby question this received (and unsustainable) wisdom. They argue that some quality initiatives are likely to pay off and others will not. Accounting systems may be one way of increasing the chances of identifying successful initiatives and of jettisoning unsuccessful ones. Their case rests on the idea that, at some stage, service quality expenditures (like most other expenditures) result in decreasing returns and a point will be reached at which the costs of additional service outweigh the benefits. The authors introduce a model which may be used to guide the development of information systems by focusing upon the key costs and benefits of service quality initiatives. They emphasise the importance of both monetary and non-monetary outcomes (e.g., referrals). The model involves allocating costs directly to individual customers and measuring the benefits associated with each customer. Service quality initiatives are then actively targeted at the customers who are most likely to respond positively to those initiatives. Rather than haphazardly feeding slot machines, information is used to target selectively the machines that are likely to pay a jackpot. Naturally, this model relies upon being able to identify which customers are most likely to benefit the organisation. In addition, the authors emphasise that data relating to past custom alone is likely to be insufficient, it is the future benefits of a customer that count. The methodology is unlikely to be valuable in situations where the customer is anonymous or it is impossible to target initiatives at specific customers. Industries that appear most amenable to their methodology include airlines and financial institutions.

This appears quite sensible, but if life were that simple, it would be necessary only to construct an information system to find that lucrative one-armed bandit, and then become infinitely rich. The argument for measuring the costs and benefits of service quality initiatives becomes transposed into an argument for measuring the costs and benefits of information systems: these costs and benefits will in turn hinge upon the anticipated costs and benefits of the service initiatives — a vicious circle of economic calculation. Barnes and Cumby break this circle by proposing a five-stage model of cost-benefit identification. Additional investment in information systems is contingent upon demonstrating that particular customer groups are already likely to offer substantial benefits to the firm. The benefit of additional information systems is the opportunity to segment those customers further and achieve a finer partitioning of the beneficiaries of service quality initiatives. This partitioning decreases the costs of service quality since it ensures that high levels of service quality are targeted only at customers who will offer substantial future benefits to the firm.

Eamonn Walsh
University of Limerick
Ireland

1. INTRODUCTION

The *service quality* concept, which seems to have become one of the business buzzwords of the 1990s, focuses on maximising profitability through increased customer satisfaction. Guided by the belief that a contented customer will strengthen an entity's financial performance, firms have jumped on the bandwagon and adopted a myriad of service quality initiatives; however, the experience with such programmes has been varied. Some firms abandon their service quality efforts when times get tough or after a relatively short trial. Still others will "do whatever it takes" to keep a customer or to increase market share. Many firms have not gauged the feasibility of investments in service quality, and decisions about the levels of effort to be expended on quality programmes are often made in a haphazard fashion. Present accounting systems generally do not effectively capture all the costs associated with such programmes, or if they do, there is no evaluation made of their profitability over the long run.

Service quality programmes are characterised by huge investments of human and financial capital, yet often no formal evaluation is made of the return on service quality. What is needed is a system that incorporates costs and benefits not traditionally captured in accounting systems, but sometimes represented through non-financial measures. Further research is needed on how these measures should best be captured and presented so as to furnish decision-makers with relevant and reliable information. Such research should acknowledge that there are different levels of value associated with various market segments, and such should be the basis for the levels of service quality offered to customers. The purpose of this chapter is to discuss advancements in accounting and management information systems that are necessary to optimise investments in service quality. First, the objectives of service quality programmes will be discussed. This will be followed by presentation of the related costs and benefits, both financial and non-financial, associated with the provision of service. The chapter will conclude with a proposed model which presents the stages of customer valuation.

2. THE THREE R'S OF MARKETING

Expenditures on service quality initiatives relate to one or all of the three R's of marketing: the establishment and maintenance of long-term customer *relationships*, the development of programmes that will lead to the *retention* of customers for extended periods, and the establishment of procedures to ensure that the company can *recover* from mistakes that are made. This must not be done indiscriminately; companies must master the well-accepted art of market segmentation and identify those customer relationships that should be cultivated and those where dissolution would have a positive impact on the company's bottom line and future prospects. This represents a departure from the belief that more is better; not all customers provide utility for a company. It has been recently argued that companies should target the "right" customers — not necessarily the easiest to attract or the most profitable in the short term, but those who are likely to do profitable business with the company over time (Barnes and Cumby, 1993; Reichheld, 1993; Slywotzky and Shapiro, 1993). In order to attract and keep customers, firms need to provide the consumer with a reason to do business; this is often accomplished by escalating the level of service. However, the provision of service involves attendant costs in terms of both time and money, and such investments may be counterproductive when they are focused on customers with whom the company should actually not be doing business (Reichheld, 1993).

> Usually service investments must be traded off against other investments on direct, tangible benefits and therefore must justify themselves by directly reducing costs, increasing resources, or both (Coyne, 1989).

3. RELATIONSHIP BUILDING

The question then arises of how to identify customers who will directly or indirectly return profit and who should, therefore, be the target of service quality initiatives. How does a firm get beyond the traditional segmentation practices based on demographics or psychographics to one where the value of the customer is based not only on historic patterns, but also on future revenues and even associated non-monetary costs and revenues? Although two customers may have very similar histories with a company in terms of sales or gross margins contributed, there may well be differences between the two in the length of time they will spend with the company, or the amount that they will contribute to the firm's wealth over time. Even if the future potential of the two customers is equal when based on some present value calculation of direct net cash flows, it could be that one customer can offer more through referral sales or word-of-mouth contacts. This being the case, management should be prepared to channel its efforts towards the customer who offers the greater future promise. To maximise profitability, relationship-building should be forward-looking, not entrenched in historic monetary revenue patterns.

The development of a loyal customer base enhances a firm's profitability. It has been observed that:

> [C]ustomer loyalty has three second-order effects: (1) revenue grows as a result of repeat purchases and referrals, (2) costs decline due to lower acquisition expenses resulting from the efficiencies of serving experienced customers, and (3) employee retention increases because job pride and satisfaction increase, in turn creating a loop that reinforces customer loyalty and further reducing costs as hiring and training costs shrink and productivity rises (Reichheld, 1993).

In addition, such loyal clientèle likely contribute to increased sales through word-of-mouth advertising to their friends, and they are less likely to quibble over prices. These additional benefits can provide tremendous value to a firm over time.

In an effort to develop a loyal customer base, firms have switched from transactional marketing to relationship marketing. Customer relationships are not just there: they have to be earned (Grönroos, 1990). To foster such relationships, companies have turned to service quality as a means of developing a distinct competitive advantage in an environment where technology is often taken for granted (Barnes and Glynn, 1993). The result has been a proliferation of quality initiatives, the objectives of which may not be clearly defined, and the progress towards the achievement of these objectives may not always be monitored.

4. RETENTION STRATEGIES

Firms cannot optimise profitability merely by securing customer relationships for extended periods of time. "There appears to be little correlation between how long a customer has been retained and how loyal that customer is" (Fay, 1994). Also, the cost to keep a customer may outweigh any short-term financial benefit to be received. Even though the customer may not extract explicit costs in terms of cash outlays or rebates, the situation may be such that the staff must spend an inordinate amount of time servicing a customer, thereby detracting from what may be other, more profitable, endeavours. Management must decide then which relationships should be solidified; some customers should be allowed to defect, while others should be retained.

A profitability analysis that evaluates all costs and benefits is critical to effective customer retention. In an attempt to gauge this, some have erroneously concluded that customer satisfaction is equated with loyalty. Satisfaction is not a surrogate for customer retention, although one study did show how "customer satisfaction may be linked sequentially to individual loyalty, aggregate retention rate, market share, and profits and how the dollar value of a shift in customer satisfaction can be measured". The conclusion was that customer satisfaction should be a central issue in the new view of market share because of its association with retention rate (Rust and Zahorik, 1993). However, this strategy in itself will not ensure an increase in corporate wealth as "Customer satisfaction measurement systems are simply not designed to provide insight into how many customers stay loyal to the company and for how long" (Reichheld, 1993). This approach to market segmentation is more progressive than earlier claims that customer satisfaction can lead to higher margins because satisfied customers are more likely to tolerate price increases and that competitors will find it difficult to lure customers from the firm (Anderson, Fornell, and Lehmann, 1993). What is missing here is an evaluation of the costs involved in bringing the customer to a certain satisfaction level and a recognition that changes in a customer's experience and expectation level may require even larger expenditures on service quality.

Market share has simplistically been seen as an indicator of customer loyalty or long-term profitability. Increases in market share may be counterproductive when gains are at the expense of lost customers who offered more potential than the recent additions. The "churn" component of market share must be evaluated to assess exactly what types of customers have been sacrificed in the name of gaining superior market position. A firm facing a significant customer turnover situation should develop strategies that seek to retain those customers who are already making or who have the potential to make a long-term contribution to corporate profits. Rather than blindly following market share, a company should be committed to developing "quality share", achieving its largest share among those customers who will provide the greatest long-term profits. "Smart choices in customer selection and timing enable companies to channel investment resources into building the highest quality of market share" (Slywotzky and Shapiro, 1993).

The development of quality market share must start with an understanding of what is important to the customer. It means avoiding situations that Gummesson refers to as "the *Peanut Syndrome*", increasing costs to give customers something that they do not care about (Gummesson, 1991). It means establishing a link between profits and surrogate measures of customer loyalty, not just fleeting moments of satisfaction. Customer satisfaction can have more of an impact on market share than on returns, given that significantly improved quality takes time to develop (Carr and Tyson, 1992). It is essential therefore, to be able to gauge the return on investments in service quality over the long term. The focus of this chapter is on identification of issues pertinent to the development of an effective measurement system, one that goes beyond historic data and into assessing all that a customer can offer a company throughout an ongoing relationship. The costs necessary to secure these relationships must be offset against the related returns, so that the value of the customer to the firm can be calculated and evaluated.

5. PROFITABLE RECOVERY STRATEGIES

The final element of the three R's of a service marketing strategy relates to a company's ability to recover from mistakes in the service area. The level to which a company will go to recover will depend primarily on two factors: the importance of the customer and the severity of the error in terms of its future impact on the relationship. Each of these factors is measured in relative terms along some continuum of importance, not at some absolute point. The level of recovery can vary from "do whatever it takes" — a strategy warranted when the mistake is severe and the customer is important, in terms of both current and potential business — to a point where the firm more or less pays lip service to dealing with the mistake, possibly by issuing only an apology. However, the strategy of "do whatever it takes" is one that firms dealing with anonymous customers — such as many retailers and fast-food restaurants — are often forced into (Quinlan, 1991) because of their inability to differentiate between customers on some valuation criterion. The recommendations of this chapter will be particularly applicable to those organisations with databases that allow the capture of information that permits discrimination among customers on the basis of their value to the company.

In assessing whether recovery is warranted, and, if so, to what level it should be taken, managers should not fall into the trap of merely looking at individual customers in terms of their past experience with the company. It may be that the failure to deliver quality service occurred early in the relationship with the customer, before any real profit had been generated, but where the potential for future returns from that alliance is significant. For example, one of Canada's national airlines has estimated the asset value of a satisfied business traveller to be more than 20 times that of a satisfied leisure traveller (Jenkins, 1992). Interestingly, the measures of asset value for each class of passenger included a multiplier effect for the number of customers gained through word-of-mouth contacts. However, there were differences between the groups in the length of time that the benefit was expected to endure. The point here is not to criticise the measurement process, but to recognise that benefits are extended, both through contacts and time, and that the level of benefit varies according to category of passenger. These should be contemplated when judging the amount and type of service quality effort to extend to a customer.

Another source of customer value comes from word-of-mouth associations. If a company does not recover effectively from mistakes in the delivery of service, the negative repercussions could far outweigh the cost of correcting the initial blunder. This is evidenced by the

> ... new rules of thumb emerging in the service industry: (1) it costs five times as much to attract a new customer as to keep an existing one; (2) it takes 12 positive service experiences to overcome one negative one;

and (3) 25 to 50 per cent of the operating expense of a company can be attributed to poor service quality — to the cost of not doing it right the first time (Liswood, 1989).

Others have found that customers who have bad experiences tell approximately eleven people about it; those with good experiences tell just six (Hart, Heskett and Sasser, 1990).

Whatever the exact costs, in terms of both monetary outlay and time of those personnel involved in compensating for the mistake, it is clear that there are significant negative consequences, both direct and indirect, associated with errors. It may be that the initial failure to deliver a quality product or service is such that the customer has unequivocally decided no longer to do business with the firm. However, the spin-off damage through word-of-mouth contacts could be mitigated through delivery of adequate compensation, even when it is clear that the original customer will not provide any future direct benefits to the company. If the management does not have a system for evaluating the future worth of a customer, it may erroneously dismiss that customer as not being worth the effort of compensation. An example of this can be found where a fast-food franchise delivers food to a new customer. If the quality of the product is unacceptable, the customer may have already decided not to do business with that company again. The customer may still choose to complain and, if this complaint is not dealt with effectively, the company may suffer extended damage as the unsatisfied customer relays the story to friends and associates.

This is not to suggest that management should escalate the level of service to the point where it goes beyond that which is expected or even deemed acceptable by the client. There are situations where the compensation may be perceived to be so excessive that the customer is left to wonder why the company went that far, or how the company will justify this extra cost. For example, airline passengers may have come to expect that if their luggage is delayed in arriving, it will be delivered to their hotel or home within a few hours of the originally scheduled time of arrival. If the airline chooses to overcompensate by not only delivering the luggage, but also offering remuneration towards the next scheduled flight, the traveller may be left wondering why this was done. Is the company desperate for business, and will this extra cost eventually translate into increased fares? From the company's perspective, management must evaluate the repercussions of their actions on future revenues and customers' expectation levels. The delivery of the luggage in a relatively prompt and courteous manner may have been an effective method of countering the error. However, it might well be the case that the extra compensation is viewed by the customer as too much, and this may translate into "negative value added" in connection with future word-of-mouth revenues.

6. MEASURING THE RESULTS OF QUALITY INITIATIVES

As discussed, referral revenues can be significant to a business but are often not captured and evaluated by accounting information systems. The traditional approach to performance evaluation assesses manage- ment on the basis of short-term results using historic measures such as net income or return on assets. There are several problems with this approach when applied to service quality. First of all, expenditures on service quality are best viewed as a contribution to the building of an asset with a long-term payback. This is because:

> The nature of the customer development process involves a lag between action and results. Investment thinking makes this time lag clear and understandable (Slywotzky and Shapiro, 1993).

This is not unlike the approach to advertising and sales promotion, which are usually evaluated against forecasted sales dollars, although the constraints of the fiscal year concept dictate that these items be charged to expense immediately. Many marketing efforts will produce future economic benefit to the firm. Therefore, the idea of treating these efforts as expenses is inconsistent with the concept of an asset. A quality report issued by the General Accounting Office (GAO) in the US con- cludes that "it takes an average of 2.5 years for firms to begin realising significant benefits from their quality management systems" (Armitage, 1992). This extended benefit period supports the argument for treating service quality expenditures as an investment.

Another problem with conventional information systems is that the benefits from service quality may be far-reaching and difficult to measure. Monetary returns may be long-lived as is the case when a firm has been successful in solidifying a relationship with a customer. It has been found that:

> Loyal customers do a lot of talking over the years and drum up a lot of business. One of the leading home builders in the United States has found that more than 60 per cent of its sales are the result of referrals (Reichheld and Sasser, 1990).

This is the positive return associated with a loyal customer. Un- fortunately, most systems cannot link profits with loyalty or customer value. Accounting systems "... can show the benefits of the one-year magic cure but not of programmes and practices that take three to five years or longer to affect profits" (Reichheld, 1993). Given the difficulty of linking inputs (service quality expenditure) with outputs (referral business) a true evaluation of service efforts is often not performed.

Also, the benefits of service quality initiatives may be indirect and even non-monetary, as is the case with improved corporate image or extended goodwill. Some such benefits are discussed in this book (Lewis, Chapter 3). Many firms will actively recruit a customer because of that person's prominent position in society, such as a high court judge. The belief is that it "looks good" to have this customer on their books. It is difficult to measure the value associated with such practices and accordingly such items are often ignored when evaluating related expenditures. This is another reason why quality initiatives may be prematurely evaluated as unsuccessful: the return is either not immediate or it is not measured using traditional financial measures. Lack of information can lead to costly decisions related to the provision of service.

Management does not allow for feedback that is traditionally not allocated to specific customers or is non-monetary in nature, but instead assesses expenditures against allocatable financial returns. Under this myopic approach, undertakings in the quality area may be labelled as unprofitable and hastily dismissed. There is a need to incorporate non-financial measures into the evaluation criteria. However, a principal weakness of non-financial performance indicators is the lack of explicit linkage to the financial numbers. It is on the latter that managers and companies are ultimately judged. Until there is a clear link between financials and non-financials, there is a risk that the non-financials will be viewed as at least slightly fluffy (Singleton-Green, 1993) and will be dismissed as too soft to be meaningful. Traditional information systems only provide objective assessment of monetary allocatable returns. Non-monetary benefits are often not quantified through surrogate measures, and many monetary returns are not captured because establishing a link with a specific customer or market segment can prove to be arduous. The model below (Table 7.1) details some of the monetary and non-monetary benefits associated with service quality initiatives. The benefits are from the perspective of the firm providing the service. Allocatable benefits are those that can be directly linked with an individual customer or a customer segment.

In order for a company to optimise its earnings and its return from service quality initiatives over the long term, it must have some way of measuring the total benefits and costs associated with a customer. This information will assist management in deciding which customer relationships should be pursued, so as to create a "quality share" of loyal clientèle. In order truly to maximise the wealth of the company, management must ascertain the total cost of providing customers with quality service, and then segment markets on the basis of monetary and non-monetary paybacks. Strategic management would dictate that once a link between service quality and long-term profits has been established, the company would channel its efforts toward attracting and keeping the "right" customers, and responding appropriately to any errors that might occur when dealing with members of this high-quality target segment of the market. Given that the level of effort required to satisfy customers changes from one person to the next, and for a given customer over time, effective profitability analysis must measure and allocate significant service quality costs.

TABLE 7.1: TOTAL CUSTOMER BENEFITS MODEL

Allocatability/ Type of Benefit	Monetary	Non-Monetary
Allocatable	• Current Sales • Historic Sales	• Customer Satisfaction • Word-of-Mouth Revenues • Benefit by Association • Reference Group Affiliation
Not Allocatable	• Referral Sales • Repeat Business • Growth in Sales • Earning Power Projections	• Loyalty/Goodwill • Corporate Image • Positioning

7. THE COSTS OF QUALITY

It has been acknowledged in some quarters that there is a cost to providing quality. Yet there is much debate over how to measure that cost and whether or not "quality is free", or if it actually represents a significant investment that must be monitored and measured over the long term. Measuring any cost is always the first step in evaluating its ability to contribute to or detract from an organisation's value. The concept of measuring the costs of service quality is not new and has its base in the manufacturing sector which identifies four categories of operating quality costs: prevention, appraisal, internal failure, and external failure. A resultant cost emerges when a purchase price reflects the supplier's operating quality costs; this has been labelled as an indirect quality cost. In order to prevent errors and appraise quality in the manufacturing sector, an investment in appropriate capital equipment becomes necessary, and this is quantified in equipment quality costs (Feigenbaum, 1961).

More recently, the definitions of the costs of quality have been tailored to the delivery of services (Harrington, 1991). These have been grouped under various subheadings, one of which distinguishes poor quality costs (PQC) from both the perspective of the provider of service (direct PQC), and the recipient of that service (indirect PQC). Direct PQC has both controllable (prevention and appraisal) and resultant components (internal error and external error) (Harrington, 1991). Prevention costs are sometimes referred to as a "cost-avoidance investment" because they relate to the cost of doing it right the first time. Within the services area, the focus would be on human resources. Regardless of the effort expended at this first stage, it is often necessary to spend time evaluating the success of the initial attempt. Appraisal costs would include examples such as proof-reading letters, and other situations where services are checked before delivery.

No matter how well things are planned and checked, the reality is that errors will occur especially when dealing with the human side of service. Internal errors are identified at the appraisal stage, before the service is delivered to the customer. Internal error costs would include such things as the time required to retype letters and additional costs incurred because bills were paid late. However, sometimes the error is not caught and unacceptable service is delivered to the customer. External error costs would include the time involved in handling complaints and missed sales (Harrington, 1991), although others have defined the latter point as an opportunity cost. It has been argued that there is another category of quality costs: the cost of overspending in areas where it is not possible to solidify a relationship with the customer, or where the cost to keep the customer outweighs future associated revenues (Barnes and Cumby, 1993).

Xerox in the US has defined three categories of quality costs:

1. The costs of conformity (prevention and appraisal)

2. The costs of non-conformity (failure to meet customer requirements before and after delivery)

3. The costs of lost opportunities.

The costs of lost opportunities includes the profit not earned resulting from lost customers and reduction in revenue because of non-conformity (Carr, 1992). These and other classifications of the costs of quality are summarised in the Definitions of Costs of Quality table below. Recent work by Youngdahl and Kellogg (1994) classifies the service quality costs of prevention, appraisal, internal failure and external failure from the customer's perspective. While these costs are critical to a comprehensive understanding of relationship marketing, they are not factored into the cost and valuation models presented in this chapter.

TABLE 7.2: DEFINITIONS OF COSTS OF QUALITY

Authors	Date	Cost Categories	
Feigenbaum	1961	• Prevention • Appraisal • Internal Failure	• External Failure • Indirect Quality • Equipment Quality
Dale and Plunkett	1991	• Prevention • Appraisal • Internal Failure • External Failure	• Warranty • Other (e.g., quality performance reporting)
Harrington	1991	Direct Poor Quality Costs: • Prevention • Appraisal • Internal Error • External Error • Equipment	Indirect Poor Quality Costs: • Customer-Incurred • Customer-Dissatisfaction • Loss-of-Reputation
Carr, Lawrence, and Tyson	1992	Voluntary Costs: • Prevention • Appraisal	Involuntary Costs: • Indirect Failure • Intangible Failure (opportunity costs of lost goodwill, reduced market share, and unrealised future profits)
Xerox (Carr)	1992	Costs of Conformance: • Prevention • Inspection/Appraisal	Costs of Non-Conformance: • Failure to Meet Customer Requirements • Exceeding Customer Requirements • Lost Opportunities

8. LINKING QUALITY COSTS WITH THE THREE R'S

Regardless of the way in which the costs of quality are defined and categorised, the real task for management is to measure each of these costs and to evaluate their effectiveness in returning a benefit to the company. A firm spends time and money on service quality in order to secure a long-term profitable relationship with its customers. But at what juncture does a firm escalate its level of service to the point where the return is just not there? Once costs of quality have been measured, it will be necessary to associate them with one of the three R's of marketing, which represent the goals of service quality initiatives.

Within the service sector, prevention costs can be considerable and generally relate to the human resources area: time spent on recruiting, hiring, and training personnel to recognise what it is that customers are demanding, and how best to meet these needs the first time so that resources are not wasted on redelivery. It is often the front-line personnel who must deal with the "moments of truth" for each customer, and whose judgment can have a critical impact on the establishment of a relationship and the likelihood that the customer will be retained, to the point of becoming loyal and ultimately lucrative for the firm. However, if these empowered employees do not have the support of a system that will help them to gauge the future potential of a customer, they may fall into the trap of "giving away the shop". The costs and benefits of empowering employees are discussed later in this book (Bowen and Lawler, Chapter 10). It is not enough to provide employees with information concerning the "value" of a particular customer; the employees' compensation and performance appraisal scheme should be such that individual employees are made accountable for how they treat the customers. It is incumbent on management to design such systems effectively because:

> [S]uccessful service managers pay attention to the factors that drive profitability in this new service paradigm: investment in people, technology that supports front-line workers, revamped recruiting and training practices, and compensation linked to performance at every level" (Heskett, Jones, Loveman, Sasser, and Schlesinger, 1994).

Heskett discusses this matter further in the final chapter of this book (Heskett, Chapter 16).

Appraisal costs incurred in the delivery of services are not nearly as extensive as in the manufacturing phase where a tangible product can be evaluated against specified criteria before it is delivered to the customer. This stage of assessment is not always possible with the provision of services, considering their intangibility, non-standardised delivery, the inseparability of production and consumption (Gummesson, 1991), and the diverse and evolving expectation levels of recipients. As discussed in the first chapter of this book:

> Unlike tangible goods, one hundred per cent quality cannot be engineered into a service, especially when even the definition of the service is in the eyes of the beholder (Fisk, Brown and Bitner, 1993, Chapter 1).

There are, however, some opportunities to evaluate whether there was adherence to the standards of performance established at the prevention stage, and if not, to utilise the opportunity to correct the error before it is evaluated by the consumer. For example, in the hotel industry, appraisal activities would include checking the status of guest rooms, banquet facilities, and conference centres to ensure they have been prepared in accordance with customer specifications and that they conform to the service level associated with the hotel (Bohan and Horney, 1991). Prevention and appraisal costs would be incurred to satisfy the service quality objectives of building and retaining relationships.

Failure costs clearly relate to the recovery stage, the premiums paid for not getting it right the first time. Remuneration can take the form of direct cash outlays, as in the situation where an airline passenger is offered £100 to compensate for the delay in delivering mislaid luggage, or it could be in the form of a foregone revenue if the compensation involves a discount on the next purchased flight. The other relevant cost is the time it takes personnel to correct the error and deliver the requisite apologies. Although the time involved may be extensive, its value is not often measured and factored into the cost of service.

9. MEASURING AND ALLOCATING COSTS

Although much time has been spent in defining and categorising the costs of service quality, the real value for practitioners comes in managing the costs. Before any cost can be managed, it must first be measured and then evaluated against meaningful criteria. Measurement is usually confined to monetary costs that are easily allocatable to individual customers or market segments. As can be seen in the Service Quality Costs Model below, these represent a minor portion of a firm's costs.

Within the context of services, many costs are non-monetary in nature. Their magnitude in terms of sheer size and ability to influence future benefits dictates that they be analysed. As Lovelock points out in Chapter 8 of this book, three key cost variables that are often ignored are: the cost of constant recruiting, hiring, and training, the lower productivity of inexperienced new workers, and the costs of constantly attracting new customers. Yet these components have been overlooked in traditional cost accounting systems which find their roots in the manufacturing sector. It is possible, however, to develop surrogate measures for non-monetary items, and this is exactly what is being done under progressive management accounting techniques where non-financial measures are supplementing traditional financial measures in evaluating performance.

TABLE 7.3: SERVICE QUALITY COSTS MODEL

Allocatability/Type of Cost	Monetary	Non-Monetary
Allocatable	• Discounts • Samples • Direct Remuneration	• Time Spent with Customers • Service Quality Efforts (specific)
Not Allocatable	• Training • Recruiting • Manager's Time Coaching Employees and Providing Feedback • Excessive Compensation	• Service Quality Efforts (general) • Motivation • Lost Goodwill • Aggravation or Grief

Once costs have been measured, what then? Is it possible to allocate them in some systematic and rational manner so as to allow for meaningful interpretations and decision-making? The desire to do this has led to the evolution of activity-based costing (ABC) which traces costs to activities instead of to products and services produced, thus providing a more accurate and correct picture of the cost consumption. "ABC is useful for management to find (i) hidden profits, and (ii) hidden losses in relationships with customers". In service firms this process is complicated by the importance of professional labour costs, the magnitude of overhead, and the difficulty of linking costs with specific services (Hussain and Kock, 1994). Although activity-based costing may not be ideal for the assessment of service quality ventures, it does serve some function. It points to the need for a system that incorporates both financial and non-financial measures, links costs with benefits, and evaluates this connection against some pre-established benchmark. Any technique used to allocate costs should be based on cause and effect; arbitrary allocations will only confuse things further, and may in fact lead to erroneous decisions concerning which relationships to build and protect, and which customers to retain.

10. MANAGERIAL IMPLICATIONS

This chapter has identified the benefits associated with building a loyal customer base, and has recognised that these benefits are optimised through the retention of a quality share of customers. It has been argued that competing on the basis of loyalty requires an understanding of the relationships between customer retention and the rest of the business, and being able to quantify the links between loyalty and corporate profits. It is the view of the authors of this chapter that there could be five stages of advancement in valuing a customer relationship, as shown in the Stages of Customer Valuation Model below (Table 7.6). These five stages would involve linking various components of a company's Total Customer Benefits Model (Table 7.4) with elements of the Service Quality Costs Model (Table 7.5). The result would be the estimation of a value, or relative worth, of a particular customer to the firm. Recognition of the fact that not all customers are the same in terms of potential profitability to the organisation would allow management and other employees to discriminate among customers in the tailoring of service offerings. This process would be inappropriate for those companies that cannot perform such calculations either because they deal with anonymous customers, or because they do not have an information system to support such decisions. The foundation of the proposed information system lies in the ability to capture information pertinent to the customers' consumption patterns, estimate related benefits from the customer, allocate relevant costs, and use that information to discriminate among customers. The problem for an organisation that deals primarily with anonymous customers, such as fast-food restaurants and convenience stores, is that they cannot economically capture pertinent customer information because they deal with customers who establish no accounts and engage in transactions which leave no records. Even if information were available as to the customers' purchasing patterns, the business is such that there is very little room for variation in the service offering. The objective of the customer valuation process is to offer employees guidance on how to deal with customers. Therefore, such a system would not be appropriate for small firms where owner/managers have an intimate knowledge of all clients and would gain little information that could supplement what they already know about the customers.

TABLE 7.4: TOTAL CUSTOMER BENEFITS MODEL

Allocatability/Type of Benefit	Monetary	Non-Monetary
Allocatable	A1	A3
Not Allocatable	A2	A4

TABLE 7.5: SERVICE QUALITY COSTS MODEL

Allocatability/Type of Cost	Monetary	Non-Monetary
Allocatable	B1	B3
Not Allocatable	B2	B4

TABLE 7.6: STAGES OF CUSTOMER VALUATION

Stage	Formula	Customer Valuation Criteria
Val 1	A1	Monetary allocatable revenues only
Val 2	A1-B1	Monetary allocatable revenues less monetary allocatable costs
Val 3	A1+A2-B1	All monetary revenues less monetary allocatable costs
Val 4	(A1+A2)-(B1+B2)	All monetary revenues less all monetary costs
Val 5	(A1+A2+A3+A4)-(B1+B2+B3+B4)	All revenues less all costs: a full-cost analysis that incorporates monetary and non-monetary components whether or not they have traditionally been allocated

Many organisations that attempt to evaluate the importance of a customer operate at the "Val 1" stage; assessment is on the basis of historic sales generated directly from that customer. This preoccupation with revenues is encouraged by employee compensation schemes tied to revenues. No attempt is made to gauge the cost of serving the customer. This may prove to be harmful in that some customers will consume inordinate amounts of employee time, a key asset in the service sector.

Some more progressive firms recognise that there are certain monetary costs that can easily be traced to an individual customer, and these organisations operate at the "Val 2" stage. Information systems in financial institutions make it quite easy for a bank to determine how much a customer contributed through interest revenue and service charges, and what that customer received in interest paid on deposits.

This analysis is still constrained by the boundaries of monetary measurement.

At the "Val 3" stage, the value of a customer or market segment would be based on all monetary revenues, less all monetary allocatable costs. Because customers' purchasing patterns and expectations change over time, it is important to know not only what our experience has been with the customer, but also what we can realistically expect from that customer in the future. At the "Val 3" stage, consideration will be given to projected as well as historic revenues and benefits. Recognising that future revenues associated with a loyal customer can be significant, especially when the customer's disposable income is projected to increase dramatically over their career, many financial institutions actively recruit students early in their professional careers so as to capitalise on increases in wealth and levels of spending. It has been shown that if a "... credit card customer leaves after the first year, the company takes a $21 loss. If the company can keep the customer for four more years, his or her value to the company rises sharply. It is equal to the net present value of the profit streams in the first five years, or about $100" (Reichheld and Sasser, 1990).

Before advancing beyond the "Val 3" stage, management should group customers in categories that might, for example, range from an "A" customer, who represents the maximum in profit potential, to a "D" customer who offers the least potential profit, or who may actually be cutting into a company's earnings. These categories, or *relationship indices*, would serve to rank customers in terms of their relative worth to the firm. The relationship indices could provide guidance on appropriate levels of service to be offered, and could also serve as the basis for further analysis. For customers in the "A" and "B" categories, and possibly even the "C" categories, it would be worthwhile to collect and analyse more information relating to the customer. For customers in category "D", the potential profit is either so small or non-existent that it would be inefficient to consume more resources rating the worth of that individual.

The "Val 4" stage would establish a customer value after deducting from all monetary revenues all monetary costs, even those not traditionally allocated to specific customer segments. In order for this information to be meaningful, the allocation procedure must not be done on some arbitrary basis. There must be some cause-and-effect rationale for the allocation exercise. It has been established that significant costs incurred in the delivery of services are those related to the human resource area: prevention and appraisal costs. By their very nature, these are not directly attributable to a specific revenue-generating activity, and would therefore be ignored if customer valuation is only taken to the third level. Yet these expenditures are probably among the most critical to the success of service ventures. Failure to invest in training and human resource development may mean that the opportunity to retain the customer will never present itself: the customer will be lost before becoming loyal. Yet there exists a danger of overspending on prevention costs, or performing the little extras that do not represent a "value-added" activity for the customer. There must exist some mechanism for evaluating the pay-back from such endeavours.

The "Val 5" stage involves a full-cost analysis that incorporates all monetary and non-monetary costs and benefits. The information system in service-oriented firms could be expanded to deal with the full range of benefits secured through a healthy relationship with a customer. The objective is to link revenues with the appropriate customer or market segment, and to match costs with their related revenues, in some systematic and rational manner. The decision to supplement traditional evaluation schemes with measures for benefits and costs traditionally captured in non-monetary terms will require something of a leap of faith by management, who have typically based decisions on financial measures and personal judgment. Some non-monetary benefits that can return significant value to the firm include customer satisfaction, customer loyalty and goodwill, and corporate image. Significant costs often not quantified in monetary terms include time spent with customers, service quality efforts, and aggravation. Non-financial indicators are essential for identification of the causes of customer satisfaction, not just the effects. These point to yet another weakness of current accounting systems:

> Profit measures show the effects of non-financial activities and achievements: they do not pin down precisely what it is in your business that you are getting right or wrong (Singleton-Green, 1993).

Non-financials represent a performance appraisal by what might arguably be the most important stakeholder — the customer. Ignoring non-monetary benefits may mean that a company will cease expending effort on an individual when that person is, in fact, a source of considerable referral revenue to the company.

The installation of sophisticated systems, motivated by the link between loyal customers and profits, has been shown to have a positive impact for Banc One, in the United States, which now

> ... conducts quarterly measures of customer retention; the number of services used by each customer, or *depth of relationship*; and the level

of customer satisfaction. The strategies derived from this information help explain why Banc One has achieved a return on assets more than double that of its competitors in recent years (Heskett, Jones, Loveman, Sasser and Schlesinger, 1994).

Once surrogate measures are established for all categories of benefits and costs, what then? How do we evaluate the results? Numbers, even those based on non-financial measures, have to be interpreted with care. The degree of service to be provided could be based on the appropriate relationship index which may differ depending on the stage of valuation. At the monetary levels, "Val 1" through "Val 3", a customer may rate as a "C" customer, but once non-monetary factors are considered, that customer may move up the relationship continuum towards a "B" rating. Judgment must still factor into the decision: we are not dealing in absolutes.

This is not to suggest that all accounting systems should be replaced by integrated schemes of surrogate measures and complicated allocation formulas. Obviously, there is a cost to developing, implementing, and monitoring any information system. Management must not lose sight of what it is that they are trying to accomplish: *segmentation of customers so as to tailor the level of service to that which is expected and that which is likely to enhance profits through the retention of loyal customers.* The objective will be to determine a value at one of the five stages of customer valuation. For some customer segments, or even some organisations, it may not be economical to proceed all the way to the "Val 5" stage, but operating at the "Val 1" stage offers management little concrete information upon which to base decisions concerning investments in service quality. Decisions as to the appropriate service offering would have to factor in changes in customers' expectation levels, competitive offerings, and a given customer's history and profitability with the firm. The quality of service would correspond to the customer's classification on the relationship index. A category "A" customer would receive the optimum level of service because that person is deemed to have more long-term profit potential for the company than a customer in another relationship category.

The concept of value evolving over time is familiar to marketing practitioners. Just as the product life cycle depicts the sales volume and profit over the life of a product, and differs from product to product, so too will the shape of a *customer life cycle* change according to the type of relationship secured and the particular market segment evaluated. It is envisaged that the customer life cycle curve will be S-shaped, with losses incurred by the company as it builds a relationship with a customer. The situation should become profitable as the relationship matures. The key will be to avoid unnecessary retention and recovery efforts that would position the firm at the down-turn of the customer life cycle curve. A detailed information system could alert management to changes in a customer's purchasing pattern that may indicate movement along the customer life cycle. Professional judgment will still be required to determine which relationships should be allowed to dissolve, and which ones should be maintained, and at what levels of service. The role of the customer valuation system will be to provide employees at various levels of an organisation with the same sense of customer worth that managers have. It would then be incumbent on employees to take a proactive role in adjusting the levels of service provided to customers.

11. CONCLUSION

This chapter has recognised that not all customers are equal. Some customers are here to do business in a "once-off" fashion; they will switch loyalties to the next best deal that comes along. However, a large number of customers can become loyal customers if they are treated properly. Firms must give customers a reason to do business with them. Value for customers often comes in the form of quality initiatives which carry with them significant costs. The key to optimum profit is to manage these costs carefully and to direct efforts towards those customers who can return a positive net benefit over an extended time frame. This would require a radical expansion of current cost accounting information. Surrogate measures would have to be established for non-financial items, and a meaningful allocation process would have to be established. This would enable the monitoring of a customer's value over time according to a relationship index. Armed with detailed information, management and front-line employees would be able to decide more effectively which relationships should be harvested so as to optimise the value of the company.

REFERENCES

Anderson, Eugene W., Claes Fornell and Donald R. Lehmann, "Economic Consequences of Providing Quality and Customer Satisfaction", *Marketing Science Institute Working Paper*, 93–112, 1993, p. 6.

Armitage, Howard M., "Quality Pays", *CGA Magazine*, Vol. 26, No. 1, 1993, pp. 30–37.

Barnes, James G., and Judith A. Cumby, "The Cost of Quality in Service-Oriented Companies: Making Better Customer Service Decisions Through

Improved Cost Information", in *Organizational and Regional Restructuring*, Proceedings of the 23rd Annual Conference of the Atlantic Schools of Business, Saint John, New Brunswick, Canada, (November) 1993, pp. 241–50.

Barnes, James G., and William J. Glynn, "The Customer Wants Service, Why Technology is No Longer Enough", *Journal of Marketing Management*, Vol. 9, No. 1, 1993, pp. 43–53.

Bohan, George P., and Nicholas F. Horney, "Pinpointing the Real Cost of Quality in a Service Company", *National Productivity Review*, Vol. 10, No. 3, 1991, pp. 309–17.

Booth, Rupert, "Activity Analysis and Cost Leadership", *Management Accounting — London*, Vol. 70, No. 6, 1992, pp. 30–32.

Carr, Lawrence P., "Applying Cost of Quality to a Service Business", *Sloan Management Review*, Vol. 33, No. 4, 1992, pp. 72–7.

Carr, Lawrence, and Thomas Tyson, "Planning Quality Cost Expenditures", *Management Accounting*, Vol. 74, No. 4, 1992, pp. 52–6.

Coyle, Kevin P., "Achieving a Sustainable Service Advantage", *Journal of Business Strategy*, Vol. 14, No. 1, 1993, pp. 3–10.

Coyne, Kevin, "Beyond Service Fads — Meaningful Strategies for the Real World", *Sloan Management Review*, Vol. 30, No. 4, 1989, pp. 69–76.

Cronin, J.J., and S.A. Taylor, "Measuring Service Quality - A Reexamination And Extension", *Journal of Marketing*, Vol. 56, No. 3, 1992, pp. 55–68.

Dale, Barrie G., and James J. Plunkett, *Quality Costing*, Chapman and Hall, London, 1991.

Develin, Nick, and Max Hand, "Total Quality: Accounting for Human Behaviour", *Management Accounting*, Vol. 71, No. 7, 1993, pp. 39–40.

Fay, Christopher J., "Royalties From Loyalties", *Journal of Business Strategy*, Vol. 15, No. 2, 1994, pp. 47–51.

Feigenbaum, A.V., *Total Quality Control*, McGraw-Hill Book Company, Inc., New York, 1961.

Fisk, Raymond P., Stephen W. Brown and Mary Jo Bitner, "Tracking the Evolution of the Services Marketing Literature", *Journal of Retailing*, Vol. 69, No. 1, 1993, pp. 61–103.

Grönroos, Christian, "Relationship Approach to Marketing in Service Contexts: The Marketing and Organizational Behavior Interface", *Journal of Business Research*, Vol. 20, 1990, pp. 3–11.

Grönroos, Christian, "Facing the Challenge of Service Competition: Costs of Bad Service", in Ton van der Wiele and Joanna G. Timmers (Eds.), Proceedings of the *Workshop on Quality Management in Services*, European Institute for Advanced Studies in Management, Brussels, Belgium, 16–17 May, 1991, pp. 288–301.

Gummesson, Evert, "Truths and Myths in Service Quality", *Journal for Quality and Participation*, Vol. 14, No. 4, 1991, pp. 28–33.

Gummesson, Evert, "Relationship Marketing: A New Way of Doing Business", *European Business Report*, Vol. 20, Autumn, 1993, pp. 52–6.

Harrington, H. James, *Business Process Improvement: The Breakthrough Strategy For Total Quality, Productivity, and Competitiveness*, McGraw-Hill, Inc., New York, 1991.

Hart, Christopher W.L., James L. Heskett and W. Earl Sasser, Jr., "The Profitable Art of Service Recovery", *Harvard Business Review*, July/August, 1990, pp. 148–56.

Heskett, James L., Thomas O. Jones, Gary W. Loveman, W. Earl Sasser Jr., and Leonard A. Schlesinger, "Putting the Service-Profit Chain to Work", *Harvard Business Review*, March/April, 1994, pp. 164–74.

Hussain, Md. Mostaque and Sören Kock, "Activity-Based Costing in Service Management", in *Quality Management in Services II*, Van Gorcum, Assen/Maastricht, The Netherlands, 1994.

Jenkins, Kevin J., "Service Quality in the Skies", *Business Quarterly*, Vol. 57, No. 2, 1992, pp. 13–18.

Liswood, Laura A., "A New System for Rating Service Quality", *The Journal of Business Strategy*, Vol. 10, No. 4, 1989, pp. 42–5.

Morse, Wayne F., "A Handle on Quality Costs", *CMA Magazine*, Vol. 67, No. 1, 1993, pp. 21–4.

Myer, Randy, "Suppliers — Manage Your Customers", *Harvard Business Review*, November/December, 1989, pp. 160–68.

Plunkett, J.J., and B.G. Dale, "A Review of the Literature on Quality-Related Costs", *International Journal of Quality and Reliability Management*, Vol. 4, No. 1, 1987, pp. 40–52.

Quinlan, Michael R., "How Does Service Drive the Service Company?" (letter), *Harvard Business Review*, November/December, 1991, pp. 146–50.

Reichheld, Frederick F., and W. Earl Sasser, Jr., "Zero Defections: Quality Comes to Services", *Harvard Business Review*, September/October 1990, pp. 105–11.

Reichheld, Frederick F., "Loyalty-Based Management", *Harvard Business Review*, March/April, 1993, pp. 64–73.

Rust, Roland T., and Anthony J. Zahorik, "Customer Satisfaction, Customer Retention, and Market Share", *Journal of Retailing*, Vol. 69, No. 2, 1993, pp. 193–215.

Shaffer, James C., "Quality Where it Doesn't Count", *Across the Board*, Vol. 29, No. 10, 1992, pp. 11–12.

Shapiro, Benson P., V. Kasturi Rangan, Rowland T. Moriarity and Elliot B. Ross, "Manage Customers for Profits (not just sales)", *Harvard Business Review*, September/October, 1987, pp. 101–108.

Singleton-Green, Brian, "If It Matters, Measure It!", *Accountancy*, Vol. 111, No. 1197, 1993, pp. 52–3.

Slywotzky, Adrian J. and Benson P. Shapiro, "Leveraging to Beat the Odds: The New Marketing Mind-Set", *Harvard Business Review*, September/October 1993, pp. 97–107.

Treacy, Michael, and Fred Wiersema, "Customer Intimacy and Other Value Disciplines", *Harvard Business Review*, January/February, 1993, pp. 84–93.

Youde, Richard K., "Cost-of-Quality Reporting: How We See It", *Management Accounting*, Vol. 72, No. 7, 1992, pp. 34–8.

Youngdahl, William E., and Deborah L. Kellogg, "Customer Costs of Service Quality: A Critical Incident Study", in Teresa A. Swartz, David E. Bowen, and Stephen W. Brown (Eds.), *Advances in Services Marketing and Management, Vol. 3.*, JAI Press Ltd., Greenwich, CT, 1994, pp. 149–73.

Zemke, Ronald, "Cost of Quality: Yes, You Can Measure It", *Training*, Vol. 27, No. 8, 1990, pp. 62–3.

8

MANAGING SERVICES:
The Human Factor

Christopher H. Lovelock
Lovelock Associates
Massachusetts, USA

PRÉCIS

In this chapter Christopher Lovelock examines the management of personnel working to provide a service. His focus is on those employees who have a high degree of contact with service customers. Drawing on a "system view" of service management, Lovelock contends that in service management the operations, marketing and human resource functions are inextricably intertwined. This means that the handling of a series of human resource policy concerns has major repercussions beyond HRM itself. The core HRM policy concerns identified are: hiring, training, job design and employee involvement/empowerment. The main challenge facing human resource management in services is to handle these areas effectively in the case of relatively junior "front-stage" personnel, as this becomes the key to ensuring consistency of service quality across transactions. Human resource management in services must focus on both technical and behavioural dimensions of service excellence. This affects recruitment strategies, training possibilities, priorities in job design, and it should also be the basis for employee empowerment. Lovelock explores how "virtuous cycles", "vicious cycles" and "cycles of mediocrity" can set in in service management, involving different dynamics linking modes of human resource management with customer perceptions and service performance.

William K. Roche
University College Dublin, Ireland

1. INTRODUCTION

Almost everybody can recount some horror story of a dreadful experience they have had with a service business — and usually, they love to talk about it! If pressed, many of these same individuals can also recount a really good service experience, too. In most instances, service personnel will play prominent roles in such dramas — either as un-caring, incompetent, mean-spirited villains or as individuals who went out of their way to anticipate customer needs, behaving in a helpful and empathetic manner, and proving highly effective in solving any prob-lems or special requests. The human factor in services basically involves two groups of players: employees and customers. Both groups need to be managed, although this chapter focuses on employees, leaving the issue of managing customers to other authors. By way of illustration and to inject an element of the real world, examples and short case histories have been provided from a variety of industries, notably airlines, retail banking, telecommunications, health care, and entertainment.

The field of human resource management (HRM) is potentially a vast one — although the literature on the HRM-customer service link is surprisingly limited (Schneider, 1994). Key HRM elements include not only recruiting, selecting, training, managing and motivating employees, but also such associated activities as pay and benefits administration, job design, labour relations, and union negotiations. Further extension within the field of organisational behaviour includes human behaviour in organisations and organisation design. Clearly, it is not possible to cover all of these topics in a single chapter.

Even a more limited focus on HRM practices within effective orga-nisations would be a daunting task. For example, Pfeffer (1994) high-lights no fewer than 16 such practices for managing people, culled from both academic and popular sources and applicable to both manufactur-ing and service businesses. Grouped by category, the first 15 are: long-term perspective, selectivity in recruiting, employment security, and promotion from within; high wages, incentive pay, and employee ownership; information sharing, participation and empowerment, teams and job redesign; training and skill development, cross utilisation and cross training; symbolic egalitarianism and wage compression; and then measurement of the impact of HRM efforts. The final factor is an over-arching philosophy that "not only provides a way of connecting the various individual practices into a coherent whole [but] also permits people in the organisation to persist and experiment when things don't work out well" (Pfeffer, 1994).

Rather than attempt such a wide-ranging review, this chapter examines a subset of HRM issues that have particular relevance for managing the most distinctive type of service employees — those whose jobs entail extensive contact with customers. The coverage begins with a systems view of service management, in which marketing, operations, and human resource management are seen as interdependent functions. Interactions between these three functions are at their most pronounced in the case of high-contact services, posing special challenges in job design, recruitment, and training. Further challenges and opportunities result from the need to re-engineer traditional jobs to take advantage of advances in information technology and telecommunications.

Since there can be advantages to customers as well as to the firm from creating positive attitudes and long-term relationships, HRM specialists need to understand the vicious cycles that lead to high turnover and/or unresponsive service in high contact services. Breaking out of these cycles and creating a "cycle of success" may require a holistic approach to management that involves reworking the sociology of the workplace to empower employees and increase their levels of involvement and discretion. These are, of course, an integral part of implementing a total quality management programme. The topic of quality is discussed elsewhere in this book (Parasuraman, Chapter 6).

Finally, this chapter looks briefly at some of the challenges involved in managing human resources in a multicultural environment, illustrating this topic with a case example from Euro Disney. The chapter concludes with suggestions for future research.

2. WHERE DO PEOPLE FIT IN SERVICE PROCESSES?

2.1. A Trinity of Management Functions

In a service company or non-profit institution, three management functions play a central and interrelated role: marketing, operations, and human resources. The interdependence of these three functions, first conceptualised by Langeard et al. (1981), actually grew out of Eiglier and Langeard's (1977) "servuction" systems model of how services are created and delivered. This interdependence between functions has encouraged researchers in the field of service management to cross functional boundaries, leading both marketing and operations specialists to involve themselves in human resource issues to a degree that would have been unthinkable when the study of management was dominated by a manufacturing mind-set. In fact, as Vandermerwe (1993) points out, getting away from an industrial model in which labour is seen as a "cost" to a new model in which employees are seen as partners and contributors has been a central theme of the service management literature.

Specialists in operations management have long recognised that customer involvement in operating systems is one of the key factors distinguishing service processes from manufacturing ones (Sasser et al, 1977; Fitzsimmons and Sullivan, 1982). Writing from a marketing perspective, Gummesson (1979, 1991) has emphasised that the work of the marketing department embraces only a small fraction of the overall marketing function in a service business — a distinction also underlined by Grönroos (1980, 1991). In a manufacturing firm, by contrast, the marketing department controls most marketing activities. Similarly, specialists in organisational behaviour and human resource management have found themselves actively involved with marketing and operations issues that relate to their field (Bowen and Schneider, 1985; Chase and Tansik, 1983). None of this is likely to surprise most line managers in service businesses, since much of their work involves juggling the sometimes conflicting demands of these three functions.

2.2. Service as a System

As shown in Lovelock's (1994) extension of the Eiglier and Langeard servuction model, any service business represents a system, comprising service operations — where inputs are processed and the elements of the service product are created — and service delivery, where final "assembly" of these elements takes place and the product is delivered to the customer (see Figure 8.1). Parts of this system are visible (or otherwise apparent) to customers; other parts are hidden from view in what is sometimes called the technical core, and the customer may not even know of their existence. As Figure 8.1 makes clear, there are many possible opportunities for customers to interact with service personnel — not only during delivery of the core service, but also through a variety of other contact points, ranging from market research surveys to sales calls and from phone conversations to billing and payment.

Customer contact with service providers takes place at two levels. The first level concerns delivery of the core product — which can be either a physical item or a service — that the customer is purchasing. The second level concerns what may be termed the peripheral or supplementary services that surround that core (Eiglier and Langeard, 1977). A wide array of supplementary services are offered by manufacturers, service firms and service intermediaries to facilitate purchase transactions and add value to the core product itself; these supplementary elements may serve as important points of brand differentiation when the core is close to a commodity. Lovelock (1992, 1994) has categorised them into eight clusters:

- Information

- Consultation
- Order-taking
- Hospitality
- Care-taking
- Exceptions
- Billing
- Payment.

In a small business, one person may both deliver the core product and provide all the supplementary services offered to customers. As the scale of the operation increases, there is often a separation between delivery of core and supplementary services as well as a degree of specialisation between provision of the many different supplementary services. Even where the core product is low contact, some of these supplementary activities may involve a higher degree of contact.

Consider, for instance, a guest's experience in using a hotel. Either the hotel chain's own reservation centre or an independent intermediary (travel agent) may deliver such pre-arrival supplementary services as providing information and advice ("consultation") as well as handling room reservation ("order-taking"). On arrival at the hotel, valets may help with baggage and park the guest's car ("caretaking"), while a receptionist checks in the guest and provides further information about the hotel. A carefully trained concierge may be on hand to deal with problems and special requests ("exceptions"), while restaurant servers and room service personnel will be in charge of meals and bar service ("hospitality"). On leaving, a guest may have the option of getting the bill from a cashier and paying it immediately or using an express check-out system. However, responsibility for the core service — preparing the room and making up the bed is in the hands of the housekeeping staff, whose contact with guests may be limited to a polite greeting when passing in the corridor.

Each interaction is what Normann has called a "moment of truth, when the service provider and service customer confront one another in the arena" (Normann, 1984, 1991). The management challenge in such instances is to ensure consistency of quality (and sometimes, style) across the array of different interactions. Carlzon (1987) centred his turnaround of Scandinavian Airlines System (SAS) on this philosophy. Most customer contact with service employees involves relatively low-level personnel, not managers. Corporate customers may fare a little better in getting to deal with senior officers, but the route to the executive office still tends to be via parking lot attendants, security guards, receptionists and executive assistants. To the extent that service experiences depend heavily on the performance of relatively junior front-stage personnel, it makes sense to think very carefully about how they are recruited, trained, and motivated.

2.3. How the Nature of the Service Affects the Extent of Customer–Employee Contact

Chase (1978) argues that services can be arrayed along a continuum from "high contact" to "low contact" according to the extent of the customer's physical presence within the service system. The greater the customer contact with the system, the greater the likelihood that customers will be dealing directly with service personnel. This contact creates a fundamental distinction between the jobs of front-line service workers and those of the workers in the back offices of service firms or in manufacturing plants. Chase and Tansik (1983) note that customer-contact employees are engaged in a three-way interaction between themselves, customers, and the relevant production process or technology, as opposed to the two-way interaction that prevails between factory workers and technology. There is, of course, another category of employee who engages in a three-way interaction to provide internal services, often supporting — in the back office — the efforts of front-line colleagues who are serving the customer directly. (For a discussion of so-called "internal marketing" activities see Gilmore and Carson, Chapter 11.)

Customer contact has traditionally taken place primarily through face-to-face encounters. Increasingly, however, contacts are taking place through the medium of the telephone, creating new challenges for HRM specialists. Finally, certain services that were formerly delivered by employees may now be delivered through self-service machines, thus replacing employees altogether, except for those responsible for dealing with machine malfunctions and related customer problems.

3. THE SPECIAL CASE OF HIGH-CONTACT SERVICE ENCOUNTERS

In what types of services are customers most likely to encounter a high degree of contact with service employees (and vice versa)? The nature of the service process tends to shape the extent to which customers need to be involved in the service system and, by extension, their contact with employees. Rather than talking loosely about managing "the human factor in services" as though all services were more or less alike, it should be clarified that service management tasks are likely to vary from one process to another and that the impact of new operational technologies may be felt more keenly in certain service jobs than in others. The "core" product that a business offers will be considered first.

A useful way of categorising services from the standpoint of human interactions is to consider what is being processed and whether the nature of these processes is tangible or intangible (Lovelock, 1983). Two broad categories of things are processed in services: people and objects. In many cases, ranging from passenger transportation to education, customers themselves are the principal input to the service process; in other instances, the key input is an object like a computer in need of repair, or a piece of financial data. And what about the nature of the process? In some services, as in all manufacturing, the process is physical: something tangible takes place. But in information-based services, the process can be intangible.

By looking at services in this way from a purely operational perspective, we see that they can be categorised into four broad groups, with significantly different implications for the nature and extent of the contacts between customers and service personnel (Table 8.1). Only one of these four categories — what might be termed "people processing", actually requires face-to-face contact between customers and the service system. In each of the other categories, such contact is largely optional, reflecting tradition, preferences, and the existing design of operational processes. Consequently, the percentage of all employees engaged in serving customers tends to be highest in people-processing businesses, with important implications for the culture of the organisation. Although we still find employees in possession-processing and information-based businesses who have high-contact jobs — that is, jobs in which a high proportion of the employees' time is spent in customer contact, advances in telecommunications technology are stimulating a long-term trend away from physical contact with customers to arm's length transactions. So, when examining HRM practices in service businesses, we need to draw a distinction between managing face-to-face contacts and managing telephone contacts. In both instances, the task of managing those employees will continue to be different from that of managing employees in the "back office".

3.1. People as Part of the Product

The more involved customers become in the service delivery process, the more they tend to encounter service personnel (and often fellow customers, too). As a result, other people become part of any customer's service experience.

TABLE 8.1:
UNDERSTANDING THE NATURE OF THE SERVICE ACT

What is the Nature of the Service Act?	Who or What is the Direct Recipient of the Service?	
	People	*Possessions*
Tangible Actions	**Services directed at people's bodies, e.g.** 　　Passenger Transportation 　　Health Care 　　Lodging 　　Beauty Salons 　　Restaurants/Bars 　　Haircutting	**Services directed at physical possessions, e.g.** 　　Repair and Maintenance 　　Warehousing/Storage 　　Janitorial Services 　　Laundry/Dry Cleaning 　　Landscaping/Lawn-care 　　Freight Transportation
	High levels of interaction between customers and service personnel are often necessary throughout service delivery, especially in "high service" contexts.	*Personal contact between customers and service personnel may not be necessary (or limited to initiating and concluding a transaction).*
Intangible Actions	**Services directed at people's minds, e.g.** 　　Entertainment 　　Management Consulting 　　Education 　　Psychotherapy 　　Religion 　　Voice Telephone	**Services directed at intangible assets, e.g.** 　　Accounting 　　Banking 　　Data Processing 　　Insurance 　　Legal Services 　　Securities Investment
	Personal contact can be replaced by broadcasting or telecommunications in many instances. One-way communications can be recorded for later replay.	*Many interactions with service personnel can be replaced by self-service and other personal contacts handled by telecommunications.*

Customer contact personnel have an important operational responsibility in terms of helping to "manufacture" the service output. At the same time, they may also be responsible for marketing it (for example, "We've got some nice desserts to follow your main course" or "We could clean your machine at the same time that we repair the motor" or "Now would be a good time to open a separate account to save for your children's education"). In the eyes of their customers, service personnel may also be seen as an integral part of the service experience. As Berry and

Parasuraman put it: "For most services, the server cannot be separated from the service" (Berry and Parasuraman, 1991). In short, the service person may perform a triple role as operations specialist, marketer, and part of the service product itself (Lovelock, 1981). This multiplicity of roles — known as boundary spanning, may lead to role conflict among service employees, especially when they feel as physically and psychologically close to customers as they do to their managers and other employees (Bowen and Schneider, 1985).

The people factor in services complicates management's task, since it means that customers may be evaluating the quality of employees' appearance and social skills as well as their technical skills. Customers are also making judgments about other customers. Businesses involving extensive service encounters tend to be harder to manage than those without such encounters, because of the human element. And consistent execution becomes that much harder to achieve, thereby complicating the task of those responsible for quality improvement efforts.

Many firms now recognise what a few have always known: that nurturing the skills and motivation of their people can create a source of competitive advantage — not least when there is a high degree of contact between employees and customers. Sadly, as Pfeffer (1994) notes, many firms do little more than pay lip service to this notion. Hal Rosenbluth (1992), owner of a chain of successful travel agencies, argues in his book, *The Customer Comes Second*, that a company's first focus should be on its employees: "Only when people know what it feels like to be first in someone else's eyes can they sincerely share that feeling with others" (p. 25).

Tansik (1990) lists several special characteristics that may be important for high-contact employees. These include interpersonal skills, appearance, selling capabilities, and skills in co-production (that is, working jointly with customers to create the desired service). Additional characteristics, particularly valuable in selling situations, include monitoring non-verbal clues (such as the customer's body language), and adjusting one's behaviour in the context of social situations. "Both technical and interpersonal skills are necessary but neither alone is sufficient for optimal job performance" (Tansik, 1990).

3.2. The Dramaturgy Analogy

As Shakespeare wrote in *Henry V*:

> All the world's a stage and all the men and women merely players.
> They have their exits and their entrances and each man in his time plays
> many parts.

The stage is, in fact, a good metaphor for services and can provide useful insights for service managers (Grove and Fisk, 1983; Grove, Fisk and Bitner, 1992). What is being offered to customers, after all, is typically a performance rather than a thing. Alternatively, it may consist of a performance around some physical object (such as the serving of a restaurant meal). Some service dramas are tightly scripted and highly ritualised; others are improvisational. Customer contact personnel are members of a cast, playing roles as actors in a drama, and supported by a backstage production team. In some instances, they are expected to wear special costumes when on stage (uniforms supplied by management) or to conform to grooming standards and a dress code. Depending on their work, they may be required to learn and repeat specific lines, ranging from a basic telephone greeting to a sales message, or from recitation of government-mandated safety information to a trite parting salutation such as "Have a nice day!"

Actors need training, coaching, and direction. So do employees. Elocution and voice control can be taught (use of the voice is especially important for service personnel who make public announcements and deal with customers by telephone). Scripting often prescribes actors' behaviour as well as their lines. Eye contact, smiles, and handshakes may be required in addition to a spoken greeting. Other rules of conduct may include bans on smoking, drinking, or chewing gum while on duty. In highly ritualised services, such as serving in a restaurant, "blocking" may prescribe how the actors should move relative to the stage, items of scenery, and other actors. Telecommunication links offer an alternative performance environment, allowing customers to be involved in the drama from a remote location, much as in radio or TV theatre.

Some people use the terms "front office" and "back office" in referring to the visible and invisible parts of the operation. Others, notably the Walt Disney Company, talk about "on stage" (or "front stage") and "backstage" (see Figure 8.1). The theatrical analogy implies performance rather than administration and bureaucracy. It also suggests that employees should be selected with reference to the roles that they will be playing. The visible components of the service operations system can be divided into those relating to the actors (or service personnel) and those relating to the stage set (or physical facilities and equipment). As with live theatre audiences, customers may sometimes be called upon to be active participants, rather than passive observers.

What goes on backstage is of little interest to most customers. Like any audience, they evaluate the production with reference to their experiences during service delivery and, of course, to the perceived service outcome. Nevertheless, if backstage workers fail to perform their support tasks properly, the impact will quickly be felt by audience members — either in individual service encounters or as part of a broader group experience. For instance, an individual diner at a restaurant may find that menu items are not available — because someone forgot to go to the fish market that morning — or that food is overcooked — because the ovens were not adjusted properly. All patrons might be aware of a backstage failure if smoke were to start pouring out of the kitchen and they were forced to leave the building. Users of repair services may experience delays in getting their equipment back if technicians don't report for work or spare parts are out of stock. And hotel guests may be awakened early by banging as thoughtless maintenance personnel start work on repairs to the heating system.

FIGURE 8.1:
THE CUSTOMER'S VIEW OF THE SERVICE ORGANISATION

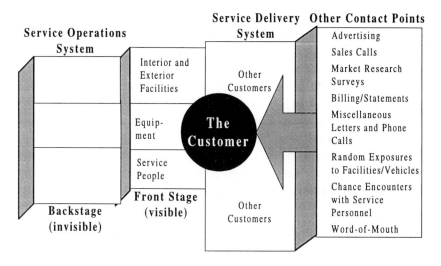

Source: Lovelock, 1994, p. 91.

The theatrical analogy has its limits (like any analogy), but it's worth thinking about how good directors get great performances. The task starts with casting: recruiting the right actors for specific roles — a topic we shall return to later. An important point to note is that performers sometimes depend on technical props, ranging from a magician's box of tricks to a musician's instrument or a singer's microphone. Without the right props, in good working order, they simply cannot give a high quality performance. Service workers are often in the same situation: There are limits to their ability to perform well without the tools of their trade, and to their ability to please customers when they must contend with poor working conditions and inferior or improperly maintained equipment. Understanding employee needs in this respect is vital.

3.3. Emotional Labour

Service encounters entail more than just correct technical execution of a task. They also involve such human elements as personal demeanour, courtesy, and empathy. This brings us to the notion of emotional labour, defined by Hochschild (1983) as *the act of expressing socially desired emotions during service transactions*. Hochschild notes that attempting to conform to customer expectations on such dimensions can prove to be a psychological burden for some service workers who perceive themselves as having to act out emotions they do not feel.

Ashforth and Humphrey (1993) have refined Hochschild's concept. They argue that service providers are expected to comply with required norms of expression — so-called "display rules" — through surface acting, deep acting, and the expression of spontaneous and genuine emotion. Display rules, they state, generally reflect the norms imposed not only by society, but also those of given occupations and organisations. For instance, the expectations of nurses are different from those of bill collectors. Expectations may also be situation-specific.

Surface acting involves simulating an emotion that one does not actually feel, accomplished by careful presentation of verbal and non-verbal cues, such as facial expression, gestures, and voice tone — skills that may be innate or learned. Deep acting, by contrast, involves trying to psyche oneself into experiencing the emotion that one wishes to display.

> Just as the performances of professional actors vary in quality so too does the quality of emotional labour vary across service providers and across service episodes for a given service provider (Ashforth and Humphrey, 1993).

Finally, service providers may spontaneously experience the expected emotion without any need for acting, as when a nurse feels sympathy for an injured child.

The concept of emotional labour has important implications for human resource managers, who need to be aware that performing such labour, day after day, can be stressful for employees as they strive to display towards customers emotions that they do not feel. However, failure to display the expected emotions can be damaging from a marketing standpoint. The challenge is to determine what customers expect, and then to recruit the most appropriate employees and train them well.

4. JOB DESIGN AND RECRUITMENT

The goal of job design is to study the requirements of the operation, the nature of customer desires, the needs and capabilities of employees, and the characteristics of operational equipment in order to develop job descriptions that strike the best balance between these sometimes conflicting demands.

Many of the most demanding jobs in service businesses are so-called boundary-spanning positions, where employees are expected to be fast and efficient at executing operational tasks, as well as courteous and helpful in dealing with customers. Bateson (1985) sees service encounters as potentially "a three-cornered fight" between the needs of partially conflicting parties: the customer, the server, and the service firm. If the job is not designed carefully, or the wrong people are picked to fill it, there's a real risk that employees may become stressed and unproductive.

There has been much discussion in recent years of the importance of empowering employees to use their own discretion to serve customers better. This literature is also reviewed elsewhere in this book (Bowen and Lawler, Chapter 10). Job designs should reflect the fact that service personnel may encounter customer requests for assistance in remote sites at any hour of the day and night. Providing employees with greater discretion (and training them to use their judgment) may enable them to provide superior service without referring to rule books or higher authority.

4.1. Recruiting the Right People for the Job

There's no such thing as the perfect, universal employee. First, some service jobs require prior qualifications, as opposed to giving employees the necessary training after they are hired. A nurse can apply for a job as a hotel receptionist, but the reverse is not true unless the applicant has nursing qualifications. Second, different positions — even within the same firm — are best filled by people with different styles and personalities. It helps to have an outgoing personality in many front-stage jobs that involve constantly meeting new customers; a shy, retiring person, by contrast, might be more comfortable working backstage and always dealing with the same people. Someone who loves to be physically on the go might do better serving in a restaurant or as a courier than in a more sedentary job as a reservation agent or bank teller. Finally, as Levering and Moskowitz (1993) stress:

> No company is perfect for everyone. This may be especially true in good places to work since these firms tend to have real character ... their own culture. Companies with distinctive personalities tend to attract — and repel — certain types of individuals.

Recruitment criteria should reflect the human dimensions of the job as well as the technical requirements. This brings us back to the notions of emotional labour and service as theatre. The Walt Disney Company, which is in the entertainment business, actually uses the term casting and assesses prospective employees in terms of their potential for on-stage or backstage work. On-stage workers, known as cast members, are assigned to those roles for which their appearance, personalities, and skills provide the best match.

4.2. Who Must be Hired *v.* What Can be Taught

As part of its turnaround efforts in the early 1980s, British Airways started paying more attention to its passengers' concerns and opinions. When research findings showed that travellers desired warmer, friendlier service from flight attendants, the airline first tried to develop these characteristics through training, But human resource managers soon concluded that while good manners and the need to smile could be taught, warmth itself could not. So the airline changed its recruitment criteria to favour candidates with naturally warm personalities (Lovelock, 1994). It has also changed its recruitment advertising to capture the challenges of the work, instead of emphasising the glamour of travel. For instance, a recent ad shows a drawing of a small child sitting in an airline seat and clutching a teddy bear. The headline reads: "His mother told him never to talk to strangers. So what's he having for dinner?"

In a study of 14 outstanding service performers, Fromm and Schlesinger (1994) observe:

> [W]hat makes these people so special are things that cannot be taught, qualities that are intrinsic to the people, qualities they would bring with them to any employer.... Energy ... cannot be taught, it has to be hired. The same is true for charm, for detail orientation, for work ethic, for neatness. Some of these things can be enhanced with on-the-job training ... or incentives.... But by and large, such qualities are instilled early on (pp. 315–6).

The logical conclusion is that service businesses which are dependent on the human qualities of their front-line service personnel should devote great care to attracting and hiring the right candidates.

Southwest Airlines, a very successful short-haul carrier in the US, believes that the selection process starts not with the candidate but with the individuals responsible for recruiting (Lovelock, 1994). Everyone hired in recent years to work in the airline's People Department — Southwest doesn't use the terms "human resources" or "personnel" — has come from a marketing or customer-contact background. "In order to continue the culture", remarked Ann Rhoades, the airline's vice president–people, "we decided that we had to hire people who really, really thought about marketing to internal and external customers." This marketing orientation is displayed in internal research on job descriptions and selection criteria, whereby each department is asked: "What are you looking for?" rather than told: "This is what we think you need!" Southwest invites supervisors and peers (with whom future candidates will be working) to participate in the in-depth interviewing and selection process. More unusually, it invites its own frequent flyers to participate in the initial interviews for flight attendants and to tell candidates what they value. The People Department admits to being amazed at the enthusiasm with which busy customers have greeted this invitation and at their willingness to devote time to this task.

4.3. Challenges and Opportunities in Recruiting Workers for Technology-Based Jobs

It used to be thought that only manufacturing jobs could be exported. Today, however, technology allows both backstage and front-stage service jobs to be located around the world. American insurance companies, for instance, have recruited workers in Ireland to process claims. Paperwork is flown in daily from the US and digitised information transmitted back to mainframe computers on the other side of the Atlantic (because of the five-hour time difference, the Irish are using those mainframes at times when they would normally be under-utilised).

Barbados, Jamaica, Singapore, India, and the Philippines are emerging as other potential English-speaking locations for telecommunications services, not only for backstage work but also for such front-stage supplementary services as airline reservations and technical helplines. Customers may be quite unaware of where the service person they are talking to is located. The key issue is that they deal with people who have the personal and technical skills — plus the enabling technological support — to provide high quality service.

Expert systems can be used to apply employees' skills to perform work that previously required higher qualifications, more extensive training, or simply years of experience. Some systems are designed to train novices by gradually enabling them to perform at higher levels. Sisodia (1992) notes:

> Many expert systems capture and make available to all the scarce expertise of outstanding performers. American Express uses a well-known expert system called Authoriser's Assistant (originally called Laura's Brain, after a star authoriser), which contains the expertise of its best credit authorisers. It has improved the quality and speed of credit decisions dramatically, and contributed enormously to corporate profitability.

An expert system contains three elements: a knowledge base about a particular subject; an inference engine that mimics a human expert's reasoning in order to draw conclusions from facts and figures, solve problems, and answer questions; and a user interface that gathers information from — and gives it to — the person using the system. Like human experts, such systems can give customised advice and may accept and handle incomplete and uncertain data.

Rapid developments in information technology are permitting service businesses to make radical improvements in business processes and even to re-engineer their operations completely (Davenport, 1993; Hammer and Champy, 1993; Quinn, 1992). These developments have resulted in sometimes traumatic changes for existing employees. In other instances, firms have redefined jobs, created new employee profiles for recruitment purposes, and sought to hire new employees.

4.4. Case Example: New Software Redefines Skill Needs at Singapore Airlines

Normally, it takes three weeks to train a check-in agent for an international airline. Much of the training centres on correct use of the computer terminals employed to confirm (or make) reservations and assign seats. Older reservations systems need to be literally programmed by the agents, who require a certain amount of technical skill to perform this time-consuming task.

Recently, Singapore Airlines (SIA) was having trouble in recruiting and retaining check-in agents for its home base at Singapore's Changi Airport (Vandermerwe and Lovelock, 1991). With wages rising in this island nation, it was getting harder to recruit people with the necessary skills at the wages SIA was willing to offer. And once they were on the job, many agents found it rather unchallenging. The predictable result: relatively high turnover and constant repetition of the expensive recruitment and training process. As part of a major programme to update its departure control systems, SIA computer specialists worked to create new software for check-in procedures, featuring screen formats with pull-down windows, menu-driven commands, and other innovations on the video terminal displays — all designed to speed and simplify usage. The net result is that SIA has been able to lower the educational criteria for the check-in position. The job is now open to people who would not previously have qualified and who consider the work and the wages fairly attractive. Because the new system is so much easier to use, only one week's training is needed — a significant saving to SIA. Employee satisfaction with this job is up, and turnover is down. Finally, agents are able to process passengers faster, making the former more productive and the latter happier.

4.5. Case Example: Recruiting Employees Who Work by Phone at BT

A growing number of customer-contact employees work by telephone, never meeting customers face to face. As with other types of service work, these jobs can be very rewarding or they can place employees in what Garson (1988) has called "the electronic sweatshop". Recruiting people with the right skills and personalities, training them well, and giving them a decent working environment are some of the keys to success in this area.

BT (formerly British Telecom) is not only a major supplier of telecommunication services, but also an active user of its own medium, the telephone, for managing relationships with its business accounts (Bliss and Lovelock, 1992). Like a growing number of firms that do business by phone, it is very dependent for its success on recruiting and retaining employees who are good at telephone-based transactions with customers whom they never see. Executives responsible for BT's telephone account management (TAM) operation, serving small business customers, are highly selective in their recruitment efforts. They look for bright, self-confident people who can be trained to listen to customers' needs and use structured, probing questions to build a database of information on each of the 1,000 accounts for which an account manager is responsible.

BT begins its recruitment process with a telephone interview, to see if candidates have the poise, maturity, and speaking voice to project themselves well and inspire trust in a telephone-based job. (Curiously, most recruiters of telephone-based employees leave this all-important telephone test until much later in the process.) Those who pass this screen proceed to written tests and personal interviews. The selection process concludes with psychometric scaling of each candidate.

Successful candidates receive intensive training. BT has built special training schools to create a consistent approach to customer care. Would-be account managers receive 13 weeks of training over a 12-month period, interspersed with live front-line experience at their home bases. They must develop in-depth knowledge of all the services and customer-premises equipment that BT sells, as well as the skills needed to build relationships with customers and to understand their business needs. Modern telecommunications technology is bewildering, for so much is changing so rapidly. Customers need a trusted advisor to act as consultant and problem-solver. And it is this role that BT's TAM programme has succeeded in filling. For all the impressive supporting technology, the programme would fail without good people at the other end of the phone line.

4.6. Case Study: Job Design and Recruitment in Firstdirect's Re-engineered Bank Environment

Firstdirect has gained prominence as the world's first, all telephone bank, operating 24 hours a day, 365 days a year. Launched in the UK in 1989, it represents a total re-engineering of traditional banking concepts, substituting telephone and post for the face-to-face customer contacts of the usual retail banking environment. In designing the new bank (legally a division of Midland Bank), managers had to enable a single telephone link to replace the functions normally delivered by five or six employees in different departments. Moreover, as one officer put it, "We had to be able to respond in seconds, not minutes — normal banking procedures simply did not apply. We had to create a workable system that would be the servant, not the master, of those who would be using it. It had to be a high performance system that was both flexible and easy to use. To the maximum possible extent, customer transactions, questions, and problems had to be handled within a single phone call."

From an employee standpoint, providing banking services by telephone was seen as a very different job from traditional branch office positions. The average bank cashier working in a branch has to be something of a jack-of-all-trades, handling large quantities of cash, working with both a computer terminal and paper-based transactions, and spending most of the day in face-to-face contact with customers. Customers with specialised banking requirements have to be directed to an enquiry desk. Telephone banking would be very different, Firstdirect management concluded. There would be no need for someone who was great at counting out stacks of bank notes, examining customer deposit slips, or spotting forged signatures in the front office. Since normal banking methods just didn't apply, neither would normal banking job descriptions.

"Banking representatives" — as Firstdirect decided to call its front-line employees — would need strong communication capabilities and excellent listening skills. These skills would be more important than banking experience. Neither customers nor banking representatives (BRs) would see each other, let alone know the other person, so it was all the more vital to create trust and confidence. BRs would have to sound friendly and well-informed over the phone, and be able to access and input data accurately and efficiently. Speed would be important, not only to achieve productivity goals but also to meet customers' expectations of prompt service. However, a customer must not feel unduly rushed.

Hiring criteria stressed maturity; Firstdirect would not employ school-leavers since they lacked good telephone presence. What recruiters looked for was confident people with a positive attitude who could project themselves well over the phone and convey a sense of energy. "If you're not putting that over," remarked one human resource manager, "you're lost!" Strong listening skills were seen as particularly important, because customers wanted reassurance that their needs were understood, particularly when seeking advice as to what type of service would best meet their own situations. Finally, recruiters were looking for systematic, well-organised people who could work together in teams.

Successful applicants receive six weeks intensive training, three of which are classroom-based. Topics include product knowledge, relevant banking procedures, and technical skills in using the equipment and understanding the screens — the different displays that appear on the monitors. New recruits also learn personal skills to help them to develop effective telephone techniques. Voice control involves the development of physical skills in pitch, tone, and authority. After all, telephone-based personnel are like actors in a radio drama who never see their customers — everything from friendliness to competence must be conveyed through the voice. And, finally, they learn customer development skills, such as spotting potential opportunities to sell new services. In this task, they are aided by the computer, which prompts for certain products based on analysis of that customer's characteristics.

All employees currently work in a single industrial building in Leeds, sharing 100,000 square feet (9,300 square metres) of space, with an additional 80,000 square feet under construction at a nearby site.

Although Firstdirect employees never see their customers, everyone is smartly dressed. There's no one here in sweaters and jeans. "We want to maintain a sense of professionalism," explains the director of operations. On the other hand, professionalism does not mean stuffiness. The building is open plan, with just low partitions to muffle the sound of numerous conversations. The mood is friendly and democratic, with everyone — from BR to chief executive — on first name terms. That's quite a contrast to traditional banking culture, especially in Britain. When taking calls, employees are seated in stations that handle a cluster of four people. These clusters, in turn, are grouped into teams of around a dozen people for the purpose of mutual support, mentoring, and competition with other teams. The floor is divided into different areas of specialisation, with teams working in areas such as customer service, financial services and lending, mortgages, investment services, Visa credit cards, and foreign services.

Although employees cannot see customers entering the system, as they might in a branch, call volumes are carefully monitored to minimise delays and ensure adequate staffing. Large electronic screens on the wall display current performance levels. The goal is to answer 80 per cent of calls within 20 seconds or less. The screens display for all to see the percentage of calls meeting that time goal during the past five minutes, together with the number of customers currently waiting to speak with someone in that group. If waits start to rise significantly, co-ordinators will summon all available personnel to staff the phones, even if this means recalling people from the cafeteria.

About 85 per cent of calls (20,000 a day in late 1993) can be handled by BRs; most calls last between two and six minutes. More specialised needs are referred to one of the other groups. In a nice touch, customers are told how long they may expect to wait on the line to speak with someone in another group, asked whether they wish to hold or be called back later, and — if they elect to hold — given a choice between listening to recorded music or simple silence.

5. SERVICE JOBS AS RELATIONSHIPS

Marketing theory argues that successful relationships are built on mutually satisfying exchanges in which both customers and suppliers gain value from their mutual transactions (Kotler, 1972). This same notion of value can be applied to any employee who has a choice of whether or not to work for a particular organisation (and the best employees usually do have opportunities to move on, if dissatisfied). The net value of a job is the extent to which its benefits exceed its associated costs. When discussing such benefits, the first things that come to mind are pay, health insurance, and pension funding. However, most jobs also generate other benefits. Some offer learning or experience-building opportunities; some positions provide deep satisfaction because they are inherently interesting or provide a sense of accomplishment; still others provide companionship, a valued chance to meet other people, feelings of dignity and self-worth, opportunities to travel, and the chance to make a social contribution.

However, working in any job has its costs, too, beginning with the time spent on the job and travelling to and from work. Most jobs also entail some monetary costs, ranging from special clothes to commuting to child-care. Stress can be a psychological and physical cost in a demanding job. Unpleasant working conditions may involve exposure to noise, smells and temperature extremes. And, of course, some jobs require intense physical or mental effort. Decisions to change the nature of the service operation frequently affect employees, too. The perceived value of their jobs may go up or down as a result. But not everybody has the same priorities and concerns — there is segmentation among employees as well as among customers. Part of the human resources challenge is to match round pegs to round holes of the right diameter.

Front-stage service jobs add another dimension: frequent customer contact — sometimes but not always involving extended relationships with the same customers. Depending on the employee's personality, such encounters may be seen in the abstract as a benefit to enjoy or a cost to be borne. In reality, good training, good support, and satisfied customers should increase the pleasure (or diminish the pain), while the reverse will also be true.

Job design cannot be restricted to ensuring that the firm gets its money's worth out of employees. It must also consider the design of the working environment, asking whether employees have the tools and facilities they need to deliver excellent service. Shrewd human resource managers know that if a job is changed through redesign, then it will become more or less attractive to certain types of employees — and they can usually predict which ones. To an increasing degree, health and safety legislation is requiring changes in the workplace to eliminate physical and even psychological hazards, but only management can create a positive working climate — and that takes a long time. Reducing the negative aspects of the job and improving its positive ones may make it easier for firms to hire and retain the best available employees, without having to pay premium salaries and load up on conventional "benefits". Employees who enjoy their work are more likely than unhappy ones to give good service to customers.

5.1. Employee Relationships and Customer Relationships

Schneider and other researchers (Schneider, 1994) have found strong correlations between employees' attitudes and perceptions of service quality among customers of the same organisation. In a retail banking study, Schneider, Parkington and Buxton (1980) showed that when employees reported a service imperative in their bank branch, customers reported that they received higher quality service. In a subsequent replication, Schneider and Bowen (1985) also found that customer intentions to switch to a competitor could be predicted, based on employee perceptions of the quality of service delivered. These two researchers also found that employee turnover probabilities were predictable, based on customer perceptions of service quality: Simply put, where customers reported high service quality, employees were less likely to leave. A reasonable inference is that it is not very rewarding to work in an environment where service is poor and customers dissatisfied. Schneider (1994) also cites a study, focusing on a truck rental service business, which found that higher levels of employee satisfaction were related to both lower turnover and lower workers' compensation claims.

Businesses with high employee turnover are frequently stuck in what Schlesinger and Heskett (1990) call the "Cycle of Failure". When jobs are low-paid, boring, and repetitive, with minimal training, service is poor and turnover high. Poor service generates high customer turnover, too, making the working environment even less rewarding. As a result, the firm spends all its resources trying to recruit both new customers and new employees. Loyal employees, by contrast, know the job and, in many cases, the customers too. To the extent that long-term employees are customer-oriented, knowledgeable, and remain motivated, better service and higher customer retention should result. Although there is conflicting evidence on the correlation between business profitability and positive attitudes among employees and customers (Schneider, 1991), researchers have been able to quantify the economic value of customer retention (see, for example, Reichheld and Sasser, 1990).

Now attention is turning to quantifying the value of employee retention (Reichheld, 1993; Fromm and Schlesinger, 1994). "Many companies," says Reichheld, "diminish their economic potential through human resource strategies that ensure high employee turnover, in part because they can't quantify the economics of retaining employees". The same logic applies to independent contractors, like insurance agents. He attributes the ongoing success of State Farm Insurance Companies in the US to the interactive effect of both customer and agent retention. According to industry studies, State Farm's customer retention rate exceeds 90 per cent, consistently the best performance of all national insurers selling through agents. At the same time, more than 80 per cent of newly appointed agents remain associated exclusively with State Farm through their fourth year, compared with only 20–40 per cent for other companies in the industry. Further, the average State Farm agent has 18 years of tenure compared to between six and nine years for competitors.

The underlying synergy at State Farm arises from the fact that agents who are committed to building a long-term relationship with the company are more likely to build lasting relationships with customers, too. In turn, it's easier for agents to work with (and sell to) loyal customers whose needs, lifestyles, and attitudes to risk they know well. "Agents' experience plus the fact that they spend more time servicing and selling to proven customers, raises agents' productivity to 50 per cent above industry norms (Reichheld, 1993).

5.2. Cycles of Failure, Mediocrity, and Success

Levering and Moskowitz (1993), long-time researchers of the quality of work life, claim that "most companies still offer dreadful work environments". The problem is that, all too often, such situations translate into dreadful service, with employees treating customers the way their managers treat them. Schlesinger and Heskett (1991) write of the potential for both vicious and virtuous cycles in service employment.

5.2.1 The Cycle of Failure

In many service industries the search for productivity is on with a vengeance. One solution is to simplify work routines and hire workers as cheaply as possible to perform repetitive work tasks that require little or no training. Schlesinger and Heskett's cycle of failure captures the potential implications of such a strategy. There are actually two concentric but interactive cycles: one involving failures with employees; the second, with customers (Figure 8.2a).

The *employee cycle of failure* begins with a narrow design of jobs to accommodate low skill levels, emphasis on rules rather than service, and use of technology to control quality. The design of fast-food kitchens has long been cited — both admiringly and despairingly — as an example of using technology to channel human behaviour in a service setting (although it's really a quasi-manufacturing operation). A strategy of low wages is accompanied by minimal effort on selection or training.

Consequences include bored employees who lack the ability to respond to customer problems, become dissatisfied, and develop a poor service attitude. Outcomes for the firm are low service quality and high employee turnover. Because of weak profit margins, the cycle repeats

itself with hiring of more low-paid employees to work in this unrewarding atmosphere.

FIGURE 8.2(a): THE CYCLE OF FAILURE

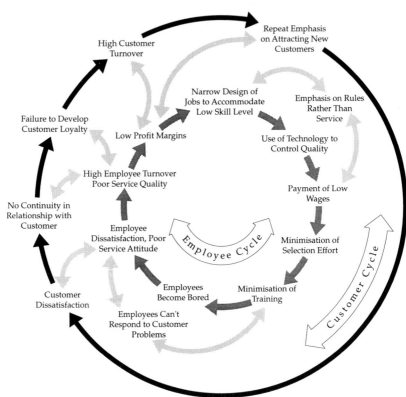

Source: Schlesinger and Heskett, 1991.
© 1991 *The Sloan Management Review* Association.

The *customer cycle of failure* begins with repeated emphasis on
attracting new customers who, becoming dissatisfied with employee
performance and the lack of continuity implicit in continually changing
faces, fail to develop any loyalty to the supplier and turn over as rapidly
as the staff, thus requiring an ongoing search for new customers to
maintain sales volume. This churn of discontented customers is
especially worrying in the light of what we now know about the greater
profitability of a loyal customer base. For managers of conscience, the
social implications of an enormous pool of nomadic service employees

moving from one low-paying employer to the next, experiencing a stream of personal failures with employers who are unwilling to invest in efforts to break the cycle, must surely be deeply disturbing.

Schlesinger and Heskett (1991) report hearing a veritable litany of excuses and justifications for perpetuating this cycle:

- "You just can't get good people nowadays."

- "People just don't want to work today."

- "To get good people would cost too much and you can't pass on these cost increases to customers."

- "It's not worth training our front-line people when they leave you so quickly."

- "High turnover is simply an inevitable part of our business. You've got to learn to live with it."

Too many managers are making short-sighted assumptions about the financial implications of low-pay/high turnover human resource strategies. Part of the problem is failure to measure all relevant costs. Often omitted are three key cost variables: the cost of constant recruiting, hiring, and training (which is as much a time cost for managers as a financial cost), the lower productivity of inexperienced new workers, and the costs of constantly attracting new customers (requiring extensive advertising and promotional discounts). Also ignored are two revenue variables: future revenue streams that might have continued for years but are lost when unhappy customers take their business elsewhere; and potential income from prospective customers who are turned off by negative word of mouth. Finally, Whiteley (1991) adds two less easily quantifiable costs: disruptions to service while a job remains unfilled, and loss of the departing person's knowledge of the business (and its customers).

5.2.2   The Cycle of Mediocrity

There is another vicious employment cycle, not discussed by Schlesinger and Heskett, but still a powerfully negative factor in creating both poor service and unrewarding working experiences. Here it is called the *Cycle of Mediocrity* (Figure 8.2b). This cycle is most likely to be found in large, bureaucratic organisations often typified by state monopolies, industrial cartels, or regulated oligopolies — where there is little incentive to improve performance and where fear of entrenched unions may discourage management from adopting more innovative labour practices.

FIGURE 8.2(b): THE CYCLE OF MEDIOCRITY

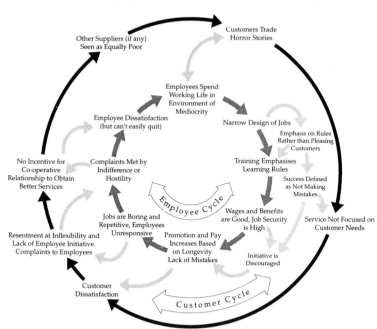

Source: © 1995 Christopher H. Lovelock.

In such an environment, service delivery standards tend to be prescribed by rigid rule-books, oriented toward standardised service, operational efficiencies, and prevention of either employee fraud or favouritism toward specific customers. Further rigidity may be imposed by union work rules. Employees often expect to spend their entire working lives with the organisation. Job responsibilities tend to be narrowly and unimaginatively defined, tightly categorised by grade and scope of responsibilities, and further rigidified by union work-rules. Salary increases and promotions are based on longevity, with successful performance in a job being defined in terms of not making mistakes, rather than on high productivity or outstanding service to customers. Training, such as it is, focuses on learning the rules and the technical aspects of the job, not on improving human interactions with customers and co-workers. Since there are minimal allowances for flexibility or employee initiative, jobs tend to be boring and repetitive. However, in contrast to cycle-of-failure jobs, most positions provide adequate pay and often good benefits, combined with high security — thus making employees reluctant to leave. This lack of mobility is compounded by absence of marketable skills that would be valued by organisations in other fields of endeavour.

Customers find such organisations frustrating to deal with. Faced with bureaucratic hassles, lack of service flexibility, and unwillingness of employees to make an effort to serve them better on grounds such as "That's not my job", users of the service may become resentful. However, there is often nowhere else to take their business — either because the service provider has a monopoly, or because all other available players are perceived as being as bad or worse. We can hypothesise that under such circumstances, dissatisfied customers may increasingly display hostility toward service employees who, feeling trapped in their jobs and powerless to improve the situation, will then protect themselves through such mechanisms as withdrawal into indifference, playing overtly by the rule-book, or countering rudeness with rudeness. The net result: a vicious cycle of mediocrity in which unhappy customers continually complain to sullen employees (and also to other customers) about poor service and bad attitudes, generating ever greater defensiveness and lack of caring on the part of the staff. Under such circumstances, there is little incentive for customers to co-operate with the organisation to achieve better service.

5.2.3 The Cycle of Success

Some firms reject the assumptions underlying the cycles of failure or mediocrity. Instead, they take a long-term view of financial performance. Schlesinger and Heskett cite service firms that have prospered by investing in people to create a *Cycle of Success* (Figure 8.2c). Their examples come from banking (Wells Fargo and Fidelity Bank of Philadelphia), maintenance, food and janitorial services (ServiceMaster), and quick-service restaurants (Au Bon Pain).

As with failure or mediocrity, success applies both to employees and to customers. Broadened job designs are accompanied by training and empowerment practices that allow front-stage personnel to control quality. With more focused recruitment, more intensive training, and better wages, employees are likely to be happier in their work and to provide higher quality, customer-pleasing service. Regular customers also appreciate the continuity in service relationships resulting from lower turnover, and so are more likely to remain loyal. Profit margins tend to be higher, and the organisation is free to focus its marketing efforts on reinforcing customer loyalty through customer retention strategies, which are usually much less costly to implement than strategies for attracting new customers.

FIGURE 8.2(c): THE CYCLE OF SUCCESS

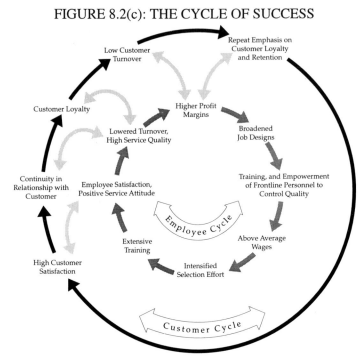

Source: Schlesinger and Heskett, 1991.
© 1991 *The Sloan Management Review* Association.

At the same time, deregulation, privatisation, opening up of new competition, and more inspired leadership of public agencies have also been instrumental in extricating organisations from the cycle of mediocrity. Both British Airways and BT provide striking examples of once mediocre public corporations which have undergone radical culture changes in the wake of privatisation and exposure to a more competitive environment. A slimming down of the ranks (usually resulting in retention of the more dynamic and service-oriented employees), redefinition of performance criteria, intensive training, and major reorganisation have created service firms that are much better placed to offer customers good service.

6. EMPOWERMENT OF EMPLOYEES AND THE SOCIOLOGY OF THE WORKPLACE

In recent years, the concept of empowering service workers has been advocated with almost religious fervour, often in the context of total quality management. From a humanistic standpoint, the notion of encouraging employees to exercise initiative and discretion is an appealing one. Empowerment looks to the performer of the task to find solutions to service problems and to make appropriate decisions about customising service delivery. It depends for its success on what is sometimes called enablement — giving workers the tools and resources that they need to take on these new responsibilities.

Advocates claim that the empowerment approach is more likely to yield motivated employees and satisfied customers than the "production-line" alternative, in which management designs a relatively standardised system and expects workers to execute tasks within narrow guidelines. But is the choice between these two approaches really so obvious?

Bowen and Lawler (Chapter 10) suggest that different situations may require different solutions, declaring that the key is to choose the management approach that best meets the needs of both employees and customers. But payoffs from greater empowerment, they note, must be set against increased costs for selection and training, higher labour costs, slower service (as customer-contact personnel devote more time to individual customers), and less consistency in service delivery. They also warn against being seduced into too great a focus on recovery, at the expense of service delivery reliability, noting that it is possible to confuse good service with inspiring stories about empowered employees excelling at the art of recovery.

The production-line approach to managing employees is based upon the well-established "control" model of organisation design and management, with its clearly defined roles, top-down control systems, hierarchical pyramid structure, and assumption that management knows best. Empowerment, by contrast, is based upon the "involvement" (or "commitment") model, which assumes that most employees can make good decisions — and produce good ideas for operating the business — if they are properly socialised, trained, and informed. It also assumes that employees can be internally motivated to perform effectively and that they are capable of self-control and self-direction. Although broad use of the term "empowerment" is relatively new, the underlying philosophy of employee involvement is not. In the US, for instance, the concept of participatory management known as the Scanlon Plan was created during the 1930s, and subsequently adopted by a number of manufacturing firms. Its originator, Joseph Scanlon, was a steelworker and union leader who believed that within a given company, the employer, the workers and the unions shared a common interest in its success (Beer et al., 1985).

In the control model, four key features are concentrated at the top of the organisation:

1. Information about organisational performance (e.g. operating results and measures of competitive performance)
2. Rewards based on organisational performance (e.g. profit-sharing and stock ownership)
3. Knowledge that enables employees to understand and contribute to organisational performance (e.g. problem-solving skills)
4. Power to make decisions that influence work procedures and organisational direction (e.g. through quality circles and self-managing teams).

In the involvement model, by contrast, these features are pushed down through the organisation.

Bowen and Lawler argue that the empowerment and production-line approaches are at opposite ends of a spectrum that reflects increasing levels of employee involvement as "additional knowledge, information, power, and rewards are pushed down to the front line". Empowerment can take place at several levels. Suggestion involvement empowers employees to make recommendations through formalised programmes, but their day-to-day work activities do not really change. Job involvement represents a dramatic opening up of job content. Jobs are redesigned to allow employees to use a wider array of skills, and this is often accomplished through use of teams. To cope with the added demands accompanying this form of empowerment, employees require training, and supervisors need to be reoriented from directing the group to facilitating its performance in supportive ways. Finally, high involvement gives even their lowest-level employees a sense of involvement in the total organisation's performance. Information is shared. Employees develop skills in teamwork, problem-solving, and business operations, and they participate in work-unit management decisions. There is profit-sharing and employee ownership of stock in the business.

In summary, there's no such thing as a single best way to manage service employees. Instead, human resource managers should be evaluating the nature of the organisation to determine how much empowerment is appropriate. They should also recognise that not all employees are eager to be empowered. Many employees do not seek personal growth within their jobs and may prefer to work to specific directions rather than having to use their own initiative.

6.1. Case Example: Reworking the Sociology of the Workplace at Beth Israel Hospital

Boston's Beth Israel Hospital (BI) is a major teaching hospital affiliated to Harvard Medical School which also serves the local community. At

BI, managers are trying to rework the sociology of the workplace in ways that are appropriate to the complex environment of a caring hospital — rather than introducing somebody else's formulation of "total quality management". As Laura Avakian, BI's vice-president for human resources, points out, such a task cannot be accomplished through a quick fix. "You can't just tell employees: 'Congratulations, you're empowered!'" she declares (Lovelock, 1994). In fact, changing the sociology of the workplace is a slow process which takes years of constant effort. Moreover, it must reflect the culture and values of the institution itself.

In 1986, the BI began creating its own version of the Scanlon Plan, which it calls PREPARE/21 ("Prepare for the 21st Century"). The plan seeks to expand and deepen employee participation, improve quality, and find ways to cut costs. As a non-profit organisation, the hospital cannot offer stock ownership, but employees do share 50 per cent of all cost savings, referred to as "gains". The plan has been in full operation since October, 1989 (Rabkin and Avakian, 1991).

PREPARE/21 includes formalised training, of course. However, much of management's task involves creating the right environment for employees. This, in turn, requires good measurement and communication systems. According to Dr Mitchell T. Rabkin, the hospital's president: "Deming [the quality pioneer] understood the importance of measuring in order to empower employees to know what was going on, thus allowing an employee to recognise before the boss that something was coming unstuck."

The BI has also focused on developing good internal communication systems, including an informal weekly newsletter written by Dr Rabkin. He remarks:

> Knowledge is empowering. When customers and visitors ask, the employees know what is going on and why. They feel they are the hospital, rather than answering "They don't tell me nothing!" If you don't tell them, if they don't know, then distorted rumours start circulating. Worse yet, they feel excluded and not a true part of the hospital. Employees, in general, are well motivated and want to do well. Furthermore, no one knows the job better than individual employees themselves. Therefore, if you create an environment in which they feel comfortable enough, knowledgeable enough, about the business to feel that they own the business in a sense, they will contribute — providing, of course, that their capacity to contribute is enhanced by a responsive upper structure of the organisation (Rabkin and Avakian, 1991).

Rabkin and Avakian are strong believers in the importance of enlightened managers who can coach employees in their use of quality tools and who can engage them in active problem solving. All Beth Israel supervisors participate in an intensive 40-hour leadership development track. One problem that top management has sought to address is that of uneven buy-in to PREPARE/21, particularly by physicians. However, these individuals are becoming more involved as they realise that the hospital's management is not assailing the quality of their care. Rabkin and Avakian note: "Physicians will buy in when we talk about improving quality of care through improving the quality of the systems by which they deliver care."

Although it may take time and effort to persuade existing employees to change their orientation and working habits, there is less of a problem with newcomers. In recruiting new employees, the hospital uses "value-based" interviewing, so that job applicants may be screened for participation and teamwork skills as well as for credentials.

6.2. The Role of Unions

If they are to achieve their full potential, many innovations in human resource management require the co-operation of employees. The power of organised labour is widely cited as an excuse for not adopting new approaches in both service and manufacturing businesses. "We'd never get it past the unions," managers say, wringing their hands and muttering darkly about restrictive work practices. Unions are often portrayed in the media as the "bad guys", especially when high profile strikes inconvenience millions: examples of particularly disruptive industrial disputes range from British, French, and Japanese railway workers to employees of specific American airlines, and from Irish bank personnel to Canadian postal workers.

American managers have a reputation for being especially antagonistic toward unions,. Pfeffer (1994) observes wryly that "the subject of unions and collective bargaining is … one that causes otherwise sensible people to lose their objectivity" and urges a pragmatic approach to this issue (p. 160). He emphasises that "the effects of unions depend very much on what management does" (p. 163). In reviewing numerous studies of the impact of unions (across many US industries), he notes that unions do raise wage levels — especially for low-wage workers — as well as reducing turnover, improving working conditions, and leading to better resolution of grievances. They also have a positive impact on productivity — but only in those companies where both management's and labour's leadership skills are strong. These improvements in productivity, he suggests, may reflect the greater selectivity in recruitment that is possible when jobs pay better and thus attract more candidates, together with the lower turnover often found in unionised firms and the resulting presence of a more experienced workforce. Clearly we are talking about cycles of success here, not cycles of mediocrity!

The United States is a useful site for comparative research on the impact of unions, since firms in the same industry vary widely in the extent of unionisation. Among the 100 best companies to work for in America, Levering and Moskowitz (1993) include 27 that are strongly unionised, including such successful service firms as Alagasco (natural gas distribution), Avis (car rentals), Knight-Ridder (newspaper publishing), Northwestern Mutual Life (insurance), Preston Trucking (freight transportation), Southwest Airlines, and US West (telecommunications).

Perhaps the most striking contrasts in American consumer service businesses are to be found among the airlines. Among the better regarded national carriers, American Airlines is unionised while Delta is not. Management–union confrontations contributed heavily to the collapse of unpopular Eastern Airlines. But compare this situation with that of Southwest Airlines, which is almost 90 per cent unionised yet boasts the lowest costs per mile, highest profits, best on-time performance, best baggage handling, and highest customer satisfaction of any American airline. Commenting on this performance, *Fortune* magazine noted that "None of the airline's achievements would be possible without its unusually good labour-management relations, a direct result of (Southwest chairman) Kelleher's hands-on efforts" (Labich, 1994). Significantly, the one area on which management will not negotiate is work rules. And in sharp contrast with the "cycle of failure" approach to hiring, Southwest devotes enormous effort to recruiting, selecting, and training new employees, as well as to internal transfers and promotions. It is also worth noting that 30 per cent of Southwest employees own 10 per cent of the company's stock.

The inescapable conclusion is that the presence of unions in a service company is not an automatic barrier to high performance and innovation, unless there is a long history of mistrust, acrimonious relationships and confrontation. However, management cannot rule by fiat: consultation and negotiation with union representatives are essential if employees are to buy-in to new ideas (conditions that are equally valid in non-unionised firms, too).

7. HUMAN RESOURCE MANAGEMENT IN A MULTICULTURAL CONTEXT

The trend toward a global economy means that more and more service firms are operating across national frontiers. Two other important trends are increased tourism and business travel, and substantial immigration of people from different cultural backgrounds into developed economies such as those of the US, Canada, Australia, and many European countries. The net result is pressure on service organisations not only to serve a more diverse array of customers, bearing different cultural expectations and perhaps coming from different language backgrounds, but also to recruit a more diverse workforce into what may once have been a culturally homogenous working environment.

Striking a balance between diversity and conformity to common standards is hardly a simple task. Societal norms vary across cultures. For instance, Ashworth and Humphrey (1993) note that when McDonald's opened a fast-food restaurant in Moscow, management trained staff members to smile at customers. However, this particular norm did not exist in Russia and some patrons concluded that staff members were mocking them. Another example of how transferring American standards to European operations may run into cultural conflicts comes from the troubled history of Euro Disney. Part of the challenge is to determine which performance standards are central and which should be treated more flexibly, as exemplified in the willingness of some public service agencies in Britain (and elsewhere) to allow Sikh employees to wear a uniformed turban with badge, whereas others have generated conflict by insisting on the use of traditional uniform caps. Multiculturalism may also impose a requirement for new skills. Thus, the decision to be more responsive to customers (and even employees) whose first language is not English may require changes in recruiting criteria and/or language training (Lovelock, 1994).

7.1. Case Example: Euro Disney and the Challenges of Multiculturalism

Few service ventures of recent years have attracted as much media comment and coverage as the Walt Disney Company's latest venture, Euro Disney, near Paris. Although most of the financial losses stem from real estate problems and low occupancy in the hotels, the cultural difficulties of creating and running Euro Disney, an American-style theme park in the heart of Europe, have been widely publicised. Since Euro Disney replicates three successful Disney theme parks, top management's objective has been to ensure that the park adapts itself to European conditions without losing the American feel that has always been seen as one of its main draws. For Disney officials, Euro Disney represented even more of a challenge than their first foreign theme park, Tokyo Disneyland, which opened in Japan in 1983. Unlike the

California, Florida, or Tokyo parks, no one nationality dominates at Euro Disney. So, handling languages and cultures has required careful planning, not least in terms of employee recruitment, training, and motivation (Lovelock and Morgan, 1994).

Knowledge of two or more languages has been an important criterion in hiring "cast members" (front-line employees). Recruitment centres were set up not only in France, but also in London, Amsterdam, and Frankfurt. During the 1992 season, approximately two-thirds of those hired were French nationals; the balance comprised another 75 nationalities, principally British, Dutch, German, and Irish. Some knowledge of French is required of all employees; in the park's opening year, about 75 per cent of employees spoke French fluently, another 75 per cent spoke English, roughly 25 per cent spoke Spanish and 25 per cent, German.

The reservations centre caters to people of many tongues, with special phone lines for each of 12 different languages. The main information centre in the park, City Hall, is staffed by cast members speaking a broad cross-section of languages. Special procedures have been instituted at the medical centre to handle medical emergencies involving speakers of less commonly encountered languages. With over 70 nationalities represented among its employees, there is a high probability that a cast member can be found somewhere on site to interpret in such a situation. Euro Disney has noted the language capabilities of every employee, can access them by computer (who is on duty who speaks Turkish?), and can page them immediately by beeper or walkie-talkie.

However, Euro Disney has encountered many cultural problems in training and motivation. The company's 1990 Annual Report announced that "a leading priority was to indoctrinate all employees in the Disney service philosophy, in addition to training them in operational policies and procedures". The apparent goal was to transform all employees, 60 per cent of whom were French, into clean-cut, user-friendly, American-style service providers. Since the founding of Disneyland in 1958, Disney has been known for its strict professional guidelines. "The Look Book", for example, dictated that female employees should wear only clear nail polish, very little — if any — make-up, and, until recent years, only flesh-coloured stockings. Men could not wear beards or moustaches and had to keep their hair short and shaped. Guests should be greeted within 60 seconds of entering a facility and helped as needed.

According to media reports, a key challenge has been training the French employees. The park's manager of training and development for Disney University, was quoted as saying: "The French are not known for their hospitality. But Disney is." During the first four months of operations, more than 1,000 employees left. According to management, half quit, and the rest were asked to leave. The women's grooming guidelines were modified because "what is considered a classic beauty in Europe is not considered a classic beauty in America." At Euro Disney, the rules were changed to allow female cast members to wear pink or red nail polish, red lipstick and different coloured stockings as long as they "complement [the] outfit and are in dark, subdued colors".

Another Disney trademark is to smile a lot. Yet as one observer commented, "If the French are asked to smile they will answer 'I'll smile if I want to. Convince me.'" The training had to be adapted in order to suit the European work force. Although Disney stressed total customer satisfaction, in the eyes of some employees the company had imposed controls that had made that goal impossible to deliver.

8. CONCLUSION AND OPPORTUNITIES FOR FUTURE RESEARCH

It is probably harder to duplicate high-performance human assets than any other corporate resource. To the extent that employees understand and support the goals of an organisation, have the skills needed to succeed in performing their jobs, work well together in teams, recognise the importance of ensuring customer satisfaction, and have the authority and self-confidence to use their own initiative in problem solving, the marketing and operational functions should actually be easier to manage.

The study of human resource management (HRM) in service organisations is still a young field. Curiously, it has not attracted the same level of academic attention as has research into the closely-related functions of service operations and service marketing. On the one hand, many human resource management specialists have apparently chosen not to specialise in services as such, as opposed to addressing specific issues across a broader array of organisations. On the other hand, interesting insights and contributions have come from academics who, whatever their original functional background, have elected to undertake cross-functional research involving, *inter alia,* the human side of services. One suspects that much of what is known about HRM in services remains confidential, confined to corporate executives who have conducted internal tests and studies or commissioned proprietary research from consulting firms. Such organisations might be able to advance broader understanding of human resource issues if they were willing to release some of their data for re-analysis by university researchers.

8.1. Suggestions for Future Research Projects

What direction should future academic and other publishable research take? Reflecting the issues discussed in this chapter, nine suggestions are offered below. Research methods might include: controlled experiments (for instance, comparative studies of different sites), surveys of managers, employees, and customers; and case studies of practices in different organisations). Comparative international research would be particularly advantageous, suggesting the need for collaborative efforts between researchers in different countries.

1. *Recruiting Procedures.* What is the economic relationship between investments in recruiting and on-the-job performance? What are key personality criteria (as opposed to technical skills) for performance in specific types of front-stage jobs. What are the most effective recruiting procedures for specific types of jobs and guidelines for how to implement them well?

2. *Economic Impact of Customer and Employee Retention.* There is a need both to replicate past research and to conduct new research into the relationship between (a) employee and customer satisfaction (b) employee and customer retention and (c) the value thereof.

3. *Economic Impact of Training and Reward Systems.* How cost effective is investment in both initial and ongoing employee training? What is its impact on such factors as (a) employee retention, (b) operational productivity, (c) customer satisfaction and retention, and (d) service profitability?

4. *Working with Unions to Achieve High Performance.* Unions are often used as a convenient excuse for not introducing innovative human resource management practices. Yet many successful service firms are, in fact, unionised. What can be learned from a cross-section of such firms in different industries about how to work well with unions to achieve higher standards of service?

5. *Use of Teams in Service Delivery.* What are the different ways in which teams can be used (a) to enhance service delivery and (b) to provide internal support and motivation for both front-stage and backstage employees? Which industries and companies use team-based organisations most effectively?

6. *Telephone-Based Service Employees.* What are the key success factors in recruiting, training and motivating telephone-based employees? What is the personality profile of a successful telephone-based service representative? What are the most effective designs for working conditions? Does absence of direct customer contact lead to

longer or shorter tenure of telephone-based jobs as opposed to similar positions involving face-to-face encounters?

7. *Use of Expert Systems in Service Delivery.* What are the opportunities to gain leverage for employee performance through expert systems in different types of service jobs? Under what circumstances can expert systems enable (a) existing employees to offer more sophisticated service, faster service, or cheaper service, and (b) employees with lower educational skills (or less experience) to meet or exceed established performance levels?

8. *Offering Service in a Multicultural Environment.* How should service firms gear up to recruit, train, motivate, and retain employees from non-traditional cultural backgrounds? What are the success factors in achieving integration of the front-stage service workplace without hurting employee morale, long-term productivity, or customer satisfaction? What are the success factors in providing good service to customers from a variety of cultural/linguistic market segments? Which companies are role models for different types of services?

9. *Key Factors in Transforming Mediocre Work Forces.* What role is played by outside forces — such as competitive threats, technology, privatisation, or deregulation — and what by internal factors such as new leadership, departure of unproductive employees, new approaches to training existing employees, new compensation schemes, and so forth? To what extent is there an interactive effect between several different elements? What can be learned from the experience of companies that have transformed mediocre work forces into high performing ones?

REFERENCES

Ashforth, Blake E. and Ronald W. Humphrey, "Emotional Labor in Service Roles: The Influence of Identity", *Academy of Management Review,* Vol. 18, No. 1, 1993, pp. 88–115.

Bateson, John, "Perceived Control and the Service Encounter", in Czepiel, J.A., M.R. Solomon and C.F. Surprenant, *The Service Encounter,* Lexington Books, Lexington, MA, 1985, pp. 67–82.

Beer, Michael, Bert Spector, Paul R. Lawrence, D. Quinn Mills and Richard E. Walton, *Human Resource Management: A General Manager's Perspective,* The Free Press, New York, 1985.

Bliss, Martin and Christopher H. Lovelock, "BT: Telephone Account Management" (IMD case, 1992), reprinted in S. Vandermerwe and C. Lovelock with

M. Taishoff, *Competing Through Services: Strategy and Implementation,* Prentice-Hall, Hemel Hempstead, UK, 1994.

Bowen, David E. and Benjamin Schneider, "Boundary-Spanning Role Employees and the Service Encounter: Some Guidelines for Management and Research", in J.A. Czepiel, M.R. Solomon, and C.F. Surprenant, *The Service Encounter,* Lexington Books, Lexington, MA, 1985, pp. 127–48.

Carlzon, Jan, *Moments of Truth,* Ballinger Books, Cambridge, MA, 1987.

Chase, Richard B., "Where Does the Customer Fit in a Service Operation?" *Harvard Business Review,* November/December, 1978.

Chase, Richard B. and Tansik, David A. "The Customer Contact Model for Organizational Design", *Management Science,* Vol. 29, 1983, pp. 1037–50.

Davenport, Thomas H., *Process Innovation: Reengineering Work through Information Technology,* Harvard Business School Press, Boston, MA, 1993.

Eiglier, Pierre and Eric Langeard, "Services as Systems: Marketing Implications", in P. Eiglier, E. Langeard, C.H. Lovelock, J.E.G. Bateson and R.F. Young, *Marketing Consumer Services: New Insights,* Marketing Science Institute, Cambridge, MA, 1977, pp. 85–103.

Fitzsimmons, James A., and Robert S. Sullivan, *Service Operations Management,* McGraw-Hill, New York, 1982.

Fromm, Bill and Len Schlesinger, *The Real Heroes of Business,* Currency Doubleday, New York, 1994.

Garson, Barbara, *The Electronic Sweatshop,* Simon and Schuster, New York, 1988.

Grönroos, Christian, "Designing a Long Range Marketing Strategy for Services", *Long Range Planning,* Vol. 13, April, 1980, pp. 36–42.

Grönroos, Christian, *Service Management and Marketing,* Lexington Books, Lexington, MA, 1991.

Grove, Stephen J. and Raymond P. Fisk, "The Dramaturgy of Services Exchange: An Analytical Framework for Services Marketing", in L.L. Berry, G.L. Shostack and G.D. Upah (Eds.), *Emerging Perspectives in Services Marketing,* American Marketing Association, Chicago, IL,1983.

Grove, Stephen J., Raymond P. Fisk, and Mary Jo Bitner, "Dramatizing the Service Experience: A Managerial Approach", in T.A. Schwartz, D.E. Bowen and S.W. Brown (Eds.), *Advances in Services Marketing and Management,* Vol. 1. JAI Press, Greenwich, CT, 1992, pp. 90–122.

Gummesson, Evert, "The Marketing of Professional Services: An Organizational Dilemma", *European Journal of Marketing,* Vol. 13, No. 5, 1979, pp. 308–18.

Gummesson, Evert, "Marketing-orientation Revisited: The Crucial Role of the Part-Time Marketer", *European Journal of Marketing,* Vol. 25, No. 2, 1991, pp. 60–75.

Hammer, Michael and James Champy, *Reengineering the Corporation,* Harper Business, New York, 1993.

Hochschild, A.R., *The Managed Heart: Commercialization of Human Feeling,* University of California Press, Berkeley, CA, 1983.

Kotler, Philip, "A Generic Concept of Marketing", *Journal of Marketing,* Vol. 36, April, 1972, pp. 48–9.

Langeard, Eric, John E.G. Bateson, Christopher H. Lovelock and Pierre Eiglier, *Services Marketing: New Insights from Consumers and Managers,* Marketing Science Institute, Cambridge, MA, August, 1981, Report No. 81–104.

Labich, Kenneth, "Is Herb Kelleher America's Best CEO?" *Fortune,* 2 May, 1994, pp. 44–52.

Levering, Robert and Milton Moskowitz, *The 100 Best Companies to Work for in America,* Currency Doubleday, New York, 1993.

Lovelock, Christopher H., "Why Marketing Management Needs to be Different for Services", in J.H. Donnelly, and W.R. George (Eds.), *Marketing of Services,* American Marketing Association, Chicago, IL, 1981.

Lovelock, Christopher H., "Classifying Services to Gain Strategic Marketing Insights", *Journal of Marketing,* Vol. 47, Summer, 1983, pp. 1–20.

Lovelock, Christopher H., "Cultivating the Flower of Service", in S.W. Brown, R. Johnston, B. Schneider, P. Eiglier, and E. Langeard (Eds.), *Marketing, Operations and Human Resources Insights into Services,* proceedings of 2nd International Research Seminar in Service Management, IAE, Université d'Aix-Marseille, Aix-en-Provence, France, 1992, pp. 295–316.

Lovelock, Christopher, *Product Plus: How Product + Service = Competitive Advantage,* McGraw-Hill, New York, 1994.

Lovelock, Christopher H., and Ivor P. Morgan, "Euro Disney", in C.H. Lovelock, *Services Marketing,* 3rd Edition, Prentice-Hall Englewood Cliffs, NJ (forthcoming).

Normann, Richard, *Service Management: Strategy and Leadership in Service Businesses,* John Wiley and Sons, Chichester, UK, 1984; 2nd Edition, 1991

Pfeffer, Jeffrey, *Competitive Advantage Through People,* Harvard Business School Press, Boston, MA, 1994.

Quinn, James Brian, *Intelligent Enterprise,* The Free Press, New York, 1992.

Rabkin, Mitchell T. and Laura Avakian, "Participatory Management at Boston's Beth Israel Hospital", *Academic Medicine,* Vol. 67, May, 1992, pp. 289–94.

Reichheld, Frederick F., "Loyalty-Based Management", *Harvard Business Review,* March/April, 1993, pp. 300–09.

Reichheld, Frederick F. and W. Earl Sasser, "Zero Defects: Quality Comes to Services", *Harvard Business Review,* September/October, 1990, pp. 105–11.

Rosenbluth, Hal E., *The Customer Comes Second,* William Morrow, New York, 1992.

Sasser, W. Earl, R. Paul Olsen and D. Daryl Wyckoff, *Management of Service Operations: Text, Cases, and Readings,* Allyn and Bacon, Boston, MA, 1978.

Schneider, Benjamin, "Service Quality and Profits: Can You Have Your Cake and Eat It, Too?" *Human Resource Planning,* Vol. 14, No. 2, 1991, pp. 151–7.

Schneider, Benjamin, "HRM — A Service Perspective: Towards a Customer-focused HRM?" *International Journal of Service Industry Management,* Vol. 5, No. 1, 1994, pp. 64–76.

Schneider, Benjamin, and David E. Bowen, "Employee and Customer perceptions of Service in Banks: Replication and Extension", *Journal of Applied Psychology,* Vol. 70, 1985, pp. 423–33.

Schneider, Benjamin, J.J. Parkington and V.M. Buxton, "Employee and Customer Perceptions of Service in Banks", *Administrative Science Quarterly,* Vol. 25, 1980, pp. 252–67.

Schlesinger, Leonard L. and James L. Heskett, "Breaking the Cycle of Failure in Services", *Sloan Management Review,* Spring 1991, pp. 17–28.

Sisodia, Rajendra S., "Expert Marketing with Expert Systems", *Marketing Management,* Spring 1992, pp. 32–47.

Tansik, David A., "Managing Human Resource Issues for High Contact Service Personnel", in D.E. Bowen, R. B. Chase, T.G. Cummings, and Associates, *Service Management Effectiveness,* Jossey-Bass, San Francisco, CA, 1990, pp. 152–76.

Ulrich, Dave, Richard Halbrook, Dave Medr, Mark Stuchlik and Steve Thorpe, "Employee and Customer Attachment: Synergies for Competitive Advantage", *Human Resource Planning,* Vol. 14, No. 2, 1991, pp. 89–103.

Vandermerwe, Sandra, *From Tin Soldiers to Russian Dolls: Creating Added Value through Services,* Butterworth-Heinemann, Oxford, UK, 1993.

Vandermerwe, Sandra and Christopher H. Lovelock, "Singapore Airlines", (IMD case, 1991), reprinted in S. Vandermerwe and C. Lovelock with M. Taishoff, *Competing Through Services: Strategy and Implementation,* Prentice-Hall, Hemel Hempstead, UK, 1994.

Whitely, Richard C., *The Customer-Driven Company: Moving from Talk to Action,* Business Books, London, 1991.

9

RELATIONSHIP MARKETING:
Its Role in the Service Economy[1]

Evert Gummesson
Stockholm University, Sweden

PRÉCIS

This chapter is an eclectic overview of one of the most influential issues in academic marketing today; relationship marketing (RM). Gummesson explains the evolution of relationship marketing in terms of relationships, networks and interaction. He claims that there is a paradigm shift away from the narrow manipulative ideology of transaction marketing towards a more benign win–win strategy implicit in relationship marketing. Relationship marketing is then viewed from three different perspectives; organisational, managerial and macroeconomic. One of the most useful aspects of Gummesson's ideas is the formal articulation of the three quite distinct aspects of the market economy; competitiveness, collaboration, and regulation. Most academic marketing authors discuss only competitiveness in any depth, but Gummesson provides a much more realistic insight into the dynamics of marketing.

The enlightened reader will question the win–win strategy of relationship marketing in the light of possible coercive relationships which may arise between small- to medium-sized suppliers and large multinationals. The large numbers of different types of relationships proposed by Gummesson will undoubtedly stimulate empirical researchers to investigate the nature of relationships across the diverse constituency of marketing practitioners. In this chapter, Gummesson has given us the clearest explanation so far in this fascinating area of relationship marketing.

Andy Lowe
University of Strathclyde, Scotland

---

[1] The chapter is based on a long-term research project, presented in progress reports (Gummesson 1987, 1991, 1993, 1994b) and finally in a book (1994c).

[244]

1. INTRODUCTION

If Relationship Marketing (RM) is treated as yet another faddish technique, deprived of the context within which it operates, it will not add to marketing wisdom. The purpose of this chapter, therefore, is to put RM in an economic and social context, both on a micro and macro level. In the first part of the chapter, this author's perception of RM is presented. The second section takes an organisational view. A change that may call for RM — or which may even be the consequence of RM — is the transition from the hierarchical company with clear boundaries — "the citadel" — to the network corporation. The third section raises the question of why RM is popular among managers in many countries. What benefits do they see in RM? In the fourth section, the eyes are raised to look at the contemporary market economy, which is a service economy rather than an industrial society. Does RM really contribute to better functioning of the markets? The chapter ends with concluding remarks.

2. RM: THE MARKETING VIEW

This explanation of the marketing view of RM begins with a definition. It proceeds with a series of examples of the significance of relationships, networks and interaction, and the theoretical background. It concludes with a presentation of a structure of RM, based on 30 relationships, the 30Rs.

2.1. Defining RM

Relationship marketing (RM) is marketing seen as relationships, networks and interaction (Gummesson, 1994c).

Relationships require at least two parties who are in contact with each other. The basic relationship in marketing is that between a provider and a customer. *Networks* emerge when relationships become many and complex and when it becomes difficult to obtain an overview of them. In relationships, the parties enter into *interaction* with each other. The core interaction consists of an exchange of values and supporting joint activities.

We are surrounded by relationships in our lives: from one-night stands through long-term relationships and matrimony to divorce. Two dancing partners have a dynamic relationship. They may waltz smoothly but they might also step on each other's toes. Peters (1992, p. 17) makes it even more dramatic: "Today's global economic dance is not a Strauss waltz. It's break dance accompanied by street rap. The effective firm is much more like Carnival in Rio than A Pyramid Along the Nile". We refer to business people as being well-connected, being members of the right clubs, having influential relatives and knowing people in high places. Companies enter into alliances with customers, competitors, research laboratories and others.

2.2 Examples

A series of examples — although they only cover a limited range of relationships — will demonstrate the versatility of RM.

- Joshua Tetley in the UK controls 1,000 pubs. In order to strengthen the personal relationship to the consumer the "100 Club" was established. Eligible for membership were personnel who knew the names and habits of a minimum of 100 guests. A misgiving was expressed that no one would qualify for membership. The outcome was a great surprise. 500 employees knew the names of 600 customers or more; the champion could address 1,200 customers by name.

- Stew Leonard's — two giant fresh-food stores in Connecticut, USA — is a champion of long-term consumer relationships. When meeting Stew Leonard in 1990, he pointed to a customer approaching his store and said: "Here comes $50,000". His philosophy is that if he keeps a consumer for 10 years, spending $100 weekly the consumer ends up spending $5,000 a year and $50,000 over a 10-year period. So he treats the consumer like $50,000. The strategy is customer retention and zero defection and the customers want to stay because they like the supplier. It's a win–win relationship.

- As early as 1922, the Reader's Digest established a close relationship with its readers. The prime objective was getting and keeping subscribers, and achieving sales through retailers was only a secondary consideration. Its founders, the Wallace couple, realised the value of the names and addresses as well as the record of buying behaviour of its subscribers. They used the customer base to market related products such as books and gramophone records. Their mailing lists are structured in accordance with previous buying behaviour: subscriber, subscriber who bought one special book, subscriber who bought the quarterly condensed books, subscriber who gave a gift subscription for Christmas, etc. This long-term relationship was fundamental for their success.

The three cases above show different types of consumer relationships and a varying degree of personal closeness: the personal contact in the local pub, the long-term customer retention strategy of a large self-service store, and the ability to stay in touch through direct mail.

- In the mid-1980s, the French government decided that its telecom manufacturing industry should benefit from competition from a second source located in France. Candidates were American AT&T, German Siemens and Swedish Ericsson. Their proposals had been compared by technical experts and all complied with the required specifications, albeit with differences. The final decision rested with the politicians. US president Ronald Reagan gave discreet support to AT&T; German Bundeskanzler, Helmut Kohl, and the President of the EU Commission, Jacques Delors, to Siemens. Ericsson negotiated through its Chairman and its Managing Director who met French cabinet ministers on several occasions. Under French Premier Fabius, a decision was made to award the contract to AT&T but this was undone by a new government under Premier Chirac. The new Secretary of Industry and the Secretary of Telecommunications recommended AT&T, whereas the Secretary of Finance recommended Siemens. Ericsson was ultimately awarded the contract, possibly because it was a compromise and politically harmless.

   The situation required *megamarketing*, a term coined by Kotler (1986). It is marketing beyond the normal understanding of the concept. The phenomenon is by no means new, but has not previously earned its way into marketing theory. Without the initial "megadecision" there are no customers to address. Megamarketing is often the most important part of marketing, for example, for companies producing goods and services of infrastructural nature such as telephone systems, military equipment or nuclear power plants. It requires close relationships and interaction.

- In the early 1990s, IBM had alliances with several of its customers, major competitors and suppliers. Some of the most important were Toshiba (joint factory in Japan for colour screens), Mitsubishi (sells IBM mainframes in Japan under its own name), Intel (joint development of chips), Apple (joint development of operative systems and technology for the integration of sound, data, graphics and video), Lotus (agent for Lotus software), and Sears (joint ownership of Prodigy, software for home shopping). Furthermore, IBM North America co-operated with some 4,000 companies. These alliances partly curb competition but at the same time can be essential to quality and productivity.

- Relationships are created via full-time marketers, FTMs, and part-time marketers, PTMs (Gummesson, 1991). Those who work in marketing and sales departments — the FTMs — are professional relationship-makers. All others, who perform other main functions but yet influence customer relationships directly or indirectly, are PTMs. Professional services are mainly marketed through personal networks and ongoing interaction in assignments but there are also contributing FTMs and PTMs outside the organisation. The management consulting company, McKinsey, gets a substantial portion of its orders from former consultants. Consultants are encouraged to take on positions offered by their clients. The company organises special events for consultants when they are leaving. Former consultants are thus left feeling loyal to their former employer and more likely to keep in touch. This is also achieved through automatic membership of the alumni association.

- The tourist needs information about services that can be booked and the tourist trade needs efficient systems for disseminating information about their offerings. Global information systems have been developed by airlines, but have gradually expanded into other sectors. The dominating computer reservation systems are Galileo and Amadeus in Europe; Sabre, Apollo, System One and Worldspan in the United States; Gemini in Canada; Abacus in Asia; and Fantasia in Australia. Sabre was the first to be computerised, through an alliance between American Airlines and IBM. The initial purpose was to keep track of airline seats, but today Sabre is a general electronic booking system established in 54 countries and used by 20,000 travel agencies through 130,000 terminals. It stores timetables for 641 airlines, 57 car rental firms and 50 tour operators, and keeps track of rooms in 22,000 hotels. The number of transactions in Sabre is 2,700 per second during peak hours and 750,000 new passenger files per day (Sahlberg, 1994). Membership of an electronic network is a necessity for airlines and others in the travel arena; it is the basis of their marketing and is increasingly becoming so for other industries too.

- It is easy to become a supplier in the US but it is just as easy to be replaced. In Japan it is hard to become a supplier but once you have got the contract, the relationship is long-term. The Japanese word *keiretsu* means long-term personal and financial relationships between firms. The president of the US Chamber of Commerce in Japan summarised: "Keiretsu links, bidding cartels, and the old-boy network still present us with formidable obstacles that Japanese corporations do not face in the US market" (Faltermeyer, 1992). The personal and social networks often determine the business networks. There are even some cultures where business is solely conducted between friends and friends-of-friends.

- In order to create a long-term lasting relationship, it has become increasingly common to involve customers in various marketing programmes. Making the customer a "member" demonstrates an interest in keeping the customer. Running a frequent fliers programme has become a must for airlines throughout the world. If you are a member of British Airways' Executive Club and have been raised to Gold Card status you earn extra mileage; have access to comfortable lounges with free drinks and snacks; get a 25 per cent discount on immunisation services at 35 Travel Clinics in the UK; get priority on waiting lists; and the right to check in at a first-class desk even if you do not travel first class. Through alliances with Qantas, Singapore Airlines, USAir and others, club members can enjoy special treatment from these airlines as well. You can also earn points by staying at Mandarin Oriental, The Savoy Group and Hilton hotels or renting your car from Hertz. Memberships are offered by a large number of industries, such as retailing, among them the furniture chain Ikea with its Family Card.

- Relationships are established with human beings and with organisations, but also with symbols and images — the latter are called *parasocial relationships*. Brands can have enormous power over the minds of consumers — Coca-Cola, Mercedes, Disney, Ralph Lauren and IBM, for example. Destinations like the French Riviera, the Australian Gold Coast, the Alps, and cities like Rome, Hollywood and Rio carry connotations of romance, adventure or culture. For consumers, they create an emotional relationship and invite loyalty.

2.3 Theoretical Background

Transaction marketing refers to an occasional deal (Jackson, 1985). It can also refer to repeated deals, each being independent of the previous one and with no forecasting capacity as to the probability of a future deal.

In contrast, RM aims to create a long-term interactive relationship between providers and customers. RM reflects a current trend expressed in terms such as "retention marketing" and "zero defection" (Reichheld and Sasser, 1990). It recognises that both the customer and the seller can be active parties. They should see each other as equal partners in a win–win relationship. Ritz-Carlton Hotels, winners of the Malcolm Baldrige National Quality Award for services in 1992, express this spirit in their motto: "We Are Ladies and Gentlemen Serving Ladies and Gentlemen". RM is embedded in the whole management process; everyone is a PTM, a part-time marketer. In order to recognise this embeddedness, it is more appropriate to speak of *marketing-oriented management* than of marketing management.

Research and practice in marketing, during the past 20 years in particular, point to the significance of relations, networks and interaction. It is essential to note the contributions from various directions that in the first half of the 1990s converged into a single unifying *term*, relationship marketing. The *phenomenon* of RM, however, has been around for a long time. The originator of the term should not also get credit for inventing the phenomenon.

The more radical areas of marketing — where the RM vantage points have emerged out of empirical, inductive, theory-generating studies — are *services marketing* and the *network approach to industrial marketing*. Both research traditions gained momentum in the late 1970s. Services marketing experienced its breakthrough during the 1980s with seminal contributions from researchers and practitioners from many countries, notably Scandinavia ("The Nordic School of Services"), the UK, France and the US. For an overview of the roots and development of services marketing and its unprecedented growth and impact on marketing, see Berry and Parasuraman (1993) and Fisk, Brown and Bitner (1993). The network approach is based on studies by the IMP Group (Industrial Marketing and Purchasing Group) represented throughout Europe at major business schools; recently also in the US, Asia and Australia (see anthologies edited by Håkansson, 1982; Ford, 1990; Axelsson and Easton, 1992). Services marketing has put *service quality* on the map but contributions to RM also come from *total quality management,* TQM, which is primarily based on experience and research in manufacturing. The major contributions to TQM come from Japan and the US. TQM has had an important impact on the practice of marketing since the early 1980s, by setting *customer-perceived quality* in focus for business *offerings*.

Relationships, networks, and interaction play a limited role in the traditional *marketing mix theory*, referred to as the *4Ps* (product, price, promotion, and place) and subsequent extensions of these. The marketing mix theory is goods-focused, seeing consumer marketing as mass marketing. Originally, the marketing mix approach was based on the marketing concept and its advocacy for understanding and satisfying customer needs. However, in practice it has turned out to be more of a conspiratorial management perspective. Marketing becomes the active manipulation of the Ps in order to make the customer buy.

Customers do not buy goods or services; they buy *offerings which render services which create value*. The offering and the value consist of many components, some of them being activities (services), some being things (goods). As a consequence, the traditional division between goods and services is long outdated. It is now a matter of redefining services and seeing them from a customer perspective: activities render services, things render services. This shift in focus to services is a shift from the means and the producer perspective to the utilisation and the customer perspective. Several thinkers emphasise the importance of focusing on services and value. For Grönroos (1994a) service management is a perspective that fits contemporary society and its economy. In the eyes of Giarini and Stahel (1989), the future society is a service economy and the long-established division in agriculture, manufacturing and services is no longer viable. In the value constellation approach by Normann and Ramirez (1993), the customer is an interactive co-producer of value. For Quinn (1992), the future society derives value from managing knowledge in service-based systems, irrespective of whether this value is created through the traditional notion of manufacturing or services. According to Vandermerwe (1993):

> The inroads made by services will continue ... bringing success to those corporations which have made the transition from ... an industrial to a service ethos.

It is time to acknowledge the service society in which we live and to shift from a goods-focused to a service-focused paradigm. Additional Ps, such as people (Judd, 1987), political power, public opinion formation (Kotler, 1984), participants and process (Booms and Bitner, 1981) to some extent incorporate relationships and interaction into the marketing mix theory. Segmentation breaks the standardisation of mass manufacturing and mass marketing into semi-customised offerings. However, RM provides a more radical change in perspective, radical enough to justify the statement: *RM constitutes a paradigmatic shift in marketing*. RM goes further, leaving the industrial society behind and welcoming the service society (Grönroos, 1994a; Gummesson, 1994a). Its core is mutually beneficial and voluntary relationships where both supplier and customer remain satisfied. Both parties should be free to leave, but their incentives to break the relationships should be reduced. RM is more often focused on one-to-one relationships and interaction, and less on impersonal mass marketing. *This is a consequence of the service society replacing the industrial mass product society* (Gummesson, 1994c).

To a much larger degree than the application of the 4Ps, true RM is based on a *win–win* strategy and a *plus-sum game*. This is a benign agenda, maybe even a naïve agenda. Not all RM may be amenable to this strategy; some will remain a *zero-sum game* — for example, "value" or goods sold and bought on an exchange where each deal creates a winner and a loser. Not all people in business subscribe to this agenda: some are thrilled and challenged by winning over others, their goal being to become extremely rich or large, sometimes applying poor ethical standards. Relationships are certainly not simple and automatically harmonious. We know this from our personal life and our life in organisations. If relationships turn out to be dysfunctional, they should, of course, be broken.

Unfortunately, there are indications that the basic values of manipulative marketing have not changed. Some understand RM to be getting a firmer grip on the customer through a bag of smart tricks that help the company to trap customers and chain them to it. This may be *relationship selling* but does not qualify as relationship marketing. RM involves relationships, not just a series of repeated transactions. Interpreted in the light of the marketing mix paradigm, the inherent strengths of relationship marketing will not be exploited. Reality has already left the traditional textbook paradigm of marketing behind — if it was ever even loosely connected to it — but our theories and classroom presentations have not changed accordingly. It may be closer to the truth to say that the paradigmatic shift induced by RM is a paradigmatic shift in textbooks, classrooms and scholarly research, rather than a shift in the real world of marketing. It may be a step towards more valid marketing theories that better mirror and communicate the actual spirit of business.

2.4. Making RM Tangible and Structured

In establishing a new paradigm of marketing, it is not enough simply to present a philosophy, basic values and a theory together with illustrations. It is also imperative to specify which relationships companies should address. This author has found 30 relationships, referred to as the *30 Rs of relationship marketing* (Gummesson, 1994c). A sample of the Rs will be presented below together with some of their essential properties (the R and a number is a means of keeping track of the relationships; it does not suggest ranking order).

Three relationships can be labelled classic. These are the dyad of the supplier and customer (*R1*, which is the parent relationship and the basis for marketing); the triad of the customer, the present supplier and the competitors (*R4*) which is central for the functioning of the market economy; and the physical distribution network (*R12*).

The market relationships constitute the core of RM. These are externally oriented and apply to the market proper. Among these are the classic dyad *(R1),* the relationship between the many-headed seller and the many-headed buyer *(R2),* the service encounter and the interaction between provider personnel and customers *(R7),* the relationship to the customer's customer *(R19),* and the customer as member *(R25).*

Above the market we find *mega relationships.* These are non-market relationships which are conditional to the market relationships. Among these are megamarketing *(R3),* megaalliances *(R14),* the relationships to mass media *(R29),* and to an extent also the personal and social networks *(R16).*

Below the market relationships we have the internally directed relationships, the *nano relationships* (from Greek *nanos,* dwarf). They constitute support to the externally directed relationships and an antecedent for them to be effective. Among these intracorporate relationships are the interhierarchical and interfunctional dependency and the relationship between internal customers and internal providers *(R8),* internal marketing to reach the "employee market" *(R10),* and quality management as a link between operations management and marketing *(R15).*

The boundary between the externally and the internally directed relationships is not clear cut; it is more a matter of emphasis. For example, the physical distribution network *(R13)* is part of a logistic flow, concerning internal as well as external customers.

The relationships also concern form and content in varying ratios. The form — the conduit — is emphasised in the physical distribution network *(R4)* and the electronic relationship *(R13).* In the green relationship *(R27)* and the knowledge relationship *(R28),* focus is on content.

More characteristics of the R's can also be found. The business world is complex and consequently the Rs are multidimensional. This complexity has to be treated with respect; every effort to squeeze the relationships into a simple scale or matrix will curtail their validity. Finally, while not drawing any comparisons here, other authors may have a somewhat different approach to the definition and the content of RM (see, for example, Grönroos, 1990, 1994b; Berry and Parasuraman, 1991; Christopher, Payne and Ballantyne 1991; McKenna, 1991; Kotler, 1992; Blomqvist, Dahl and Haeger, 1993; Millman, 1993). This author contends that we have to seek alternative approaches based on the relationship theme. These may be supplementary or competitive; some may co-exist and establish their own supporters; others may die. It would not be beneficial to marketing if one single approach to RM — as today the single marketing mix approach — were to be given a monopoly status.

3. RM: THE ORGANISATION VIEW

The concept of the *network organisation* reflects the ideas of RM; RM is the marketing aspect of the network organisation. There is a chicken and egg connection between RM and the network corporation: the direction of causality is not evident. RM is a perspective on marketing, or an image or metaphor. Morgan (1986) has contributed with organisational metaphors, such as viewing a company as a machine, a brain or a psychic prison. The marketing metaphor in this definition of RM is marketing seen as relationships, networks and interaction. Its organisational corollary is the network organisation.

The basic notion of the network organisation will be explained in this section. Other designations for the new organisational structure are the *virtual organisation* (Davidow and Malone, 1992), the *imaginary organisation* (Hedberg, 1992/93) and the *boundaryless organisation*. The contents of these are basically the same, although the emphasis varies (see also Peters, 1992; and Vandermerwe, 1993).

Badaracco (1991) describes the transition away from the clearly defined traditional corporation, "the citadel":

> Firms were ... islands of managerial co-ordination in a sea of market relationships.... Companies are now breaking down barriers which, like the Berlin Wall, have endured for decades. Their managers are now working in a world that consists not simply of markets and firms, but of complex relationships with a variety of other organisations.

In fact, marketing strategy and organisation must adapt to these changing conditions of business. Gradually it is being accepted that companies are not clearly defined citadels and objects. Gustavsson (1992) warns against the reification of the organisation, making it a tangible object by regarding it as a building or an organisational chart. Organisations are fuzzy sets which take amoeba-like forms. They become borderless entities and try to be both centralised and decentralised, both large and small, both global and local. They continuously change shape by changing the customer relationships and other relationships on which they are built, and by changing the interaction within these relationships. The network corporation has diverse locations. It adapts quickly to changing needs and provides "instant" products and services in large varieties so as to cater for individual needs. "Any time, any place" has become a guiding principle (Davis, 1987). It is difficult to describe and to get an overview of the organisation. It maintains control of a core business, where it is better at adding value than anybody else, while outsourcing other activities. Its core is intellectual capital (Buck-Lew and Edvinsson, 1993) and intelligence (Quinn, 1992) rather than equipment, land and raw material. Information technology and other innovations, faster travelling and better education provide the basis for the networks. It makes it possible for new breeds of small knowledge-based companies, such as independent consultants, to utilise much larger resources than they could ever recruit to their organisation.

The network organisation has been in evidence for a long time, although our ability to define it and communicate its true content is still limited. It will grow in importance. Or rather: its development is intertwined with new approaches to management and marketing. The following examples show various aspects of the network structures:

- *Financial Services.* AFS — Assurance and Financial Services, a subsidiary of the Skandia insurance company — describes its organisation as consisting of 500,000 customers, 12,000 active and independent brokers, 1,200 employees dispersed over the globe and a corporate staff of no more than 20 people. Information technology is crucial; the borders between customers and outside providers are indeterminate; the core organisation is kept at a minimum.

- *Retailing.* The Body Shop had 1,000 outlets around the world in 1994, selling environmentally friendly cosmetics. Its expansion is primarily based on franchise agreements. In fact, its founder had no money to expand and could not get adequate bank loans to do so. But she was repeatedly approached by individuals who wanted to duplicate her concept, and franchising provided a solution. Franchises are kept together through a legal contract and shared values, knowledge and image — but not by ownership.

- *Exchanges.* The spot market for oil was once located in Rotterdam. Today it exists as activities in an electronic and global network, operating around the clock. It is based on information technology. It is everywhere, but nowhere; it fulfils the strategy at any time, any place.

- *Hotels.* Holiday Inn has almost 2,000 hotels that are operated through franchise agreements. These hotels have a central connection to a reservation network and loyalty programmes, but they also have their own local network. Small companies can be networks, too; in fact the network may be the essence of their business. The small hotel thrives on its regular customers and its close connection to local suppliers, the local bank branch, local government and others, all of which may also constitute their network of family and friends, the "familial unit"

(Lowe, 1988). In Lowe's study, the driving force behind small hotel owners and their families was both social and economic — not to get rich and big but to have a "full" life.

In order to exist in the long term, a network organisation must have a "heart", a core of competence. This core is usually associated with a unique product or service, an ability to innovate, a unique marketing method or a financial strength. From that core, a texture of alliances and contacts can be woven.

Organising a network business requires continuous creation, transformation and maintenance of dynamic processes and organisational structures. Management must defend a new type of "citadel" which successively changes character and whose boundaries differ depending on which stakeholders look at the organisation. Its strength is the ability to combine its own resources with resources from other organisations, and its ability to grow and shrink more quickly than the traditional organisation.

In Figure 9.1, three organisational designs show different facets of an organisation. The first is the traditional hierarchy.

FIGURE 9.1(a): THE TRADITIONAL HIERARCHICAL
REIFICATION OF AN ORGANISATION WITH CLEAR
BOUNDARIES

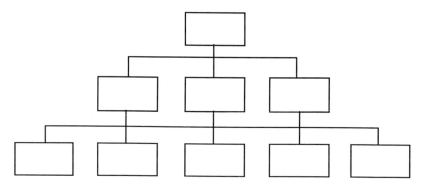

The second and third are networks as a clear structure, and then as an "amoeba". The hierarchy does not include the customer nor any other actor outside its boundaries; the network organisation does. The network diagram Figure 9.1(b) includes all types of actors and their relationships. The amoeba diagram shows two interrelated companies — which could be a customer and a provider — and stresses the fuzziness of the borders of the network.

FIGURE 9.1(b): THE NETWORK CORPORATION DESCRIBED AS
A NETWORK OF RELATIONSHIPS

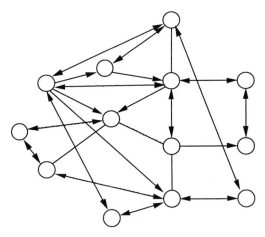

FIGURE 9.1(c): THE NETWORK CORPORATION DESCRIBED AS
AMOEBA-LIKE AND CONTINUOUSLY CHANGING SHAPES
WITH FUZZY BOUNDARIES AROUND CORE COMPETENCES

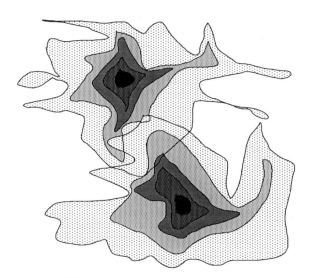

Source: Gummesson 1994c.

By integrating these three simple and incomplete sketches, we get a
glimpse of the complexity of an organisation and its interaction with
other organisations (Figure 9.2). It is within such an environment that
RM takes place.

FIGURE 9.2: INTEGRATING THE THREE APPROACHES TO THE
NETWORK ORGANISATION (its hierarchical structure, its structured
network and its amoeba-like shape of a core and fuzzy boundaries)

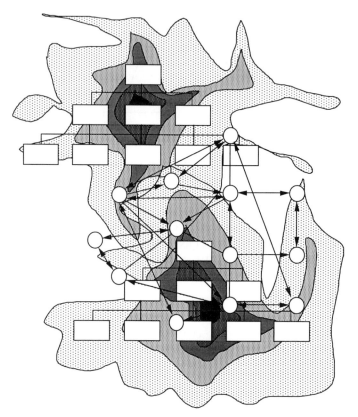

Source: Gummesson 1994c.

4. RM: THE MANAGEMENT VIEW

Current theory development and practice advocate that relationships are
basic to business. History shows that relationships have existed as pillars
of business since time immemorial. But what is the real reason behind
this? It is hoped that the following explanation, though not conclusive,
will be a stimulus for a constructive dialogue, leading to a deeper understanding of RM.

In the first place, companies need a basic degree of *security*. Security
is associated with words such as *promises, honesty, reliability, predictability, stability, freedom from fear of being swindled or let down, reduction of uncertainty and reduction of risk*. The market — customers and

competitors — as well as technological and political change and general changes in society create insecurity. Competition is considered to be a dynamic force, but it is also accepted that a certain amount of predictability through stable relationships is beneficial. It has been seen that completely planned and centralised economies, such as the former Soviet Union, as well as monopolies and sheltered industries, are dysfunctional. However, what can be planned, should be planned. No one would think that the timetable of a railway should be abandoned, leaving personnel to come to the railway each morning, scratching their heads and asking "What trains are we going to dispatch today?" It is difficult enough to get the trains to operate predictably even with elaborate planning systems. So the argument is not "either, or", either planning or complete freedom. It is "both, and", the combination of the two and an efficient ratio between them. Too much planning and collaboration creates rigidity, too much freedom and competition creates turmoil.

Furthermore, what cannot be foreseen can be better handled if the organisation has contingency planning designed into it — and is thus prepared for whatever situations occur. Everyone — both suppliers and customers — wants to make certain that promises are kept. The supplier should be reliable and deliver the right goods or services at the right time and place; just-in-time (JIT) is an extreme instance of this. The customers must be predictable in certain respects and, for example, not cancel orders or dodge payment. Security can be sought from four sources as shown in Figure 9.3.

Relationships provide security. People with a close relationship trust each other. They want to do repeat business. As has already been pointed out, business could be a *win–win* relationship with benefits to all parties in a network. If this were the case, consumerism and litigation would not be necessary, or at least would be rare. Without relationships, it is easy to fall into a "find a sucker" and "be smart" mentality. The long distance from the company to the customer can easily stimulate fraud. Blumberg (1989) explains the reasons:

> The injury done to others is often impersonal.... The people who suffer are anonymous, invisible customers far away, and as such only exist as abstractions.... People die in automobiles far from those who have designed them. Smokers die quietly far from those who manufacture and advertise cigarettes. Third world people suffer far from the plants that produced the chemicals that poison them.... The division of labour in the modern enterprise is so elaborate that each worker performs but a small part of the whole operation ... responsibility is so widely diffused throughout the firm that no one need feel responsible for anything ... in

a large bureaucratic organisation people abandon their role as full moral human beings.

Security can also be derived from the *law*, but legal security may be delusive. It is not always balanced. A powerful corporation or government can use any number of lawyers (tax deductible cost) while the private person can hardly afford legal counsel (non-deductible). The stronger party can stall and create unbearable stress for the weaker party. In the US, however, it has gone a long way in the other direction with private citizens suing companies and professionals for astronomical sums for minor or unclear damages — so called "frivolous suits" — and winning (Ramsey, 1991). The basic notion that a legal contract could cover all aspects of a business deal is often absurd, particularly when business transactions are complex.

FIGURE 9.3: SOURCES OF SECURITY

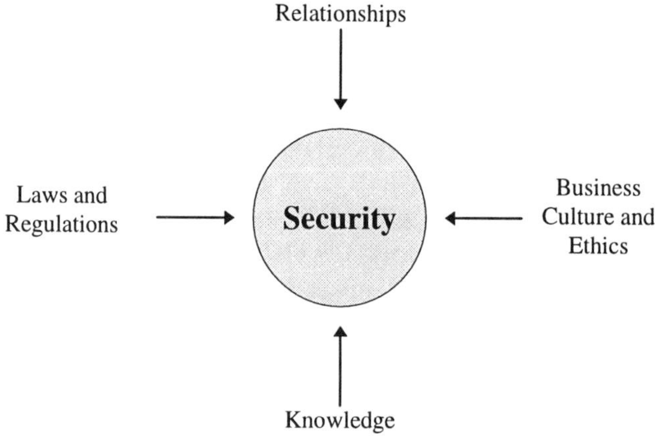

Source: Gummesson 1994c.

The United States has 25 times as many lawyers per capita as Japan. It has 5 per cent of the world's population but almost 70 per cent of its lawyers. According to Blumberg (1989):

> It is an elementary sociological fact that as the social fabric of society unravels, shared values and norms that once guided behaviour break down and are replaced by formal codes, regulations, and laws. As the sense of community withers further, social conflict intensifies and litigation proliferates as each person seeks advantage at the expense of others.

Business Culture and Ethics can also contribute to security. There can be very clear rules and ethical codes telling what is right and wrong. People abide by them and solve occasional disputes among themselves. The rules can be similar to those of a board game: if the dice shows five, you move five steps and this is not negotiable. There can be clear rewards and punishments, like becoming an outcast in the business community, if you break the code. In turbulent and immature market economies with no business culture, as in many of the East European states (Vlásek, 1994), premeditated deception, threats and violence create insecurity.

If the *Knowledge* of the customer or supplier is superior, security can be derived from this knowledge. For most of us, buying a used car poses a problem as we do not have sufficient knowledge to evaluate the quality of the car. Used car sales are also a classic area for deceit; deceit may even be the deliberate business mission. In today's society — which is often described as a knowledge-based society — knowledge is highly fragmented. We are increasingly dependent on products and service systems that we may understand how to use but without necessarily understanding how they operate. Consequently, we become dependent upon intermediaries — professionals and experts — or "brokers of uncertainty" (Giarini and Stahel, 1989). Without knowledge we are forced to make decisions based on "expert advice", impressions and symbols such as image, corporate identities and brand names.

Although it may sound like a paradox, Blumberg (1989) has concluded that the strength of the market economy — competition and the profit motive — encourages fraud. Unfortunately, conscious and systematic deception is omnipresent and we all sense this from time to time, both from work inside corporations and as private consumers. It is suppressed in the marketing books and in economic theory. The textbooks prefer the idealised picture — competition as a driver to create customer satisfaction; customer-perceived quality in focus; giving consumers what they want and are willing to pay for — and all this is claimed to generate profitability and long-term success. Customers are asked about satisfaction and quality, but their knowledge is limited. In 1271, philosopher Thomas Aquinas said that "... to determine the quality of a thing great skill is needed, which most buyers lack." It is just as true today, maybe even more true as the complexity of the offerings has grown. A marketing cynic once said: "Customers are not as stupid as you think. They are much more stupid." Maybe it is not cynicism, maybe it is true and companies use it. Obviously it is possible to create good customer relationships in spite of deception, as long as customers are ignorant. Here are some examples:

- Prices are increased before a sale and are then reduced — "50 per cent off!" — meaning that the same prices are offered as before the "cut", sometimes even a higher price.

- Taxi drivers tamper with meters and take advantage of visitors who are unfamiliar with fares, routes and customs.

- Providers take advantage of the fact that customers can be tired and distracted, for example when a party is being arranged, or can be helpless (inmates in psychiatric hospitals, for example).

- Employees sometimes look down on customers because they are easily cheated, using degrading names for them among themselves.

The four sources of security are not mutually exclusive. Even strong relationships and a high level of knowledge may require a dose of law, but the dose can be minimised. A strong business culture can consist of social relationships and personal closeness as well as being supplemented by law.

The US is an example of legal dominance and weaker relationships, while Japan is the opposite. Within countries there can exist differences between individuals or groups of business people, industries and places. It is, however, obvious how much weight companies and consumers give to relationships and how little weight has been given to them in the marketing literature. Both new theories and ancient practice supports this conclusion. The growing global competition and mass markets create anonymity and insecurity about the rules of the game and the confidence one can place in others. Swindlers are often successful just because they manage to fake the confidence and trust of close relationships; they are aptly referred to as "con men".

This author's conclusion is that relationships provide the best means of creating security, although support from other sources may be desirable. The ratio between the sources can vary. If we are extremely knowledgeable in one area, we master the situation through our knowledge and are less dependent on other sources. If the law is clear enough, it may provide adequate security, at least in well-defined and straightforward situations.

5. RM: THE ECONOMICS VIEW

This section takes a broader, societal and macro approach to RM. A working market economy can be seen as being based on the existence of three forces: *competition, collaboration,* and *regulations and institutions* (Figure 9.4).

FIGURE 9.4: THE THREE FORCES OF THE MARKET ECONOMY
WHICH STRIVE IN THE DIRECTION OF MARKETING
EQUILIBRIUM.

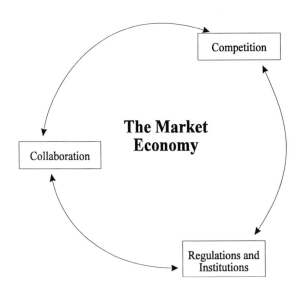

Source: Gummesson 1994c.

In market economies, competition is recognised as a driving force for economic progress and welfare. In its idealised and theoretical form, a market strives for equilibrium through the invisible hand of supply and demand, with price as the referee. From a marketing and management perspective, millions of decisions and actions taken by individuals — and today also by computers — accumulate and lead up to the *market equilibrium*.

A supplementary type of equilibrium is suggested here, based on the three forces: competition, collaboration, and institutions/regulations. It is called the *marketing equilibrium*. In marketing an effort is made to reach an equilibrium — a point of balance — between the three forces seen here as parts of the concept of RM. The emphasis on collaboration as a dynamic force is the major contribution of RM, but RM needs competition and institutions/regulations, too.

The global wave of privatisation and deregulation is a consequence of markets having become stifled by misguided state interference and obsolete regulations. The wave is an effort to turn back towards both a market equilibrium and a marketing equilibrium. There is a naïve belief that competition will do the whole trick — just as there was a naïve belief by socialists that a planned economy, controlled by institutions/ regulations, would do the trick. There is no known example of a market that works without institutions and regulations, nor is there one without competition and collaboration. In the former Soviet Union and its colonies, where the left extreme — total regulation of the markets — was replaced by the right extreme — totally free competition — the result is chaos, misery, unfairness, bribery and violence. There is need for "good institutions" which support economic activity. There are necessary elements of the market economy that are not conducive to competition and free market mechanisms. The European Union is building institutions and regulations, such as courts to handle trade discrimination and contract disputes. Whether a dinosaur bureaucracy is being born in Brussels, or whether the EU is building institutions to make the market economy functional, is under debate. Today's important contribution to deregulation is actually *re-regulation*, abandoning inadequate institutions and regulations and providing supportive ones.

One of the winners of the 1993 Nobel Prize in the Economic Sciences, Douglass C. North, has studied the significance of institutions and regulations as a necessity for a working market economy. In his Nobel Lecture, North (1993) proposed that the study of economic development has "ignored the incentive structure embodied in institutions ... it contained two erroneous assumptions: one that institutions do not matter and two that time does not matter".

North continued:

> Institutions form the incentive structure of the society and the political and economic institutions, in consequence, are the underlying determinant of economic performance. Time, as it relates to economic and societal change, is the dimension in which the learning process of human beings shapes the way institutions evolve. That is, the beliefs that individuals, groups, and societies hold which determine choices are a consequence of learning through time — not just the span of an individual's life or of a generation of a society but the learning embodied in individuals, groups and societies that is cumulative through time and passed on intergenerationally by the culture of a society.

North, being an economic historian with a longer time perspective than marketers, claims that it takes 500–600 years to implant a functioning institutional framework in a society; it is the outcome of the collective consciousness of a people.

The current dramatic changes in the telecommunications market provide an example of the efforts to strive towards a marketing equilibrium. The deregulation — or rather re-regulation — in Europe and

America has made it possible for telecommunications to expand beyond national markets. But they can hardly do it on their own. Three telecommunication companies from small countries — the Netherlands, Sweden, and Switzerland — have formed the Unisource alliance. British Telecom has joined forces with MCI Communications, the second largest operator of international telecommunications in the US. GTE, one of the largest telecommunications companies in the US, is at the same time competitor, customer and supplier to AT&T. GTE buys equipment from AT&T, competes with them on certain telephone lines but sells access to local lines to AT&T. In the early 1980s, with reference to the antitrust laws, the then dominant telecommunications company in the US, Bell, was broken up into seven regional operators, the Baby Bells. The purpose was to stimulate competition. AT&T is prohibited by law from acquiring stock in the Baby Bells. But in 1993, AT&T acquired the largest operating company in mobile telephones, McCaw. With the help of its cellular technology, AT&T can bypass the regional and local operators. They do not need the Baby Bells any longer.

The above example shows an ongoing effort to find the marketing equilibrium. When the telecommunications companies experience restrictions from regulations, they attempt to bypass these without breaking the law and by creating new alliances or utilising new technology. Competition thus takes new forms and the effects of existing regulations are nullified, revised regulations become imperative, and so forth.

6. CONCLUSIONS

In this chapter, RM is approached from a broad perspective, not just from the outlook of marketing and sales departments, but from that of organisation and management too. In addition, a societal macro perspective has been presented, discussing the impact of RM on the currently prevailing service economy.

It is advocated here that RM is a paradigmatic shift in marketing. It sets the buyer–seller interaction in focus — not having a situation where the buyer is manipulating the seller. It adds the necessity of collaboration which is often regarded with suspicion as limiting to competition. RM is not a bag of tricks to imprison the customer, nor is it just repeated transactions. It is a win–win, voluntary relationship. Although the ideal marriage rarely exists except in romantic films and novels, RM is an effort to work in the direction of a sustaining and harmonious balance of the forces in the market.

REFERENCES

Axelsson, Björn and Easton, Geoffrey, (Eds.), *Industrial Networks*, Routledge, London, 1992.

Badaracco, J.L., *The Knowledge Link*, Harvard Business School Press, Boston, MA, 1991.

Berry, Leonard L. and Parasuraman, A., *Marketing Services: Competing Through Quality*, The Free Press, New York, 1991.

Berry, Leonard L. and Parasuraman, A., "Building a New Academic Field — The Case of Services Marketing", *Journal of Retailing*, Vol. 69, No. 1, Spring, 1993, pp. 13–60.

Blomqvist, R., Dahl, J. and Haeger, T., *Relationsmarknadsföring: Strategi och metod i servicekonkurrens* (Relationship Marketing: Strategy and Method in Service Competition), IHM, Göteborg, Sweden, 1993.

Blumberg, P., *The Predatory Society*, Oxford University Press, New York, 1989.

Booms, B.H., and M.J. Bitner, "Marketing Strategies and Organisation Structures for Service Firms", in James Donnelly and W.R. George, *Marketing of Services*, American Marketing Association, Chicago, IL, 1981.

Buck-Lew, M. and L. Edvinsson, *Intellectual Capital at Skandia*, Skandia, Stockholm, Sweden, 1993.

Christopher, M., A. Payne and D. Ballantyne, *Relationship Marketing*, Heinemann, London, 1991.

Davidow, William H. and Michael S. Malone, *The Virtual Corporation*, Edward Burlinggame Books/Harper Business, New York, 1992.

Davis, Stanley M., *Future Perfect*, Addison-Wesley, Reading, MA, 1987.

Faltermeyer, Edmund, "Does Japan Play Fair?", *Fortune*, 7 September, 1992, pp. 22–9.

Fisk, R.P., S.W. Brown, and M.J. Bitner, "Tracking the Evolution of Services Marketing Literature", *Journal of Retailing*, Vol. 69, No. 1, Spring, 1993, pp. 61–103.

Ford, David (Ed.), *Understanding Business Markets: Interaction, Relationships and Networks*, Academic Press, London, 1990.

Giarini, O. and W.R. Stahel, *The Limits of Certainty: Facing New Risks in the Service Economy*, Kluwer, Dordrecht, The Netherlands, 1989.

Grönroos, Christian, "Relationship Approach to the Marketing Function in Service Contexts: The Marketing and Organization Behavior Interface", *Journal of Business Research*, No. 1, 1990.

Grönroos, Christian (a), "From Scientific Management to Service Management", *International Journal of Service Industry Management*, Vol. 5, No. 1, 1994.

Grönroos, Christian (b), "Quo Vadis, Marketing? Towards a Relationship Marketing Paradigm", *Journal of Marketing Management*, Vol. 10, No. 4, 1994.

Gummesson, Evert, "The New Marketing: Developing Long-term Interactive Relationships", *Long Range Planning*, Vol. 20, No. 4, 1987, pp. 10–20.

Gummesson, Evert, "Marketing-orientation Revisited: The Crucial Role of the

Part-time Marketer", *European Journal of Marketing*, Vol. 25, No. 22, 1991, pp. 60–75.

Gummesson, Evert, "Broadening and Specifying Relationship Marketing", invited paper for the *Monash Colloquium on Relationship Marketing*, Monash University, Melbourne, Australia, August, 1993.

Gummesson, Evert (a), "Service Management: An Evaluation and the Future", *International Journal of Service Industry Management*, Vol. 5, No. 1, 1994, pp. 77–96.

Gummesson, Evert (b), "Is Relationship Marketing Operational?", paper presented at *The 23rd EMAC Conference*, University of Limburg, Maastricht, The Netherlands, May, 1994.

Gummesson, Evert (c), *Relationship Marketing: From 4Ps to 30Rs*, Stockholm University, Stockholm, Sweden, 1994.

Gustavsson, B., *The Transcendent Organisation*, Stockholm University, Stockholm, Sweden, 1992.

Håkansson, Håkan (Ed.), *International Marketing and Purchasing of Industrial Goods*, John Wiley, Chichester, UK, 1982.

Hedberg, Bo, "Imaginära Organisationer" (Imaginary Organisations), *MTC-Kontakten*, 1992/93, pp. 12–13.

Jackson, Barbara Bund, *Winning and Keeping Industrial Customers*, Lexington Books, Lexington, MA, 1985.

Judd, V.C., "Differentiate with the 5th P: People", *Industrial Marketing Management*, November, 1987.

Kotler, Philip, "Kotler: Rethink the Marketing Concept", Interview in *Marketing News*, Vol. 18, No. 19, 14 September, 1984.

Kotler, Philip, "Megamarketing", *Harvard Business Review*, March/April, 1986, pp. 117–24.

Kotler, Philip, "Total Marketing", *Business Week Advance*, Executive Brief, Vol. 2, 1992.

Lowe, Andy, "Small Hotel Survival: An Inductive Approach", *The International Journal of Hospitality Management*, Vol. 7, No. 3, 1988, pp. 197–223.

McKenna, Regis, *Relationship Marketing*, Addison-Wesley, Reading, MA, 1991.

Millman, Tony, "The Emerging Concept of Relationship Marketing", paper presented at the *9th IMP Conference*, University of Bath, September, 1993.

Montagu-Pollock, Matthew, "All the Right Connections", *Asian Business*, 19 January, 1991, pp. 20–4.

Morgan, Gareth, *Images of Organization*, Sage, Newbury Park, CA, 1986.

Normann, R. and Ramirez, R., "From Value Chain to Value Constellation: Designing Interactive Strategy", *Harvard Business Review*, July/August, 1993, pp 65–77.

North, Douglass C., "Economic Performance Through Time", The Nobel Foundation, *Prize Lecture in Economic Science in Memory of Alfred Nobel*, Stockholm, Sweden, 9 December, 1993.

Peters, Tom, *Liberation Management*, Alfred A. Knopf, New York, 1992.

Quinn, J.B., *The Intelligent Enterprise*, The Free Press, New York, 1992.

Ramsey, R.D., "'It's Absurd': Swedish Managers' Views of America's Litigious Society", *Scandinavian Journal of Management,* Vol. 6, No. 1, 1991, pp. 31–44.

Reichheld, F. and W.E. Sasser Jr., "Zero Defections: Quality Comes to Services", *Harvard Business Review*, September/October, 1990, pp. 105–11.

Sahlberg, Bengt, "Information Systems and the Quality of Tourism", in R. Teare, M.D. Olsen and E. Gummesson (Eds.), *Service Quality in Hospitality Organizations*, Cassell, London, 1994.

Vandermerwe, S., *From Tin Soldiers to Russian Dolls. Creating Added Value through Services*, Butterworth-Heinemann, Oxford, UK, 1993.

Vlásek, V., "Services in Eastern Europe: A Neglected Child of Command Economy", in, Bo Edvardsson, and Eberhard E. Scheuing (Eds.), *Proceedings from QUIS 3 (1992)*, CTF and ISQA, Karlstad, Sweden, 1994.

10

ORGANISING FOR SERVICE:
Empowerment or Production Line?*

David E. Bowen
Arizona State University-West, USA

Edward E. Lawler III
University of Southern California, USA

PRÉCIS

This chapter examines the appropriateness of the employee empower-ment model versus the traditional management control model as applied to the service sector. The empowerment model advocates worker involvement and self-management, whereas the control model, akin to the assembly-line concept of organising work, is based on hierarchy, procedures, and work standardisation. Empowerment, already widely applied successfully to manufacturing, is now being advocated for services by many experts. After discussing the complexities of the empowerment model and performance evidence of organisations apply-ing it, versus those applying the control model, the authors decide in favour of a contingency approach, namely that different situations call for different degrees of empowerment versus control.

Empowerment is not an all-or-nothing concept. The authors suggest a continuum, ranging from total control to total empowerment. The low-est level of empowerment is "suggestion involvement" where employees make recommendations which are not binding on management. The next higher level of empowerment is "job involvement", whereby jobs are redesigned to allow employees scope to use a variety of skills to complete an identifiable piece of work, and generally to assume more

* Portions of this chapter were published previously as: Bowen, D.E., and E.E. Lawler III, "The Empowerment of Service Workers: What, Why, How and When", *Sloan Management Review*, Vol. 3, 1992, pp. 31–9.

self-management and control over their work, often in the context of teams. The highest level of empowerment entails the distribution throughout the organisation of power, information, knowledge, and rewards. Real empowerment creates an empowered "state of mind" within employees. This consists, in some measure, of the following factors: control over one's job activities; awareness of the rationale of one's job as it fits into the broad context of organisational operations; and accountability for work output.

Following a discussion of the benefits and limitations of empowerment, Bowen and Lawler delineate the sorts of business situations that call for an emphasis on empowerment, as opposed to those that call for a control orientation. They conclude that globalisation and concomitant competition have placed pressure on manufacturing companies to optimise the human resource contribution to competitiveness by empowering workers. The service sector is well placed to follow suit, but it should be discriminating by invoking empowerment only when the contingencies demand it.

Eleanor O'Higgins
University College Dublin, Ireland

1. INTRODUCTION

In the 1970s, Theodore Levitt presented a "production line approach to service" as the remedy for the sector's problems of inefficient operations and dissatisfied customers (Levitt, 1972, 1976). It was argued that the secrets of the production line approach could be discovered, quite simply, by looking at the world of manufacturing. The argument was to transfer to the service sector such industrial practices as the simplification of tasks and the substitution of technology, equipment, and systems for employees. The objective was to face the customer via standardised, tightly-controlled, procedurally-driven operations. Philosophically, service managers were encouraged to think in technocratic terms rather than humanistic terms.

In the 1990s, the "employee empowerment approach to service" is being presented as the remedy for the service sector's problems of poor customer service and inefficient operations. The guiding philosophy of empowerment is very non-bureaucratic and worker-oriented (Bell and Zemke, 1988; Schlesinger and Heskett, 1991). Empowerment is presented as the remedy that can lead to higher quality service, quicker responses to customers, and lower costs. Indeed, empowerment is often presented as a cure-all for the lagging productivity and profit problems of many service organisations.

Does the employee empowerment approach offer a better way of organising for service than the production-line approach? In this chapter, that question is first positioned as part of a more fundamental debate in business about the merits of two competing management models or paradigms: the long-standing control-oriented model versus the newer involvement-oriented model. These alternative models of organising are described briefly in order to provide a historical and theoretical context for assessing the effectiveness of an employee empowerment approach in service. This overview will also reveal that practitioners and researchers know less about the emergent involvement model (and empowerment in service, per se) and its effectiveness than they do about the long-standing control model.

Most of the chapter then details the nature of an involvement-oriented, employee empowerment approach to service. The following are described: *what* empowerment means in services; *why* to do it (there are costs, as well as benefits); *how* to do it (there are alternatives that lead to varying degrees of empowerment; and *when* to do it (the appropriate degree of empowerment should be matched to characteristics of the situation). This "when" component means that although we advocate empowerment, overall, we are most supportive of a "contingency model of empowerment".

2. THE ORGANISING DEBATE: CONTROL VERSUS INVOLVEMENT

Two very different approaches dominate the recent literature in management (Lawler, 1992). They represent competing paradigms or models of how organisations should be managed. The oldest, most-established approach has been variously referred to as top-down, pyramidal, hierarchical, mechanistic, and bureaucratic, but perhaps is best described as the control-oriented approach. The second approach has been called the commitment approach, but is now more frequently referred to as the involvement-oriented approach. As the following descriptions will reveal, the production-line approach to service (Levitt, 1972, 1976) fits the control paradigm; the empowerment approach to service (Bowen and Lawler, 1992) fits the involvement paradigm.

2.1. The Control Model

This model assumes that hierarchy and vertical relationships represents the best way to ensure productivity and quality. Its origins are in

Weber's (1947) bureaucratic model of management. It relies upon layers of hierarchy to control and co-ordinate the workplace.

The control model also has strong roots in Taylor's (1911, 1915) principles of scientific management. It claims that the work of low-level participants should be standardised, specialised, and simplified. Workers are told exactly how to do their jobs. Managers are the only ones who are expected to think, co-ordinate, and control.

The control model peaked in popularity in the 1960s and 1970s. In the US, companies like AT&T, Exxon, Kodak, IBM, and General Motors appeared to have perfected the approach *and* they prospered. They were viewed as management role models. In retrospect, however, their superior performance may have been attributable not to the control model, but other factors such as being based in the US and having limited competition (Lawler, 1992).

2.2. The Involvement Model

The key to how the involvement approach differs from the control approach is that involvement assumes that *all* employees, not just managers, are capable of thought, co-ordination, and control. The involvement approach relies much more on self-control and self-management, as supported by participatory management and training.

The involvement approach has its origins in pioneering works on participatory management by Argyris (1964), McGregor (1960) and Likert (1961). For example, McGregor made a case for Theory Y management which rests on the assumption that individuals can be trusted and motivated to perform well if they are given interesting and challenging work. Another foundation for the involvement approach was the work in the 1970s on job enrichment (Hackman and Lawler 1971; Hackman and Oldham 1976) that emphasised how task characteristics like autonomy and skill variety could be satisfying to employees with high-growth-need strength.

Despite these historical roots, it has only been in the past decade that significant numbers of firms have begun to adopt these various practices in any integrated, intensive way. The model is visible in companies like General Mills, Federal Express, Sun Microsystems, and Herman Miller.

3. THE CONTROL VERSUS INVOLVEMENT DEBATE IN SERVICE: IS PRODUCTION-LINE OR EMPOWERMENT BEST?

The control model clearly underpins Levitt's two classic articles, the "Production Line Approach to Service" and the "Industrialisation of Service". Levitt described how service operations can be made more efficient by applying the logic and tactics of manufacturing. His recommendations included:

- Simplification of tasks
- Clear division of labour
- Substitution of equipment and systems for employees
- Little decision-making discretion afforded to employees.

In short, management designs the system and employees execute it.

McDonald's is a good example. Workers are taught how to greet customers, and ask for their order (including a script for suggesting additional items). There is then a set procedure for assembling the order (for example, cold drinks first, then hot ones), placing various items on the tray, and placing the tray where the customers need not reach for it. Next, there is a script and a procedure for collecting money and giving change. Finally, there is a script for saying thank you and asking the customer to come again (Tansik, 1990). This production-line approach gives the organisation control over, and uniformity of, the customer-server interaction. It is easily learned, so workers can be quickly trained and put to work.

What are the gains from a production-line approach to service? Efficient, low-cost, high-volume profitable service operations—with satisfied customers. How? In Levitt's words, with a management rationality and set of tactics borrowed from the manufacturing sector:

> Manufacturing thinks technocratically, and that explains its success.... By contrast, service looks for solutions in the performer of the task. This is the paralysing legacy of our inherited attitudes: the solution to improved service is viewed as being dependent on improvements in the skills and attitudes of the performers of that service.
>
> While it may pain and offend us to say so, *thinking in humanistic rather than technocratic terms ensures that the service sector will be forever inefficient and that our satisfactions will be forever marginal.*

The involvement approach is evident in writings on empowering service workers. Ron Zemke and Dick Schaaf in their book *The Service Edge: 101 Companies that Profit from Customer Care* note that empowerment is a common theme running through many, even most, of their excellent service businesses, such as American Airlines, Marriott, American Express, and Federal Express. To Zemke and Schaaf, empowerment means "turning the front-line loose" — encouraging employees to exercise initiative and imagination and rewarding them for so doing.

"Empowerment in many ways is the reverse of doing things by the book" (Zemke and Schaaf, 1989). The humanistic flavour that pervades empowerment is clear in the words of advocates such as Tom Peters:

> [I]t is necessary to "dehumiliate" work by eliminating the policies and procedures (almost always tiny) of the organisation which demean and belittle human dignity. It is impossible to get people's best efforts, involvement, and caring concern for things you believe important to your customers and the long-term interests of your organisation when we write policies and procedures that treat them like thieves and bandits (as quoted in Zemke and Schaaf, 1989: p. 68).

And from Jan Carlzon, CEO of SAS Airlines:

> [T]o free someone from rigorous control by instructions, policies, and orders, and to give that person freedom to take responsibility for his ideas, decisions, and actions is to release hidden resources which would otherwise remain inaccessible to both the individual and the organisation (Carlzon, 1987).

In contrast to the logic of the industrialisation of service, empowerment very much looks to the "performer of the tasks" for solutions to service problems. Employees are asked to make suggestions for new services and products and they are asked to solve problems in a creative and effective manner.

3.1. Which Approach is Better?

This is really two questions. First, generally speaking, how does the control model perform relative to the involvement model? Secondly, more specific to services, how does the production-line approach compare to employee empowerment?

The evidence on the first question is *limited* but increasingly supportive of there being positive returns on the involvement approach (Lawler, Mohrman, and Ledford 1992). Lawler (1992) offers an important caveat when evaluating involvement versus control: control-oriented organisations are at a mature place on the learning curve with respect to their management approach, whereas involvement-oriented firms are just at the beginning stages of learning how to implement their management approach. Lawler goes on to present a strong conceptual argument that involvement, overall, will prove superior to control on four organisational performance variables: cost and productivity; quality; speed; and innovation. Nevertheless, there may be specific individual cases where the control model works best.

Turning to the question of service via the production line or empowerment, it is also difficult to pick a winner. Just look at the following test cases:

- In 1990, Federal Express became the first service organisation to win the highly coveted, Malcolm Baldrige National Quality Award. The company's motto is "people, service, and profits". Behind its brightly coloured blue, white, and red planes and uniforms, there are self-managing work teams, gain-sharing plans, and empowered employees seemingly consumed with providing quality service to their customers—whose individual needs for pick-up time and locations, and destinations, are flexibly and creatively serviced.

- At UPS, referred to as "Big Brown" by its employees, the company's philosophy was clearly stated by Jim Casey when he founded the company: "Best Service at Low Rates". Here, too, we find turned-on people and profits. But we do not find empowerment: instead we find controls, rules, a detailed union contract and carefully studied work methods. Nor do we find a promise to do all things for customers, such as handling off-schedule pick-ups and handling packages that don't fit size and weight limitations. In fact, rigid operational guidelines help to guarantee the customer reliable, low-cost service.

Federal Express and UPS present two very different "faces" to the customer and behind these faces are two different management philosophies and organisational cultures. Federal Express is a high-involvement, horizontally co-ordinated organisation which responds to customers with empowered employees who are encouraged to use their judgment above and beyond the rule-book. UPS is a top-down, traditionally controlled organisation, in which employees face customers directed by policies and procedures that are based on industrial engineering studies of how all aspects of service delivery should be carried out and how long they should take (although, lately UPS has shown signs of becoming more flexible and less bureaucratic).

At Disney theme parks, ride operators are thoroughly "scripted" on what to say to "guests", even including a listing of pre-approved "ad-libs"! At Club Med, CEO Jacques Giraud fervently believes the "magic" of the guest's experience must be real and the resorts' GOs are set-free to create this feeling spontaneously for its guests. So, which is the better approach? Federal Express or UPS? Club Med or Disney? McDonald's, which provides customers with quality, service, cleanliness, value — but no special orders — or Burger King which says "Have It Your Way?"

This mixed evidence, however, has not seemed to weaken the

apparently universal support for empowerment that we hear from service managers in all sorts of industries. All seem committed to abandoning the production line in favour of empowerment. Should they? Not without first clearly understanding the what, why, how, and when of empowerment.

4. EMPOWERING SERVICE EMPLOYEES: WHAT, WHY, HOW, AND WHEN

Deciding whether and how to empower service employees requires that managers understand the following:

- *What* empowerment really entails. Empowerment, as a relatively new approach, is imperfectly understood and variously defined. We provide a clear definition.

- *Why* to empower. They need to know the potential benefits *and* costs of empowerment.

- *How* to empower. Managers need to know the managerial practices associated with empowerment, and their options in using them.

- *When* to empower. There *do* seem to be contingencies such as the firm's basic business strategy that affect whether the gains of empowerment outweigh the costs.

4.1 What Empowerment Means

Empowerment is a "state of mind" that is produced by high-involvement management practices. Employees don't just suddenly feel empowered because managers tell them they are. Organisational policies, practices, and structures must be changed to create empowerment on a sustained basis. It is possible to give employees a brief rush of adrenaline through a speech by a charismatic leader about how they are the front line of the organisation and critical to its effectiveness, but this rush of adrenaline passes unless organisational structures, practices, and policies constantly and continually send a message that employees are empowered in order to deal effectively with customers.

Research suggests that empowerment exists when companies implement practices that distribute power, information, knowledge, and rewards throughout the organisation. This is happening most frequently in companies that have abandoned the traditional, top-down, control-oriented management model in favour of the high-involvement approach. Power can be redistributed by pushing decisions down to employees who interact directly with customers. Often this requires restructuring work so that employees as a group or team are responsible for the entire service process or for a designated group of customers. Information needs to be pushed down, through sharing customer feedback as well as through giving employees financial information about how the business is doing. Employees need to be knowledgeable concerning the goals and objectives of the business as well as the full-service delivery process of which they are a part. Finally, they need to be in a position to experience customer expectations and feedback.

Rewards should be allocated based on how effectively employees use information, knowledge, and power to improve the quality of service that customers receive and the financial performance of the organisation. This can be done in the form of stock options, profit-sharing plans, gain-sharing plans, and a host of other plans that tie employees' financial rewards into the success of the organisation.

Management practices that push down power, information, knowledge and rewards create an empowered "state of mind" within employees. This state of mind is what "comes between" management practices and the results they hope to achieve — employees who work hard to provide great service and delighted customers (see Table 10.1). Precisely specifying what any particular state of mind looks like, empowered or not, is a tricky business.

TABLE 10.1: A MODEL OF AN EMPLOYEE EMPOWERMENT APPROACH TO SERVICE

High-Involvement Management Practices that Push Down	Create in Employees an "Empowered State of Mind" in which They Feel:	That Leads to These Positive Outcomes:
Power e.g. Quality Circles Job Enrichment	More **Control** over what happens on the job	**Employees** who work hard for customers

Information
 e.g. Customer Feedback
     Unit Performance Data
     Data on Competitors
	More **Awareness** of the context in which the job is performed	**Customers** whose expectations are met or exceeded

Knowledge
 e.g. Skills to analyse business
     results
     Group Process Skills
	More **Accountability** for work output	**Organisations** that enjoy the returns from customer satisfaction and retention

Rewards e.g. Pay tied to service quality Individual and group plans		

However, based on research in the area of job design (Hackman and Lawler, 1971; Hackman and Oldham, 1976), and our work with service managers and their employees, an empowered state of mind seems to include feelings of:

- *Control* over what happens on the job, i.e. freedom of choice among different ways of doing the job; input on how the job is designed; a belief that you can handle the job; better ability to respond if something goes wrong.

- *Awareness* of the context in which the job is performed. i.e. understanding of where work fits into the "big picture"; where it fits in with various downstream and upstream activities.

- *Accountability* for work output. They recognise the linkage between the quality and quantity of their own work, and the rewards they receive at work.

Table 10.1 emphasises the importance of both management practice *and* employee state of mind for implementing empowerment. The management practice empowerment equation reads: Empowerment = Power x Information x Knowledge x Rewards. The multiplication sign, rather than a plus, highlights that if any one of the four pieces is zero — that is if nothing is happening to redistribute that ingredient — then empowerment, itself, will be zero. This formula reminds managers to avoid the common error of giving employees more discretion (power), but not providing employees with the necessary abilities (knowledge) to exercise that discretion wisely.

The kernel of empowerment is how it transforms employees' psychological experience of themselves and their work. The quality of management practices aimed at empowering employees can be judged by their success in creating an empowered state of mind. The key is structuring work situations so that employees throughout the organisation have the personal feeling that they have what they need to satisfy the customer.

In short, empowerment is not a state of mind that comes about simply through better training of service employees. It is a performance capability and state of mind that is produced by a unique set of well-designed, systematically-implemented organisational practices and procedures. This is the main reason why in fact it is difficult to produce, and once created it is hard for competitors to match, making it a sustainable source of competitive advantage.

4.2. Why to Empower: The Benefits and Costs

What gains are possible from empowering service employees?

- *Quicker on-line responses to customer needs at the point of service delivery* — Check-in time at the hotel begins at 2 p.m., but a guest asks the receptionist if she can check in at 1.30 p.m. An airline passenger arrives at the gate at 7.30 a.m., Friday, for a 7.45 a.m. departure and wants to board the plane with a special travel coupon that is good for Monday–Thursday — there are empty seats on the plane. The hostess is taking an order in a modestly-priced family restaurant; the menu says "no substitutions" but the customer requests one anyway.

  The customer wants a quick response. And the employee, facing the customer, would often like to be empowered to respond with something other than "No, it is against our rules" or "I will have to check with my supervisor". Empowering employees in these situations can lead to the sort of spontaneous, creative breaking of the rules on the front lines that can turn a potentially frustrated or angry customer into a satisfied one. This is particularly valuable when there is little time to refer the decision to a higher authority — for example, the plane leaves in 15 minutes.

- *Employees feel better about their jobs—and themselves* — Giving front-line employees the power to decide how to interact flexibly with customers heightens their feelings that they are doing meaningful work, *and* are responsible for it. Earlier, we mentioned Peters' thinking on how strict rules can belittle human dignity. Empowerment — letting employees call the shots — allows employees to feel that they have "ownership" of the job; it's not just a job description that they caretake for management. Think of the difference in how you treat your own car as opposed to one you rent. Have you ever washed a rental car? Decades of research on job design show that when employees have a sense of control and of doing meaningful work, they are more satisfied. This in turn leads to lower levels of turnover and absenteeism, and fewer union organising drives.

- *Employees will interact with customers with more warmth and enthusiasm* — Research now supports our long-standing intuitions: customers' perceptions of service quality are shaped by the courtesy, empathy, and responsiveness of service employees (Schneider and Bowen, 1985; Zeithaml, Parasuraman, and Berry 1990). Customers want employees to appear concerned about their needs. Can empowerment help to create this? Customer service research in branch banks has shown that when the tellers reported feeling good about how they were supervised, trained, and rewarded, customers thought more highly of the quality of service they received (Schneider and

Bowen, 1985). In short, when employees felt that management was looking after their needs, they were more willing to take good care of the customer.

In service encounters, employees' feelings about their jobs will "spill over" to affect how customers feel about the service they get. This is particularly important when employee attitudes are a key part of the service package that customers purchase. In banking, where the customer receives no tangible benefits in the exchange other than a savings deposit slip, a sour teller can really blemish a customer's feelings about the encounter.

- *Empowered employees can be a great source of ideas about how best to serve the customer* — Empowering front-line employees with a voice in "how we do things around here" can lead to improvements in how services are delivered and ideas for new services. In the bank study, it was found that the tellers were able to report accurately how customers saw the branches' "climate for service": for example, adequacy of staff, appearance of facilities, and how customers viewed the quality of service, overall (Schneider and Bowen, 1985).

  Front-line employees, then, can provide accurate data on how customers see the service delivery system and feel about the services they receive. And these employees are often extremely eager for someone to ask their opinion. When it comes to market research, can you imagine the difference in response rates from surveying your employees as opposed to surveying your customers?

- *Great "word-of-mouth" advertising and customer retention* — Nordstrom's advertising budget is 1.5 per cent of sales versus an industry average of 5 per cent. Why? Their satisfied-no-matter-what customers spread the word about their service and end up as repeat customers.

- *To save the best for last: empowerment improves important business outcomes* — Research indicates that firms which report higher utilisation of practices that enact empowerment/involvement (pushing down power, information, rewards, and knowledge, for example) experience numerous improvements in business outcomes. A survey of Fortune 1,000 companies found that of those firms using employee involvement activities, 61 per cent reported a positive impact on productivity, 67 per cent on customer service, 66 per cent on employee satisfaction, and 45 per cent on profitability (Lawler, Mohrman, and Ledford 1992).

What are the *costs* of empowerment?

- *A greater monetary investment in selection and training* — Employees who are effective, creative, problem-solvers on the front line are not hired on the basis of chance or mere intuition. Unfortunately, because this would be a far less expensive hiring approach than the more systematic methods necessary to screen those who are good candidates for empowerment from those who might also break the rules, but not creatively. For example, Federal Express selects customer agents and couriers on the basis of very scientifically-drawn profiles of successful performers in those jobs.

   Training is the even larger cost. An important benefit of the industrialisation approach is that workers can be easily trained — and then put to work. New recruits at SAS are formally assigned a "mentor" to help them to learn the ropes; department managers within Nordstrom understand that it is their responsibility to orient and train new members of the sales team; new customer service reps at Lands' End and L.L. Bean spend a week in training before handling their first call.

   These selection and training costs are higher, the more labour-intensive the service. Retail banking, department stores, and convenience stores are labour-intensive and so these costs can run high. Utilities and airlines are far less labour-intensive.

- *Higher labour costs* — Many consumer service organisations, such as department stores, convenience stores, restaurants, banks, and so on, rely upon large numbers of part-time and seasonal workers to meet their highly variable staffing needs. Their time with the organisation is often brief and their compensation is typically low, near minimum wage with limited benefits, or none.

   Empowerment assumes that employees are guided by the organisation's culture and values, not by attention to policies and procedures. Feeling one's way through the "ropes to know" and the "ropes to skip" when facing the customer takes time — that may not be available to the employee, the organisation, or the customer. Either the organisation invests training money to try to initiate into the culture quickly (probably unsuccessfully) employees who may not be around long enough to provide a return unless they are paid well, or it staffs with only full-time long-tenure personnel whose wage costs are higher and who may not be needed when business is slow.

   The challenges associated with empowering part-time workers have recently become more widespread as their presence in the retailing sector increases. Retail firms have turned to part-time workers to reduce costs, as well as to reshape their workforces to fit advances in information technology better. The returns on empowering part-time workers largely depend on keeping their turnover relatively low. That is, empowerment fits best with "permanent part-timers". Retaining these employees requires attractive wages, training programmes, and desirable working conditions, none of which is inexpensive.

- *Slower or inconsistent service delivery* — Let's take another look at our earlier examples of the potential benefits of empowering employees to deal with hotel guests wanting to check-in early, and airline passengers requesting special treatment at the gate. True, this is a benefit, but only for the person at the *front* of the queue! Customers at the *back* of the queue are grumbling and checking their watches. Yes, they may have the satisfaction of knowing that they too may have the opportunity for a creative problem-solving session when (if) they reach the counter, but it is small consolation if the plane has already left.

  Based on our experiences as both researchers and customers, we believe that customers will increasingly value "speed" in service delivery. Purposeful chaos may be at cross-purposes with this. It is also our belief that many customers value "fairness" and "no surprises" in service delivery. Customers may not like seeing employees cutting special deals with other customers. They also may like to know what to expect when they revisit the same service business, or patronise different outlets of a franchise. Empowerment, where service delivery is left more to employee discretion, can have pose difficulties in delivering fairness and no surprises.

- *Employees may give away the store or simply make bad decisions* — Managers are often reluctant to empower their employees for fear that they will give too much away to the customer. Perhaps they have heard the story of Willie, the doorman at a Four Seasons Hotel, who left work and took a flight to return a briefcase left behind by a guest; or they have heard of too many giveaways from empowered Nordstrom employees. For some services, the costs of giveaways are far outweighed by enhanced customer loyalty, but not for all services.

  Sometimes creative rule-breaking can cause a major problem for an organisation. There may be a "good" reason why no substitutions are allowed or why a coupon cannot be used on a certain day — an international airfare agreement, for example; if so, having an empowered employee break a rule may cause the organisation serious problems, something of which the employee may not even be aware.

In summary, management should think about "why" to empower, and whether or not it makes good business sense, before unconditionally moving ahead. A cost/benefit analysis of the proposed empowerment initiative should be conducted. At the same time, however, management should not view the additional costs associated with better selection or more training merely as expenses, but also as investments. They can be investments that yield a stream of returns in the form of more satisfied employees and customers, as well as higher profits.

4.3 How to Empower: Understanding the Options

Recall from the discussion of the *what* of empowerment that it requires organisational practices that push power, information, knowledge, and rewards in the company down to the front line. Three different approaches can be used for this redistribution which differ in the degree to which the four features are pushed down to the front line (Lawler, 1988).

4.3.1 *Suggestion Involvement*

Suggestion involvement asks employees to solve problems and to generate ideas that will affect how the work is done. Formal suggestion programmes are the most popular means of providing with a voice in how to solve work-related problems. Quality circles represent a recent version of suggestion involvement and are an important part of many total quality control programmes.

Suggestion involvement represents a small shift away from the control model. Employees are encouraged to contribute ideas via formal suggestion programmes or quality circles, but their day-to-day work activities do not really change. Also, employees are only empowered to recommend; management typically retains the power to decide whether or not to implement.

Suggestion involvement can produce some of the gains possible with empowerment, without altering the basic production-line approach. McDonald's, for example, really listens to the front line. The Big Mac, Egg MacMuffin, and McDLT were all invented by individual employees within the system; as was the system workers use to wrap burgers without leaving a thumbprint indentation in the bun. As another example, Florida Power and Light, which won the Deming quality award, defines empowerment in suggestion involvement terms.

4.3.2 *Job Involvement*

Job involvement entails important changes in the way in which work is done. Jobs are redesigned so that employees: use a variety of skills in performing them; are provided with heightened feelings that their tasks are significant; have considerable freedom in deciding how to do the work; get more feedback from their work; and handle a whole, identifiable piece of work. Research shows that employees find enriched work more internally motivating and satisfying, and they do higher quality work (Hackman and Oldham, 1980).

Often, job involvement is accomplished through the extensive use of teams and groups. Teams are often appropriate in complex service organisations such as hospitals and airlines, because individuals cannot offer a whole service or deal with a customer from the beginning to the end of their interface with the organisation. Teams can be used to empower back-office workers in banks and insurance companies as well.

Job involvement represents a significant departure from the control model because of its dramatic "opening up" of the content of employees' jobs. Employees require training to deal with the added complexity. Supervisors, who now have fewer shots to call, need to be reoriented toward supporting the front line, rather than directing it. Despite the heightened level of empowerment it brings, the job-involvement approach does not change higher-level strategic decisions concerning organisation structure, power, and the allocation of rewards. These remain the responsibility of senior management.

4.3.3 High Involvement

In a high-involvement organisation, employees at the lowest level have a sense of involvement not just in how they do their jobs or how effectively their group performs, but in the performance of the total organisation. High involvement requires that virtually every aspect of the organisation be designed differently from how it is with the control approach. There *is* job enrichment but there is also information-sharing on business performance. Employee knowledge of team skills, problem-solving, and business operations need to be developed. Employees are involved in work-unit management decisions; there is profit-sharing and employee ownership.

High-involvement designs may be expensive to implement. Perhaps most troublesome, however, is that these management techniques are relatively underdeveloped and untested. People's Express tried to operate as a high-involvement airline and the ongoing struggle to learn and develop this new organisational design was a contributor to its operating problems.

More recently, America West has tried to make the high-involvement design work. New recruits spend 25 per cent of their first year's salary in purchasing company stock. All employees receive annual stock options. Flight attendants and pilots develop their own work procedures and schedules. Employees are extensively cross-trained so they can work where they are needed.

Federal Express displays many features of high involvement. A couple of years ago, it began a company-wide push to convert to teams — including the back office. It organised its 1,000 clerical workers in Memphis into super-teams of five to ten people, and gave them the authority and training to manage themselves. These teams helped the company to cut customer service problems — such as incorrect bills and lost packages — by 13 per cent in 1989.

4.4 Setting Limits on Empowerment: Between Control and Involvement

A challenge in managing empowered acts is setting reasonable boundaries for employee heroism. This is a real key to implementing the "how" of empowerment. Empowerment may need to be procedurally-driven, to some degree.

Boundary-setting boils down to establishing the difference between "good" versus "bad" heroic acts of empowerment. Employees sometimes don't realise the impact that their heroic act has on upstream or downstream activities. The helpful hotel receptionist who allows a disgruntled guest to check-in early doesn't always think through the implications for that day's housekeeping plan. Companies can tackle this by providing employees what Xerox terms "line of sight" or "line of visibility" training, in which employees are made very familiar with where their job fits relative to upstream and downstream activities.

After increasing employees' awareness of the context for their actions, boundaries can then be set in terms of monetary limits, as illustrated by the Ritz-Carlton and Hampton Inn examples. This can even be fine-tuned so that the monetary limits vary by value of customer. The frequent business traveller guest may have a higher monetary limit than the one-time tourist. But employees must also understand *when* to do something out of the ordinary, not just how much. Marriott identifies not only the boundaries for employees, but also tries to identify "safe zones" for them — situations in which empowered actions are called for. Marriott has employees spend a day in empowerment training to hear stories of empowered employees and to discuss the merits (or demerits) of the employees' actions. A related example is Williams Sonoma which collects stories of good examples of empowered actions and makes them available to employees through electronic mail.

The real challenge, however, is to fine-tune the service delivery system so that employees don't need to scramble to recover, because they get it right the first time. Here, advocates of the employee empowerment approach may have much to learn from the production-line approach's emphasis on procedures and technology. The strength of the production-line approach to service is its delivery of reliability and consistency.

An important key for companies concerns better integration of their employee empowerment programmes (which tend to glorify recovery) with their TQM efforts (which sanctify doing it right the first time). A rule might be that the more frequent the occurrence of acts of recovery, the more the "hard" tools of TQM such as pareto analysis, fishbone diagrams, and so on, should be used.

In summary, the issue of "how" to empower involves the implementation of alternative levels of empowerment: suggestion, job, or high involvement. Also, the same firm may adopt different levels of empowerment across different departments or jobs. The firm then holds a "portfolio of empowerment approaches". Even within any one job, some aspects may be made routine within a production-line approach so that they can be done quickly and easily, thus providing employees with more latitude on other aspects of the job.

4.5 When to Empower: A Contingency Approach

The history of management thought and practice has frequently been seduced by the search for "one best way to manage". Unfortunately, the complexity of the business world does not lend itself to universal truths, only "contingency theories" of management. It is possible that empowerment is a universal truth, but the weight of the historical evidence is against it.

It is argued here that both the empowerment and production-line approaches have their advantages, and that as shown in Table 10.2, both fit certain situations. For all situations, the key is to present the face that best meets the needs of *both* employees *and* customers.

Basic Business Strategy. A production-line approach makes the most sense if your core mission is to offer high volume service, at the lowest cost. The "industrialisation of service" certainly provides leverage for volume. On the cost-side, the question is, what is the value-added from spending the additional money on employee selection, training, and retention necessary for empowerment? This question becomes even more compelling in labour-intensive services, such as fast-food, grocery stores, convenience stores, in which labour is a substantial percentage of operating costs. This is particularly true where efficient staffing requires the use of part-time and/or temporary employees.

The answer to the value-added question depends on what customers really want from the service firm — and what they are willing to pay for. Obviously, customers want good service. However, good service can be defined in several ways. Certain customer segments are just looking for cheap, quick, reliable service. Yes, they do want quality, in the sense of a warm hamburger, rather than a cold one. But they are not necessarily expecting quality in terms of the much talked about "serve me, mother me" dimension of being polite, engaging, and attentive to customers' special needs. Or, even if they wanted it, they wouldn't pay for it.

In this case, a production-line approach is the face customers prefer. A study of convenience stores even found a *negative* relationship between clerks being friendly with customers queueing and store sales (Sutton and Rafaeli, 1988). Customers wanted speed and were generally turned off by spontaneous clerks who slowed things down. The key point is that customers themselves may prefer to be served by a *non-*empowered employee. Not all customers want a flexible, creative employee to serve them. Customers of some services actually want a fast, efficient, "by the rule-book" employee.

TABLE 10.2: A CONTINGENCY APPROACH TO EMPOWERMENT

Contingency	Favours a Production-line Approach	Favours an Empowerment Approach
Basic Business Strategy	Low cost, high volume	Differentiation, customised, personalised
Tie to Customer	Transaction, short time period	Relationship, long time period
Technology	Routine, simple	Non-routine, complex
Business Environment	Predictable, few surprises	Unpredictable, many surprises
Types of People	Theory X managers, employees with low growth needs, low social needs, and weak interpersonal skills	Theory Y managers, employees with high growth needs, high social needs, and strong interpersonal skills

Source: Adapted from Bowen and Lawler, 1992, p. 37.

At Taco Bell, counter attendants are expected to be civil, but Taco Bell wants to serve customers who want low-cost, good quality, *fast* food. It hires workers with learning difficulties who can execute the production line, but are not expected or encouraged to be creative problem-solvers on the front line. Interestingly, Taco Bell also feels that as more chains move to customised, service-oriented operations, the fast, production-line, low-price approach market niche is left even more open to them.

The use of a production-line approach does not rule out using suggestion involvement. As mentioned in the case of McDonald's, employees often have ideas even when much of their work is made routine. Quality circles and other approaches can be used to capture and develop them.

On the other hand, SAS has a targeted market segment: the frequent business traveller, who wants the quality "serve me" dimension more than speed and cost (most business travellers do not even pay their own way). Consequently, Jan Carlzon took the approach of looking at every ingredient of the company's service package to see if it fitted this customer segment's definition of service quality, and, if so, whether or not they would pay for it. The analysis has led to SAS being sure that the frequent business traveller pays the training and other costs associated with empowerment.

4.5.1 Business Strategy and Service Recovery

There are two main ingredients in customer service. One is delivering the service — checking a guest into a hotel room, for example. The other is recovery — relocating the guest from a smoking floor to the non-smoking room requested when the reservation was made. Can recovery be programmed, or do even production-line approaches to service delivery require an empowered approach to service recovery?

All service organisations need to take recovery seriously, regardless of their basic business strategy. Customers may differ in their preferences for speed versus customisation in service delivery, but *all* customers feel service businesses ought to fix things when service is delivered improperly.

At the same time, service managers should not be seduced into too great a focus on recovery. We say "seduced" because it is possible to confuse good service with heroics and inspiring stories about empowered service employees excelling in the art of recovery. Recovery has more sex appeal than dealing with the nitty-gritty detail of building quality into every seemingly mundane aspect of the service delivery system, but an organisation that relies on recovery may end up losing out to firms that do it right the first time.

The primary importance of delivery is evident in the research data which show that reliability, "doing it right the first time", is the most important dimension of service quality in the eyes of customers (Zeithaml, Parasuraman and Berry, 1990). It matters more than dimensions such as the employees' customer responsiveness, courtesy, competency, empathy or the attractiveness of the service setting. Regrettably, the same data show that a sample of large, well-known firms are more deficient on reliability than on these other dimensions. The value of recovery is that putting things right can turn a dissatisfied customer into a satisfied, even loyal, customer. Yet, for customers, recovery still comes in second to doing it right the first time.

The two aspects of service — delivery and recovery — can each be offered with an empowerment or production-line approach. McDonald's operates with a production-line approach to both delivery and recovery. A customer who complains that a burger is cold, gets another one, unconditionally. But given the high reliability of the production line, how often does a customer get a cold hamburger?

Clearly, companies like SAS and Nordstrom operate with empowered delivery and recovery. The "mixed modes" (different approaches for service and recovery) are more complex cases. UPS and many utility companies appear to face the customer with a production-line approach to delivery, but rely on empowered recovery. Much less common are organisations that operate in an empowered mode with delivery but rely on production for recovery. It might be appropriate when recovery needs to be very rapid because of an emergency situation and needs to involve the co-ordinated action of several employees — for example, in a fire or aeroplane emergency.

In many respects, the "mixed" models represent the greatest management challenge. In order for them to be effective, managers need to do a good job of gaining acceptance of the need to use two approaches and also to establish clearly when each applies. Even when this is done well, there is likely to be conflict when the organisation needs to use its recovery style (assuming this is used less often) because it is likely to be in conflict with the organisation's day-to-day practices concerning information, power, knowledge and rewards.

4.5.2 Nature of the Tie to the Customer

Empowerment is the best approach when service delivery involves managing a relationship. This is in contrast to simply performing a transaction. There are times when the service firm wants to establish a relationship with customers in order to build loyalty and to get ideas from them about how to improve the service delivery system, or what new services to offer. A flexible, customised, problem-solving face can help to establish the relationship and get the ideas flowing.

The returns on empowerment and relationship-building are higher with at least modestly sophisticated services and delivery systems. An empowered service employee in the international air freight industry is more likely to learn from a relationship with customers than is the empowered petrol pump attendant.

The relationship itself can be the principal valued commodity that is delivered in many services and here, again, empowerment is the best way to face the customer. When no tangibles are delivered, as in the case of inheritance planning or management consulting, the service provider often *is* the service in the customer's eyes and empowerment allows the employee to customise the service to fit the needs of the customer.

The more enduring the relationship, and the more it is an important piece of the service package, the stronger the case for empowerment. Remember the earlier example of how Disney tightly scripts its ride operators, but Club Med encourages the spontaneity of its GOs? The reason for this, as explained by Club Med's CEO, is that Disney employees relate to their guests in thousands of very brief encounters; GOs, on the other hand, have week-long close relationships with a more limited number of guests. The valuable service they sell is "time".

4.5.3 Technology

The kind of technology used by the service firm, and the kinds of jobs that go with it, are a key contingency. It is very difficult to build challenge, feedback, and autonomy (the characteristics of enriched work) into a telephone operator's job, given the way in which the delivery technology has been designed. The same is true of many fast-food operations. In these situations, the technology limits empowerment to only suggestion involvement and ultimately may remove individuals almost completely from the service delivery process, as has already happened with ATMs.

When technology is a constraint on empowerment, service managers can, nonetheless, support front-line employees in ways that enhance their satisfaction and the quality of service they provide customers. For example, if the jobs themselves cannot be enriched, then supervisors can at least show employees consideration and care. Also, managers can communicate and show employees how much their jobs matter to the success of the organisation. In other words, managers can try to do a better job of making the old management model work!

Routine work can be engaging if those doing it are convinced that it matters to something they care about. An extreme example of this is how volunteers will spend hours licking envelopes in a fund-raising campaign for their favourite charity. A less extreme example is the employees of Disney theme parks who, though tightly controlled, perform repetitive work admirably, partly because of a belief in the values, mission and show business magic of Disney.

4.5.4 Business Environment

Service businesses that operate in an environment of "surprises" benefit from empowerment. Airlines face an environment full of unpredictable challenges to their operations: bad weather, mechanical breakdowns, and competitors' actions. They serve passengers who often make a wide variety of requests for special services. In response, flexible and creative problem-solving employees are needed. It is simply impossible to anticipate many of the situations that will occur and to "programme" employees to respond to them. Employees trained in purposeful chaos are right for unpredictable environments.

Fast-food restaurants, however, operate in stable environments. Operations are fairly fail-safe; customer expectations are simple and predictable. In this environment, the service-business can face the customer with a production-line approach. The stability of the environment allows, even encourages, managing operations through policies and procedures, because most of the situations that occur can be predicted and the best response identified.

4.5.5 Value Systems

Empowerment and production-line approaches demand different types of managers and employees. For empowerment to work, particularly the high involvement form of it, managers need to have Theory Y participative beliefs that their employees can exercise self-control for the benefit of both the organisation and customers. If the management ranks are filled with Theory X autocratic types, who believe that employees only do their best work when closely supervised, then the control-oriented, production-line approach may be the only feasible alternative unless the organisation changes its managers.

Employees will respond positively to empowerment only if they have strong needs to grow and to deepen and test their personal competencies at work. A chequered history of job enrichment efforts has taught us not to assume that everyone wants more autonomy, challenge or responsibility, at work. Some employees simply prefer a production-line approach.

Lastly, empowerment that involves teamwork such as self-managing work-groups requires that employees are also interested in dealing with their social and affiliation needs at work. It also requires that employees have good interpersonal and group process skills.

5. THE FUTURE OF SERVICE WORK

The debate over control versus involvement models of organising has clearly moved into the service sector. Should the empowerment approach to service replace production-line approaches? How likely is it that more and more service businesses will choose to face the customer with empowered employees? Will the high-involvement, employee-centred management philosophy of empowerment be embraced by service managers over the more control-oriented, production-line approach?

The most likely scenario would seem to be that more service organisations currently operate on the control end of our continuum than is called for by the business situation they face and the strategies they have adopted. The results of a recent survey of companies in the "Fortune 1,000" offer some support for this view (Lawler, Mohrman and Ledford, 1992). It revealed that manufacturing firms tend to use significantly more employee-involvement practices than do service firms. For example, quality circles, participation groups, and self-managing work teams are used by manufacturing firms far more than by service firms.

Why are the various approaches to empowerment more frequently applied in manufacturing? Our explanation is that global competition has placed more pressure to change on the manufacturing sector — automotive, electronics, and steel, for example. This has created more dissatisfaction with the old control-oriented way of doing things. Also, it can be easier to see the payoffs from different management practices in manufacturing than in service. Often, increases in objective measures of productivity are more visible and clearly connected to profitability than are improvements in customer perceptions of service quality. However, these differences are now blurring as competition in services increases and service companies become more sophisticated in tracking the benefits of customer-service quality.

As service businesses consider empowerment, they can look at high-involvement manufacturing organisations as "labs" in which the various empowerment approaches have been tested and developed. Many lessons have been learned in manufacturing about how best to use quality circles, enriched jobs, and so on. And the added good news for service businesses is that many of them are ideally suited to applying and refining these lessons. Multi-site, relatively autonomously-run service operations afford their managers an opportunity to customise, and then evaluate first-hand, the effectiveness of empowerment efforts.

In summary, the newest approaches to managing the production line can serve as role models to be applied in many service businesses, but should not be used in all service businesses. Before service organisations rush into empowerment they need to see if it fits their situation. If it does, then they need to determine which type of empowerment fits best.

REFERENCES

Argyris, Chris, *Integrating the Individual and the Organization*, John Wiley, New York, 1964.

Bell, Chip and Ron Zemke, "Terms of Empowerment", *Personnel Journal*, September, 1988.

Bowen, David E. and Edward E. Lawler III, "The Empowerment of Service Workers: What, Why, How, and When", *Sloan Management Review*, Vol. 33, 1992, pp. 31–9.

Carlzon, Jan, *Moments of Truth*, Ballinger, New York, 1987.

Hackman, J. Richard and Edward E. Lawler III, "Employee Reactions to Job Characteristics", *Journal of Applied Psychology Monograph*, Vol. 55, 1971, pp. 259–86.

Hackman, J. Richard and Greg Oldham, "Motivation Through the Design of Work: Test of a Theory", *Organizational Behavior and Human Performance*, Vol. 16, 1976, pp. 250–79.1

Hackman, J. Richard and Greg Oldham, *Work Redesign*, Addison-Wesley, Reading, MA, 1980.

Lawler, Edward E., III, *High Involvement Management*, Jossey-Bass, San Francisco, CA, 1988.

Lawler, Edward E., III, *The Ultimate Advantage: Creating the High-Involvement Organization*, Jossey-Bass, Inc., San Francisco, CA, 1992.

Lawler, Edward E., III, Susan A. Mohrman and Gerald E. Ledford Jr., *Employee Involvement and Total Quality Management: Practices and Results in Fortune 1,000 Companies*, Jossey-Bass, Inc., San Francisco, CA, 1992.

Levitt, Theodore, "Production-Line Approach to Service" *Harvard Business Review*, September/October, 1972, pp. 41–52.

Levitt, Theodore, "Industrialization of Service" *Harvard Business Review*, September/October, 1976, pp. 63–74.

Likert, Rensis, *New Patterns of Management*, McGraw-Hill, New York, 1961.

McGregor, Douglas, *The Human Side of Enterprise*, McGraw-Hill, New York, 1960.

Schlesinger, Len and James L. Heskett, "Enfranchisement of Service Workers", *California Management Review*, Vol. 33, 1991, pp. 82–100.

Schneider, Benjamin and David E. Bowen, "Employee and Customer Perceptions of Service in Banks: Replication and Extension", *Journal of Applied Psychology*, Vol. 70, 1985, pp. 423–33.

Sutton, Robert J. and Anat Rafaeli, "Untangling the Relationship Between Displayed Emotions and Organizational Sales: The Case of Convenience Stores", *Academy of Management Journal*, Vol. 31, 1988, pp. 461–87.

Tansik, David, "Managing Human Resource Issues for High-Contact Service Personnel", in D.E. Bowen, R.B. Chase and T. Cummings (Eds.), *Service Management Effectiveness*, Jossey-Bass, Inc., San Francisco, CA, 1990, pp. 152–76.

Taylor, Frederick W., *The Principles of Scientific Management*, Harper Collins, New York, 1911.

Taylor, Frederick W., *Shop Management*, Harper Collins, New York, 1915.

Weber, Max, *The Theory of Social and Economic Organization*, The Free Press, New York, 1947.

Zeithaml, Valarie, A. Parasuraman and Leonard L. Berry, *Delivering Quality Service: Balancing Customer Perceptions and Expectations*, The Free Press, New York, 1990.

Zemke, Ron and Dick Schaaf, *The Service Edge: 101 Companies That Profit from Customer Care*, New American Library, New York, 1989.

11

MANAGING AND MARKETING TO INTERNAL CUSTOMERS

Audrey Gilmore and David Carson
University of Ulster — Jordanstown
Northern Ireland

PRÉCIS

To date, much has been written about internal marketing. It is widely recognised as an important concept that has evolved through services marketing, but which has extensive applicability to all marketing organisations. The purpose of internal marketing is to find and retain customer-conscious employees. It is also a means of developing and maintaining a "service ethos", which has often been used as a competitive advantage for organisations when they can get it to work! Considerable attention is paid in the literature to the potential benefits of successful internal marketing programmes. The difficulties associated with designing and implementing such programmes, however, are also clearly identified and shortfalls are apparent in current approaches advocated. There has been a tendency to rely on translating techniques and concepts designed for implementing external marketing programmes which may not be appropriate for internal customers, and which may fail to take on board the need for an integrated management approach within the organisation. The difficulties and shortfalls relating to well-tried attempts to implement internal marketing are examined by the authors who pose the question, "how can managers and staff be developed in order to improve their internal marketing performance within the context of their organisational role?"

This chapter reviews key influences on the evolution and development of the internal marketing concept. The scope and parameters of internal marketing are discussed, and specific issues addressed relating to the internal and external marketing interface. Particular attention is given to the difficulties associated with the practical implementation of internal marketing programmes from an organisational perspective. The authors focus on the human factors which impact on successful internal marketing; the concept of the internal customer; inter- and intra-functional relationships; the role of staff training and development; and human resource management issues. They present a view of internal marketing which goes beyond a set of marketing-type activities and pro-grammes: the idea of managing internal customers within an integrated management focus which draws on new developments in marketing, operations and human resources management. In response to the ques-tion raised earlier, the authors refer to the growing literature concerned with the development of management competencies for the specific roles and tasks of individual managers as a route to improved performance. They identify appropriate management competencies essential for suc-cessful internal marketing and provide practical examples to illustrate implementation of internal marketing through competency development. This chapter provides a useful exploration of the internal marketing concept and the practical issues concerned with managing and market-ing to internal customers. The authors present interesting proposals for a new, competency-based approach to managing internal customers based on contemporary marketing thought.

Helen Woodruffe
University of Salford, England

1. HISTORY, ORIGINS AND EVOLUTION OF INTERNAL MARKETING

1.1. Introduction

Internal marketing as a term has been widely used in varying contexts such as manufacturing process management, Human Resource Manage-ment, Total Quality Management and Services Marketing. However much confusion surrounds what it actually entails.

Internal marketing evolves from the idea that employees represent an internal market within the organisation. This market needs to be edu-cated and informed about the organisation's mission, the benefits of its products and services and the expectations of its customers. Successful marketing to this group will contribute significantly towards achieving ultimate success in the delivery of all marketing activity to external customers. Internal marketing can be seen as one way of achieving a "balance" between operational efficiency and sales.

This chapter considers the scope and nature, body of knowledge, current issues and future development of internal marketing in relation to its origins, the organisation and management of services marketing activity; and the relevant issues relating to a services marketing situation. The chapter concludes with some discussion about future developments in internal marketing by describing an alternative approach to managing internal customers based on some contemporary marketing management thought.

1.2. The Concept of Internal Customers: Origins

Although the term "internal marketing" emerged from the services marketing literature, the issue of managing internal activities has always been of interest to organisations. Various research has focused entirely on internal processes, operations and activities of employees (see for example, Weiss and Jacobson, 1955; Christopher, 1986; Sacker, 1988; Lundberg, 1990). This includes research surrounding:

- Organisational development
- Improving manufacturing and distribution deadlines
- human resource management, training and development
- Improving employee motivation through better communication, involvement and participation
- Many other internal initiatives to improve organisational output and efficiencies

During the past two decades, the term "internal marketing" has been widely used in organisations loosely to describe many of those managerial initiatives aimed at improving the effectiveness and efficiency of organisational resources. The use of the term "marketing" in this context does not mean simply the application or performance of marketing activity, but, more specifically, means a focus on marketing concepts and theories that are inherently directed towards a philosophy for customer satisfaction, both in the obvious external situation and, increasingly, in the context of the internal customer.

1.2.1 Evolution of Internal Customers

The concept of internal customers has emanated from the context of manufacturing industry and the area of operations management and quality. As early as the 1950s, one of the initiators of TQM used the slogan "the next process is your customer" (Ishikawa, 1985) to resolve hostility between workers from different backgrounds.

During the increased growth and development of the service sector in the 1970s, the recognition of the workforce as a resource became a prerequisite to employee performance improvement in their dealings with external customers. Consequently, this extended the interpretation of "customer" to mean the employees of the organisation. These employees are the people who are involved in the organisation's transactions and provide the service to external customers.

So, although it builds upon earlier organisational and management concepts, the concept of the internal customer emerged in the literature on services marketing (Sasser and Arbeit, 1976; Thompson, Berry and Davidson, 1978; Berry, 1981) and later in the service management literature (see for example, Normann, 1984; George, 1984; Compton, George, Grönroos and Karvinen, 1987; Carlson, 1987; Grönroos, 1990). The notion of internal customers has also entered the literature on industrial marketing (Grönroos and Gummesson, 1985; Gummesson, 1987) where each company's suppliers are considered to be internal customers.

Moreover, Heskett (1987) observes that successful service firms have achieved their position by "turning the strategic service vision inward", where they target key employee groups and customers, rather than customers only. So, although internal marketing in its full scope of meaning began in service organisations, the concept now has a much wider application in different industries and types of organisations today and is showing indications of being expanded further into such areas as public health and government organisations.

1.2.2   Other Influences on the Concept of the Internal Customer

The Total Quality Management (TQM) approach contributed to a significant expansion of the concept of internal marketing. This approach focuses not upon the relationship between the organisation and the employee, but on the relationship between the employees themselves. The idea of the internal customer in TQM means that every person is both a supplier and a customer, and the working of an organisation can be thought of as a series of transactions between customers and suppliers.

More recently, another alternative approach to marketing and management has emerged which has impacted upon the concept of the internal customer. There has been considerable interest in a longer-term approach to marketing through a closer examination of the role of relationships in the industrial marketing and services contexts (Berry, 1983; Jackson, 1985). Studies which concentrated on customers' perspectives of marketing (Grönroos, 1990) emphasised the importance of "interactive marketing" or "interactive relationships" in the industrial arena (Håkansson, 1982) and when applied to services, as seen in the work of the "Nordic School" (Grönroos and Gummesson, 1985). Whichever term is chosen, customer relationships lie at the centre of these concepts, and internal marketing is consequently of paramount importance to ensuring employee participation and involvement.

A further extension to the notion of internal customers and internal marketing could include the company's relationships with dealers and distribution channels, strategic partnerships and social contracts. These relationships are based on interdependencies and co-operation. For example, the just-in-time logistic system (JIT) stresses the significance of networks and long-term relationships. Although the network/interaction theory's empirical background is in industrial marketing, it has a wider application, where it may apply to concentrated consumer markets. For example, when a company sells through a limited number of outlets, the buyer may work out specifications for the standard of raw materials involved and details relating to the service delivery, together with the service manager involved. This theory stresses the importance of the "extended" internal customer. A network is gradually built around these interactive relationships over the long term (Gummesson, 1991).

It is generally accepted today in many companies that internal marketing is a prerequisite for successful external marketing performance (Grönroos, 1985; Compton, George, Grönroos and Karvinen, 1987).

2. DEFINITION OF INTERNAL MARKETING
2.1. What is Internal Marketing ?

The discussion so far has suggested that internal marketing has been used to describe a variety of internal management activities, which, although not new in themselves, have "offered a new approach to developing a service orientation and an interest in customers and marketing among all personnel" (Grönroos, 1990). As such, its parameters seem to be vague and ambiguous. Recent literature suggests that there is still no single unified notion of what is meant by internal marketing (Foreman and Woodruffe, 1991; Rafiq and Ahmed, 1993) and it is still an ill-defined concept which offers a "philosophy for managing the organisation's human resources based on a marketing perspective" (George and Grönroos, 1990). Although this offers a philosophical definition, it does not offer a specific definition at an operational level.

We can find some clearer understanding when considering it from the perspective of management. The management philosophy that is internal marketing calls on management to create, encourage continuously, and enhance an understanding and appreciation of the roles of employees in the organisation. The aim of this activity is to achieve a motivated work-force made up of employees who take responsibility for their own tasks within the context of the organisational goals. When given a freedom and empowerment, employees may go a long way to establishing, main-taining and developing an internal marketing philosophy, but the orga-nisational environment must be conducive to this circumstance. This is discussed in some depth earlier in this book (Bowen and Lawler, Chapter 10). There are many organisations where staff motivation is stifled because of a rigid structure, a poor working environment or other organisational problems. These human issues are also considered else-where in this book (Lovelock, Chapter 8). So where and how can the internal marketing philosophy exist operationally?

Gummesson (1991) suggests that there are at least four phenomena that can be labelled internal marketing and where internal customers exist. These include: the customer–supplier relationship between em-ployees inside a company; the application of marketing know-how to the personnel (particularly in services marketing); the activities involved in getting a company to be marketing-oriented; and the marketing that takes place between profit-centres inside a decentralised company.

A speculative definition of the concept of internal marketing might involve "the spreading of the responsibility for all marketing activity across all functions of the organisation, and the proactive application of marketing principles to 'selling the staff' on their role in providing cus-tomer satisfaction within a supportive organisational environment". In turn, this should have an effect on the marketing to external customers (Lewis Chapter 3; Payne and Clark, Chapter 12).

This definition argues that the central aspect and purpose of internal marketing revolves around the creation and delivery of the internal marketing message and managing the communication of this message. Firstly, the message must illustrate how the marketing philosophy can be applied to the various functions of the organisation. All managers, con-tact and support staff need information to be able to perform their tasks as leaders and managers and as service providers to both internal and external customers. Consequently, they will need information about job routines, the features of goods and services, the implications of the promises given to customers by advertising campaigns and salespeople and how that impacts upon their roles. Communication must occur not only from the top down, but also from the bottom up and across functional boundaries. For example, employees need to be able to communicate about their needs, requirements, views on how to improve performance and their interpretations of what customers want. There-fore, the internal marketing message needs to take account of educating, understanding, stimulating and informing employees at all levels. Moti-vating employees and influencing their attitudes is central to internal marketing, and the communication message is thus very important.

Therefore, a further definition of internal marketing might include the creation of an internal environment where all functions of the orga-nisation proactively communicate, understand and inform each other in relation to all marketing activity, so that all activity can be performed in an integrated and co-ordinated way. Thus, sound internal marketing can be practised when joint responsibility is taken by all functional depart-ments, with key people from each function leading from the front.

2.2. Scope and Parameters of Internal Marketing

There has been considerable scope and variety in the type of internal marketing activity that has been used by many companies. These activities include:

- The internal and external marketing interface

- The application of the marketing mix to internal customers

- The use of marketing training and internal communication methods to sell the staff on their role within the context of the organisation

- The involvement and empowering of staff to allow them to make decisions in relation to dealing with customers

- The development of managers' and employees' role responsibility and cross-functional participation

- The functional responsibility of the organisation for internal market-ing integration.

These aspects of internal marketing are discussed below.

2.2.1 The Internal and External Marketing Interface

If internal marketing is so integral to marketing, why then is it not always present or performed? The absence of managing and marketing to internal customers can find expression in one or a combination of the following circumstances:

- A "performance gap", where there is a gap between what the external customer expects from a company and what the customer actually perceives by way of service experienced during and after the transaction

- The "human factor", which is the consequence of the interpersonal contact or relationship between contact staff and the external customer.

A gap occurs when an organisation's service standards are not defined on the basis of customer expectations. There is a considerable literature in this area which is reviewed and discussed in this book (Parasuraman, Chapter 6). When customers compare their expectations prior to receiving a product or service with the actual experience they have had, they will form either a positive or negative opinion of that product or service and of the company. Parasuraman, Zeithaml and Berry (1985) call this discrepancy the "performance gap".

The "human factor" impacts crucially on customers' experience and their overall perceptions of the organisation. Whether customers feel that they have received sufficient customer care or service depends heavily on what has happened during the actual time spent interacting with the company's staff. The interpersonal behaviour of the front-line staff, their knowledge and competence, their responsiveness and willingness to help is obviously important from the customers' perspective. The main problem occurs when senior management in organisations overlooks the underlying importance of inter-relationships between staff, their departments and the customer contact environment. For example, in British Airways "Putting People First" campaign, the senior development projects manager noted that before the launch top management tended to "overlook the fundamental inter-relatedness of people with themselves and with their environments" (Bruce, 1988). Furthermore, managers tended to break problems into little parts, categorise significant factors and then concentrate on fixing the offending factor. This often led to a short-term reprieve of the situation but, because relations and interactions were ignored and the integrative functioning of the whole organisation had not been considered, the problem issue often re-emerged in another form.

2.2.2   *Using the Marketing Mix to Target the Internal Customer*

Piercy and Morgan (1989/90) contend that the easiest way to make practical progress with internal marketing is to use the same structures that are used for planning external marketing. Thus, consideration should be given to integrating the elements needed for an internal marketing mix based on the analysis of the opportunities and threats in the internal marketplace of a specific company.

However, there is some concern that this concept of the internal customer may be too simplistic, does not take account of some important aspects of the requirements of employees in relation to their jobs, and therefore may not represent a realistic view of organisational life. Fundamental to this argument is the issue of customer choice: where external customers have choice, internal customers may not. The internal product comprises the marketing strategies and the marketing plan and needs to be sold to employees as the values, attitudes and behaviours which are needed to make the marketing plan work effectively. These internal products that employees are being sold may be unwanted or may have a negative utility. In addition, the internal product can be defined at a strategic and tactical level, and so a new marketing strategy may lead to a new tactical procedure which involves new performance measures or new ways of dealing with customers which may not be acceptable to employees.

Therefore although the marketing mix concept can be used loosely to give some framework to inwardly directed marketing techniques, on its own it would appear to be insufficient. The simple or ad hoc transfer of marketing concepts and techniques is not likely to address all management- and employee-related internal issues in their quest for more successful external marketing activity.

2.2.3 Staff Roles: Training, Communicating and Selling the Concept

In an attempt to improve the performance of staff, some companies have tried schemes that involve treating their employees as customers through the use of internal marketing training. Training programmes have been used to improve communication and understanding by bringing multi-disciplinary groups together. This can provide considerable benefits to employees as individuals as, particularly if looking after the external customer is recognised as a skill and employees can then measure their own improvement, they will have a greater sense of achievement.

However, training programmes alone are not enough as people may quickly forget the training they received or find themselves out of phase with other employees. Thus, many internal training programmes and internal communication initiatives have failed to achieve an integrative approach to the internal performance of an organisation. Internal marketing success will depend upon finding a means of developing staff to create an environment of communication and inter-relationship on a continuous rather than an ad hoc basis.

2.2.4   *Empowerment and Involvement of Staff*

Some companies have tried empowering and involving staff by authorising them to use discretion in order to deliver a better quality service to their customers. The aspect of empowerment in service organisations is included elsewhere in this book (Bowen and Lawler, Chapter 10). Empowerment means that the organisation must create the right circumstances and environment in which employees can operate. This will include: providing information about the organisations' performance; providing rewards based on the organisations' performance; providing knowledge that enables them to understand and contribute to organisational performance; and giving them power to take decisions that influence organisational direction and performance (Bowen and Lawler, 1992).

However, many organisations have failed or have met with internal opposition and barriers in their quest to create empowerment, mainly because it is seen as a threat to the existence of the role of middle managers and because there is an overall fear of delegating power and authority, and sometimes a reluctance on the part of operational staff to accept the increased responsibility and accountability that empowerment engenders. Such opposition is often most common in established, bureaucratic organisations.

2.2.5   *Functional Responsibility for Internal Marketing*

There is still some confusion about the formalisation of whether internal marketing is predominantly the preserve of the personnel function or whether it should belong to marketing (see, for example, Barnes, 1989; Berry, 1981; Collins and Payne, 1991; Flipo, 1986; George, 1977 and 1990; Grönroos, 1981, 1985, and 1990; Piercy and Morgan, 1989/90, Sasser and Arbeit, 1976; Winter, 1985; Rafiq and Ahmed, 1993). This implies that it is generally considered to be either a function of human resource management or a marketing activity.

However, the interface of all functional managers in an organised, systematic way would not only contribute to the integration of all the functions, but would also provide guidance for the development of each function in relation to its correct role and in relation to the other business functions. In this context, internal marketing activity can be deemed to be an intra-organisational concern transcending all functional boundaries, largely dependent on the degree of integrative activity within company functions, with key managers taking responsibility for the development of internal marketing initiatives and leading cross functional communication. It can also refer to inter-organisational activities, for example, in the business-to-business sector (de Burca, Chapter 14; Fynes, Ennis and Negri, Chapter 13).

2.2.6 Summary of the Scope and Parameters of Internal Marketing

The scope and parameters of internal marketing rely upon and involve management and employee role responsibility and cross-functional participation. The need for role responsibility and interfunctional dependency is implicitly accepted as being a prerequisite to successful organisational and marketing activity. All activities in a company are inter-related; therefore, all organisational functions need to behave in an inter-related way. If companies do not consider the linkages between all functions, their overall performance will be uncoordinated and fragmented. Functional barriers to co-ordinated activity occur in many forms. Some examples are: the organisational structures in which managers operate and the impact of conflicts of interests with other functions; the inter-action between organisational structure and the effectiveness of marketing activities; and the manipulation of marketing information (Piercy, 1990).

Organisational structures must be conducive to internal services marketing concepts and philosophies. It may be necessary to break down interfunctional barriers and emphasise the merging of the functions of departments such as Human Resource Management and Marketing into an overall internal services marketing activity, so that internal marketing is practised throughout the organisation in some form as a "joint" function, which is representative of all departments.

Functional integration is necessary for long-term organisational success. It needs to permeate all levels of the workforce so that co-ordination and co-operation will occur at all levels. Judd (1987) categorises different levels of staff within an organisation depending on the degree and type of contact with external customers:

- "Contactors" who have direct frequent or periodic customer contact

- "Modifiers" who have less direct frequent or periodic customer contact (usually not fact-to-face)

- "Influencers" who traditionally have no direct contact with customers although they may make many decisions in relation to customers

- "Isolateds" who have no customer contact at all.

Judd emphasises that the "contactors" are not the only people involved in service delivery, as all the other types of staff have important internal roles to play in the delivery of customer service and in helping the front-line staff to be more effective. Referring to these as part-time marketers, Gummesson (1991) argues that their role is also very important, as although they do not belong to the marketing and sales department, they influence customer relations, customer satisfaction, customer-perceived quality and revenue. Therefore, the importance of everyone's role in an organisation is emphasised.

3. DIFFICULTY OF IMPLEMENTING INTERNAL MARKETING AND SHORTFALLS IN CURRENT APPROACHES

Attempts to implement internal marketing have included initiatives such as: informal and ongoing internal training, the encouragement of informal interactive communication, periodic newsletters or updates, internal marketing segmentation, and internal market research. Although there is agreement in the literature that an internal marketing programme should be executed on strategic policy and tactical levels, the demarcation between strategic and tactical activities is often blurred (Richardson and Robinson, 1986; Tansuhaj, Randall and McCullough, 1991).

To date, the implementation of internal marketing in practice has received little success (Rafiq and Ahmed, 1993). Another reason for lack of success in applying internal marketing in practice may be that many attempts have structured activity around the McCarthy 4Ps framework which in itself is too general and non-specific in relation to dealing with internal customers' requirements and expectations from their employment (McCarthy, 1964). Similarly, the lack of a clear recognition of which function or department should have overall responsibility for internal marketing may have contributed to no real ownership being taken for the implementation of initiatives. The holistic adoption of internal marketing poses some problems, particularly in relation to the context of implementation. To date, there are very few models of how internal marketing should be *implemented*. Thus, the issue of implementation is perhaps the most significant aspect of internal marketing that needs to be addressed.

Clearly, the discussion so far illustrates that attempts to improve external activity through internal marketing initiatives have fallen short of achieving a holistic, organisation-wide, action-oriented result. In particular, the shortfalls identified are:

- Although the use of some marketing techniques will help, on their own they will not produce results until there is some precise specification of how the marketing concept can be put into operation in the internal context.

- From an organisational point of view, there is no easy standardised approach to managing internal customers. Organisations cannot plan for every eventuality. By acknowledging the role of customers as co-producers, and consequently the fact that even if employees' behaviour could be standardised, the behaviour and expectations of customers cannot.

- The nature of organisational inter-relationships and interactions in the context of daily life needs to be recognised. Organisations are internal networks of interacting groups where power dependencies and relationships occur between internal departments (Mastenbroek, 1993). Therefore, relying on organisational structure alone is not sufficient. Informal networks are required for effective activity and internal marketing. In addition to this, the use of key managers or gate-keepers is not enough. The interactive nature of all marketing activity throughout an organisation and in relation to external customers and suppliers means that every member of staff needs to have the ability to manage all situations. The ownership of managing internal customers must lie with every individual within an organisation, particularly in a services situation where the production, delivery and marketing are partially simultaneous and are partially carried out by the same employees who are partially in direct contact with the customer who partially consumes the service in interaction with the service provider.

- Strategic and tactical approaches may be too abstract in themselves and have some difficulty in succeeding if the actual implementation issues of specific action plans and responsibility for activities are not addressed. Managing internal affairs will involve encouraging members to ensure that organisational goals are met and that plans and standards are followed. That is, "members make the internal adjustments necessary to see that their intentions become actualities" (Lundberg, 1990).

Any new approach needs to take account of these issues and understand the basic inter-relationships between the employee in a particular job and the abilities, skills and knowledge required in order to fulfil that role. Thus, a holistic, actionable, implementable approach is required.

4. THE INFLUENCE OF NEW THEORETICAL DEVELOPMENTS ON INTERNAL MARKETING

Where does internal marketing fit in relation to some of the new developments in marketing and management? The "new approaches" of the 1990s include relationship marketing, the use of networks and inter-actions and a re-emphasis on total quality management. Unlike the tradi-tional marketing concept which focuses on the external customers, these theories also stress the importance of the internal customer.

Any alternative approach to the management of internal customers should of course go a long way to overcoming the shortfalls of the approaches highlighted above. The essence of an alternative approach will be, firstly, to borrow from some of the fundamental concepts of the "new approaches" to marketing and management and to consider how these may impact upon the overall management of internal marketing and, secondly, to contribute to the development of internal customers in relation to their specific roles.

Relationship marketing captures the essence of the new develop-ments in marketing. This is discussed at some length elsewhere in this book (Gummesson, Chapter 9). Interaction has become the key concept referring to the contact between the service provider's staff and the con-sumer in the services marketing arena, and the contact between producers and purchasers in the arena of industrial markets. Conse-quently, the interaction and relationship between the two parties in any of these contexts has been explicitly recognised as being vital for the long-term survival of each company.

Total Quality Management focuses on customers as suppliers, thus emphasising that everyone contributes to organisational success or lack of success. Consequently, TQM has become the integrator between production-orientation and marketing-orientation, between technology-driven and market-driven behaviour, thus creating a more holistic per-spective of organisational purpose.

By drawing from the fundamental and holistic aspects of TQM and relationship marketing, internal marketing management could be con-sidered and redefined as a more holistic, systemic and organisation-wide concept. In particular, the new approaches to managing marketing focus on the following:

- Internal customers in the context of their influence over external customers

- A holistic perspective of organisational purpose and activity

- The importance and necessity of organisations without boundaries

- Individual responsibility for activities

- The continual training, development and involvement of all staff.

Therefore, any new approach to managing and marketing to internal customers needs to build on these approaches and focus on the continual development of management and staff as the organisation continually evolves and adapts to suit the changing environment. Particular emphasis will be on who should manage internal marketing inside the company; and the development of their leadership skills will be crucial to the cross-functional dimensions of holistic internal marketing management (Heskett, Chapter 16).

So how can managers and staff be developed in order to improve their internal marketing performance within the context of their organisational role? Current developments in the management literature focus on the development of management competencies for the specific roles and tasks of individual managers in order to improve performance. Although much has been written about management competencies (see for example, Wrapp, 1967; Mintzberg, 1973; Katz, 1974; Rugman, 1984), consideration of which competencies are most suitable for marketing has only recently been given attention (see for example, Carson, 1993; Carson, Hill and Magowen, 1993; Gilmore and Carson, 1994). However, the specific roles of the organisation's marketing managers and the areas of decision-making which most concern them should be taken into account if the most suitable management competencies are to be recognised and developed in such a way as to build on each manager's experience, knowledge and expertise. In addition, the focus of competence-development recognises and promotes the existence of "learning" managers who are continually improving their competence in relation to their specific role, rather than assuming that training programmes should teach managers how to think and behave.

5. MARKETING MANAGEMENT COMPETENCIES FOR INTERNAL MARKETING

There is increasing recognition that managers should have competence in their relevant functional area and that the development of management competencies is the key to improved management performance (Boyatzis, 1982; Carson, 1993). This is no less relevant in the context of internal marketing. Management and staff must have appropriate competencies for successfully implementing internal marketing, particularly in a services situation where all staff are part of the service process. Firstly, in considering the notion of marketing management competencies for internal marketing, we need to have a brief working definition of management competencies for managing and marketing to internal customers and then give some consideration to which competencies are most appropriate for marketing, focusing specifically on which are most appropriate for internal customers in a services context.

5.1. Competencies for Marketing Services

The literature has provided many descriptions of competencies. For the purpose of this discussion a competency is defined as a management skill. Such competencies will consist of a range of attributes which are given relevance in a task environment as being appropriate for the particular activities of managers.

From the descriptions in the literature of "general management competencies" those which are frequently mentioned include competencies such as those for managing peers, decision-making under ambiguity, conflict-resolution, information-processing, resource-allocation, leadership, entrepreneurship and introspection. However, the question remains as to whether these competencies are appropriate for marketing and indeed marketing services. The answer is that all are appropriate in some combination or other. However, when taking account of the characteristics of marketing and services, it is possible to envisage a list of specific competencies which will focus more on marketing-related decisions and activities. Carson (1993) offers a list of competencies which relate specifically to marketing decision-making. These are illustrated on the left column in Figure 11.1 under the heading "Marketing Management Competencies". When considered in relation to services' specific marketing decision-making, some of these competencies may be more appropriate than others. For example, competencies relating to people management such as leadership and communication may have particular importance in a services marketing situation. Furthermore, some of these competencies may require a particular emphasis in a services situation. Leadership focused on the concept of internal services management across functions will be important. Communication may also be vital in motivating staff to ensure that some action is taken in relation to the service delivery. So, we can say that marketing management competencies will become more refined and specific depending on the marketing situation in which the company operates. Thus, it is conceivable to produce a list of "Services Marketing" competencies, which is naturally derived from the more general, but still relevant, marketing management competencies. We have illustrated this in Figure 11.1, under the heading "Services Marketing Competencies".

However, some of the services marketing competencies may be more fundamental than others. That is, core competencies may be required in order to provide a basis for building and developing further refined and specific competencies. These core competencies will include the inherent or basic competencies of knowledge, experience, expertise and judgment. It is contended here that competency in these four attributes will enable a manager in a services marketing situation to perform services marketing effectively. These competencies may be used as a basis for building on the more specific competencies dictated by the manager's role responsibilities. The core competencies for services marketing can be seen in Figure 11.1.

FIGURE 11.1: CORE COMPETENCIES FOR EXTERNAL SERVICES MARKETING

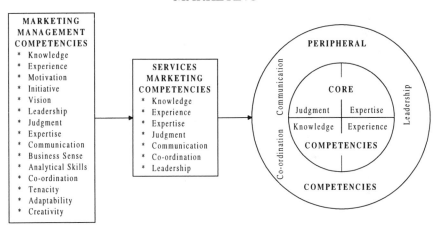

Our rationale for these attributes representing core competencies is that managers will possess some competency in relation to knowledge, experience, expertise and judgment in the context of their management responsibilities. These core competencies of knowledge, experience, expertise and judgment are considered below.

5.1.2 Knowledge

A knowledge competency includes clear understanding of the specific details and requirements of the job, the company's markets, competitors, and different customers. In particular, managers need to have a knowledgeable understanding of the processes and activities required for the successful integration of the service delivery, how each process impacts upon the other and specific details of the job including every aspect of the service delivery and the issues that may affect it. The inter-dependencies between staff and departments must be known and under-stood as they have an impact upon how the service will be delivered.

Furthermore, managers need to have knowledge. This is obtained by gathering information about their markets, different customers' require-ments for core services and their priorities in relation to different service products and how they are delivered. In the case of developing new service products, the internal management team will need to recognise when to extend its service product range and when to delete or modify old service products without losing or disappointing the core market.

This is particularly important in a services situation where each cus-tomer will have varying needs and requirements which may call for some careful adaptation of the service to suit each situation. For example, some customers may need more specific guidance and direc-tion than others in relation to the use of a more complex or unfamiliar service. Some management team motivation and initiative development will be needed in order to benefit from everyone's knowledge of the service delivery so that new service products can be well thought through in terms of core customers' likes and dislikes. Supervisors and managers can perhaps develop responsibility and motivation by allowing front-line staff to apply their knowledge in leading the development of new products.

5.1.3 Experience

The depth and width of experience of all managers will contribute to the quality of internal marketing. The depth of experience relates to the circumstances of working in the same area over a period of time and allowing detailed concentrated involvement and understanding of specific tasks. This will contribute to a manager's experience. The width of experience is also important in relation to allowing managers to trans-fer their experience to other situations, contributing to the building and development of their overall performance. Managers need to be allowed to experiment, try out new ideas, learn from experience and have the ability to develop and expand their experience to build to the future. The variety of experience is also important in order to develop vision to see and understand all other possibilities in service development. For example, some customers may prefer to receive more attention from staff than others. Such staff will need to be experienced. In addition, dealing with customer complaints in a services situation often means having the ability to make an instant decision and to take a corrective course of action on the spot. Experience will allow more considered decisions and will reduce the risk of them being wrong.

5.1.4 *Expertise*

An expertise competency may be built up over time by managers taking the initiative to try out new ideas, having commitment and involvement, learning from their mistakes, and adapting accordingly. Continual development in expanding the depth and width of expertise will ensure that the organisation develops and changes to suit external environmental changes. The depth of expertise contributes to the suitability of managerial actions, decisions and responses to particular situations, and to how well managers can actually *do* the job. The width of expertise manifests itself in the transfer of expertise to different situations and the ability to manage each issue within the perspective and context of the organisational purpose. That is, the expertise to *do* other jobs, or wider job dimensions. Expertise is required in relation to both technical expertise, such as possessing the specific skills or ability to do a job and managerial expertise, which calls for the ability to manage a situation, facilitate the process and allow the service to happen. As the customer is involved in the whole delivery of the service product, each member of staff must be encouraged to develop their expertise.

5.1.5 *Judgment*

A competency for judgment is built upon knowledge, experience and expertise. Good judgment will be based on knowledge of the job, experience in the industry and the development of expertise in the particular area of services management. It involves the ability to analyse the results of a prescribed course of action or the impact of certain decisions and to learn from this experience.

These competencies of knowledge, experience, expertise and judgment are clearly suitable for external services marketing activity, but they are equally important for internal marketing in a services firm. We will now consider the marketing tasks and activities of a services company and the emphasis of each of the competencies in internal marketing activity.

5.2. Competencies for Managing Internal Marketing in a Services Context

The services manager's activities and tasks for external decision-making must be matched with the services' specific competencies for these tasks — described in the previous section. The services marketing management role involves the integration of service activities and processes; managing customer and staff interactions; people management; accessibility and timing; managing the intangible nature of services; and service differentiation. In particular, service managers need to manage the intangible nature of the product and how customers perceive and understand this product, to ensure that they get the most from it and are satisfied with it; and they need to manage the whole service delivery process from the beginning to the end of the customers' interaction with the company. The core services marketing competencies and services marketing activities are illustrated together in Figure 11.2.

If these two dimensions represent the essence and scope of services marketing management, it is expected that the same dimensions should be applicable in an internal marketing situation within a service company. However, it is necessary to enhance these dimensions by introducing other specific competencies. The competencies required for the internal management of service tasks and responsibility for the service delivery will thus revolve around internal communication, namely, primarily communication with a focus on co-ordination and leadership. Communication is the link-pin of these three, because without it co-ordination and leadership could not exist. This is described below.

5.2.1 Communication

In order to build on and develop knowledge, experience and expertise a communication competency is necessary. In fact it could be argued that by their nature, the development of all management competencies depend upon communication. Communication is about achieving the sharing of ideas, in order to contribute to the holistic organisational viewpoint and progress.

FIGURE 11.2: CORE COMPETENCIES FOR INTERNAL SERVICES
MARKETING

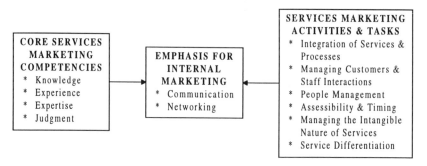

A communication competency may manifest itself in the creation of suitable brochures, promotional literature and materials, selecting effective media, and face-to-face messages for communication. More importantly, however, it can contribute to management activity in an action-oriented way as a method of achieving co-ordination and leadership. A communication competency will provide the vehicle for cross-functional participation in the integration and co-ordination of activities throughout the organisation; contribute to successful direction and implementation ensuring that everyone knows what is involved and their role in the whole activity; and aid leadership, as a services manager who is a good persuader and makes good presentations to staff will win over their allegiance.

A communication competency in a services situation is necessary in order to maintain a consistent and continuous level of service and to help avoid fragmentation — when maintaining consistent customer–staff interactions and ensuring complete service delivery, for example.

5.2.2 Networking

Internally, it is important to recognise the significance of using and listening to both formal and informal networks. Encouraging the development of networks within the organisation, between key managers, supervisors and members of staff in different departments and positions will help build on managers' external competencies of knowledge, experience, expertise and judgment by concentrating on internal communication, particularly in relation to co-ordination and leadership of activities. This will aid staff empowerment and lead to a motivated workforce and overall improved service performance.

To summarise, competency development for managing internal customers in a services marketing context should build upon the experience, expertise, knowledge and judgment already in existence by focusing on developing communication competencies and building networks between internal customers within the company. This, in turn, will contribute to a suitable environment for empowerment and staff responsibility. However, it is acknowledged that these core competencies are essentially those competencies required for managing services in the general sense and aiding the development of internal staff operating in a services marketing context. They require different emphasis in order to carry out various specific services marketing functions and activities effectively. Because of this different emphasis, it can be argued that, in this context of managing internal customers, they should be viewed as uniquely *core internal marketing management competencies for services*. These competencies are clearly activity- or action-oriented.

6. IMPLEMENTATION OF INTERNAL MARKETING THROUGH COMPETENCY DEVELOPMENT: A CASE EXAMPLE

The improvement of external marketing activity has been the impetus for many internal marketing programmes. Two examples from a company operating internationally in the hotel and catering industry are given here to illustrate this point. The company in question has recently experienced a major reorganisation. The established traditions and procedures have been abandoned and there have been many personnel changes. Our case focuses on two managers in two similar divisions of this company. One, new to management, is charged with developing external and internal marketing in his division; the other manager is experienced in the company, but has been moved to a new division about which he has no experience and little knowledge. These examples focus on the development of competencies which build on individuals' competency strengths in such a way as to overcome their existing competency weaknesses.

6.1. Scenario 1

This describes the circumstance of a young manager in his early twenties. His competency strengths were his wide knowledge of the industry, having worked in it for six years, and his expertise in dealing with various aspects of the activities and tasks of the day-to-day running of the business. His competency weaknesses were his lack of judgment and overall experience in management. His competency development process evolved through using proactive communication with other managers and outside agencies in order to share ideas and develop his scope and perspective of his managerial activity. In addition, he built up networks with key managers within the local division, with other branches of the same company and with head office decision-makers, in order to gain advice and guidance and gather a number of opinions on various aspects of managerial activities and tasks. In the short term, the young manager was able to rely on opinions and advice from his more experienced and senior peers to help him make decisions. Over a relatively short space of time, this manager's competency weaknesses of judgment and experience were overcome, and in the process he had succeeded in creating a marketing focus and emphasis across the company. He now has a standing of sound dynamic decision-making and evidence of results performance. His "experience" and "judgment" are perceived to be contemporary and modern and his subordinates are keen and motivated to work with and to be associated with him. The internal marketing in this division has a clear focus and purpose.

6.2. Scenario 2

This circumstance describes a senior manager with responsibility for a new division within the reorganised company. His competency strengths were his judgment and experience which had been gained over some years in a variety of senior management positions within the company. However, his weaknesses were his knowledge and expertise in relation to his new management responsibility. His competency development process occurred through setting up structures and systems which would stimulate communication, bringing key managers together, informing and involving staff in each functional area in the development process. For example, he created the environment for groups of staff to suggest new ideas for improving their activity in relation to service delivery, allowed them to try out their ideas and solicit feedback from customers. Throughout this process, he communicated both formally and informally with staff members. This developed his knowledge and expertise in operational service activities and encouraged staff by his interest in their work. In addition, he used his networking experience to direct others and gather information and feedback on all new activities and initiatives in order to develop his knowledge and expertise in relation to his new responsibilities. Not only has he rapidly gained "knowledge" and "expertise", he has the respect and motivation of his staff, which has enhanced the whole internal marketing aspect of the division.

This manager also encouraged the use of networking as a means of achieving company improvement at operational level. Key managers from each specific service location — such as chefs, waiters and cashiers — were identified for their depth and width of knowledge, experience and expertise in their chosen field, and were requested to collaborate with their teams of staff in order to identify how they might improve some aspect of service for which they had responsibility. The focus was on improving the competencies of service staff through giving them the responsibility for decision-making and activities so that they could constantly improve service delivery practices. Small groups of staff worked together to address specific issues. These "quality groups" were formed according to their area of work responsibility and interest. For example, the restaurant management team incorporated all personnel who were involved in decisions relating to any aspects of the restaurant service delivery —food service managers, waiters and chefs, for example. Each group was requested to deal with an appropriate identified problem area, focusing on issues to address and the specific tasks involved. The process of implementation involved an interactive exchange of views and opinions. Restaurant managers, chefs, cashiers and waiters from each service area met regularly as equals without superior–subordinate authorities, to consider each particular quality issue and how it was impacted upon by internal activities and personnel. Over time, new initiatives were developed in relation to the service delivery and a *modus operandi* was established for company development. Thus, all external marketing improvement was built on improved internal marketing activity, particularly in relation to the development of internal communication and networking competencies.

7. CONCLUSION

There is little doubt that the role of marketing and management is undergoing change. The new organisations of the 1990s emphasise partnerships and networking between firms, multiple types of ownership and partnering within the organisation, teamwork among members and sharing of responsibility. Consequently, the role of marketing is changing within the context of the organisation. Marketing management activity may occur in a company without boundaries where suppliers are not outsiders, internal functions begin to overlap and blur, and all staff are integral to the service delivery. This clearly has an effect on the management of internal customers.

This chapter has considered the scope and nature of internal marketing in relation to current thinking in this area. The influence of the new theoretical developments of the 1990s such as relationship marketing, network/interaction theory and the re-emphasis of total quality management on internal marketing have been discussed. Although many of the current approaches to internal marketing have had considerable success in improving some organisations' external activity, the problem of achieving a holistic, organisation-wide, action-oriented implementation of internal marketing still remains.

The final section of this chapter has argued that the development of management competencies is the key to improved internal marketing management performance. The competency development approach takes account of managers' current strengths and uses these to develop their areas of weakness. This occurs in the context of their specific role responsibility within the organisation. Knowledge, experience, expertise and judgment in relation to specific managerial roles are of fundamental importance to good decision-making in relation to external marketing activity. By using proactive communication and networking, managers can build on their strong competencies to develop and strengthen their weaker attributes.

REFERENCES

Barnes, J.G., "The Role of Internal Marketing: If the Staff Won't Buy it Why Should the Customer?", *Irish Marketing Review*, Vol. 4, No. 2, 1989, pp. 11–21.

Berry, L.L., "The Employee as Customer", *Journal of Retail Banking*, Vol. 3, No. 1, March, 1981, pp. 33–40.

Berry, L.L., "Relationship Marketing", in L.L. Berry, G.L. Shostack and G.D. Upah, (Eds.), *Emerging Perspectives on Services Marketing*, American Marketing Association, Chicago, IL, 1983, pp. 25–8.

Bowen, D.E. and E.E. Lawler III, "The Empowerment of Service Workers: What, Why, How and When", *Sloan Management Review*, Spring, 1992, pp. 31–9.

Boyatzis, R., *The Competent Manager. A Model for Effective Performance,* John Wiley, New York, 1982.

Bruce, M., "Managing People First: Bringing the Service Concept to British Airways", *Industrial and Commercial Training*, March/April, 1988, pp. 21–6.

Carlzon, J., *Moments of Truth*, Ballinger, Cambridge, MA, 1987.

Carson, D., "A Philosophy for Marketing Education in Small Firms", *Journal of Marketing Management*, Vol. 9, No. 2, April, 1993, pp. 189–204.

Carson, D., J. Hill and P. Magowan, "Effective Marketing Education Provision for SME Executives: A Radical Approach", Symposium of Marketing and Entrepreneurship: Research at the Marketing Entrepreneurship Interface, San Francisco, CA, August, 1993.

Christopher, M., "Reaching the Customer: Strategies for Marketing and Customer Service", *Journal of Marketing Management*, Vol. 2, No. 1, 1986, pp. 63–71.

Collins, B. and A. Payne, "Internal Marketing: A New Perspective for HRM", *European Journal of Marketing*, Vol. 9, No. 3, 1991, pp. 261–70.

Compton, F., George, W.R., Grönroos, C and Karvinen, M., "Internal Marketing", in J.A. Czepiel, C.A. Congram, and J. Shanahan (Eds.), *The Service Challenge: Integrating for Competitive Advantage,* American Marketing Association, Chicago, IL, 1987.

Foreman, S. and H. Woodruffe, "Internal Marketing: A Case for Building Cathedrals", Marketing Education Group Proceedings, Cardiff, UK, July, 1991, pp. 404–22.

Flipo, J.P., "Service Firms; Interdependence of External and Internal Marketing Strategies", *European Journal of Marketing*, Vol. 20, No. 8, 1986, pp. 5–14.

George, W.R., "The Retailing of Services — A Challenging Future", *Journal of Retailing*, Vol. 53, Fall, 1977, pp. 85–98.

George, W.R., "Internal Marketing for Retailers. The Junior Executive". in J.D. Lindqvist (Ed.), *Developments in Marketing Science,* Academy of Marketing Science, Miami, FL, 1984.

George, W.R., "Internal Marketing and Organisational Behaviour: A Partnership in Developing Customer — Conscious Employees at Every Level". *Journal of Business Research*, Vol. 20, 1990, pp. 63–70.

George, W.R. and C. Grönroos, "Developing Customer-Conscious Employees at Every Level: Internal Marketing", in C.A. Congram and M.L. Friedman (Eds.), *Handbook of Services Marketing"* AMACON, New York, 1990.

Gilmore, A. and D. Carson, "Marketing Management Competencies in a Services Context", European Institute for Advanced Management Studies, Quality in Service Management Workshop IV, *Proceedings*, Marne La Vallée, Paris, France, 12–13 May, 1994.

Grönroos, C., "Internal Marketing — Theory and Practice", in T.M. Bloch, G.D. Upah, and V.A. Zeithaml (Eds.), *Service Marketing in a Changing Environment*, American Marketing Association, Chicago, IL, 1985.

Grönroos, C., "Internal Marketing — An Integral Part of Marketing Theory", in J.H. Donnelly, and W.E. George (Eds.), *Marketing of Services*, American Marketing Association Proceedings Series, 1981, pp. 236–8.

Grönroos, C., *Service Management and Marketing: Managing the Moments of Truth in Service Competition,* Lexington Books, Lexington, MA, 1990.

Grönroos, C. and E. Gummesson, *Service Marketing — Nordic School Perspectives,* Stockholm University, Sweden, 1985.

Gummesson, E., "Using Internal Marketing to Develop a New Culture — The Case of Ericsson Quality", *Journal of Business and Industrial Marketing*, Vol. 2, No. 3, Summer, 1987, pp. 23–8.

Gummesson, E., "Marketing-Orientation Revisited: The Crucial Role of the Part-time Marketer", *European Journal of Marketing*, Vol. 5, No. 2, 1991, pp. 60–75.

Heskett, J.L., "Lessons in the Service Sector", *Harvard Business Review*, March/April, 1987.

Ishikawa, K., *What is Total Quality Control? The Japanese Way*, Prentice-Hall, Englewood Cliffs, NJ, 1985.

Jackson, B.B., "Build Customer Relationships that Last", *Harvard Business Review*, November/December, 1985, pp. 120–8.

Judd, V.C., "Differentiate with the 5th P: People", *Industrial Marketing Management*, Vol. 16, No. 4, 1987, pp. 241–7.

Katz, R.L., "Skills of an Effective Administrator", *Harvard Business Review*, September/October, 1974, pp. 90–102.

Lundberg, C.C., "Towards Mapping the Communication Targets of Organisational Change", *Journal of Organisational Change Management,* Vol. 3, Part 3, 1990, pp. 6–13.

McCarthy, E. Jerome, *Basic Marketing*, Richard D. Irwin, Homewood, IL, 1964.

Mastenbroek, W.S., *Conflict Management and Organisational Development*, John Wiley, New York, 1993.

Mintzberg, H., *The Nature of Managerial Work,* Harper and Row, New York, 1973.

Normann, R., *Service Management,* John Wiley, New York, 1984.

Parasuraman, A., V.A. Zeithaml, and L.L. Berry, "A Conceptual Model of Service Quality and its Implications for Future Research", *Journal of Marketing*, Vol. 49, Fall, 1985, pp. 41–50.

Piercy, N., "Marketing Concepts and Actions: Implementing Marketing-led Strategic Change", *European Journal of Marketing*, Vol. 24, No. 2, 1990, pp. 24–42.

Piercy, N and N. Morgan, "Internal Marketing Strategy: Leverage for Managing Marketing-Led Strategic Change", *Irish Marketing Review*, Vol. 4, No. 3, 1989/90, pp. 11–28.

Rafiq, M. and P.K. Ahmed, "The Scope of Internal Marketing: Defining the Boundary between Marketing and Human Resource Management", *Journal of Marketing Management*, Vol. 9, No. 3, 1993, pp. 219–32.

Richardson, B.A. and C.G. Robinson, "The Impact of Internal Marketing on Customer Service in a Retail Bank", *International Journal of Bank Marketing*, Vol. 4, No. 5, 1986, pp. 3–30.

Rugman, N., "What is a Marketer?" *Marketing*, Vol. 6, No. 7, 16 February, 1984, p. 37.

Sacker, F., "Customer Service Training in Context", *Personnel Management*, March, 1987, pp. 34–7.

Sasser, W.E. and S.P. Arbeit, "Selling Jobs in the Service Sector", *Business Horizons*, June, 1976, pp. 61–5.

Tansuhaj, P., D. Randall and J. McCullough, "Applying the Internal Marketing Concept within Large Organisations: As Applied to a Credit Union", *Journal of Professional Services Marketing*, Vol. 6, No. 2, 1991, pp. 193–202.

Thompson, T.W., L.L. Berry and P.H. Davidson, *Banking Tomorrow — Managing Markets through Planning*, Van Nostrand Reinhold, New York, 1978.

Wrapp, H.E., "Good Managers Don't Make Policy Decisions", *Harvard Business Review*, Vol. 45, No. 5, September/October, 1967.

Weiss, R.S. and Jacobson, E., "A Method for the Analysis of the Structure of Complex Organisations", *American Sociological Review*, Vol. 20. 1955, pp. 661–8.

Winter, J.P., "Getting your House in Order with Internal Marketing: A Marketing Prerequisite", *Health Marketing Quarterly*, Vol. 3, No. 1, 1985, pp. 68–72.

12

MARKETING SERVICES TO EXTERNAL MARKETS

Adrian Payne and Moira Clark
Cranfield University, England

PRÉCIS

In this chapter, Payne and Clark focus their attention on marketing services to external markets, emphasising that there are a number of external markets, as well as internal markets within the organisation, to which marketing frameworks and principles can be applied. The authors accept a broader integrated view of markets with which a service organisation interacts, and propose a "six markets model". A framework for managing services marketing strategically is then developed and the three key steps in creating business focus — business definition, segmentation and positioning — are outlined. Considering the particularities of services, the authors follow the stream of thought of those who support the view that there is an important need to redefine the marketing mix in a manner more applicable to the service sector. They argue that, although imperfect, an augmented marketing mix consisting of seven key elements is a useful approach to managing services marketing. The "people" element of the marketing mix is emphasised by internal marketing.

The need for services marketers to pay attention to relationship-building and cross-functional activities is highlighted. The lack of co-ordination across functions, departments and tasks is identified as a major problem which demands new, more improved and decentralised organisational forms. Undoubtedly, this study opens new directions for further research, but in so doing, one might suggest that it would be of importance to separate marketing activities that are directed to customers from the ones that are directed to publics.[1]

An additional point of reflection is that, whilst the need for internal marketing is well understood, very few organisations apply the concept in practice. Moreover, a series of questions emerge: does a single unified notion of the meaning of internal marketing exist? Can marketing concepts and tools be applied to the internal market? In addition, problems arise with the definition of the internal product: what are internal customers buying? How are they paying? Can employees really be treated as customers? The key difference between internal and external customers remains that internal customers can be "coerced" into "buying".[2] *This is the result of the contractual nature of employment that gives the personnel function the coercive power to enforce compliance. If this policy is to be adopted, then it is bound to lead to conflict between marketing, human resource management and operations management and other directly affected departments. Therefore, further research is required, which examines the extent to which this broad view of marketing replaces the domain of other disciplines such as management or occupational theory.*

The proposal supported by Payne and Clarke provides a valuable conceptual framework integrating many variables that historically have been considered independently in marketing services to external markets. This chapter identifies numerous issues in an evolving field and beckons the reader to explore this exciting area further.

George G. Panigyrakis
Athens University of Economics and Business
Greece

---

[1] Consumer demand refers to the characteristics and needs of the final consumers, industrial consumers, channel members, government institutions, international markets, and non-profit institutions. Public's demand refers to the characteristics and needs of employees, unions, stockholders, consumer groups and other internal and external forces that affect company operations: Kotler P., "A Generic Concept of Marketing", *Journal of Marketing*, Vol. 36, April, 1972, pp. 346–54.

[2] Rafiq M. and Ahmed P., "The Scope of Internal Marketing: Defining the Boundary Between Marketing and Human Resource Management", *Journal of Marketing Management*, Vol. 9, 1993, pp. 219–32.

1. INTRODUCTION

The dynamics of most services markets have changed from having low levels of competition to having vigorous and intense competition. With many services organisations facing ever-increasing competition, marketing is becoming a key differentiator between success and failure.

This chapter examines some key issues in marketing services. It begins by considering a broader view of markets, which goes beyond traditional customer markets — the six markets model. A framework for managing services marketing strategically is then developed and the three key steps in creating business focus — business definition, segmentation and positioning — are outlined. The role of the marketing mix in the context of service businesses is then considered and the seven elements of the services marketing mix are examined in detail.

The creation of a services marketing mix and marketing plan is necessary, but not sufficient, for success in services marketing. As pointed out in other chapters in this book, successful service management requires the integration of operations and human resources with marketing. This requires a marketing approach that incorporates the traditional elements of marketing — service and product decisions, distribution, pricing and promotion — but also needs to include the newer elements of people, processes and customer service. It sees marketing as primarily relationship-oriented (rather than transaction-oriented), but also operates outside the narrow functional perspectives of marketing. The final section of this chapter discusses the new cross-functional process orientation that is starting to be adopted by services companies, one that is being increasingly utilised to provide a source of competitive advantage.

The intensifying interest in services has been accompanied by considerable disagreement and debate as to whether services marketing is a distinct subject area. Many authors have sought to develop definitions of what a service is, yet no adequate definition has emerged. Examples of services which do not fit any existing definition can be readily found. However, given the diversity of services, it seems unlikely that any description of services can be developed which is fully comprehensive. This notion of the diversity of services is very important. It highlights the question: "Is the marketing of services similar to or different from that of consumer or industrial products?". The answer to this question, is, arguably, both yes and no. This reply, rather than being evasive, is intended to highlight the following:

- At a strategic level, the theory of marketing is relevant to all exchange relationships. The same principles and issues apply.

- At the industry sector and operational levels the characteristics of services may dictate the need to place more emphasis on some marketing elements and/or apply other marketing elements in a different way.

As pointed out in Chapter 1, services have specific characteristics which differentiate them from conventional goods (Fisk, Brown and Bitner, Chapter 1). However, the specific characteristics of a given service business are frequently so different from one another that generalisations about "the service sector" can be misleading. There is a need, therefore, to understand the specific dimensions of a given service industry thoroughly before applying general marketing principles.

1.1. Understanding the Heterogeneous Nature of Services

Broad assumptions that services are homogeneous are clearly incorrect. There is a need for managers to understand how service industries differ and to what extent they share common characteristics. If managers are to learn from best practice in other service businesses, they need guidelines as to which other service industries are relevant to their organisation.

Many of the early classification schemes developed for services were purely descriptive and did not assist managers in identifying relevant marketing strategies that could be used within their industry. More recently, researchers have sought to classify services in a manner more meaningful to the services marketer. They have been concerned with the development of classification schemes that give insight into the strategic dimensions of services marketing. Lovelock (1983) has developed classification schemes which attempt to answer a number of specific questions. These questions include:

- What is the nature of the service act?

- What style of relationship does the service organisation have with its customers?

- How much room is there for customisation and judgment?

- What is the nature of the demand for the supply of this service?

- How is the service delivered?

These questions are examined by Lovelock in a series of matrices which characterise key dimensions of each question. This approach is based on the idea that appropriate combinations of classification schemes are more likely to lead to improved strategic marketing insights than are classification schemes based on using only one variable at a time.

These classification systems provide a framework for managers of service businesses to consider both the nature of their businesses and to what extent they share common characteristics with other service businesses which may be seemingly unrelated. It also provides them with an opportunity to look outside their own industries for successful approaches to solving marketing problems that are transferable to their own service businesses. This approach helps those interested in services marketing to consider their businesses in a more appropriate context, avoiding the generalities of broad assertions about services and at the same time transcending the inherently narrow perspective of considering services on a single industry basis.

1.2. Services Marketing — Not Just for Services Organisations

A distinction also needs to be made between services marketing and service industries. Services marketing is not just concerned with organisations in the services sector. With the exception of a few commodities, almost all products have a service component. Today, many manufacturing companies need to focus on managing their services, just as service companies do. As others have pointed out (Grönroos, 1990), it may be more useful to discuss service and manufacturing *activities* rather than service and manufacturing *industries*. The confusion about services is compounded by arbitrary categorisation. Consider the high-cost activity of large jet engine overhaul. If Pratt and Witney overhaul their own aircraft engines, this is part of a manufacturing company's activity and falls within the manufacturing sector. If the engine overhaul is carried out by one of the emerging global companies specialising exclusively in engine overhaul, such as Standard Aero of Canada, it is a service activity and falls within the service sector.

In a world where competitive imitation is increasing in manufacturing organisations, services are becoming the main instrument for creating differentiation. Grönroos points out that every firm, irrespective of whether it is a service firm by today's definition, has to learn how to cope with these new forms of service competition. Thus, manufacturing businesses are now increasingly looking at service businesses in an effort to gain new insights.

Services have become a vital means of competition in all forms of business — services *and* manufacturing — and offer the potential to achieve significant competitive advantage. Services and manufacturing have now evolved to a stage where they are highly inter-related and complementary and the dividing line between traditional manufacturers and classic service companies has become less clear. Whilst the discussion in this chapter focuses on services in the context of service industries, much of the discussion is also applicable to services in manufacturing companies.

2. MARKETING SERVICES: THE SIX MARKETS MODEL

Just as the boundaries around "What is a service?" are being questioned, so too is the issue of "What is a market?" A broader view of markets with which a service organisation interacts is now emerging. In addition to customer markets, the organisation also needs to be concerned with the development and enhancement of more enduring relationships with other external markets, including suppliers, recruitment, referral and influence, as well as internal markets. The "six-markets model" (Christopher, Payne and Ballantyne, 1991), illustrated in Figure 12.1, suggests that organisations have six key market areas with which they should consider directing marketing activity and where the development of detailed marketing plans may be appropriate.

FIGURE 12.1: THE SIX-MARKETS MODEL: A BROADER VIEW OF MARKETING

- *Customer Markets* — Customers must remain the prime focus for marketing activity. This focus needs to be less on "transaction marketing" and more on "relationship marketing" — the building of long-term customer relationships. Whilst a relationship focus has been adopted by some service organisations, it is mostly absent in others.

- *Referral Markets* — Referral markets consist of two main categories — your existing customers and intermediaries. Frequently, the best marketing is that done for you by your own customers, which is why the creation of positive word-of-mouth referral, through delivering outstanding service quality, is essential. Intermediaries — other parties who may refer your organisation to prospective customers — are also a critical market to be addressed. For example, in one division of a commercial bank, an analysis showed that over 70 per cent of new business was gained through referrals from intermediaries and existing satisfied customers.

- *Supplier Markets* — The relationship between organisations and their suppliers is undergoing considerable change, partly as a result of the influence of Japanese companies. The old adversarial relationship is giving way to one based much more on partnership and collaboration. Marks and Spencer provide a good example of this. From a marketing point of view, one key issue is the selling of the new attitudes implicit in such a collaborative relationship both to suppliers and, of equal importance, to the company's own staff.

- *Influence Markets* — "Influence" markets vary according to the industry sector. Companies involved in selling infrastructure services such as communications or utilities will place government departments and regulatory bodies high on their list of influence markets. Other influence markets include: financial analysts, stockbrokers, shareholders, business journalists and consumer groups. Whilst this activity is often carried out within public relations or corporate affairs, it is important that it is recognised as being an essential element of overall market activity and that appropriate resources are devoted to it.

- *Recruitment Markets* — The scarcest resource for many service businesses, even during times of recession, is skilled people — perhaps the most vital element in the delivery of service quality. Service organisations as diverse as Disney, Nordstroms and the Ritz Carlton chain of hotels have built a reputation for service quality that is largely a product of their approach to employee recruitment. In particular the organisation should focus on being an "organisation of first choice" amongst the target audience of prospective employees it wishes to attract.

- *Internal Markets* — Marketing activity has traditionally been focused on external markets. More recently, attention has been directed at internal marketing within the organisation. Internal marketing plays an important role in employee motivation and retention — an issue which is discussed elsewhere in this book (Lovelock, Chapter 8; Gilmore and Carson, Chapter 11) and will be addressed in more detail later in this chapter

Not all of these six markets require equal levels of attention and resources. A decision on the appropriate level of attention required by each market can be determined by:

- Identification of key participants in each market

- Determination of expectations and requirements of these key participants

- Review of current and proposed level of effort and resources applied to each market

- Formulation of a marketing strategy and, where appropriate, a marketing plan for each market.

The six-markets model above shows how service organisations need to consider each of these markets. In this chapter, our discussion will be primarily directed at customer markets. However, it should be recognised that the broad approach now outlined will be appropriate for each of the other markets.

3. MANAGING SERVICES MARKETING STRATEGICALLY: A FRAMEWORK

As noted earlier, successful services management requires the successful integration of operations, human resources and marketing. Other chapters in this book focus on issues such as service quality, measuring productivity and efficiency, service mapping and boundary spanning (Glynn and Lehtinen, Chapter 4; Heskett, Chapter 16; Kingman-Brundage, Chapter 5; Lewis, Chapter 3; Parasuraman, Chapter 6). In this section, we focus on one aspect of service management — the development of a strategic approach to the management of the traditional marketing activity. We then examine how these elements need to be better integrated and used to better advantage, how marketing activities need to emphasise relationships and how they need to be managed in a broader cross-functional context.

It should be recognised, however, that management of the traditional functional marketing activity represents only one of the key elements of success in services management. A number of writers have suggested that an overemphasis has been placed on the development of a marketing mix to the exclusion of other important issues such as service quality. This view would appear to be largely accurate. However, many examples have been encountered where the lack of marketing success can be attributed firmly to poor performance in the domain of traditional marketing. It is appropriate, then, to consider these elements and how they should be expanded, integrated and used to better advantage.

FIGURE 12.2: MANAGING SERVICES MARKETING STRATEGICALLY

A framework for managing services marketing strategy is shown in Figure 12.2. The framework outlines four stages which need to be addressed:

- *Understanding the Market, Environment and Key Relationships* — This stage involves the analysis of the customer, competitive and general environmental arenas. Successful marketing is based on a rigorous analysis in these areas. This analysis is common to all areas of marketing — not just services — and is covered well in any standard marketing text (Kotler, 1994, for example), so is not expanded on here.

- *Identifying Business Focus* — This stage consists of three steps: defining the scope of the service business, identifying market segments to be serviced and the positioning to be adopted.

- *The Services Marketing Mix: Strategies to Achieve the Business Focus* — This stage addresses the seven key elements of the services marketing mix, namely: the service product, pricing, place, promotion, people, customer service and processes.

- *Developing a Marketing Plan* — this stage consists of developing a logical framework to establish how the company can best use its resources to match the needs of its chosen markets. Again, the approach to marketing planning is well documented (see McDonald, 1989) and only a brief overview will be made in this chapter.

We will now address the two central stages of marketing strategy development — identifying business focus and the services marketing mix.

4. IDENTIFYING BUSINESS FOCUS

This stage comprises three inter-related tasks: defining the scope of the service business; identifying market segments to be served; and determining the positioning to be adopted. This critical set of activities in services marketing ensures that subsequent marketing activities are focused on achieving the service organisation's corporate objectives.

4.1. Business Definition

The development of an effective business definition is especially important in services because of the need for strong focus and differentiation in service sector businesses. Given the intangibility of services and the significance of people in service operations, organisations need to develop a clear statement of purpose or "mission" to ensure that the appropriate attention is directed at the key elements of their service strategy.

We define a mission as follows:

A mission is an enduring statement of purpose that provides an animated vision of the organisation's current and future business activities, in product, service and market terms; its values and beliefs, and its point of differentiation from competitors.

A mission helps to determine the relationships with each of the key markets with which the organisation interacts, and provides a sense of direction and purpose leading to more correct independent decisions being made at all levels of the organisation.

Such a mission statement should explicitly reflect the underlying beliefs, values, aspirations and strategies of the organisation. However, many organisations' mission statements display a bland similarity and consist of "motherhood" generalisations rather than reflecting a unique commitment to the values and corporate direction that is intended. Organisations' purposes in writing a mission may vary. While some do it for public relations purposes, it is seen here as a key means of strategically focusing the business activities of the service organisation.

Relatively little research has been undertaken on the nature of mission statements. It has been observed that relatively few service organisations have developed effective missions, and there is considerable evidence to support the poor quality of mission statements. One study examined 157 mission statements and concluded that most were written so broadly that they had very little meaning.

Those service companies which have taken the development of a mission statement seriously have benefited. The president and CEO of the Hospital Corporation of America pointed out the value of an effective mission:

> I cannot stress enough how important the development of our written mission and philosophy has been to this company ... far more important than any value received from the external public knowing our mission and philosophy has been the internal discipline and direction it has provided our employees throughout all levels of the organisation (Brown, 1984, pp. 44–52).

Most significant service companies believe it is important to have a formal business definition to help guide staff's actions to achieving them. Many missions make the mistake of focusing on shareholders, customers and managers and do not attempt to motivate the non-managerial workforce. Companies should focus on the employee as a high priority in their mission statements, as in a service organisation the collective behaviour of the employees is critical to success.

4.2. Services Market Segmentation

The concept of market segmentation within the services sector is often under-utilised. The process of market segmentation is one of dividing a total market up into a series of sub-markets (or market segments). The marketing segmentation approach is concerned with first considering the alternative bases for segmentation; second, choosing specific segments (or a single segment) within that base; and finally determining appropriate service levels for these segments.

There are at least seven broad bases which have been traditionally used in market segmentation, including: geographic, demographic, psychographic, benefit, usage, loyalty and occasion segmentation. These bases apply equally to product and services marketing and are widely discussed in the marketing literature (see Weinstein, 1987). However, one area of potential which has received little attention is the consideration of how customers respond to varying service offerings. In a sense, this may be considered a subset of benefit segmentation, but here it is felt to be of sufficient importance to merit being addressed separately.

4.2.1 Segmentation by Service

The various elements of customer service that can be offered, and possible differentiation in terms of service levels within these elements, represent considerable opportunity for designing service packages appropriate to different market segments. Segmenting markets by service involves addressing these issues:

- Can groupings of customers be identified with similar service requirements?
- Can we differentiate our service offering?
- Do all our products require the same level of service?

In a study of the scientific instrument and supplies industry, Gilmour (1977) examined the response of five customer segments to a range of nine customer service elements. The results showed disparity between the customers' perception, and that of their suppliers, of the importance of certain customer service elements, particularly in the areas of sales service and back-up and efficient telephone handling of orders and queries. There were also very marked differences between market segments in the importance attached to a wide range of service elements including availability, after-sales service and back-up, ordering convenience, competent technical representatives and demonstrations of equipment. By explicitly measuring the perceived importance of different customer service elements across market segments, the supplier is much better placed to respond to that segment's identified needs and to allocate the service offering appropriate to it.

Studies such as this emphasise that decisions to increase or reduce customer service levels should not be made equally across the entire customer base or across service factors. Considerable potential exists in many companies to reduce customer service costs and/or to improve levels of service to the customer by adopting an approach that recognises differentiated service requirements by customer segment.

The identification and selection of a particular market segment for targeting with a distinctive service offering may depend on many factors, but size of the segment, its special needs, the extent to which these needs are already being met by the service company or the competition and whether the service company has the resources to meet the service requirements are particularly important. Market segmentation will, therefore, determine the basic segments of the market to be targeted with a particular service. The service offered to these segments then needs to be positioned in the minds of the customer.

4.3 Positioning

Positioning offers the opportunity to differentiate any service better. Each service company and its goods and services have a position or image in the consumer's mind and this influences purchase decisions. Positions can be implicit and unplanned and evolve over a period of time, or can be planned as part of the marketing strategy and then communicated to the target market. The purpose of planned positioning is to create a differentiation in the customer's mind which distinguishes the company's services from the competition's services. It is important to establish a position of value for the product or service in the minds of the target market — in other words, it must be distinguishable by an attribute, or attributes, that are important to the customer. These attributes should be factors that are critical in the customer's purchase decision.

There is, therefore, no such thing as a commodity or "standard" service. Every service offered has the potential to be perceived by a customer as different. Buyers have different needs and are therefore attracted to different offers. Thus, it is important to select distinguishing characteristics that satisfy the following criteria (Kotler, 1991):

- *Importance* — The difference is highly valued to a sufficiently large market.

- *Distinctiveness* — The difference is distinctly superior to other offerings that are available.

- *Communicability* — It is possible to communicate the difference in a simple and strong way.

- *Superiority* — The difference is not easily copied by competitors.

- *Affordability* — The target customers will be able and willing to pay for the difference. Any additional cost of the distinguishing characteristic(s) will be perceived as sufficiently valuable to compensate for any additional cost.

- *Profitability* — The company will achieve additional profits as a result of introducing the difference.

Positioning is a critical part of developing marketing strategy, but has not been widely discussed in the services literature. For some exceptions, see Easingwood and Mahajan (1989); Lovelock (1990); Payne (1993). It is a strategic marketing tool which allows managers to determine what their position is now, what they wish it to be and what actions are needed to attain that position. Positioning permits market opportunities to be identified, by considering positions which are not met by competitors' products. It therefore helps influence both product development and the redesign of existing products. It allows consideration of competitors' possible moves and responses so that appropriate action can be taken. Positioning involves giving the target market segment the reason for buying your services and thus underpins the whole marketing strategy. It also offers guidelines for the development of a marketing mix with each element of the mix being consistent with the positioning.

5. THE SERVICES MARKETING MIX — STRATEGIES TO ACHIEVE THE BUSINESS FOCUS

Traditionally the marketing function has been considered as consisting of three key components:

- *The Marketing Mix* — The key elements that make up the organisation's marketing programme.

- *Market Forces* — These are external opportunities or threats which an organisation must take into account when developing a marketing programme.

- *The Matching Process* — This is the strategic and managerial process that ensures that the marketing mix and supporting internal tactics and strategies take into account market forces.

Part of the role of the marketing manager in developing a marketing programme is to develop a marketing mix that ensures the best match between the internal capabilities of the organisation and the external marketing environment.

Traditionally, marketers have considered four basic components or elements of the marketing mix: product, place, price and promotion. However, such a list has long been considered restrictive by marketers working both within the services sector, and elsewhere (Payne and Clark, 1994). This framework, known as the 4Ps, was largely developed in the context of fast-moving consumer goods markets. In recent years there has been considerable dissatisfaction with the limited comprehensiveness and utility of marketing strategies based on such a restrictive number of elements. Many authors including de Ferrer (1986), Gummesson (1987) and Grönroos (1990) point out that the traditional marketing paradigm based on this marketing mix, was developed using the assumptions that were based principally on studies of a huge North American market for consumer goods, with its nationwide media coverage and extensive distribution systems. In particular, the mix can be criticised in terms of its short-term transaction focus, which is inappropriate for many services markets, and its failure to concentrate sufficiently on the longer-term relationships with customers that are critical to organisational success. Authors such as Brownlie and Saren (1992) have pointed to difficulties with implementation as grounds for questioning the validity of the concept. Undoubtedly, the lack of a relationship focus has been responsible for the marketing efforts of a number of service organisations being sub-optimal.

The origins of the marketing mix concept are to be found in Borden (1965), who originally suggested a list of twelve elements that should be considered when developing a marketing programme. Over the years, the listing of the marketing mix elements was simplified under the headings of the 4Ps, which has formed the basis of many textbooks, especially within North America. This fixed list of four elements became enshrined in marketing theory, although it must be said less so in the marketing practices adopted by leading service organisations. However, whilst leading service organisations have adopted a more sensible and pragmatic approach, it should be said that the 4Ps have offered a seductive sense of simplicity to some students, teachers and practitioners of marketing. Further, the lack of empirical study into key marketing variables and how they are perceived and used by marketing managers, together with the focus on structure rather than processes (Kent, 1986), has resulted in sub-optimal marketing activity.

In reality, the 4Ps comprise a whole collection of sub-activities. The use of a simplified list can, therefore, be misleading in that it focuses attention on the generic categories of product, price, place and promotion, rather than emphasising attention on the most relevant sub-activities and their components. As such, the basic 4Ps model does not sufficiently capture the extent and complexity of services marketing, or the essential inter-relationships between the elements of the mix and the potential to integrate tactical marketing elements into a strategically focused marketing plan.

Many authors have now suggested a modification of the existing 4Ps framework. For example, Brookes (1988) has argued for the inclusion of customer service as a fifth element. In the services marketing literature, the seven elements suggested by Booms and Bitner (1981) are probably best known. They suggest that the existing four elements of the marketing mix need to be extended to include three additional areas — people, processes and physical evidence. In the context of marketing overall, rather than services marketing, Baumgartner (1991) suggests fifteen elements to be included for a complete specification of the marketing mix.

It is disputed here that the dogmatism with which many authors argue a given number of marketing mix elements is misplaced. Whilst a generic list of relative marketing mix elements is useful, the natures of services businesses vary greatly and they are not nearly as homogeneous as is frequently argued. As the earlier discussion of Lovelock's (1983) work on classifying services pointed out, the specific contexts of services vary greatly. Thus, a critical issue is to determine the appropriate marketing mix for a particular service firm in a particular marketplace context.

Grönroos (1989) has emphasised that Borden indicated that his original list of twelve marketing mix elements probably had to be reconsidered in every given situation. However, it is apparent that in many service businesses, this is not done. Whilst there are generic elements that should usually be considered by most service marketers, managers should use their own judgment to decide whether a specific ingredient deserves a separate existence in a marketing mix for their organisation. Majaro (1982) has identified three factors to help determine if an individual marketing mix element deserves a separate existence. These are:

- The level of expenditure on a given ingredient of the marketing mix

- The perceived level of elasticity in customer responsiveness

- Allocation of responsibilities.

These guidelines, whilst not all-encompassing, nevertheless support the argument that attention needs to be given to deciding which particular elements are relevant to a given service organisation.

The authors' experience, in working with many services managers, gives considerable support to the 7Ps suggested by Booms and Bitner (1981), although an argument is made for the modification of this by excluding physical evidence as a major element and replacing it with "customer service". Whilst this results in one element not being a "P", it can be argued that a preoccupation with finding elements beginning with the letter "P", may be counterproductive and for those fixated with Ps, we suggest "proactive customer service" (see Figure 12.3).

It should be noted that the emphasis here is to use the marketing mix elements to create, develop and sustain relationships, rather than to regard them as existing as an end in themselves. Before moving to a more detailed discussion of the marketing mix elements for services, it is appropriate to comment briefly on why these additional three elements are important.

- *People* — In this book, the importance of managing and marketing internal customers is emphasised. People are an essential element of both the production and delivery of most services, and increasingly are becoming part of the differentiation of service organisations to create, add value and gain competitive advantage (Gilmore and Carson, Chapter 11; Lovelock, Chapter 8).

- *Processes* — Processes are procedures, mechanisms and routines, by which a service is created and delivered to a customer. Processes are both functionally and cross-functionally based. Service mapping is a key aspect of process management and is fully discussed elsewhere in this book (Kingman-Brundage, Chapter 5).

- *Customer Service* — There are several justifications for including customer services as an important and separate element in a services marketing mix. These include the trend to more demanding customers requiring higher levels of service, the increased importance of customer service because of competitors increasingly seeing service as a competitive weapon to differentiate themselves, and the need to build closer and more enduring relationships with customers. Customer care in services is also discussed elsewhere in this book (Lewis, Chapter 3).

FIGURE 12.3: EXPANDED MARKETING MIX FOR SERVICES

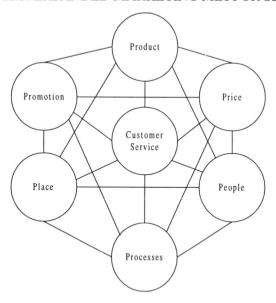

Given the diversity of the services sector and the emphases that are inevitably required in marketing activity, it may be necessary to vary this list. Nevertheless, it is considered sufficiently robust to cover most service situations. It is equally clear that the 4Ps model does not capture the full complexity of services marketing in practice. Further, the 4Ps model does not recognise the cross-functional relationships in service businesses. The three additional marketing mix elements — people, processes and customer service — represent elements of services marketing that are cross-functional in character and that are typically more concerned with keeping the customer (relationship marketing) than catching the customer (transaction marketing).

These seven key elements of the services marketing mix will now be addressed. Emphasis will be placed on some specific issues of relevance to services or considered by these authors not to be sufficiently emphasised in many marketing texts. For the reader wishing to explore these general themes of marketing mix in more detail, see Dibb et al. (1991) or Kotler (1994).

6. MARKETING MIX 1: THE SERVICE PRODUCT

Of the many issues that could be discussed relating to the service product, we will focus on four of them — differentiation and branding, physical evidence, service product decisions, and managing the service offer — which are of special relevance in services. However, before discussing these issues, the nature of "what the customer buys" should be considered.

Customers do not buy goods or services — they buy specific benefits and value from the total offering. This total offering to customers is referred to here as "the offer" — it represents those benefits that customers derive from the purchase of goods or services. An offer can be visualised as having a nucleus or core in the centre surrounded by a series of both tangible and intangible features, attributes and benefits which cluster around the core product. These include packaging, advertising, financing, availability, advice, warranty, reliability, etc. It has been suggested (Levitt, 1983) that the offer can be viewed at several levels:

- *The Core or Generic Product* — This consists of the basic service product, for example, a bed in a hotel room for the night.

- *The Expected Product* — This consists of the generic product along with the minimum purchase conditions which must be met. When customers buy an airline ticket, they expect, in addition to a seat on the aeroplane, a range of additional elements, including a comfortable waiting area, prompt in-flight service and good quality meals.

- *The Augmented Product* — This is the area which enables one product to be differentiated from another. For example, Dell have a reputation for excellent customer service, although they may not have the most technologically advanced core product. They differentiate by "adding value" to their core product in terms of reliability and responsiveness.

- *The Potential Product* — This consists of all potential added features and benefits that are or may be of use to buyers.

Thus, a service product is a complex set of value satisfactions. People buy services to solve problems and they attach value to them in proportion to the perceived ability of the service to do this. Value is assigned by the buyers in relationship to the benefits they receive. Augmentation of the expected product represents a means of creating product differentiation and thus added value from the customer perspective.

6.1. Differentiation and Branding

Differentiation is achieved by adding value to the basic core service product. For example, the core product may represent 70 per cent of the cost of providing the service, but may only have 30 per cent of the total impact on the customer. By contrast, the augmented product or product surround may represent perhaps 30 per cent of the cost, but may account for 70 per cent of total customer impact.

The research findings on service quality support this view (Berry, Parasuraman and Zeithaml, 1988). Perceived service quality depends more on reliability, responsiveness, assurance and empathy than on tangibles. This means that service markets should give increased attention to how they can differentiate the product surround, and how they enlarge it. The larger the product surround, the greater the potential for differentiation of a company's brand offering from those of its competitors.

The brand name also becomes an important element of the augmented product. Brands can be a major determining element in the purchase of services and an important means of adding differentiation. Dobtree and Sage (1990) illustrate the considerable efforts made by service organisations to establish distinctive brands in virtually every service sector.

A key issue in the context of differentiation and brands is the brand to commodity continuum. This continuum is shown in Figure 12.4. At one extreme, the service product consists of a speciality — often a highly differentiated brand — and at the other extreme, a commodity. When a totally new product or service is introduced it is, by definition, a speciality. Over time, as new competitors emerge, there is a tendency as it moves through the product life cycle for it to move towards commodity status. This results in considerably reduced product image and differentiation, lowered prices and increased competition. Berry and Parasuraman (1991) have indicated some key issues that service managers should consider with respect to their organisations' branding and how to avoid the shift to commodity status.

FIGURE 12.4: THE BRAND TO COMMODITY CONTINUUM

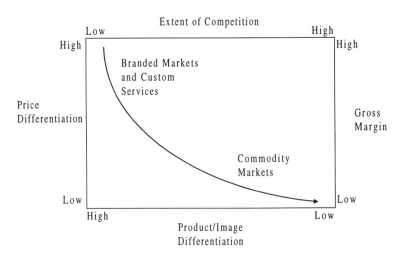

Competition in commodity markets is primarily based on prices and terms. By contrast, competition in speciality branded services and goods is based on the other elements of the marketing mix and sub-mixes including customer service, advertising, brand name, packaging, guarantees, warranties, etc. Service firms need to consider how to halt (or reverse) this transition to ensure that service products remain differentiated, rather than sliding into the commodity category.

6.2. Physical Evidence

Physical evidence is a key element (although, we do not believe that it justifies existence as a separate part of the marketing mix), which helps to reinforce the brand and strengthen the product surround. Physical evidence consists of the service firm's physical environment where the service is created and where the service provider and customer interact, plus any tangible elements that are used to communicate or support the role of the service. In a service business, the marketer should seek to compensate for the intangibility dimension by providing physical clues to support the positioning and image and to enhance the product surround.

Researchers have divided physical evidence into two types: essential and peripheral. Essential evidence represents, for example, the design and layout of a building, the type of aeroplanes to be used by an airline, the ambience of a reception room. These can be used to add significantly to the product surround. Peripheral physical evidence has little value on its own. A railway ticket has no independent value in itself, but represents a right to experience the service at a later point in time. Peripheral evidence adds tangibility to the value of the service, provided that it is valued by the customer.

6.3. Service Product Decisions

Service organisations will often wish to offer a range of products and services. Decisions on the range of services to be offered need to be considered in the context of both the company's positioning strategy and the competitors' services offerings. The range of strategic growth options can be considered using the Ansoff matrix (Figure 12.5 shows an example of these growth options for a management consulting firm), which looks at four fundamental growth options for the service provider:

FIGURE 12.5: GROWTH OPTIONS FOR A MANAGEMENT CONSULTING FIRM

	Existing Products	New Products or Services
Existing Markets	**Market Penetration** * Repeat Business * Increased Frequency * Depth Consulting	**Product or Service Development** * New Products & Services * New Image * Consultant Involvement on Boards
New Markets	**Market Development** * Industry Groups * Segmented Growth * Internationalisation	**Diversification** * Venture Capital * New Businesses * Acquisitions

- *Market Penetration* — Market penetration is concerned with how company's should exploit their current position in the marketplace better. This can be achieved by more focused segmentation, a more clearly defined positioning strategy, or through better application of the marketing mix elements. Two aspects — customer retention and increasing frequency of use — are of particular importance. Customer retention strategies aim at keeping customers and can be assisted by loyalty programmes. Increasing frequency of usage involves encouraging customers to use the services more frequently.

- *New Product/Service Development* — New service development, or new product development for service businesses, is a relatively new area of research. Lovelock (1984) has suggested six categories of service innovation, including: major innovations, start-up businesses, new products for the market currently served, product line extensions, product improvements and style changes. These categories provide guidelines as to where new service development activities can be considered.

- *Market Development* — Market development seeks new groups of buyers with a firm's current service offerings. For example, many banks have opened international offices in order to attract foreign clients. This strategy is riskier than the two strategies above, and may require in-depth market research to ensure that the needs of international customers are understood. Market extension can be more safely adopted if the service is to be used by existing customers in the different market.

- *Diversification — New Services to New Markets* — This is the riskiest strategy, as a service firm is not building on any of its existing strengths. It is most typically adopted within a mature service industry, where growth cannot be achieved in any other way. It is hard to achieve success with such a strategy, as each business has very different critical success factors.

6.4. Managing the Service Offer

Grönroos (1990) outlines four steps that the services marketer needs to manage in providing a service offer:

- *Developing the Service Concept* — The basic concept or intention of the service provider.

- *Developing a Basic Service Package* — The core service, facilitating services and goods, and supporting services and goods.

- *Developing an Augmented Service Offering* — The service process and interactions between the service provider and customers, including the service delivery process. It includes a consideration of the accessibility of the service and the degree of customer participation.

- *Managing Image and Communication* — So that they support and enhance the augmented service offer. This is the interface between the promotion and product marketing mix elements.

A consideration of these steps makes clear some of the linkages with other elements of the marketing mix. Once the basic service offer has been established, attention can then be directed towards development of other ingredients of the marketing mix.

7. MARKETING MIX 2: PRICING THE SERVICE

Price plays a pivotal part in the marketing mix of a service, because pricing attracts revenue to the business. Pricing decisions are significant in determining the value for the customer and they play a role in the building of an image for the service. Price also gives a perception of quality. Pricing decisions are often made by adding a percentage mark-up on cost. This approach, however, loses the benefits that a pricing strategy can offer within the marketing strategy. Service firms, at least within deregulated markets, need to use pricing more strategically to help gain competitive advantage.

Pricing decisions have an impact on all parts of the supply/marketing channels. Suppliers, salespeople, distributors, competitors and customers are all affected by the pricing system. Pricing decisions for services are particularly important given the intangible nature of the product. The price charged for a service not only affects the customers perceptions of the service offered, but also signals to customers the quality of the service that they are likely to receive. Thus, a restaurant that places its menu in the window for prospective customers to view is giving customers information about what they can expect in terms of quality of food and service levels as well as cost.

Special pricing considerations also apply to services by virtue of the immediacy of delivery and the importance of availability. Thus, pricing decisions for services may involve premium pricing at maximum demand times and discounted pricing in order to attract additional customers when demand is low. This has given rise to complicated pricing of services within the package holiday market, railway and airline industries, entertainment and leisure services, media advertising services and many utilities.

7.1. Pricing Decisions

The decision on the pricing of a new service must take into account many relevant features. The most important of these is that the pricing decision must be consistent with the overall marketing strategy. The charging of different prices in different markets may also need to be considered. In addition, the specific price to be charged depends on the type of customer to whom the service is sold. Value is not determined by price, but by the benefits the buyer perceives the service to offer relative to its total acquisition cost, and the price of alternative services which are competing with it.

A simple cost-plus price structure loses many of the advantages which can be gained by a properly researched and well-managed pricing policy. Services have an intrinsic value for the customer and it is this rather than the costs of performing the service that a pricing policy should consider. Pricing thus needs to be viewed from a market-oriented perspective.

The experience curve can be a useful tool in helping managers to understand cost behaviour in a service industry and make informed pricing decisions. Figure 12.6 shows an experience curve for electronic banking compared with paper processing of cheques. The experience curve is an empirically derived relationship which suggests that, as accumulated sales or output double, costs per unit (in real terms) typically fall by between 20 and 30 per cent. Many financial service organisations have moved from paper-based processing which offers no real economies of scale, to mechanisation and electronic processing which offer considerable potential for scale economies.

The experience curve can help marketers to understand the cost dynamics of their own organisations and those of their competitors in the future, and it provides a more informed rationale for subsequent determination of pricing.

7.2. Pricing Methods

Pricing starts with a consideration of pricing objectives and a review of demand, cost, competitors' prices and costs, and other relevant factors. The services marketer then needs to consider the method by which prices will be set. Such methods vary considerably in the services sector and typically include the following:

- *Cost Plus Pricing* — A given percentage mark-up is sought.
- *Rate of Return Pricing* —Prices are set to achieve a given rate of return on investments or assets. This is sometimes called "target return" pricing.

- *Competitive Parity Pricing* —Prices are set on the basis of following those set by the market leader.

- *Loss Leading Pricing* — This is usually applied on a short-term basis, to establish a position in the market or to provide an opportunity to cross-sell other services.

- *Value-based Pricing* —Prices are based on the service's perceived value to a given customer segment. This is a market-driven approach which reinforces the positioning of the service and the benefits that the customer receives from the service.

- *Relationship Pricing* —Prices are based on considerations of future potential profit streams over the life-time of customers.

FIGURE 12.6: EXPERIENCE CURVE FOR ELECTRONIC BANKING

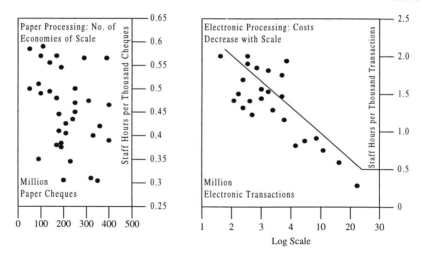

Source: Channon, 1988, p. 307, based on material from Boston Consulting Group.

It is clear that cost-plus based pricing is unacceptable as customers are interested in their own costs, not those of the supplier. Also, costs in many service businesses can be extremely hard to estimate, as companies offer a range of services which typically make use of the same resources.

Relationship pricing would appear to be the most appropriate form of pricing where there is an ongoing contact between the service provider and the customer. Relationship pricing follows closely the market-oriented approach of value-based pricing, but takes the life-time value of the customer into account. It is based on value considerations of all the services provided to the customer and makes an assessment of the potential profit stream over a given period of time — often the customer's life time. Whilst value-based pricing, which emphasises benefits, drives this pricing philosophy, it allows the firm to use loss-leader, competitive or marginal costing at appropriate points in time on relevant services, for both strategic and tactical purposes.

The value-based relationship approach to pricing is aimed at helping to position the service, and reflects the fact that customers are willing to pay extra for the perceived benefits provided by both the core product and the product surround in terms of brand image, brand values and service quality. This concept is shown in Figure 12.7. The size of the price premium is not meant to be to scale; in fact, the premium provided by the surround could be greater than the core product.

FIGURE 12.7: VALUE-BASED PRICING

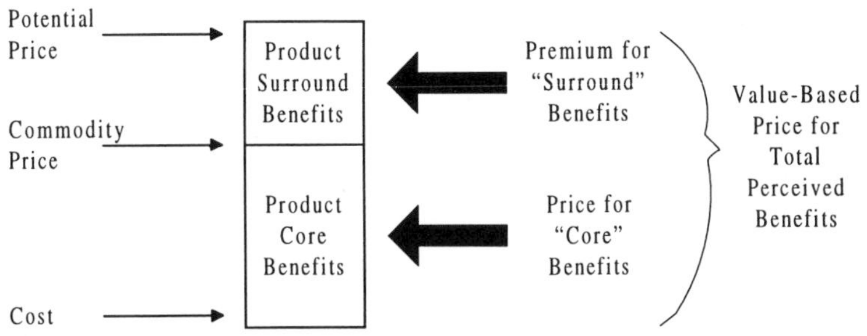

As with other marketing mix elements, the pricing of services also needs to take into account the delivery mechanism — which we shall now address.

8. MARKETING MIX 3: PLACE — SERVICE LOCATION AND CHANNELS

The location and channels used to supply services to target customers are two key decision areas. Location and channel decisions involve considering how to deliver the service to the customer and where this should take place. This has particular relevance to services, as very often they cannot be stored and will be produced and consumed at the same point.

The diversity of services makes generalisation about "place" strategies difficult. Addressing this issue involves a consideration of the nature of the interaction between the service provider and the customer, and the decision on whether the service organisation has single or multi-site locations.

Service marketers should seek to develop appropriate service delivery approaches that yield competitive advantage for their firms. Some of the issues relating to location and channels that need to be considered when seeking to develop such delivery approaches will now be examined.

8.1. Location

Location is concerned with decisions a firm makes about where its operations and people are situated. The importance of location for a service depends upon the type and degree of interaction involved. Lovelock (1983) discusses three types of interaction between the service provider and the customer: the customer goes to the service provider; the service provider goes to the customer; the service provider and customer transact business at arm's length.

When the customer has to go to the service provider, site location becomes very important. For multi-site service operators, the optimum location becomes a critical decision. Such organisations take great care in selecting appropriate sites, and a number of sophisticated computer models have been developed which can be used to assess site desirability.

Where the service provider can go to the customer, site location becomes much less important, provided that it is sufficiently close to the customers for good service quality to be received. In some circumstances, certain services must be provided at the customer's premises. For example, lift repair, pest control and cleaning services. In other cases, service providers can decide at their own discretion whether to offer their services at the customer's or their own premises. Some garages, for example, now offer car tuning and servicing at the customer's home or office.

However, when the customer and service organisation transact at arm's length, location may be largely irrelevant, particularly where efficient postal or electronic communications are in place. In some cases, certain services can be provided at arm's length but others need physical interaction between the service provider and customer. A bank can provide routine home banking services or remote ATM, but a customer may wish to arrange a mortgage in person at the bank premises.

The importance of location varies according to the service concerned.

Cowell (1984) has summed up some of the key considerations that should be addressed by the service marketer:

- What does the market require? If service is not provided in a convenient location, will purchase of the service be postponed or use delayed? Will poor location lead to do-it-yourself decisions by the customer? Are accessibility and convenience critical factors in service choice (for example, bank choice)?

- What are the trends within the sector of service activity? Could some competitive advantage be obtained by going against the norms operating in the sub-sector?

- How flexible is the service? Is it technology based or people based? How do these factors affect flexibility in location and relocation decisions?

- Does the organisation have an obligation to locate in convenient sites (for example, public health care services)?

- What new systems, procedures, processes and technology can be harnessed to overcome weaknesses of past location decisions (for example, growth of banking by post)?

- How critical are complementary services to the location decision? Are customers seeking service systems or service clusters? Does the location of other service organisations reinforce any location decision taken?

A consideration of these questions will help the service marketer with the location decision.

8.2. Channels

The second type of decision relates to who participates in the service delivery. There are three kinds of participant: the service provider, intermediaries and customers. Traditionally, it has been argued that direct sales is the most appropriate form of distribution for services. Whilst this form of distribution is common in some service sectors — for example, professional services — companies in other areas of the service sector are increasingly seeking additional channels to achieve improved growth and to fill unused capacity. Many services are now being delivered by intermediaries.

The broad channel options for services include:

- *Direct Sales* e.g., accounting and management consulting services

- *Agent or Broker* e.g., insurance broker, estate agent and travel agent

- *Sellers and Buyers Agent or Broker* e.g., stockbrokers and affinity groups

- *Franchises and Contracted Service Deliverers* e.g., fast food, car services and dry-cleaning.

This illustrates that although many services are intangible and inseparable and although direct sales may be the appropriate channel, services can be distributed through a considerable number of other channel options.

8.3. Location and Channel Choice

The choice of both location and channels for services largely depends on the particular requirements of the market and the nature of the service itself. Technology has, in some instances, changed the advantage to be gained by proximity of a service to the customer market. For example, a number of writers have pointed out that electronic banking has removed some of the need for personal contact with customers, for banks to be located on high streets and also for long opening hours to deliver their services. Technology has allowed changes in the location decision in many service industries but the decision on where and how to distribute services is often still dependent on the needs of the customer.

Service delivery channels are often the service providers. This highlights the importance of the selection of the appropriate delivery channel. If a franchised delivery system is chosen, then the choice of franchisee is of great importance to ensure the quality of the service. Stringent requirements are therefore often required to maintain the standard of service. Training is essential to provide consistency of quality. This poses a particular problem to those services where service providers may have relatively low qualifications and may not remain in one job for long — for example, the hotel and catering trade.

9. MARKETING MIX 4: PROMOTION AND COMMUNICATION OF SERVICES

The promotion element of the services marketing mix forms a vital role in helping to communicate the service to customers and other key relationship markets. The promotion of services encompasses a number of major areas. These areas, known as the communications mix or promotions mix can be used in a communications programme and include:

- Advertising
- Personal Selling
- Sales Promotion
- Public Relations
- Word-of-Mouth
- Direct Mail.

The choice of medium is determined by decisions on how to create the most favourable awareness amongst the target audience. The steps to integrate the communications mix within a promotion and communication programme comprise:

- Identification of target audience
- Determination of promotion objectives
- Development of the message
- Selection of the communications mix.

It has been argued that several factors impact on the communications mix and the emphasis placed on different elements within it (Rathmell, 1974). These include whether:

- The service is in the profit or non-profit sector
- Constraints exist, as in some professions
- Competitive intensity is high or low
- The geographic spread is large or small
- The custom within a specific service sector dictates promotional practice
- Managers are sophisticated or not.

9.1. Guidelines for Services Communications

Six guidelines for services advertising have been identified (George and Berry, 1981) which, as Gronröos (1990) points out, really are applicable to most elements of the communication mix . These apply to a wide range of service industries, but not, because of the heterogeneous nature of services, to all of them.

1. *Provide Tangible Clues* — Tangible elements within the product surround can be used to provide tangible clues.

2. *Make the Service Understood* — Because of the intangibility of services, tangible attributes of the service can be used to help to understand better the service offered. For example, Legal and General use an umbrella to symbolise the shelter and protection offered by their insurance policies.

3. *Communications Continuity* — This is important to help achieve differentiation and present a unifying and consistent theme over time. The black horse used by Lloyds Bank, the McDonald's and Disney logo, signs, symbols, packaging and advertising provide good examples of such continuity.

4. *Promising What is Possible* — Service firms must deliver on their promises. If a promise such as fast delivery cannot be consistently met, it should not be made at all. British Rail's "We're getting there" advertising campaign suffered when operations could not deliver a significant perceived improvement in their services.

5. *Capitalising on Word-of-Mouth* — The variability inherent in services contributes to the importance of word-of-mouth. Word-of-mouth is a vitally important communications vehicle in services, as evidenced by the way in which we seek personal recommendations for lawyers, accountants, doctors, hairdressers and bankers.

6. *Direct Communications to Employees* — In high-contact services, advertising should be directed at employees to build their motivation and *esprit de corps*, as well as to customers. The notion behind this is closely tied to internal marketing, which we will discuss shortly under the "people" element of the marketing mix.

9.2. The Communication Mix

Having described the basic elements of the communication programme and guidelines for services communications, we will now briefly discuss each of the main categories within the communications mix.

9.2.1 *Advertising*

Advertising is one of the main forms of impersonal communication used by service firms. The role of advertising in services marketing is to build awareness of the service, to add to the knowledge of the customer about the service, to help persuade the customer to buy and differentiate the service from other service offerings. Relevant and consistent advertising is therefore of great importance to the success of the marketing of the service.

9.2.2 Personal Selling

Personal selling has a vital role in services, because of the large number of service businesses which involve personal interaction between the service provider and the customer. Many customers of service firms have a close and ongoing relationship with the service providers. Whilst advertising can create knowledge of the firm, targeted and effective personal selling and motivated staff are needed to bring in the revenue. Under these circumstances selling has a pivotal role in the communications mix, and in certain services is the pre-eminent element in the communications mix.

9.2.3 Sales Promotion

A number of activities can be undertaken which aim at providing incentives to encourage sales. Patronage awards schemes such as green stamps, and British Airways' Airmiles and Latitudes Programmes, and other frequent user programmes, are further examples of promotions activity. Point of sale promotion includes brochures, information sheets and other materials made available to customers.

9.2.4 Public Relations

Public relations (PR) is defined as "The planned and sustained effort to establish and maintain goodwill between an organisation and its publics". These "publics" represent all groups of people and organisations which have an interest in the service company and are broadly equivalent to the six markets described earlier, particularly the "influence" markets.

9.2.5 Word-of-Mouth

One of the most distinctive feature of promotion in service businesses is the greater importance of referral and word-of-mouth communications. Customers are often closely involved in the delivery of a service and then go and talk to other potential customers about their experiences. They are glad to offer advice on service providers and, indeed, some businesses are specially established in order to offer such services. Research points to personal recommendations through word-of-mouth being one of the most important information sources and one which can, in fact, sometimes have more impact than other mass or personal communications mix elements.

9.2.6 Direct Marketing

In recent years, more sophisticated approaches to direct marketing have been adopted. Companies such as British Telecom, American Express, Royal Mail and most banks and airlines are using direct marketing to build profitable business with their customer base. Developments in electronic media, telecommunications, and computers are now presenting greater opportunities for developing an integrated programme of direct marketing activities. These can be used in conjunction with each other to reinforce the personal selling, advertising and other promotional elements.

10. MARKETING MIX 5: PEOPLE

People are increasingly becoming part of the differentiation by which service companies seek to create added value and gain competitive advantage. Within the overall services marketing mix, employees play a vital role in acquiring customers, building long-term customer relationships and ensuring customer satisfaction. It is surprising, therefore, that until recently, attempts to view employees as part of a service organisation's marketing mix have been notably absent from academic and marketing literature.

The success of marketing a service is tied closely to the selection, training, motivation and management of employees There are many examples of services failing or succeeding as a consequence of the ineffective or effective management of people. One of the most famous examples is the turnaround of British Airways during the 1980s. Faced with declining profits, greater customer complaints, employee dissatisfaction and increased competition, British Airways launched a series of programmes to refocus on the people within the organisation. Employees were trained to develop new attitudes towards customers by emphasising that the airline was in business to satisfy their needs. In turn, the company made employees feel wanted and cared for, building on the principle that those who are looked after will pass on this caring attitude. The success of this new direction for the airline was made apparent by increased profits, matched by greater customer and employee satisfaction.

10.1. Internal Marketing

The importance of people within the marketing of services has lead to greater interest in internal marketing. This recognises the importance of attracting, motivating, training and retaining customer-conscious employees at every level. Schneider and Bowen (1985) have found that, when employees identify with the norms and values of an organisation, they are less inclined to leave and, furthermore, customers are likely to be more satisfied with the service. Satisfied employees are also able to communicate the service values and norms to newcomers and successive generations of service providers. Employee satisfaction in internal markets is thus a prerequisite to customer satisfaction in external markets.

There are two main aspects to internal marketing:

- Every employee and every department within an organisation has roles both as internal customers and internal suppliers. To help to ensure high-quality external marketing, every individual and department within a service organisation must provide and receive excellent service.

- Staff must work together in a way that is aligned with the firm's mission, strategy and goals. This has become particularly important within high-contact service firms where there are high levels of interaction between the service provider and customer.

In practice, internal marketing is concerned with communications, developing responsiveness, responsibility and unity of purpose. The fundamental aims of internal marketing are to develop internal and external customer awareness and remove functional barriers to organisational effectiveness. The idea is to ensure that all members of staff provide the best possible contribution to the marketing activities of the company and successfully complete all interactions with customers in a way that adds value to the service encounter.

An increasing number of companies have recognised the need for internal marketing programmes, and the implementation of these programmes has gained momentum in recent years. Perhaps the most famous examples being British Airways and Scandinavian Airlines System (SAS). In fact, some organisations have started to view internal marketing as a strategic weapon to help to retain customers through achieving high-quality service delivery and increased customer satisfaction (George, 1977; Berry, 1983; Band, 1988; George and Grönroos, 1989).

10.2. Differing Roles of People

An essential aspect of viewing people as an element of the marketing mix is recognising the different roles in which people affect both the marketing task and customer contact. This issue has been identified by Gummesson (1987) in his concept of the "part-time marketer". Judd (1987) has developed a categorisation scheme based on the degree of frequency of customer contact and the extent to which staff are involved with conventional marketing activities, as shown in Figure 12.8.

FIGURE 12.8: EMPLOYEE INFLUENCE ON CUSTOMERS

	Involved With Conventional Marketing Mix	Not Directly Involved With Marketing Mix
Frequent or Periodic Customer Contact	**Contractors**	**Modifiers**
Infrequent or No Customer Contact	**Influencers**	**Isolateds**

Source: Judd, 1987.

- *Contactors* — These people have frequent and regular customer contact and are typically involved with conventional marketing activities, for example, customer service and selling. They need to be well trained, prepared and motivated to serve the customer. They should be recruited based on their potential to be responsive to customer needs and be evaluated and rewarded on this basis.

- *Modifiers* — People such as receptionists, credit department and switchboard personnel. Whilst they are not involved with conventional marketing activities, they nevertheless have frequent customer contact. They have a vital role to play in service businesses. Modifiers need high levels of customer relationship skills. Training and monitoring performance are especially important.

- *Influencers* — While involved with the traditional elements of the marketing mix, they have infrequent or no customer contact. They include those with roles in product development, market research, and so forth. In the recruitment of influencers, those with potential to develop a sense of customer responsiveness should be favoured. They should be evaluated and rewarded according to customer-oriented performance standards.

- *Isolateds* — These people perform various support functions and have neither frequent customer contact nor a great deal to do with conventional marketing activities. However, as support people their activities critically affect performance of the organisation's activities. Staff falling within this category include those in the purchasing department, personnel and data processing. Such staff should be sensitive to the fact that internal and external customers have needs that must be satisfied.

This categorisation suggests that people form an important part of the differentiation in service organisations which can create added value for the external customer. By viewing people as a separate element in the marketing mix, the appropriate level of attention can be directed to maximising the impact of their activities, motivating them to make the desired contribution and rewarding them for so doing.

11. MARKETING MIX 6: CUSTOMER SERVICE

A major differentiating factor for services companies is the quality of customer service. Customers are much more sophisticated and demanding than they were 30 years ago. Not only do they *require* higher standards of service, but they also *expect* them. Many major services companies are finally waking up to the need to improve customer service. They recognise that warranties, unconditional service guarantees and free phone-in advice centres are critical in order to compete in today's highly competitive service environment.

11.1. The Role of Customer Service

A wide range of views and perspectives exists as to the definition of customer service. Here customer service is defined as being concerned with the building of bonds with customers and other markets or groups to ensure long-term relationships of mutual advantage which reinforce the other elements of the marketing mix. The provision of high levels of customer service involves understanding what the customer buys and determining how additional value can be added to the offer. Customer service can therefore be seen as an activity which provides time and place utilities for the customer and which also involves pre-transaction

and post-transaction considerations relating to the exchange process
with the customer. Some of the key elements are shown in Figure 12.9.

FIGURE 12.9: ILLUSTRATION OF ELEMENTS OF CUSTOMER
SERVICE

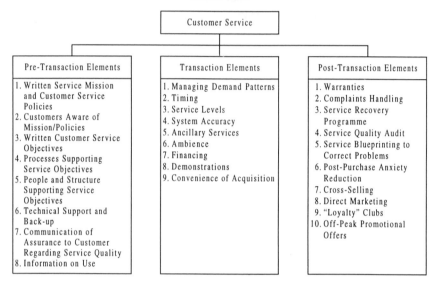

11.2. Customer Service Strategy

There are four key steps in creating a customer service strategy, as
outlined by Christopher (1992):

1. *Identifying a Service Mission* — A service company should articulate
   its service commitment and values within its corporate mission, and/
   or in a separate customer service mission statement which reflects the
   company's philosophy and commitment to customer service.

2. *Setting Customer Service Objectives* — This involves answering
   questions such as: "How important is customer service compared
   with the other marketing mix elements?" "Which are the most
   important customer service elements?" In considering levels of performance in setting these objectives, service companies must consider the importance of service quality variables such as reliability,
   responsiveness, assurance, empathy and tangibles (see Berry,
   Parasuraman and Zeithaml, 1988).

3. *Customer Service Strategy* — Most markets consist of market
   segments which seek different combinations of benefits. As all

custcmers do not require the same level of service, segmentation can be a powerful means of creating appropriate service packages for each relevant market segment. Christopher's approach to developing a service-based strategy consists of four parts: identify service segments; identify most important products and customers; prioritise service targets; and develop the service package.

4. *Implementation* — Once the most effective service package has been developed for each segment, it should then become part of an integrated marketing mix.

A service organisation should focus especially on customer service and keep customer satisfaction levels under constant review. Usually there is a need for a complaint system which allows unhappy customers to be identified and corrective action to be taken. Above all else, a service company must stay in touch with the changing needs of its customers in terms of its customer service offering.

12. MARKETING MIX 7: PROCESSES

The processes by which services are created and delivered to the customer is a major factor within the services marketing mix, as services customers will often perceive the service delivery system as part of the service itself. Thus, decisions on operations management are of great importance to the success of the marketing of the service. In fact, continuous co-ordination between marketing and operations is essential to success in most services businesses.

All work activity is process. Processes involve the procedures, tasks, schedules, mechanisms, activities and routines by which a product or service is delivered to the customer. They also involve policy decisions about customer involvement and employee discretion.

While the people element is critical in the services marketing mix, no amount of attention and effort from staff will overcome continued unsatisfactory process performance. If the processes supporting service delivery cannot, for example, quickly repair equipment or provide a meal within a defined period, an unhappy customer will be the result. This suggests that close co-operation is needed between the marketing and operations staff who are involved in process management.

In reviewing the role of processes, two issues are worthy of particular attention: how processes can be seen as structural elements that can be altered to help achieve positioning strategy; and how marketing and operations should be managed to achieve synergy between them.

12.1. Processes as Structural Elements

Shostack (1987) has suggested that processes are structural elements that can be engineered to help deliver a desired strategic positioning. She points out that a process-oriented approach involves the following:

- Breaking down the process into logical steps and sequences to facilitate its control and analysis

- Taking into account the more variable processes, which may lead to different outcomes because of judgment, choice or chance

- Deviation or tolerance standards which recognise that processes are real time phenomena which do not perform with perfect precision, but function within a performance band.

Services processes can also be analysed according to their complexity and divergence. Complexity is concerned with the nature of the steps and sequences that constitute the process, while divergence refers to the "executional" latitude or variability of the steps and sequences. The processes in services can be depicted by developing service blueprints, which reduce the processes to interactive steps and sequences.

Processes can be changed in terms of complexity and divergence to reinforce the positioning or establish a new positioning. The four options outlined by Shostack are as follows:

- *Reduced Divergence* — This tends to reduce costs, improve productivity and make distribution easier. It can also produce more uniform service quality and improved service availability. However, negative effects may include a perception of limited choice and a rejection of the highly standardised service.

- *Increased Divergence* — This involves greater customisation and flexibility, which may command higher prices. This approach suggests a niche positioning strategy based less on volume and more on margins.

- *Reduced Complexity* — This usually means a specialisation strategy. Steps and activities are omitted from the service process and this tends to make distribution and control easier.

- *Increased Complexity* — Greater complexity is usually a strategy to gain higher levels of penetration in a market by adding more services. Supermarkets, banks and building societies tend to follow this approach.

Each of the above options has its advantages and disadvantages, as well as providing opportunities to alter customers' perceptions and positioning.

12.2. Balancing Marketing and Operations

Once the appropriate levels of complexity and divergence for processes to achieve a desired strategic position have been configured, it is then essential to ensure that a balance is achieved between marketing and operations perspectives.

Within services, marketers should be vitally concerned with the operations and service-delivery processes. This balance becomes especially important in services which involve a high level of customer contact, such as hotels, restaurants and airlines. However, many service businesses are frequently dominated by the operations function. The marketing staff are often relatively new to the function and do not have a full understanding of processes and operations. Marketers must take the initiative and fully understand the implications of the cost-benefit trade-offs of changes in processes, and their impact on both the marketing and operations areas.

Lovelock (1992) points out that whilst many services firms are seeking to develop an effective marketing function to act as a bridge between the organisation and the environment in which it operates, the introduction of a marketing orientation may be resisted by operations executives who see marketing as a costly add-on function. They see marketing as being confined to consumer research and communications activity and resent it when marketers seek to become involved in product design and service delivery.

There is a critical interplay between processes, marketing and human resources. A clear understanding of configuring processes in terms of complexity and divergence, and a balance of marketing and operations activities, are key inputs for improving service systems.

13. MARKETING MIX INTEGRATION AND MARKETING PLANNING

Seven elements of the services marketing mix have now been considered. Each of these mix elements interact with each other and they should be developed so that they are mutually supportive in obtaining the best possible match between the internal and external environments of the organisation. In developing a marketing mix strategy, service marketers need to consider the relationships between the elements of the mix. It has been pointed out that there are three degrees of interaction between the marketing mix elements (Shapiro, 1985):

- *Consistency* — This occurs where there is a logical and useful fit between two or more elements of the marketing mix.

- *Integration* — This involves an active harmonious interaction between the elements of the mix.

- *Leverage* — This involves a more sophisticated approach and is concerned with using each element to best advantage in support of the total marketing mix.

Each of the elements of the services marketing mix and their sub-elements need, therefore, to focus on supporting each other in terms of consistency, integration and leverage, reinforcing the positioning and delivery of service quality required by the market segment (or segments) that are targeted, as shown in Figure 12.10.

FIGURE 12.10: A RELATIONSHIP-ORIENTED MARKETING MIX FOR SERVICES

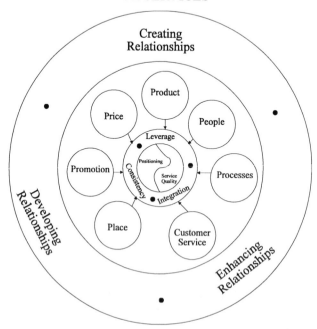

Source: Payne and Clark, 1994.

In developing a marketing mix strategy, we need to consider the impact of each marketing mix element on the market segments selected. This implies ensuring that there is:

- A fit between the marketing mix and each target segment

- A fit between the marketing mix and the company's strategic capabilities, emphasising its strengths and minimising the impact of its weaknesses

- A recognition of competitors' capabilities, which involves evading their strengths and capitalising on their weaknesses.

To achieve this, a strategic marketing plan should be developed which shows how the marketing mix strategy is to be developed and implemented. This involves organising marketing resources, deciding levels of marketing expenditure and determining the expected results.

The purpose of marketing planning is to provide a logical framework to establish how the organisation can best use its resources to match the needs of its chosen markets. One approach that has proven robust in service firm marketing planning is the framework developed by McDonald (1989). The planning framework has four phases which in turn break into ten major steps. The four major phases are:

- Strategic Context

- Situation Review

- Marketing Strategy Formulation

- Resource Allocation and Monitoring.

These four phases, together with the associated steps, are shown in Figure 12.11 below.

14. SERVICES MARKETING: FROM FUNCTIONAL TO CROSS-FUNCTIONAL ORIENTATION

In this chapter, our focus has been on some of the key tasks which need to be managed in marketing services. We have emphasised that traditional marketing mix management *by itself* is not likely to result in positions of superiority for service organisations. Whilst service organisations need to manage and undertake the traditional 4Ps — product, price, promotion and place — they also need to understand and address the critical role of the expanded marketing mix elements of people, processes and proactive customer service.

FIGURE 12.11: THE MARKETING PLANNING PROCESS

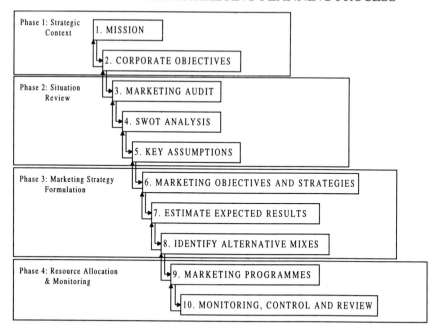

A consideration of these other elements of the marketing mix raises two important issues for service management. First, the traditional 4Ps are primarily functionally oriented around the marketing department and are largely concerned with catching the customer — transaction marketing. Second, the additional three elements are not only concerned with functional activities which fall within the domain of the marketing department — they are also cross-functional in nature and involve the other functions within the organisation; further, they are primarily concerned with developing an ongoing dialogue with the customer — relationship marketing. This raises the question of whether these should be the 7Ps of services marketing or the 7Ps of services management.

Viewing marketing solely from a functional perspective, shown in Figure 12.12, even if it does focus on all these marketing mix elements, will result in sub-optimal performance. Increasingly it is being recognised that traditional vertical organisations which are hierarchically structured and functionally oriented often optimise individual functions at the expense of integration across the whole business — and true customer orientation through which the whole organisation is focused on the customer.

The core problem is the lack of co-ordination across functions, departments and tasks. This functional approach often means that while problems manifest themselves in one part of the organisation, their root cause may remain unattended elsewhere. This results in low levels of corporate performance and even lower levels of customer satisfaction, as customers are passed from one functionally-focused department to the next in the quest for a solution to their problems. Unfortunately, performance measurement systems often exacerbate these problems and lead to even more functional emphasis.

FIGURE 12.12: MARKETING AS A FUNCTIONAL ACTIVITY

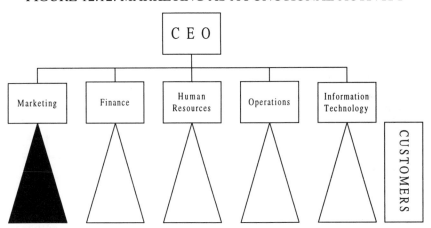

Increasing competition in service businesses and fast-changing markets has meant that flexibility and co-ordination across organisations have become as important as functional performance within departments. Companies need to achieve excellence in quality, service levels, cycle times and other performance measures. These challenges require managers to rethink the way in which companies interact with their supplier, channels and customers. Hence, what is necessary is an approach that organises the flow of work around company-wide *processes* — as opposed to *functions* — that ultimately link with customer needs. This market facing approach is illustrated in Figure 12.13.

These processes include activities such as new product development, marketing planning and marketing information systems, and the management of customer relationships.

A fundamental aspect of cross-functional processes is that they add customer value. As Christopher (1994) points out, this means that the service offering becomes more attractive to the customer because of the way in which we do things. However, the sources of customer value are time, place and form utilities. In other words, the ways in which we

deliver services to meet customers' requirements and the way in which
we make it easy for customers to do business with us are all components
of customer value.

FIGURE 12.13: MARKETING AS A CROSS-FUNCTIONAL
ACTIVITY

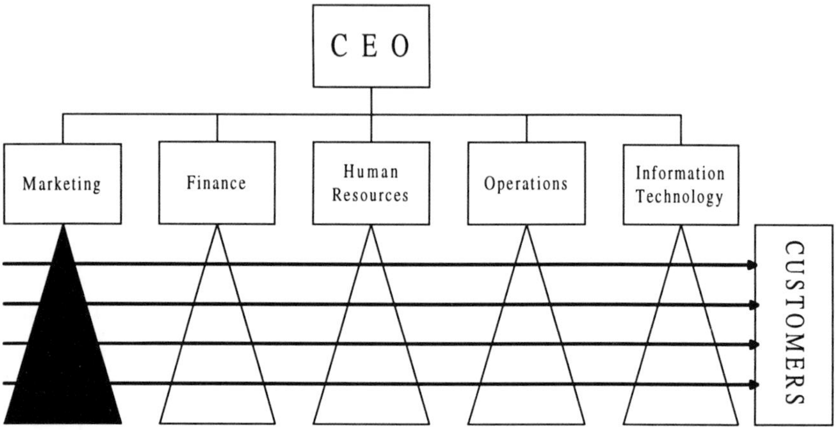

In market-facing service organisations, key players are drawn together in
multidisciplinary teams or groups that seek to marshal resources to
achieve relationship-based objectives and increased customer satisfaction. The functions may still exist but they are now seen as "pools of
resources" from which the market-facing teams draw expertise. Ostroff
and Smith (1992) emphasise the value of this approach: "there is real
performance leverage in moving toward a flatter, more horizontal mode
of organisation, in which cross-functional, end-to-end work flows link
internal processes with the needs and capabilities of both suppliers and
customers".

We will conclude with a final comment on the concept of the marketing mix. It is acknowledged that this framework does not do full justice
to the complexity of services management. Services management is still
an evolving field. Although this field has been characterised as "walking
erect" (Fisk, Brown and Bitner, Chapter 1), Gummesson (1994) points
out that a human being "walks after the first year and then lives another
80 years" and concludes: "the service management journey has just
begun". It is to be expected that a consolidation of "work to date" will
occur within the services sector over the next five years, and with this
consolidation some improved integrative frameworks for services

management will be developed. Until such time, the 7Ps remain as an important part of services management, but one that needs to be devoted to the creation, development and enhancement of relationships — relationship marketing — rather than as a set of "stand-alone" functionally-oriented activities.

REFERENCES

Band, W., "Customer Satisfaction Studies Changing Marketing Strategies", *Marketing News*, Vol. 22, 12 September, 1988, p. 14.

Baumgartner, J., "Nonmarketing Professionals Need More than Four Ps", *Marketing News*, 22 July, 1991, p. 28.

Berry, L., "Relationship Marketing", in L. Berry, G.L. Shostack and G.D. Upah (Eds.), *Emerging Perspectives on Services Marketing*, American Marketing Association, Chicago, IL, 1983, pp. 25–8.

Berry, L.L., A. Parasuraman, and V.A. Zeithaml, "The Service Quality Puzzle", *Business Horizons*, Vol. 31, No. 4, September/October 1988, pp. 35–43.

Berry, L.L. and A. Parasuraman, *Marketing Services: Competing through Quality*, The Free Press, New York, 1991.

Booms, B.H. and M.J. Bitner, "Marketing Strategies and Organisation Structures for Services Firms", in J. Donnelly and W.R. George (Eds.), *Marketing of Services*, American Marketing Association, Chicago, IL, 1981, pp. 47–51.

Borden, N.H., "The Concept of the Marketing Mix", in G. Schwartz (Ed.), *Science in Marketing*, John Wiley, New York, 1965, pp. 386–97.

Brookes, R., *The New Marketing*, Gower Press, London, 1988.

Brown, J.K., "Corporate Soul Searching: The Power of Mission Statements", *Across the Board*, March, 1994.

Brownlie, B. and M. Saren, "The Four Ps of The Marketing Concept: Prescriptive, Polemical, Permanent and Problematical", *European Journal of Marketing*, Vol. 26, No. 4, 1992, pp. 34–47.

Channon, D.F., *Global Banking Strategy*, John Wiley, New York, 1988.

Christopher, M., *The Customer Service Planner*, Butterworth Heinemann, Oxford, UK, 1992 .

Christopher, M., "Customer Service and Logistics Strategy", in M. Baker (Ed.), *The Marketing Book*, Heinemann, Oxford, UK, 1994.

Christopher, M., A. Payne and D. Ballantyne, *Relationship Marketing: Bringing Quality, Customer Service, and Marketing Together*, Butterworth Heinemann, Oxford, UK, 1991.

Cowell, D., *The Marketing of Services*, Heinemann, London, 1984, p.199.

de Ferrer, R.J., "A Case for European Management", *International Management Development Review*, Vol. 2, 1986, pp. 275–81.

Dibb, S., L. Simkin, W. Pride and O. Ferrell, *Marketing*, Houghton Mifflin Company, Boston, MA, 1991.

Dobtree, J and A.S. Sage, "Unleashing the Power of Service Brands in the 1990's", *Management Decision*, Vol. 28, No. 6, 1990, p. 21.

Easingwood, C.J. and V. Mahajan, "Positioning of Financial Services for Competitive Advantage", *Journal of Product Innovation Management*, Vol. 6, 1989, pp. 207–19.

George, William R., "The Retailing of Services: A Challenging Future", *Journal of Retailing*, Vol. 53, Fall, 1977, pp. 85–98.

George, W.R. and L.L. Berry, "Guidelines for the Advertising of Services", *Business Horizons*, Vol. 24, No. 4, July/August 1981, pp. 52–6.

George, W.R. and C. Grönroos, "Developing Customer Conscious Employees at Every Level — Internal Marketing", in Carole A. Congram, and Margaret L. Friedman (Eds.), "Handbook of Services Marketing", AMACON, New York, 1989.

Gilmour, P., "Customer Segmentation: Differentiating by Market Segment", *International Journal of Physical Distribution*, Vol. 7, No. 3, 1977, pp. 141–8.

Grönroos, C., "Defining Marketing: A Market-Orientated Approach", *European Journal of Marketing*, Vol. 23, 1989, pp. 52–60.

Grönroos, Christian, *Service Management and Marketing: Managing the Moments of Truth in Service Competition*, Heath Lexington Books, Lexington, MA, 1990.

Gummesson, E., "The New Marketing — Developing Long-Term Interactive Relationships", *Long Range Planning*, Vol. 20, No. 4, August, 1987, pp. 10–20.

Gummesson, Evert, *Relationship Marketing: From 4Ps to 30Rs*, Stockholm University, Stockholm, Sweden, 1994.

Judd, V.C., "Differentiate with the Fifth P: People", *Industrial Marketing Management*, Vol. 16, 1987, pp. 241–7.

Kent, R.A., "Faith in the Four Ps: An Alternative", *Journal of Marketing Management*, Vol. 2, No. 2, 1986, pp. 145–54.

Kotler, P., *Marketing Management: Analysis, Planning, Implementation and Control*, Prentice-Hall, Englewood Cliffs, NJ, 7th Edition, 1991.

Kotler, P., *Marketing Management: Analysis, Planning, Implementation and Control*, Prentice-Hall, Englewood Cliffs, NJ, 8th Edition, 1994.

Levitt, T., *The Marketing Imagination*, The Free Press, New York, 1983.

Lovelock, C. H., "Classifying Services to Gain Strategic Marketing Insights", *Journal of Marketing*, Vol. 47, Summer 1983, pp. 9–20.

Lovelock, C.H., "Developing and Implementing New Services", in W.R. George, and C. E. Marshall (Eds.), *Developing New Services*, American Marketing Association, Chicago, IL, 1984, p. 45.

Lovelock, C., *Services Marketing: Text, Cases and Readings*, Prentice-Hall, Englewood Cliffs, NJ, 1990.

Lovelock, C., "Seeking Synergy in Service Operations: Seven Things Marketers Need to Know about Service Operations", *European Management Journal*, Vol. 10, No. 1, March, 1992, pp. 22–9.

Majaro, S., *Marketing in Perspective*, George Allen and Unwin, London, 1982.

McDonald, M., *Marketing Plans: How to Prepare Them, How to Use Them*, Butterworth Heinemann, Oxford, UK, 2nd Edition, 1989.

Ostroff, F. and Smith, D., "The Horizontal Organisation", *McKinsey Quarterly*, Winter 1992, pp. 148–67.

Payne, A.F.T., *The Essence of Services Marketing*, Prentice-Hall, Hemel Hempstead, UK, 1993.

Payne, A.F.T. and M.K. Clark, "The Marketing Mix: Is It Valid for Services", Working Paper, Cranfield School of Management, Cranfield, UK, 1994.

Rathmell, J., *Marketing in the Service Sector*, Winthrop Publications, Cambridge, MA, 1974, pp. 92–103.

Schneider, B. and D.E. Bowen, "Employee and Customer Perceptions of Service in Banks: Replication and Extension", *Journal of Applied Psychology*, Vol. 70, 1985, pp. 423–33.

Shapiro, B., "Rejuvenating the Marketing Mix", *Harvard Business Review*, September/October, 1985, pp. 28–33.

Shostack, G.L., "Service Positioning through Structural Change", *Journal of Marketing*, Vol. 51, January, 1987, pp. 34–3.

Weinstein, A., *Marketing Segmentation*, Probus Publishing Company, Chicago, IL, 1987.

13

SERVICE QUALITY AT THE MANUFACTURING–MARKETING INTERFACE:

From *Kaizen* to Service-Driven Logistics

Brian Fynes
University College Dublin, Ireland

Sean Ennis
University of Strathclyde, Scotland

Lionello Negri
Consiglio Nazionale delle Ricerche, Italy

PRÉCIS

This chapter examines the series of rapid changes affecting manufacturing-industry procedures and organisations in recent years. Amongst the issues dealt with by the authors are the moves towards lean production, the growing importance of logistics, the increasing search for quality production and the drive for World Class Manufacturing. The chapter includes a case study of Microsoft Ireland and, based upon the findings of this case-study, draws important conclusions regarding the potential of modern processes to facilitate manufacturing location and expansion in peripheral locations such as Ireland. The chapter pays particular attention to the importance of "service-driven logistics", and throughout the presentation there are constant references to the importance of services and service-inputs as drivers of change in manufacturing-industry processes and procedures.

Modern industrial development depends upon an increasing array of service inputs to ensure quality products, efficient production and the increased customisation of output, as well as to ensure comprehensive and continuing post-production after-sales service.

In a world where up to 75 per cent of the value-added of a manufacturing product can derive from embodied services,[1] the tradi-tional dichotomy between goods and services is proving meaningless. Recent developments have witnessed an integration of goods and services in an effort to provide customers, not with products or with services, but with solutions.[2] In turn, this gives rise to final "products" which are no longer clearly identifiable as either a good or a service. This convergence of goods and services is also transforming the organisation of work. Segmentation of the workplace and the blurring of the divisions between job-functions is yielding to modern integrated production systems, an emphasis on teamwork, multi-skilling and the need for shared flexible work spaces.

The outcome of such processes and the implications of the con-vergence of services and manufacturing are well seen in the case of Microsoft which is described below. Such trends may prove especially beneficial for Ireland which is a small, peripheral and relatively under-developed economy. Given the time and costs of goods transportation to mainland Europe, efficient production and the elimination of delays and lead times are crucial. Ireland is better suited to the production of high-value products which are the consequences of the service-industry mix, especially having regard to this country's strengths in areas such as education, telecommunications, quality of life and interpersonal commu-nication skills.

Michael J. Bannon
University College Dublin, Ireland

1. INTRODUCTION

The growth in the quality movement over the last 20–30 years has been well documented. In the manufacturing/production management litera-ture, contributions by individuals such as Deming (1986), Juran (1986), Crosby (1979), and Schonberger (1990) have been discussed, dissected and, occasionally, disparaged. Likewise in the services and marketing

---

[1] See Pauli, G., *Double Digit Growth: How to Achieve it with Services*, Pauli Publishing, Belgium, 1991, p. 148.

[2] See Vandemerwe, S., "The Market Power is in Services: Because the Value is in the Result", European Management Journal, Vol. 1, No. 8, December, 1990, pp. 464–73.

literature, the contributions of Lewis (1991), Grönroos (1988), and Parasuraman, Zeithaml and Berry (1988) have been widely reported. The purpose of this chapter is to focus on a sometimes neglected interface between both bodies of literature: the service dimension to manufacturing. More recently, authors such as Mathe and Shapiro (1993) and Chase and Garvin (1989) have begun to address this very issue. In this chapter we highlight the evolution of manufacturing in recent times and its implications for marketing. At the interface, we focus on the area of enhanced and personalised customer service in the area of logistics and how it has developed. In addition, we present details of a case study at Microsoft's European manufacturing plant, tracing the route from lean production to lean logistics and the implications of such a journey for the interface between manufacturing and marketing/service support.

2. MANUFACTURING IN PERSPECTIVE

2.1. Introduction

Womack, Jones and Roos (1990) have documented the evolution of manufacturing since the early 1900s with particular regard to the car industry (Figure 13.1). At the turn of the century, there was a very wide range of products on sale, as each vehicle was a one-of-a-kind, custom built to the requirements of the owner. Volumes, however, were quite low and cars were only purchased by those on high incomes. Under the mass production principles of standardisation, interchangeable parts and division of labour, developed by Henry Ford, volumes of the ubiquitous Model T rose to 2 million units per year, yet product variety fell to just a few dozen offerings: "You can have any colour as long as it is black". Mass production was characterised essentially by economies of scale. Later, Alfred Sloan at General Motors succeeded in offering greater variety (different models and extra features) as customers became more demanding, but it was only with the emergence of the Japanese car producers and their lean production strategies (because they use less resources to offer far greater choice) that economics of scope (both volume and variety) were achieved.

Lean production, in effect, combines the best features of both craft and mass production, with Womack suggesting that:

> Lean production will supplant both mass production and the remaining outposts of craft production in all areas of industrial endeavour to become the standard global production system of the twenty-first century.

FIGURE 13.1: THE PROGRESSION OF PRODUCT VARIETY AND
PRODUCTION VOLUME IN THE CAR INDUSTRY

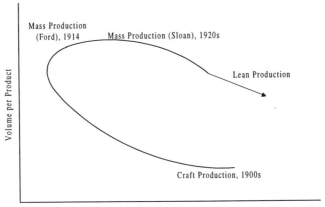

Source: Adapted from Womack, Jones and Roos, 1990.

A number of important factors are currently playing a major role in influencing the further diffusion of lean production. They include:

- Increasing product and market complexity

- Greater service content

- More choice and customisation

- The ability to produce quality products at low cost

- Shorter product life cycles

- Getting product more quickly to the marketplace.

2.2. Lean Production and World Class Manufacturing

Roth, Giffi and Seal (1992) broadly define world class manufacturing as follows:

> A dynamic process that provides unique value, competitive advantage and delight to customers and suppliers through the development of internal operations capabilities that foster continuous improvements in human assets, technology, materials and information flows, that are synergistic with the total business, and that provide a sustainable competitive position in the firm's target markets.

The DTI/PA Consulting Group Study (1990) identified the achievement of excellence as being a critical ingredient for the development of business strategy in the 1990s. The word excellence is used here in the context of "high standards of customer satisfaction, plus total quality and reliable delivery; all at low cost, in circumstances where people will be difficult to attract and retain, and where environmental considerations will also have to be catered for". Before examining the specific components of world class manufacturing, it is prudent to inject a cautionary note into the discussion. Terms like "WCM", "manufacturing excellence" and "high-performance businesses" (see Scott-Morgan, 1992) are pejorative because they convey a vague, simplistic notion about what is required on the part of manufacturing strategy to achieve such positions of eminence. A key prerequisite for understanding such terminology is that it is aspirational in nature and as a consequence, the onus is on the company to place a strong degree of emphasis on continuous improvement as a way of moving towards the desired or ideal position. In this regard, Hall (1987) is quite clear when he contends that "one interesting aspect of manufacturing excellence is that if such a thing is attainable at all, it will be by those who realise that no such condition exists."

Continuous improvement and elimination of waste (any operation that does not add value) are two key principles of manufacturing excellence as identified by Huge and Anderson (1988). They also pinpoint lower cost, higher quality, better service and more flexibility than competitors as key success factors. However, the adoption of techniques and tools alone does not guarantee success. Organisations must establish an ethos or corporate culture which is conducive to the acceptance of such changes This needs to be driven not just through the workforce and management, but also among its stakeholders, suppliers and customers. Such a change in culture is only possible if a number of essential prerequisites are in place. These include: commitment at all levels; union co-operation (if relevant); sufficient time; the need for someone to champion the process; and the provision of necessary financial support.

2.3. The Manufacturing-Marketing Interface

The adoption of lean manufacturing and logistics strategies presents organisations with the opportunity to achieve many typical marketing objectives. Much of the recent marketing literature has stressed the importance of speed to market, customer service, quality management and internal customers (see Vesey, 1992; Morgan and Piercy, 1992; Brooks and Wragg, 1992; Lancaster, 1993). If a company wishes to achieve improvements in areas such as delivery, order scheduling, depth and variety of product line, and ultimately move towards what West-brook and Williamson (1993) have labelled *mass customisation*, it can only do so if manufacturing policy and procedures are aligned to those emanating from the marketing department.

This calls for substantial co-operation between the various functions operating within the business. There is, therefore, a major requirement on the part of senior management within the company to accept and recognise the need to integrate the often conflicting objectives which can emerge from within the departments. In many ways, while this may be difficult to achieve initially, it is being forced on manufacturing and marketing personnel, as the former require the latter to make accurate estimates of each product line whereas marketing requires products to be produced as and when required by the customer.

In summary, the manufacturing–marketing interface should not be viewed as a battleground which encourages conflict. Quite the reverse. As Sweeney (1993) notes, "the ultimate goal of the world class manu-facturer is to be the least cost operator of a highly differentiated product range." Thus, if a company can achieve such a position through the adoption of advanced manufacturing techniques, then it can compete more favourably in the marketplace and, more importantly, allow the marketers to achieve substantial improvements in areas such as customer-driven logistics.

3. THE QUALITY MOVEMENT IN MANUFACTURING

While quality impacts on everything a company does, it has proven difficult to fit a clear, concise definition to the overall concept. Defi-nitions are applied according to the circumstances of the particular busi-ness situation. The traditional view of quality was based on the physical characteristics of the product. According to this "product-based" approach, quality reflects differences in measurable attributes of the product, thereby implying that more of one attribute in a product may be desirable to more of another. This view is balanced somewhat by the "manufacturing-based" view, where the quality of a product is measured by its conformance to a predetermined set of specifications.

Ishikawa (1985) suggests that, broadly interpreted, quality means quality of work, quality of service, quality of system, quality of information, quality of people, quality of process and quality of objec-tives: companies must address the issue in its every manifestation. He goes on to argue that quality control is carried out for the purpose of realising the quality which conforms to customer requirements. This involves:

- Identifying the true quality characteristic, namely, the customers' actual need or perceived benefit, and deciding to measure it to determine the quality standard for it

- Next, identifying the substitute characteristics of the production processes which are likely to have an effect on the true characteristic, by the use of cause-and-effect diagrams

- Finally, determining the relationship between these substitute characteristics and the true characteristic by test and experiment.

Standards can then be set for the substitute characteristics to ensure that the standard for the true characteristic is constantly attained. Continuing analysis is then used to improve both the level and the economics of delivering on the true characteristics, thereby delighting the customer.

Deming (1986) expands on this topic by reference to operational definitions which put communicable meaning into concepts such as "safe", "round" or "reliable". Communicable implies that it has the same meaning for supplier and purchaser at all times. Recognising the difficulty of establishing operational definitions, he suggests a 14-point action strategy for improving quality:

1. Establish a constant objective of improvement for product and service.

2. Adopt a philosophy of quality control.

3. Use statistical methods to prove that quality is built-in.

4. Develop long-term relationships with a few suppliers.

5. Constantly improve the process to eliminate waste.

6. Train effectively on the job.

7. Improve supervision.

8. Remove hierarchical barriers of communication between managers and employees.

9. Promote communications between departments, suppliers and customers.

10. Eliminate numerical goals for the workforce.

11. Eliminate work standards.

12. Give workers the tools to evaluate their own work and to take pride in it.

13. Institute a vigorous programme of education and training.

14. Create a top management structure that will support these points.

Deming emphasises that quality is primarily the result of senior management actions and decisions. Managers can allocate resources, provide training for employees, select the technology, and provide the work environment that will foster and nurture a quality culture. He stresses that it is the system of work that determines how the work is performed, and only managers can create that system.

Juran (1986) argues that quality is fitness for use rather than conformance to specification. This implies that it is up to the individual company to determine customer requirements, and to produce a product that meets these needs. He suggests a cost-of-quality accounting system, focusing on internal and external failure costs, appraisal costs and prevention costs. In addition, he advocates that quality planning, control and improvement be closely linked with their financial counterparts and advocates the following "breakthrough sequence" for quality improvement:

1. Create a climate for change.

2. Identify breakthrough projects.

3. Organise for breakthroughs in knowledge.

4. Conduct in-depth diagnostic analysis.

5. Determine how to overcome resistance to change.

6. Institute the change.

7. Institute controls.

Like Deming, Crosby's (1979) approach to quality is directed at management. He contends that it is management's lack of understanding that contributes to a large extent to problems with quality. He advocates the zero defects approach, defining quality as the absence of defects, and faults and problems that arise are essentially ones of non-conformance. Again like Deming, he suggests a 14-point plan for achieving zero defects:

1. Obtain management commitment to quality.

2. Establish a quality improvement team.

3. Take measurements of existing quality.

4.   Estimate the cost of quality.

5.   Encourage action to correct quality problems.

6.   Spread awareness throughout the company.

7.   Establish a zero defects programme committee.

8.   Train supervisors in zero defects programmes.

9.   Train and get commitment for zero defects for workers.

10. Have each employee or group set goals for improving their work.

11. Remove causes of error.

12. Recognise employee achievements.

13. Establish a company-wide quality council.

14. Do it all again, so that commitment is reinforced.

The approaches of Deming, Juran and Crosby are summarised in Figure 13.2 below. Irrespective of the variation in approaches of Deming, Juran and Crosby, Maxon (1991) notes that they all agree on five critical issues: firstly, that quality is management's responsibility; secondly, that an open, participatory management style is necessary; thirdly, that companies cannot improve in isolation from their suppliers; fourthly, that there are no short cuts to continuous improvement; and finally, that the process is never-ending.

4. LOGISTICS IN PERSPECTIVE

4.1 Recent Trends in the Management of Logistics

It is becoming increasingly clear that addressing quality issues solely from a manufacturing perspective reflects primarily what Hill (1993) terms qualifying criteria (getting to the starting line) rather than order-winning criteria (being first to the finishing tape). Instead, as Fuller, O'Conor and Rawlinson (1993) contend, the emphasis in the 1990s is on the ease of doing business with a company by way of logistics differentiation, rather than the on the quality of its products per se. They do, however, suggest that the principles of lean production which improve the flow of goods through the factory can be adapted to improve the flow of manufactured goods through the logistics pipeline, and ultimately to enhance customer service.

FIGURE 13.2: COMPARING DEMING, JURAN AND CROSBY

	Background	Timescales	Definition	Philosophy	Method	Suppliers	Knocks	Known For
DEMING	Statistician Author American Deming Prize Japan	Thirty years for the West to get to where Japan is now	Whatever the customer needs and wants	Constant objective of improvement	Use of SPC and customer research	Single sourcing selected on the basis of SPC	Multi-sourcing Mass inspection Motivation programmes	14 Points Deming chain SPC
JURAN	American Engineer Lawyer Author Japan	Significant progress in 3-5 years	Fitness for use and conform to specification	Need to manage HR and systems for quality	Project by project, massive training & quality circles	Make part of team & multi-source key ones	Single sourcing & lack of project-by-project approach	10 Steps Quality Trilogy: Improve Control Plan
CROSBY	American Quality Specialist Hands-On Experience Author	Attitude change will not be achieved in this generation	Zero defects and conform to requirements	Prevent rather than detect ... right first time	Use of groups	Use rating scales & clear lines of communication	Quality audits of suppliers, SPC & accepting inherent defects	14 Steps Quality is free Cost of quality Zero defects

Source: Maxon, 1991.

While this chapter addresses the issues of total quality implementation and customer-driven manufacturing, the primary emphasis is on how enhanced logistics service quality can create value-added beyond the factory gates. Logistics have become increasingly important to overall strategy because products are not just things-with-features: they are things-with-features coupled with services or "envelopes around a product" (Fuller, O'Conor, and Rawlinson, 1993).

Marrodt and Davis (1992) have documented the evolution of such "envelopes" since the 1960s. The total cost concept, first suggested by Lewis, Culliton and Steele. (1956), emphasised the role of physical distribution management. The objective was to minimise the total cost associated with physical distribution, not the individual costs that made up the total. Trade-offs were explicit and the focus of the organisation was cost control rather than service delivery. However, the advent of the 1970s forced logisticians to re-examine their traditional role in the light of inflation, fuel shortages and increased interest rates.

Lambert and Stock (1982) have suggested four reasons for the emergence of a more integrated approach to logistics management. They are:

- A more scientific approach to management

- Advances in computer technology

- The importance of logistics in providing increased levels of customer satisfaction

- The potential profit leverage from increased efficiency.

Nevertheless, the integrated or systems approach to logistics was still primarily internally driven, reflecting a traditional production-led philosophy of business. However, as the customer-service concept began to attract attention, logistics became increasingly more concerned with customer and market considerations. Definitions of custom service at this time began to proliferate and are comprehensively summarised by Heskett (1971). He includes:

- The elapsed time between the receipt of an order at the supplier's warehouse and the shipment of the order from the warehouse

- The minimum size of order, or limits on the assortment of items in an order which a supplier will accept from its customers

- The percentage of items in a supplier's warehouse which might be found to be out-of-stock at any given point of time

- The proportion of customer orders filled accurately

- The percentage of customers, or volume of customer orders, which describes those who are served (whose orders are delivered) within a certain time period from the receipt of the order at the supplier's warehouse

- The percentage of customer orders which can be filled completely on receipt at a supplier's warehouse

- The proportion of goods which arrive at a customer's place of business in saleable condition

- The elapsed time between the placement of an order by a customer and the delivery of goods ordered to the customer's place of business

- The ease and flexibility with which a customer can place their order.

4.2. Service-Driven Logistics

Marrodt and Davis (1992) suggest, however, that customer service was still essentially reactive and firm-oriented in the 1970s and 1980s: the majority of the above definitions (with the exception of the last two) are essentially "supplier-oriented" rather than "customer-oriented". They contend that moving from a position where service measurements are determined by what the company was capable of, and not by what individual customers actually wanted, is caused by factors such as the globalisation of business, structural changes in organisations, changes in the political legal environment and advances in information and communication technologies.

Instead of focusing on shifting product, service response logistics emphasises the role of delivering benefits that the customer desires — in other words, logistics will become increasingly concerned with managing the implementation of customised delivery strategies. Fuller, O'Conor and Rawlinson (1993) have applied the term "tailored logistics" to this philosophy, arguing that:

> Logistics have the potential to become the next governing element of strategy as an inventive way of creating value for customers, an immediate source of savings, an important discipline on marketing, and a critical extension of production flexibility.

As the scope for gaining further competitive advantage in manufacturing becomes increasingly narrow, the authors suggest that remaining sources of value creation such as the development of "logistically distinct businesses" serving distinct customers is the next source of competitive advantage. In effect, as has occurred in manufacturing, logistics will become leaner and more menu-driven.

The next section of this chapter presents a detailed study of how one company, Microsoft Ireland, addressed the problem of how to provide better levels of service to its customer base. As a consequence, senior management had to reconsider all aspects of their business operations — from its manufacturing strategy and its marketing policies right through to its logistics strategy.

5. MICROSOFT CORPORATION

5.1. Introduction

Microsoft grew exponentially in the 1980s to become the world's leading software company with a market value of $21 billion, even greater than that of General Motors. Founded by chairman Bill Gates in 1975, Microsoft emerged in the 1990s, according to *Business Week*, as "clearly the most important single force in the entire computer industry".

The company introduced 48 new products in 1992, including well over 100 international versions. Most phenomenal of all was the introduction of Microsoft Windows 3.1. Now running on more than 12 million systems worldwide, Windows has become the fastest-selling graphical user interface ever. In the two years since its introduction, these figures represent a new customer every 10 seconds. Other leading software products include Microsoft Word, Excel, PowerPoint and Project. The company's manufacturing facilities are located at Bothell in the United States (serving North America and the rest of the world), Hunacao in Puerto Rico (serving North and South America) and in Dublin (serving the European market).

5.2. Microsoft Ireland

Microsoft Ireland is the European manufacturing base of Microsoft Corporation. Located in Dublin since 1985 on an 80,000-square-foot facility, the company employs 350 people at this manufacturing site. From this facility, the company supplies software packages to all major European markets, with Britain, Germany and France accounting for in excess of 60 per cent of all sales.

The ability of companies such as Microsoft Ireland to provide enhanced logistics service support in the European marketplace must be considered in terms of the disadvantages associated with a peripheral island location (see Fynes and Ennis, 1994a). The overall cost of sending freight between Ireland and other European Union (EU) member states and the time-to-market involved, are adversely affected by Ireland's geographical situation and the fact that it is isolated from the main centres of the market.

5.3. Manufacturing at Microsoft Ireland: 1985–88

When initially established in Ireland, the plant was allocated direct responsibility for manufacturing and shipping to UK and European destinations. Marketing, customer service and technical support were provided by each national sales subsidiary (of which there were 13 in Europe). The manufacturing process at Microsoft Ireland was (and still essentially is) a two-stage one. The first stage was the duplication of software packages from master disks. The second stage of the process was the assembly of the finished software package. The assembly process was labour-intensive and consisted of placing the duplicated disks, manuals, licence agreement and packing material in the appropriate carton. These were then shrink-wrapped to await shipment.

Initially, Microsoft operated like most other manufacturers — long production runs, large inventories, lengthy set-up times, quality control problems and multiple suppliers — in other words, the manufacturing process was based on traditional production principles. From a total product range of 280 products, high-volume lines such as Word would be produced in batches of 10,000 units once a week, with lower-volume lines being assembled just once a month. This traditional approach was based on the primary objective of minimising costs associated with long set-up times. Such a process necessitated bulk deliveries of raw materials from their suppliers, and required a warehouse of 40,000 square feet, capable of housing eight weeks of inventory with associated storage costs. At the end of a production run, the finished goods were moved back to the finished-goods warehouse where they awaited shipment. Delivery to customers occurred at the end of the month. This approach resulted in a three-week order cycle and lent itself to stock-outs as production capacity was locked into a given line for considerable periods of time.

The structure of the distribution channel at this time was typical of the industry in general. Microsoft Ireland would ship large batches intermittently to the warehouses of the 13 sales and support subsidiaries around Europe who were responsible for onward logistics. For example, in Britain, Microsoft Ireland shipped product directly to the UK subsidiary's warehouse. From there, Microsoft UK would ship to a mix of about 200 distributors and dealers using contract delivery for large distributors, and couriers for smaller orders to dealers. Back-order rates were typically of the order of 15 per cent of total orders.

5.4. The Journey to Lean Production: 1988–90

In 1988, Microsoft Ireland decided to confront these problems of working capital tied up in inventory, quality and product availability. They commissioned a study which highlighted that, on average, Microsoft's process lead-time was 151 days — 60 days in raw material, 1 day in work-in -progress and 90 days in finished goods. On the other hand, the product received value for only 4 minutes (the time it took the package to be assembled on the line) during a normal production run. Faced with a value-added to non-value-added ratio of 4 minutes to 151 days, the company's response was immediate: emphasising throughput, a policy decision was taken to manufacture smaller lots more frequently. The objective was to receive supplies daily and build (assemble) daily. The company identified four critical dimensions in the implementation process:

5.4.1 Supplier Reduction

The company's supplier base included indigenous printing companies (manuals), packaging manufacturers, disk manufacturers and freight forwarders. Microsoft decided to initiate a process of selecting strategic partners. In return for providing their suppliers with a long-term commitment, standardisation of product design and rolling sales forecasts, Microsoft received assurances with regard to mutual cost reduction and daily deliveries. These commitments were not based on legally binding contractual agreements, but rather on the basis of "gentlemen's agreements" coupled with quarterly reviews. The result of cutting its supplier base by 70 per cent led to a significant reduction in transaction and communication costs.

5.4.2 Production Batch Sizes

These were cut in half to facilitate shorter production runs, lower inventories and the assembly of all products on a JIT basis; set-up times had, therefore, to be dramatically reduced. Set-up involved ensuring that all the disks, manuals and packaging were available at the appropriate work-station for assembly. The company came up with an imaginative and novel approach to eliminating lengthy set-up times. While many exponents of JIT suggested that U-shaped production lines facilitated the process, Microsoft replaced the traditional assembly lines with 15 dual-level carousels or "round-tables" (see Figure 13.3). While operatives assembled from one level of the carousel, individuals who had completed their tasks for that run set up the other carousel for the next production run. In addition to eliminating set-ups, quality control was facilitated by this approach — for example, in a production batch of 10 units, it became immediately obvious at the end of the process if any disks or manuals were not included in the carton as they would remain highly visible on the carousel. By producing in smaller batches, quality problems were immediately and clearly identified.

FIGURE 13.3: MANUFACTURING CELLS WITH CAROUSELS

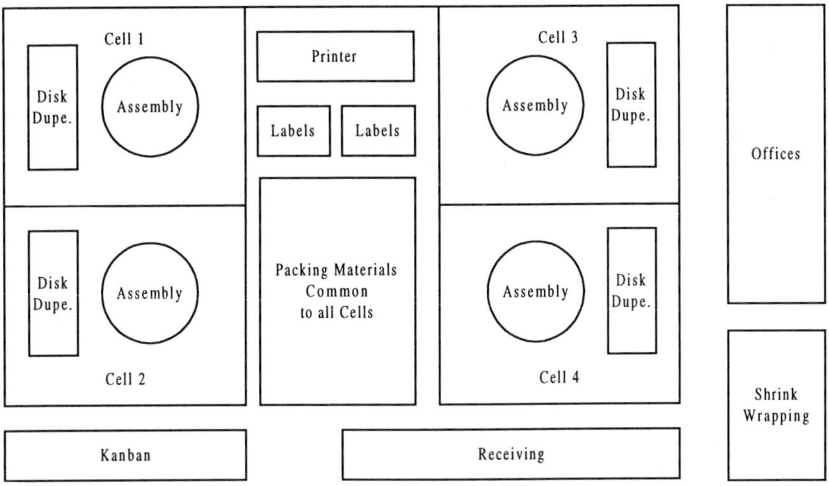

5.4.3 *Employee Involvement*

The solution to overcoming resistance to change on the shop floor required a radical change in the way in which individuals were managed. The company identified employees who they felt would be suitable facilitators in the training of operatives in JIT/TQM techniques. Employees were now to be paid on the basis of the number of new skills they acquired by way of in-company training. Considerable resources were devoted to education and training. Quality-focused teams were introduced to brainstorm on how the manufacturing process could be improved. The Japanese concept of *kaizen* or continuous improvement was seen as critical to the success of such teams. A measure of this change was the 3,700 suggestions forwarded to the company's suggestion scheme in the first two years of operation. Richard Schonberger, on a visit to the plant, was later to remark that this was the highest rate of contribution he had observed in *any* western manufacturing plant.

5.4.4 *Focused Factories*

Wickham Skinner (1974) pioneered the concept of focus in manufacturing in the 1970s. He argued that a plant would perform better if it
limited itself to a focused number of tasks, processes or products. Within
Microsoft it was decided that a customer-driven approach must form the
basis of organising "factories within the factory". The requirements of
the marketplace were now to have an impact on the manufacturing process. Since the geographic destinations of the software packages were
language-related, four factories within the plant were introduced —
Britain and English language products (Euro), Germany, France and the
Rest of Europe (multilingual). Each focused factory was now charged
with dealing with specific geographic markets and had its own independent manufacturing cells, production equipment (duplicating
machines and carousels) and work teams (see Figure 13.4).

FIGURE 13.4: PLANT LAYOUT WITH FOCUSED FACTORIES

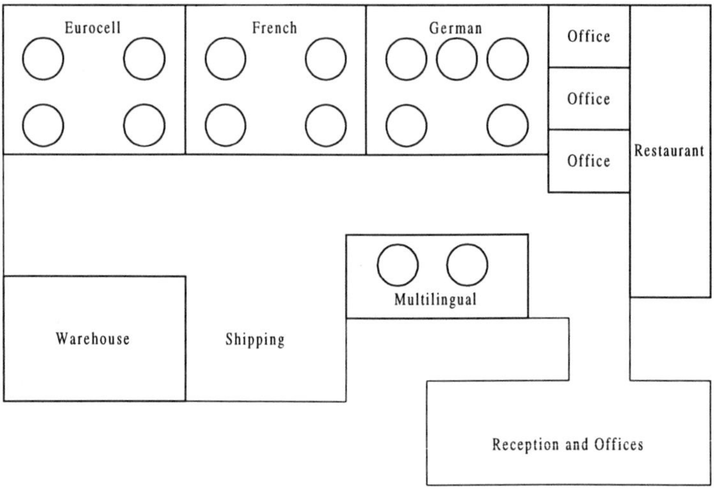

In addition, the possibility of extra paperwork and administration was
eliminated by extending the concept of focus to suppliers. A printing
supplier would now typically deliver to only one focused factory. The
national flags of the destination markets were in evidence at each
focused factory, highlighting the market-driven nature of the approach.

Within months, cost of goods sold had been reduced by 25 per cent,
while inventory levels in the plant had been cut by 70 per cent and, more
importantly from the customers' point of view, lead times could now be
reduced to just one day.

5.5. Changes in Channel Structure in the UK

As the radical changes in operations in the Dublin plant were beginning to impact positively on manufacturing performance, a series of developments and trends began to emerge in the channels of distribution:

5.5.1 Relocation of Microsoft UK's Headquarters

In 1990, Microsoft UK (the sales and service subsidiary in Britain) was in the process of relocating its headquarters to a new site at Winnersh in the south-east of England. As there was a lack of suitable warehousing space at this new headquarters, the parent company felt it was now opportune to evaluate the future warehousing requirements for the UK. There was some concern that the phenomenal growth rates being experienced in the industry could lead to customer-service problems and have significant cost implications for the company. As a result, the company decided to evaluate the possibility of separating the warehousing function from the marketing and technical support functions currently being performed by Microsoft UK.

5.5.2 The Emergence of a Low-Cost Channel of Distribution

Approximately nine major distributors accounted for 80 per cent of Microsoft's business in the UK. The remaining 20 per cent included smaller dealers, educational establishments and original equipment manufacturers (OEMs). A notable feature of the industry is that channel structure has been historically based on the computer hardware sector. In the mid-1980s, distributors concentrated on the sale of PCs where high margins were readily obtained. However, this situation changed considerably in the early 1990s as low-cost equipment began to appear on the market. The mystery surrounding the use of PCs began gradually to evaporate with the spread of interfaces such as Windows. Hardware manufacturers now began to use more direct forms of distribution to high-street retailers as lower-cost distribution channels became the norm. Similarly, Dell Computers began to pioneer direct marketing approaches such as mail order and toll-free telephone ordering. Ever narrowing margins on PCs became less attractive to major distributors and their primary focus of attention moved to turnover of software products and ancillary hardware equipment such as printers.

5.6. From *Kaizen* to Service-Driven Logistics: 1990–92

In the light of these developments Microsoft Europe felt it would be timely to examine logistics strategy with particular emphasis on warehousing requirements and changes in the nature and structure of the channels of distribution. Following a comprehensive analysis of possible future options with regard to logistics strategy, Microsoft Europe's eventual decision was to relocate the UK distribution hub at the manufacturing plant in Ireland (Fynes and Ennis, 1984b). While this might appear to have been a very radical decision in terms of locating at a more peripheral and distant site, the selection highlighted the need to view the decision in the wider context of logistics and channel strategy, rather than just simply warehouse location. This broader rationale for selecting Microsoft Ireland included the following:

- The realisation that there were significant logistical implications of rate-based manufacturing: *the ability to manufacture on a daily basis now offered the opportunity to deliver on a daily basis.*

- Locating the UK warehouse in Dublin facilitated the adoption of "one-touch" inventory — in other words, once finished goods were shipped from the production line in Dublin (one-touch), there were no further intermediate stocking points at Microsoft UK.

- The emergence of the more direct, low-cost channel structure, coupled with a rationalisation of the company's distribution network in the UK from 200 down to just nine major distributors, acknowledged that it would be more efficient to ship directly to a small concentration of distributors as against a large number of geographically dispersed dealers.

- The implementation of lean production principles with just-in-time delivery from suppliers released an extra 40,000 square feet of warehouse space (by default rather than design) at the Dublin manufacturing site (Figure 13.4). Previously used for storing raw materials, this space could now be used for managing the distribution hub.

5.7 Managing Service Logistics from the Edge

Microsoft Ireland were conscious that the relocation of the UK warehouse to Dublin presented the company with a number of interdependent challenges associated with supplying the large UK market from a seemingly peripheral site. They included the following:

5.7.1 Control of Inventory and Customer Service Levels

One of the major factors that had to be considered was the perceived loss of control by Microsoft UK over the entire warehousing function.

Concern had been expressed about separating the sales and warehousing functions and the implications that this might have for customer-service levels in Britain.

5.7.2 Loss of Visibility

In addition to a perceived loss of control, any physical relocation of the UK warehouse could potentially eliminate inventory visibility for Microsoft UK. Warehouse managers and supervisors generally prefer to be actually able to see current inventory levels for all stock-keeping units (SKUs). Some means of counterbalancing this "fear factor" with a "comfort factor" in the event of relocation needed to be examined.

The issue of customer service was addressed by following a phased implementation plan, initially allowing Microsoft UK to define customer-service measurements and levels. In addition, the "comfort factor" was provided by daily E-mail updates between Ireland and the UK. Finally, any manufacturing–marketing interface difficulties relating to customer service that arose were addressed at weekly problem clinics at the UK headquarters.

Within a year, the impact of leaner logistics (relocation, direct shipment and one-touch inventory) on performance was as significant as that achieved when the company adopted world class manufacturing principles. In a marketplace where rapid product introductions and revisions mirrored the importance of time-based competitive strategies, the company was able to record the following improvements in logistics performance:

- Delivery lead times were cut to one day.

- Inventory savings of the order of £3m were achieved in the first year of operation.

- Back-order levels fell from 15 to just 5 per cent of total orders.

Furthermore, from Microsoft UK's perspective, they were now able to devote greater attention and resources to their core competence: marketing and technical support.

6. CONCLUSION

This case has illustrated how the management of logistics service was transferred to a geographically remote manufacturing location, but with a significant improvement in performance and service levels. While logistics decisions have frequently been a source of conflict in the often-times adversarial relationship that exists between marketing and manu-facturing, Microsoft's experience demonstrates that it is possible for manufacturing and sales personnel to understand their respective func-tional requirements. A key element in this understanding is *trust*: the sales and service subsidiary were confident that logistics could not only be effectively managed by manufacturing, but could also be effectively managed from a peripheral location.

The case also illustrates the interaction between distribution-channel developments and the management of logistics. There is, in fact, a wide range of channels of distribution to be serviced by Microsoft, each requiring different approaches. Furthermore, the channels are in a far-from-steady state, so flexible strategies are necessary. Indeed, Stern, Sturdivant, and Getz (1993) argue that, ultimately, organisations like Microsoft "instead of merely watching their channels develop organi-cally or playing the reactionary game of catch-up, must think creatively about how they can deliver superior value to their customers". Increased product customisation will drive the concept of "tailored channels", which in turn will drive differentiation logistically. And it is logistics, La Londe and Powers. (1993) contend, which will ultimately integrate the product-service chain in the next century.

REFERENCES

Brooks, R. and T. Wragg, "Channelling Customer Loyalty", *TQM Magazine,* December, 1992, pp. 361–3.

Chase, R.B., and D.A. Garvin, "The Service Factory", *Harvard Business Review,* July/August, 1989, pp. 61–9.

Crosby, P.B., *Quality is Free,* McGraw-Hill, New York, 1979.

Deming, W.E., *Out of the Crisis,* MIT Centre for Advanced Engineering Study, Cambridge, MA, 1986.

DTI/PA Consulting Group, *Manufacturing into the Late 1990s,* HMSO, London, 1990.

Fuller, J.B., J. O'Conor, and R. Rawlinson, "Tailored Logistics: The Next Com-petitive Advantage", *Harvard Business Review*, May/June, 1993, pp. 87–98

Fynes, B. and S. Ennis, (a) "Beyond World Class Manufacturing: Microsoft Ireland", *Irish Marketing Review,* Vol. 7, 1994, pp. 7–16.

Fynes, B. and S. Ennis, (b) "From Lean Production to Lean Logistics: The Case of Microsoft Ireland", *European Management Journal,* Vol. 12, No. 3, 1994, pp. 322–31.

Grönroos, C., "Service Quality: The Six Criteria of Good Perceived Service Quality", *Review of Business,* Vol. 9, No. 3, 1988, pp. 10–13.

Hall, R.W., *Attaining Manufacturing Excellence,* Dow Jones-Irwin, Homewood, IL, 1987.

Heskett, J., "Controlling Customer Logistics Service", *International Journal of Physical Distribution,* Vol. 1, No. 3, 1971, pp. 140–5.

Hill, T., *The Essence of Operations Management,* Prentice-Hall, London, 1993.

Huge, E.C. and A.D. Anderson, *The Spirit of Manufacturing Excellence: An Executive's Guide to the New Mind Set,* Dow Jones-Irwin, Homewood, IL, 1988.

Ishikawa, K., *What is Total Quality Control? The Japanese Way,* Prentice-Hall Inc., Englewood Cliffs, NJ, 1985.

Juran, J.M., "The Quality Trilogy", *Quality Progress,* Vol. 19, No. 8, 1986, pp. 19–24.

La Londe, B.J. and R.F. Powers, "Disintegration and Re-Integration: Logistics of the Twenty-First Century", *International Journal of Logistics Management,* Vol. 4, No. 2, 1993, pp. 1–12.

Lambert, D.M. and J.R. Stock, *Strategic Physical Distribution Management,* Richard D. Irwin, Homewood, IL, 1982.

Lancaster, G., "Marketing and Engineering — Can there ever be Synergy?", *Journal of Marketing Management,* Vol. 9, No. 2, 1993, pp. 141–53.

Lewis, H.T., J.W. Culliton and J.D. Steele, *The Role of Air Freight in Physical Distribution,* Harvard Business School, Boston, MA, 1956.

Lewis, B.R., "Service Quality: An International Comparison of Bank Customers' Expectations and Preferences", *Journal of Marketing Management,* Vol. 7, No. 1, 1991, pp. 47–62.

Marrodt, K.B. and F.W. Davis, "The Evolution to Service Response Logistics", Vol. 22, No. 9, 1992, pp. 3–10.

Mathe, H. and R.D. Shapiro, *Integrating Service Strategy in the Manufacturing Company,* Chapman and Hall, London, 1993.

Maxon, J., "Total Quality Management", in *International Manufacturing Strategy Resource Book,* Strategic Direction Publishers, Zürich, Switzerland, 1991, pp. 189–202.

Morgan, N.A. and N.F. Piercy, "Market Led Quality", *Industrial Marketing Management,* Vol. 21, No. 2, 1992, pp. 111–18.

Parasuraman, A., V.A. Zeithaml and L.L. Berry, "SERQUAL: A Multiple Item Scale for Measuring Consumer Perceptions of Service Quality", *Journal of Retailing,* Vol. 64, No. 1, 1988, pp. 14–40.

Roth, A.V., C.A. Giffi and G.M. Seal, "Operating Strategies for the 1990s: Elements Comprising World Class Manufacturing" in C. Voss (Ed.), *Manufacturing Strategy — Process and Content,* Chapman and Hall, London, 1992.

Schonberger, R.J., *Building a Chain of Customers: Linking Business Functions to Create the World Class Company,* The Free Press, New York, 1990.

Scott-Morgan, P.B., "Removing the Barriers to Becoming a High Performance

Business", *Prism,* First Quarter, 1992, pp. 1–12.

Skinner, W., "The Focused Factory", *Harvard Business Review,* May/June, 1974, pp. 113–21.

Stern, L.W., F.D. Sturdivant and G.A. Getz, "Accomplishing Marketing Channel Change: Paths and Pitfalls", *European Management Journal,* Vol. 11, No. 1, 1993, pp. 1–8.

Sweeney, M., "Strategic Manufacturing Management: Restructuring Wasteful Production to World Class", *Journal of General Management,* Vol. 18, No. 3, 1993, pp. 57–62.

Vesey, J.T., "Time to Market: Put Speed in Product Development", *Industrial Marketing Management,* Vol. 21, No. 2, 1992, pp. 151–8.

Westbrook, R. and Williamson, P., "Mass Customisation: Japan's New Frontier", *European Management Journal,* Vol. 11, No. 1, 1993, pp 38–45.

Womack, J.P., D.T. Jones and D. Roos, *The Machine that Changed the World,* Macmillan, New York, 1990.

14

SERVICES MANAGEMENT IN THE BUSINESS-TO-BUSINESS SECTOR:
From Networks to Relationship Marketing

Seán de Burca
University College Dublin, Ireland

PRÉCIS

The Network Perspective has provided rich insights into how business is co-ordinated, and it is credited with being an important reservoir of ideas that have given rise to developments in the traditional services marketing literature. This chapter traces the genesis of the network approach and maps the characteristics of that approach and the assumptions on which it is grounded.

The theoretical foundations of the network perspective lie very much with the work of the IMP Group. Ground-breaking research at Uppsala helped to define the major marketing problem of firms as being concerned with the establishment, development and maintenance of lasting business relationships with the firms' customers, suppliers and other important actors. The insights generated by this research focused on interaction in business relationships. The emergent interaction model placed emphasis on the parties, the environment and atmosphere, and the elements and processes of the interaction.

The network perspective assumes that there is an erosion of the distinctive boundary between a firm and its environment. There is a continuous flow of interactions between the firm and its environment involving individuals at every level. Relationships are heterogeneous in nature, in the resources they employ and in the demands they meet. The characteristics of networks are detailed. Networks are made up of relationships which in turn are regarded as consisting of four key elements cumulatively developing over time — mutual orientation, dependency, bonds and the investments they mutually exchange. The networks are essentially dynamic in character with the dialectical forces related to competition and co-operation. In a network, indirect relationships mediated through a third player may be crucial. Boundaries are arbitrary and the network itself is opaque in that no individual player can have a clear view of relationships other than the ones within which they themselves are. It follows that the main marketing emphasis in the network approach is to establish, develop, maintain and/or destroy relationships whereas the traditional marketing mix was concerned with optimisation by the sole pro-active player — the seller.

The rise of service marketing and the clear inadequacy of the managerial approach led inevitably to the search for an alternative paradigm to the traditional four Ps. The reigning paradigm was perceived as incomplete and manipulative and not adequately addressing the needs of services marketing and business-to-business marketing. Relationship marketing, partly grounded in network theory, and building on the assumptions and characteristics implicit in that approach, contributed significantly to a solution. The network perspective contributed to the rise of relationship marketing through its emphasis on interaction, contextuality and time, its stress on relationships as the primary unit of analysis, and its achievement of a more holistic view by bringing into play indirect relationships.

However, the relationship marketing concept is generic in nature and there must be doubt as to whether it is specific enough to comprehend adequately both inter-firm and consumer relationships. The very origins of relationship marketing lie in dissatisfaction with the tool utilised by the consumer marketing approach. The network perspective clearly implies that relationships have to be managed. Managing those relationships raises issues of strategic choice in the areas of limitation and handling. What relationships does the firm engage in, given the limitations imposed by technology, structure, knowledge, resources and time? The handling problem is concerned with issues of dependency and co-operation/conflict, and seeks efficient ways of managing the different exchange processes and different groups of customers. This automatically becomes a revenue and productivity issue for the company. This area of difficulty prompts the author to raise the key question of whether the relationship marketing concept is developed enough to distinguish between the marketing of consumer services and industrial services and the further difficulties arising from the handling of production services versus maintenance, repair and operating services.

Paul O'Sullivan
Dublin Institute of Technology, Ireland

1. INTRODUCTION

The development of the interaction approach and network perspective has provided a rich source of new ideas, especially in the business-to-business marketing area. These ideas are the source of new thinking in the services marketing literature. Both business-to-business and services marketing have remained underdeveloped as a consequence of the application of the traditional marketing concept, developed in a consumer goods context, to business-to-business and services marketing problems. Fresh insights and approaches are needed to capture the unique dynamics of business-to-business marketing and services marketing. The network perspective has emerged as one source of new thinking in the business-to-business marketing literature, and has also been credited as the origin of the new relationship marketing approach in the service management literature. This chapter describes the network perspective and the concept of relationship marketing, and looks at the contribution and conflicts which the network perspective holds for relationship marketing.

2. THE NETWORK PERSPECTIVE

2.1. Theoretical Foundations

The network perspective has a number of theoretical foundations. This section draws on three sources: empirical studies of the Industrial Marketing and Purchasing (IMP) group; social exchange theory; and resource dependence theory. In empirical research at the university of Uppsala about Swedish industrial firms in international competition, it was found that major marketing problems in firms concerned establishment, development and maintenance of lasting business relationships with customers, suppliers and other important actors. This observation led a number of researchers, who became known as the IMP group, to engage in a line of research focusing on interaction in business relationships. Prior to this, the predominant viewpoint in marketing was characterised by an "organisational system perspective", and is exemplified in the so-called "managerial approach" to the study of marketing.

The prevailing view in the literature is of an active marketer, assembling a mix of variables for passive consumers, who may or may not respond to the offering. This view of marketing simply did not reflect the experience of the researchers. The traditional approach to marketing, which was developed in a consumer context, was transferred to the analysis of business-to-business marketing (Ford, 1990). This automatic transfer neglected a number of factors identified in previous research. Firstly, both buyer and seller are active participants in the market. Secondly, the relationship between buyer and seller is frequently long term, close and involving a complex pattern of interaction between and within each company. Thirdly, the links between the buyer and seller often become institutionalised into a set of roles that each party expects the other to perform (Håkansson, 1982).

These three factors take their theoretical foundations from inter-organisational studies that are based on several organisations where the firm is seen as part of a group of interacting units. In order to obtain necessary resources, the organisation is seen to develop relations with a number of other organisational units, and thus it enters into a network of relationships:

> The interaction between buying and selling companies occurs within the context of a relationship between the companies. This relationship may be distant and impersonal, but is often close, complex and long-term. The relationship is built out of the history of the companies' dealings with each other, and can be described in terms of adaptations, commitments, trust and conflict (Ford, 1990).

2.2. IMP Studies

The initial focus of the IMP group took the dyadic buyer–seller relationship as its unit of analysis. Empirical data was collected on over 1,000 relationships in European markets. The results of the IMP project demonstrated the existence of stable, long-term buyer–seller relationships, and identified four groups of variables that describe and influence the interaction between buying and selling companies (Håkansson, 1982). These variables describe the parties involved, the elements and process of interaction, the environment within which the interaction takes place and the atmosphere affecting, and affected by, the interaction. The main components of the interaction model developed by the IMP-project are illustrated in Figure 14.1 below.

However, the interaction approach, which focused on single dyadic relationships, provided only a partial view of how companies interact. The inappropriateness of focusing solely on single dyadic relationships led to the realisation that firms are embedded in a range of relationships. Business in any given relationship is often conditioned by relationships with third parties, such as the customer's customers, the supplier's suppliers, consultants, competitors, supplementary suppliers, middle-men, as well as public or semi-public agencies (Forsgren and Johanson, 1992). This concept of the network of relationships between firms provides a compelling reason for using inter-organisational relationships as a research perspective. It is concerned to understand the totality of relationships among firms engaged in production, distribution and the use of goods and services in what might best be described as an industrial system (Easton, 1992).

FIGURE 14.1: AN ILLUSTRATION OF THE INTERACTION MODEL

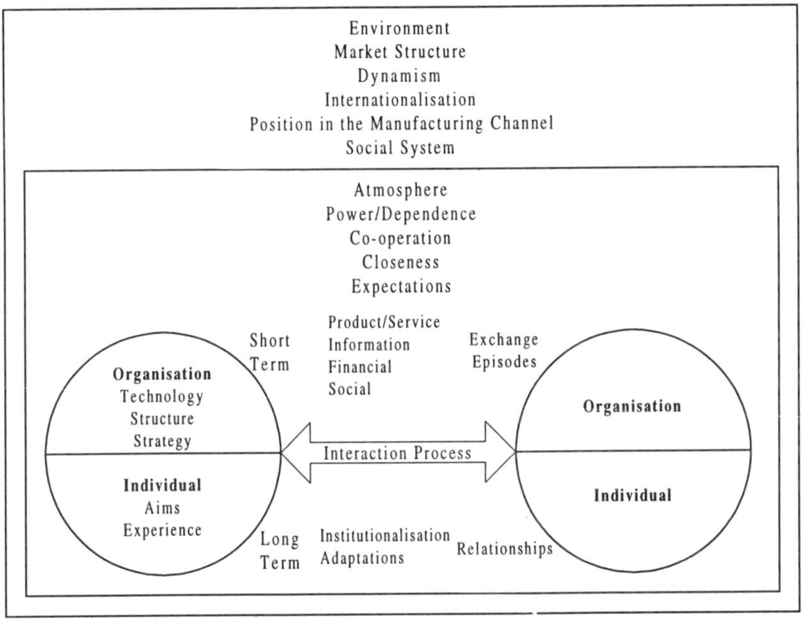

Environment
Market Structure
Dynamism
Internationalisation
Position in the Manufacturing Channel
Social System

Atmosphere
Power/Dependence
Co-operation
Closeness
Expectations

Short Term   Product/Service   Exchange Episodes
Information
Financial
Social

Organisation
Technology
Structure
Strategy

Interaction Process

Organisation

Individual
Aims
Experience

Individual

Long Term   Institutionalisation   Relationships
Adaptations

Source: Håkansson, 1982.

2.3. Social Exchange Theory

In addition to the empirical studies outlined above, the network perspective also draws its roots from social exchange theory. Cook and Emerson (1984) describe the primary focus of social exchange theory as being "the explanation of the emergence of various forms of social structure, including networks and corporate groups". Specifically, theories of social exchange are primarily interested in explaining the operation of network phenomena. When firms interact and exchange, the nature of the connection between them is contingent upon the interdependency between them and the other interdependent relationships that they might have. Therefore, the unit of analysis can move beyond the dyad to the network of both direct and indirect relationships that a firm might have.

2.4. The Resource Dependency Model

The resource dependency model provides another perspective on inter-organisational relationships (Pfeffer and Salancik, 1978). The model concentrates on the actions of a single firm, and attempts to describe the multiplicity of relationships from a focal organisational point of view. The basic assumption is that organisations use these relationships in order to gain access to the resources which are vital to their continuing existence. The resource dependency model mainly focuses on the way in which firms handle individual relationships. The unit of analysis is different from the network approach because it focuses on the actions of a single firm, and the working of the network is seen to be of secondary importance (Easton, 1992).

3. NETWORK ASSUMPTIONS

A basic assumption in the network perspective is that the individual firm is dependent on resources controlled by other firms. Because of the interdependencies of firms, the use of an asset in one firm is dependent on the use of other firms' assets (Johanson and Mattsson, 1987). This dependency between firms has to be co-ordinated. Co-ordination takes place through firms interacting in the network — in contrast to the traditional market model where co-ordination is achieved by organisational hierarchy, or through the price mechanism.

In the atomic perspectives typically assumed by economics, individual actors are depicted as making choices and acting without regard to the behaviour of other actors. This ignores the social contexts within which the social actors are embedded (Knoke and Kuklinski, 1982). The network perspective places greater emphasis on context and time and incorporates two significant assumptions about social behaviour. Knoke and Kuklinski describes these assumptions as follows: firstly, "any actor typically participates in a social system involving many other actors, who are significant reference points in one another's decisions", and thus their relationship may affect each other's perceptions, beliefs and actions; and secondly, "emphasising the relationship between actors, within which individual actors are embedded, allows social phenomena that have no existence at the level of the individual actor to be detected." Therefore, firms' activities are not performed in isolation. They are more or less embedded in the wider web of business activities. These business activities are co-ordinated through interactions between firms. This interaction process develops over time.

The traditional business literature places the single firm as the unit of analysis. The firm is assumed to have a distinct boundary which separates it from its environment. In contrast, the network model assumes that business takes place in a network setting, where different business actors are linked to each other through direct and indirect relationships. The network of relationships is the unit of analysis, not the individual firm.

The network perspective assumes that there is no distinct boundary between the firm and its environment. The environment is not transparent to managers. Rather than viewing the environment as a set of separate political-legal, competitive, cultural and social forces, managers perceive the meaning of these forces through enactment (Forsgren and Johanson, 1992). This enactment occurs through the everyday interaction between firms, and is not based on single discrete decisions. The interaction involves individuals within firms on every level and lacks the traditional dominant top management perspective. These individuals have different interests, and, within the context of interacting with other individuals, have great opportunities and possibilities to pursue their interest. Therefore, the firm as a whole entity is not assumed or taken for granted, rather it is the relationship between firms that is important.

Another basic assumption of the network perspective is that networks are essentially heterogeneous in nature (Hagg and Johanson, 1983). The sources of heterogeneity are rooted in matching heterogeneous resources to heterogeneous demands, given that individuals or individual firms' needs can be met in a variety of different ways. An additional source of heterogeneity lies in the firms involved in the network. Each firm is individual in its structure, employer preferences, history and resources, and the role it chooses, or may be forced, to play in the transformation process will be determined partly by these factors (Easton, 1992).

Finally, the network perspective is based on a different ontological and epistemological orientation from the traditional market model. The network perspective is a combination of both subjective and objective orientations, with the nature of man viewed as primarily voluntarist, in contrast to the market model's objective world view, realistic ontology and deterministic orientation.

In conclusion, the combined assumptions of the network perspective present an alternate platform to the analysis of how business is co-ordinated. The dependency assumption between firms motivates firms to co-ordinate their interactions in relationships. Therefore, all their activities are considered in the context of these relationships. These relationships cannot be made overnight, they take time to develop. The development of those relationships is activated by individuals at all levels of the firm, and not just by top management. Everyday interaction between individuals, focusing on current activities and not single discrete decisions, is the means by which relationships are developed. The unit of analysis is the network of relationships that the firm has, and the firm is not considered separate from its environment. The alternative platform of the network perspective cannot be denied by the traditional dominant market model perspective, because it is based on a different ontological and epistemological orientation.

4. THE CHARACTERISTICS OF THE NETWORK PERSPECTIVE

The characteristics of a network are described by Cook and Emerson (1984) as "sets of connected exchange relationships between actors controlling business activities". The emphasis on connection is important because networks emerge and develop as a consequence of interactions. Business activities are co-ordinated through interactions between firms in the network. When firms interact with each other they exchange resources, products and services. Through interaction, they influence and adapt to each other's ways of performing activities. This interaction process develops over time, parties have to learn about each other's ways of doing and viewing things and how to interpret each other's acts (Håkansson and Johanson, 1988).

Relationships form the context in which interactions take place. Johanson and Mattsson (1985) distinguished between inter-firm relationships and interaction behaviour. The relationship elements of behaviour tend to be long-term in nature, and comprise the processes by which firms adjust products, production and routines, whereas interactions represent the day-to-day exchanges of a business.

4.1. Networks as Relationships

Relationships are the *sine qua non* of the network perspective, and comprise four elements: *mutual orientation, dependency, bonds* and *investments* (Easton, 1992). Inter-firm relationship is a *mutual orientation* of two firms towards each other. This implies that the firms are prepared to interact with each other and expect each other to do so (Johanson and Mattsson, 1987) A number of reasons have been identified to explain this mutual orientation. Hagg and Johanson (1983) suggest that "relationships allow a more effective acquisition of resources and sale of product", exploiting the complementary aspects. A second set of rationale for mutual orientation concerns a firm's ability to exploit network access (Easton, 1992). Such relationships allow access to resources consisting of physical , financial and human assets.

Dependence is the second element used to describe networks as relationships, and in some senses may be regarded as the price a firm may have to pay for the benefits that a relationship bestows. It also brings with it the problems of power and control (Easton, 1992).

The third element describing the characteristics of networks as relationships is the *bond* between firms. Bonds of various kinds are developed between firms: technical, planning, knowledge, socio-economic and legal. These bonds can be exemplified by product and process adjustments, logistical co-ordination, knowledge about the counterpart, personal confidence and liking, special credit arrangements and long-term contracts (Johanson and Mattsson, 1987).

Johanson and Mattsson (1986) identify *investment* as the fourth element of networks as relationships, and define investments as being "processes in which resources are committed in order to create, build or acquire assets which can be used in the future".

If relationships are the *sine qua non* of the network perspective, then: "the character of business relationships is a consequence of the interaction strategies of the parties" (Cunningham and Homse, 1982). Firms have different interaction strategies towards each other depending on the nature of the relationships. Interacting with each other to develop or solve a technical problem is different from the interaction that takes place emphasising sales volume. Therefore, both interaction strategies and relationships are intertwined.

The four elements described above are inter-related and imply that a firm's activities are cumulative processes. Because of the cumulative nature of business activities, the network position of a firm is an important concept. Mattsson (1984) defines a position as a role "that the organisation has for other organisations that it is related to, directly or indirectly". Such positions are the result of mutual orientation, dependency between firms, different kinds of bonds and investments.

4.2. Position

Position is inherently a dialectical concept, in the sense that it provides the development possibilities and constraints of the firm in the network. A firm's current position is determined by earlier activities in the network, both by the firm itself and by other firms. Thus, history is important.

Mattsson (1984) outlines four characteristics of position:

1. The role the firm has for the other firms

2. The identity of the other firms with which the firm has direct relationships and indirect relations in the network

3. The importance of the firm in the network

4. The strength of the relationships with the other firm.

The position concept provides a metaphor to describe network dynamics and change. A change in position for any one firm will change, the relative positions of other firms.

Network positions are also the result of the different power some actors have over the activities. Power (the ability to influence the decisions or actions of others) is the central concept in network analysis (Thorelli, 1986). Many relationships are asymmetrical with respect to power. The power structure dictates the way in which the network both operates and develops.

4.3. Dynamic

The assumption that business networks consist of lasting exchange relationships does not suggest that network structures can be characterised as static. On the contrary, the structure changes continually as new relationships are established. Existing relationships can be further developed or terminated. Gradual changes are made and accumulate over the years, resulting in a radical change to the structure of the network. These changes reflect the dynamic characteristics of networks. Therefore, while network structures are considered stable, they are not static. Instead, they evolve gradually in response to changes external and internal to the network.

4.4. Competition and Co-operation

Two dialectical processes in networks are competition and co-operation (Easton, 1992). While the network perspective emphasises co-operation, the reality is that in every exchange relationship there is potential conflict between the actors. Hagg and Johanson (1983) argue that: "potential conflict or competition in the traditional sense is replaced by rivalry for the control of resources." This rivalry is necessary because for a network to exist there must be at least a partial overlap in domain (Thorelli, 1986). Thorelli defines the domain of any organisation in terms of five dimensions:

1. Product (or service) offered the environment

2. Clientèle served

3. Functions performed

4. Territory

5. Time.

Should there be total domain overlap, then we would have a case of head-on competition. Therefore, complete overlap implies competition, while partial overlap implies networking.

4.5. Indirect Relationships

Indirect relationships are another important characteristic of networks to be considered. Easton (1992) defines indirect relationships as "the relationship between two firms which are not directly related but which is mediated by a third firm with which they both have relationships". Mattsson (1986) identifies seven dimensions which can be used to characterise indirect relationships. They are:

1. Distance from a focal firm

2. Vertical or horizontal nature

3. Complementary or competitive

4. Narrow or wide connection

5. The strength, kind and content of the direct bonds concerned

6. The interdependency of the direct relations concerned

7. The value-added of a focal firm's direct relationship.

The importance of indirect relationships can be seen in the way in which they affect the structure of the network. Firms control resources directly and indirectly. Thus, in every network, there is a power structure where different firms can influence the action of other firms, which ultimately affects the development of the network. The dynamic combination of direct and indirect business relationships leads to the important conclusion that markets are more or less stable networks of business relationships (Hagg and Johanson, 1983).

4.6. Boundary

The assumption that there is no distinct boundary between the firm and its environment gives the network the characteristic whereby boundaries are arbitrary and depend on the perspectives, intentions and interpretations of the actors (Håkansson and Johanson, 1986). Boundaries can be drawn for analytical purposes on the basis of technology, product, process, country or focal organisation.

4.7. Opacity

Networks are opaque. Everybody is aware of the existence of business relationships, but no one can have a clear view of relationships other than their own. This is particularly true of indirect relationships. It is difficult to view relationships from the outside because they are subtle phenomena, in that intentions, interpretations and expectations are important. Håkansson and Johanson (1986) claim that the opacity of networks has to do with the complexity, fluidity and unequivocal nature of the interaction; actors have a clear view of their own interaction and bonds with other actors, even if the views of interacting actors are not necessarily consistent.

Finally, the network approach can be further distinguished by comparing the approach to the traditional marketing mix model. The exchange partners to the network approach are active and mutually dependent, in contrast to the passive, independent approach of the marketing mix model. Both buyer and seller initiate exchange in the network approach. The main marketing emphasis is to establish, develop, maintain and sometimes break-up relationships as distinct from the optimisation focus of the marketing mix approach.

5. A MODEL OF INDUSTRIAL NETWORKS

The network model developed by Håkansson and Johanson (1992) based on earlier works such as Hammarkvist, Håkansson and Mattsson (1982), Hagg and Johanson (1983), Håkansson (1982), and Mattsson (1984), consists of three components:

- Actors
- Activities
- Resources.

Actors are defined as those who perform activities and/or control resources. In activities actors use certain resources to change other resources in various ways. Resources are means used by actors when they perform activities. Through these circular definitions, a network of actors, a network of activities and a network of resources are related to each other (Håkansson and Johanson, 1992). the basic structure of the model is given in Figure 14.2 below.

5.1. Actors

Actors can be defined as individuals, firms or industries. Håkansson and Johanson (1992) describe five characteristics of actors. Firstly, "they perform and control activities", secondly, "through exchange processes actors develop relationships with each other", thirdly, "actors base their activities on control over resources", fourthly, "actors are goal oriented", to increase their control over the network, and finally, "actors have differential knowledge about activities, resources and other actors in the network." In summary, each actor attempts to increase their control in the network by using their experience and knowledge of the network, as well as their relationships with others, in order to improve their position.

FIGURE 14.2: BASIC STRUCTURE OF THE MODEL

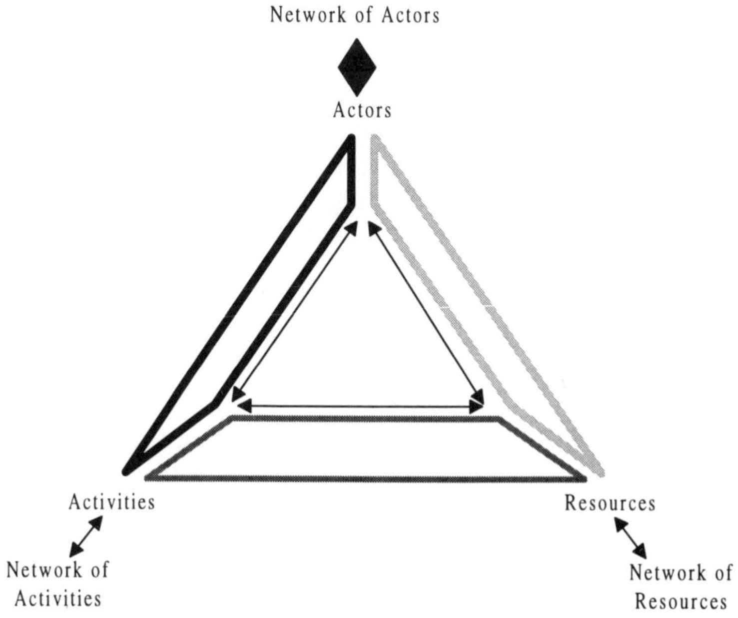

Source: Håkansson and J. Johanson, 1992.

5.2. Activities

According to Håkansson and Johanson (1992): "an activity occurs when one or several actors combine, develop, exchange or create resources by utilising other resources." The authors distinguish between two main kinds of activities. Resources can be changed and improved by transformation activities. Such activities can be carried out within the control of one actor. Transfer activities transfer direct control over a resource from one actor to another and are not controlled by one actor. Together, transformation and transfer activities complete the cycle between actors and this complete cycle is never controlled by a single actor. Each activity is a link in the chain of the activity cycle. While there is strong interdependency between actors and activities, single actors and activities are never indispensable, because the network of relationships will adjust to take over any vacant gap.

5.3. Resources

Performing transformation and transfer activities requires resources (Håkansson and Johanson, 1992). Because resources are heterogeneous, their combination, by actors with different knowledge and experience of resources, can lead to different use and value of resources.

In summary, therefore, the relationship between the three components of the model form structures that can be described as networks. All actors, activities and resources are interconnected or interdependent. They are interwoven in a total network. However, there are some specific forces that bind the elements together. Håkansson and Johanson (1992) suggest that these forces include the following:

- *Functional Interdependence* — Actors, activities and resources together form a system where heterogeneous demands are satisfied by heterogeneous resources. They are functionally related to each other.

- *Power Structure* — On the basis of control of activities and resources, there are important power relations between the actors. The performance of the activities is, to some extent, organised on the basis of those power relations.

- *Knowledge Structure* — The design of the activities and the use of the resources are bound together by the knowledge and experience of present and earlier actors. The knowledge of these actor is related one to another.

- *Inter-temporal Dependence* — The network is a product of its history in terms of all memories, investments in relationships, knowledge, routines, etc. Changes of the network must be accepted by at least large parts of the network. Therefore, all changes will be marginal and closely related to the past.

6. TRADITIONAL PERSPECTIVES ON SERVICES MARKETING

The "Relationship Marketing" concept has a number of progenitors. The motivation for one such source arises out of the dissatisfaction with the traditional consumer goods literature. In particular, this dissatisfaction centres on its inability to absorb new developments, especially in the services and business-to-business marketing area. It is important to articulate this dissatisfaction as it provides the background to the development of the relationship marketing concept. This section attempts to describe how concepts developed in the consumer goods area have failed to reflect the dynamics of services management.

The traditional approaches to the study of services marketing and business-to-business marketing have been a poor relation within the broad family of attempts to understand marketing. Traditional marketing thinking has developed in a consumer goods context, and has been transferred directly to the analysis of services and business-to-business marketing problems. The most prominent concepts have been the "marketing mix" and the "marketing concept." The marketing mix concept, introduced by Borden (1965), has damaged marketing, in the sense that it fails to capture the unique dynamics of services marketing. These dynamics are primarily concerned with the development of long-term interactive relationships. Borden intended that the various variables of the marketing mix would be blended into an integrated marketing programme. Instead, the traditional approach to marketing has primarily concerned itself with the mass-marketing of standardised consumer goods, and the active manipulation of the 4Ps in order to make the customer buy. The marketing concept postulates that, once you know your customers, through market research or otherwise, you can design, price, promote and distribute a product that matches these needs. The assumption here is that the seller is the active party, and the customer, having to be persuaded to buy, is passive.

Attempts have been made to overcome the deficiencies of the 4Ps approach by extending the number of Ps. In the service marketing literature, Booms and Bitner (1982) have added three additional Ps: people, physical evidence and process. Kotler (1986) has extended the mix to include public relations and politics. Judd (1987) suggests that the addition of one new P, people, is sufficient to capture the dynamics of services marketing. Regardless of these attempts, the traditional marketing mix concept is still promoted as a general theory of marketing.

A number of researchers in service marketing reject the prevailing view of services in the literature. Gummesson (1987) suggests that: "the theories and models that constitute the present marketing concept are too limited in scope, exaggerate some aspects of marketing and suppress others. The old marketing concept needs to be replaced." The debate within the services literature has concentrated too much energy on the goods–services division. Customers do not buy goods or services in the traditional sense, they buy an offering that renders services, which in turn create value for the customer. Therefore, the traditional division between goods and services is outdated. It is a matter of redefining services and seeing them from a customer's perspective (Gummesson, 1994).

The goods-marketing versus services-marketing debate represented a fundamental challenge to the right of the services marketing field to exist (Fisk, Brown and Bitner, Chapter 1). These authors have pointed to the one-sidedness of the debate. This is because virtually all services marketing authors during the 1970s felt compelled to argue that services marketing was different. However, few felt compelled to publish their arguments.

The concept of "marketing myopia" was introduced to the marketing literature by Levitt (1960). The concept describes a common marketing disease: sellers who concentrate on the product instead of the customer's needs are said to suffer from the disease "marketing myopia". Gummesson (1994) suggests that services management is suffering from a similar disease — "services marketing myopia" — and describes the phenomenon as "watching the customer's navel without reflection". He describes how managers

> passively rely on what the customer says. By giving the customers what they say they want brings no real closeness to the customer [sic]. Rather it manipulates the customers into an external state of ignorance. Myopia has thus moved from one extreme to the other, from the inside to the outside.

Grönroos (1994) further extends the argument that the marketing mix concept as a universal truth has damaged marketing in the sense that marketers and salespeople have become isolated in their organisation. Therefore, the marketing department concept is obsolete because it prevents the spreading throughout the organisation of a market orientation and an interest in the customer.

Finally, the marketing-mix approach to marketing has dominated the way in which marketing knowledge is presented in internationally widespread textbooks. Gummesson (1993) raises six objections to the way in which marketing is presented in these traditional textbooks:

1. The textbook presentations of marketing are based on limited real-world data.

2. Goods account for a minor part of all marketing, but the textbook presentations are focused on goods; services are treated as a special case.

3. Marketing to consumers dominates textbooks, while industrial/business marketing is treated as a special case.

4. The textbook presentations are a patchwork: new knowledge is piled on top of existing knowledge but not integrated with it.

5. The textbooks have a clever pedagogical design: the form is better than the content.

6. The Europeans surrender to the US and its marketing gurus, and do not adequately promote their own original contributions.

Classifying marketing knowledge as such compounds the marketing-mix approach to marketing, and prevents new thinking and paradigm shifts from occurring. Services will continue to be referred to as residuals, intangibles and invisibles, and have one chapter dedicated to them in traditional textbooks.

In summary, the reigning paradigm that dominates the traditional marketing texts has been criticised for being incomplete and manipulative, not bearing in mind the needs of the customer and disregarding services and business-to-business marketing (Gummesson, 1994). It has damaged marketing because it has failed to capture the dynamics of services marketing and has placed too much emphasis on the goods–services division. The management of services is suffering from "service marketing myopia". Finally, marketers and salespeople have become isolated in their organisation, leaving the marketing department concept obsolete. The old marketing concept needs to be replaced. The new marketing concept should be seen as relationship management: creating, developing and maintaining long-term interactive relationships (Gummesson, 1987).

7. RELATIONSHIP MARKETING

Relationship marketing, inspired by new thinking in the services marketing literature, the network perspective and the interaction model developed in the business-to-business marketing area, has emerged as the new perspective in the management of services. Marketing can be seen as relationship management: creating, developing and maintaining relationships. Relationships require at least two parties who are in contact with each other. The basic relationship in marketing is that between a provider and a customer (Gummesson, Chapter 9). This relationships aspect of marketing captures several unique characteristics of services. These unique characteristics according to Gummesson (1987) are:

• The importance of interactions

- The emphasis on person-to-person interaction

- The fact that internal relations are stressed as a prerequisite for successful external relations

- The fact that the significance of the external relations is reflected in the expression "moments of truth", which stresses that each customer contact creates a moment that influences the firm's relations

- The fact that the emphasis is on the long-term perspective.

The new concept of "relationship marketing" has the ability to absorb new developments in marketing. A number of issues have emerged that have reflected these new developments. They have emerged through the study of services and industrial marketing, and through the experiences of practitioners. These issues have been recognised and are absorbed by the new concept of relationship marketing. Gummesson (1987) summaries these issues as follows:

- The terms buyer and seller can refer to any number of contacts between representatives from buying and selling organisations.

- The real customer does not necessarily appear in the marketplace.

- The customer can be a co-producer who interacts with the seller as well as with systems, the physical environment and other customers, and that marketing can become an integral part of the production as well as the consumption process.

- Market mechanisms can be curbed in the external market, but also, the market mechanisms have been brought inside the firm.

- Customer relations are influenced by "part-time marketers" from all sorts of functions within the firm, and consequently, the interfunctional dependency within the firm must be emphasised.

- The internal processes can be better handled by introducing the notions of the internal customer and process management.

- Efficient internal marketing is a prerequisite for successful external marketing.

- Relational quality is part of customer-perceived quality.

To develop relationships, firms have to interact with each other. The concept of the interactive marketing function was introduced by Grönroos (1979) to cover the marketing impact on the customer during the consumption process, where the consumer of a service typically has to interact with various parts of a firm. Grönroos suggests that these parts should be considered separately as interactive functions and supporting functions. The interactive part of the firm consists of the contact people, systems and physical environment. These are the visible parts to the customers. The contact people are considered the most powerful aspects of the interaction, as the other parts are more or less fixed. Consequently, the contact people act as "part-time marketers" (Gummesson, 1991). These "part-time marketers" are motivated by the systems with which they have to work, and the physical environment in which the interactions take place. Relationships are created via full-time marketers, FTMs, and part-time marketers, PTMs (Gummesson, Chapter 9).

Given the inseparability of the service production and delivery process, customers have the opportunity to interact with one another, which in turn influences the interaction process. The invisible supporting part of the firm, which is non-interactive, influences the outcome of the interactions, because the better the management support and material support, the better the interactive performance by the contact people. A customer-based view of the interactions and of the sources of interactions is illustrated in Figure 14.3.

FIGURE 14.3: A CUSTOMER-ORIENTED INTERACTION
APPROACH

	Supporting Part	Interactive Part	
Invisible Part	Technology and Systems Know-How Systems Support	Systems	**Customers**
	Managers and Supervisors Management Support	Human Resources (Salespeople and Contact People)	
	Supporting Functions and People Material Support	Physical Environment (Physical/Technical Resources)	

Source: Grönroos and Gummesson, 1986, p. 23.

The service company should recognise the immense importance of the interactive marketing functions, and should give high priority to developing this marketing function, because the relational quality is part of customer-perceived quality. During these interactions, the customer has the opportunity to form an impression of the service supplier. These interactions have both short-term effects and longer-term cumulative effects on the all-important customer relationships. Ensuring the successful outcome of every moment of truth through good interactive marketing is the primary objective of the services marketing strategy (Glynn and Lehtinen, Chapter 4).

The relationship marketing concept recognised that both the customer and seller can be active parties, that everyone is a "part-time marketer", and that marketing is not confined to a marketing and sales department. This implies that the interactive marketing function has important consequences for the firm. Relationship marketing requires the support of all people in all other departments and business functions to be effective and successful. Parasuraman, Zeithaml and Berry (1986) speculate that: "perhaps the most precious asset that service firms can acquire is a single-minded dedication on the part of all its employees towards satisfying its customers."

The concept of internal marketing has been developed as a means of empowering and enabling employees to manage the interaction process effectively (Grönroos, 1981 and Berry, 1983).

Internal marketing as a phenomenon starts from the notion that the employees are the first internal market of the firm and if the jobs cannot be marketed to this target group, the external marketing performance will probably be less successful (Sasser and Arbeit, 1976). Although the term "internal marketing" emerged from the services marketing literature, the issue of managing organisational activities has always been of interest to organisations (Gilmore and Carson, Chapter 11).

8. CONTRIBUTIONS TO AND CONFLICTS WITH RELATIONSHIP MARKETING

The main contribution of the network perspective to the relationship marketing concept rests on the emphasis placed on the interaction between firms in business relationships. This interaction approach advocates that marketing should not be seen purely as a proactive process, which emphasises the active part played by the marketer, assembling a mix of variables for passive consumers who may or may not respond to the offering. Instead, both producer and consumer are active participants in service marketing, as much as buyers and sellers are in industrial marketing. The active participation between the parties transcends the traditional notion of inseparability, and refers to the consumer as a co-producer who interacts directly with the contact people, systems, physical environment, and indirectly with the supporting part of the firm.

The network perspective makes an additional contribution to the relationship marketing concept by placing greater emphasis on context and time. Each service encounter or "moment of truth" can involve many other people who are significant reference points in one another's decisions and can affect each other's perceptions, beliefs and actions. The importance of this for service management is that relational quality is part of customer-perceived quality. Therefore, the move away from the atomic perspective where individuals are depicted as making choices and acting without regard to the behaviour of other individuals, is significant, as it recognises the importance of the context of the relationship in which individuals are embedded.

The network perspective postulates that relationships form the context in which these interactions develop over time. These relationships are formed because of the interdependencies of firms and are played out through the everyday interactions of individuals within these firms on every level. This idea compliments the concept in relationship marketing that everyone is a "part-time marketer", and that marketing is not confined to a marketing and sales department. The focus on everyday interaction between individuals challenges the traditional dominant top management perspective in the literature and also challenges the assumption that the firm as a whole is not assumed or taken for granted.

The network perspective takes the relationships between firms as the unit of analysis, which contributes to the overall objective of relationship marketing, which is seen as relationship management: creating, developing and maintaining long-term, interactive relationships.

Indirect relationships are another important characteristic of the network perspective. Similarly, the relationship marketing concept realises that the real customers do not necessarily appear in the marketplace, and that any exchange relationship has to take account of the indirect relationships that all firms have with a number of publics.

While recognising the enormous contribution of the network perspectives to the development of relationship marketing ideas, it is important to consider the unresolved conflicts that have emerged. A major source of conflict arises out of the generic nature of the relationship marketing concept. The essence of the conflict centres on whether the relationship marketing concept is specific enough to cover both inter-firm and consumer relationships. This is not a request to return to the tired debate of consumer versus industrial marketing, but rather an acknowledgement that the network perspective was born out of the inadequacy of traditional consumer goods marketing to capture the dynamics of the close, complex and long-term relationships that reflect inter-firm activities. These inter-firm relationships are built out of a history of firms dealing with each other and can be described in terms of adaptations commitments, trust and competition. The overall implication of the network perspective for inter-firm relationships is that these relationships have to be managed. Managing them can give rise to two types of problem: the limitation problem and the handling problem (Håkansson, 1982). The limitation problem concerns itself with the strategic question of what relationships the firm wishes to be engaged in. The nature of inter-firm relationships implies that firms have to decide to which relationships they are going to limit their activities, given the demands on the firm's technology, organisation, knowledge, resources and time. Some relationships will place very high demands on the quality and performance of the product, while other relationships will be based on a standard quality, as cheap as possible. The other aspect to the limitation problem concerns itself with the question of whether all relationships should be treated in a uniform way or whether some relationships should get special treatment. Barnes and Cumby (Chapter 7) suggest that:

> This must not be done indiscriminately; companies must master the well-accepted art of market segmentation and identify those customer relationships that should be cultivated and those where dissolution would have a positive impact on the company's bottom line and future prospects.

The handling problem concerns itself with handling the power-dependence and the co-operation/conflict aspects of the relationship over the long term. Sometimes this means close co-operation and sometimes it may mean conflict. In the short term, the handling problems are primarily related to attaining an efficient way of handling the different exchange processes with individuals, as well as groups of customers. The relationship marketing concept recognises these problems and considers them to be a revenue and productivity issue.

This revenue and productivity issue has major implications for the relationship marketing concept. The key question raised by the limitation and handling problems is whether the relationship marketing concept is developed enough to distinguish between the marketing of consumer services and industrial services. There are key differences between the management of consumer services and that of industrial services, just as there are key differences between the management of consumer products and that of industrial products. A number of authors have noted the key differences between industrial and consumer marketing. Jackson and Cooper (1988) identified the major differences that have an impact on the marketing of industrial products. These are presented in Table 14.1.

TABLE 14.1: HOW INDUSTRIAL PRODUCTS AND PROCUREMENT DIFFER FROM CONSUMER PRODUCTS

1.	There are relatively fewer buyers in the marketplace.
2.	The buyers that are there tend to buy in larger quantities.
3.	Much of the demand in industrial purchasing is derived demand.
4.	A relatively larger amount of the demand in the industrial market is inelastic.
5.	The products in the industrial market are usually of a more technical nature.
6.	There is multi-use of products in the industrial market as different buying influences within a purchasing company may use the same product for a different use.
7.	Industrial buyers stockpile products for production inventories as opposed to immediate use.
8.	There is a predominance of raw and semi-finished goods found in the industrial market — these products are sold into the consumer market on rare occasions.
9.	There is tremendous emphasis on the importance of product service after the sale in the industrial market.
10.	There is also tremendous significance placed in the industrial market on pre-sale servicing and technical assistance in setting up and operating products in the customer's plant.
11.	Packaging in the industrial market is generally more protective in nature, as opposed to promotional, although instances of the latter can be found, especially with distributor items.
12.	There is tremendous emphasis placed in the industrial market on promptness and certainty of delivery of products, because of the effects of delays on production-line operations, and so forth.
13.	Industrial customers do not always have to purchase the products they require, but can sometimes produce them with their own production facilities — this is very rare in the consumer market.

The main progenitor of the relationship marketing concept is the network perspective. The network perspective challenges the traditional dominance of the consumer goods literature. This traditional consumer literature fails to capture the unique dynamics of the business-to-business market. Likewise, the management problems associated with consumer services are different from the management problems associated with industrial services. The main difference is largely accounted for by the limitation and handling problems discussed earlier. The network perspective in its entirety can embrace the management problems associated with industrial services. In contrast, this chapter suggests that the network perspective is inappropriate to the management of consumer services. Given the nature of the limitation and handling problems in consumer services, the development and maintenance of relationships in that context would appreciably differ from the development and maintenance of relationships in an industrial services context. To treat the development and maintenance of these relationships in a similar way has major implications for revenue and productivity in management of consumer services. Relationship marketing does not distinguish between the management of these relationships in a consumer or industrial context.

This revenue and productivity issue is further exacerbated when we turn to consider how industrial services are classified and the impact of this classification on the relationship marketing concept. Jackson and Cooper (1988) found that the discussion that industrial services has received is limited, and appears to be restricted to the marketing of services used in the maintenance or operation of the business. Ignored are the services used in the production process, which, in effect, become part of the product. This division of industrial services into maintenance, repair and operating (MRO) services and production services has implications for the relationship marketing concept. Jackson and Cooper suggest that two further additional characteristics should be added to the common four characteristics (intangibility, inseparability, heterogeneity and perishability) normally discussed in the literature These characteristics are specialisation and technology. Specialisation can best be characterised by the level of customisation to customers' needs, especially with regard to production services which are often specialised on a per job basis. This level of specialisation in production services gives rise to additional limitation and handling problems as discussed above. Relationship marketing does not distinguish between how to manage MRO-type services and how to manage production-type services. The failure to distinguish between the two types of service gives rise to further revenue and productivity issues.

To date, the relationship marketing literature has not adequately addressed the issue of how a stream of revenue, both direct, and indirectly from a single customer, may meet the productivity demands necessary to survive, especially in consumer services marketing. The relationship marketing literature must address the issue of how to put into operation the relationship concept between consumer services marketing and industrial services marketing.

Apropos of the interaction between service quality, productivity and profitability, the first EIASM international workshop on service productivity was held in Brussels in October 1994. This workshop addressed the question of the connection between service quality, service productivity and profitability.

REFERENCES

Berry, L., "Relationship Marketing", in L. Berry, L.G. Shostack and G. Utah (Eds.), *Emerging Perspectives in Services Marketing*, American Marketing Association, Proceedings Series, Chicago, IL, 1983.

Booms, B.H. and M.J. Bitner, "Marketing Strategies and Organisations Structures for Service Firms", in J. Donnelly and W. George, *Marketing of Services,* American Marketing Association, Chicago, IL, 1982.

Borden, N.H., "The Concept of the Marketing Mix", in G. Schwartz (Ed.), *Science in Marketing*, Wiley and Sons, New York, 1965.

Cook, K.S. and R.M. Emerson, "Power, Equity and Commitment in Exchange Networks", *American Sociological Review,* Vol. 43, 1978, pp. 721–39.

Cunningham, M.T. and E. Homse, "An Interaction Approach to Marketing Strategy", in H. Håkansson (Ed.), *International Marketing and Purchasing of Industrial Goods: An Interaction Approach,* John Wiley, Chichester, UK, 1982.

Easton, G., "Industrial Networks: A Review", in B. Axelsson, and G. Easton (Eds.), *Industrial Networks — A New View of Reality,* Routledge, London, 1992.

Ford, D., "IMP and the Interaction Approach", in D. Ford, *Understanding Business Markets*, Academic Press, London, 1990.

Ford, D., H. Håkansson and J. Johanson, "How do Companies Interact?", *Industrial Marketing and Purchasing*, Vol. 1, 1986, pp. 26–41.

Forsgren, Mats and Jan Johanson, "Managing Internationalisation in Business Networks", in Mats Forsgren and Jan Johanson (Eds.), *Managing Networks in International Business*, Gordon and Breech Science Publishing, Philadelphia, PA, 1992.

Gadde, L.E. and L.M. Mattsson, "Stability and Change in Network Relationships", *International Journal of Research in Marketing*, Vol. 4, 1987, pp. 29–41.

Grönroos, C., "An Applied Theory for Marketing Industrial Services", *Industrial Marketing Management*, Vol. 8, 1979, pp. 45–50.

Grönroos, C., "Internal Marketing: An Integral Part of Marketing Theory", in J.H. Donnelly, and W.R. George (Eds.), *Marketing of Services*, American Marketing Association, Proceedings Series, Chicago, IL, 1981.

Grönroos, C., "An Applied Theory for Marketing Industrial Services" *Industrial*

Marketing Management, Vol. 8, 1979, pp. 45–50.

Grönroos, C., "Quo Vadis, Marketing? Towards a Relationship Marketing Paradigm", *Journal of Marketing Management*, Vol. 10, No. 5, 1994, pp. 347–60.

Grönroos, C and E. Gummesson, "Service Orientation in Industrial Marketing", in M. Venkatesan Diane M. Schmalensee and Claudia Marshall (Eds.), *Creativity in Services Marketing: What's New, What Works, What's Developing*, American Marketing Association, Proceedings Series, Chicago, IL, 1986.

Gummesson, E., "The New Marketing — Developing Long-Term Interactive Relationships", *Long Range Planning*, Vol. 20, No. 4, 1987.

Gummesson, E., "Marketing Orientation Revised: The Crucial Role of the Part-Time Marketer", *European Journal of Marketing*, Vol. 25, No. 2, 1991, pp. 60–75.

Gummesson, E., "Marketing According to Textbooks: Six Objections", in D. Brownlie, M. Saren, R. Wensley and R. Whittington (Eds.), *Rethinking Marketing: New Perspectives on the Discipline and Profession*, Warwick Business School, Coventry, UK, 1993.

Gummesson, E., "Service Management: An Evaluation and The Future", *The International Journal of Service Industry Management*, Vol. 5, No. 1, 1994, pp. 77–96.

Hagg, I and S. Johanson, *"Firms in Networks"*, Business and Social Research Institute, Stockholm, Sweden, 1983.

Håkansson, H., "An International Approach", in H. Håkansson, (Ed.), *International Marketing and Purchasing of Industrial Goods*, John Wiley, Chichester, UK, 1982.

Håkansson, H. and J. Johanson, "Formal and Informal Co-operation Strategies in International Industrial Networks", in F.J. Contractor and P. Lorange (Eds.), *Co-operative Strategies in International Business, Joint Ventures and Technology Partnerships Between Firms,* Lexington Books, Lexington, MA, 1988.

Håkansson, H. and J. Johanson, "A Model of Industrial Networks." in B. Axelsson and G. Easton (Eds.), *Industrial Networks — A New View of Reality*, Routledge, London, 1992.

Hammarkvist, K.O., H. Håkansson and L.G. Mattsson, *Marketing for Competitive Power,* Liber, Malmø, Sweden, 1982.

Jackson, R.W. and P.D. Cooper, "Unique Aspects of Marketing Industrial Services", *Industrial Marketing Management*, Vol. 17, 1988, pp. 111–18.

Johanson, J., "Swedish Special Steel in Foreign Markets", Department of Business Studies, Uppsala, Sweden, 1966.

Johanson, J and L.G. Mattsson, "Interorganisational Relations in Industrial Systems: A Network Approach Compared with the Transactions–Cost Approach", *International Studies of Management and Organisations*, Vol. 17, No. 1, 1987, pp. 34–48.

Johanson, J. and L.G. Mattsson, "Marketing Investments and Market

Investments in Industrial Networks", *International Journal of Research in Marketing,* Vol. 2, No. 3, 1985, pp. 185–95.

Judd, V.C., "Differentiate with the Fifth P: People", *Industrial Marketing Management,* Vol. 16, November, 1987, pp. 241–7.

Knoke, D. and J.H. Kuklinski, *Network Analysis,* Sage, London, 1982.

Kotler, P., "Megamarketing", *Harvard Business Review*, March/April, 1986, pp. 117–24.

Levitt, T., "Marketing Myopia", *Harvard Business Review,* July/August, 1990, pp. 45–56.

Mattsson, L.G., "Indirect Relationship in Industrial Networks: A Conceptual Analysis of their Significance", Third IMP International Seminar, IRE, Lyon, France, 1986.

Mattsson, L.G., "An Application of a Network Approach to Marketing in Changing the Course of Marketing: Alternative Paradigms for Widening Marketing Theory", *Research in Marketing*, Supplement 2, 1985, pp. 263–88.

Mattsson, L.G. and J. Johanson, "Network Positions and Strategic Action — An Analytical Framework", in B. Axelsson and G. Easton (Eds.), *Industrial Networks — A New View of Reality,* Routledge, London, 1992.

Parasuraman, A., V.A. Zeithaml and L.L. Berry, "A Conceptual Model of Service Quality and its Implications for Future Research", *Journal of Marketing*, Vol. 49, 1985, pp. 41–50.

Pfeffer, J. and G. Salancik, G., *The External Control of Organisations,* Harper and Row, New York, 1978.

Sasser, W.E. and S. Arbeit, "Selling Jobs in the Service Sector", *Business Horizons*, Vol. 19, June, 1976.

Smith, P. and G. Easton, "Network Relationships: A Longitudinal Study", Third International IMP Research Seminar, IRE., Lyon, France, 1986.

Thorelli, H.B., "Networks: Between Markets and Hierarchies", *Strategic Management Journal,* Vol. 7, 1986, pp. 37–51.

15

THE SERVICE FIRM IN INTERNATIONAL MARKETING

Frank Bradley
University College Dublin
Ireland

PRÉCIS

In the mid-1980s, 40 per cent of the world's total direct foreign investment stock of about $700 billion was in services, compared to about 25 per cent in the early 1970s, and less than 20 per cent in the early 1950s. Direct foreign investment in services became the fastest-growing component of overall direct foreign investment flows. By the end of 1985, more than half of all direct foreign investment flows — about $50 billion annually — were in services, with about two-thirds of it in Finance and trade-related activities. Service is also the fastest-growing component of international trade. In 1992, services accounted for 20 per cent of total world trade, and notably 30 per cent of American exports. In 1995, it seems safe to say that the benign period, during which service companies were relatively sheltered locally from foreign competition, is most definitely over, even in industries such as utilities or telecommunications, which used to be, but no longer are, protected by regulations and monopoly status. Economic and cultural interdependencies between countries, political and economic policies such as deregulation and protectionism, and dramatic developments in communications and information technology, intensify international competition in service industries. As much as companies the world over recognise, and indeed are participants in, the accelerating pace of exchange in services, numerous firms find themselves grappling with questions about how to provide international marketing. The cost of marketing a service globally can be considerable — for example, in the express transport or credit card business. Extensive advertising is needed to create initial awareness in a new market. Currently, there are substantial sums of money being *earmarked for this purpose in many service sectors. These companies may well increase their promotional activity as international competition intensifies. It is a widely-held opinion throughout the express transport industry, for example, that there will be a major price war within the next couple of years, led by leading integrated operators. This will tend to squeeze out less efficient operators. A similar situation can be observed in the airline business where extensive resources are also committed to support advertising campaigns.*

Interest in service marketing has reached a considerable high in recent years, both as a field for action in firms and as a major area of academic research. The unique status of the international marketing of services offers rich potential for creative new approaches and analysis. In this chapter, Frank Bradley adds a significant contribution to this domain. As is shown, most of the growth that has occurred in international services has been primarily concentrated in a few key sectors, such as advertising, accounting and financial services. Other services, such as transportation, retailing, and most recently health-care, are becoming important targets for international marketing investment. Factors such as low cost and the ability to compete in many activities, such as data processing and software development, are contributing to this trend in these services. The need for the management of trade-offs in the international marketing of services is highlighted in this chapter. The author argues that unless service marketing is perceived by managers to be at least as important as product marketing, opportunities in the international marketplace will continue to be lost. A number of other issues regarding the future of international services marketing and management are also addressed, including: global service delivery systems; effects of technology; scale and cultural aspects; impact of synergy in diversification in international markets; foreign market entry considerations; and barriers to internationalisation of services.

Hervé Mathe
ESSEC, France

1. INTRODUCTION

There are three reasons stemming from the international marketing of products which promote the growth and internationalisation of service firms. First, a manufacturing firm which pursues an international strategy requires detailed information on the size, composition and trends in foreign markets — services which are usually provided by specialised firms. Second, where it is essential to modify the product, the firm will require engineering and design services and, frequently, after-sales maintenance and servicing facilities. Third, as products moving across borders meet more obstacles than sales within the domestic market —for example, distance, language, customs, laws and regulations — there is a growing demand for services to remove these barriers. Many of the added costs of internationalising in manufacturing are service costs. Services are independent of, but related to, developments in product-markets. The ideas discussed in this chapter are a development of Bradley (1991).

2. INTERNATIONALISING THE SERVICE FIRM

With few exceptions — Cowell (1984), Normann (1984), for example — to find any discussion of services in an international context, it is necessary to examine the work of economists on the structure of indus-tries in the world. A random sample of a great many well-known stan-dard international marketing textbooks shows that little space is devoted to the treatment of service marketing, let alone a consideration of the international dimension. The overall picture presented by the economists is, as Inman (1985) puts it, "a world economy predominantly involved in producing and trading services". Yet, it is difficult to find a more appa-rent neglect than that which the international marketing of services has suffered at the hands of marketing theorists (Cowell, 1984).

Many commentators believe that the principles of services marketing internationally are the same as those applied to domestic markets. Differences occur when considerations of environmental factors such as cultural, legal, social and political factors are taken into account. Such beliefs have served product marketing reasonably well. With regard to services, however, an important difference needs to be examined. While domestic and international services are characterised by their range and complexity, the pattern of domestically-traded services is, however, very different from that of those traded internationally (Staltson, 1985). Cit-ing the US as an example, Staltson explains that the two major domestic service sectors — government and social services — hardly figure in the international arena where such services as transport, financial services and tourism are much more significant, even more so than in the US itself. Staltson adds that high-tech sectors such as communications and data processing are likely to account for a significantly greater propor-tion of service revenues from abroad than of domestic ones.

In 1970 and 1987, the US was the largest exporter of services. In 1970, the US exported $56 billion worth of services, which represented

11.2 per cent of total world exports of services. Other important export-
ers were France, the UK, the Federal Republic of Germany and Italy. In
1987, West Germany replaced the US as the largest importer of services.
In that year, West Germany imported $64 billion worth of services or
12.4 per cent of the total world imports. With the addition of Japan, the
same countries dominated import activities. Worldwide services trade increased from $300 billion in 1980 to $775 billion in 1990 (Figure 15.1).

FIGURE 15.1: WORLD GROWTH IN SERVICES TRADE, 1980–90

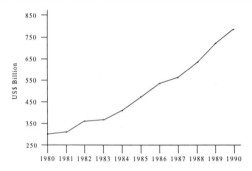

Source: Commission of the European Communities , 192, p. 66.

Europe is responsible for approximately 32 per cent of world service
exports (Figure 15.2). The next largest exporter is the US with 20 per
cent of world exports. Tourism accounts for about 28 per cent of world
export of services while transportation accounts for about 20 per cent, of
which maritime transport is the most important (Figure 3).

FIGURE 15.2: WORLD FLOWS OF SERVICE CREDITS
(1986–88 AVERAGE)

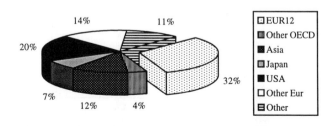

Source: Commission of the European Communities, 1992, p. 67.

FIGURE 15.3: EUROPEAN UNION EXPORTS OF SERVICES, 1988
(ECU BILLION)

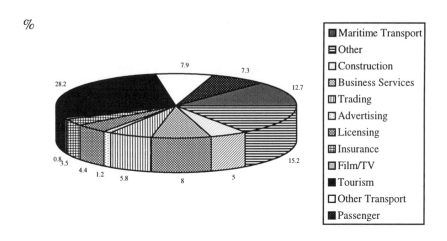

World exports of commercial services were worth $505 billion in 1987. The most important category was private services and income which includes financial services. These accounted for 40 per cent of the total in 1987. Travel and shipping were the other important categories. The fastest growing category is private services and income, the average growth of which was 14.5 per cent between 1970 and 1987. In the period 1980–87 passenger services was dominant in terms of growth (Table 15.1).

TABLE 15.1: WORLD EXPORTS OF COMMERCIAL SERVICES

Service Category	Share in Exports of Commercial Services		Average Annual Change in Value	
	1970 (%)	1987 (%)	1980–7 (%)	1970–87 (%)
Shipment	22	13	1.5	9.5
Passenger Services	5	6	7.5	14.0
Port Services	12	11	0.0	12.0
Travel	29	30	6.5	13.0
Other Private Services & Income	24	40	6.5	14.5
Total Commercial Services (%)	100 = $64 bn	100 = $505 bn	5.0	13.0

Sources: General Agreement on Tariffs and Trade, 1989; *International Trade* 1988–89, pp. 23–4; World Bank, 1988, p. 30.

2.1. Basis for Internationalising the Service Firm

In many cases, the service offering is not conducive to "going international" or it is necessary to start out "large" — the airline industry and some corporate banking activities, for example. The international service marketing firm often cannot draw from small-scale domestic experience, whereas the product marketing firm usually can develop the domestic market first — before going abroad.

The product marketing firm can also "test the waters" — that is, start into export markets initially by exporting a limited or reduced product line. Gradually, as success gathers momentum, the full product line can be introduced abroad. Market commitment can be extended by setting up overseas production units and subsidiaries. The process continues, constantly building from a position of strength. It is very different for the service marketing firm. It will have to "plunge straight in" as a service cannot be exported. Normann (1984) explains that few services can be exported without exporting the full "service delivery system" also. Basically, the service offering must be available in full from the day of entry to the market.

Among the many reasons why product marketing firms go international are: stagnant domestic market; growth in the market abroad; matching domestic competitors as they internationalise; opportunism; counteracting foreign firm action, i.e., threat in the domestic market; and exploiting a competitive advantage. These reasons also apply to service firms as they attempt to enter and develop international markets. Normann (1984) highlights two additional reasons:

- A personal challenge to senior people in the firm

- The need to service customers who have internationalised.

Unless three conditions are fulfilled, however, the full potential of international markets can never be realised (Normann, 1984):

- A competitive advantage must exist in the service management system.

- There must be a strong desire or ambition among senior management to internationalise.

- The service firm must provide adequate commitment of time and resources.

The involvement of people in the process usually means that there is a degree of variability not experienced by the product marketing firm. Cultural diversities and social norms quickly come into focus in service marketing. The effect of these elements obviously varies with the degree of intangibility of the service offering.

3. RECENT TRENDS IN INTERNATIONAL MARKETING OF SERVICES

The growth in services internationally may be attributed to two principal factors: changing life styles affected by affluence, leisure time and women in paid employment; and the changing world, affected by the increased complexity of life, ecological concerns and the variety and complexity of products available on the market.

World trade in services is increasing in importance. To date, developed countries have held the dominant position in the international trade of services. According to GATT sources, however, the differences between the relative importance of services in developed and developing countries may be a result of the lower prices of many services in the latter group. Market services account for nearly 50 per cent of the GDP in the EU, and services in general provide employment for 60 per cent of the EU workforce. About 200 of the top 500 companies in the EU are service companies (Commission of the European Community, 1987).

Commercial services in international markets may be divided into three groups:

- Transport Services

- Travel Services

- Other Private Services.

The third group is now seen as the most dynamic. It embraces such areas as financial services, communications, management and other professional services, including medical and healthcare services. Between 1970 and 1990, the value of trade in this group is estimated to have increased by an average of 15 per cent per year, outperforming of the other categories. As a result, it is now the single most important category of commercial services trade.

While information on this category is quite limited, it is noteworthy that labour income is the category of earnings from commercial services in which developing countries have the largest share, whereas the more developed countries record greater earnings from commercial services than from licensing, franchising, trademarks, technology and other forms of intangible property. This has important implications for the development of international trade in health and similar services, for example, in developing countries, given the importance of the human resource element.

In addition, it is important to look beyond the statistics and examine how services contribute to the globalisation of world markets and the expansion of world trade — in other words, how transport and tele-communications have facilitated trade in other services. Developing countries attempting to embark on trading services internationally need to be sure of rapid access to technological innovations which would facilitate their trade and enhance their competitiveness.

To some extent, the difference in the relative importance of services in developed and developing countries may be due to the lower prices of many services in developing countries (General Agreement on Tariffs and Trade 1989). Services are very important in the gross domestic product (GDP) of most countries. In 1970, services represented 55 per cent of the GDP in developed countries and 45 per cent in developing countries. By 1987, these proportions had risen to 63 per cent and 49 per cent respectively. Among developed countries it appears that services are proportionately more important in the smaller countries.

In some countries, the shift to a service economy has not been very pronounced but the composition of services has changed dramatically. Finance, business and government services have gained share at the expense of personal and distribution services (General Agreement on Tariffs and Trade, 1989). The importance of the various kinds of services varies somewhat between developed and developing countries and among service categories. In developed countries, the wholesale and retail trade and restaurants and hotels were responsible for 15 per cent of GDP in the period 1980–84. Government services were of the same magnitude while financial services were 14 per cent of GDP. The wholesale, retail, restaurant and hotel category was more important in developing countries, and government services were less significant.

3.1. Types of Services in International Markets

Services marketing is very heterogeneous and consists of many disparate activities. Services are provided by private and public firms which use low- and high-skilled labour. Services provided are sold to final consumers and to the industrial market. In the US, firms in healthcare, education and retailing sell more than 90 per cent of their output to consumers. In contrast, over 80 per cent of the output of accounting, engineering, advertising, equipment rental, computer and data processing, freight and air transport is sold to industrial buyers (General Agreement on Tariffs and Trade, 1989). According to this study, the transportation of merchandise and people — i.e., shipping, port and passenger services — accounts for about 30 per cent of world trade in commercial services. Expenditure by travellers at their destinations accounts for a further 30 per cent, and other private services and income account for about 40 per cent (General Agreement on Tariffs and Trade, 1989).

Three types of services have been described by Stern and Hoekman (1987):

- No movement of providers or customers

- Movement of providers only

- Movement of customers only.

The first category covers the separated services (Sampson and Snape, 1985) which are "pure" or independent services in that they can be traded like products without any requirement for a physical presence in the foreign country. Many separated services complement trade in products, especially industrial products. The second type of service requires the physical proximity of customer and provider. Capital and/or labour must move internationally for provision to be feasible. The transfer mode may be through foreign direct investment or some form of competitive alliance. It is not necessary that all factors move abroad. Management may remain in the home country but support foreign production through management, manufacturing and marketing guidelines. In the third stage, the services are provided in the home country of the providers. Tourism, education and medical services are prime examples.

The Uruguay Round of GATT in its basic agreement uses a variant of the Stern and Hoekman approach to define the scope of services as:

- Services supplied from the territory of one party to the territory of another

- Services supplied in the territory of one party to the consumers of any other

- Services provided through the presence of service-providing agents of one party in the territory of another

- Services provided by nationals of one party in the territory of any other.

An example of the second-type list is tourism, while banking and financial services generally would fit the third category. Construction and engineering projects and management consultancy are examples of the fourth category.

Two factors which influence the international marketing of services are the extent of personal contact involved and the number of customers served in a typical period (Figure 15.4). Professional services involve very extensive personal contact and a small number of customers served. At the other extreme, mass services such as banking through ATMs and credit cards typically involve much less personal contact but much larger number of customers served. In between these extremes are service shop operations such as car hire. The degree of personal contact and the number of customers served has clearly defined consequences for attempts to internationalise a service business.

FIGURE 15.4: SERVICE CLASSIFICATION

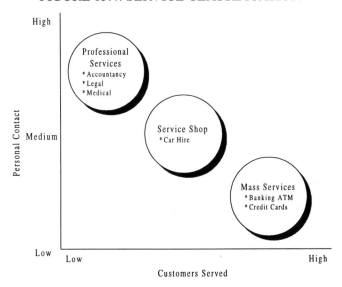

4. INTERNATIONAL MARKETING OF SERVICES

Services differ from products in that international marketing transactions frequently require consumers and providers to be at the same place at the same time. One result of this is that restrictions on market access for services may involve both barriers to the international exchange of services and policies affecting the actual entry of service providers into the markets where the customers are located.

Because services tend to be intangible and non-storable when they are traded, they must be embodied in products, information flows or people which are transported from one country to another (Feketekuty, 1988). Furthermore, it is frequently necessary for providers and consumers of services to co-operate if the service is to be provided. The interaction or exchange requirement can be met through sets of modes of delivery (Sampson and Snape, 1985).

4.1. Role of Technology in the Internationalisation of Services

Technology has the potential to make service industries more cost-effective and it also supports quality control. Other potential benefits highlighted by Cowell (1984) include the ability to handle large volumes of services, to offer a wider range of services, and potential increases in management efficiencies. Employees also benefit considerably. Technological improvements enhance the status and motivation of employees (Normann, 1984). For example, secretarial work has become less tedious as word processors have been introduced.

Services involve social actions and considerable customer interactions. Both are heavily dictated by cultural and social norms. With the introduction of technology, social interaction may be removed. The potential benefits from employing new technology will only be realised if they are favourably perceived by potential customers. For instance, many customers have reacted adversely to the introduction by banks of "faceless" ATMs. The banks may have a more efficient and controlled service, but in many cases, customers do not welcome such developments.

Once again, it is necessary to be constantly aware of the delicately and balanced service process and management system. Any changes must be skilfully introduced and positioned to increase the likelihood of their trouble-free acceptance. According to Normann (1984), "if the new technology could be skilfully employed to enhance and promote rather than to disturb the kind of social process that typifies effective service organisations, then the potential would be very great".

4.2. Productivity in Services

Regarding productivity, it has been noted that higher services productivity is clearly the key to securing a rising national standard of living. Moreover, it is a critical factor in improving a country's competitiveness and shrinking the trade deficit. Services are just as productive as manufacturing, or are becoming so. Services traditionally were protected by restrictive practices but are now being liberalised and freed to competition. Privatisation and deregulation have forced airlines, telecommunications, and financial institutions to become more efficient.

Services, it is often argued, are not susceptible to international marketing and competition. It is difficult to envisage dry-cleaning services, financial advice and hotel accommodation being the subject of international marketing. But many services *are* tradable and more are becoming so. Through cross-border sales, joint ventures and foreign direct investment, financial services, legal and business services, consultancy, telecommunications and recreation companies experience international marketing opportunities. Indeed, by combining or incorporating services in products, companies have discovered that it is easier to export services. Two sources of labour productivity in services are high technology investment and international competition (Figure 15.5).

FIGURE 15.5: SOURCES OF LABOUR PRODUCTIVITY IN
SERVICES

It is generally believed that, while both investment in technology and international competition contribute to improved productivity in services, the latter is the more effective. Labour productivity is the most accurate measure of economic performance in an economy. Productivity growth means higher living standards, and the faster the rate of productivity growth, the faster the economy can grow without inflation. It is often argued that productivity in services lags behind that in manufacturing but it is not certain whether this is a measurement issue or a result of lack of technology or lack of competition. The level of technology available to workers has risen dramatically in recent years, which has resulted in a shake-out in services industries. Furthermore, services have until recently been sheltered from international competition. Much of the shake-out in services has been a consequence of government deregulation in industries such as telecommunications and airlines, and increased foreign direct investment in services. Productivity differences in services are caused as much by open international competition and improved labour configurations as by investment in technology.

It has been argued that the growth of services internationally is as much a result of the failure of the services sector to modernise as of the increase in consumer demand for services. Employment growth is higher in services, it is argued, because productivity growth is lower. With expansion of an economy, services would absorb more labour than, say, manufacturing. One school of thought argues that productivity in services is low because of poor training and insufficient skills. The difficulty may reflect the very wide variety of activities contained within services. It would be necessary to relate growth to the different classes of services and the evolution in the pattern of demand for each.

4.2.1 Strategic Determinants of Service Productivity

In order to understand service productivity, it is necessary to examine the factors that influence its production:

- The cost of input resources
- The efficiency of transforming the resources
- The utilisation of the transformed resources.

The importance of services in the US may be judged by observing that service firms account for more than 70 per cent of private employment. As a result, it is argued that "higher services productivity is clearly the key to securing a rising national standard of living. Moreover, it's a critical factor in improving the nation's competitiveness and shrinking the trade deficit" (*Business Week*, 22 May 1989). Pressure for increased productivity in services comes from the customers of services; the manufacturing firms who must also compete in international markets. Productivity in service firms has increased at different rates in different countries mainly because of differential investment levels in new technology to support workers in service firms.

Between 1979 and 1986, services output per person in Japan, the Federal Republic of German, France, Sweden and the UK increased by about 2 per cent per year compared with only 0.4 per cent in the US. The increased capital investment in services industries in Europe has been driven by the high level and relative inflexibility of pay in service firms. While US private service workers in 1989 were paid only 67 per cent of manufacturing wages, in Japan they received 93 per cent as much and in West Germany 85 per cent as much (*Business Week*, 22 May 1989).

Thomas (1978) discusses the apparent difficulty in service-based offerings of availing of economies of scale. The perishable quality of a service creates a need to decentralise the service production process to a local level. However, a little imagination provides considerable scope, — for example, by introducing wide-bodied jets, airlines could fly twice as many passengers with the same number of high-salaried pilots.

Service systems with high customer contact are more difficult to control and to rationalise than those with lower customer contact (Chase, 1978). In high-contact systems, the customer can affect the time of demand, the exact nature of the service and the quality of the service, since, by definition, the customer becomes involved in the process itself. In fact, it is frequently better to view the marketing of services as the marketing of a system. The system consists of products which produce explicit benefits, and services which produce tacit benefits. Emphasis on individual components of the system is associated with transportation, financial and personal services. Emphasis on the system itself arises in education and professional services.

In services where the customer must be present, satisfaction with the service will be influenced by the interactions between customers and the service facilities themselves, and perhaps also by others using the system (Lovelock, 1983). At the opposite end, where the customer does not come in contact with the service facility, the outcome of the service remains very important but the process of service delivery may be of little interest — bank credit cards, for example.

Service managers must be aware of the drawbacks of intangibles, or pure services, in any attempt to increase productivity through commonly accepted methods such as standardisation or economies of scale. Many writers warn of the implications of bringing a highly intangible dominated "market offering" to the market. Such an approach must be weighed against the benefits of driving towards a more "tangible intangible" (Chase, 1978). Contrary to what managers might believe, service marketing has a lot of discretion in making this transformation both through the service marketing mix and by thinking creatively about the nature of the services provided. Chase provides two classic examples here: the use of ATMs by the financial service industry, and the UK's Open University system. The former transformed the delivery of certain traditional banking services from a human delivery mode, people-based and intangible, to a machine delivery mode, equipment-based and very tangible. Hence, by weighing up the costs and benefits of a particular positioning on the scale, transformations involving a movement along the product service continuum can be made.

4.3. Potential for International Marketing of Services

The unique status of the marketing in services offers rich potential for creative new approaches and analysis. Interest in services marketing has reached a considerable height. Unless service marketing is perceived by managers to be at least as important as product marketing, opportunities in the international marketplace will continue to be lost.

The problems in service marketing which frequently arise are caused by a number of factors:

- Physical display is impossible.

- Patent protection is impossible.

- Demonstration gives the service away.

- Provision of warranties is difficult.

- Packaging is marginal.

In recent years there has been a very considerable growth in the international marketing of services. Many of the motives for international product marketing can be found in services marketing. Most of the growth which has occurred in international services has been concentrated in a few key sectors, such as advertising, accounting and financial services. Healthcare and medical services are a relatively new phenomenon in the international marketplace.

To examine how best to approach the international marketing of services, it is necessary to return to the unique characteristics of services: intangibility, inseparability, heterogeneity, perishability and ownership. It is because services are performed, rather than produced, that they have several distinguishable characteristics which present the service firm with many problems.

In purchasing products, the product and its features provide enough evidence of what is being offered. In the case of a service, the "management of evidence" is vital (Shostack, 1977). This refers to the tangible cues surrounding the seller's capabilities to deliver the service. The literature is extensive on the importance of situational characteristics in purchase decisions for services (Shostack, 1977; Berry, 1980). Such things as the physical, environmental setting — e.g., doctors' waiting rooms — and the appearance of service — e.g., clothes and presentation — should receive very high management priority.

4.4. Diversification in the Services Firm

When a service firm reaches a certain size or has spare capacity, it may consider diversification as a growth strategy. The most common form of service companies diversification is client-based diversification (Normann, 1984). The importance of establishing the confidence and trust of the client has already been discussed. This relationship with the client is an integral asset of a service firm. If clients indicate a need for complementary or additional services, this may be a strong motivator to the service firm to provide them. This is clearly illustrated in the financial services industry. Major companies such as Citicorp and Chase Manhattan now offer a complete range of banking or financial services.

Grönroos (1978 and 1987) provides the setting for the second form of diversification discussed by Normann: main and auxiliary services. Viewing a service as more than just a "core" or "main" offering, diversification into auxiliary support and peripheral services makes good business sense. In some cases, as Normann points out, these auxiliary services can grow in importance in their own right. A third common form advanced by Normann is the situation where basic knowledge exists in the company, making it capable of catering for different market segments. Such situations occur where there is no ambiguity in the image that the company presents to the public and employees. In many ways, the diversification of a services business is similar to diversification in a product market. Service-market diversification involves developing a new range of services for existing customers and transferring existing services to new customers in international markets.

As in product markets, basic to the concept of growth through diversification, is the idea of synergy. Synergy is usually based on financial benefits to the firm, better services to the established customer base or complementariness in services offered. Financial synergy arises when the service firm develops different businesses which have complementary cash-flow patterns. As in many other areas of marketing, the established customer base constitutes a most valuable asset for the firm. In recent years, banks, insurance companies and building societies have each extended the kind of service they provide. It is reasonably easy for a transaction-type business to diversify into providing several types of service based on such transactions.

The third type of diversification arises when a service firm develops an auxiliary service for its own core business, and then commercialises this auxiliary business so that a wider customer group has access to it. Several examples may be cited to demonstrate the nature of this diversification. Airlines have developed their own catering, aircraft service and repair systems to such an extent that they are offered to other users including competitors. American Express has developed a "front-office" and a "back-office" business. In the front office, the traditional American Express business is carried on, while in the back office the company has developed its card-billing and payments-processing business to serve other proprietary credit card businesses. In these situations the service firm is using the same basic knowledge to cater for different market segments.

When a firm in the service business attempts to internationalise, it must transfer an entire system abroad. It is not simply a matter of adapting a product to the needs of customers in international markets. It is necessary to transfer the entire system, and the problem becomes one of adapting the system to new combinations. The issue of intangibility makes this process difficult to achieve. As in product markets, internationalisation of a service business is frequently a condition for holding on to important customers.

4.5. Scale and Cultural Effects

There are certain scale and cultural effects in the international marketing of services which must be considered when diversifying into international markets. Some services businesses respond to scale operations, while others do not. The provision and marketing of some banking services, recorded music, films, video, computer software, information services and some forms of advertising are examples of services which have associated scale effects (Figure 15.6). Medical services, legal and accountancy services, market research, theatre, personal care and education are examples of services where the scale effects are low.

FIGURE 15.6: SCALE AND CULTURAL EFFECTS IN
INTERNATIONAL MARKETING

		Low Cultural	High Cultural
SCALE EFFECTS	**High**	* Banking ATM * Recorded Music * Computer Software * Car Hire * Information Services	* Film, Video * Fast Food * Advertising

	Low	* Medical Services
		  (e.g., Cardiology)
		* Legal
		* Accountancy
		* Market Research
			* Medical Services
			  (e.g., Gynaecology)
			* Theatre
			* Personal Costs
			* Education

		Low	High

CULTURAL EFFECTS

The important point, however, is that services are also influenced by cultural factors. Some services are highly culture-bound and demand is strongly influenced by the culture of the society. Many medical services, personal care, education programmes, films, video and selected advertising are strongly influenced by culture. Many banking services, computer software, some medical services and professional services are not as strongly affected by culture.

5. MARKET ENTRY MODES FOR SERVICES

5.1. Impact of Coterminality of Production and Consumption of Services

In general, the production of services and of products are usually very closely linked together. It has been argued by Vandermerwe and Chadwick (1989) that modes for service internationalisation are influenced by a combination of the nature of the service — i.e. the degree of interaction between service provider and service consumer — and the way in which it is delivered — i.e., the degree to which the services are embodied in or delivered through goods. For example, telecommunications services cannot be produced without the support of extensive technical equipment. Distribution services are essential for manufacturing to take place. For international exchange to occur in services that require the physical proximity of provider and consumer, it is necessary that one visit the other. The coterminality in production and consumption of many services, requiring both the supplier and consumer to be present for the service transaction to take place, has made them difficult to trade by conventional means (Miles, 1993). If physical proximity is not required, other possibilities exist. The interaction requirement may be met through physical movement, through the use of telecommunication and computer technology or through the postal services. Computer- and telecommunications-based information technology makes it possible to separate the location and timing of the provision of a service and its delivery which gives rise to a "mode of presence" range on a continuum from greater to lesser intimacy (Miles, 1993; Posthuma, 1987). The greatest degree of intimacy is obtained with foreign direct investment and the least with exporting.

Because of the frequent need for temporary visits by providers or foreign direct investment in competing in foreign markets, the international marketing of services involves a greater number of dimensions than is the case with products. Market access for services may involve the full range of market-entry modes, whereas access for products can be achieved through one — exporting, for example. In health services, for example, where the customer-patient must be present, satisfaction with the service will be influenced by the interactions between customers and the health service facilities themselves, and perhaps also others using the system.

In purchasing products, the product and its features provide enough evidence of what is being offered. In the case of a health service, the management of the evidence is vital. This refers to the tangible cues surrounding the healthcare provider's capabilities to deliver the service. As emphasised by Berry (1980), it is vital to get the "how" of service distribution right. The distribution and delivery of medical services is a particularly difficult issue to manage across cultures and requires a high degree of cultural sensitivity in the management of health services.

5.2. Choosing the Entry Mode

In respect to market-entry strategies, the options open to the service firm are similar to those available for the product marketing firm:

- Exporting

- Competitive Alliances

- Acquisitions/Direct Investment.

5.2.1 Exporting Product-Embodied Services

Exporting has already been shown to be difficult for the service market-ing firm since the service delivery system must accompany the service which cannot be exported alone. By embodying services in a product, it is possible to access foreign markets. This is a particularly attractive option when barriers to trade in services are greater than barriers on merchandise trade. By embodying services in products, the company is moving towards the tangible dominant part of the product–service con-tinuum (Shostack, 1977). Service contracts sold as part of an equipment-purchase package are an example of how Levi Strauss embodies a design service in the famous denim jeans, which is branded and sold in many markets. Benetton similarly embodies design and style in clothing sold through leading retailers throughout the world.

Forms of competitive alliance such as joint ventures abound and are used more often than in product marketing because of the cultural element of services and the different people involved. Locals can over-come many barriers confronting the service marketing firm.

5.2.2 Licensing of Services

The licensing of a service operation has never been as widespread as it is for products but the franchising of services operations is growing. Many are of the opinion that because of the very nature of services, a service firm cannot have patents or exclusive "manufacturing" processes to protect its offering, hence it is considered unsuitable for licensing. To overcome this problem, Winter (1970) demonstrates the need for the service firm to offer a substantial quid pro quo in return for the licence fee. He suggests that to avoid the foreign counterpart "taking the idea and going it alone", an acceptable arrangement should include:

- A strong name
- A well-designed marketing strategy
- A complete "manualised" operation system
- Substantial opportunity for profit.

The name of the firm and the goodwill attached to the trademark are crucial elements in the service offering process. When a product is taken to international markets, these markets are generally quite familiar with the product. For a service marketing firm, such will not be the case: the firm's name and reputation are critical to selling the service successfully, and these must be given much attention and be advertised or communicated in some way to the new market, before purchase of the service can begin. The confidence of the prospective client must initially be won. The firm's name and existing experience may not be sufficient, however, and the conditions in the marketing environment must be conducive.

In designing an international licensing agreement, Winter (1970) strongly advises that minimum sales performance standards be included. Otherwise, the licensee is unlikely to put much effort into the programme. Because of the nature of services, the licensee will need considerably greater legal, personnel, management and promotional support. The distance factor, language barriers and differences in business customers can often cause problems between the licensor and licensee. There may be a requirement for strong regional management structures, constantly able to guide the licensee.

Franchising appears to be even better for service companies, affording a greater degree of control over the elements of the service component as described by Grönroos (1978 and 1987). Franchising is frequently used in the fast-food industry.

5.2.3 Acquisitions and Foreign Direct Investment

Acquisitions and foreign direct investment decisions for service firms, in the form of a branch or subsidiary, must consider the costs of the investment compared with other market entry modes, on the one hand, and the obvious scope for greater control, particularly quality control, on the other.

6. PUBLIC POLICY RESTRICTIONS ON INTERNATIONAL MARKETING OF SERVICES

Restrictions come into play much more rapidly for service firms than is usually the case for product-based firms. We have already dealt with two potential problems facing the international services firm:

- The risk of plunging straight into the foreign market

- The need to adapt to the new market.

Another problem more strongly felt by service firms than by product firms, is that of barriers to trade and government restrictions. Restrictions by governments and public agencies are much more common for service firms than for product firms. After primary resources, host governments see services as a way by which foreign companies can "take the most out of a country and leave little" (Carman and Langeard, 1979). The special nature of some services prompts governments into taking action — particularly when the service has some cultural, political or security sensitivity.

Staltson (1985) illustrates the extent of government regulation of services in the US by drawing attention to "a voluminous inventory compiled by the Office of the US Trade Representative". She also highlights the service equivalent to tariff barriers used against products. Services can be controlled by measures such as licences, fees and special taxes. Administrative and investment-related barriers are quite common and are examined in detail in Cowell (1984). Administrative barriers may be in the form of:

- Delays in granting licences

- Failure to certify certain professional services

- Discriminatory implementation of statutory regulations

- Inadequate access to local judicial bodies.

Among barriers listed as investment-related are:

- Employment requirements that control the personnel practices of the foreign firm

- Restrictions on the extent of foreign ownership permitted

- Biased government regulation against foreign service companies
- Limitations on the firm's access to advertising and communications failures
- Discriminatory practices against specific service industries (i.e. higher reserve requirements for foreign bank subsidiaries or special capital requirements for foreign insurance firms).

7. INTERNATIONALISATION IN SELECTED SERVICE INDUSTRIES

7.1. Advertising Services in International Markets

Any service marketing firm attempting to tackle the complexities of advertising unequipped with a thorough understanding and appreciation of the uniqueness and abstract nature of a service, is bound to pay a very heavy price as it attempts to advertise. The product marketing firm enters the arena with a principal tangible product to which the advertising process adds abstract qualities to enhance and sell the product. The service marketing firm enters with an intangible offering which cannot be physically evaluated or accessed. When combined with further abstract and intangible qualities by the advertising process, the result may be confusion, even a "money-for-nothing" image (Shostack, 1977). Shostack urges the service marketing firm to understand the need to make the service offered more "concrete" through advertising, rather than more "hazy". Merrill Lynch has developed a strong association between itself and the bull symbol. Also, its advertisements show photographs of tangible physical booklets, and the TV screenings of most advertisements finish by inviting customers to write for them. In this regard, Merrill Lynch successfully associated their intangible service with some "tangible evidence" working against the media's abstracting qualities. Both domestic and international services marketing firms are well advised to acquaint themselves with Shostack's concluding principle: "Effective media representation of intangibles is a function of establishing non-abstract manifestations of them" (Shostack, 1977).

The advertising agency world has gone through a number of changes in recent years, many of which can be attributed to international market trends and company responses. Many advertising agencies find that to service their clients properly they must follow them abroad. The European top 10 advertising agencies were dominated by the Saatchi and Saatchi group in 1988, with its two networks, Backer Spielvogel Bates Worldwide and Saatchi and Saatchi Advertising Worldwide (Table

15.2). Other very large agencies are Ogilvy and Mather, McCann-Erickson and Young & Rubican, each of which is reported to earn more than £200 million each year from European operations alone (*Sunday Times*, 12 March 1989).

It is not just the large agencies which have internationalised. Many smaller firms are also seeking partners and other ways into international markets. The smaller agencies seek partnerships principally because of the squeeze placed on them by the size of their clients, on the one hand, and the size of the international media groups on the other. The concentration of advertiser strength and the development of large media groups together are forcing many small- and medium-sized advertising agencies to internationalise by seeking competitive alliances abroad. Other factors are also important in opening up international markets to advertising agencies. Deregulation of the television industry in Europe indicates that further growth in advertising is expected. Liberalisation tends to increase the size of the market, rather than just draw advertising away from other media such as newspapers or magazines. Satellite television also contributes to the growth in the international advertising market. Advertisers have access through satellite television to new and wider markets. The market in Europe is, however, at different stages of maturity, depending on the country. The UK is still the largest market for advertising (Table 15.2).

TABLE 15.2: EUROPE'S TOP TEN COUNTRIES AND COMPANIES
IN ADVERTISING

Advertising Budgets, 1988			Advertising Gross Income, Europe, 1987		
	Country	$ Million		Agencies	$ Million
1.	United Kingdom	11,894	1.	Backer Spielvogel Bates	248
2.	West Germany	9,522	2.	Saatchi & Saatchi AW	230
3.	France	6,843	3.	Ogilvy & Mather	218
4.	Italy	4,981	4.	McCann Erickson	215
5.	Spain	4,407	5.	Young & Rubicam	201
6.	Netherlands	2,438	6.	Lintas: Worldwide	186
7.	Switzerland	1,985	7.	J. Walter Thompson	175
8.	Finland	1,443	8.	BBDO Worldwide	171
9.	Sweden	1,571	9.	Publicis	162
10.	Belgium	981	10.	Grey Advertising	151

Source: The Sunday Times, 12 March 1989.

It will continue to be difficult to consolidate the European advertising industry for two reasons. Many of the advertising agencies sought as partners are private companies, and are therefore difficult to acquire through share purchases. Furthermore, mergers or co-operative alliances between advertising agencies are intrinsically difficult to establish and maintain. Manufacturers of industrial or consumer products combine to serve a common purpose: to sell a product. The advertising agency is a service business where success depends greatly on its next campaign. There is no product to hold potential partners together. The need is greater for a coalition of people and perceptions and how they work together. It is the human factor and the nature of the business which can cause disharmony and instability in such partnership relations. A further complicating factor is that an agency joining with another agency to serve a particular market can easily fall into the trap of a conflict of interest among customer groups. Rarely will competitor clients agree to being served by the same agency. In such circumstances, the newly formed joint groups frequently lose valued customers.

7.2. Financial Services in International Markets

For financial services, the ability to engage in international marketing of such services and the ability to establish a physical presence in foreign markets is important, as some financial services require establishment whereas others do not (Hoekman, 1992).

Between 1984–5 and 1986–7, the number of mergers and acquisitions recorded by the EC Commission Directorate General for Competition in distribution, banking and insurance increased from 67 to 112. Most of these acquisitions occurred within the same EC country, which is similar to the situation in manufacturing. In 1986–7, EC cross-border acquisitions and mergers accounted for only 15 of the total, while non-EC firms were involved in only 18 situations. Most of these acquisitions were in distribution, followed by banking and insurance.

Acquisitions and mergers in financial services have increased quite dramatically. As was seen above, the purpose of these acquisitions and mergers appears to be a broadening of the product range and market expansion. Financial institutions are able through mergers and acquisitions to offer their customers quickly an international network based on a wider range of services, and at the same time to reduce operation costs.

Scale economies are not a key determinant of acquisitions in financial services, as labour and interest expenses represent the most important costs of operation. Nevertheless, the EU is attempting to liberalise the financial services market. Recent directives are expected to turn the

EU into a single financial market. Mergers and acquisitions, however, are not the easiest way of obtaining the benefits of integration of large financial markets like the EU. Friendly competitive alliances involving cross-selling of selected products or joint ventures could be an attractive alternative.

Financial service companies are major users of telecommunication services and computer technology. In many cases, international marketing of financial services cannot occur if companies do not have access to telecommunications networks, as these are the delivery vehicles for their services.

7.3. Internationalising Accountancy Services

Accountancy firms are also going through a dramatic period of change for similar and different reasons. The growth of individual firms among the "Big Eight" accountancy firms has led to much comment. The announcement by Ernst and Whinney and Arthur Young that they planned to merge has focused attention on firms within and outside the "Big Eight". The subsequent announcement by Price Waterhouse and Befec — part of the European based BDO Binder group — that they would also merge, raised the question of survival for smaller European firms. The importance of Befec to Price Waterhouse lies in the area of the market for audits. Price Waterhouse has a strong base in the UK and the US, but very little representation elsewhere in Europe. In 1988 in the US, Price Waterhouse had an audit market share approaching 20 per cent of the market. In the UK, its share was 15.5 per cent. But in other European markets its share was just over 9 per cent (Table 15.3).

Since audits change among companies very infrequently, success by Price Waterhouse in attracting firms like Befec, complete with its own client bases, is a key way of building market position in the core accountancy business in Europe. When the merger is complete, the share positions in the table will change. Two other interesting factors emerge from the table. First, two firms in the "Big Eight" already have very strong positions in Continental Europe; KPMG and Coopers and Lybrand. Second, the planned merger between Ernst and Whinney and Arthur Young will make the new firm dominant in the US market, but only the third largest in Europe (Table 15.3).

8. CONSTRAINTS OF THE GROWTH OF THE INTERNATIONAL SERVICE FIRM

International service industries are fragmented. There are low entry barriers to service businesses, as manifested by the many small firms sharing each market. There are few scale economies because of the relatively simple process involved — e.g., warehousing — or the inherently high labour content — e.g., personal care. In services business, there are frequently very high transportation costs, since services are usually produced at the customer's premises, or the customer must visit the provider. Because inventory is impossible, services businesses' premises are usually frequented. The problem is exacerbated for services with fluctuating demand. Firms with large-scale facilities have no advantage.

TABLE 15.3: AUDIT MARKET SHARES OF LEADING ACCOUNTANCY FIRMS, EUROPE AND THE UNITED STATES.

Firm	Audit Market Share Among:		
	US Fortune 500 Firms (%)	UK Times Top 1,000 Firms (%)	European Financial Times Top 500 (%)
Arthur Andersen	17.0	6.7	4.3
Arthur Young	8.6	6.4	5.7
Coopers & Lybrand	11.6	8.1	12.5
Deloite Haskins and Sells	8.8	8.9	8.1
Ernst and Whinney	14.6	7.3	6.4
KPMG	13.6	19.1	18.7
Price Waterhouse	19.4	15.5	9.4
Touche Ross	4.8	4.7	6.0
Other	1.6	23.3	28.9
Total	100.0	100.0	100.0

Source: Adapted from *The Financial Times*, Thursday, 1 June 1989.

In many instances, diseconomies of scale exist in service businesses. Small firms are more efficient where personal service is the key to the business. Individualised, responsive service declines with size after reaching a threshold — e.g., beauty care and management consulting.

Market needs in regard to services are diverse. Buyer tastes for many services are fragmented. This fragmentation arises because of local and regional differences in market needs. There is a large need for customised products and services — most fire engines sold are unique, for example. The problem with fragmentation in the marketing of services is that in an industry in which no firm has a significant market share, no firm can strongly influence the industry outcome. There is also considerable indeterminacy in the industry since there are no market leaders with the power to shape industry events.

It is the accessibility of the service that counts. A service may be intangible, but the resources — human and equipment — influencing its accessibility transform the service into a concrete offering. A number of simple illustrations demonstrate how accessibility is evaluated by customers in comparison with competing offerings:

- Location of a bank and its interior

- Means of transportation and their condition

- Exterior of a restaurant and the waiters.

Stressing accessibility isolates direct distribution as just one way of reaching customers:

- Insurance vending machines

- Hotel and restaurant franchising.

As with all aspects of marketing, it is necessary for the service firm to research the market, identify its target customers very carefully and aim its products and services at customer needs. For a retailer, this means merchandising to meet consumer requirements.

People are very important in service marketing. The administration of human resources is a key way of competing. Most people in a service firm act in a selling capacity: all are engaged in the personal market communication effort of the firm. In such circumstances, marketing training, especially in the areas of communications and selling, is essential for success. As all people in the service firm are engaged in marketing tasks, the firm must recognise the internal marketing task of service firms. The service must be successfully marketed to the people in the firm itself. This helps to avoid the possibility that the service might fail in its ultimate target markets. The staff are simultaneously the producers and sellers of the service.

REFERENCES

Berry, Leonard L., "Service Marketing is Different", *Business*, May/June, 1980, pp. 24–8.

Bradley, Frank, *Trade in Health Services in Developing Countries: A Discussion Document,* Technical Co-operation Programme, Department of Marketing, University College Dublin, Ireland, December, 1990.

Bradley, Frank, *International Marketing Strategy*, Prentice-Hall, Hemel Hempstead, UK, 1991.

Carman, James and Eric Langeard, "Growth Strategies for the Service Firm", paper presented to the Eighth Annual Meeting of the European Academy for Advanced Research in Marketing, Groningen, The Netherlands, 10–12 April, 1979.

Commission of the European Communities, *The EC and the Uruguay Round*, Brussels, Belgium, November, 1992.

Chase, Richard B., "Where Does the Customer Fit in a Service Operation?" *Harvard Business Review*, November/December, 1979, pp. 137–42.

Cowell, Donald W., *The Marketing of Services,* Heinemann, London, 1984.

EC Commission, *Seventeenth Report on Competition Policy*, Brussels, Belgium, 1988.

Feketekuty, G., *International Trade in Services: An Overview and Blueprint for Negotiations,* Ballinger Publications, Cambridge, MA, 1988.

General Agreement on Tariffs and Trade, "Guidelines for Advertising of Services", *Business Horizons*, July/August, 1989.

Grönroos, Christian, "A Service-Orientated Approach to the Marketing of Services", *European Journal of Marketing*, Vol. 12, No. 8, 1978, pp. 588–601.

Grönroos, Christian, "Developing the Service Offering — A Source of Competitive Advantage", Working Paper 161, Swedish School of Economics and Business Administration, Helsinki, Finland, 1987.

Hoekman, Bernard, "Market Access Through Multilateral Agreement: From Goods to Services", *The World Economy*, Vol. 15, No. 1, January, 1992, pp. 707–27

Inman, Robert P., *Managing the Service Economy, Prospects and Problems*, Cambridge University Press, Cambridge, MA, 1985.

International Trade, Vol. 1, Geneva, 1988–89.

Lovelock, Christopher H., "Classifying Services to Gain Strategic Marketing Insights", *Journal of Marketing*, Vol. 47, Summer, 1983, pp. 9–20.

Miles, Ian, "Services in the New Industrial Economy", *Futures*, July/August, 1993, pp. 653–72

Normann, Richard, *Service Management*, John Wiley and Sons, Chichester, UK, 1984.

Posthuma, A., *The Emergence of Offshore Services*, Occasional Paper No. 24, Science Policy Research Unit, Brighton, UK, 1987.

Sampson, G. and R. Snape, "Identifying the Issues in Trade in Services", *The World Economy*, Vol. 8, 1985, pp. 171–81

Shostack, G. Lynn, "Breaking Free from Product Marketing", *Journal of Marketing*, April, 1977, pp. 73–80.

Staltson, H., "US Trade Policy and International Services Transactions" in Robert P. Inman (Ed.), *Managing the Service Economy*, Cambridge University Press, Cambridge, MA, 1985.

Stern, Robert M. and Bernard M. Hoekman, "Issues and Data Needs for GATT Negotiations on Services", *The World Economy*, Vol. 10, No, 1, March, 1987, pp. 39–59

Thomas, Dan R.E., "Strategy is Different in Service Business", *Harvard Business Review*, July/August, 1978, pp. 158–65.

Vandermerwe, Sandra and Michael Chadwick, "The Internationalisation of Services", *Services Industries Journal*, Vol. 9, No. 1, January, 1989, pp. 79–93

Winter, Elmer L., "How to License a Service", *Columbia Journal of World Business*, September/October, 1970, pp. 83–5.

World Bank, *World Development Report*, Oxford University Press, Oxford, UK, 1988.

16

STRATEGIC SERVICES MANAGEMENT:
Examining and Understanding It

James L. Heskett
Harvard University, USA

PRÉCIS

In this chapter, Heskett sets out to review what he refers to as a very small portion of significant contributions to strategic management thinking, and to raise questions about future directions of research in Services Management. In his review, he covers three areas of contribution and three conceptual models. The three areas of contribution are: service quality, customer loyalty/retention, and service mapping. In reviewing the contributions of service management to strategic management thinking he notes the multifunctional nature of the service encounter and the implications of this for organisation structures, selection, training and compensation. In discussing the service quality contributions he notes that this topic is the domain of researchers in marketing, operations and human resource management. Research deals with process as well as function, thus illustrating the multifunctional and multifaceted aspects of services management. In his second contribution area —customer loyalty/retention — he notes that the shift in focus, from market share to customer retention as a driver of profitability, originated in services management. In his third example, service mapping, he notes that the currently in-vogue topic of re-engineering is simply a development of blueprinting from services management, and that this is simply a marriage of operations and marketing. The three conceptual frameworks for integrating ideas are: the strategic service vision; the cycle of failure; and the service profit chain, all of which combine elements of marketing, operations, and human resource management. A feature of this chapter is the excellent examples provided to illustrate each of these conceptual frameworks. Heskett's graphic description of the cycle of failure deserves special mention.

His most thought provoking ideas relate to what he calls a set of challenges for future research:

- *The need for further development of ways of measuring the "fit" not just between a company and its competitive environments, but also among the internal elements of each strategy.*

- *Measuring the individual element of each framework — for example, how do we define customer and employee loyalty and satisfaction?*

- *Assessing inter-relationships between phenomena: in this regard the effects of individual elements of the service strategy working in concert are clearly not additive, and while holding all variables but one constant may constitute good research in a scientific sense, it may be totally inappropriate in examining results produced by different systems of organisation elements.*

- *Factoring concepts of focus, leadership and culture into the research, he suggests that aspects such as these may need to be given greater emphasis — instead of those commonly emphasised in "five forces analysis".*

- *Applying the results of the work or translating results into practice, the natural tendency of managers to opt for a "quick fix" sometimes leads to frustration and disappointment in regard to applying research results. Some key questions to consider here relate to the extent to which the important relationships between profit-oriented phenomena and management actions have been made clear, and also the degree to which the appropriate caveat has been attached to research findings.*

Overall, Heskett provides us with a most thought-provoking and challenging set of issues for future research.

James J. Ward
University College Galway, Ireland

1. INTRODUCTION

Over the past 20 years, the pioneering work of investigators of service management phenomena, many of whom are represented in the chapters of this book, has greatly influenced our thinking about management in general. Specifically, it has had an increasing impact on the study and management of marketing, operations, and human resources (Fisk, Brown and Bitner, Chapter 1; Wright, Chapter 2).

This work has evolved from important efforts to describe phenomena ranging from the service encounter to other initiatives with stronger prescriptive components, such as research associated with service quality. Its focus has shifted from the application of concepts of manu-facturing management to the service sector to ways in which service management concepts can be used to advantage in manufacturing firms. (Fynes, Ennis and Negri, Chapter 13). It has matured, starting from an emphasis on the contrasts between services and manufacturing to a more holistic view of businesses as composites of both, with an increasing emphasis on information as an important element of the business mix and a source of profit. And, finally, it has both inspired and benefited from an increasing emphasis on inter-functional research and study that reflects trends already taking place in practice.

The objectives of this chapter are to review a very small portion of the significant contributions to strategic management thinking resulting from this work, while raising questions about future directions of the research itself. This will be done in the context of three integrative frameworks, the strategic service vision, the cycle of failure and the service profit chain.

2. CONTRIBUTIONS TO STRATEGIC MANAGEMENT THINKING

Because of the simultaneous nature of service creation and marketing in many services, practice and theory in the service sector has been multi-functional, anticipating more recent trends in all organisations. The very idea of a service encounter, comprising one or more so-called "moments of truth", is multifunctional in character, requiring comprehensive analysis and, in many cases, the creation of new forms of organisation, selection, training, and compensation. It defies description in traditional functional terms (Payne and Clark, Chapter 12). Many possible illus-trations of this observation are available, encompassing work in service quality, customer loyalty or retention, and service mapping.

2.1. Service Quality

Early research in service quality disclosed its subjective, relative nature, essentially casting an entirely new light on a subject formerly dominated by sampling and statistical analysis of products in the process of being manufactured. In 1974, for example, a research team of which this author was a part attempted to ascertain why consumers of a major car manufacturer's dealer services believed that their best car service providers were, in order of quality, the corner mechanic, large retail chains, and finally the authorised manufacturer's dealer. Several years later, the concept of service quality as the result of differences between actual and expected levels of service began to emerge. We then witnessed investigations leading to the development of a service quality measurement process such as SERVQUAL, consisting of instrumentation rooted in a focus on service *process* as an important, sometimes dominant, determinant of quality alongside the focus on *function* that was our legacy from the study and management of quality in manufacturing-oriented organisations (Parasuraman, Zeithaml, and Berry, 1985 and 1988; Zeithaml, Parasuraman, and Berry, 1990; Parasuraman, Chapter 6). For example, there is growing proprietary evidence that failures in the process of delivering results in medical services (reliability, responsiveness, authority, empathy, and tangible evidence, to use the basic SERVQUAL dimensions) are several times more important than results (whether the patient lives or dies) in prompting legal suits for medical malpractice in the US.

The development of effective ways of measuring service has allowed us to turn to questions concerning the impact of quality on profitability. This has included efforts to measure the costs of both good and poor quality (Barnes and Cumby, Chapter 7) And it has encouraged the development of models to estimate the profit impact of service quality improvements (Rust, Zahorik, and Keiningham, 1994). This body of work confirms that the delivery of high quality in service is not the domain of those interested exclusively in marketing, operations, *or* human resources. It is the domain of *all three* groups.

2.2. Customer Loyalty or Retention

The decade of the 1970s was dominated by fallout from the PIMS studies (Schoeffler, Buzzell, and Heany, 1974; Buzzell and Gale, 1987), whose conclusions associating market share with profitability sent literally thousands of organisations off in a quest to build portfolios liberally sprinkled with, or even limited to, so-called "star" businesses with large relative market shares and high profits, all the while "milking cows", businesses with low growth but high profits, and "shooting" or otherwise disposing of businesses identified as low-growth, low-profit "dogs". Two decades later, documentation of the favourable impact on profits resulting from customer retention in service businesses helped managers to turn from buying and selling businesses to building a more loyal cadre of customers in those they already operated (Reichheld and

Sasser, 1990). Similarly, marketing budgets and incentives to sales and service people were developed, which began stressing the importance of customer retention as well as customer attraction. It should not be surprising that the investigators most often associated with this important set of marketing concepts, Earl Sasser and his former student Fred Reichheld, had no marketing management backgrounds; Sasser's previous work was almost entirely associated with operations management.

This work has led directly to the development of an understanding of market share quality, the proportion of a company's business represented by loyal customers registering repeat sales. Market share quality often results directly from efforts to build the satisfaction and loyalty of service workers who are in direct contact with customers. Employee satisfaction results from initiatives to match attitudes and skills with jobs, train and recognise people, rethink work, and provide technological support to increase the capability to deliver results to customers. It clearly requires attention to both operating and human resource management issues, once again a bridging of functions.

2.3. Service Mapping

Recently we have observed a great deal of interest in a concept called re-engineering, the study and radical redesign of processes to shorten response times dramatically, improve quality, and improve productivity (Hammer, 1990). Re-engineering concentrates on following work flow through its various stages, within and across organisations. Concepts of service blueprinting or mapping have been put forth to ask how such processes look and feel to customers, where their fail points are most often found, and how to correct them to provide desired, seamless services to customers both inside and outside the organisation (Shostack, 1984 and 1987; Shostack and Kingman-Brundage, 1991; Kingman-Brundage, Chapter 5). The operations orientation of re-engineering is bonded to marketing management and the customer's point of view, to produce a truly valuable cross-functional approach to process redesign.

These examples of research and application in the service sector are not only characterised by their cross-functional orientation, they also represent some of the more important contributions to management thinking in the past two decades.

3. CONCEPTUAL FRAMEWORKS FOR INTEGRATING IDEAS

During this same time period, many efforts to synthesise the work of others in service-management-related topics into useful conceptual schemes have been set forth. This author and his colleagues in the Service Management Interest Group at Harvard have engaged in this activity as well. Because they are illustrative of, but not necessarily superior to, a much larger number of efforts, three of these efforts will be described very briefly in terms of their components, the implied hypotheses they comprise, and the ways in which they help to provide perspective to much of the collective work. They are the strategic service vision, the service profit chain and the cycle of failure, shown in Figures 16.1, 16.2 and 16.3, respectively. All combine elements of marketing, operations, and human resource management in an effort both to describe and influence competitive strategies.

3.1. The Strategic Service Vision

This conceptual framework (Heskett, 1986) resulted from experiences in organising and teaching a course designed to integrate elements of previously-offered service marketing and service operations courses at the Harvard Business School. Its development coincided with the creation by others of similarly broad conceptual schemes (Norman, 1984).

Distinguishing features of the strategic service vision are that it is centred around:

- Target market segments, defined as much in terms of psychographics as demographics

- A service concept, defined in terms of results produced for targeted customers rather than services, products, or processes

- The positioning of the service concept in relation to the needs expressed by members of targeted market segments and the ability of competitors to meet those needs. (This was later expanded into the concept of value addressed in the service profit chain described in Figure 16.2 below.)

- An operating strategy comprising marketing, operating, and human resource policies, procedures, organisations, and controls designed to act as leverage for results produced for customers (and the value associated with such results) over the costs of service production, a basic determinant of bottom line results

- A service delivery system comprising networks, systems, facilities, and other physical assets to complement the operating strategy.

FIGURE 16.1: BASIC AND INTEGRATIVE ELEMENTS OF A STRATEGIC SERVICE VISION

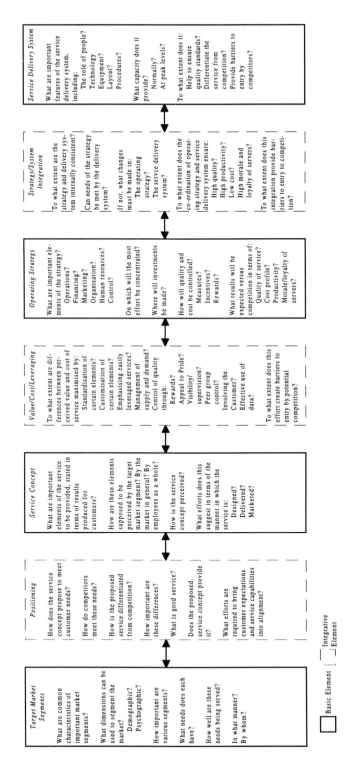

Source: Heskett, 1986, p. 30.

FIGURE 16.2: THE SERVICE PROFIT CHAIN

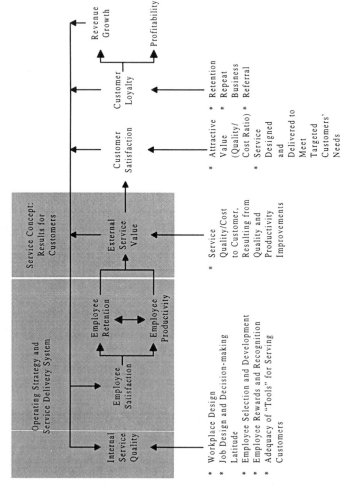

Basic objectives for setting forth a strategic service vision are to foster a new way of thinking about the question, "What business are we in?", while encouraging both a marketing and operating focus. A hypothesis implicit in the strategic service vision is that a very good business can be built on either extraordinary marketing focus or operating focus. Truly outstanding businesses, on the other hand, feature both.

Thus, outstanding multinational service enterprises such as IKEA, United Parcel Service, and Benetton were built around ingenious ideas that provided simultaneously high levels of marketing and operating focus to those companies. At IKEA, affordable, attractive ways of furnishing a home were made available to a new generation of relatively young European consumers who were, in increasing numbers, in the process of forming households; who held less traditional ideas about how to furnish their houses; and who were willing to handle and assemble their own furniture. The target was very clear. Value for potential customers was created through a unique concept of producing, handling, and selling furniture in components in partially assembled form to reduce many of the most important costs of furniture production and retailing associated with the inventorying and handling of assembled furniture. Easily accessed locations with unusual amounts of parking (for Europe) were the central feature of the service delivery system.

Similarly, United Parcel Service (Sonnenfeld and Lazo, 1987) has built by far the most profitable transportation service in the world by focusing its attention on retailers in need of dependable, low-cost methods of package delivery (market focus) and carefully restricting package sizes to allow the development of highly efficient and productive handling machinery, delivery cars, and driver-deliverers (creating operating focus). Through a set of operating policies and procedures of a paramilitary character, combined with liberal opportunities for employee ownership, United Parcel Service provides the tools that insure worker capability to create results for customers and the incentive to do so.

Benetton, characterised some years ago by its managing director as a "service system", was founded on the service concept of making "industrial,' that is to say affordable and easily produceable, fashion available to young consumers in their mid-teens to mid-twenties who are interested in colour and comfort (Signorelli and Heskett, 1984). Young entrepreneurs capable of relating to the target market were selected as shop owner/licensees, with a priority given to those with no previous retailing experience. By the early 1980s the company had developed the well-publicised manufacturing process that allowed it to assemble woven garments in undyed form and dye them later to order to provide a rapid response inventory replenishment capability to retailers that was not available to their competitors operating under more traditional fashion manufacturing and retailing systems. Although the proportion of wool and cotton garments processed in this fashion never exceeded 30 per cent (and at times has fallen far short of this percentage with the introduction of more intricate colour designs), it provided a competitive edge that enabled the company's shop owner/licensees to succeed, particularly in those parts of the world that had not been touched by advanced retailing practices. It represented an operating strategy that gave value a strategic advantage to customers over cost, and produced substantial profits for Benetton.

3.2. The Cycle of Failure

Growing concerns about interventions that produce effective operating strategies led to a concept based on pioneering empirical research (for example, Shostack, 1985; Schneider and Bowen, 1985; Parkington and Schneider, 1979; Lawler, 1973; and Johnson and Seymour, 1985) that investigated inter-related components of what we called the cycle of failure, shown in Figure 16.3. Very simply, the cycle of failure describes ways in which well-meaning managers insure "poor service by design" by systematically taking steps to guarantee that front-line service workers will be unable to deliver results desired by customers, thereby reducing job satisfaction, employee loyalty and productivity, and ultimately customer satisfaction and loyalty (Schlesinger and Heskett, 1991).

At the heart of many manager-created cycles of failure is a basic lack of belief that front-line service workers are motivated to deliver good service or even that they want to work. This leads to the design of front-line service jobs that tightly constrain the service worker, offering little opportunity for latitude in delivering results to customers; require little training; are boring; and pay low wages. A predictable result is lack of employee interest in the job, high employee turnover, an inability to build relationships with customers, and ultimate customer dissatisfaction and loss. (An important variation on this concept, the "cycle of mediocrity", is presented by Lovelock, Chapter 8).

Proposed antidotes for the cycle of failure have shaped our data collection and analysis efforts. They include:

- Finding ways to enfranchise front-line service workers by providing them with increased latitude (within clearly specified limits) for delivering results to customers and paying them for their performance (as opposed to their effort) in doing so, particularly in the delivery of services requiring real-time customisation and judgment on the part of front-line service workers.

- Developing ways of selecting people who respond well to enfranchisement, and then encouraging them to help in selecting their co-workers with the primary emphasis on attitudes and a secondary emphasis on skills required for the job.

- Providing training and development that emphasise both job and life skills to a group of people who may have experienced little training in the past.

- Restructuring organisations in radical ways that enable organisations to operate with greatly increased spans of control, fewer levels of management, lateral (as opposed to vertical) promotion for service workers with good performance, and a larger proportion of total compensation paid to those actually serving customers.

- Developing counterintuitive management philosophies such as paying individual front-line service workers more, in order to reduce labour costs in relation to sales while at the same time insuring greater continuity and longevity in relationships between front-line service workers and customers.

- Designing technologically-based support and information systems that enhance front-line service worker capability in delivering results to customers.

At about the same time that seminal work was being done on component relationships within the cycle of failure, Leonard Schlesinger, had the unique opportunity to test various ways of combating the cycle of failure as the operating head of a US-based French bakery café chain called Au Bon Pain (Lytle and Sasser, 1987). Elsewhere, organisations as far-flung as the Marriott Corporation in the US and the Ito Yokado retailing empire in Japan were taking steps to implement many of the same concepts (Wylie and Salmon, 1989).

At Au Bon Pain, these ideas were advanced to the store management level through the vehicle of a so-called Partner/Manager Program. The programme invited selected managers to sign "contracts" with the company under which they would agree to meet performance requirements regarding the quality of core services, the preservation of the company's brand equity, and the achievement of an agreed level of operating profit. They could then engage in any profit-enhancing activity they thought appropriate for their particular stores, including such things as modest expansions, outside catering, and even wholesaling of product. The resulting increment in operating profit over the previously agreed amount was split equally between the company and the store's management. Ingenious store managers extended the concept to the front line, in some cases eliminating positions in order to provide the typical employee with extended hours (up to 50 and 60 hours per week) and much higher pay, in exchange for greater productivity and improved relations with customers. (In one store, this led to a reduction in the turnover of front-line service workers from more than 100 per cent to less than 10 per cent per year.) Store-level operating profits for the company were found to improve dramatically, in some cases doubling in a short period of time.

FIGURE 16.3: THE CYCLE OF FAILURE

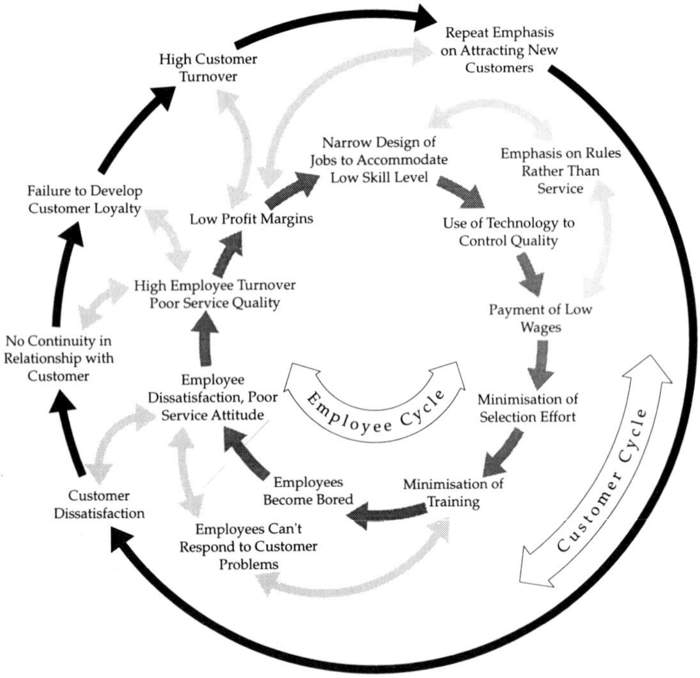

Source: Schlesinger and Heskett, 1991.

Similarly, Marriott's Fairfield Inn economy hotel chain in the US was designed around ways of combating the cycle of failure in a venture developed to deliver to so-called "road warriors" (frequent regional business travellers) the world's cleanest rooms and friendliest employees (and little more) for a very low price (Ray and Heskett, 1989). A simple inn design was complemented by an innovative human resource strategy intended to provide the latitude to employees to deliver on the company's promise to customers. One element of this strategy was the implementation of a guest feedback device called Scorecard which electronically solicited answers to just four questions from each guest on departure. Based on responses, the cleanliness of rooms and friendliness of employees could be traced back to individual employees to allow for them to be paid in part on a variable compensation basis. Thus, housekeepers found their compensation based in part on the perceived cleanliness of rooms they cleaned. Further, they were invited to *earn* leave (as opposed to *receive* vacation) by their perfect attendance on the job or their ability to provide an acceptable substitute when they found they could not be at the job, a practice aimed at the biggest problem in managing many front-line employees — absenteeism. This required the development of new devices to insure the selection of housekeepers who would respond to performance measurement, pay-for-performance, and increased responsibility for staffing their respective positions.

Ito Yokado, a large Japanese retailing organisation with operating performance levels far higher than its competition, adapted these same concepts for the management of activities such as retail inventory management. Instead of full-time professionals devoted to the task of reordering supplies for its food businesses, Ito Yokado's management elected to employ inventory managers from a growing pool of capable people — many of them women — available on a part-time basis in Japan. By supporting them with outstanding inventory management technology and extensive training on the job, and paying them in part on the quality of their results, the company has developed a cadre of people each of whom is knowledgeable about and capable of quite effectively managing on a regular part-time basis a very small number of inventoried items.

In each of these cases, extraordinary results were achieved through integrated strategies comprising a number of internally consistent elements that were designed to address a specific set of customers' and servers' needs. This is an important point to which we will return.

3.3. The Service Profit Chain

The convergence of work being carried out by Reichheld and Sasser on customer loyalty with that associated with the cycle of failure in front-line human resources management led to the creation of a broader framework with day-to-day management relevance. In particular, work on customer loyalty provided a link between customer and employee satisfaction, on the one hand, and profit and growth, on the other. The result was the service profit chain (Schlesinger and Heskett, 1991; Heskett, Jones, Loveman, Sasser and Schlesinger, 1994), shown in Figure 16.2, describing a series of not-fully-proven hypotheses that:

- Profit and growth in a service organisation are most directly related to customer loyalty, customer satisfaction, the value of services delivered to customers, employee loyalty, employee productivity, employee satisfaction, and the internal quality of services (work life) made available to employees.

- Each component of the service profit chain is influenced primarily by the components following it in the chain.

- The chain is circular in that customer satisfaction, for example, is a contributor to employee satisfaction and loyalty.

- The value of a service is a function of results produced for customers, as well as the quality of the process by which they are produced, all in relation to the cost to the customer not only of the service but of the effort to acquire it.

- The internal quality of service made available to employees is the sum of practices described in reversing the cycle of failure, that is, latitude (within limits) in delivering results to customers as well as rewards for doing so and support mechanisms such as technology that contribute to what we call employee capability — perhaps the most important determinant of employee satisfaction in many service settings.

Two examples of the service profit chain at work, which have been studied in some depth, are provided by the ServiceMaster Company and Taco Bell. These examples are instructive because they not only illustrate relationships within the chain but also involve sophisticated efforts to measure the relationships.

3.3.1 ServiceMaster

ServiceMaster was built on a core business providing management services to hospitals, schools, and industrial firms for housekeeping, catering, equipment maintenance, and related support services (Heskett, 1987). In this business, personnel performing these activities remain on the payroll of the client but work under ServiceMaster's management. This formula has been applied in a number of countries outside the US, most notably Japan, Jordan, and the UK. Given one of ServiceMaster's most important objectives, to "help people develop", the company has gone to great lengths to develop materials, methods, equipment, and training routines to help front-line service employees become more productive at what they do. One important objective is to raise job satisfaction by restoring the dignity of employees previously ignored in their jobs. As a result, employee loyalty rises along with productivity and quality of work, enabling ServiceMaster to contain costs for its clients. This requires the assiduous development and use of various productivity and quality measures, based largely on the inspection of work, such as cleaning, which was previously regarded as largely invisible. This, coupled with an effort by the company to encourage "horizontal" promotions through increased responsibilities on the same site or multi-site job expansion, has produced a record of high loyalty among ServiceMaster's site managers, in turn fostering the highest rate of loyalty in the industry among ServiceMaster's institutional clients. Measurement is at the heart of ServiceMaster's strategy. In one of the company's subsidiaries, Merry Maids, offering home cleaning services through franchised operators, measurement of and management by service profit chain elements is being given one of its most significant tests thus far.

3.3.2 Taco Bell

Taco Bell, a subsidiary of PepsiCo, has perhaps carried measurement as far as any service organisation in a strategy that has evolved from that of a Mexican ethnic fast-food chain to one of feeding people wherever they may need food, both prepared and packaged. This strategy has created the fastest growing major chain of its kind in North America, with 250,000 points of distribution sought by the year 2000. Having developed a strategy based on extensive customer research, it has continued to measure service profit chain elements assiduously, including those of customer and employee satisfaction built around the concept of value (results achieved for customers through product and process in relation to the cost of product and related acquisition costs) resulting from high employee loyalty and productivity as well as product and service quality. It calls some of these measures, particularly those related to customers' reactions and quality, "safety nets". In order to deliver value to customers, Taco Bell is in the process of reducing administrative costs in relation to sales by 75 per cent, through actions suggested by the service profit chain measurements:

- Increasing the latitude of employees who are now trained to function as self-managed work groups, while providing them with state-of-the-art information systems

- Completely re-engineering the organisation to reduce the ranks of managers, while changing their jobs from commanders and supervisors of employees to coaches and consultants to self-managed work groups

- Providing unprecedented high levels of incentive-based compensation to all the remaining levels of management.

Monthly measurements conducted on a unit-by-unit basis among company-owned units (60 per cent of Taco Bell's outlets) suggest that these developments have been accompanied by rising levels of customer and employee satisfaction, higher productivity and quality, and increasing profits and growth.

In total, work carried out thus far by this author and his colleagues, including in-depth studies and the development of extensive data bases in more than 20 organisations, has not produced any major contradictions of the hypotheses implied in the strategic service vision, cycle of failure, or service profit chain. But it has raised a number of questions concerning the relative importance of each of the hypotheses under various conditions. (For other comments concerning contingent characteristics of service profit chain elements, see Bowen and Lawler, Chapter 10 and Wright, Chapter 2.) And it has suggested a number of challenges to be faced in future efforts to explore related ideas embedded in these and similar multi-element conceptual frameworks.

4. CHALLENGES FOR FUTURE RESEARCH

The conceptual frameworks described here are based on and intended to integrate the findings of other researchers. While the second and third of these were intended to explore ways of implementing strategies suggested by the first, all require important strategic decisions of those who would employ them. All are also broad-based, complex, and multi-functional. Herein lies a set of challenges for those who would research them as well as implement them in practice. They include:

- The need for further development of ways of measuring the "fit" not just between a company and its competitive environment, but also among the internal elements of its strategy

- The need to measure individual elements of each framework

- The even more challenging task of assessing inter-relationships among phenomena
- The need to factor concepts of focus, leadership, and culture into our assessments
- The careful translation of result into practice.

They produce a series of questions that we will increasingly have to ask ourselves as both researchers and practitioners.

4.1. The Measurement of "Fit"

The strategic service vision is intended as a device for designing and assessing strategy. It is more internally-oriented than other concepts to which it is related (for example, Porter, 1980). It and related concepts are especially interesting to us today as strategies elected by service companies are introduced across national and cultural boundaries. Work based on these ideas will have to deal with questions such as the following:

- To what degree does the success of a given strategy result from "positioning" in relation to customer needs, competitor capabilities, and strengths in dealing with suppliers and others, as opposed to internal phenomena such as market or operating focus?
- What are the "core" elements of a given strategy? How are they determined?
- To what extent should managers be given the latitude to change core elements as a strategy is implemented across markets, various related services, or national or cultural boundaries? (See, for example, Langeard and Eiglier, 1983).

Increasingly, we are developing an understanding of how to "position" a service in relation to the needs of a particular "segment" of customers. Now we will have to turn more attention to how to satisfy the same customer over time, as expectations for services in a given setting change with repeated experiences. It is clear that research addressing these questions will require the in-depth examination of companies operating in different businesses and environments, largely resulting in anecdotal evidence that can be tested further.

4.2. Measurement of Framework Elements

Thus far, our discussion has assumed that measures and the data they produce are readily available in service-producing companies today.

While measurement is improving, those of us who have had an opportunity to explore in-company data bases know that they present real problems of definition, comprehensiveness and reliability. In part, until concept and practice converge — as we are observing in organisations like Merry Maids, cited earlier — there will be little incentive for management to develop the kind of database that will enable us to test the validity of our ideas with any degree of assurance. And at that point, it will be necessary to ask whether the result will only display a self-fulfilling prophecy. Before we reach that point, other questions will occupy us:

- How are elements such as customer and employee loyalty and satisfaction defined?

- To what extent does the way in which they are defined affect an analysis of relationships between phenomena?

- What efforts are made to discourage the natural tendencies of managers and customers to bias data, particularly with respect to satisfaction levels?

- How do incentives provided to managers influence the reporting and accuracy of data?

Clearly, in contrast to multi-company research investigating questions of strategic "fit", this research will be carried out largely within individual multi-site service companies, in which both cross-sectional and longitudinal data can be analysed in depth. This raises additional questions concerning the effects of local conditions on the data for particular operating units and the extent to which care is taken to compensate for them in the preparation of the data base.

4.3. Assessing Relationships Between Phenomena

To date, the most careful work carried out by the rules of scientific investigation has produced some highly misleading results, primarily because of the failure, firstly, to ascertain just what is being measured; and secondly, to recognise and adjust research efforts to reflect complex inter-phenomena relationships.

For example, efforts to relate customer satisfaction and customer loyalty have yielded sometimes puzzling results, suggesting little or no relationship. Increasingly in such situations, we have to ask what is being measured and whether the measures used for customer satisfaction are those most important in influencing customer loyalty. The same principle applies to attempts to measure other relationships in the service profit chain.

The effects of individual elements of a service strategy working in concert clearly are not additive. The effects increase geometrically with increasing internal consistency through changes across the company of the type suggested by practices in firms in our sample. For example, the more narrowly a group of potential customers is targeted, the more effective a specifically-designed operating strategy to create value for that group of customers will be. This phenomenon is illustrated by the relationships between elements in a human resource strategy on which a growing body of research is being performed.

The most careful of this research emphasises the need to consider issues regarding such things as selection, training and compensation in the context of an organisation system comprising, for example, organisation structure, reporting relationships, communication methods, and even the organisation and design of the workplace. Mahoney, for example, has argued and set forth alternative arrangements for matching pay methods, work characteristics, and organisational arrangements, cautioning that: Careful matching of compensation systems and organisational systems, rather than implementation on the basis of fad interest, provides the opportunity to truly reinforce organisational strategy (Mahoney, 1989; see also Lawler, 1981, and Sears, 1984).

Holding all variables but one constant may constitute good research in the scientific sense. But it may be totally inappropriate in examining results produced by different systems of organisation elements, research that requires that as many things be varied concurrently as possible. It probably accounts for reports of unexpectedly weak relationships between human resource management variables such as the careful selection of employees *or* pay-for-performance *or* increased job latitude *or* increased involvement in job-related decisions and performance. One summary of research to-date suggested only small positive long-term effects on productivity from pay schemes that reward individual or group performance, even when individuals participate in the design of the schemes (Blinder, 1990). Other variables — such as nature of the work; working conditions; the structure of the organisation in which the work was being carried out; or selection, training, and recognition practices — either were held constant in the interest of good science or were ignored. In their work on the impact of worker participation in job-related decisions on productivity, Levine and Tyson describe very well the nature of the problem:

> ... few empirical studies provide quantitative assessments of the effects of substantive participation in work teams on productivity. Most studies

of work teams yield qualitative assessments of their effects in particular cases. Quantitative evaluations are extremely difficult to make because teams are usually associated with several other important changes in the workplace, including new technology, more training, new team or group reward structures, and greater representative participation (Levine and Tyson, 1990).

Narrow, "blinkered" scientific research has produced curious results in recent years. For example, one respected and oft-quoted study attempting to control all relevant variables but those under investigation actually concluded that money lowers employee motivation by reducing the "intrinsic rewards" that an employee receives from the job (Deci, 1972). Another concluded that merit-pay systems are counterproductive because, among other things, "people see themselves as being controlled by a reward" (Kohn, 1988).

Of course, the conceptual frameworks described earlier suggest that change must be made on a wholesale basis if the internal consistency of strategy elements is to be preserved. This requires a change in the way in which we design and carry out much of our research, as suggested by the following questions:

- In our research, are all relevant and related variables allowed to vary?

- Do our techniques of analysis allow us to measure multivariate effects?

- To what extent have we designed our work to allow for an evaluation of the self-reinforcing relationships between sets of variables?

These questions suggest an important role for field-based case research of complex phenomena such as those in the service profit chain, as well as the collection and analysis of data from more highly controlled situations involving smaller numbers of variables.

4.4. Factoring Concepts of Leadership, Culture, and Focus Into Our Work

Concepts of leadership, culture, and focus in the service sector both benefit from and contribute to more general work in competitive strategy. Recent work suggests that there is a direct relationship between corporate performance and the development of cultures encouraging an adaptive approach to constituencies served by the firm (Kotter and Heskett, 1992).

For example, based on in-depth studies of outstanding service producers, this author and his colleagues have concluded that they deliver value by simultaneously creating low-cost service of extraordinarily high quality to those market segments to which they are targeted. So, while costs at Southwest Airlines, a regional US carrier, may have been 20 per cent below those of its lowest full-service competitor before the advent of minimum-service competitors, the airline's culture of service is so effective that its passengers, who expect and value exactly what they get in terms of on-time arrivals and friendly service, give it the highest marks on quality (fewest complaints per volume of travel) among major US airlines. The resulting value in the eyes of Southwest's passengers is incomparable and sets new standards for sustainable competitive advantage.

An important factor in the ability of Southwest and other outstanding service providers to realise their achievements is focus. In the case of one of the examples cited earlier, United Parcel Service has built the world's most successful transportation service by offering one thing to all customers — its fast, efficient handling of packages of strictly limited size and weight — allowing it to achieve one of the most highly focused operating strategies at very low costs for those customers who can make use of it. Culture again plays a major role in the success of UPS. Its combination of military-like discipline (critical to the implementation of a focused operating strategy) and extensive employee ownership insure that UPS's productivity ranks higher than that of other comparable freight carriers.

Organisational culture is critical to the success of all of these companies, suggesting that elements other than those commonly emphasised in "five forces" and other analyses of competitive opportunity must be given much greater emphasis when examining factors leading to winning strategies in the service sector. Further, it is the leadership of these organisations that is responsible for developing and maintaining both the culture and focused strategies. Leaders of organisations cited as examples here speak a different language from their counterparts in other organisations. They speak, as does Herb Kelleher at Southwest Airlines, of "the patina of spirituality" with which employees are selected and the fact that hiring at Southwest is "almost a religious experience". Similarly, Bill Pollard at ServiceMaster is fond of emphasising the importance of all managers being "teacher/learners" and of his being a "servant leader". Thus we must ask ourselves:

- Where cross-company research is being performed, how have attempts been made to quantify or otherwise take into consideration matters such as leadership, culture, and focus?

- To what degree are these relevant factors in the interpretation of results?

4.5. Applying the Results of the Work

Managers have a natural tendency to opt for the "quick fix" at times when they are confronted with performance shortfalls. Given the complexity of the relationships described earlier, this can often lead to frustration and disappointment. Armed with this knowledge, the following questions are those which we will have to address as our work becomes increasingly relevant to everyday management practice:

- To what extent have the importance of relationships between profit-oriented phenomena and management actions been made clear?

- Have the appropriate caveats been attached to research findings to discourage managers from concluding that any one change will produce the desired results, when, in fact, many changes are needed simultaneously?

5. CONCLUSION

The examination of strategic service management has led to the development of a new set of multifunctional, integrative hypotheses with importance for practitioners. It has raised significant questions concerning both measurement and analysis. It has provided insights into management in multi-site, multi-country business operations. By refocusing our attention on the importance of customer and employee satisfaction and loyalty, it has already produced results of importance for managers in both product- and service-producing organisations, whether in the for-profit or not-for-profit sectors.

Precisely because this work has such high managerial relevance, we will be challenged to redouble our efforts to assess the fit between various strategies and their environments; to create more valid measures of the variables under examination; to assess carefully the relationships between many phenomena simultaneously; to factor considerations of the impact of leadership, culture, and focus more prominently into our work; and to provide appropriate caveats to managers looking for easy solutions to their problems in our findings and recommendations.

Efforts to understand elements critical to the achievement of competitive advantage in services will not only continue to provide invaluable inputs to future efforts to formulate strategy, but will influence day-to-day management practice as well. It would be unfortunate if, confronted with this unusual opportunity to achieve high levels of managerial relevance and credibility in our research, we were to settle for anything less.

REFERENCES

Blinder, Alan S., *Paying for Productivity*, The Brookings Institute, Washington, DC, 1990, pp. 1–13.

Buzzell, Robert D. and T. Gale Bradley, *The PIMS Principles*, The Free Press, New York, 1987.

Deci, Edward, "The Effects of Contingent and Non-contingent Rewards and Controls on Intrinsic Motivation", *Organizational Behavior and Human Performance*, Vol. 8, 1972, pp. 217–29.

Hammer, Michael, "Reengineering Work: Don't Automate, Obliterate", *Harvard Business Review*, July/August, 1990, pp. 104–112.

Heskett, James L., *Managing in the Service Economy,* Harvard Business School Press, Boston, 1986, pp. 27–43.

Heskett, James L., Thomas O. Jones, Gary W. Loveman, W. Earl Sasser, Jr. and Leonard A. Schlesinger, "Putting the Service-Profit Chain to Work", *Harvard Business Review*, March/April, 1994, pp. 164–74.

Heskett, James L., "ServiceMaster Industries Inc.", Harvard Business School, Publishing Division, Boston, MA, 1987.

Johnson, Eugene M. Johnson and Daniel T. Seymour, "The Impact of Cross Selling on the Service Encounter in Retail Banking", in John A. Czepiel, Michael R. Soloman, and Carol F. Surprenant (Eds.), *The Service Encounter*, D. C. Heath, Lexington, MA, 1985, pp. 225–39.

Kohn, Alfie, "Incentives Can be Bad for Business", *INC.*, Vol. 10, No. 1, January, 1988, pp. 93–4.

Kotter, John P. and James L. Heskett, *Corporate Culture and Performance,* The Free Press, New York, 1992.

Langeard, Eric and Pierre Eiglier, "Strategic Management of Service Development", in Leonard L Berry, G. Lynn Shostack, and Gregory D. Upah (Eds.), *Emerging Perspectives on Services Marketing,* American Marketing Association, Chicago, IL, 1983, pp. 68–72.

Lawler, Edward E., III, *Motivation in Work Organisations,* Brooks/Cole, Monterey, CA, 1973, pp. 153–65.

Lawler, Edward E., III, *Pay and Organisation Development,* Addison-Wesley, Reading, MA, 1981.

Levine, David I. and Laura D'Andrea Tyson, "Participation, Productivity, and the Firm's Environment", in Alan S. Blinder (Ed.), *Paying for Productivity*, The Brookings Institution, Washington, DC, 1990, pp. 191, 196.

Lytle, Lucy N. and W. Earl Sasser Jr., "Au Bon Pain: The Partner/Manager Program", Harvard Business School, Publishing Division, Boston, MA, 1987.

Mahoney, Thomas A., "Multiple Pay Contingencies: Strategic Design of Compensation", *Human Resource Management,* Vol. 28, No. 3, Fall, 1989, pp. 337–47.

Normann, Richard, *Service Management: Strategy and Leadership in Service Businesses,* John Wiley and Sons, Chichester, UK, 1984, pp. 97–8.

Parasuraman, A., Valarie A. Zeithaml and Leonard L. Berry, "A Conceptual Model of Service/Quality and Its Implications for Future Research", *Journal of Marketing*, Vol. 63, Fall, 1985, pp. 41–50.

Parkington, J.J. and Benjamin Schneider, "Some Correlates of Experienced Job Stress: A Boundary Role Study", *Academy of Management Journal,* Vol. 22, 1979, pp. 270–81.

Porter, Michael E., *Competitive Strategy*, The Free Press, New York, 1980.

Ray, Kenneth and James L. Heskett, "Fairfield Inn", Harvard Business School, Publishing Division, Boston, MA, 1989.

Reichheld, Frederick F. and W. Earl Sasser Jr., "Zero Defections: Quality Comes to Services", *Harvard Business Review*, September/October, 1990, pp. 105–11.

Rust, Roland T., Anthony J. Zahorik and Timothy L. Keiningham, *Return on Quality*, Probus, Chicago, IL, 1994.

Schlesinger, Leonard A. and James L. Heskett, "Breaking the Cycle of Failure in Services", *Sloan Management Review,* Vol. 32, Spring, 1991, pp. 17–28 .

Schlesinger, Leonard A. and James L. Heskett, "How Does Service Drive the Service Company?" *Harvard Business Review*, November/ December, 1991, pp. 146–158 .

Schneider, Benjamin and David E. Bowen, "New Services Design, Development and Implementation and the Employee", in W.R. George and C. Marshall (Eds.), *New Services*, American Marketing Association, Chicago, IL, 1985, pp. 82–101.

Schoeffler, Sidney, Robert D. Buzzell and Donald F. Heany, "Impact of Strategic Planning on Profit Performance", *Harvard Business Review*, March/April, 1974 .

Sears, D., "Make Employee Pay a Strategic Issue", *Financial Executive*, October, 1984, pp. 40–3.

Shostack, G. Lynn, "Designing Services That Deliver", *Harvard Business Review*, January/February, 1984, pp. 133–9.

Shostack, G. Lynn and J. Kingman-Brundage, "How to Design a Service", in *The American Management Association Handbook of Marketing for the Service Industries*, American Management Association, AMACOM, New York, 1991, pp. 243–61.

Shostack, G. Lynn, "Planning the Service Encounter", in John A. Czepiel,

Michael R. Soloman and Carol F. Surprenant (Eds.), *The Service Encounter*, DC Heath, Lexington, MA, 1985, pp. 243–53.

Signorelli, Sergio and James L. Heskett, "Benetton (A)", Harvard Business School, Publishing Division, Boston, MA, 1984.

Sonnenfeld, Jeffrey and Meredith Lazo, "United Parcel Service (A)", Harvard Business School, Publishing Division, Boston, MA, 1987.

Wylie, David and Walter J. Salmon, "Ito Yokado", Harvard Business School, Publishing Division, Boston, MA, 1989 .

Zeithaml, Valarie A., A. Parasuraman and Leonard L. Berry, *Delivering Quality Service*, The Free Press, New York, 1990.

INDEX

THE WAY

WORD

FOR

WINDOWS™

WORKS